Global Themes and Local Variations in Organization and Management

Global Themes and Local Variations in Organization and Management: Perspectives on Glocalization offers a broad exposition of the relations between the global and the local with regard to organizational and managerial ideas, practices, and forms. This edited volume forges ahead to capture the complexity of modern management and organization that results from the processes of glocalization.

Universality is among the core underlying principles of the management of organizations, as well as of organization and management science itself. Yet, reality reveals enormous variation across social and cultural contexts. For instance, multinational corporations must adjust their management practices to adhere to national regulation and local standards; manufacturers and service providers routinely tailor their products to suit the local preferences of consumers; and non-profit organizations amend their advocacy agenda to appeal to local sentiments. The work assembled here goes beyond merely describing such patterns of variation and adaptation in organization and management; research and commentary engage directly with the tensions between homogeneity and heterogeneity, convergence and divergence, global and local.

With contributions from leading scholars in the field of comparative organization studies, this collection offers a substantive contribution to the investigation of organization and management, as well as providing a valuable resource for students of organization studies, international business, and sociology.

Gili S. Drori is Associate Professor of Sociology and Anthropology at The Hebrew University of Jerusalem, Israel.

Markus A. Höllerer is Lecturer of Organization Theory at the Australian School of Business, University of New South Wales in Sydney, Australia.

Peter Walgenbach is Professor for Organization, Leadership, and Human Resource Management at the Friedrich Schiller University of Jena, Germany.

Global Themes and Local Variations in Organization and Management

Perspectives on Glocalization

Edited by Gili S. Drori, Markus A. Höllerer, and Peter Walgenbach

NEW YORK AND LONDON

First published 2014
by Routledge
711 Third Avenue, New York, NY 10017

Simultaneously published in the UK
by Routledge
2 Park Square, Milton Park, Abingdon, Oxon OX14 4RN

Routledge is an imprint of the Taylor & Francis Group, an informa business

© 2014 Taylor & Francis

The right of Gili S. Drori, Markus A. Höllerer, and Peter Walgenbach to be identified as authors of the editorial material, and of the authors for their individual chapters has been asserted by them in accordance with sections 77 and 78 of the Copyright, Designs and Patents Act 1988.

All rights reserved. No part of this book may be reprinted or reproduced or utilised in any form or by any electronic, mechanical, or other means, now known or hereafter invented, including photocopying and recording, or in any information storage or retrieval system, without permission in writing from the publishers.

Trademark notice: Product or corporate names may be trademarks or registered trademarks, and are used only for identification and explanation without intent to infringe.

Library of Congress Cataloging in Publication Data
Global themes and local variations in organization and management : perspectives on glocalization / edited by Gili S. Drori, Markus A. Höllerer, and Peter Walgenbach.
    pages cm
  Includes bibliographical references and index.
  1. Organizational change. 2. Management. 3. Globalization.
  I. Drori, Gili S.
  HD58.8.G586 2013
  658–dc23   2012050212

ISBN: 978-0-415-80760-9 (hbk)
ISBN: 978-0-415-80768-5 (pbk)
ISBN: 978-0-203-13948-6 (ebk)

Typeset in Bembo
by HWA Text and Data Management, London

Printed and bound in the United States of America by
Edwards Brothers Malloy

Contents

List of Figures	*viii*
List of Tables	*ix*
List of Contributors	*x*
Preface	*xv*

PART I
Introduction   1

1 The Glocalization of Organization and Management: Issues, Dimensions, and Themes   3
   Gili S. Drori, Markus A. Höllerer, and Peter Walgenbach

2 Situating Glocalization: A Relatively Autobiographical Intervention   25
   Roland Robertson

PART II
Revisiting Glocalization   37

3 The Travel of Organization   39
   Göran Ahrne and Nils Brunsson

4 Global Themes and Institutional Ambiguity in the University Field: Rankings and Management Models on the Move   52
   Kerstin Sahlin

5 Storytelling: A Managerial Tool and its Local Translations   65
   Barbara Czarniawska

6 'Re-localization' as Micro-mobilization of Consent and Legitimacy   79
   Renate E. Meyer

Contents

7	Competition Regulation in Africa Between Global and Local: A Banyan Tree Story *Marie-Laure Djelic*	90

PART III
Ideas, Structures, and Practices — 105

8	Boomerang Diffusion at a Global Bank: Total Quality Management and National Culture *David Strang*	107
9	Rhetorical Variations in the Cross-national Diffusion of Management Practices: A Comparison of Turkey and the US *Şükrü Özen*	119
10	Toward a Multi-layered Glocalization Approach: States, Multinational Corporations, and the Transformation of Gender Contracts *Michal Frenkel*	133
11	Words Fly Quicker Than Actions: The Globalization of the Diversity Discourse *Iris Barbosa and Carlos Cabral-Cardoso*	146
12	New Public Management and Beyond: The Hybridization of Public Sector Reforms *Tom Christensen*	161
13	Adoption and Abandonment: Global Diffusion and Local Variation in University Top Management Teams *Danielle M. Logue*	175
14	Decoding Localization: A Comparison of Two Transnational Life Insurance Firms in China *Cheris Shun-ching Chan*	189

PART IV
Actors and Influences — 201

15	Cosmopolitans, Harlequins, or Frankensteins? Managers Enacting Local, Global, and Glocal Identities *Giuseppe Delmestri*	203
16	Personal Rule in Asia's Family-controlled Business Groups *Michael Carney*	219
17	The Glocalization of Academic Business Studies *Lars Engwall*	232
18	Gender in Times of Global Governance: Glocalizing International Norms Around Money and Power, Violence and Sex in Peru *Miriam Abu-Sharkh*	248

19 Europeanization of National Administrations in the Czech Republic and Poland: Assessing the Extent of Institutional Change   264
Christoph Knill and Jale Tosun

20 From Historical Roots to Hybrid Identities: The Transformation Challenge of French Grandes Ecoles de Commerce   278
Farah Kodeih

21 Governance of Science in Mediatized Society: Media Rankings and the Translation of Global Governance Models for Universities   295
Josef Pallas and Linda Wedlin

PART V
Processes and Mechanisms   309

22 Micro-strategies of Contextualization: Glocalizing Responsible Investment in France and Quebec   311
Eva Boxenbaum and Jean-Pascal Gond

23 Projecting the Local into the Global: Trajectories of Participation in Transnational Standard-setting   325
Olga Malets and Sigrid Quack

24 The Changing Factors of ISO 9001 Adoption among Korean Firms   339
Hokyu Hwang, Yong Suk Jang, and Ki Tae Park

25 The Localization of Carbon Markets: Negotiated Ambiguity   355
Anita Engels and Lisa Knoll

26 Managing Illicit Flows: The Formation of Global Anti-money Laundering Regulations   369
Anja P. Jakobi

27 Subsidiary Initiative-taking in Multinational Corporations: The Role of Issue-selling Tactics   383
Christoph Dörrenbächer, Florian Becker-Ritterspach, Jens Gammelgaard, and Mike Geppert

28 Cosmopolitanism and Banal Localism: The Domestication of Global Trends in Finnish Cities   396
Pertti Alasuutari

PART VI
Concluding Remarks   411

29 Empowered Actors, Local Settings, and Global Rationalization   413
John W. Meyer

Index   *425*

Figures

15.1	Italian managers espousing distinct role identities according to firm nationality	208
15.2	Brazilian managers espousing distinct role identities according to firm nationality	208
15.3	Chinese managers espousing distinct role identities according to firm nationality	208
15.4	German managers espousing distinct role identities according to firm nationality	208
15.5	An expanded model of acculturation to local communities and the world society	212
24.1	The number of companies adopting ISO 9001 in Korea	341
24.2	The number of newspaper articles on ISO standards and certification	343
24.3	The adoption pattern among the 300 Korean firms in the sample	347
26.1	Anti-money laundering regulations and related organizational change	377
28.1	Net expenditures of cultural activities in 2007, € per citizen	402

Tables

1.1	The glocalization of organization and management: an analytical grid	14
9.1	The rhetorical strategies for management practices	122
9.2	The rhetorical strategies and the origin of the practices	123
9.3	The rhetorical strategies and the countries	124
11.1	The affiliates' major attributes	150
11.2	The affiliates' external and internal diversity discourses	155
11.3	The affiliates' diversity practices	157
13.1	Proportion of universities in sample with position listed in TMT	179
13.2	Adoption and abandonment of positions by region	181
13.3	Examples of leadership positions at individual universities 1918–2008	183
17.1	Origin of the literature in eight Nordic business schools in the mid-1990s	234
17.2	Titles that were used most in the eight Nordic business schools in the mid-1990s	234
17.3	Share of international students and share of international faculty for the global MBA programs	236
17.4	Average share of international students and faculty by region for the 65 institutions	237
17.5	Fifteen management top journals with impact factors, 1985 and 2009	239
17.6	Share of author origin in the fifteen top journals, 1981–1992 and 2005–2009	240
17.7	The twenty top institutions in the fifteen top journals, 1981–1992 and 2005–2009	241
17.8	Top twenty-five citations in the fifteen journals, 1981–1992 and 2005–2008	242
17.9	Ten most cited authors in the fifteen journals, 1981–1992 and 2005–2009	243
20.1	Institutional logics in the French Grande Ecole de Commerce (FGEC) field	282
22.1	Micro-strategies of contextualization: definition and illustrations	316
24.1	Variable description and descriptive statistics	348
24.2	Factors associated with the adoption of ISO 9000 among Korean firms, 1992–2006	349
26.1	Global and regional standard-setting against money laundering	375
27.1	Detailed information on the cases mentioned	388

Contributors

Miriam Abu-Sharkh is a consulting associate professor at the Stanford Center for International Development, USA, and on the faculty at the Development Studies Institute, London School of Economics and Political Science, UK. She is the principal investigator on a large research grant by the European Research Council on gender and global governance. Her current research interests include labor-related international human rights, especially child labor and (non-)discrimination, social movements, and work satisfaction.

Göran Ahrne is professor emeritus of sociology at Stockholm University, Sweden. His main research interests are the organization of social interaction and the role of theories of organization for theories of society.

Pertti Alasuutari is academy professor at the University of Tampere, Finland. His current research interests are the global spread and domestication of worldwide trends, particularly the synchronization of national policies, and the role of the media in policy making.

Iris Barbosa is professor of organizational behavior and HRM at the University of Minho, Portugal. Her main research interests are the management of human diversity at the workplace, the dissemination and local translation of management knowledge, and the dynamics between management discourse and practice.

Florian Becker-Ritterspach is professor of international business at the German University in Cairo (GUC), Egypt. Alongside issues of politics and learning in multinationals, his recent research has focused on both multinationals in emerging markets and the internationalization of emerging market firms.

Eva Boxenbaum is professor of management science at École des Mines de Paris, France, and professor with special responsibilities in organizational theory and institutional innovation at Copenhagen Business School, Denmark. Her main research interests are the adoption and translation of managerial innovations from foreign countries, and the role of embedded actors in processes of institutional change.

List of Contributors

Nils Brunsson holds the chair in management at Uppsala University, Sweden, and is also affiliated to Score (Stockholm Centre for Organizational Research). He currently leads a research program on the organization of markets.

Carlos Cabral-Cardoso is professor of management at the University of Porto, Portugal. His current research interests are in the relationship between work and other life spheres, privacy issues at the workplace, the management rhetoric and action in HRM, and ethical issues in academia.

Michael Carney is research chair in strategy and entrepreneurship at Concordia University in Montréal, Québec, Canada. His research focuses on family firms, business groups and the comparative analysis of business, financial and governance systems, and their influence upon the development of firm capabilities and strategic assets.

Cheris Shun-ching Chan is associate professor of sociology at the University of Hong Kong. Her main research interests are culture and economy, globalization of modern capitalism, new religious movements, guanxi and Chinese society, and medical professionalism in China.

Tom Christensen is professor of organization theory and public administration at the Department of Political Science, University of Oslo, Norway, and also adjunct professor at the University of Bergen and the City University of Hong Kong. His main research is in the field of comparative public sector reform.

Barbara Czarniawska holds the chair in management studies at GRI, School of Business, Economics and Law, at the University of Gothenburg, Sweden. She takes a feminist and constructionist perspective on organizing, recently exploring the connections between popular culture and practice of management, and the organization of news production. She is interested in methodology, especially in techniques of fieldwork and in the application of narratology to organization studies.

Giuseppe Delmestri is professor for organization and global management education at Johannes Kepler University in Linz, Austria. His main research interests are institutional organizational theory, international comparative research, and the global diffusion and contestation of modern management practices.

Marie-Laure Djelic is professor of management at ESSEC Business School, France. Her main research interests are comparative capitalism, globalization, diffusion and institutionalization, the role of the corporation, and transnational governance.

Christoph Dörrenbächer is professor of organizational design and behavior in international business at the Berlin School of Economics and Law, Germany. His current research focus is on subsidiary role development, headquarters-subsidiary relationships, and careers in multinational corporations.

Gili S. Drori is associate professor of sociology and anthropology at The Hebrew University of Jerusalem, Israel. Her main research interests are the globalization of science, technology, innovation, and higher education, as well as issues of organization and rationalization.

List of Contributors

Anita Engels is full professor of sociology at Universität Hamburg, Germany. Her main research interests are economic sociology, corporate greening, and social science research on climate change.

Lars Engwall is professor of business administration at Uppsala University, Sweden. His research has been directed towards structural analyses of industries and organizations as well as the creation and diffusion of management knowledge by business schools, consultants, and the media.

Michal Frenkel is senior lecturer of sociology and anthropology at The Hebrew University of Jerusalem, Israel. Her main research interests are cross-national transfer of ideas and practices, postcolonial organization, and work–family reconciliation.

Jens Gammelgaard is associate professor at Copenhagen Business School, Denmark. His main research interests are the strategic development of subsidiaries, as well as mergers and acquisitions, and strategic alliances. Furthermore he researches into the brewery sector.

Mike Geppert is professor of comparative international management and organization studies at the University of Surrey in Guildford, UK. His current research focuses on socio-political issues in and around multinational companies, and on comparative studies of management, organization, and employment relations of internationally operating grocery retailers and airlines.

Jean-Pascal Gond is professor of management at Cass Business School, City University London, and senior visiting fellow at the International Centre for Corporate Social Responsibility at Nottingham University Business School, UK. His main research interests are the social construction of corporate social responsibility, the emergence of responsible investment, and the organizational study of performativity.

Markus A. Höllerer is lecturer of organization theory at the Australian School of Business, University of New South Wales in Sydney, Australia. His research interests are the dissemination and local adaptation of global managerial concepts, in particular the heterogeneous theorizations and local variations in meaning, and the relationship between different bundles of concepts and their underlying governance and business models.

Hokyu Hwang is senior lecturer at the Australian School of Business, University of New South Wales, in Sydney, Australia. His main research interests are the causes and consequences of organizational rationalization, the nonprofit sector, as well as the proliferation of actors.

Anja P. Jakobi is senior research fellow at the Cluster of Excellence "Normative Orders" and the Peace Research Institute Frankfurt, Germany. Her main research interests are world society theory, international organizations, and policy diffusion.

Yong Suk Jang is associate professor of public administration at Yonsei University in Seoul, Korea. His current research interests include macro-comparative analyses of nation-states and organizations, governance, and neo-institutionalism.

List of Contributors

Christoph Knill is professor at the University of Konstanz, Germany. His current research interests are in comparative public policy with a particular emphasis on morality issues, Europeanization, public administration, and institutional organizational theory.

Lisa Knoll holds a postdoctoral position in sociology at Universität Hamburg, Germany. Her main research interests are economic sociology, the French Convention School, and social science research on climate change.

Farah Kodeih is assistant professor in strategy at Reims Management School, France. Her current research interests are institutional theory, organizational identity, and the interplay between both, as well as the globalization of management education and business schools.

Danielle M. Logue is lecturer at the University of Technology, Sydney, Australia. Her current research interests are in the diffusion of innovations, drawing on institutional theory to examine implications for organizational performance, structure and management, and broader processes of social change.

Olga Malets is lecturer at the chair of forest and environmental policy, Technische Universität München, Germany. Her current research interests are the local implementation of transnational private standards of corporate environmental and social responsibility, particularly in the forest sector.

John W. Meyer is professor of sociology, emeritus, at Stanford University, USA. He has contributed to organizational theory and the sociology of education, developing institutional theory. He studies the world human rights regime, world curricula in education, and the global spread of formal organization.

Renate E. Meyer is professor of public management and governance at WU Vienna University of Economics and Business, Austria, and permanent visiting professor at Copenhagen Business School, Denmark. Her main research interests are visual and discursive framing strategies, ambiguity as response to institutional complexity, and new forms of governance in the public sector.

Şükrü Özen is professor of organization theory at Yıldırım Beyazıt University in Ankara, Turkey. His main research interests are in institutional organizational theory, cross-national diffusion and translation of managerial practices, and social movements and institutional change.

Josef Pallas is senior lecturer at the Department of Informatics and Media, Uppsala University, Sweden. His main research focuses on mediatization of different parts of society and the implications this has for the way modern organizations are organized and governed.

Ki Tae Park is doctoral student at the Department of Sociology, University of Hawaii, Manoa, USA. His main research interests are globalization and its impact on East Asian societies, and economic and organizational sociology.

List of Contributors

Sigrid Quack is head of the research group "Institution Building across Borders" at the Max Planck Institute for the Study of Societies, and professor of sociology at the University of Cologne, Germany. Her main research interests are transnational institutions, social mobilization, and organization.

Roland Robertson is distinguished service professor of sociology emeritus at the University of Pittsburgh, USA, and emeritus professor of sociology and global society at the University of Aberdeen, Scotland.

Kerstin Sahlin is professor of management at Uppsala University, Sweden. She was the deputy vice-chancellor of Uppsala University between 2006 and 2011. Her main research interests are transnational governance, university governance, the role of corporations in global society, and public–private relations.

David Strang is professor of sociology at Cornell University, USA. His main research interests concern diffusion and learning in the business and political arenas, and institutional models of organization.

Jale Tosun is research fellow at the University of Mannheim, Germany. Her main research interests are in comparative public policy with a focus on environmental and energy policies as well as risk regulation, international political economy, and Europeanization.

Peter Walgenbach is professor for organization, leadership, and human resource management at the Friedrich Schiller University of Jena, Germany. His main research interests are in institutional organizational theory, structuration theory, international comparative research, and the diffusion and application of modern management concepts.

Linda Wedlin is associate professor of business studies at Uppsala University, Sweden. Her main research interests include organizational and institutional transformations of higher education and the scientific field, and the construction and diffusion of transnational governance models and practices.

Preface

It is often unclear where the starting point of something is exactly; this endeavor to compile research and commentary on the glocalization of organization and management is, in this respect, no different. We, the editors, have known each other for quite some time; we had met on several occasions here and there, and we therefore knew that we share an interest in the themes the work included in this volume considers. Initially, the junction between something as broad as institutional theory, issues and concepts of organization and management, and what had been labeled as "globalization"/"glocalization", was illusive. Nevertheless, in 2008 we decided to propose a sub-theme for the 2010 EGOS Colloquium in Lisbon, Portugal. This sub-theme, titled "Management and glocalization: global dissemination and local adaptation of managerial concepts", sparked not only the interest of numerous colleagues, but also caught the attention of Routledge. The thoughtful paper presentations and the lively discussions in Lisbon further encouraged us to seize this opportunity and bring together the leading scholars on matters related to the glocalization of organization and management. And even in the midst of advanced editorial work, we continued these scholarly discussions in yet another sub-theme at the 2012 EGOS Colloquium in Helsinki, Finland.

Now, with this collection of compelling research and thoughtful commentary in your hands, we wish to express our gratitude to all who have shared in making this project possible. We, foremost, thank the contributing authors, for offering their important work to build this volume – as well as for reviewing the chapters of fellow contributors in a thorough, thoughtful, and constructive way. We thank the editorial team of Routledge, especially Sharon Golan, for their guidance and support. And we thank our friends and colleagues who provided critique and comments at various stages of the editorial process. In particular, we are grateful to John W. Meyer for joining us as a discussant in Lisbon, and for his insightful and inspiring commentaries on the work herein. We also highly appreciate Roland Robertson's introductory commentary which, together with the concluding chapter by John W. Meyer, frames the array of chapters included in this volume. It is our hope that the discussions offered here – on the many dimensions of global and cross-national variation-cum-similarity – will further encourage conceptual and empirical research on the glocal dimensions of organization and management.

Gili S. Drori, Markus A. Höllerer, and Peter Walgenbach
Jerusalem, Sydney, and Jena, December 2012

Part I
Introduction

1

The Glocalization of Organization and Management

Issues, Dimensions, and Themes

Gili S. Drori, Markus A. Höllerer, and Peter Walgenbach

A dramatic wave of globalization throughout the 20th century – spurred by information and communication technology, and imprinted primarily by North American hegemony – resulted in a world that seems neither "flat" nor "spiky". Globalization has not resulted in worldwide homogeneity; likewise, it has also not fully preserved national differences, let alone led to increasing cross-national divergence. Rather, globalization has revealed itself as "glocalization": as a complex process that fuses the global and the local, and interlaces worldwide similarity with cross-national variation.

Such realization has also struck scholars of organization and management, even if they have so far hardly referred to the very term "glocalization". At its core, their discipline is founded upon assumptions of universality: decision-making criteria in the management of organizations are assumed to follow law-like patterns that confirm theories of the *homo oeconomicus*. Still, even the most rational choice-inspired studies recognize that the global spread of organization and management is accompanied by great variation across social and cultural contexts. For instance, multinational corporations need to adjust their organizational practices in order to adhere to national regulation and standards; producers routinely tailor their products to suit local consumers' tastes; and non-profit organizations amend their advocacy agenda to appeal to local sentiments. While numerous studies describe such patterns of variation and adaptation, few offer the conceptual and analytic depth that is signature of the domains of globalization scholarship and organization studies. Drawing upon the richness of research on the diffusion of organizational and managerial ideas, we therefore reframe these adjustments in terms of the glocalization of organization and management.

With this, we ask: What are the antecedents – organizational and global, strategic and cultural alike – that account for context-specific adjustment of organization and management? What are the themes that diffuse on a global scale, remain local, or become glocal? Further, what are the mechanisms that underlie these processes of globalization, localization, and glocalization? And finally, who are the actors who propel the glocalization of organization and management? The collection of academic research in this volume explores these issues in great detail.

Issues

Especially during the past two decades, the globalization of organization and management has emerged as a prominent topic of research and commentary. In this still-evolving field of scholarship, organizing and managing are described as both exemplars of globalization patterns and as principal forces behind broader globalization processes. Much like research on globalization in general, organization and management studies drew attention to the two core dimensions of globalization, namely cross-national diffusion of ideas and concepts and the consolidation of the global.

First, studies of organization and management robustly illustrate the global, cross-national diffusion of rationalized ideas of governance (e.g., Aguilera and Jackson, 2010; Drori, Jang, and Meyer, 2006; Haxhi and van Ees, 2010). Other studies illustrate the global, cross-organizational diffusion of intensively rationalized organizational and managerial concepts such as, for instance, quality management and ISO standards (e.g., Guler, Guillén, and Macpherson, 2002; Albuquerque, Bronnenberg, Corbett, 2007), or codes of (good) corporate governance (e.g., Aguilera and Cuervo-Cazurra, 2004; Vogel, 2008), and the importance of American hegemony in setting the tone for such cross-national diffusion (Djelic, 1998). Second, research addresses the consolidation of a global model of organization and management, specifying the form and logic of global governance (e.g., Sahlin-Andersson and Engwall, 2002; Djelic and Quack, 2003; Djelic and Sahlin-Andersson, 2006). Both streams of research point at mechanisms of diffusion and institutionalization of global models of organization and management, and, most importantly, describe resulting patterns of isomorphism and variation. Still, the idea of glocalization – and with it the explicit acknowledgement of the simultaneous and interrelated impact of global and local forces – remains largely absent. This seems problematic insofar as it downplays the role of empowered locals, the authoritative voice of global models, and the impact of their co-existence.

Applying the notion of glocalization to the study of organization and management, we tend to the complexity of globalization as well as the synergetic nature of related processes and their outcomes. In addressing such complexity, as do the studies compiled in this volume, we intersect between several important issues.

Global and Local

By the mid-1980s, discussions of globalization had quickly transitioned, much to our relief, from the futile debate on whether globalization is good or bad, to a more nuanced realization that, whatever its outcome, globalization is one of the most profound and sweeping processes of our time. Still, such realization has not quieted the discussion of whether globalization is "flattening" the world or resulting in variations and ever-expanding gaps (see Friedman, 2005; Florida, 2005; for discussion, see also Tempel and Walgenbach, 2007). For a decade or so, debates about globalization were then stuck on this polarity between convergence and divergence.

The divide between "global" and "local" shadowed this conversation: convergence was understood to emerge from a focus on overarching global processes, whereas the focus on local conditions seemed to highlight worldwide differences and processes of divergence. In addition, a series of similar dichotomies emerged, each emphasizing a particular axis of difference. On the one hand, local was conflated with indigenous, autochthonous, authentic, and bottom-up, as well as with peripheral and marginalized; on the other, global came to mean foreign, Western or North American, capitalist, and top-down, as well as core and hegemonic. Each dichotomy, or set of opposing characterizations, was regarded as incommensurable, and scholars were judged and tagged as standing for one position or the other.

Roland Robertson saved the field of globalization studies from this mired debate by problematizing the divide between the global and the local and by coining the term "glocalization" within our broader field of scholarship. Engaging the conversation on hybridity and modernity, Robertson (1995; see also Chapter 2) conceived glocalization as creating synergies across time and space, thus resulting in an amalgamation across cultural, national, and regional divides, as well as across historical (dis-)continuities. Glocalization, as described also by Courchene (1995), Tomlinson (1993), Ritzer (2003), or Roudometof (2005), suggests that the global and local are mutually constitutive: the so-called global is a collage of local practices, behaviors, and tastes, while the so-called local is increasingly constructed within the scripts drafted by global forces. In this sense, the then emergent discussion on glocalization was an assault on binary thinking in general. Therefore, in its focus on fusion into a new form, glocalization implies more than the multiplicity, diversity, and assemblage of globally scattered elements (see Sassen, 2006), but rather asserts the co-constitutive nature of global–local relations, and is revealed as a conjuncture of identity and form.

Building on Robertson's notion of fusing global and local, Bartelson (2000) summarizes the critique of post-realist approaches to globalization by distinguishing between three approaches to globalization studies: *transference*, which views globalization as an exchange among entities; *transformation*, which centers discussions on globalization on the change that comes to such entities through the exchange process; and *transcendence*, which – in distinction from the previous two approaches – highlights the dissolving of the "divide between inside and outside" (Bartelson 2000: 189), or the porousness of the boundaries of such entities that results from the transference and transformation that globalization brings. In this fashion, Robertson's call for looking beyond divides in time and space is echoed in envisioning glocalization essentially as a process of transcendence of various social and cultural boundaries.

The synergetic approach implied by glocalization is reflected in a series of similarly minded terms or labels. Such terms, many of which are principal to the work compiled in this volume, highlight unique dimensions of glocal synergies. Some of them imply heterogenization and processes of translation, editing, and adaptation. Specifically, the terms "indigenization" (e.g., Appadurai, 1990), "creolization" (e.g., Hannerz, 1989, 1996; Eriksen, 2003), and "domestication" (e.g., Alasuutari, Chapter 28) each highlight the adaptation of a global theme to its (new) local host environment, in a manner reminiscent of Latour's notion of contextualization (see, 1996: 133; see also, R.E. Meyer, Chapter 6; Boxenbaum and Gond, Chapter 22). Other terms – most notably "transculturation" (e.g., Lull, 2000), "global localization" (e.g., Beck, 2000), and hybridization (e.g., Pieterse, 1994; Kipping, Üsdiken, and Puig, 2004; Christensen, Chapter 12) – highlight the fusion of global and local into a new form (as well as the inherent duality that results in such a new form). Lastly, the term "glonacal" (e.g., Marginson, 2004) reorients this terminological discussion towards the issue of levels by highlighting the multiplicity of spheres that are now interlaced, specifically combining global, national (or field-level), and more local spheres.

We take the term glocalization to stand for this range of issues, recognizing the dialectics between the global and the local (or any other intermediate level). Most importantly, we recognize that global and local are dependent on each other, and regard any essentialist approach as myopic. Glocalization is, therefore, an ontological matter. Following Robertson

(1994, 1995; see also Chapter 2), the notion of glocalization, in its broadest sense, refers to the simultaneity and interdependence of particularizing and universalizing tendencies of globalization, and the co-presence of heterogenization and homogenization as imprints of global processes. "The local is a *global* phenomenon," assert Robertson and Khondker (1998: 30; italics in original text), thus describing the globally constituted character of the local. Therefore, rather than global and local standing in dialectic opposition to each other, and rather than seeing globalization and localization as complementary processes, glocalization touches upon imbued meanings: global models instill agency into empowered locals, who in turn enact and thus reinforce such global scripts. The co-organization of global and local *per se* does not imply conflict or crisis.

Organization and Management

While the term glocalization was effectively applied to the study of a variety of social phenomena – from Argentinian riots (Auyero, 2001) to issues of environmentalism (Brand, 1999) to migrant soccer fans (Giulianotti and Robertson, 2007) – it has hardly been made relevant to organization and management research. This volume acknowledges and highlights the importance and relevance of the notion of glocalization to this specific field of scholarship. We argue that the transcendence of social and cultural boundaries is particularly valuable for a research field in which numerous practices are simultaneously universalized and customized.

Universality has been one of the core underlying principles of organization and management science: social laws of organization and administration have been assumed to remain constant, similar to natural laws, across equivalent contexts. With that, ideas, practices, and skills of organizing and managing have been accepted as transferable to, and applicable for, societies and organizations worldwide (see, e.g., Drucker, 1989). It is because of this axiomatic understanding that, for instance, accounting and budgeting instruments, human resource management techniques, strategic management, performance measures and indicators, or marketing tools are similarly applied to the management of organizations that are as different as for-profit firms and public sector agencies, large multinational corporations and small regional start-ups, or organizations in Western and non-Western contexts. Such a principle of universality and its application naturally turned the eye of researchers to the isomorphic features of worldwide organizational forms and managerial practices and to related institutional dynamics (Kostova, Roth, and Dacin, 2008; and the canonized DiMaggio and Powell, 1983).

In spite of this grip of the universality principle, locality and authenticity – and with these terms the concept of particularization – remain powerful images for organization and management, especially among the more critical schools of organization studies (see, for instance, Frenkel and Shenhav, 2006). For example, Ul-Haq and Westwood (2011) describe Islamic management knowledge, which is "informed by the philosophical, ethical and epistemological principles of Islam", as an exemplar of the marginalized knowledge of the "Global South" – despite its historic role as the source of capitalist mercantilism and monetization. Similar claims of authenticity and then marginalization have been made, for instance, regarding Latin American (e.g., Alcadipani and Rosa, 2011; Ibarro-Colado, 2011), Indian (e.g., Srinivas, 2011), the "Atlantic divide" between American and European management and organization studies scholarship (Meyer and Boxenbaum, 2010; Üsdiken, 2010), or for different versions of European management knowledge (e.g., Delmestri and Walgenbach, 2009; Beck, Kabst, and Walgenbach, 2009). Yet, as argued eloquently by Srinivas

(2011), such claims of authenticity and relevance further reinforce the prevalent feeling of epistemic inferiority because of the definition of such authenticity being inevitably done in reference to hegemonic (notably Western, and principally North American) management knowledge.

We argue here that the divide between universalization and particularization is difficult to sustain both empirically and conceptually. For one, the glocalization of organization and management has strategic implications for practical matters – from where a company's headquarters should be located, to whether a single branding strategy for all subsidiaries is required, to what main hiring criteria should be, among many others. In making such practical decisions, multinational organizations wrestle with matters of identity and of operations that are simultaneously global and local. In addition to these strategic and practical implications, the glocalization of organization and management also adds a conceptual dimension to comparative studies and to commentaries on diffusion, governance, and structuration.

Substantively, the comparative interest in organization studies blends investigations of management and managing (i.e., as a set of administrative and executive practices; see, for instance, Delmestri and Walgenbach, 2005; Delmestri, Chapter 15), of organizations (i.e., as both loci of action and structural forms; see, e.g., Ahrne and Brunsson, Chapter 3), of organization and organizing (i.e., as the ideal model of rationalized administration; see Drori, Jang, and Meyer, 2006; Drori, Meyer, and Hwang, 2009), and of managerialism (i.e., as a professionalized administrative logic; see, e.g., Logue, Chapter 13). In this volume, tales from all such foci are gathered.

The Objective: Juncture

Drawing on the transcendental essence of glocalization, our objective here is to describe the complexity of global organization and management further. As noted in detail above, the potent concept of glocalization, recognizing the transcendental nature of social processes, has not been applied broadly to organization and management research. In addition, the growing field of comparative organization studies, while blooming with transcendental notions of translation or hybridity, has only just started to engage these with the study of global organization.

The diverse chapters in this volume bring together far separate lines of research. In the following section, we propose a scheme to integrate current discussions of global–local relations with the research agenda on organization and management.

Multi-dimensionality: The Main Axes of Glocalization

Recognizing the complexity inherent to the glocalization of organization and management, we present an analytical framework that conceptually outlines institutional patterns of sameness-cum-variation. Glocalization (in its broad sense as the duality of sameness and variation), we propose, involves various dimensions and concerns transcendence: (a) between the global and the local, i.e., across "vertically" nested categories; (b) within and between regions, sectors, fields, or organizations, i.e., across "horizontally" equivalent entities; and (c) over time when past ideas and practices imprint subsequent forms, i.e., across different points in time, or across historical eras. Our proposed scheme is therefore multi-dimensional, stretching along these three main axes: vertically across hierarchical levels; horizontally across equivalent entities; and over time.

The Vertical Axis

With its imagery of hierarchical relations between nested categories (so-called levels), the vertical axis is the one most frequently referred to. It is a taken-for-granted matter that globalization occurs through top-down and bottom-up processes between the distinct levels of global and local. Commonly, it is the global-to-local path, where universalized ideas and models diffuse to embedded entities, that is noted as the prime direction of flows and influence (e.g., Strang and Meyer, 1993; Guler, Guillén, and Macpherson, 2002; Walgenbach and Beck 2002; Brannen, 2004; Drori, Jang, and Meyer, 2006; Meyer and Höllerer, 2010). With the exception of a few who also elaborate on recursive effects (notably, in this volume, R.E. Meyer, Chapter 6; Djelic, Chapter 7; Strang, Chapter 8; Dörrenbächer, Becker-Ritterspach, Gammelgaard, and Geppert, Chapter 27), less attention has been given to the bottom-up processes that feed into universalized models (but see Djelic and Quack, 2003), or to the "boomerang" or "re-localization" trajectory of "global-to-local-and-back-to-global". Nevertheless, such bottom-up "rebound" similarly unfolds along the same vertical path.

Scholarly discussions on glocalization, in spite of their obvious challenge to prevailing dichotomies in the debate on globalization, have not abolished the imagery of levels, and of hierarchical and nested relations. Rather, the notion of glocalization, while essentially calling for the transcendence of the boundaries between these levels (Bartelson, 2000), also worked to reify the global, the local, and the tiered relations between them. This bias is addressed by such terms as "glonacal" (Marginson, 2004), highlighting the intervening national level (see also Frenkel, Chapter 10), or by the study of the role of regional agencies (e.g., Abu-Sharkh, Chapter 18).

The Horizontal Axis

In observing global–local patterns of sameness-cum-variation, one notes similar configurations across similar entities, meaning across the boundaries of such entities as regions, sectors, fields, or organizations. It is in this way that we also observe glocalization being manifested along a horizontal axis.

The diffusion of universalized ideas and models essentially entails the notion of equivalency of entities across cultural boundaries. This calls attention to the diverse translation processes that occur when ideas and models travel between divergent regions, sectors, fields, or organizations. For instance, Palmer and Dunford (2001) report that – to the extent that private firms and state-owned enterprises share a similar vision of their environment – both private and public sector organizations adopt the same set of innovation strategies; in a similar vein, Meyer and Hammerschmid (2006) observe that executives of public agencies increasingly replace their legalistic-bureaucratic identity with a managerial identity that mirrors private sector management practice. Learning and diffusion of ideas and models with regard to organization and management also occur cross-regionally, among nations, and across fields, populations, sectors, or industries. Examples here include processes of glocalization among national governments and administrations (e.g., Christensen, Chapter 12; Knill and Tosun, Chapter 19), or among higher education organizations (e.g., Logue, Chapter 13; Engwall, Chapter 17; Kodeih, Chapter 20).

The transcendence of regional, sectoral, field-level, or organizational boundaries through diffusion and related processes of adoption and adaptation is clearly facilitated by partnerships and networks of all kinds, as well as by the features and adoptive capacity of the local "receptor site" (Frank, Hironaka, and Schofer, 2000) and the degrees of fidelity and extensiveness in the relevant population (Ansari, Fiss, and Zajac, 2010). Among these, as Strang and Meyer (1993) argue, the principal driving mechanism is powerful theorization that envelops both the notions of universality and equivalency, thus only enabling emulation and diffusion.

The Temporal Axis

Principles of universality and equivalency can also be extended over time, allowing for transcendence and diffusion to occur across historical eras. The axis of time, while implicitly included in any process model, differentiates among historic eras and marks the relations of abstraction-equivalency-adoption (and -adaption) between such eras. Three definitions of time apply here. First, historical time describes the adoption and adaptation of era-specific concepts and "fashions" (for instance, the transformation of Taylorism into post-industrial models of human resource management). In this way, time plays into the process of defining (non-)variation. Second, since a process in the social sciences is by definition a timed sequence of acts, adoption and adaptation may themselves be sequenced. Indeed, as further discussed in the forthcoming chapters, variation in the degree of adaptation and implementation is evident between early- and late-adopters of a theorized idea, structure, or model (e.g., Jang, 2006; Ansari, Fiss, and Zajac, 2010). Third, time may be one of the dimensions by which modification occurs: in adopting and adapting universalized ideas and models, some locals impute a past-looking or future-looking translation. It is in this regard that path dependence also influences glocalization: much of the adaptation – and thus also much of glocalization – of organization and management is shaped by preceding forms, enduring arrangements, and their legacies.

Interlocking the Dimensions

Together, these three axes form the multiple paths of diffusion, adoption, and adaptation of universalized ideas and models. They somehow echo Robertson's (1994, 1995) definition of glocalization as the transcendence of time and space. Both vertical and horizontal axes, referring to levels and equivalent entities, shadow Robertson's notion of space, while the third axis obviously refers to Robertson's notion of time. It is along each of these three axes, and in the junctures between them, that processes of transcendence and co-constitution occur.

But how do ideas and models move across different levels, across entities on the same level, or over time? Strang and Meyer (1993), in their seminal paper, point to the crucial role of abstraction through theorization. Theorization, they argue, contributes to diffusion in several ways – "in accounts of adopters, in accounts of practices, and in diffusion mechanisms" (Strang and Meyer, 1993: 495). Commenting specifically on the global processes of diffusion, they state that "global theorization defocuses individual variability, assuming equivalences that are perceptively inaccurate given the local information" (Strang and Meyer, 1993: 500). As "a strategy for making sense of the world" (Strang and Meyer, 1993: 493), theorization also takes an ontological role in interpreting and then projecting – hence in constructing – social reality.

When explaining theorization as an essential component of diffusion, Strang and Meyer (1993) consider the role of experts as "legitimated theorists", the content of theorized constructs, and the issue of levels. In regard to the latter, they especially emphasize the impact of global models on local situations, meaning top-down influence. "[F]orms of 'bottom-up' theorizing," on the other hand, "should impact diffusion, but in rather local ways" (Strang and Meyer, 1993: 493); individual-specific theories or theories specific for a locality might affect the individual's adoption patterns or the adoption patterns of local inhabitants; they may homogenize actors involved, but not larger populations.

For ideas and models to move horizontally across regions, sectors, fields, or organizations, two prerequisites have to be met. First, equivalency needs to be constructed across the respective entities and established within the theorization of the idea or model. With this, the paths for adoption and adaptation open up. Second, theorized ideas and models must be translated and edited to fit with the local adoptive and enacting locale (e.g., Czarniawska and Joerges, 1996; Sahlin-Andersson, 1996; Brannen, 2004; Sahlin and Wedlin, 2008; see also R.E. Meyer, Chapter 6; Boxenbaum and Gond, Chapter 22).

Most importantly, the vertical, horizontal, and temporal axes intersect, thus compounding the impact of theorization, equivalency, and translation. Horizontal transference of ideas and models is bound to vertical transference: cross-region, cross-sector, cross-field, or cross-organization adoption and adaptation essentially require an understanding of equivalency across these entities – and such theorization generally occurs at the macro (i.e., global, or somehow more general) level. For example, adoption and adaptation across organizations may occur, "arching" through the field level, as in an industry; such arching may occur at the regional/national level, as in Europeanization (e.g., Knill and Tosun, Chapter 19); and arching can yet occur through the global sphere, as it does through the work of international organizations (e.g., Ahrne and Brunsson, Chapter 3; Abu-Sharkh, Chapter 18). Such interlocking of the vertical and horizontal axes further dissolves the boundedness of entities such as sectors, fields, and organizations. And it further problematizes the definition of global and local by suggesting that these are not fixed levels but are rather defined in relation to each other.

Specifying Glocalization as a Process

In their emphasis on diffusion, and in their focus on abstraction and equivalency, theorization and glocalization are similar. Indeed, theorization is the mechanism that enables glocalization. Still, theorization is only a part of the overall process: on the one hand, glocalization also involves translation – as does theorization – in order to adjust ideas, structures, and models to new and different social and cultural domains. In addition, theorization – as originally conceived – emphasizes top-down influence, whereas part of the dynamic nature of transcendental glocalization is a rebound effect and influence, where locally enacted ideas and models influence the globally theorized schemes bottom-up. Overall, glocalization creates dynamic, often oscillating, relations between global and local levels, among equivalent entities, and also among ideas and models of different eras.

We therefore detail the process of glocalization as encompassing four distinct phases: (a) *abstraction* through theorization (i.e., moving from an idea or model as a particular problem-solution to a typified problem-solution); (b) based on such abstraction, *construction of equivalency* across boundaries on a more macro level (or in other words: extrapolating similarity between entities or contexts); (c) adoption and *enactment* of the "globally" theorized idea or model through translation, adaptation, re-contextualization, or otherwise modification to fit the local context; and (d) *rebound* of the locally adapted and enacted ideas and models onto the theorized templates. Together, these four phases articulate the process of glocal diffusion, as it intersects vertical, horizontal, and temporal axes of variation and similarity.

Several stipulations bind this articulation of glocalization as a phased process. First, while abstraction occurs at a higher level than the theorized entity or category, there is no rigid specification of what these distinct levels are. Rather, abstraction may occur at various levels: what is "global" from one perspective might be "local" when observed from another perspective. For example, both an entire organizational field *and* the individual organization may be regarded as local contexts for the diffusion of globally established standards and norms, such as, for instance, international accounting standards or codes of good governance. Likewise, nation states are local in the context of, for example, theorization on a pan-European level – while simultaneously serving as the "global" context in which ideas and models are theorized, and then diffused, for public sector agencies within each national domain. Therefore, "global" and "local" are relative categories; and similarly, sectoral, organizational, and temporal boundaries are socially determined. Second, the recoiled feature of glocalization, where the localized rebounds to influence the globalized sphere, presupposes change as an integral component of the process of glocalization. Any idea, structure, or model is, therefore, potentially in a constant state of flux. Third, the combination of relative levels and fluid categories brings much flexibility to the world of organization and management. As a result, theorized and glocalized ideas and models do not necessarily emanate from the hegemon. The global diffusion of total quality management (TQM) exemplified the glocalization of a management tool that, while propelled further and legitimated by American management gurus, is regarded as Japanese in origin and cultural character. And therefore while some of TQM's core ideas were misaligned with individualist cultural orientations in Western societies (see, Strang, Chapter 8), other TQM ideas (namely statistical quality control) were developed in the US (where they have been applied in mass production) and imported after World War II to Europe and Japan, where they were adopted and transposed (Walgenbach, 2000). Thus, the example of TQM nicely illustrates the continuous rebounding of locally adapted and enacted ideas and models onto globally theorized templates.

Overall, the discussion of the three axes of glocalization extends Robertson's pioneering work in conversation with contemporary studies of global themes and local variations in the domain of organization and management. The contributions in this volume engage with both globalization scholarship and organization and management studies, by wrestling the tensions between homogeneity and heterogeneity, convergence and divergence, and global and local. Such engagement is of both conceptual (e.g., by relating to notions such as translation, contextualization and re-localization, bricolage, and, of course, glocalization) and empirical nature (e.g., by detailing case analyses of specific managerial practices or specific managerial groups). Methodologically, the aspiration to study organization and management globally is, as noted by Drori, Meyer, and Hwang (2009), quite ambitious. Indeed, a formal research strategy for a comparative and longitudinal study that also pays attention to the manifold axes of variation remains a target rather than a manageable outline for research. Nevertheless, the range of comparative studies and work featured in this volume is rich with strategies for empirical research: from a single case study (Djelic, Chapter 7) to case comparisons (e.g., Barbosa and Cabral-Cardoso, Chapter 11; Christensen, Chapter 12; Abu-Sharkh, Chapter 18; Knill and Tosun, Chapter 19; Kodeih, Chapter 20; Boxenbaum and Gond, Chapter 22; Malets and Quack, Chapter 23), from case history method (e.g., Carney, Chapter 16) to gathering and analyzing large amounts of numeric data (e.g., Engwall, Chapter 17; Hwang, Jang, and Park, Chapter 24), and from participatory (Sahlin, Chapter 4) to archival (e.g., Özen, Chapter 9; Logue, Chapter 13) to interview-based research strategies (e.g., Dörrenbächer, Becker-Ritterspach, Gammelgaard, and Geppert, Chapter 27), to mention just a few. In its analytic rigor, the work in this volume goes a long way in describing the glocalization of organization and management.

Describing Glocalization Through its Themes

Glocalization envelops multiple dimensions of variation: extending along the three distinct axes outlined above, it recognizes variation in the nature of diffusion mechanisms and processes (e.g., translation, embedding, and interpretation) and in the matter that is diffused (e.g., ideas, structures, or practices). This complexity obviously compounds the ambiguity associated with the phrase. With the aim of dissipating such vagueness, we build on a simple framework by which we configure glocalization for the purpose of this volume. The study of the glocalization of organization and management, we argue, invariably comprises three main elements of glocalization, which we label the "what", the "who", and the "how" of glocalization.

"What?": Glocalized Ideas, Structures, and Practices

A first element of glocalization refers to the ideas, structures, and practices that are glocalized – in other words, the model that diffuses on a global scale and gets translated, adapted, and enacted in local contexts. The "what" refers to the item that is glocal. Research compiled in this volume highlights ideas, structures, and practices that are as diverse as international standards (Ahrne and Brunsson, Chapter 3), rankings (Sahlin, Chapter 4), story telling (Czarniawska, Chapter 5), TQM (Strang, Chapter 8; Özen, Chapter 9), diversity management (Frenkel, Chapter 10; Barbosa and Cabral-Cardoso, Chapter 11), public sector reforms (Christensen, Chapter 12), management positions (Logue, Chapter 13), and life insurance (Chan, Chapter 14).

Such ideas, structures, and practices travel at different degrees of coherence: some are theorized to the point of being relatively tight bundles of meanings and practices; others, whose diffusion occurs through a copy-and-paste technique, are highly fragmented. Still, diffusion and especially isomorphism can occur only when they exceed a certain – even if undefined – threshold of theorization: prior to sufficient abstraction, by which typical features are identified and meanings are assigned, the item is not adequately defined or articulated. Yet, coherence does not equate similarity across contexts: while a certain coherence is inherent to the abstraction phase of glocalization, on the "tail end" of the glocalization process we accept variation as an inherent feature of re-contextualization, localization, and domestication, and as a probable outcome of translation and interpretive processes.

"Who?": Actors and Influences

The second element of glocalization refers to the advocates for, or carriers of, globally diffusing models. Such "agents of glocalization", be they individuals, organizations, or nation states, are understood to carry the institutional work that is involved in the glocalization-related processes of diffusion, translation, and advocacy (see also Lawrence and Suddaby, 2006). A special role among these agents is reserved for the experts and professionals whose hold on universalized knowledge, and through it on theorization, is key to glocalization – and, in particular, to the glocalization of organization and management (e.g., Greenwood, Suddaby, and Hinings, 2002). Research compiled in this volume highlights, for instance, the role of managers (Delmestri, Chapter 15), academia that credentials professionals (Engwall,

Chapter 17; Kodeih, Chapter 20), regional agencies (Abu-Sharkh, Chapter 18), supranational organizations and national administrations (Knill and Tosun, Chapter 19), and the media (Pallas and Wedlin, Chapter 21).

In emphasizing agency, several distinct foci for research emerge: first, taking an explicitly political perspective, in order to investigate power and the political allegiance that builds a path of influence; second, to address not only the role of individual actors but also relations among them, i.e., the specific constellations (or coalitions) of actors; and, third, in examining the context, in order to describe not only the hosts of global models, but also the source and reference cases in which globalized models are conceived and consolidated, and from which such models are adopted.

"How?": Processes and Mechanisms

The third element of glocalization refers to the nature of glocalization as a process. Such a standpoint calls for a thorough investigation of the very stages of the process: Czarniawska (Chapter 5) and R.E. Meyer (Chapter 6), for instance, highlight the sequence of de-contextualization, abstraction, and re-contextualization; Strang (Chapter 8) and J.W. Meyer (Chapter 29) emphasize theorization as a critical step. Process perspectives are to be differentiated between those that focus on change and agency, and those that focus on persistence, order, or reproduction. Obviously, time – historic era and process duration – serves as the main axis for such process perspectives, with change being an elementary principle.

The complexity of glocalization is evident in the broad variety of terms that are used to describe the nature of its underlying process. Research compiled in this volume conceives glocalization as (re-)localization or (re-)contextualization (R.E. Meyer, Chapter 6; Boxenbaum and Gond, Chapter 22), sedimentation and layering (Christensen, Chapter 12), or internationalization (Engwall, Chapter 17), and focuses on processes such as standardization (Ahrne and Brunsson, Chapter 3; Malets and Quack, Chapter 23; Hwang, Jang, and Park, Chapter 24) or regulatory processes (Engels and Knoll, Chapter 25; Jakobi, Chapter 26).

Glocalization as Interlocked Elements

Describing glocalization through the analytic framework of "what", "who", and "how" reveals how tightly interwoven these three elements are. Such tight interweaving shows that glocalization – and with it the diffusion of global ideas and models into various local contexts – is not merely a process of relocation, but rather such diffusion necessitates institutional work and praxis. In this regard, both coupling and inertia come into play. First, the glocal form is a loosely coupled or sediment form, where one model is attached to, or layered onto, another model, as evidenced in the co-occurrence of ideas and practices that come from different "worlds". In this sense, an organization in general appears glocal as it is an internal collage of global and local components. Second, discussions of the glocal as a recombinant form require a consideration of which components of which models get redeployed, are erased, persist, or trigger resistance. It is indeed a challenge to decipher why some parts of a system become abstracted and diffuse, whereas other parts of the same system remain rather local. The resulting glocal form need not bear any traces of contention or dysfunction, but rather the glocal reveals itself as maintaining local agency while also being current on global themes.

Gili S. Drori, Markus A. Höllerer, and Peter Walgenbach

Structure of this Edited Volume

Overall, and against the backdrop of the volume at hand, it is important to hold that the breakdown of glocalization into these three discrete elements – the "what", the "who", and the "how" – is for the sake of analytic distinction only. Empirical studies commonly bring together these three, even if one element is accentuated over the other.

The contributions to this volume originate from fields and communities of research in organization studies that all share a common interest in the glocalization of organization and management. Many of the authors touch upon broad issues in this scholarly domain (such as, for instance, global governance, universal management concepts, or the nature of management knowledge in various fora). With that, the various chapters build towards the main theme of this volume, examining a particular dimension of organizational or managerial activity, analyzing particular factors that describe the observed patterns, and relating their insights to the core concepts and discussions of the field.

For an overview of the book, we would like to suggest an analytical grid that places individual research as it addresses both the three axes/dimensions of glocalization and the three constituting elements/themes, as described in Table 1.1. The studies included in this volume exemplify the cells in this 3 × 3 matrix, even if most studies transcend these analytic categories in order to describe and comment on the various dimensions of the process of glocal diffusion of organization and management.

The structure of the volume at hand broadly follows this analytical grid. In the introductory chapter, we presented the overall motivation for this volume: the need to deepen and broaden our understanding of the essential dimensions, elements, and mechanisms of glocalization. Following this articulation of the challenge of intersecting glocalization research with organization and management studies, Roland Robertson (Chapter 2) spearheads the list of contributors with his comprehensive overview and evaluation of more than three decades of

Table 1.1 The glocalization of organization and management: an analytical grid

Conceptual focus of research on glocalization	"What?" Glocalized ideas, structures, and practices	"Who?" Actors and influences	"How?" Processes and mechanisms
Vertical axis – across nested categories (i.e., levels)			
Horizontal axis – across equivalent entities			
Temporal axis – across time and historical eras			

academic writing on glocalization. Part II, then, revisits glocalization from various conceptual perspectives, carving out core topics and challenges for research. Part III through Part V explore glocalized ideas, structures, and practices; actors and influences; and the process of glocalization. Finally, in Part VI, John W. Meyer (Chapter 29) shares his thoughts and impressions upon reading the individual chapters, and draws insightful conclusions from this broad range of cutting-edge research in the field of glocalization.

It is for editorial reasons that the chapters in this volume include only brief methodological explanations. However, their solid foundation in empirical research allows for comprehensive study and rich commentaries on the "glocalized", the "glocalizers", and the very process of glocalization.

Revisiting Glocalization

The collection of papers in this part of the volume all contain theoretical-conceptual considerations aiming at a better understanding of the phenomenon of glocalization. While taking stock and outlining the current research agenda in the field, they do, however – as most other papers in this volume – address one or more of the constituting elements of glocalization outlined above as well.

Göran Ahrne and Nils Brunsson (Chapter 3) highlight the ongoing global organization in the form of partial organization and meta-organizations. Partial organization, such as international standards, rankings and rating systems, and international meta-organizations, such as the European Union, the International Association of Universities, or the International Chamber of Commerce, Ahrne and Brunsson state, offer fruitful compromises between a local and a global order. The authors go beyond studying the diffusion and translation of ideas among organizations, and shed light on two alternative routes to glocalization.

Kerstin Sahlin (Chapter 4) focuses on university rankings. Recently, university rankings have multiplied, expanded in order to assess more aspects of university performance, and moved into the very heart of academic governance systems. Universities have responded to these developments with extensive organizing efforts. Sahlin argues that, in combination with nationally driven reforms, these recent changes have resulted in a global academic landscape conceptualized as a market, and characterized by intensified rationalization and homogenization. These developments give rise to institutional ambiguity, which turns out to be an important source of local variation within a global theme.

Barbara Czarniawska (Chapter 5) looks at globalization as a process of "translocalization", i.e., as the spread of local practices, ideas, customs, and technologies all over the globe with the supporting mechanism of translation. However, she then asks: "What happens if translation stops? Why can translation not reach a certain locality, even though it concerns an idea that is traveling globally?" Czarniawska focuses on storytelling – a fashionable management technique that is applied in most Scandinavian organizations, with the exception of Swedish organizations. She thus presents a case where full glocalization does not happen, and offers speculations as to why the repeated attempts of management consultants to embed storytelling in the Swedish context seem to have had no effect.

Renate E. Meyer, in Chapter 6, emphasizes that although diffusing ideas, structures, and practices are shaped and determined by broader global models, they nonetheless have to gain legitimacy on the local level before potential adopters can actually implement and enact them. Usually, the diffusing models and their theorizations are substantially altered in the processes underpinning glocalization. Meyer focuses on mechanisms of discursive micro-mobilization and examines a variety of accounts that actors use to align with locally existing values and beliefs. For illustrative purpose, she uses the example of translation of shareholder value "into Austrian".

According to Marie-Laure Djelic (Chapter 7), globalization is always localized, but the local also becomes inscribed in global dynamics. Empirically, she focuses on the regulation of competition and a transnational region that research in our discipline has so far largely neglected: Africa. The notion of competition, and the concepts and tools associated with the regulation of competition, have entered this region only recently, as Djelic puts it, as foreign objects coming from the global/transnational "galaxy." In her chapter, she explores the ways in which the global interacts with different nationals/locals, in particular through the structuring mediation of regional initiatives. Her study well illustrates the interconnectedness of different levels of glocalization that we outlined above.

Ideas, Structures, and Practices

Several chapters of this volume make their core contribution by exploring, in particular, the nature of the very ideas, structures, and practices – i.e., the universalized models – that are glocalized, as well as by examining the local outcomes of the glocalization process. However, these insights entail important implications for other constituting elements of glocalization.

David Strang (Chapter 8) focuses on the widespread managerial strategy of TQM and traces its adoption by various branches of an American-headquartered multinational bank. The practice of TQM and its global diffusion have received much attention also by others (e.g., Westphal, Gulati, and Shortell, 1997; Walgenbach, 2000; Kennedy and Fiss, 2009), chiefly due to its origination in Japan; these non-Western roots challenge Strang to explain why a Manhattan-based bank would promulgate managerial practices so ill-suited to American social psychology. The explanation offered reveals that contrary to expectations of a liability of foreignness, TQM was utilized most vigorously in peripherally located businesses, thus the pattern of global diffusion is robustly linked to national culture. Strang situates the American quality movement within a broader pattern of borrowing from Japan and then considers how Japanese practices were translated for an American audience.

Şükrü Özen (Chapter 9) compares the rhetorical strategies used to legitimate TQM and multidivisional form in the United States with those used to legitimate TQM and holding structures in Turkey. He not only focuses on two important ideas in the field of organization and management, but also addresses the very process of glocalization. Findings indicate that the rhetorical strategies for foreign practices contain more ethos and pathos and less logos justifications than those for indigenous practices. Also, Özen shows that rhetorical strategies contain more ethos and pathos and less logos appeals in Turkey compared with the United States. The author traces the rhetorical strategies back to variations in the diffusion processes of foreign and indigenous practices, and to differences between the political economies of the two countries.

Michal Frenkel (Chapter 10) analyzes "gender contracts" in Israeli companies, showing that work–family arrangements (such as parental leave or flexible work arrangements) are negotiated among the state, organizations, and individuals. This case study challenges the binary distinction between "global" and "local" that is implicit in glocalization discussions by calling attention to the multiplicity of sites in which such encounters between local and international agents and ideas occur. Frenkel introduces the notion of "multi-layered glocalization", and examines how states, organizations, and individuals independently incorporate, hibernate, and translate global trends in their conceptualization of gender relations, and how they reconstruct new gender contracts at the intersections between the different layers of global influence.

Iris Barbosa and Carlos Cabral-Cardoso (Chapter 11) examine the way diversity is perceived and managed in affiliates of international companies that are located in Portugal – i.e., in a context with so far only limited sensitivity to diversity issues. The authors describe two distinct responses to outside pressures: when perceiving coercive pressure from headquarters but limited relevance of diversity issues to the local context, affiliates seem to be more prompt in developing a superficial, decoupled, and locally unadjusted adoption of the parental discourse and practices; when parental mimetic mechanisms gain relevance, affiliates appear to be more willing to develop a "glocal" version of the headquarters' diversity strategy, and increasingly couple discourse and practices.

Tom Christensen (Chapter 12) uses a comparative perspective to discuss the concepts of complexity, hybridity, and layering in public sector reform processes, and relates them to the notion of glocalization. Christensen explores examples, effects, and outcomes of hybridity and layering in countries with different political-administrative systems; his empirical evidence is primarily taken from comparative works on public sector reforms in New Zealand, Australia, China, and Norway.

In Chapter 13, Danielle M. Logue explores the diffusion of key leadership positions in universities throughout the last century. The author shows that, on the one hand, overall changes in such positions provide evidence of a wave of managerialism washing over universities; on the other hand, when disaggregated to a more local level, a considerable amount of variation remains. Logue examines the universalizing and particularizing tendencies of glocalization tracing, for an impressive empirical sample, both the adoption and abandonment of organizational practices. Revealing patterns with regard to the presence or absence of key leadership positions, her research provides insights into the scale, nature, and translation of managerialism within the global population of universities.

Localization is the process by which practices and concepts are modified according to the specific conditions of the locale. Cheris Shun-ching Chan (Chapter 14) aims at further decoding what "local" exactly means. Her key argument is that localization is a relative concept that is highly dependent on how local is defined: differences in the delineation of what counts as local, she argues, result in different conclusions about the extent and the form of localization. Empirically, she compares the localization strategies of two transnational life insurance firms in China. Chan adds to the literature on glocalization by demonstrating that practices by transnational firms require relatively little effort to appear localized in specific locales, depending on the extent to which they have gone through multiple levels of localization.

Actors and Influences

The following contributions to the volume primarily focus on the "who", i.e., the advocates for, or carriers of, the ideas, structures, and practices that are glocalized.

"Cosmopolitans, harlequins, or Frankensteins? Managers enacting local, global, and glocal identities" – Giuseppe Delmestri aims at answering this provocative question that is an element of the title of Chapter 15. Focusing on managers as important actors in the process of glocalization, he suggests that considering the global and local identifications of managers is not sufficient to understand the blending of global and local into glocal modes of management. He proposes a tripartite model that considers the identification with the values of world society, the identification with the native local culture, and the acceptance for, and adaptability to, other local cultures.

Michael Carney (Chapter 16) investigates the glocalized form of Asia's family-controlled business groups (FBGs) that adopt Western corporate practices while maintaining the traditional personal-rule authority structure. The persistence of personal-rule through industrialization and globalization of Asia's large conglomerates, explains Carney, results in a hybrid of Eastern (personal-rule authority) and Western (professional management or multi-divisional structure) organization. With that, Carney paints a nuanced picture of glocalization: as property rights are well-protected in Asia, FBGs have adopted an array of practices emanating from the West, but do not imitate Western forms of corporate governance.

Lars Engwall (Chapter 17) draws attention to the sort of training that managers receive, thus analyzing the glocal nature of business school programs. By investigating program ranking, publication targets, research orientation, and the composition of student and faculty bodies, Engwall reveals that while rhetoric associated with global competitiveness and internationalization is prime among business educators, few are the kind of business school that is truly global in terms of student body and faculty. Rather, business studies are glocal in character: they are embedded in local labor markets but are influenced through globally distributed textbooks and teaching materials. As the template for the rest of the world, the US programs appear particularly limited in their globalization.

Miriam Abu-Sharkh (Chapter 18) traces the influence of international and Latin American organizations on the discourse and legal practice of gender rights in Peru. Through the examination of four key gender issues (labor market discrimination, political representation, violence against women, and reproductive rights), Abu-Sharkh shows that the more institutionalized a women's issue is at the global level, the more isomorphic it becomes across Peru. Still, a major role in this translation is reserved to the Organization of American States (OAS), whose influence on women's rights issues is felt both in the capital Lima and in remote Amazonian regions.

Christoph Knill and Jale Tosun (Chapter 19) explore how international pressures affect institutional arrangements at national level. Their research is based on a model that relates nation states on the local level to an overarching entity (i.e., the European Union [EU]) on the global level. Knill and Tosun ask to what extent the EU has induced events of institutional change in the new member states, the Czech Republic and Poland, analyzing the tensions between tendencies toward harmonization on the one hand, and national variation on the other. Their empirical findings reveal that institutional change has taken place in both local contexts, even in constellations in which the theoretical literature tends to predict stability. The authors argue that taking into account local conditions for institutional change will help to better understand the more general logic of glocalization.

In Chapter 20, Farah Kodeih examines how French Grandes Ecoles de Commerce (FGECs) came under pressure to adapt to the growing internationalization of business education and to adopt increasingly dominant global standards. While attempting to redefine themselves as international business schools, FGECs continue to value their historical identity – which still forms the basis of their local legitimacy in France. Based on a comparative and longitudinal approach, Kodeih illustrates how the identities of four FGECs have been impacted and hybridized as a result of simultaneously responding to both local and global pressures.

Josef Pallas and Linda Wedlin (Chapter 21) call attention to the media as an arena of translation and to the mediatized form as a mode of organization. Analyzing the media ranking of academic institutions, Pallas and Wedlin present such ranking as a global model of academic governance. This mediatized practice entails three forms of translation processes: simplification, standardization, and popularization. These forms of translation have implications not only for the stakeholders' perceptions of universities, and for what ideals and aspirations are incorporated into university governance, but also for the way we understand the processes in which glocalization takes place.

Processes and Mechanisms

Next, a range of authors explicitly addresses individual mechanisms and processes of glocalization.

In Chapter 22, Eva Boxenbaum and Jean-Pascal Gond examine how individuals contextualize global concepts and business practices in order to fit the local setting in which they are implemented. The authors expound on three micro-strategies of contextualization – filtering, reframing, and bricolage – and illustrate how entrepreneurial individuals utilize these to adapt the notion of responsible investment (RI) to local contexts in France and Quebec. Boxenbaum and Gond empirically show that such efforts can result in different glocalized versions of an idea or practice. With its focus on micro-strategies of contextualization, this chapter advances current insights into the process of glocalization.

Olga Malets and Sigrid Quack (Chapter 23) explain why and how a set of global ideas of stakeholder/constituency participation, inclusiveness, and fair representation is built into transnational standard-setting organizations' structures and procedures. The authors not only show that this does not occur in one single manner across various governance fields, but also identify two trajectories along which transnational governance fields emerge and develop: monopolistic and pluralistic. Two case studies are used to demonstrate how three sets of factors – initial organizational design, challenges and contestation, and organizational responsiveness – shape these trajectories.

Hokyu Hwang, Yong Suk Jang, and Ki Tae Park (Chapter 24) utilize a longitudinal dataset on the largest 300 Korean corporations between 1992 and 2006 to analyze different factors that facilitated the spread of ISO 9001. The authors find that the process of diffusion, in the early period, exhibits familiar institutional processes. After a critical event (i.e., the Asian financial crisis of 1997), driving forces within this process shift, and functional necessities and economic efficiency become the primary motivation for the adoption of the global standard.

Beyond doubt, carbon trading is a globalized management topic. The price of carbon is regarded as a global signal based on which companies in various local contexts develop carbon management strategies. However, as Anita Engels and Lisa Knoll (Chapter 25) state, the diffusion of market-based policy instruments to govern the earth's atmosphere lacks a clear guiding orientation for organizations. Based on case studies, the authors provide insights into the complex and sometimes contradictory processes through which employees in organizations struggle for orientation and rationalization in the institutional "universe" of carbon management. They suggest that the local negotiations over legitimate forms of carbon management are the key processes through which this practice becomes manageable and through which the dominant mode of global environmental governance is localized.

Anja P. Jakobi (Chapter 26) points to the importance of the United States and the Financial Action Taskforce (FATF) in institutionalizing, diffusing, and enforcing the global managerial idea of anti-money laundering. In specifying anti-money laundering regulations, these agencies set global standards of proper governance. Furthermore, in building a global network of financial monitors, which also includes national Financial Intelligence Units fostered worldwide by FATF, these agencies further reinforce the legitimacy and enforceability of these standards of proper governance worldwide, even if these standards originate mainly from a US effort to internationalize its national regulations.

Christoph Dörrenbächer, Florian Becker-Ritterspach, Jens Gammelgaard, and Mike Geppert (Chapter 27) focus on the instruments and tactics that subsidiaries and their key managers use to integrate local initiatives within the global strategy-making processes that take place in a multinational company (MNC). In their study, they show that overall strategies of MNCs – whether they are global, local, or glocal – are negotiated constructs of headquarters' will and subsidiaries' issue-selling tactics and bargaining power. The authors illustrate the bottom-up process that builds the universalized models that are thought to be globally enacted.

Pertti Alasuutari (Chapter 28) analyzes the government's cultural activities development project in Finnish cities, which unifies the accounting system for city culture policy. While the project report described the initiative in cosmopolitan terms, reports of this initiative in local newspapers highlighted concerns of the local community. This results in the emphasizing of local anxieties and the forming of a sense of "banal localism", which while expressing the unique lived experience of local community members, also conceals the similarity of concerns and of initiatives taken locally in response to global policy trends.

Concluding Remarks

John W. Meyer (Chapter 29) concludes – based on his reading of the individual chapters – with insightful thoughts on the overall theme of glocalization of organization and management. Meyer highlights the importance of rationalization, professionalization, and actorhood in explaining the worldwide layout of organization, or of formal organizations and their management. He argues that both conformity with global models of organization and variation in organization are shaped by the rapidly expanding world polity: the glocal is a mode of authority that draws from global models and empowers locals (who are themselves constructed as agents). In such glocalization, the role of professionals, who hold the authority for theorization, is of prime importance. Meyer's commentary boldly wraps discussions of the glocalization of management and organization with world society theory.

In summary, this volume takes advantage of the potency of the term glocalization, which envelops the dual – and presumably contradictory – notions of commonality and variation (Robertson, 1994, 1995). The focus on organization and management, which are among the most universalistic and scientized of globally diffusing themes, allows for particularly insightful analyses of the dual tendencies of globalization, namely global models that also diffuse worldwide by their refraction through local prisms. In this emphasis on the duality that is inherent to the notion of glocalization, the work in this volume marries two important traditions of scholarship in our field: organization and management studies, and globalization research.

References

Aguilera, R.V., and Cuervo-Cazurra, A. (2004). 'Codes of good governance worldwide: what is the trigger?' *Organization Studies*, 25: 415–443.

Aguilera, R.V., and Jackson, G. (2010). 'Comparative and international corporate governance'. *Academy of Management Annals*, 4: 485–556.

Albuquerque, P., Bronnenberg, B.J., and Corbett, C.J. (2007). 'A spatiotemporal analysis of the global diffusion of ISO 9000 and ISO 14000 certification'. *Management Science*, 53: 451–468.

Alcadipani, R., and Rosa, A.R. (2011). 'From grobal management to glocal management: Latin American perspectives as a counter-dominant management epistemology'. *Canadian Journal of Administrative Sciences*, 28: 453–466.

Ansari, S.M., Fiss, P.C., and Zajac, E.J. (2010). 'Made to fit: how practices vary as they diffuse'. *Academy of Management Review*, 35: 67–92.

Appadurai, A. (1990). 'Disjuncture and difference in the global cultural economy'. *Public Culture*, 2: 1–23.

Auyero, J. (2001). 'Glocal riots'. *International Sociology*, 16: 33–54.
Bartelson, J. (2000). 'Three concepts of globalization'. *International Sociology*, 15: 180–196.
Beck, N., Kabst, R., and Walgenbach, P. (2009). 'The cultural dependence of vocational training'. *Journal of International Business Studies*, 40: 1374–1395.
Beck, U. (2000). *What is globalization?* Cambridge: Polity Press.
Brand, K.W. (1999). 'Dialectics of institutionalisation: the transformation of the environmental movement in Germany'. *Environmental Politics*, 81: 35–58.
Brannen, M.Y. (2004). 'When Mickey loses face: recontextualization, semantic fit and the semiotics of foreignness'. *Academy of Management Review*, 29: 583–616.
Courchene, T.J. (1995). 'Glocalization: the regional/international interface'. *Canadian Journal of Regional Studies*, 18: 1–20.
Czarniawska, B., and Joerges, B. (1996). 'Travel of ideas', in: B. Czarniawska, and G. Sevón (eds), *Translating organizational change*. Berlin: de Gruyter, 13–48.
Delmestri, G., and Walgenbach, P. (2005). 'Mastering techniques or brokering knowledge? Middle managers in Germany, Great Britain and Italy'. *Organization Studies*, 26: 197–220.
Delmestri, G., and Walgenbach, P. (2009). 'Interference among institutions and technical-economic conditions: the adoption of the assessment center in French, German, Italian, UK, and US-American multinational firms'. *International Journal of Human Resource Management*, 20: 885–911.
DiMaggio, P.J., and Powell, W.W. (1983). 'The iron cage revisited: institutional isomorphism and collective rationality in organizational fields'. *American Sociological Review*, 48, 147–160.
Djelic, M.-L. (1998). *Exporting the American model: the postwar transformation of European business*. Oxford: Oxford University Press.
Djelic, M.-L., and Quack, S. (eds) (2003). *Globalization and institutions: redefining the rules of the economic game*. Cheltenham: Edward Elgar.
Djelic, M.-L., and Sahlin-Andersson, K. (eds) (2006). *Transnational governance: institutional dynamics of regulation*. Cambridge: Cambridge University Press.
Drori, G.S., Jang, Y.S., and Meyer, J.W. (2006). 'Sources of rationalized governance: cross-national longitudinal analyses, 1985–2002'. *Administrative Science Quarterly*, 51: 205–229.
Drori, G.S., Meyer, J.W., and Hwang, H. (2009). 'Global organization: Rationalization and actorhood as dominant scripts', in: R. Meyer, K. Sahlin, M. Ventresca, and P. Walgenbach (eds), *Research in the sociology of organizations: ideology and institutions*, 27: 17–43.
Drucker, P. (1989). 'What business can learn from nonprofits'. *Harvard Business Review*, 67: 88–94.
Eriksen, T.H. (2003). 'Creolization and creativity'. *Global Networks*, 3: 223–237.
Florida, R. (2005). 'The world is spiky'. *The Atlantic*, 296: 48–51.
Frank, D.J., Hironaka, A., and Schofer, E. (2000). 'The nation-state and the natural environment over the twentieth century'. *American Sociological Review*, 65: 96–116.
Frenkel, M., and Shenhav, Y. (2006). 'From binarism back to hybridity: a postcolonial reading of management and organization studies'. *Organization Studies*, 27: 855–876.
Friedman, T.L. (2005). *The world is flat: a brief history of the twenty-first century*. New York: Farrar, Straus and Giroux.
Giulianotti, R., and Robertson, R. (2007). 'Forms of glocalization: globalization and migration strategies of Scottish football fans in North America'. *Sociology*, 41: 133–152.
Greenwood, R., Suddaby, R., and Hinings, C.R. (2002). 'Theorizing change: the role of professional associations in the transformation of institutionalized fields'. *Academy of Management Journal*, 45, 58–80.
Guler, I., Guillén, M.F., and Macpherson, J.M. (2002). 'Global competition, institutions, and the diffusion of organizational practices: the international spread of ISO 9000 quality certificates'. *Administrative Science Quarterly*, 47: 207–232.
Hannerz, U. (1989). 'Notes on the global ecumene.' *Public Culture*, 12: 66–75.
Hannerz, U. (1996). *Transnational connections*. London: Routledge.
Haxhi, I., and van Ees, H. (2010). 'Explaining diversity in the worldwide diffusion of codes of good governance'. *Journal of International Business Studies*, 41: 710–726.

Ibarro-Colado, E. (2011). 'Organization studies and epistemic coloniality in Latin America: thinking otherness from the margins'. *Organization*, 13: 463–488.

Jang, Y.S. (2006). 'Transparent accounting as a world societal rule', in: G.S. Drori, J.W. Meyer, and H. Hwang (eds), *Globalization and organization: world society and organizational change*. Oxford: Oxford University Press, 167–195.

Kennedy, M.T., and Fiss, P.C. (2009). 'Institutionalization, framing, and diffusion: the logic of TQM adoption and implementation decisions among US hospitals'. *Academy of Management Journal*, 52: 897–918.

Kipping, M., Üsdiken, B., and Puig, N. (2004). 'Imitation, tension, and hybridization: multiple "Americanizations" of management education in Mediterranean Europe'. *Journal of Management Inquiry*, 13: 98–108.

Kostova, T., Roth, K., and Dacin, T. (2008). 'Institutional theory in the study of MNCs: a critique and new directions'. *Academy of Management Review*, 33: 994–1007.

Latour, B. (1996). *Aramis, or the love of technology*. Cambridge: Harvard University Press.

Lawrence, T.B., and Suddaby, R. (2006). 'Institutions and institutional work', in: S. Clegg, C. Hardy, W.R. Nord, and T. Lawrence (eds), *Handbook of organization studies*. 2nd edn, London: Sage, 215–254.

Lull, J. (2000). *Media, communication, culture: a global approach*. 2nd edn, Cambridge: Polity Press.

Marginson, S. (2004). 'Competition and markets in higher education: a "glonacal" analysis'. *Policy Futures in Education*, 2: 175–244.

Meyer, R.E., and Boxenbaum, E. (2010). 'Exploring European-ness in organization research'. *Organization Studies*, 31: 737–755.

Meyer, R.E., and Hammerschmid, G. (2006). 'Changing institutional logics and executive identities: a managerial challenge to public administration in Austria'. *American Behavioral Scientist*, 49: 1000–1014.

Meyer, R.E., and Höllerer, M.A. (2010). 'Meaning structures in a contested issue field: a topographic map of shareholder value in Austria'. *Academy of Management Journal*, 53: 1241–1262.

Palmer, I., and Dunford, R. (2001). 'The diffusion of managerial innovations: a comparison of Australian public and private sector take-up rates of new organizational practices'. *International Public Management Journal*, 4: 49–64.

Pieterse, J.N. (1994). 'Globalization as hybridization'. *International Sociology*, 9: 161–184.

Ritzer, G. (2003). 'Rethinking globalization: glocalization/grobalization and something/nothing'. *Sociological Theory*, 21: 193–209.

Robertson, R. (1994). 'Globalisation or glocalisation?' *Journal of International Communication*, 1: 33–52.

Robertson, R. (1995). 'Glocalization: time-space and homogeneity-heterogeneity', in: M. Featherstone, S. Lash, and R. Robertson (eds), *Global modernities*. London: Sage, 25–44.

Robertson, R., and Khondker, H.H. (1998). 'Discourses of globalization: preliminary considerations'. *International Sociology*, 13: 25–40.

Roudometof, V. (2005). 'Transnationalism, cosmopolitanism and glocalization'. *Current Sociology*, 53: 113–135.

Sahlin-Andersson, K. (1996). 'Imitating by editing success: the construction of organizational fields', in: B. Czarniawska, and G. Sevón (eds), *Translating organizational change*. Berlin: de Gruyter, 69–92.

Sahlin-Andersson, K., and Engwall, L. (2002). 'Carriers, flows, and sources of management knowledge', in: K. Sahlin-Andersson, and L. Engwall (eds), *The expansion of management knowledge: carriers, flows, and sources*. Stanford: Stanford Business Books, 3–32.

Sahlin, K., and Wedlin, L. (2008). 'Circulating ideas: imitation, translation and editing', in: R. Greenwood, C. Oliver, K. Sahlin, and R. Suddaby (eds), *The SAGE handbook of organizational institutionalism*. Los Angeles: Sage, 218–242.

Sassen, S. (2006). *Territory, authority, rights: from medieval to global assemblages*. Princeton: Princeton University Press.

Srinivas, N. (2011). 'Epistemic and performative quests for authentic management in India'. *Organization*, 19: 145–158.

Strang, D., and Meyer, J.W. (1993). 'Institutional conditions for diffusion'. *Theory and Society*, 22: 487–511.

Tempel, A., and Walgenbach, P. (2007). 'Global standardization of organizational forms and management practices? What new institutionalism and the business-systems approach can learn from each other'. *Journal of Management Studies*, 44: 1–24.

Tomlinson, J. (1993). *Globalization and culture*. Chicago: University of Chicago Press.

Ul-Haq, S., and Westwood, R. (2011). 'The politics of knowledge, epistemological occlusion and Islamic management and organization knowledge'. *Organization*, 19: 229–257.

Üsdiken, B. (2010). 'Between contending perspectives and logics: organization studies in Europe'. *Organization Studies*, 31: 715–735.

Vogel, D. (2008). 'Private global business regulation'. *Annual Review of Political Science*, 11: 261–282.

Walgenbach, P. (2000). Die normgerechte Organisation. Stuttgart: Schäffer-Poeschel.

Walgenbach, P., and Beck, N. (2002). 'The institutionalization of the quality management approach in Germany', in: K. Sahlin-Andersson, and L. Engwall (eds), *The expansion of management knowledge: carriers, flows, and sources*. Stanford: Stanford Business Books, 145–174.

Westphal, J.D., Gulati, R., and Shortell, S.M. (1997). 'Customization or conformity? An institutional and network perspective on the content and consequences of TQM adoption'. *Administrative Science Quarterly*, 42: 366–394.

2
Situating Glocalization
A Relatively Autobiographical Intervention

Roland Robertson

Globalization, paradoxically, has led to a strengthening of local ties, allegiances, and identity politics within different nation-state formations, even though what may emerge is what Stuart Hall calls that more 'tricky version' of 'the local' which operates within, and has been thoroughly reshaped by 'the global' and operates largely within its logic.

(Wilson and Dissanayake 1996: 5)

(G)lobalization makes national boundaries porous as people, goods and signs move from one part of the world to another with greater velocity and ubiquity… In the process, categories of the local and the global, which previously appeared to be distinct, now become increasingly interwoven and reproduce each other.

(Ray and Srinivas 2012: 5)

Coffeehouses can recreate and symbolize the global influence of Western coffee culture while expressing the uniqueness of a specific locale or cultural context. The coffee shop I patronize in Guatamala City created an atmosphere reminiscent of a Starbucks, but used ceramic mugs more than paper cups, and featured photos with themes of rural Guatamala and Mayan peoples in coffee fields. The combination acknowledged global coffee culture and Guatamalan coffee traditions at once.

(Tucker 2011: 9)

[U]nder the vast expansion of global capitalism and its accelerating volatility, culture has now become the contested focus of complex economic and political transformations. These shifts irrevocably alter the culture concept as anthropologists have used it in the past, and in less complex contexts.

(Weiner 1995: 18)

Introduction

It would probably be most fruitful to begin with a small number of empirical examples of the subject in hand, a number of which do not specifically invoke the concept of glocalization:

Dance (Savigliano 1995 on Tango; Wulff 1998 on ballet); Food and beverages (Ray and Srinivas 2012 on curry; Ritzer 1993; 2002 on fast food restaurants; Tucker 2011 on coffee; Warde 2000 on ethnic food; Watson 1997 on fast food restaurants); Exhibitions, festivals, and theme parks (Hendry 2000; Moeran and Pedersen 2012); Art genres (Howard 1996 on painting); Music (Inglis and Robertson 2005); Academic disciplines (Barth, Gingrich, Parkin, and Silverman 2005 on anthropology; Robertson 1992: 32–48 on sociocultural theory); Medicine (Payer 1996); Migration (Morawska 2011); and Sports (Giulianotti and Robertson 2007, on soccer). Other substantive areas to which the idea of glocalization has been applied, implicitly or explicitly, include language, beauty, translation, tourism, map-making, and management. However, my general claim is much more inclusive. In fact, I want to argue that disciplinarity has blinkered our eyes to much of what is now addressed under the heading of *glocalization*. In that sense, what follows constitutes an attempt to become truly transdisciplinary and, as part of this endeavor, to coordinate much of the recent work of sociologists, geographers, anthropologists, cultural studies specialists, and other conventionally labelled 'disciplinarians.' More succinctly, I will maintain that glocalization and the associated concept of *glocality* are the most appropriate ways of comprehending life on Planet Earth and beyond.

The concept and theme of glocalization developed primarily out of the widespread concern with globalization that gained great political and academic force during the 1980s and 1990s (Franklin, Lury, and Stacey 2000a; Robertson 1992: 54, 173–174; Ruijter 2001). For the most part, the discourse of globalization was centered upon economic policies; policies that stressed the necessity for deregulation, privatization, free trade, and marketization. Indeed, much business, economic, and political discourse up to the present still has these characteristics and has long been known as neoliberalism (Harvey 2005; Steger and Roy 2010). Much of this approach to globalization was characterised by its emphasis on homogenization—more specifically, the thesis concerning global Americanization. Nevertheless, since the early 1980s, a slightly less conspicuous and more academic discourse of globalization has been emerging. This stressed the multidimensionality of that phenomenon, expanding the discourse so as to include social and cultural factors. The inclusion of the latter dimensions—particularly the cultural (Robertson 1992; Robertson and Chirico 1985)—turned out to be a major opening to the increasing use of the term *glocalization*. This chapter is a further elaboration upon my previous lengthy contributions to this subject (Robertson 1995a; Robertson and White 2004). I was among those who strongly advocated the expansion of the study of globalization and the latter's use as a symbol of new political and economic policies.

It is necessary here to remark that the topic of glocalization has received a significant amount of attention in a clearly cross-disciplinary manner in Italy. In this respect, Italy is rather unique. The Association Globus et Locus (AGL) was apparently established in 1997 in Milan, and its present officials claim that it arose because of the deepening problems arising from glocalization, a word which they explicitly used. Much more recently, the AGL has been involved in the establishment of an on-line journal devoted to this very topic—again in a cross-disciplinary—or better, transdisciplinary—mode.

In speaking of multidimensionality, it is the cultural facet that should be given special, but not exclusive, emphasis. This is due to the fact that much of the discussion of glocalization involves relating the cultural to the economic. Bielby and Harrington (2008) have, in fact, directly addressed the issue of the connection between cultural sociology and organizational sociology. More generally, the interpenetration of the cultural and the economic is a hallmark of the current transdisciplinary study of globalization. Moreover, but surprisingly to many, it is the functioning of late-twentieth century capitalism(s) that has heightened the interest in, and visibility of, culture in general (Franklin, Lury, and Stacey 2000a). This constitutes a major theme of the present contribution. Put simply, modern capitalism in all of its forms has involved increasing sensitivity to the variety of cultures and culture in general, including the concept of world culture (Krücken and Drori 2009; Lechner and Boli 2005). At the same time, capitalism has promoted and facilitated vested interests in the advocacy of cultural difference. In short, the connection between the economic and the cultural has become of pivotal significance in the world as a whole, not to speak of everyday life at the so-called micro level. It should be noted, en passant, that the old Marxist conception of the economic base determining the cultural superstructure is hereby being undone. In fact, this culture-promoting outcome of contemporary capitalism may well be leading to its thorough transformation.

For the most part, the political-economic conception of globalization has more than a temporal tinge, whereas the concept of glocalization has a very definite spatial thrust. It is on the basis of the latter characteristic that geographers became increasingly concerned with glocalization. In fact, there have by now been literally hundreds of geographers who have worked with and used this concept. Unfortunately, the sociological and the geographical sides of the discourse of glocalization have been kept relatively segregated from each other—at least until very recently. I became particularly conscious of this when I attended a conference at Emory University, at which the late Neil Smith—an anthropologist as well as a geographer—invoked the word *glocalization* to the apparent surprise of the mainly sociological audience, the members of which had only become familiar with this term through my own writings (cf. Smith 2005). After the relevant session, Smith took me aside and explained that this concept was used quite widely in the geographical profession. Retrospectively, this should have been a cause for some embarrassment because the problematic tone of the relationship between the local and the global has been rather widely dealt with in anthropology (e.g., Friedman 1994; Hannerz 1996; Long 1996; Tsing 2005). Without doubt, Swyngedouw (e.g., 1992; 1997; 2004) has been one of the most influential geographers in this respect, but there are many others of the same discipline who have contributed, including Brenner (1997; 2004), Taylor (2004), Sack (1986), and Massey (2005). In the background, so to speak, lies the formidable figure of Henri Lefebvre (1991).

The significant overlap between the work of geographers, anthropologists, and of course, sociologists with respect to the relationship between the local and the global should now be clear. One should remark that, in the present endeavor, what began as a relatively straightforward genealogical exploration of the specific concept of glocalization has evidently become vastly more extensive. Moreover, issues concerning hybridity, creolization, indigeneity, multi-raciality, and multi-ethnicity have yet to be confronted and interwoven with the concept of glocalization. Much of this broadening of focus has to do with contemporary problems concerning authenticity, the fashionability of fakeness, and more generally, the invention and commodification of cultures, a core feature of which is the phenomenon of branding (Boli and Elliott 2008; Franklin, Lury, and Stacey 2000b).

All things considered, at this point in time, it would seem that the collage of human society is more 'normal' than unusual. This is a major thesis of the somewhat overlooked book by McNeill, *Polyethnicity and National Unity in World History* (1986). According to McNeill's perspective, polyethnicity and multiculturality are the human norm, with homogeneity being historically and anthropologically unusual, indeed aberrational. In this respect, that which has led to our current awareness of glocalization and associated concepts and processes is the result of a break in the norm of plurality and difference by the standardizing processes of the period that has lasted from the mid-eighteenth century to the near present. We are, in other words, rediscovering our past but doing this under new circumstances. The latter centers upon increasing world unicity—or world compression—not to speak of the multiverse that we inhabit.

Briefly stated, then, glocalization refers to the process in which phenomena that spread, flow, or are diffused from one 'place' to another have to be, and indeed are, adapted to the new locality where they arrive. This process of adaptation constitutes the pivotal motif of the very idea of glocalization. In fact, it stands in a tradition concerning diffusion as an anthropological idea and as one that was developed in the field of rural sociology. In the latter, diffusion was intimately related to the theme of innovation. Specifically, in American rural sociology (e.g., Rogers 2003) practitioners were mainly concerned with the ways in and the degrees to which new ideas were adopted and transferred from one context to another. It would not be too much to say that the diffusion of innovations literature was the indirect foundation for much of the contemporary and more empirically wide-ranging theme of glocalization.

It should also be emphasized that the actual concept of glocalization was greatly inspired by Japanese business practices. Strictly speaking, the Japanese term for glocalization is *dochakuka*, a word that literally means *to indigenize*. This tradition of the Japanese conception of production generally, and undoubtedly, was the reason why Japanese business practices became so prominent in the 1980s and early 1990s. Both Robertson and Swyngedouw gained much of their inspiration in using the term *glocalization* from this source. During that period, when Japan seemed to be in the vanguard of modernization, when Japan was 'No 1' (Vogel 1979), and there was much fear of rapid Japanese success among Americans, it became increasingly clear that Japanese elites had acquired very sophisticated skills with respect to American tastes (partly by industrial espionage). In contrast, it was quite common during this period for American business journals and newspapers to complain about Japanese culture being unreceptive to American exports and, so, arguing that Japanese people were too short, houses and cars were too small, Japanese streets were too narrow, and their car parks too limited in space. Of course, the 'exotic' nature of Japan was greatly admired—an exoticism that Japan itself strongly promoted (Hendry 2000). In a nutshell, in that period, Japan had a particular ability, or so it seemed, to be hypersensitive to the demands of glocalization, whereas US elites were more blasé—indeed demanding—with respect to the problem of adaptation. From the American standpoint, Japan should change its culture and social practices in order to play its part in world society and, in particular, facilitate the import of American goods and services.

Needless to say, it is China, rather than Japan, that is now the principal rival to the US (Mishra 2012). However, China is much less concerned with the issue of being sensitive to the sociocultural characteristics of 'the Other'. To put this differently, apparently China seeks to override the glocalization trend, and this may well be a case of what Ritzer (2003) calls *grobalization*. Moreover, as China is rapidly becoming a major imperial power, the question is raised as to the ways in which different imperial projects have involved different styles of glocalization (or even, grobalization). Clearly, such relatively recent imperial projects—such as the British, French, Portuguese, and American—have displayed significant trajectories of 'coping' with 'native' cultures and practices. Indeed, the study of imperialism promises to be one of the most useful sites for the application of what I would call *methodological glocalism* (cf. Holton 2005; 2008).

As has been emphasized, the invocation of the concept of place does not have a specific, essentialistic geographical connotation. Undoubtedly, in any case, in modern geography the notion of place is much more fluid and constructed than many 'outsiders' would recognize. Nevertheless, in a sociological or anthropological framework, the idea of place can have a very constructivist connotation. Specifically, sociologists draw increasing attention to the construction of 'audiences' and potential clients of particular products or services. To put this differently and more concretely, the promotion and advertisement of goods and services increasingly involves the 'invention' and calibration of new or latent markets. For example, it is not easy to see whether the increasing recognition of gays as consumers is actually based upon the recognition of already existing, natural gayness or whether, at the other extreme, gayness is promoted for financial gain or personal power. The same could well be said of numerous other constructed 'needs'. In this sense, when we speak of glocalization involving adaptation to a place, we should not be misled into attributing to adaptation a too essentialistic meaning. The idea of adaption is much more fluid than this. Indeed, it would probably be more appropriate to say that the place has to be adapted to the phenomena that flow. (Unfortunately, space considerations preclude the exploration of the degree to which what is usually now called *gender bending* has relevance in the present context.)

Clearly, everyday practitioners in the field of production and advertising have had a much more pragmatic and, in a sense, realistic view of the relation between the local and the global than have strictly 'academic people'. There have been scores, if not hundreds, of interrogations of the so-called problem of the relationship between the local and the global. However, such deliberation has little or no effect on the management of corporations, big or small. The latter have apparently simply taken it for granted that they have to deal with the issue of a product that they wish to sell widely. Inevitably, or at least in most cases, this involves a variety of cultures and social contexts—not to speak of different personnel. Therefore, it is not surprising at all that many well-known global products are advertised and sold in different forms and with different recipes. To take but a few examples, there is a great variety of ways in which such products as Starbucks coffee, Coca-Cola and Pepsi-Cola drinks, McDonald's food, and Heineken beer are produced, distributed, and consumed. Of particular significance here is the United Colors of Benetton, whose magazine, *Colors*, is proudly dedicated to global diversity, which is ironic for, in this case, a seemingly homogeneous global brand proclaims that it is heterogeneous (Lury 2000). More succinctly, manufacturers and distributors simply take it for granted that they must cater to a variety of markets and, moreover, widen those markets in the same process. It is of more than incidental interest that anthropologists are frequently employed in the role of not merely recognizing but also providing nuance to what appear superficially to be standardized products. In this regard, they are following and promoting the maxim that 'difference sells' (Lamont and Fournier 1992; cf. Sacks 2003), as does exoticism.

As the drift toward a multidimensional conception of globalization gained strength in the late 1980s and early 1990s, the question arose as to the degree to which globalization inevitably involved standardization. Indeed, in some circles—both academic and political—the idea of globalization as standardization still prevails. Moreover, until very recently, globalization was conceived as not merely a form of standardization but even more narrowly by the term *Westernization*. It has not been until very recently that the idea of American decline and Chinese climb has become globally significant (and, in my view, greatly exaggerated). An intriguing aspect of the contrast and difference between the US and China is that each side—particularly the Chinese one—tends to consider that the 'opponent', or rival, has some kind of superiority and, thus, is to be envied, indeed copied, in certain respects. This is but one among numerous examples that could be offered concerning the interpenetration of national and regional identities.

Localization

In the last ten years or so, there has been an increasing stress on and valorization of locality. Indeed, one could well argue that locality has been globalized—that the very idea of the local has been intensified by so-called globalization (Robertson 1997; Wilson and Dissanayake 1996). This apparent paradox is pivotal to the present discussion. The globalization of the local has gone hand in hand with the idea of *globalization from below*. This theme became particularly prominent following the much-publicized demonstrations against the World Trade Organization (WTO) in Seattle, USA in late 1999. (These demonstrations may now be seen as constituting a forerunner of the contemporary Occupy movement.) The WTO was regarded by many activists as the enemy—a world of corporate domination and globalization in the economic sense. However, it soon came to be seen in the early 2000s that those who were allegedly opposing globalization were actually participants in and promoters of that very phenomenon. Hence, the 'excuse' was created that one could have globalization from below rather than a hegemonic form of *globalization from above*. The latter has recently come to be labelled as grobalization (Ritzer 2003). In fact, Ritzer seems to regard grobalization as the very opposite of glocalization. In other words, whereas glocalization involves accommodation to the local, grobalization supposedly involves the invasion of or the destruction of the local and particular. The major limitation of this perspective is that it appears to be merely a reaction to the concept of glocalization. Moreover, grobalization appears to be a way of shoring up Ritzer's many writings on the theme of McDonaldization, a concept which is used, many times, to support his thesis that the world as a whole is being homogenized, standardized, and routinized. Ideas of the latter kind have been applied to a vast range of phenomena, from theme parks to brothels and religious institutions to magazines (Ritzer 2002).

It can be usefully reiterated that I had a very pertinent experience when, after a rather long absence from Japan, I returned in the early 2000s and was immediately confronted by a copy of the *Japan Times* that stated on its front page that a new concept, glocalization, had arrived that gave hope to those who wished to defend Japanese traditions. Needless to say, I found this to be extremely ironic, for I had first used the concept of glocalization following my initial encounter with the Japanese concept of dochakuka in the early 1990s (Robertson 1992). Irony, of course, resided in the fact that I had more or less obtained the idea of glocalization from Japan itself. In any case, it should be emphasized that glocalization now seems to have become embedded in Japanese social science (Yui 2006).

Reflexive Glocalization

As various institutional leaders have become increasingly aware of the issue of diffusion and flows, and the relative advantages of some kinds of glocalization over others, a much greater awareness has developed of the importance of adaptability and the forms adaptability can take. This can usefully be labelled *reflexive glocalization*, meaning that glocalization increasingly becomes a way of outdoing 'glocalizers'. Put differently, as practitioners become increasingly conscious of the apparent success of glocalization projects, it becomes the norm, in contrast to standardization. Moreover, contrary to the emphasis on standardization and routinization that has been central to the McDonaldization thesis, people have become increasingly aware of the value of difference. In fact, it would not be too much to say that 'being different' is one of the major motifs of our time. For example, a prominent theme of women's magazines—and probably the everyday life of women—is that one of the worst things that can happen to a woman is to arrive at a social occasion and discover that at least one other woman is wearing the same dress! From a different perspective, glocalization can be seen to be in the tradition of Freud's idea concerning the narcissism of minor differences. Freud, of course, emphasized that the greater the standardization, the greater the need for difference. This can be clearly seen in the case of fashion. On the surface, most 'fashionistas' appear to be clones, whereas the perceptive observer will notice slight but crucial differences. The latter are particularly significant for the wearer and are meant to be observed by the discerning. The intention is to be simultaneously different and the same—different within the in-group, but the same to outsiders.

Merry White's (2012) cogent argument that coffee, as opposed to tea, is an icon of Japanese culture, and that Japan is the third largest consumer of coffee in the world, will surprise many. However, coffee actually entered Japan in the early twentieth century following a slump in global sales of coffee in Brazil, resulting in Japan being targeted by the Brazilian coffee industry as a new market. This was largely facilitated by the fast-growing traffic of labor from Brazil to Japan. (Here it should be remarked that the tension between Japan and the US, occasioned by the antagonistic attitude of the local San Francisco School Board towards Japanese children, led to the diversion of emigration from Japan to Brazil and Peru—hence, the part of Sao Paulo named Liberdade, a Japanese enclave. One of the most striking features of Liberdade—at least in the late 1990s—is its untidiness. It is, in one important sense, basically 'non-Japanese'.) This is a classic example of the ways in which certain practices take on different forms as they move from place to place. In the Japanese case of coffee, one finds that coffee is consumed very quietly, with no 'clinking or clanking'. Moreover, traditionally, coffee has been consumed in Japan, or so White (2012) argues, as a form of 'dry inebriation' in a very erotic manner, including 'subway service' (oral sex under the table) and customers fondling waitresses through slits below the waist in kimonos. In these respects, female sexuality was regarded as fundamentally modern, in the sense that women were participating in the public sphere for the first time, so as to appear more Western. This is but one of many examples of the manner in which a phenomenon that moves from one place to another may well become a vehicle of localization. Watson (1997) provides numerous examples of this in his study of McDonald's in various East Asian locations, where there is considerable variation in menus and social practices. McDonald's is apparently about to open a vegetarian restaurant in Amritsar, near the Sikh temple, while the most popular burger, also in India, is the McAloo Tikka. In China there is the Full Three Taels, in the Middle East the McArabia, in Japan the MegaTerryaki, in Thailand jasmine rice patties. Moves are afoot to incorporate classic French cheeses into the McDonald's brand in France.

These considerations bring to the forefront the problematic relationship between glocality and hybridity. In fact, there has been an on-going debate—if somewhat implicit—as to the relationship between these two concepts (Pieterse 1995, 2004). In fact, it would seem that different corporations and chains take calculated decisions as to whether to 'go hybrid' or to glocalize. For example, in the UK, a chain of restaurants has opened, called Las Iguanas, which apparently and self-consciously glocalizes the hybridity of Latin American cultures. A typical 'local' menu in a Las Iguanas restaurant includes a mix of alcoholic and non-alcoholic beverages from Chile, Peru, Brazil, Cuba, Mexico, Honduras, and other Latin American countries. The same applies to its selections of food. The fact that Las Iguanas concentrates on selling Latin American food and beverages is particularly significant in view of the fact that, for many, Latin America is the home of hybridity (Burke 2009). Indeed, in contrast, Pieterse (1995) argues unconvincingly that globalization is hybridization.

This also raises the question of authenticity and what some have called *strategic authenticity*; the latter indicating the deliberate presentation of something as being authentic when it is widely known to be inauthentic. All of this centers upon the fashionability—on an almost worldwide basis—of fakeness, or 'fauxness' (cf. Boli and Elliott 2008).

Concluding Remarks

A particularly important consequence of glocalization has not by any means been fully addressed in this chapter, although it is of great importance in the larger context of the consideration of globalization. My proposition is that globalization is, when viewed through the lens of glocalization, basically self-limiting—indeed, self-defeating. In fact, as I have remarked elsewhere on a number of occasions, there are good reasons for using the term *glocalization* as a substitute for *globalization*. A particularly important aspect of this idea is the way in which 'hyperglobalization'—in effect, increasingly reflexive glocalization—would result in the whole world becoming, literally, a mass of individuals, or even, individuals with multiple selves (Boli and Elliott 2008).

Finally, it should be stressed that there appears to be a great deal of convergence across the world with respect to localization as being facilitated by standardizing globalization (e.g., Kennedy 2010). Somewhat unfortunately, localization has acquired an increasingly ideological connotation. For example, this is a very prominent feature in a policy of the British Conservative Party, although the fact that this so-called localization comes from above confirms the general thesis concerning glocalization as discussed in the present chapter.

One final comment is in order—one that is of great importance in the modern world. The rapidly expanding use of CCTV surveillance, camera-carrying drones, Google Earth, and related phenomena means that the old distinctions between the local and the global, as well as the private and the public, are being obliterated.

References

The list that follows includes several items that are not cited in the text above. They are, nonetheless, included because they are directly relevant to the discussion of the general theme.

Anderson, P. (1968). 'Components of the National Culture'. *New Left Review*, 50: 3–57.
Appadurai, A. (1996). *Modernity at Large: Cultural Dimensions of Globalization*. Minneapolis, MN: University of Minnesota Press.
Barth, F., Gingrich, A., Parkin, R., and Silverman, S. (2005). *One Discipline, Four Ways: British, German, French, and American Anthropology*. Chicago, IL: University of Chicago Press.
Bastide, R. (1978). *The African Religions of Brazil: Toward a Sociology of the Interpenetration of Cultures*. Baltimore, MD: Johns Hopkins University Press.
Baumann, G. (1999). *The Multicultural Riddle: Rethinking National, Ethnic, and Religious Identity*. New York, NY: Routledge.
Beugelsdijk, R., and Maseland, R. (2012). *Culture in Economics: History, Methodological Reflections, and Contemporary Applications*. Cambridge, UK: Cambridge University Press.
Bhabha, H. (1994). *The Location of Culture*. London, UK: Verso.
Bielby, D.D., and Harrington, C.L. (2008). *Global TV: Exporting Television and Culture in the World Market*. New York, NY: New York University Press.
Boli, J., and Elliott, M.A. (2008). 'Façade Diversity: The Individualization of Cultural Difference'. *International Sociology*, 23: 540–560.
Brenner, N. (1997). 'Global, Fragmented Hierarchical: Henri Lefebvre's Geographies of Globalization'. *Public Culture,* 10: 135–167.
Brenner, N. (2004). *New State Spaces: Urban Governance and the Rescaling of Statehood*. Oxford, UK: Oxford University Press.

Brotton, J. (2012). *A History of the World in Twelve Maps*. London, UK: Allen Lane.
Brown, M.F. (2003). *Who Owns Native Culture?* Cambridge, MA: Harvard University Press.
Burke, P. (2009). *Cultural Hybridity*. Cambridge, UK: Polity Press.
Campbell, L. (2011). *Historical Linguistics: An Introduction*. Cambridge, MA: MIT Press.
Canclini, N.G. (1995). *Hybrid Cultures: Strategies for Entering and Leaving Modernity*. Minneapolis, MN: University of Minnesota Press.
Cantle, T. (2012). *Interculturalism: The New Era of Cohesion and Diversity*. Basingstoke, UK: Palgrave Macmillan.
Castells, M. (1996). *The Rise of the Network Society*. Oxford, UK: Blackwell.
Comaroff, J.L., and Comaroff, J. (2009). *Ethnicity, Inc.* Chicago, IL: University of Chicago Press.
Comaroff, J.L., and Comaroff, J. (2012). *Theory from the South: Or, How Euro-America Is Evolving toward Africa*. London, UK: Paradigm Publishers.
Cowen, T. (2002). *Creative Destruction: How Globalization Is Changing the World's Cultures*. Princeton, NJ: Princeton University Press.
Dirlik, A. (2001). 'Place-based Imagination: Globalism and the Politics of Place', in R. Prazniak and A. Gurlik (eds), *Places and Politics in an Age of Globalization*. Lanham, MD: Rowman and Littlefield.
Escobar, A. (2008). *Territories of Difference: Place, Movements, Life*. Durham, NC: Duke University Press.
Evans, G. (2012). 'No Clinking' [Review of White (2012)]. *Times Literary Supplement*, 23: 29.
Franklin, S., Lury, C., and Stacey, J. (2000a). 'Introduction', in S. Franklin, C. Lury, and J. Stacey, *Global Nature, Global Culture*. London, UK: Sage, 1–16.
Franklin, S., Lury, C., and Stacey, J. (2000b). *Global Nature, Global Culture*. London: Sage.
Friedman, J. (1990). 'Being in the World: Globalization and Localization', in M. Featherstone and R. Robertson (eds), *Global Culture: Nationalism, Globalization and Modernity*. London, UK: Sage, 311–328.
Friedman, J. (1994). *Cultural Identity and Global Process*. London, UK: Sage.
Giddens, A. (1991). *Modernity and Self-Identity*. Cambridge, UK: Polity Press.
Giulianotti, R., & Robertson, R. (2007). *Globalization and Sport*. Oxford: Blackwell.
Hannerz, U. (1992). *Cultural Complexity*. New York, NY: Cambridge University Press.
Hannerz, U. (1996). *Transnational Connections: Culture, People, Places*. London, UK: Routledge.
Harvey, D. (2005). *A Brief History of Neoliberalism*. Oxford, UK: Oxford University Press.
Hendry, J. (2000). *The Orient Strikes Back: A Global View of Cultural Display*. Oxford, UK: Berg.
Hines, C. (2000). *Localization: A Global Manifesto*. London, UK: Earthscan.
Holton, R.J. (2005). *Making Globalization*. Basingstoke, UK: Palgrave Macmillan.
Holton, R.J. (2008). *Global Networks*. Basingstoke, UK: Palgrave Macmillan.
Holton, R.J. (2009). *Cosmopolitanisms: New Thinking, New Directions*. Basingstoke, UK: Palgrave Macmillan.
Howard, J. (1996). *Art Nouveau: International and National Styles in Europe*. Manchester, UK: Manchester University Press.
Inglis, D., and Robertson, R. (2005). 'World Music and the Globalization of Sound', in D. Inglis and J. Hughson (eds), *The Sociology of Art: Ways of Seeing*. Basingstoke, UK: Palgrave Press, 156–170.
Kennedy, P. (2010). *Local Lives and Global Transformations: Towards a World Society*. Basingstoke, UK: Palgrave Macmillan.
Kornberger, M. (2010). *Brand Society: How Brands Transform Management and Lifestyle*. Cambridge, UK: Cambridge University Press.
Kraidy, M.M. (2005). *Hybridity: Or the Cultural Logic of Globalization*. Philadelphia, PA: Temple University Press.
Krishnendu, R., and Srinivas, T. (eds). (2012). *Curried Cultures: Globalization, Food, and South Asia*. Berkeley, CA: University of California Press.
Krücken, G., and Drori, G.S. (eds). (2009). *World Society: The Writings of John W. Meyer*. Oxford, UK: Oxford University Press.

Kunitake, K., Tsuziki, C., and Young, R.J. (eds). (2009). *Japan Rising: The Iwakura Embassy to the USA and Europe 1871–1873*. Cambridge, UK: Cambridge University Press.

Lamont, M., and Fournier, M. (1992). *Cultivating Differences: Symbolic Boundaries and the Making of Inequality*. Chicago, IL: University of Chicago Press.

Latour, B. (1993). *We Have Never Been Modern*. Hemel Hempstead, UK: Harvester Wheatsheaf.

Lechner, F., and Boli, J. (2005). *World Culture: Origins and Consequences*. Oxford, UK: Blackwell.

Lefebvre, H. (1991). *The Production of Space*. Oxford: Blackwell.

Long, N. (1996). 'Globalization and Localization: New Challenges to Rural Research', in H.R. Moore, *The Future of Anthropological Knowledge*. London, UK: Routledge, 37–59.

Lury, C. (2000). 'The United Colors of Diversity: Essential and Inessential Culture', in S. Franklin, C. Lury, and J. Stacey, *Global Nature, Global Culture*. London, UK: Sage, 146–187.

Massey, D.B. (2005). *For Space*. London, UK: Sage.

McNeill, W.H. (1986). *Polyethnicity and National Unity in World History*. Toronto: University of Toronto Press.

Mishra, P. (2012). *From the Ruins of Empire: The Revolt Against the West and the Remaking of Asia*. London, UK: Allen Lane.

Moeran, B., and Pedersen, J.S. (eds). (2012). *Negotiating Values in the Creative Industries: Fairs, Festivals and Competitive Events*. Cambridge, UK: Cambridge University Press.

Moore, S.F. (1989). 'The Production of Cultural Pluralism as a Process'. *Public Culture*, 1: 26–48.

Morawska, E. (2011). *A Sociology of Immigration: (Re)Making Multifaceted America*. Basingstoke, UK: Palgrave Macmillan.

Payer, L. (1996). *Medicine and Culture: Varieties of Treatment in the United States, England, West Germany, and France* (Revised edn). New York, NY: Henry Holt.

Pieterse, J.N. (1995). 'Globalization as Hybridization', in M. Featherstone, S. Lash, and R. Robertson (eds), *Global Modernities*. London, UK: Sage, 45–68.

Pieterse, J.N. (2004). *Globalization and Culture: Global Melange*. Lanham, MD: Rowman and Littlefield.

Potts, J. (2012). *Creative Industries and Economic Evolution*. London, UK: Edward Elgar.

Pym, A. (1998). *Method in Translation History*. Manchester, UK: Jerome.

Ray, K., and Srinivas, T. (eds). (2012). *Curried Cultures: Globalization, Food, and South Asia*. Berkeley, CA: University of California Press.

Rhinesmith, S.H. (1993). *A Manager's Guide to Globalization*. Alexandria, VA: American Society for Training and Development.

Ritzer, G. (1993). *The McDonaldization of Society*. London, UK: Sage.

Ritzer, G. (ed.). (2002). *McDonaldization: The Reader*. London, UK: Sage.

Ritzer, G. (2003). *The Globalization of Nothing*. London, UK: Sage.

Robertson, R. (1992). *Globalization: Social Theory and Social Culture*. London: Sage.

Robertson, R. (1993). 'Globaliseringens Problem'. *GRUS*, December: 6–31.

Robertson, R. (1994). 'Globalisation or Glocalisation?'. *Journal of International Communication*, 1: 33–52.

Robertson, R. (1995a). 'Glocalization: Time-Space and Homogeneity-Heterogeneity', in M. Featherstone, S. Lash, and R. Robertson (eds), *Global Modernities*. London, UK: Sage, 25–44.

Robertson, R. (1995b). 'Theory, Specificity, Change: Emulation, Selective Incorporation and Modernization', in B. Grancelli (ed.), *Social Change and Modernization: Lessons from Eastern Europe*. Berlin, Germany: Walter de Gruyter, 213–231.

Robertson, R. (1997). 'Values and Globalization: Communitarianism and Globality', in L.E. Soares (ed.), *Identity, Culture and Globalization*. Rio de Janeiro, Brazil: UNESCO, 73–97.

Robertson, R. (2003a). 'The Conceptual Promise of Glocalization: Commonality and Diversity', in *Proceedings of the International Forum on Cultural Diversity and Common Values*. Seoul, South Korea: Korean National Commission for UNESCO, 76–89.

Robertson, R. (2003b). 'Epilogue: Rethinking Americanization', in U. Beck, N. Sznaider, and R. Winter (eds), *Global America?: The Cultural Consequences of Globalization*. Liverpool, UK: Liverpool University Press, 257–264.

Robertson, R. (2007a). 'Diffusion', in R. Robertson and J.A. Scholte (eds), *Encyclopedia of Globalization*. New York, NY: MTM/Routledge, 318–320.

Robertson, R. (2007b). 'Glocalization', in R. Robertson and J.A. Scholte (eds), *Encyclopedia of Globalization*. New York, NY: MTM/Routledge, 545–548.

Robertson, R. (ed.). (2013). *European Glocalization in Global Context*. Basingstoke, UK: Palgrave Macmillan.

Robertson, R., and Chirico, J.A. (1985). 'Humanity, Globalization and Worldwide Religious Resurgence: A Theoretical Exploration'. *Sociological Analysis*, 46: 219–242.

Robertson, R., and White, K.E. (2004). 'La Glocalizzazione Rivisitata ed Elaborate' [Glocalization Revisited and Elaborated], in F. Sedda (ed.), *Glocal: Sui Presente a Venire*. Rome, Italy: Luca Sossella Editore, 13–41.

Rogers, E.M. (2003). *Diffusion of Innovations* (5th edn). New York, NY: Simon Schuster.

Rosenau, J.N. (2003). *Distant Proximities: Dynamics beyond Globalization*. Princeton, NJ: Princeton University Press.

Roudometof, V. (2003). 'Glocalization, Space and Modernity'. *The European Legacy*, 8: 37–60.

Roudometof, V. (2005). 'Transnationalism, Cosmopolitanism and Glocalization'. *Current Sociology*, 53: 113–135.

Ruijter, A. de. (2001). 'Globalization: A Challenge to the Social Sciences', in F.J. Schuurman (ed.), *Globalization and Development Studies: Challenges for the 21st Century*. London, UK: Sage, 31–43.

Sack, R.D. (1986). *Human Territoriality: Its Theory and History*. Cambridge, UK: Cambridge University Press.

Sacks, D. (2003). *The Dignity of Difference: How to Avoid the Clash of Civilizations*. London, UK: Continuum.

Savigliano, M.E. (1995). *Tango and the Political Economy of Passion*. Boulder, CO: Westview Press.

Schwarz, R. (1992). *Misplaced Ideas: Essays on Brazilian Culture*. London, UK: Verso.

Smith, N. (2005). *The Endgame of Globalization*. New York, NY: Routledge.

Soja, E.W. (1989). *Postmodern Geography: The Reassertion of Space in Critical Social Theory*. London, UK: Verso.

Sollors, W. (1989). *The Invention of Ethnicity*. New York, NY: Oxford University Press.

Steger, M.B., and Roy, R.K. (2010). *Neoliberalism: A Very Short Introduction*. Oxford, UK: Oxford University Press.

Swyngedouw, E. (1992). 'The Mammon Quest: "Glocalization", Interspatial Competition and the Monetary Order: The Construction of New Scales', in M. Dunford and G. Kafkalis (eds), *Cities and Regions in the New Europe: The Global-Local Interplay and Spatial Development Strategies*. New York, NY: Wiley, 39–67.

Swyngedouw, E. (1997). 'Neither Global nor Local: "Glocalization" and the Politics of Scale', in K. Cox (ed.), *Spaces of Globalization: Reasserting the Power of the Local*. New York, NY: Guilford, 137–166.

Swyngedouw, E. (2004). 'Globalisation or "Glocalisation"? Networks, Territories and Rescaling'. *Cambridge Review of International Affairs*, 17: 25–48.

Taylor, P.J. (2004). *World City Network: A Global Urban Analysis*. London, UK: Routledge.

The Economist. (2012). 'Nightclubs: Getting Down Globally: Western Nightclubs Eye Asia, and Clever Technology'. *The Economist*, June 2: 72.

Tomlinson, J. (1991). *Cultural Imperialism: A Critical Introduction*. Baltimore, MD: Johns Hopkins University Press.

Tomlinson, J. (1999). *Globalization and Culture*. Cambridge, UK: Polity Press.

Tsing, A.L. (2005). *Friction: An Ethnography of Global Connections*. Princeton, NJ: Princeton University Press.

Tucker, C.M. (2011). *Coffee Culture: Local Experiences, Global Connections*. New York, NY: Routledge.

Vogel, E. (1979). *Japan as Number One: Lessons for America*. Cambridge, MA: Harvard University Press.

Warde, A. (2000). 'Eating Globally: Cultural Flows and the Spread of Ethnic Restaurants', in D. Kalb, M. van de Land, R. Staring, B. van Steenbergen, and N. Wilterdink (eds), *The Ends of Globalization: Bringing Society Back In*. Lanham, MD: Rowan and Littlefield, 299–316.

Watson, J.L. (ed.). (1997). *Golden Arches East: McDonald's in East Asia*. Stanford, CA: Stanford University Press.
Watson, J.L., and Caldwell, M.L. (eds). (2005). *The Cultural Politics of Food and Eating: A Reader*. Malden, MA: Blackwell.
Weiner, A. (1995). 'Culture and Our Discontents'. *American Anthropologist*, 97: 14–40.
Wellman, B. (2004). 'The Glocal Village: Internet and Community'. *Ideas: The Arts and Science Review*, 1: 26–30.
Werbner, P., and Modood, T (eds) (1997). *Debating Cultural Hybridity*. London, UK: Zed.
Westney, D.E. (1987). *Imitation and Innovation: The Transfer of Western Organizational Patterns to Meiji Japan*. Cambridge, MA: Harvard University Press.
White, M. (2012). *Coffee Life in Japan*. Berkeley, CA: University of California Press.
Wilson, R., and Dissanayake, W. (eds). (1966). *Global/Local*. Durham, NC: Duke University Press.
Wilson, R., and Dissanayake, W. (1996). 'Introduction: Tracking the Global/Local', in R. Wilson, R., and W. Dissanayake (eds), *Global/Local*. Durham NC: Duke University Press, 1–18.
Wulff, H. (1998). *Ballet across Borders: Career and Culture in the World of Dancers*. Oxford, UK: Berg.
Yui, K. (2006). 'Hikaku Kindaikaron to Gurokarukaron' [Comparative Modernization Theory and Glocalization]. *The Japanese Sociological Review*, 57.

Part II
Revisiting Glocalization

3
The Travel of Organization

Göran Ahrne and Nils Brunsson

Globalization and Organization

In our contemporary world, people interact and communicate at greater distances than ever before, and interaction and communication reinforce and are reinforced by strong global similarities. It is increasingly difficult to find differences in appearance and life at various places; even long-distance air travel can lead us to distant but amazingly similar cities. An increasing number of categories are now being used worldwide. States, firms, and unions, for example, can be found virtually everywhere, and they tend to nurture similar ideas and behave in similar ways. Their very similarity makes it possible to differentiate among them according to status—there are global status orders providing world champions in sports, universities, and cities. Organizations that are geographically separated tend to introduce similar structures and procedures. And an increasing number of organizations depend more on the coordination of their activities with organizations in other parts of the world than with organizations in their local community.

Such characteristics of the contemporary world are easily observed. They may be truly global, involving the entire world, or they may be global in a more restricted sense, affecting only large parts of the planet. The processes that lead to them are more difficult to observe, and sometimes remain unnoticed. It is usual to subsume these processes under the general concept of globalization, but that should not hinder us from observing significant differences among them. Globalization is far from a unitary process that shapes everything in its way into the same form (Therborn 2011). There are various paths to a globalized world; they are more or less visible and they each exert a different impact on the outcome.

There is a distinct lack of concepts in social sciences for analyzing globalization. In most traditions, it has long been taken for granted that each state is a 'society' separated from other 'societies', each having its own social structure; its own culture, institutions, and politics, its own class structure, and its own people. Because of their focus on a distinct state, such concepts are not particularly useful in an analysis of globalization and a global world. The concept of organization, on the other hand, has had no prominent place in traditional social theory. Organizations, however, are social actors that frequently move and expand across the borders of separate societies. There is also organization that extends beyond formal organizations.

The traditions of organization studies hold several theories about the relationships between organizations and their environments and what happens when organizations expand or move to new environments—both the effect of the new environment on the organization and the effect of the organization on the new environment (Pfeffer and Salancik 1978; Scott 2001). Thus, organization theory has the potential to contribute in new ways to an understanding of how and why globalization happens—a potential that has not been fully exploited so far.

There are two well-established traditions in organizational research that have contributed to our understanding of globalization: the *travel of ideas among organizations* and the *expansion of multinational corporations*. In this context, the latter type of study can be described as the travel of formal organizations. But there are other aspects of organization that have been virtually neglected in research on globalization. There is an ongoing global organization of organizations in the forms of *partial organization* and *meta-organizations*. These forms are necessary to understand if we are to explain the full range of the contribution of organization to globalization. In this chapter, we discuss how these forms of organization contribute to globalization and how they differ from the travel of ideas and formal organizations. We restrict the discussion to a single, albeit significant, aspect of globalization processes: the conflict between the global and the local.

The Global and the Local

Although people may talk and behave in similar ways without knowing each other or having contact with each other (Brunsson 2000), it is fair to assume that much of the global homogenization that we see today results from knowledge of and contact with distant others. And the other aspects of globalism mentioned above presuppose such knowledge and contact. Therefore, most globalization implies that people embedded in a local order adapt to conditions with a foreign origin. Although globalization has been intensified over the past fifty-some years, there is no such thing as a global world. There are still various local idiosyncrasies and many contradictions and conflicts between the global and the local. Furthermore, the local and the global are not neutral categories. The origin of something is still a relevant issue; whether a new idea, practice, or product is perceived as foreign or local has implications for its evaluation.

In some contexts and under some circumstances, foreignness generates a negative value, whereas local innovations trigger greater prestige; the syndrome *not invented here* that has been said to characterize some organizations serves as a good example. But more generally, modern individuals and organizations are constructed as entities that are and should be autonomous and unique. They are expected to find their own ways of doing things rather than imitating others, which makes the importing of innovations somewhat problematic for their identity. Modern states claim the same characteristics: they request and pretend sovereignty and have actively propagated ideas of the uniqueness of their 'nation' (Krasner 1999; Billig 1995).

Sometimes, it is the other way around. People with little respect for their local organizations may find innovations suggested or tried elsewhere more prestigious than ideas suggested at home. In malfunctioning or new states, citizens may prefer administrative forms used by prestigious foreign states rather than accepting those invented by their own governments (Badie 2000). The same goes for firms. Japan was actively and explicitly imitating state structures and procedures from the West in the 19th century, and firms in the West were trying to imitate what came to be known as 'Japanese management' during Japan's business success in the 1980s (Boyer et al. 1998; Westney 1987).

Localness and foreignness are perceptual categories. Although an external observer may categorize an innovation introduced into a local context as emanating from the outside, people within that context are more likely to think that it was created within the local community. An innovation may even become institutionalized: people take it for granted rather than thinking about its origin and how things could be different.

The visibility of the local and the global varies, depending on the processes involved: the travel of ideas among organizations or the travel of formal organizations, partial organization or meta-organizations. These organizational forms have different potentials for combining the local with the global, and therefore, different potentials for contributing to globalization.

We next describe some findings from the extensive literature on the travel of ideas and the travel of formal organizations that are relevant in this context. We then discuss how partial organization and meta-organizations affect tension between the local and the global, comparing them with each other and with the other forms.

The Travel of Ideas

In organization studies, the travel of ideas among organizations is a well-studied phenomenon, not least in the tradition of institutional analysis. Ideas may travel long distances (Czarniawska-Joerges and Joerges 1996), an example being the spread of management recipes (Sahlin-Andersson and Engwall 2002; Røvik 2007). Ideas may slowly diffuse in networks of organizations or in organizational fields, as organizations imitate each other (DiMaggio and Powell 1983). Global networks and fields, when they exist, may produce a great diffusion of ideas. But the spread of ideas does not presuppose contact among organizations, or even that the members of one organization have knowledge of the other organization. The main source of foreign ideas in modern societies is probably the various mass media covering events far from home. New and old ideas fly easily to every corner of the globe. Or there are mediating organizations or people who fly; management ideas can be spread by management consultancies, for example, or by management gurus who, like a modern St Paul, travel from one organization to another preaching the gospel.

As long as ideas are merely ideas—perceptions of a situation and what can or should be accomplished—they are highly flexible. In order for them to affect organizational practice, they must be translated into a local context (Czarniawska-Joerges and Joerges 1996; Sahlin-Andersson 1996), and their origin or any similarity to their origin may become highly ambiguous during that process. The propagator of an idea has considerable leeway in choosing to present it as being related to ideas in distant places or as being firmly rooted in or even invented in the local context. In fact, as all scholars know, it is no trivial task to determine if or to what extent one's ideas originated in one's own mind or in someone else's. It is clear to external observers, for example, that public sector administrative reforms across many countries were strikingly similar during the 1980s and 1990s; observers even gave them the common name of New Public Management (Hood 1995). But at least in the Swedish debate, reformers have rarely presented their ideas as originating in other countries. And it is conceivable that they were, in fact, local inventions in each country (Brunsson 2000). The flexibility of ideas makes them difficult to criticize on the grounds that they are foreign or local. On the other hand, flexibility may be a hindrance to globalization. The ideas can be given an interpretation far from their original meaning and one that is different in different local contexts. At the extreme, they may be interpreted as describing the existing local order, so it is the ideas rather than the local context that are adapted.

The basic notion in institutional analysis is that ideas travel and organizations stay at home. The travel of ideas is, without a doubt, one path of globalization with significant consequences for organizations, but globalization happens not only through the travel of ideas among organizations, but also through the organizations' travels. The travel of organizations, however, is another kind of journey.

Travel of Organizations

Earlier in the history of globalization, it usually occurred through the travel of formal organizations. States were conquering other states or colonizing areas with little previous state organization. These processes had significant consequences for the building of similarities, coordination, and communication among distant places—sometimes exceedingly distant.

The contemporary equivalent of conquests and colonization is the expansion of multinational corporations that establish subsidiaries or buy existing firms far from their home base. These corporations provide systems for communication and interaction at great distances and create similarities in locations scattered across the globe. Some multinational corporations have become symbols of rapid globalization. McDonald's and IKEA, for example, have spread their businesses to many corners of the world in a relatively short time, and both have high visibility. They are examples of companies with innovative and clear concepts of what products to sell and how to sell them. They are associated with new lifestyles, and in their local contexts, they have been seen as something new with a clear foreign origin.

The last 20 years have witnessed substantial growth in possibilities for coordinating the various parts of global firms through the implementation of new advanced systems and practices of communication and control (Boussebaa, Morgan, and Sturdy 2012). Like all organizations, firms are decided orders (Luhmann 2000; March and Simon 1958) with access to the organizational elements of membership, hierarchy, rules, monitoring, and sanctions (Ahrne and Brunsson 2011). Multinational corporations introduce their own version of a decided organizational order into a local context. Centrally placed top managers in McDonald's make significant decisions about what should be done in their local units. They apply the same rules in their foreign restaurants as they apply at home, and they decide to monitor and sanction employees in the same way (Ritzer 1993). McDonald's establishments are remarkably similar all over the world, as are those of IKEA and many other multinational retail firms; they form foreign enclaves in scores of local contexts.

On the other hand, multinational corporations cannot always control their subsidiaries effectively in other countries (Morgan, Kristensen, and Whitley 2001). Not all corporations are as successful in this respect as McDonald's and IKEA have been. There are many obstacles for the travel of formal organizations, which Zaheer (2002) has called 'the liability of foreignness'—a concept that summarizes the many disadvantages confronting companies attempting to expand into a new business environment. These disadvantages are highly significant, because multinational corporations, unlike conquering states, tend to meet lasting domestic competition. There are 'structural costs' in the form of poorer access to local information and a lack of networks and linkages to key local actors. There are also 'institutional costs' having to do with legitimacy and acceptance.

When the organizing of foreign firms is in conflict with local values and norms, these foreign firms may become seen as unwelcome intruders into an order that exists in the home locale. And their character of decided orders makes them easy victims of objections and protests. Because organizational structures and procedures have been decided upon, it becomes obvious that the order could be different—that managers of the foreign firms *could* decide to adapt their rules, monitoring, and sanctions to local values and norms. So in that sense, the objections are valid. And because specific people are responsible for having made these 'wrong' decisions, there will be someone to whom objections can be directed. In fact, McDonald's *has* met with such objections, even to the extent of street protests (Smart 1999).

These effects make it tempting to expand in less visible ways than McDonald's and IKEA have done, that is, to expand by acquiring local firms and allowing them to maintain their original names and brands, as Electrolux and Unilever have done (Jones 2005). In a local context, the process of globalization may remain unnoticed by everyone except insiders—employees of the company, for instance. Yet, it does constitute the travel of formal organizations, and if the new conditions are revealed, similar reactions may be aroused.

In comparison with ideas, organizations are not as free-floating and flexible. Their origin is clearer and more difficult to hide. It is easier to mobilize protests against an organization than it is to attack an idea. Travelling organizations always have a connection to their roots; their origin and history tend to be well known and their records may be investigated. Their foreignness may create obstacles to their expansion. Furthermore, expansion requires significant resources. We can therefore expect the travel of organizations to be slower and less frequent than the travel of ideas.

Multinational corporations are not the only examples of contemporary organized globalization, however. There are other ways of spreading organization globally, and other organizations are involved. Instead of expanding a formal organization, one or a few organizational elements that can travel more easily can be decided upon in a process we call partial organization. Or organizations may participate in global journeys by joining global meta-organizations. These forms of global organization form the topics of the next two sections.

Partial Organization

Organization need not be confined to formal organizations, such as states or firms. It is both possible and common to use one or a few organizational elements at a time in order to organize people or organizations. Most importantly, people or organizations may set rules for others, monitor others, or sanction them. Even though these elements are used outside the context of a formal organization, they have all the characteristics of organization. They are decided upon from among several options, they are connected to people who are responsible for the decisions, and they are open to contestation (Ahrne and Brunsson 2011). They constitute a form of partial organization.

One example of partial organization is the creation of global standards for measures, products, or organizational structures and procedures. Many such standards are set by international standard organizations like the International Organization for Standardisation (ISO), European Telecommunications Standards Institute (ETSI), or Comité Européen de Normalisation (CEN). Unlike a multinational corporation setting rules for its subsidiaries, standardization organizations do not have the hierarchical authority to set binding rules for anyone. On the other hand, their standards reach far beyond a single formal organization. International standards have a huge impact on the creation of worldwide similarities in industrial products and organizations. Many of these similarities are essential for achieving coordination over long distances (Brunsson and Jacobsson 2000; Tamm Hallström and Boström 2010).

Standards are sometimes complemented and reinforced by other organizational elements. Various monitoring activities provide checks on whether standards are complied with or not. And when they are, the standard follower may be given certifications or accreditations, which can be interpreted as positive sanctions. Companies can allow others to inspect their quality or environment work in order to become certified for compliance with ISO 9000 or ISO 14000, for example. States are observed by Human Rights Watch to ensure that they comply with standards for human rights and to criticize them publicly if they fail to do so. This combination of standards and monitoring sometimes creates global status orders; who is best at complying with certain standards becomes known, thereby conferring prestige upon the person or organization. Such global status orders have long been organized in sports, and later spread to other areas, as exemplified in the search for 'best practice' among firms around the world.

Monitoring can also be conducted with little or no relation to standards, as with some university rankings and the activities of such financial rating institutes as Moody's or Standard and Poor's. Sanctions can be given in the form of prizes and awards, which are common phenomena in many industries.

Local Reactions

Although the purpose of ranking and awards is to highlight differences, it also creates similarities. Awards often make people and organizations eager to demonstrate their advantages in the dimensions emphasized by global organizers. By choosing to comply with global standards or accepting monitoring, certifications, and awards with a global reach, a local organization can create or reinforce a global identity. By complying with a global standard for environmental protection, for instance, a company can demonstrate that it belongs to the category of environmentally aware firms, a category known around the world. By accepting a ranking in the 'business school' category, a school can claim this global identity.

In other cases, organizations defend their local particularities against partial organization by trying to avoid standards, monitoring, or sanctions. For example, the production and effects of international standards can be counteracted in at least three ways. First, large corporations in many industries expend great effort at influencing standard decisions in order to obtain standards that fit the individual corporation's needs, production processes, or product development plans. Second, they may participate in standardization processes in order to stop decisions about international standards (Tamm, Hallström and Boström 2010). Third, they may refuse to comply with a standard they do not like – not to say that they always succeed. In many cases, they end up having to comply with product standards in their own products in order to coordinate their production with that of other firms or with such organizational standards as ISO 9000 or ISO 14000, in order to be considered a respectable or at least an acceptable partner by foreign organizations.

For people and organizations that are not directly involved in international standard setting, some international standards may go largely unnoticed. For instance, consumers of mobile phones may not reflect on the fact that most of the phones' components are determined by international standards, even if the phone is produced in their home country. Yet there are situations in which the foreignness of international standards and any ensuing monitoring and sanctioning activities and their effects on local life are easily observed—for example, when organizations publish certifications to demonstrate that they comply with global standards.

Like complete formal organizations, partial organization stimulates and directs objections. But it is less clear who can be blamed. Standards require two decisions: the standard setters' decision to set a certain standard and the individual organization's decision to comply with it. Thus, responsibility is diluted by being shared between setter and adopter. And there are, in fact, fewer institutionalized structures and procedures for complaints about standards than there are for binding rules in organizations. The same responsibility dilution and its effects arise for monitoring and sanctioning activities that are partly decided by the organization that is monitored or sanctioned—organizations that seek certification, for example. And even those that are given a prize for which they have not applied may be seen as partly responsible because they are seen as having the ability to refuse or accept.

In conclusion, when globalization is initiated by organizational elements outside one formal organization, foreignness tends to become somewhat less visible and somewhat more difficult to object to than when formal organizations expand across the globe. They do not constitute such a brutal reminder of global similarities, connections, and interdependencies, as do states or multinational firms invading local contexts with alien practices.

But in comparison with the diffusion of mere ideas, there are still significant differences. Foreign organizational elements tend to be stronger reminders of global connections than foreign ideas do. It is more difficult to hide the origin of partial organization from those who are really interested. Both local and foreign decision-makers can be held responsible. And organizational elements are less flexible: there is less room for local translation. Someone has decided about these elements, and this party is interested in the effects, as are others. The standard setters and other standard compliers have an interest in the way organizations claiming standard compliance actually comply with it, for example.

Meta-organizations

Partial organization can be directed towards individuals or formal organizations, but most partial organization with a global reach is directed towards organizations. Furthermore, the organizers are most often organizations themselves, as examples in the previous section indicate. Organizations may also organize in a more complete form by creating a common organization in which they are members—a meta-organization, having a membership comprising other organizations rather than individuals (Ahrne and Brunsson 2005, 2008). Well-known meta-organizations such as the United Nations (UN), the European Union (EU), the Fédération Internationale de Football Association (FIFA), and the International Chamber of Commerce (ICC) are essential drivers of globalization, as are thousands of less well-known international meta-organizations, such as the International Association of Universities (IAU), the International Fertilizer Industry Association (IFA), and the United Cities and Local Governments (UCLG).

Meta-organizations are associations, which means that membership is voluntary and that all members are considered equal (Warren 2001). The members of meta-organizations are not necessarily associations, however; they are often other types of organizations like states, as in so-called international government organizations or firms in national industry associations. On the international level, the members are typically other meta-organizations: firms or sports associations, for instance, form a national meta-organization which then becomes a member of the international one.

Like all formal organizations, a meta-organization has access not only to the organizational elements of rules, monitoring, and sanctions, but also to membership and hierarchy. The members of meta-organizations are still autonomous organizations, however, and they have the option of leaving the meta-organization at will. Meta-organizations do not have the right to close down one of their members or to move it to a new location.

Membership in an international meta-organization offers organizations unique opportunities to participate in a process of globalization without expanding their own businesses or moving their boundaries. In contrast to the travel of organizations, the formation of a meta-organization does not mean that local organizations move to new places. As members of meta-organizations, local organizations remain local and keep their local identity, while simultaneously becoming part of an expanding organization with a global or at least regional reach. For organizations that have little chance to expand or move, meta-organizations offer a welcome means for attaining external contacts and for the opportunity to influence distant others. A member can use its membership to influence the decisions of the meta-organization and thus, indirectly, the practices of other members.

For most contemporary states, the conquering of other states is not an option. But states have a large number of meta-organizations that they can join—approximately 2,000, in fact. Or they can found new ones; the number of international governmental organizations has long been expanding. In contrast, empires are no longer popular, and some empires have been turned into meta-organizations—the British Empire (now the Commonwealth of Nations) or the Soviet Empire (now the Commonwealth of Independent States [CIS]), for instance. States are still key actors in the contemporary world, but arguably, for most states, membership in international government meta-organizations provides the main form through which they influence global or regional affairs.

Organizations sometimes form or join a meta-organization in order to seek protection from partial organization. Meta-organizations can choose their own rules and their own systems of monitoring and sanctions, thereby decreasing their vulnerability to the organizing attempts of other less supportive organizations. In order to defend themselves, organizations can refer to the organizational elements provided by the meta-organization, which makes other forms of organization unnecessary. The founding of a global meta-organization can be an attempt to seek protection from partial organization with a global reach or to avoid local organizers such as national governments. When the Swedish labor market was deregulated in 1993 and private firms were allowed to recruit and lease workforces, the newly established companies soon founded a meta-organization to institute their own rules. In order to increase its legitimacy, this meta-organization, the Swedish Staffing Agencies, has become a member of the International Confederation of Private Employment Agencies (CIETT) (Garsten 2008: 33–4). Even governmental agencies may use the same strategy. It is fair to assume that some international governmental meta-organizations have been initiated by state agencies mainly for defending their sector and expert interests rather than for some general state interest. Through membership in the International Association of Universities (IAU), for example, national universities can seek to defend academic values against political interference in their home states.

Meta-organizations contribute to globalization in many ways. Within their respective fields, many meta-organizations are active in facilitating interaction and communication among their members, as the International Telecommunications Union (ITU) has done since 1868 and the Universal Postal Union (UPI) has done since 1874. The efforts of a great number of such meta-organizations have created much of our present global interconnectivity. Furthermore, these efforts have often required a certain harmonization among the members, thus producing similarities not only in techniques, but also in organizational structures and administrative processes (Jacobsson 2006).

Some meta-organizations contribute to global or regional status orders by restricting their membership; just because an organization clearly belongs to the relevant category may not automatically accord its acceptance as a member. Only the 'best' business school in each country can become members of Commaunauté Européenne de Management Schools (CEMS). Other meta-organizations invest a great deal of work into providing global status orders by distributing awards to successful members (the International Egg Commission's Golden Eggs, for instance) or, as in sports, by arranging world championships to advertise which of their members or their members' members are the best.

Balancing the Local and the Foreign

For international meta-organizations, the balance between foreign and local is fundamental. The tension between these two levels is built into the organization itself: the meta-organization represents the global aspect and the members represent the local aspect. The tension now becomes partly one of competition among organizations, but within the framework of one organization. Because both the members and the meta-organization are organizations, they compete with each other and must strike a balance as to which organization is the most relevant in various situations. Should the international meta-organization that is foreign in all local contexts be the one with greatest authority and visibility, or should the local member organizations be the significant ones?

The purpose of international meta-organizations is to constitute workable connections between the local and the global. Members of meta-organizations need to appear autonomous and independent in the eyes of their own members and customers in the local community, both of which expect them to be able to make their own decisions. Thus, the authority of a meta-organization vis-à-vis its members must be limited compared with the authority of an organization such as a multinational firm vis-à-vis its individual members. Even if a meta-organization has the right to use all the organizational elements expected of formal organizations, its members may not allow it to use them. In order to balance between the authority of the meta-organization and the authority of its members, it is common that qualified majorities be required for decision making, or even that members have veto rights. Members who want to block decisions on certain rules, monitoring, or sanctions are likely to succeed. Therefore, meta-organizations tend to make little use of their right to hierarchy, avoiding binding decisions and allowing members to decide if they will comply. Rules are often formulated as standards, monitoring is voluntary, and negative sanctions are avoided.

Thus, the influence of a meta-organization on specific members is restricted in many ways, in comparison with the usual level of influence of organizations that have individuals as their members. The local order is under less threat than it is when states and multinational corporations move. But over time, the members tend to influence each other in order to interact more effectively. The similarities in what they do and how they do things tend to increase, thus stripping member organizations of some of their local characteristics. The influence of an international meta-organization on single members is a process that explains much globalization.

There is great variation among meta-organizations, however, in the influence they can exert on their members. The number of members, their similarity, and the purpose and scope of the meta-organization all play a role. Although all these characteristics are subject to change, at any given time, there are meta-organizations that exert little impact on their members and that can be described as a type of club in which organizational elements other than membership are rarely used. A possible example is United Cities and Local Governments (UCLG). Still, such meta-organizations may contribute to globalization by establishing links among their members and an awareness of common interests and issues. In other cases, several members have joined a meta-organization in order to prevent the organization from becoming too powerful. The International Labour Organization (ILO) seems to have been the victim of such strategies at times (Brännström 2005). Other meta-organizations, like the EU, the WTO, FIFA, and NATO, have more positive members and exert a stronger impact by adapting their members to the purpose and tasks of the meta-organization—most often by creating similarities among them to facilitate co-ordination, communication, or common forceful action. Such meta-organizations are among the most significant contributors to globalization. In some cases, they may, over time, even assume some of the characteristics of individual-based organizations (which is the case of the contemporary EU), or even turn into an individual-based organization (as the US did between 1787 and 1862).

Meta-organizations affect the identity of their members—how they are perceived by internal and external parties. Most meta-organizations—car producers and football clubs, for example—recruit members with a similar identity, an identity that is reinforced rather than threatened by membership. In most meta-organizations, there is no significant division of labor among members, and the core activities of the members remain intact. They do not change what they do, but how they do it. So an organization that becomes a member of a meta-organization maintains its old, local identity, while adding a new, global identity.

Having access to two identities gives members the opportunity to manipulate the way they are viewed in their local community. If the management of an organization believes that foreign connections would create suspicion or protests, it can use only its local identity in relationships with its members, customers, or other external parties. Then its membership and new, extra global identity need not generate much attention, and its global connections may remain almost unnoticed. If, on the other hand, the member wants to demonstrate its foreign connections, it can emphasize its membership in an international organization.

How significant this membership appears to others also depends on the meta-organization and whether or not it attempts to become highly visible. Some meta-organizations de-emphasize their significance by avoiding the label of organization; rather, they hide behind weaker labels such as 'fora', 'networks', or 'alliances', trying to suggest that they are relatively insignificant. Others present themselves in a manner similar to that of firms and states: as forceful actors. The Commonwealth of Nations seems less powerful or threatening than NATO, and it is more difficult to criticize membership in the first organization than the second. But no international meta-organization can completely conceal its global aspect.

Meta-organizations and Partial Organization

In comparison with partial organization, membership in a meta-organization provides a stronger new identity. Adding membership to other elements, such as rules or monitoring, increases the trustworthiness of the new identity because it implies that the organization has been recognized as an equal by similar organizations. It becomes easier to convince others about a certain identity and may even generate higher status. Liberal International, for example, helps political parties to ensure or stabilize their identity as liberal parties (Smith 1997).

Members often find it more difficult to reject even a voluntary organizational element advanced by their meta-organization than to reject a voluntary element not connected to membership but advanced by parties seen as wholly external. Yet member organizations cannot translate and use the rules of the meta-organization as they please, without expecting reactions from the other members. If the interpretations of a member organization are too far-reaching, it may even be excluded from the meta-organization, as has happened to some political parties belonging to Liberal International and Socialist International (Christensen 1992; Smith 1997).

On the other hand, if the members agree, a meta-organization can, in practice, soften the organizational elements of the meta-organization more easily than they can soften externally imposed organization. Organizations are highly capable of maintaining a gap between what they do and what they say (Brunsson 2006, ch. 1). To some extent, meta-organization standards may be less restrictive, the monitoring less vigilant, and the sanctions less draconic than they claim to a skeptical audience that may have preferred strong external interventions.

Meta-organizations provide vital roads to globalization, thanks to their unique way of connecting the local with the global. And many meta-organizations may become key global actors in the long run and develop into supra-territorial corridors of order, linking geographically distant organizations and weakening local orders. The traditional multifunctional and geographically bounded states are undermined and partly replaced by global meta-organizations that are based on such various narrow functions as the production of eggs or soft drinks, auditing or football (Ahrne and Brunsson 2008, ch. 9).

Conclusions

Organizations and organization are significant factors explaining many of the global similarities and interactions that we see in the contemporary world. Two processes within organization studies have raised considerable attention: the travel of ideas among organizations and the travel of firms. It seems unlikely, however, that these processes alone would create as much similarity and connectedness as we observe in the world today. Without partial organization and meta-organizations, the world would be much less homogeneous than it currently is, and it would be appreciably more difficult to interact and communicate globally. The increase in similarities, interaction, and communication over the past fifty years has followed a sizeable increase in both partial organization and meta-organizations. The International Standards Organization, for example—just one of several international standardization organizations—has produced 18,500 standards since its inception in 1947. Almost 1.5 million organizations in 178 countries have received a certification that complies with the ISO's management standards (including ISO 9000 and ISO 14000). Moody's have rated more than 33,000 organizations in 110 countries. There are now dozens of different global ranking systems of universities. Almost all of the more than 10,000 international meta-organizations that exist today were founded over the past fifty years, and approximately one-quarter of them over the last decade. The ongoing expansion of these forms of organization is likely to make the world even more homogeneous and connected in the future.

Partial organization and meta-organizations derive some of their significance from the fact that they may offer fruitful compromises between a local order and a global one. Local organizations can choose the extent to which they relate to them. They are not as likely to be brutal reminders of a foreign influence as expanding multinational corporations are; they are softer forms, which makes them more mobile. Yet they are less free-floating and less open to local translation than ideas are. And even though they may attempt to conceal it, it is difficult to avoid noting their foreign origin.

By distinguishing among the four types of globalization processes related to organization, we can also discern their interaction. They may compete, but they may also reinforce each other. Organization facilitates the travel of ideas. Multinational corporations are arenas in which ideas about innovations float more freely than they do in the world outside (Kogut and Zander 1993). Within meta-organizations, people with common interests have the opportunity to exchange ideas about the situation of their organization and what to do about it. Meta-organizations constitute a common structure for the travel of ideas to all their members; they are a kind of global track for safer and more predictable journeys of common ideas.

Moreover, organization may influence ideas about categories in a relatively silent and unobtrusive way. Organizers make decisions on categories of people, organizations, and situations to which their organization element applies. If a category is less visible than the organizational element itself, it may draw less criticism, its origin becoming unclear or forgotten. Specific standards or rankings for business schools may be contested, for example, whereas the Anglo-Saxon concept of business school may become a taken-for-granted label for various schools in different contexts and with different traditions and orientations. There may be criticisms of ISO's standard 9000 whether, in fact, it improves quality, while the relevance and definition of quality may remain uncontested. In the same way, by defining who can be a member, meta-organizations also create or reinforce certain categories, thereby spreading the same identities all over the world.

Any discussion of organization raises questions of institutionalization. To what extent can we expect the extreme degree of acceptance of ideas or organization that is represented by their institutionalization? And to what extent do the different forms vary in this respect? On the one hand, the greater possibility of adapting ideas to local needs and values should facilitate a process by which they and their ensuing practices become taken for granted, and their origin is forgotten or becomes irrelevant. On the other hand, less flexibility of organizational elements does not wholly prevent them from becoming institutionalized as well. Many international standards are no longer perceived as decisions with options, but are taken for granted in many local contexts (David 1986). Some aspects of new technical products may even become almost immediately institutionalized. It is taken for granted, for instance, that a mobile phone should look and function largely the way it does. It is more difficult to imagine how formal organizations, whether multinational firms or international meta-organizations, could become taken for granted and their origin forgotten.

We believe that knowledge about organizations and organization is necessary for understanding the increasing globalization of the contemporary world—not least, knowledge about partial organization and meta-organizations. These forms offer a challenging arena for research by students of organization with an interest in globalization.

References

Ahrne, G., and Brunsson, N. (2005). 'Organizations and meta-organizations'. *Scandinavian Journal of Management, 21*(4): 429–49.

Ahrne, G., and Brunsson, N. (2008). *Meta-organizations*. Cheltenham: Edward Elgar.

Ahrne, G., and Brunsson, N. (2011). 'Organization outside organizations: the significance of partial organization'. *Organization, 18*: 83–104.

Badie, B. (2000). *The imported state: the westernization of the political order*. Stanford, CA: Stanford University Press.

Billig, M. (1995) *Banal nationalism*. London: Sage.

Boussebaa, M., Morgan, G., and Sturdy, A. (2012). 'Constructing global firms? National, transnational and neo-colonial effects in international management consultancies'. *Organization Studies, 33*: 465–86.

Boyer, R., Charrion, E., Jurgens, U., and Tolliday, S. (1998). *Between imitation and innovation: the transfer and hybridization of productive models in the international automobile industry*. Oxford: Oxford University Press.

Brännström, L. (2005). 'Reglering i en metaorganisation – fallet ILO', in G. Ahrne and N. Brunsson (eds), *Regelexplosionen*. Stockholm: EFI.

Brunsson, N. (2000). 'Standardization and uniformity', in N. Brunsson and B. Jacobsson (eds), *A world of standards*. Oxford: Oxford University Press.

Brunsson, N. (2006). *Mechanisms of hope. Maintaining the dream of the rational organization*. Malmö: Copenhagen Business School Press.

Brunsson, N., and Jacobsson, B. (eds). (2000). *A world of standards*. Oxford: Oxford University Press.

Christensen, S. (1992). *Nye mål i en ny verden: Socialistisk Internationale 1976–1992*. Köbenhavn: Fremad.

Czarniawska-Joerges, B., and Joerges, B. (1996). 'Travels of ideas', in B. Czarniawska-Joerges and G. Sevón (eds), *Translating organizational change*. Berlin: de Gruyter.

David, P.A. (1986). 'Understanding the economics of QWERTY: the necessity of history', in W.N. Parker (ed.), *Economic history and the modern economist*. London: Basil Blackwell.

DiMaggio, P.J., and Powell, W. (1983). 'The iron cage revisited: institutional isomorphism and collective rationality in organizational fields'. *American Sociological Review*, 48: 147–60.

Garsten, C. (2008). *Workplace vagabonds. Career and community in changing worlds of work*. Basingstoke: Palgrave.

Hood, C. (1995). 'The new public management in the 1980s: variations on a theme'. *Accounting, Organizations and Society*, 20: 93–109.

Jacobsson, B. (2006). 'Regulated regulators: global trends of state transformation', in M.-L. Djelic and K. Sahlin-Andersson (eds), *Transnational governance*. Cambridge: Cambridge University Press.

Jones, G. (2005). *Renewing Unilever. Transformation and tradition*. Oxford: Oxford University Press.

Kogut, B., and Zander, U. (1993). 'Knowledge of the firm and the evolutionary theory of the multinational corporation'. *Journal of International Business Studies*, 24(4), 1993.

Krasner, S.D. (1999). *Sovereignty: organized hypocrisy*. Princeton, NJ: Princeton University Press.

Luhmann, N. (2000). *Organisation und Entscheidung*. Opladen: Westdeutscher Verlag.

March, J., and Simon, H. (1958). *Organizations*. New York: Wiley.

Morgan, G., Kristensen, P.H., and Whitley, R. (2001). *The multinational firm: organizing across institutional and national divides*. Oxford: Oxford University Press.

Pfeffer, J., and Salancik, G. (1978). *The external control of organizations: a resource dependence perspective*. New York: Harper and Row.

Ritzer, G. (1993). *The McDonaldization of society*. London: Pine Forge Press.

Røvik, K.A. (2007). *Trender og translasjoner. Idéer som former det 21. århundrets organisasjon*. Oslo: Universitetsforlaget.

Sahlin-Andersson, K. (1996). 'Imitating by editing success: the construction of organization fields', in B. Czarniawska-Joerges and G. Sevón (eds), *Translating organizational change*. Berlin: de Gruyter.

Sahlin-Andersson, K., and Engwall, L. (eds). (2002). *The expansion of management knowledge*. Stanford: Stanford University Press.

Scott, R. (2001). *Institutions and organizations*. Thousand Oaks: Sage.

Smart, B. (ed.). (1999). *Resisting McDonaldization*. London: Sage.

Smith, J. (1997). *A sense of liberty: the history of the Liberal International 1947–1997*. London: Liberal International.

Tamm Hallström, K., and Boström, M. (2010). *Transnational multi-stakeholder standardization. Organizing fragile non-state authority*. Cheltenham: Edward Elgar.

Therborn, G. (2011). *The world. A beginner's guide*. Cambridge: Polity Press.

Warren, M.E. (2001). *Democracy and association*. Princeton, NJ: Princeton University Press.

Westney, D.B. (1987). *Imitation and innovation: the transfer of western organizational patterns to Meiji Japan*. Cambridge, MA: Harvard University Press.

Zaheer, S. (2002). 'The liability of foreignness, redux: a commentary'. *Journal of International Management*, 8(3): 351–358.

4

Global Themes and Institutional Ambiguity in the University Field

Rankings and Management Models on the Move

Kerstin Sahlin

A Rising Interest in the Management and Governance of Universities

When organizational scholars started to explore the increased similarity among organizations across countries and societal sectors (Meyer and Rowan 1977; Meyer and Scott 1983) in the context of what later became known as the new institutionalism (Powell and DiMaggio 1991) or organizational institutionalism (Greenwood, Oliver, Sahlin, and Suddaby 2008) more extensively, they based the theory on studies of different organizations, including, for example, schools, museums, the biotech industry, and public agencies. One important source for this increased homogenization was the adoption of widely diffused management techniques and management ideals (Sahlin-Andersson and Engwall 2002). At the time, universities were largely absent as an object of study in the main publications that paved the way for this line of research (e.g., Meyer and Rowan 1977; Powell and DiMaggio 1991; Meyer and Scott 1983).

Today, as this volume clearly exemplifies, studies of universities form an essential part of research on the global proliferation of organization and management. In parallel, we have also seen a global rise in interest in the management and organization of universities among university leaders, policy-makers, and international organizations, and, indeed, a more active reformation of these aspects of universities. Universities appear to be somewhat of a latecomer when it comes to global waves of management reforms, but they are now clearly the object of extensive organizational, governance, and management reforms and ideas, very much in line with developments in other sectors of society.

Many studies have shown a global expansion of management and organizing efforts across countries and across societal sectors (e.g., Sahlin-Andersson and Engwall 2002; Drori, Meyer, and Hwang 2006; Greenwood et al. 2008; Power 2008). This general knowledge will not be repeated here, but is described in detail in other chapters of this volume. In this chapter, I follow two globally diffused themes of university management and governance, and

I explain how these themes have evolved and proliferated. I focus primarily on developments in Europe, and especially Sweden, but we need to go beyond the borders of Europe to follow some of the dynamics of these global themes.[1] Even though this chapter focuses on worldwide transformation of universities, references to institutional literature will show that there are broader lessons to be drawn from this particular sector. The university case displays some of the general patterns and dynamics of the expansion of management and organization.

My argument is not that universities did not change, or were not subject to globally diffused models before these recent global themes developed. From the very beginning, universities have been subject to rationalizing efforts and have been modeled on globally diffused ideas, ideals, and regulations. Historical studies point to distinct eras when universities have been shaped by certain ideas and ideals (e.g., Nybom 2006). Of special importance is the global wave of mass education and the increased emphasis on governance and planning that followed in the 1960s and 1970s. More recently, however, we have witnessed a rising interest—globally—in the governance and management of universities. This global theme has co-evolved with a proliferation of rankings.

The recent changes have resulted in a global landscape characterized by intensified rationalization and homogenization, as well as ambiguity. As the themes co-evolve, they are blended and translated into various local practices and models. Moreover, they are integrated in historically rooted modes of organizing and governing universities. I end this chapter by showing how this development gives rise to institutional ambiguity; I will briefly discuss the implications of this ambiguity for management, governance, and further changes of the university field. First, however, I describe the two global themes and their dynamics.

A Wave of Rankings

In 2011, the World Bank published an edited volume entitled, *The Road to Academic Excellence. The Making of World-Class Research Universities* (Altbach and Salmi 2011). The making of world-class universities has been a popular theme worldwide for the last decade. The 2011 World Bank volume reports on world-class initiatives from several developing and transition countries around the world. The ambition to build world-class universities can be detected behind many reforms of governance of universities in Europe as well, with the introduction of performance-based resource allocation models in many countries, including Great Britain and the Nordic countries, and specific excellence initiatives like the one in Germany.

World-class initiatives are closely linked to rankings. This is clearly demonstrated in the above-mentioned volume. The first chapter extensively discusses rankings and the second chapter is written by professor Liu, the director of the Center for World-Class Universities at Shanghai Jiao Tong University in China and the founder of the well-known *Academic Ranking of World Universities*. The volume also argues for the importance of management and leadership for the building of world-class universities.

A couple of decades ago, rankings of universities and academic disciplines were seldom talked about and did not at all affect the daily work of most university professors and leaders. At least this was true for European universities, although talk about rankings that appeared now and then on the American scene sometimes caught the attention of European media reporters. During the past decade, however, we have witnessed what appears to be an explosion in rankings. This development includes three aspects: (1) the number of rankings has multiplied; (2) rankings have spread globally with the proliferation of international rankings—and with the global attention also paid to national rankings; and (3) rankings have moved into the very heart of university governance systems (Wedlin, Sahlin, and Hedmo

2009; Sahlin 2012). Discussions about and criticism of rankings have expanded with this development. Many organizational changes in universities have been initiated with reference to rankings (Wedlin 2006; Sauder and Espeland 2009; Kehm and Stensaker 2009). Rankings even impact the very logic of governing and performing research (Espeland and Sauder 2007; Shin, Toutkushian, and Teichler 2011; Hazelkorn 2011).

The first international ranking that caught global attention was the *Academic Ranking of World Universities,* also widely known as the Shanghai rankings, first published in 2003 by the Center for World-Class Universities and the Institute for Higher Education at Shanghai Jiao Tong University. The Shanghai ranking was initially developed by Liu as a response to the Chinese projects, starting in the late 1990s, to build world-class universities (e.g., Wang, Wang, and Liu 2011). Liu knew about rankings from his years of PhD training in Canada, and now, back in China, he constructed an international league table based on available official data in order to indicate the current global standing of Chinese top universities and to inform the Chinese world-class project of what characterizes the top universities in the world (www.arwu.org and personal communication June 2006). This league table soon attracted the attention of university leaders and policymakers throughout the world, and has since become the most widely cited international ranking list.

A number of rankings followed. The *Times Higher Education Supplement World University Ranking* came in 2004 (later renamed the *Times Higher Education Ranking*). The European University Association recently reviewed 13 international rankings (Rauhvargers 2011), which shows not only the global expansion of rankings, but also the diversity of rankers. Several league tables have been formed by university-based research centers. Media organizations are also active rankers, as are intergovernmental organizations.

New rankings have been formed in reaction to existing ones. According to the EUA report, the *Times Higher Education Ranking* was formed as a European response to the Shanghai rankings, since very few European universities (only 19) were found among the top 100 on this list. A similar pattern was observed by Wedlin (2006) in her studies of business school rankings. These rankings proliferated globally somewhat earlier than the university rankings. A main motive behind the first international European-based business school ranking (published by *Financial Times*) was the fact that very few European schools made it to those lists.

New rankings have also been formed as a result of the criticism of the narrowness of previous rankings. The CHE rankings and the EU multi-rank are both multidimensional, and hence, seek to cover more aspects of the universities than the Shanghai type of rankings, which had a pronounced focus on research performance. Interestingly, the Shanghai group is now in the process of developing a multi-rank. Clearly, this is a reaction to the reactions. With these developments, rankings have become more global, both in the sense that rankers are now appearing in many parts of the world and in the sense that they cover wider aspects of university operations. Driving this development is also a revised view on what rankings are for. While the Shanghai rankings were first developed to inform politicians and policymakers about what comprises a world-class university, rankings are today largely described as ways to inform students about where to study and to inform university leaders about with whom to form partnerships. Media also report that such uses have increased over the years. Rankings, in other words, have come to be regarded as the main reputation measure, and currency, on a global university market.

A third aspect of the expansion is that the use and production of rankings have moved into the very heart of university governance. The EU has planned its own ranking project, Multi-rank. A few years ago, the Swedish government considered the construction of its own ranking list, but later gave up the idea. Governments repeatedly refer to rankings and express concerns when the universities of their respective countries do not appear high enough on the league tables; they try to initiate policies to enhance the chances of their universities to advance. In turn, rankers, apparently as a way of boosting their alleged growth and to compete with other rankers, continuously refer to the use of the rankings by governments.

Rankings have not only moved closer to governments, they have also been privatized. Since 2009, the ARWU, which has been published by the Shanghai Ranking Consultancy, is described on the ARWU website as a fully independent organization that also offers tailored services to individual universities and policymakers. Clearly, a market for rankers and for services addressing the rankings is in the making.

All rankings are partly based on bibliometrics, either Web of Science provided by Thompson Reuters or Scopus provided by Elsevier. These publishing houses are also active participants in the many international conferences on rankings. They take an active part in the constructing, editing, and proliferation of rankings across the globe, and they have developed tailored services that are sold to university leaders as a means of using bibliometrics in their strategic management efforts. Hence, we find a clear mix of private corporate interests and global intergovernmental interests, which also means that boundaries between private and public are becoming increasingly blurred. The use of bibliometrics for assessment purposes goes far beyond ranking lists. Systems of quality-based resource allocation models have been introduced throughout Europe. Even though they differ in their design, the arguments, as well as the assessments of them, are all at least partly based on bibliometrics. It is actually difficult today to find reviews, resource allocation models, and peer reviews that do not, at least in some way, use and refer to bibliometric measures.

Rankings and bibliometrics are two of the many assessment technologies that have proliferated during the past few decades. We can see a more general diffusion of evaluations and assessments of individual research performance, universities, and of various aspects of national systems of higher education; the field of higher education is, like other sectors of organized society, subject to extensive auditing and evaluation (cf. Power 1998, 2008).

Most European countries have set up special quality assurance agencies. These agencies are, in turn, members of the ENQA (the European Association for Quality Assurance in Higher Education), an organization that disseminates information about quality assurance in higher education and also reviews European national quality assurance agencies (cf. Stensaker and Harvey 2011). There is also a growing interest in assessing and auditing universities as organizations. So-called institutional evaluations are focusing on the way in which universities are organized and managed. Risk management is another diffused management technique that is now subject to extensive organizing and scrutinizing efforts (Power et al. 2009). During the past few years, we can see what could be described as a market for audits—that is, assessments and evaluations. In Sweden, where universities are public agencies, they are also subject to assessments and evaluations that reach across the public sector. For example, the national audit office is nowadays very active when it comes to auditing universities, not only concerning their use of resources but also their academic performance. In addition to the several units concerned with audit, evaluation, and assessments, there are a growing number of think tanks worldwide, and these, too, are being ranked (cf. www.gotothinktank.com/2011-global-tank-index)!

Rankings—and assessments more generally—have spurred extensive organizing efforts. Many universities have set up special units with the task of following the rankings, suggesting appropriate management responses and ensuring that fair and favorable data is submitted to the rankers. Some universities have set a goal of climbing the rankings, and they have developed strategies for how to do so. We also see further structural reforms among universities in response to these broadly diffused rankings and assessments, such as the formation of alliances and mergers, as well as reorganizations.

Conferences on rankings are held regularly by most international organizations concerned with universities. Reports on rankings have been written, among others, in the frameworks of some of the most influential international organizations—the World Bank and the OECD. I have already referred above to the report issued by the European University Association. On its website, this organization states that the monitoring of rankings is one of its most essential tasks. A special expert group, the International Ranking Expert Group (IREG), was formed in 2004 by the UNESCO European Centre for Higher Education (UNESCO-CEPES) in Bucharest and the Institute for Higher Education Policy in Washington DC. At their second meeting in 2006 in Berlin, they formulated *The Berlin Principles on Ranking of Higher Education Institutions*. These Berlin principles have been widely disseminated. The group has continued to hold conferences on a regular basis, and they have a website where they issue news on rankings and provide an audit of rankings. Hence, in this area, as in most parts of contemporary society, we find proliferating soft regulations, available for actors in global society to more or less voluntarily subscribe to and for others to use as a basis for their scrutiny, regulation, and reorganizing efforts (cf. Mörth 2004; Djelic and Sahlin-Andersson 2006).

The aforementioned Shanghai unit hosts biannual international conferences on world-class universities. The fourth such conference in November 2011 was attended by university leaders, policymakers, and rankers from around the world; it was sponsored by Thompson Reuters. Presentations dealt with how universities and national bodies worked to encourage or establish 'world-class universities' and how they sought to improve their ranking positions. The conference and its composition can be seen as a sign that the 'world-class university' has developed into a world phenomenon. However, there were critical presentations and remarks, too, summarized with expressions like 'WCU disease', 'the danger of homogenization', and 'the danger of complacency'.

In this section, I have shown how rankings have developed into a global theme and have spurred extensive organizing efforts. Ranking models have been subject to translation by individual persons, organizations, and networks of various kinds. Translations and expansion have followed when rankings have been taken up in new contexts, and when new rankings have been formed in reaction to and resulting from critique of previous ones. The critical debate on rankings is integrated into, or co-opted by, the main missionaries of these same assessment techniques. The global theme of rankings has been closely related to other forms of measuring and assessing the performance of universities, and they relate to efforts of creating world-class universities. This idea was behind the first rankings and has found further fuel as rankings have developed into a global theme.

Management Reforms

Extensive reforms of the governance of universities have been pursued worldwide, partly in response to the emerging rankings and assessments and partly driving such efforts. Academic management has caught the attention of many think tanks, policymakers, and academic leaders. With this development, universities have come to build elaborate organizational and management structures (e.g., Frank and Meyer 2007); they have become managed organizational actors (e.g., Ramirez 2006, 2010; Krücken and Meier 2006; Brunsson and Sahlin-Andersson 2000). Universities, in other words, have been formed as goal-directed entities with their own formulated strategies, clear boundaries, and hierarchies for management control. As universities have been restructured into becoming organizational actors, research results tend to be increasingly attributed to the entire university—and to university management—rather than to the individual researcher. In line with this development, successful universities are given the resources and responsibilities to develop further—that is, to become 'world-class'.

Ramirez (2010) showed that 'US universities underwent earlier organizational rationalization and differentiation in part because they were less differentiated from other social institutions' (p. 55). If we follow this trend globally, we find that developments came first in the US, then in Europe, and later in Asia, Latin America, and Africa. This pattern is also reflected in themes, for example, at global conferences, in rankings, and in publications, where a regional focus follows this order. However, this should not automatically lead to the conclusion that the entire university sector is being Americanized. Instead, the global wave of university reforms follows a more mediated pattern, where parts of the American system are being imitated and translated as other regions are being reformed. Hence, it is much too simple to describe the entire transformation as one of Americanization (Krücken 2012). American role models are present on all levels of this transformation (not least because top positions on the ranking lists are dominated by US schools), but they rather appear as regional constructions of American models (cf. Maasen and Olsen 2006; Mazza, Sahlin-Andersson, and Strandgaard Pedersen 2005).

The construction of universities as managed organized actors has also followed on a number of national political reforms. The financing and regulation of universities was subject to many reforms throughout the world, from the mid-1990s and onward, in what has been described as efforts to enhance their autonomy (Musselin 1997; Ramirez 2006, 2010; Frank and Meyer 2007). These reforms came together with or followed in the wake of reforms of the public sector more generally, to the extent that public services have come to be organized as rational actors with clear boundaries, hierarchies, rational control measures, and identities (Brunsson and Sahlin-Andersson 2000). While public service used to be organized largely as professional communities or as agents, they were restructured to form into more corporate-like organizations through a number of organizational reforms inspired by private management or corporate models of organization. Hence, much of the restructuring of universities is driven not directly by policies for research and higher education, but by management policies for the public sector as a whole (Sahlin 2012). In addition, in countries where universities are somewhat more distanced from the government—formed as specific associations or foundations—the transformation of universities has followed more general organizational trends, often summarized as following the trends of the New Public Management (e.g., Ramirez 2010; Elzinga 2010). The introduction of block grants, accounting regulations for universities similar to those found in the private sector, the introduction of individual salaries, and the quest for strategies and profiles for individual universities, all sprang from the corporate ideal and came to reshape the very identity of these units. Comparisons with and references to private management are today commonplace among university leaders. Universities all over Europe extended their management structures, many with layers of vice-rectors, often appointed by the rector and placed above faculties and with responsibilities over specific areas (e.g., vice-rector for internationalization, vice-rector for academic affairs, vice-rector for research, vice-rector for innovation, etc.).

Although rectors (or vice-chancellors or presidents—terminology still differs across the world) and deans are still being elected in many places (for an overview of different rules and practices regarding appointments, see Estermann, Nokkala, and Steinel 2011), management systems are mixtures of appointed and elected leaders. The basic principle of *primus inter pares* is replaced by a management culture with extensive management training and where experiences in management positions—inside and outside academia—is increasingly taken into account when appointing academic leaders. Academic leadership has become a career in itself where many rectors climb the career ladder by moving from one university to the next and where a clear distinction between those who manage and those who are being managed evolves (Engwall 2012). In Sweden, the overall governance of universities has clearly been remodeled on corporate governance with external chairs and external members (many of them representing the business community) on the university boards. In line with this model, the government is depicted as an owner—compared with owners of business corporations. What started as external pressure to reform university governance, organization, and management has developed into a transformed identity and identification with continuous pressures for management reforms from within. Hierarchical models of decision-making and control came more into focus, as did specific procedures for quality assurance and control—in several places using industrial models, such as ISO. Consultants have been brought in to set up the most efficient management and organization. In Sweden, the recruiting of academic leaders, including rectors, is nowadays routinely done with the assistance of head-hunting consultants.

We also see, more recently, a privatization of the university sector worldwide. In many parts of the world, the number of private universities is clearly on the rise. Across the whole sector, research and education are increasingly being defined as private rather than public goods (e.g., Calhoun 2006) and the whole university field has been characterized in terms of academic capitalism (Slaughter and Leslie 1999). As I already pointed out, the assessment and ranking systems are also largely run by private bodies.

The transformed identity and ideal type structure of universities has followed from a number of reforms and individually diffused organizational elements. The adoption of some elements and ideas has given rise to requests for further organizational change, eventually combined with a revised organizational structure and a revised organizational identity. As is shown by Brunsson and Sahlin-Andersson (2000), once public bodies come to be viewed and managed as organizations, they tend to become more receptive to the many globally diffused management recipes and organization elements. In other words, this development has not followed a grand plan, but has evolved in small, self-reinforcing steps. Universities formed into managed organizational actors, and the adoption of generic management models followed. The development also meant the construction of university systems as markets. Of course, competition is nothing new in the university world, but the central competitive dimension of the recent ranking explosion and organizational transformation is that universities are perceived primarily as organizations on a market. The expansion of organization is not only apparent at the level of universities. With the described development, the university field has become more densely organized. Interest and intermediary organizations have been mobilized and expanded with these developments, and new organizations have been formed. This development drives the global themes as the newly formed and mobilized organizations engage in them.

A recent example is an 'autonomy scorecard,' issued by the European University Association (Estermann and Nokkala 2009; Estermann et al. 2011) in collaboration with rectors' conferences in Poland and Germany, the association of universities in Denmark, and the University of Jyväskylä. The study is financed by the European Commission. Autonomy was measured along four dimensions: organizational autonomy, financial autonomy, staffing autonomy, and academic autonomy. The survey dealt with the autonomy of the university primarily vis-à-vis the state, and the scoring and comparisons concerned national university systems. Again, universities were treated as unified social actors, and it was the autonomy of this actor—not, for example, the autonomy of the individual academic—that was in focus. This survey was performed against the backdrop of a series of normative statements issued by the EUA, formulated in the form of a series of declarations, all emphasizing the importance of autonomy and accountability.

An Institutional Transformation Characterized by Ambiguity

With the two interrelated global themes, universities are going through institutional transformation. The field is being restructured with more marketized relations and a more densely organized landscape. Universities have become organizational actors, seen less as unique social formations, but increasingly discussed and assessed as a variant of a more generic organizational type. With this development, universities have become increasingly receptive to globally diffused management ideas so that their restructuring has evolved in self-sustaining spirals.

At first glance, the described emergent global themes appear quite clear-cut, with specific assessment criteria and labels such as autonomy, accountability, quality, excellence, and world class. However, earlier studies of such management models and ideas have portrayed widely disseminated management knowledge as being simultaneously highly ambiguous. Management models build on many sources, and carriers edit models, ideas, and experiences in various ways as they circulate, so their use and practical implications vary with time and space (cf. Sahlin and Wedlin 2008). This combination of ambiguity and precision means that they can travel and, at the same time, seem capable of being applied in many settings; it is one explanation for their success as global management models (Sahlin-Andersson and Engwall 2002; Czarniawska and Sevón 2005). However, for the individual organization, leader, or researcher, this also entails ambiguity. Many participants at conferences and writers of newsletters and reports also express such ambivalence. I referred above to the critical debate on rankings and to the many questions posed—at conferences, among individual universities, and in reports from the many international organizations—on the implications of rankings. How important are they, and to what extent should one apply those success criteria as one's own? The stepwise development of the global themes adds to the ambiguity; discussions on the importance for individual initiatives as well as for where the field is heading are commonplace. Furthermore, I have pointed to autonomy, deregulation, and universities and strategic actors as important drivers for and implications of the global themes. At the same time, the European university field is highly politicized with national excellence initiatives, earmarked research funding schemes, and the like. Therefore, reforms and discussions on autonomy are ambiguous, too. Does it, for example, mean more or less political control of the university sector? Hence, we can also see the many reports, conferences, and newsletter items on university management and on rankings as a sign of the ambiguity that these global themes bring.

Ambiguity also follows from the interplay of the two global themes. I have shown how the two themes intertwine and partly build on and reinforce each other. However, there are also fundamental differences. The described management reforms emphasize universities not as specific kinds of coordinated bodies, but rather as any kind of public agency or any kind of organization. Even though the rankings were fueled and framed by a more generally emerging audit society where governance by numbers is proliferating (Power 1998, 2008; Miller and Rose 1990; Rose 1991), the measures and quality indicators are specific to universities, and comparisons are kept within the university sector. In the interplay of the two themes, an ambiguity evolves concerning the extent to which universities are unique bodies in society and the extent to which they can be managed and measured in generic modes—as any kind of organization.

Institutional ambiguity shows even more clearly when we view the global themes in the broader institutional context in which they emerge, diffuse, and impact. It is not difficult to find criticism against the themes. Some of this criticism, as I described above, is integrated into the processes and actually contributes to the expansion. For example, new rankings were started as a result of critiquing the existing ones; individual universities and university associations formed special groups with a task of monitoring developments and reflecting upon them. At the same time, such organizing efforts directed more attention to the phenomena and in this way further fueled the proliferation.

However, there is also a more fundamental critique (e.g., Berman 2012; Bok 2003; Ginsberg 2011; Halsey 1992; Kirp 2003; Mirowski 2011; Schrecker 2010; Washburn 2005), largely based on different visions and models for how universities should be governed and, in fact, on what universities are and what they are for (cf. Boulton and Lucas 2008; Collini 2012). The critique in focus is largely formulated from more traditionally rooted visions of the university and its governance than the one implied in recent management, governance, and organizing measures described above. I summarize it here as collegiality. Collegiality, as an organizing principle, ideally includes a management structure with elected leaders (elected as *primus inter pares*), peer review, ongoing and critical seminars, and a continuous critical dialogue among academics, all based on the belief that knowledge should be continually tested and reviewed. It is through peer review and critical dialogue that high-quality teaching and research can be ensured. To avoid personal conflicts and dependencies, peer review transcends organizational boundaries, and thus limits management control within organizations. Collegiality is not only a basis for criticism, but collegial forms of governing and organizing are certainly still active in the field—for example, with the maintenance of more or less powerful senates and faculty boards, ideals of *primus inter pares* and elected leaders, the extensive use of peer review, and legal backings of academic freedom, even though they have been challenged by the more recently emerging themes. This critique and the continuation of collegial models of governance and decision-making suggests that the transformation of the field is not as univocal and clear-cut as it may have appeared when we followed individual emergent global themes above. Moreover, these themes may not be as dominant in the field as some of the recent policy rhetoric may suggest. Instead, the university field is characterized by multiple institutions.

Richard Scott and his colleagues (2000) remind us that institutional transformations do mean that not only do the new institutions become dominant, but also the old ones become deinstitutionalized. Even where profound institutional change is demonstrated, developments do not need to follow a straight line with clear-cut phases. Scott et al. (2000) conclude that different modes of governance can be simultaneously active in the field, although to different degrees. Hence, it is not the case that one kind of governance disappears or is abandoned when a new type of governance is introduced. Instead, it is rather a question of new ideals and principles being added to the old; they complement and challenge previous principles.

The university field is thus characterized by institutional pluralism (Kraatz and Block 2008), where multiple modes of governance are at play, where universities are ascribed multiple identities at the same time, as emphasized by Kerr (1963) in the expression 'multiversity', and where modes of governance and identities mix differently in different settings (Clark 1986). In analyzing the university dynamics in Europe, Maasen and Olsen (2006) distinguished between four models of university governance and university visions: a rule-governed community of scholars, an instrument for national political agendas, an internal representative democracy, and a service enterprise embedded in competitive markets. They show a development away from the first model, where universities are viewed as an institution in their own right and where the university operations are assumed to be best governed and controlled in a collegial mode, to the other three, where universities are instruments for various societal interests and groups. Most profoundly, they emphasize the increased business orientation of management and governance—similar to my emphasis in this chapter. Again, they show how collegiality—or the vision of universities as a rule-governed community of scholars—is challenged and translated as it interplays with the above-described themes. It does not disappear, but it is challenged, and it may not be as much talked about as the more recently evolving themes. The newly introduced principles in the university field tend to be more clearly formulated, while the earlier principle of collegiality is often taken for granted ('that's what we've always done', etc.). This partly follows from how ideas spread. Moreover, once established in a context, certain organizational ideals easily become taken for granted and are therefore perhaps not always perceived to be so important to document and explain. When existing or previously dominating governing principles are not described and explained to the same extent, but rather referred to as old habits, there is the risk that they will be considered passé, uninteresting, unimportant, and simply not very relevant—or they may stay, but the way in which they are to be combined with newly introduced principles is not spelled out.

While public reports and consultancy reports on universities write extensively about the agency and management ideals, collegiality may be mentioned but not really spelled out. Many books written by former deans, vice-chancellors, and presidents, on the other hand, based on their own experiences as university leaders, devote considerable space and thoughts to professional and collegial systems. These books typically have at least some chapters on the importance of collegiality and of the free pursuit of knowledge as the main principle for the organizing of universities (e.g., Cole 2009; Kennedy 1997; Rosovsky 1990; Russel 1991; Sundqvist 2010; see also Goodall 2009).

A reading of these 'reports from the field' together with the reforms, policies, and models of the newly emerging themes gives an image of the institutional ambiguity of the field. Collegial principles are still fundamental to universities for their capacity to produce high-quality research and teaching. However, individual leaders appear many times to learn about these principles largely through experience when seeking to manage, despite newly introduced systems of governance that are often based on the other governing principles. Collegial models for the governing and organizing of universities, and the vision of the role of universities on which they rest are certainly alive in the field, but if and how these competing modes of governing and the competing visions of the university can be combined remains to be seen.

In short then, the university field is evolving in the intersection of several fundamental notions of what universities are and hence how they should be organized and governed. These institutions mix differently across levels and in different places.

Previous writings present rather contradictory implications regarding the impact of institutional ambiguity for the further development and dynamics of the university field. On the one hand, this ambiguity may drive the expansion of the newly formed global themes further. DiMaggio and Powell (1991) point to ambiguity as a main driver for organizational imitation (see also Sahlin-Andersson 1996). Hence, we might expect that those more clearly and generally formulated management models—circulated by the many carriers working across universities—will come to dominate, reshape, and homogenize the field further.

Rooted in the theoretical tradition of ambiguity and organizational change, as developed primarily by James March and Johan P. Olsen (1976, 1972; March 1981), Kraatz and Block

(2008) show that institutional pluralism may, in fact, lead to more as well as less change and to more as well as less locally grounded change. Individuals, groups, and organizations may be lost in translation and, in fact, caught in the conflicting dynamics of the diverse institutions, which may lead to inertia and less change, at least locally. Another possibility is that ambiguity and institutional pluralism is exploited and used strategically by individuals, groups, or organizations, so that they find space and ways of pursuing their own ideas and changes. Indeed, institutional ambiguity can drive global themes as well as local variations.

Acknowledgments

I would like to thank Thorsten Nybom, John Meyer, Johan Olsen, Chiqui Ramirez, Bjørn Stensaker, Åse Gornitzka, and Patricia Bromley, participants at seminars at the University of Oslo, INCHER at the University of Kassel, Linköping University and Uppsala University, and the editors and reviewers of this volume for valuable comments on earlier drafts of this chapter.

Note

1   The data presented here is based on participant observation at conferences on rankings and world-class initiatives, analysis of policy reports, previous publications on rankings and organizing of universities, and a review of Web-based newsletters from rankers and international university associations. In analyzing these data, I also make use of my five and a half years of experience as deputy vice-chancellor of Uppsala University.

References

Altbach, P.G., and Salmi, J. (eds). (2011). *The road to academic excellence. The making of world-class research universities*. Washington: World Bank.
Berman, E.P. (2012). *Creating the market university. How academic science became an economic engine*. Princeton, NJ: Princeton University Press.
Bok, D. (2003). *Universities in the marketplace. The commercialization of higher education*. Princeton, NJ: Princeton University Press.
Boulton, G., and Lucas, C. (2008). *What are universities for?* LERU report.
Brunsson, N., and Sahlin-Andersson, K. (2000). 'Constructing organizations: the example of public sector reform'. *Organization Studies*, 21(4): 721–46.
Calhoun, C. (2006). 'The university and the public good'. *Thesis Eleven*, 84, February: 7–43.
Clark, B. (1986). *The higher education system: academic organization in cross-national perspective*. Berkeley, CA: University of California Press.
Cohen, M.D., March, J.G., and Olsen, J.P. (1972). 'A garbage can model of organizational choice'. *Administrative Science Quarterly*, 17(1).
Cole, J.R. (2009). *The great American university: its rise to preeminence, its indispensable national role, why it must be protected*. New York: Public Affairs.
Collini, S. (2012). *What are universities for?* Harmondsworth: Penguin Books.
Czarniawska, B., and Sevón, G. (eds). (2005). *Global ideas: how ideas, objects and practices travel in the global economy*. Lund: Liber and Copenhagen Business School Press.
Djelic, M-L., and Sahlin-Andersson, K. (2006). 'Introduction: a world of governance. The rise of transnational regulation', in M.-L. Djelic and K. Sahlin-Andersson (eds), *Transnational governance. Institutional dynamics of regulation*. Cambridge: Cambridge University Press, 1–28.
Drori, G., Meyer, J., and Hwang, H. (eds). (2006). Globalization and organization: world society and organizational change. Oxford: Oxford University Press.
Elzinga, A. (2010). 'Globalisation, new public management and traditional university values'. Keynote at the 1st NIRPA workshop, Swedish Science Council (VR), Stockholm, 7–8 April 2010.

Engwall, L. (2012). 'The making of a market for academic leaders'. Paper for the workshop 'The organization and re-organization of markets' at SCORE, Stockholm, Sweden, 12–13 January, 2012.

Espeland, W., and Sauder, M. (2007). 'Rankings and reactivity: how public measures recreate social worlds'. *American Journal of Sociology*, 113(1): 1–40.

Estermann, T., and Nokkala, T. (2009). *University autonomy in Europe—exploratory study*. Brussels: European University Association.

Estermann, T., Nokkala, T., and Steinel, M. (2011) *University autonomy in Europe II—the scorecard*. Brussels: European University Association.

Frank, D., and Meyer, J.W. (2007). 'University expansion and the knowledge society'. *Theory and Society*, 36(4): 287–311.

Ginsberg, B. (2011). *The fall of the faculty. The rise of the all-administrative university and why it matters*. Oxford: Oxford University Press.

Goodall, A. (2009). *Socrates in the board room. Why research universities should be led by top scholars*. Princeton, NJ: Princeton University Press.

Greenwood, R., Oliver, C., Sahlin, K., and Suddaby, R. (2008). *The SAGE handbook of organizational institutionalism*. London: SAGE.

Halsey, A.H. (2004/1992). *Decline of donnish dominion: the British academic professions in the twentieth century*. Oxford: Oxford University Press.

Hazelkorn, E. (2011). *Rankings and the reshaping of higher education: the battle for world-class excellence*. New York: Palgrave Macmillan.

Kehm, B.M., and Stensaker, B. (eds). (2009). *University rankings, diversity, and the new landscape of higher education*. Sense Publishers.

Kennedy, D. (1997). *Academic duty*. Cambridge, MA: Harvard University Press.

Kerr, C. (1963). *The uses of the university*. Cambridge, MA:. Harvard University Press.

Kirp, D.L. (2003). *Shakespeare, Einstein, and the bottom line. The marketing of higher education*. Cambridge, MA: Harvard University Press.

Kraatz, M.S., and Block, E.S. (2008). 'Organizational implications of institutional pluralism', in R. Greenwood, C. Oliver, K. Sahlin, and R. Suddaby (eds), *The SAGE handbook of organizational institutionalism*. London: Sage, 243–75.

Krücken, G. (2012). '"Americanisation" of European universities is not on the cards'. *University World News*, 206.

Krücken, G., and Meier, F. (2006). 'Turning the university into an organizational actor', in G.S. Drori, J.W. Meyer, and H. Hwang (eds), *Globalization and organization: world society and organizational change*. Oxford: Oxford University Press.

Maasen, P., and Olsen, J.P. (eds). (2006). *University dynamics and European integration*. Berlin: Springer.

March, J.G. (1981). 'Footnotes to organizational change'. *Administrative Science Quarterly*, 26: 563–77.

March, J.G., and Olsen, J.P. (1976). *Ambiguity and choice in organizations*. Bergen: Universitetsforlaget.

Mazza, C., Sahlin-Andersson, K., and Strandgaard Pedersen, J. (2005). 'European constructions of an American model: developments of four MBA programs'. *Management Learning*, 36(4): 471–91.

Meyer, J., and Rowan, B. (1977). 'Institutionalized organizations: formal structure as myth and ceremony'. *American Journal of Sociology*, 83: 340–63.

Meyer, J., and Scott, W.R. (1983). *Organizational environments*. Beverly Hills, CA: Sage.

Miller, P., and Rose, N. (1990). 'Governing economic life'. *Economy and Society*, 19(1): 1–31.

Mirowski, P. (2011). *Science-Mart. Privatizing American science*. Cambridge, MA: Harvard University Press.

Mörth, U. (2004). *Soft law in governance and regulation*. Cheltenham: Edward Elgar.

Musselin, C. (1997). 'State/university relations and how to change them: the case of France and Germany'. *European Journal of Education*, 32(2): 145–64.

Nybom, T. (2006). 'A rule-governed community of scholars. The Humboldt vision in the history of the European university', in P. Maasen and J.P. Olsen (eds), *University dynamics and European integration*. Berlin: Springer.

Powell, W., and DiMaggio, P. (1991). *The new institutionalism in organizational analysis*. Chicago: University of Chicago Press.

Power, M. (1998). *The audit society: rituals of verification*. Oxford: Oxford University Press.

Power, M. (2008). *Organized uncertainty: designing a world of risk management*. Oxford: Oxford University Press.

Power, M., Scheytt, T., Soin, K., and Sahlin, K. (2009). 'Reputational risk as a logic of organizing in late modernity'. *Organization Studies*, 30(2 & 3), 165–88.

Ramirez, F. (2010). 'Accounting for excellence: transforming universities into organizational actors', in V. Rust, L. Portnoi, and S. Bagely (eds), *Higher education, policy, and the global competition phenomenon*. New York: Palgrave Macmillan.

Ramirez, F.O. (2006). 'The rationalization of universities', in M. Djelic and K. Sahlin-Andersson (eds), *Transnational governance: institutional dynamics of regulation*. Cambridge, UK: Cambridge University Press.

Rauhvargers, A. (2011). *Global university rankings and their impacts*. Brussels: European University Association.

Rose, N. (1991). 'Governing by numbers: figuring out democracy'. *Accounting, Organizations and Society*, 16(7): 673–92.

Rosovsky, H. (1990). *The university. An owner's manual*. New York: Norton.

Russel, C. (1991). *Academic freedom*. New York: Routledge.

Sahlin, K. (2012). 'The interplay of organizing models in higher education. What room is there for collegiality in universities characterized by bounded autonomy?' in B. Stensaker, J. Välimaa, and C.S. Sarrico (eds), *Managing reform in universities: the dynamics of culture, identity and organisational change*. London: Routledge.

Sahlin, K., and Wedlin, L. (2008). 'Circulating ideas: imitation, translation and editing', in R. Greenwood, C. Oliver, K. Sahlin, and R. Suddaby (eds.), *The Sage handbook of organizational institutionalism*. Thousand Oaks, CA: Sage.

Sahlin-Andersson, K. (1996). 'Imitating by editing success: the construction of organizational fields', in B. Czarniawska and G. Sevón, (eds), *Translating organizational change*. Berlin: Walter de Gruyter, 69–92.

Sahlin-Andersson, K., and Engwall, L. (eds). (2002). *The expansion of management knowledge*. Stanford: Stanford University Press.

Sauder, M., and Espeland, W. (2009). 'The discipline of rankings: tight coupling and organizational change'. *American Sociological Review*, 74(1): 63–82.

Schrecker, E. (2010). *The lost soul of higher education. Corporatization, the assault on academic freedom, and the end of the American university*. New York: New Press.

Scott, W.R., Ruef, M., Mendel, P., and Caronna C. (2000). *Institutional change and healthcare organizations*. Chicago: University of Chicago Press.

Shin, J.C., Toutkushian, R.K., and Teichler, U. (eds). (2011). *University rankings. Theoretical basis, methodology and impacts on global higher education*. Berlin: Springer.

Stensaker, B., and Harvey, L. (eds). (2011). *Accountability in higher education: global perspectives on trust and power*. New York: Routledge.

Sundqvist, B. (2010). *Svenska universitet: lärdomsborgar eller politiska instrument?* Hedemora: Gidlunds.

Wang, Q., and Liu, N.C. (2011). 'Building world-class universities in China: Shanghai Jiao Tong University', in P.G. Altbach and J. Salmi (eds), *The road to academic excellence. The making of world-class research universities*. Washington: World Bank, 33–62.

Washburn, J. (2005). *University Inc. The corporate corruption of higher education*. New York: Basic Books.

Wedlin, L. (2006). *Ranking business schools. Forming fields, identities and boundaries in international management education*. Cheltenham: Edward Elgar.

Wedlin, L., Sahlin, K., and Hedmo, T. (2009). 'The ranking explosion and the formation of a global governing field of universities', in L. Wedlin, K. Sahlin, and M. Grafström (eds), *Exploring the worlds of Mercury and Minerva. Essays for Lars Engwall*. Uppsala: Acta Universitatis Upsaliensis. Studia Oeconomiae Negotiorum 51, 317–34.

5
Storytelling
A Managerial Tool and its Local Translations

Barbara Czarniawska

> The days of hands-on leadership are over. That's why we don't want to be manipulated, seduced. But we want to know what's going on within the organization we belong to. Shared goals, shared metaphors are part of the narrative that is an organization.
>
> (Swedish publisher, Fabelredaktionen)[1]

Most management theoreticians and practitioners would agree that 'the days of hands-on leadership are over.' Ever since Michel Foucault, many authors (e.g., Latour 2005) have noted that Jeremy Bentham's Panopticon, based on the assumption of co-presence, no longer works (even if some maintain that the Web may turn out to be one). Managers can no longer see their subordinates, and when they do, they often see them on the screen rather than in person. What is needed is technology that facilitates control at a distance, and perhaps *storytelling* is just such a technology. But do we want it? And who are 'we' anyway?

In what follows, I first present my perspective: looking at globalization as a process of translocalization, with a mechanism of translation (Czarniawska 2002). From this point of view, I try to reconstruct the emergence and spread of storytelling as a management tool. Studies of the travel of ideas, objects, and practices within the global economy tend to present successful translocalizations; however, no attention is paid to negative cases, which is understandable in light of the difficulties encountered in such fieldwork. Nevertheless, I suggest that the lack of interest in storytelling in Swedish organizations, in contrast to its popularity in other Scandinavian countries, can be treated as one such negative case. I offer some explanations for this deviance and end by considering possible consequences of the use of this management tool in work organizations.

Globalization as Translocalization

There are a great many definitions of globalization. The one that attracts me most is the suggestion that globalization can be perceived simply as *translocalization* (Czarniawska and Joerges 1996), a phenomenon consisting of the spreading of local practices, ideas, customs, and technologies to localities beyond their origin—spreading, in fact, all over the globe.

Understood in this way, globalization is hardly a contemporary phenomenon. It encompasses colonialization, in the sense of conquering new lands, as well as new markets and new domains. It includes the voluntary imitation of non-local ('foreign') practices, technologies, and customs. All of these have been known for thousands of years, but there is, indeed, one specific trait that is unique to contemporary globalization: modernization. Modernization consists of imposing or voluntarily adapting new ways of being in the name of formal rationality and technological progress (Meyer 2007).

A question as old as the phenomenon itself arises. How do ideas, practices, customs, and technologies spread beyond the localities of their origin? What is the vehicle that makes such travels possible? Traditionally, it has been suggested that the spreading of ideas, forms, and practices occurs through *diffusion*. This chemical metaphor has become extremely popular in social sciences, although its originator, Gabriel Tarde (1890/1962), did not suggest that ideas move like particles, but rather that particles move like ideas. His suggestion was based on the assumption that the social world is the one people know best, and with its help, they can understand the physical world. The main propagator of his idea, Everett Rogers (1962), remembered the details of this conception, but later followers turned the metaphor on its head.

The notion of *translation* may be of better use therefore in describing the emergence and stabilization of various kinds of connections around the globe. This notion is polysemic, too, but it is a polysemy bridging natural sciences, social sciences, and humanities. Most commonly associated with language, translation can also mean the transformation and transference of anything moved from one place to another. This notion of translation was borrowed from French philosopher Michel Serres (Serres 1982; S. Brown 2002). In Serres' reading, translation may involve the displacing of something or an act of substitution, but it always involves transformation. Indeed, biologists speak of translation of RNA into protein (http://en.wikipedia.org/wiki/Translation_(biology)).

The notion of translation has been adopted by two French sociologists of science and technology, Michel Callon (1980) and Bruno Latour (1986). Whereas Callon emphasized its homologizing effects ('Translation involves creating convergences and homologies by relating things that were previously different' [Callon, 1980: 211]), Latour emphasized the opposite effects, albeit these are mostly unintended ('the spread in time and space of anything … is in the hands of people; each of these people may act in many different ways, letting the token drop, or modifying it, or deflecting it, or betraying it, or adding to it, or appropriating it' [Latour, 1986: 267]). Research applying a translation perspective to organization studies showed that both effects occur (e.g., Czarniawska and Sevón 1996, 2005).

What sets the vehicle of translation in motion? Following Girard (1977), Callon (1980) has suggested that it is a shared desire. Behind translation there is imitation, the fundamental learning mechanism (Tarde 1890, 1962; Sevón 1996).

Yet, how do people (and organizations) know what to imitate? Tarde (1890/1962) suggested that what is imitated is allegedly superior, but how do people know what is superior? It is here that the notion of fashion, as used by Tarde and later by Simmel (1904/1971) and Blumer (1969), can be of use. Fashion is a collective choice among tastes, things, and ideas; it is oriented toward finding but also toward creating what is typical of a given time.

In management, fashion is one of the ways of introducing order and uniformity into what may seem like an overwhelming variety of possibilities. In this sense, fashion helps managers to come to grips with the present, even as it 'serves to detach the grip of the past in the moving world. By placing a premium on being in the mode and derogating what developments have left behind, it frees actions for new movement' (Blumer 1969: 289). It also introduces some appearance of order and predictability into preparations for what is, by necessity, disorderly and uncertain: the future. Fashion, in its gradual emergence, makes the surprises of the next fashion less startling and tunes in the collective by making it known to itself, as reflected in the present fashion and in the rejection of past fashions (Czarniawska and Joerges 1996).

Thus, guided by fashion, people imitate desires or beliefs that appear attractive at a given time and place, leading them to translate ideas, objects, and practices, for their own use. This translation changes what is translated and those who translate. The more imitated something is, however, the less attractive it becomes over time (Tarde 1890/1962: 210). There is always room for new fashions, therefore, and for subsequent translations. This circular, or rather spiral, process produces an enormous variety of results, many of which have been examined in relation to management and management research.[2]

One variation of the phenomenon remains less known, mostly because of the well-known difficulties in studying negative cases. What happens if translation stops? Why can translocalization not reach a certain locality, even though it concerns an idea that is travelling globally? I suggest that such an event took place in relation to one of the current management fashions—storytelling—which, traveling globally, stopped at the border of Sweden (metaphorically speaking). First, however, I trace its translocal progress.

Once upon a time, an idea began to travel …

The following excerpt, taken from the 20 April 1998 issue of *Financial Times*, signals the beginnings of the new fashion in management:

> **The consultant's tale: A new branch of management training uses the power of storytelling in an effort to improve communication (Lucy Kellaway [1998])**
> Once upon a time, there was a management consultant. He was a man of talent, with a genius for making companies part with their money. He had a friend, whom he loved dearly. Yet his friend was not happy. He wanted to be a famous writer, but so far had met with nothing but failure.
> "Nobody will publish my stories. What shall I do?" he wailed.
> "Don't worry," said the consultant. "My clients will buy anything. I'm sure they'll love your stories."
> "But your clients are big businesses. What will they want with my ramblings?"
> "Leave it to me," said the consultant.
> I have written this story to share some exciting news: a brand new branch of management training is born. Today and tomorrow a group of business people will gather in a hotel in Bedford (having each paid £600) for a conference called The Power of Story in Organisations. They will learn how to tell stories. They will find out how The Body Shop is using stories to make its communications more human. They will learn how stories can help them dream up great visions.[3]

The journalist was obviously skeptical about this news; she said later in the article that 'companies know more than enough about stories already' and pointed out that annual reports often include more narratives than facts and figures these days. Her account of the origin of the new tool is believable, even though it cannot be proved or disproved.

The first trace of storytelling as a managerial tool that I have been able to find leads to a book written by the CEO of Armstrong International, David M. Armstrong (1992), entitled *Managing by Storying Around: A New Method of Leadership*. Armstrong described how he was sitting in church listening to a sermon—a story that Armstrong did not quite follow until the minister finally explained its moral. When Armstrong looked around to check if other members of the congregation were showing agreement with the moral, he made the following discovery:

> The people who had been nodding off, or not paying much attention before the sermon began, were now wide awake.
>
> And suddenly I understood an amazing thing. *This happened every Sunday*. People who often attend church probably can recite some of these stories word for word, yet they still listen. People like to hear stories.
>
> What a great way of communicating, I thought. Why can't we do this in our company, Armstrong International? (…)
>
> Right there in the church, I decided we would tell stories in our company. We'd tell stories about our goals and objectives, stories that would explain our core values and our vision of the future, and stories that would celebrate our victories. We'd even share a few stories that would underscore what shouldn't be done.
>
> I started telling stories at Armstrong five years ago, and as I hoped, storytelling has turned out to be an amazingly effective form of communication. Rules, either in policy manuals or on signs, can be inhibiting. Through storytelling, our people can know very clearly what the company believes in, and what needs to be done.
>
> (Armstrong 1992: 2–3)

The remainder of the book consists of Armstrong Inc. stories.

In 1996, Warren Bennis, the doyen of management studies, reviewed Howard Gardner's *Leading Minds: An Anatomy of Leadership* (1995) in the *Harvard Business Review*. Gardner was a Harvard professor of pedagogy. This book is particularly well known, but the critical detail for my line of reasoning is that the title of Bennis' review was 'The Leader as Storyteller.' Then Australian Stephen Denning, of the World Bank, came out with *The Springboard: How Storytelling Ignites Action in Knowledge-era Organizations* (2001). In his later book (2005), Denning told his readers how he had visited the International Storytelling Center in Johannesburg, Tennessee, in 1998, to access professional help for narrating a story about the possible future of the World Bank. That professional helper made Denning realize that *business stories* had to be different from other narratives. Denning instructed others how to go about it, and soon an entire industry was growing around the idea. He continues to write books and give seminars (very expensive ones), although the Dane, Rolf Jensen (*The Dream Society: How the Coming Shift from Information to Imagination will Transform Your Business* [2001]), has become almost as well known (and can be engaged at a more modest fee).

The Internet and intranet have become forums for narrations. Julian Orr's (1996) study of Xerox technicians revealed that they used stories as a way of sharing knowledge about the machines the company repairs. John Seely Brown and Paul Duguid (2000) used this insight when creating the Eureka program, which can archive all such stories. In their role as consultants, Norwegian scholars from NTNU/SINTEF have introduced 'Scheherazade's divan' to the IT company Computas, a portal in which all the employees tell stories about experiences that may be relevant to their colleagues (Gisvold 2005/2006). Some of the recent books on storytelling in organizations are by Brown et al. (2004), Denning (2005/2011), Lori Silverman (2006), Anna Linda Mussacchio Adorisio (2009), and Browning and Morris (2012). The center is still in the US, but then the US still dictates management fashions.

Storytelling as a management fashion has made a strong impact in Denmark and Norway (e.g., Carlsen et al. 2004). Danish hi-fi producer Bang & Olufsen (B&O) has long used the motto 'We are a storytelling company' on its Web page. I asked the Swedish B&O salespeople what the motto meant. 'It means that they tell the same story [about the two engineers, Bang and Olufsen] over and over again,' one of them said with a laugh. The other one looked at him reprovingly and said, 'Yes, but it's never exactly the same. And by listening to the little nuances in the storytelling we have learned to figure out which way the wind is blowing.'

The word in the field of practice is that storytelling is becoming passé: B&O no longer carry the story of their origins on their Web page, and they have removed the motto. Others argue that storytelling is well established, practically institutionalized. A Danish consulting company, Workz, which originated in Lars von Trier's Zentropa, offered 'Third Generation Storytelling,' which combines semiotics, systemic theory, and dramaturgy.[4] This page no longer exists, however. Workz offers games and films 'because nothing beats the capacity of film media to tell a good story.'[5] In Norway, some companies have abandoned storytelling (for example, the company Synnøve Finden did so after a change in top management), whereas others, especially international firms such as Rolls-Royce, still see it as their primary mode of internal communication.[6]

So why has Sweden, which is well known for quickly following management fashions (Czarniawska 1993), not readily adopted storytelling as a management tool? Before addressing this issue, I must take a detour through the research community's engagement with narrative to determine what role, if any, scholars have played in discovering and popularizing the tool.

... even as the research community turned toward narrative ...

Sometime in the 1970s, narratives began to capture the interest of anthropologists and ethnologists. Two US sociolinguists, Labov and Waletzky (1967), most likely encouraged by Lévi-Strauss, adapted for their own purposes Vladimir Propp's analysis of Russian fairy tales by Russians. US historian Hayden White (1973) daringly suggested that history as a scientific field did not exist; instead, it should be called historiography—that is, the theory of how people create narratives about different places during different eras. US sociologist Richard Harvey Brown (1977) proposed a poetics for sociology, unaware that Russian formalist Mikhail Bakhtin had already advanced the same idea. By the 1980s, the 'narrative turn' had become a fact in US social sciences: Walter Fisher (1984) had introduced it to political sciences, Jerome Bruner (1986) and Donald E. Polkinghorne (1987) had brought it to psychology, and Deidre McCloskey (1990) had demonstrated that economics actually consists of stories and metaphors.

Scholars of organization theory usually refer to Ian I. Mitroff and Ralph H. Killman's article, 'Stories Managers Tell: A New Tool for Organizational Problem Solving' (1975), Joanne Martin et al.'s 'The Uniqueness Paradox in Organizational Stories' (1983), and Alan L. Wilkins' 'The Creation of Company Cultures: The Role of Stories and Human Resource Systems' (1984). Notice that Mitroff and Killman still used an earlier paradigm (problem solving), although they eventually became the main promoters of the corporate culture frame, whereas Wilkins was already employing the new paradigm. Eventually scholars, and not merely US scholars, began to speak about 'narrative approaches in organization studies' as popularized by Boje (1991, 2001), Gabriel (1991, 2000), and Czarniawska (1992, 2004). This is the way the approach has been described in a Swedish textbook on organization science:

> [A narrative approach] is a theoretical undertaking based on the assumption that narration plays a central role for understanding and communication. Within this approach, one devotes a great deal of attention to the stories that appear in organizations, in the form of myths, tall tales and jokes, for example. (…) Some consultants view stories as tools for influencing a workplace and therefore recommend that managers avail themselves of stories and cautionary tales for governing their organizations.
> (Corvellec and Holmberg 2004: 9; my translation)

Corvellec and Holmberg's text introduces a clear distinction between the theoretical undertaking and the management tool. In practice, however, the dividing line is not so obvious. Textbooks that contain narratives do teach future managers how to use stories (Corvellec and Holmberg's model was Fineman and Gabriel's UK collection of organization narratives in *Experiencing Organizations* [1996], a textbook published in many editions). Furthermore, many scholars formulate recommendations to practitioners, as did Jeff Gold (1997), for example, when he tried to convince companies in Great Britain that storytelling was an invaluable part of every learning organization. Moreover, it often happens (as it did with the Norwegian scholars in the previous example) that scholars act as consultants, or at least as action researchers. In Sweden, Margareta Bjurklo and Gunnel Kardemark experimented with *narrative accounting* (Bjurklo 2008). Earlier, Corvellec (1997) had noted that the Swedish words *redovisning* and *redogörelse* are closely related to one another, as is clearly seen in the English term for both: *account*. But I failed to discover further indications that Swedish scholars, who are undoubtedly interested in narratives, attempted to extend their interest to practice. Swedish (and other) consultants did, and yet storytelling has made no impact on Swedish companies and authorities.

… whereas Swedes are not quite convinced[7]

In 1953–1954, Volvo distributed a book to all eight-year-old children in Sweden entitled *Willy Volvo Conquers the World and Wins the Princess*.[8] It was a children's story about a Volvo car. Just in time for Christmas 2003, the Swedish chain of luxury department stores, NK, released the book, *Mr Mollgren's Unusual Christmas Journey: A tale from Nordiska Kompaniet*.[9] 'Talk about corporate storytelling!' exclaimed the consultant and author in an interview, relating the event. Does this mean that storytelling is an old, traditional tool in corporate Sweden, or that, like Molière's Monsieur Jourdain who spoke prose throughout his life without knowing it, companies employ storytelling without either giving it a name or regarding it as a tool? Most likely, it is the latter.

The consultant and her colleagues discovered storytelling in 2000 and arranged an event on 'corporate storytelling.' At the outset, companies were not interested: they wanted to present themselves through their financial facts and not through 'fuzzy' and potentially revealing stories from their own practice. But there were some people at Volvo who thought that it may be possible to use storytelling in both their internal and external marketing. The consultant and her collaborators were asked to teach people at Volvo to tell stories about Volvo, with an emphasis on quality. In preparation for the course they conducted, they undertook a round of interviews within the company, resulting in the booklet, *Tell Me: The Volvo Cars Storytelling Primer*, which was then used as instructional material in the course.

Participants in the course were chosen by Volvo to be 'brand ambassadors.' They constituted people regarded as formal and informal leaders, who were recruited from the echelons of top management and from painters on the shop floor. Their task was to use their own stories to tell visitors or new employees what Volvo stands for. The assumption behind this task was that official stories lacked credibility.

According to the evaluation, the participants were pleased with the course, yet it was not continued. Perhaps one of the reasons was that in 1999 Volvo was bought by Ford, and the new owner announced that outside consultants would no longer be engaged—a decision that took some time to implement, but implemented it was. It is hard to predict what would be Geely's stand on storytelling since its acquisition of Volvo in 2010. But the consultant involved changed her profile and now offers help in contacts with mass media.[10]

Coincidence, or something else? Danish and Norwegian organization theorists, informally interrogated about this matter, pointed to two relevant differences between Swedish managers and their Danish and Norwegian counterparts—two differences that are actually related. First, Sweden is perceived as a country where modernism, with its clear preference for logical-scientific knowledge, has become entrenched in a way that cannot be compared with that of Denmark and Norway. In the vocabulary of Charles Tilly (2006), Swedish managers look for technical cause–effect accounts. Second, my interlocutors pointed to the cultural value traditionally given to fairy tales in Denmark and Norse sagas in Norway. Narrative knowledge, then, is regarded as a significant type of knowledge in Denmark and Norway, but not in Sweden.

The 'story of storytelling' may not be quite finished in Sweden. In 2004, Inter IKEA Systems BV (which is the sole proprietor of the IKEA concept) launched a project that was later named 'IKEA Stories.' The idea for the project was based on the conviction that IKEA, as a work organization, contained many narratives that could illustrate the development of the IKEA concept and the IKEA culture. Hundreds of IKEA employees were interviewed and video-recorded in Sweden and other countries. They were asked to narrate their own experiences of working for IKEA—the challenges, the opportunities, and the successes. These narratives were to be constructed around some personally experienced event—meaning, no opinions or second-hand stories.

The project resulted in more than 1,000 filmed stories that are now available on IKEA's intranet, on DVDs, and in books.[11] IKEA used them in introductory courses for new employees and as tools in courses in learning and communication for other employees. The consultants' website with these stories still existed when I wrote this chapter, but it is clear from its homepage that storytelling seminars are now given not to managers, but to employees in communication departments.[12] Kaboodle.com used to have a forum called 'It is all about IKEA,' in which 'Amusing IKEA stories, jokes, cartoons' were posted; but since 2010, it has given the space over to other companies. Still, IKEA uses storytelling 'for internal communication,' the Web says. Is this the beginning of a new era, or merely an exception that confirms the rule? After all, IKEA is an *international* retailer—one of the first and most successful (Martenson 1987; Cassinger 2010). Its 'Swedishness' is now merely part of its brand, and even this is fading, as the company's strongly protested decision to drop famous Swedish brands in their food shops in 2011 seems to indicate.[13]

There have been other attempts within marketing. The leading Swedish academic publisher, Liber, has published a book by Emma Dennisdotter and Emma Axenbrant, entitled *Storytelling: An Effective Marketing Concept* (2008).[14] The blurb for the book said:

> By using storytelling, a company can be unique, even though its products or services are not. The company uses a story that is simple to remember, that enables an understanding of the company's values, and that can easily be passed on. And all this at a price that is a fraction of that for traditional marketing.
>
> (my translation)

This is an unusually honest description of storytelling. A reader's response can be extremely positive ('Finally someone who tells it exactly how it is!') or extremely negative ('Just another new way of conning customers and investors rather than improving the operation'). It seems, however, that the reluctant acceptance of storytelling in Swedish organizations is restricted to management and (external) communication. I was attempting to depict the spreading of fashions concerning storytelling, either as a management tool (internal communication) or as a knowledge repository.

One Tool or Three?

In his 2005 book, Denning said that while he was writing his first book, he had thought of storytelling as a tool. When he wrote his second book, he had thought of it as a toolbox. While writing this third book, he concluded that storytelling was an entire subject, a discipline. In this way, he completed the circle, as narratology is and has always been an academic discipline. Reviewing the ways in which storytelling is presented in various texts, one can conclude that it indeed comes in three guises: a management tool, a communication tool, and a marketing tool.

It could be claimed that storytelling as a management tool includes the two other uses, but I shall present them separately at first. As mentioned, storytelling as a *managerial tool* appears mainly in two variations, both of which arrived at companies following two other management fashions: 'corporate culture' and 'knowledge management.' The propagators of corporate culture were primarily interested in myths or in narratives that create stability. The adherents of knowledge were the next generation's 'learning organization' people, interested mainly in narrative knowledge as an implementation for enabling (planned) change.

The concept of corporate culture is nearly thirty years old and appears to be on the way out. (It must be noted, however, that the former Volvo AB CEO, Leif Johansson, spoke warmly of corporate culture in his honorary doctorate address at Göteborg University on 20 October 2007.) Nevertheless, even the most convinced enthusiasts seem to have realized that a culture cannot be assembled or created in a week, if it can be 'created' at all.

In Gideon Kunda's (1992/2006) well-known book, based on the study of a company that was a leading light within corporate culture, there is a section describing a course in corporate culture. Asked by a course leader (an anthropologist who wrote her dissertation on corporate culture) what culture was, one of the engineers portrayed it as an organism that grows. He added that he tried to cultivate such a culture (mold), but his dog had unfortunately eaten it. The course leader was furious, but the engineer was quite right. Cultivating a culture—of any kind—demands a great deal of time and effort, and it can vanish in an instant under dramatic circumstances. That is why most managers realize that they may be able to protect and spread propaganda for a culture, but not *create* one. Storytelling is a tool that can be used toward that end, but then it becomes a tool of communication—about culture, strategy, vision, or anything else.

Storytelling has been called a *communication tool*, but 'communication,' like 'motivation,' is a usually a euphemism for controlling. The aim of internal communication is often to prevent spontaneous changes, to unite people by instigating a feeling of belonging, to create a corps. Shared stories create a feeling of inclusion for those who know them, while excluding those who (as yet) do not; storytelling reinforces the stories and the feeling of belonging. If these stories succeed, a company may even replace family, friends, and country; storytelling is an ancient tool for creating togetherness in small societies, which the modern, rootless cosmopolites flouted and made difficult.

In contrast, stories seem to work differently when they are treated as a *repository of knowledge and competence*. Even if not everyone favors narrative knowledge (for a voice speaking against narrativity, see Strawson 2004), many people do. In any case, people with a preference for narrative knowledge were for so many years discriminated against in organizational contexts by those who preferred logico-scientific knowledge, that it would be only fair if they were now to receive privileged treatment. In principle, a repository of narratives is an excellent idea.

A problem can arise, however, as more than spontaneous storytelling is needed to create such a repository. First, courses are arranged to improve know-how about storytelling, because not everyone is a born storyteller. Consultants' or teachers' ideas about good storytelling are disseminated, and it is difficult to imagine that management did not previously approve these ideas. Second, software presents its own demands; a certain amount of standardization is unavoidable if stories are to be archived digitally. Third, it is obvious that not all stories can be made public; filtering and validation (Benkler 2006) are inescapable. These three points would seem to indicate that even stories collected in order to preserve knowledge can easily become management tools. After all, Denning (2005) admitted that he *had to go* to the International Storytelling Center because the World Bank had decided to invest in knowledge management.

A third use of storytelling—as a *marketing tool*—is perhaps the most obvious and easiest to accept. Traces of this idea can be found in nearly all descriptions of the practical employment of storytelling. It may nevertheless be the case that many Swedish managers will still think, like Lucy Kellaway does, that it is unsuitable to conceal a company's actual results behind tall tales. This is what some Polish managers in public administration thought when Czarniawska (2002) suggested that they market their company better—that it would be dishonorable to deceive the taxpayers, who should know 'how things really are.' Perhaps public administration will prove most resistant to storytelling as a managerial tool, although the aforementioned consulting company certainly attempts to enter this domain as well. In my ongoing study of the municipality in which I live now, I have seen mention of 'storytelling' being used in courses for employees, but the trace vanished—nobody remembered who mentioned it, and it was not actualized.

There is another difficulty in storytelling as marketing: storytelling requires talent. Kellaway's story of the consultant and his impoverished writer friend contains deep insight. Such a situation was prophesied early on by Swedish writer Göran Hägg, in his David Lodge-style *Doctor Elgcrantz or Faust in Boteå*[15] (1983), a hilarious novel about university life in Sweden. The novel ends with a resourceful but poor professor of literature, Dr Elgcrantz, offering his literary talents to company managers. Twenty-five years later, this fiction was realized. It is unlikely, however, that many Swedish top managers—unlike Danish top managers—will employ writers and literary theorists as management consultants.

Regardless of how storytelling entered the picture and what level of success it attains in Sweden, it will remain a management tool, at least for a while. Is that good or bad, and for whom?

Barbara Czarniawska

Dazed by Stories?

Danish literary theoretician Svend Erik Larsen distinguished between three basic types of contemporary stories: behind-the-scenes stories, anecdotes, and biographies. All three can be found in the world of management. *Behind the scenes* is a genre that scholars share with journalists, and with which even knowledge managers are familiar; the genre includes stories about everyday details in someone's work, 'the way things really are.' As Larsen (2005) noted, these stories can be as stylized as other stories, but they lay claim to authenticity.

The second genre is *anecdotes*. One can imagine that this is a particularly unwelcome genre in serious Swedish companies, but oddly enough, it turns out to be appreciated in a number of serious contexts. US scholars Holmes and Marcus (2006) discovered that both members of the Federal Open Market Committee and high officials in the Federal Reserve Banks had their networks of informers who daily imparted anecdotes that helped them to understand what was happening in the global economy. Similarly, Tarim (2009) observed that storytelling was a dominant mode of communication among brokers at the Istanbul Stock Exchange. Still, one can assume that the high-ranking officials, or Exchange directors, would not send their informers and employees to courses in storytelling. Nor would they sanction the collection of anecdotes in a Web archive, particularly because they would not want to share them with others.

Last, but not least, is the genre of *biographies*, a modern genre that blossoms forth in hero stories about the Genial Founder, the Wise Leader, the Brave Entrepreneur, and similar figures. This genre is the most popular, and although the genre itself is modern, the emplotment of its texts follows old hero stories (more on popular culture and management in Czarniawska and Rhodes 2006). Sometimes texts are stylized as if they belong to the behind-the-scenes genre, when they are actually masked hero stories. The readers or the listeners get to know what the hero's life is like on a daily basis.

Larsen claimed that contemporary stories are good at revealing specific features of our culture, but not so good at criticizing or showing its limitations. Furthermore, there are too few passage points where bad stories—of which there are many—would be rejected. He also noted that stories about democracy are neither plentiful nor particularly moving; too much consensus and too many compromises do not make for exciting intrigue.

Larsen's essay is entitled 'My Story—Or Ours?' But I would like to adapt it to this text by changing it to 'Our Story—Or Theirs?' Who were the 'we' in the initial quote—the 'we' who are supposed to share common goals and metaphors? 'An organization,' the readers are told. If 'an organization' refers to an association, the description is correct, almost by definition. But if it refers to a work organization, the situation becomes much more complex. Such organizations often become modern Golems. Like the legendary clay figure in Prague, they were created to achieve common goals, but sooner or later break free of their own creators. In the worst scenario, they turn against them, as Kunda (1992/2006) demonstrated in his ethnography of a high-tech company.

If 'we' are people who want to do something together, however, the demands will be much more modest. People do not have to have the same goal. They sometimes use the same means for different goals (as when buying an expensive machine together and using it for different purposes). And sometimes it suffices simply to agree on what is right and what is left—no common goals, values, or convictions. Rather, we merely say, 'This is a table, that is a door, and if we go this way we can carry the table through the door. We do it because the table is in the way, because I am not strong enough to carry furniture alone, and because on the other side of the door I can use it to display my books.'

At least the totalitarian society was less hypocritical when admitting that it wanted people to think alike. Brunsson (1989) convincingly argued that hypocrisy is necessary in organizations, but that one must recognize that a state of thinking the same way cannot be achieved without strong sanctions. Furthermore, being in agreement does not necessarily mean thinking alike. A society, no matter how large or small, in which everyone uses the same metaphors and tells the same stories would be appalling. Fortunately, 'we' do not have to worry so much about that, because today's problem is completely different. How can we live together, we who are so very different from one another (Latour 2005)?

From this perspective, storytelling as a management tool would seem to fit an Orwellian scenario. French author Christian Salmon (2010) has analyzed how storytelling was used by Bush and Sarkozy, and has drawn pessimistic conclusions about the political 'narrating machine' (*une machine à raconter*), which, in his view, helps to erase the difference between reality and fiction. He believes that the public imagination is being robbed when the same manipulative techniques are used in politics, the film industry, and the business community to influence opinion, create consent, and regulate behavior. One can also maintain that management's increasing inroads into storytelling are a way of reaching and draining its opponents' repertoires, as stories have always been accessible for ordinary people as tools of resistance.

Yet there is every reason to believe in the power of stories, for no matter how many workshops on storytelling are organized, contradictory stories will appear. Every free culture produces a counterculture, every story its anti-story. Telling stories will continue to be a popular tool of many uses for everybody, even when the storytelling fashion fades away. Perhaps Swedish organizations are not missing much, after all.

Notes

1. Introduction to a collection of texts on narratives, *BerättarBoxen*, Gothenburg: Fabel 2005; my translation.
2. See e.g., two special issues of *International Studies of Management & Organization*, 2008, 38 (1, 2) and the Special Themed section of *Organization Studies*, 2011, 32(5).
3. More about storytelling at The Body Shop in Collison & Mackenzie (1999).
4. http://www.workz.dk/tool_storytelling.html, accessed 2010-03-26.
5. http://eng.workz.dk/node/18, accessed 2012-05-27.
6. I thank the researchers studying storytelling at Tromsø University, Norway, for providing me with this information (2012-05-25).
7. This section is based partly on material gathered by Peter Zackariasson in 2007. He interviewed two Swedish and one Danish consultant who attempted to introduce storytelling to Swedish companies. I am grateful for his assistance.
8. *Ville Volvo vinner världen och princessan.*
9. *Herr Mollgrens sällsamma julresa, en saga från Nordiska Kompaniet.*
10. http://www.louisehamilton.se/, accessed 2012-05-27.
11. The consultants' webpage is http://www.storytellers.se/txt/2007/02/1000_ikeastorie.html (accessed 2010-03-21).
12. http://www.storytelles.se/tzt/index.php, accessed 2012-05-27.
13. http://www.thelocal.se/36748/20111014/, accessed 2012-06-01.
14. *Storytelling: Ett effektivt marknadsföringsgrepp.*
15. *Doktor Elgcrantz eller Faust i Boteå.*

References

Armstrong, David M. (1992). *Managing by storying around: a new method for leadership*. New York: Doubleday.

Benkler, Y. (2006). *The wealth of networks: how social production transforms markets and freedom*. New Haven, NJ: Yale University Press.
Bennis, W. (1996). The leader as storyteller. *Harvard Business Review*, Jan–Feb: 154–160.
Bjurklo, M. (2008). Narrative accounting: A new form of management accounting? *International Studies of Management & Organization*, 38(2): 25–43.
Blumer, H. (1969/1973). Fashion: from class differentiation to collective selection, in G. Wills and D. Midgley (eds), *Fashion marketing*. London: Allen & Unwin, 327–340.
Boje, D. (1991). The storytelling organization: a study of storytelling performance in an office supply firm. *Administrative Science Quarterly*, 36: 106–126.
Boje, D. (2001). *Narrative methods for organizational and communicational research*. London: Sage.
Brown, J.S., and Duguid, P. (2000). *The social life of information*. Cambridge, MA: Harvard Business School.
Brown, J.S., Denning, S., Groh, K., and Prusak, L. (2004). *Storytelling in organizations: why storytelling is transforming 21st century organizations and management*. Woburn, MA: Butterworth-Heinemann.
Brown, R.H. (1977). *A poetic for sociology: toward a logic of discovery for the human sciences*. New York: Cambridge University Press.
Brown, S. (2002). Michel Serres: science, translation, and the logic of paradise. *Theory, Culture & Society*, 19(3): 1–28.
Browning, L., and Morris, G.H. (2012). *Narrative theory and organizational life: ideas and applications*. New York: Routledge.
Bruner, J. (1986). *Actual minds, possible worlds*. Cambridge, MA: Harvard University Press.
Brunsson, N. (1989). *The organized hypocrisy: talk, decisions and actions in organizations*. London: Wiley.
Callon, M. (1980). Struggles to define what is problematic and what is not: the sociology of translation, in K. Knorr, R.G. Krohn, and R. Whitley (eds), *The social process of scientific investigation: sociology of the sciences*. Dordrecht: D. Reidel, 197–219.
Carlsen, A., Klev, R., and von Krogh, G. (eds) (2004). *Living knowledge: the dynamics of professional service work*. London: Palgrave Macmillan.
Cassinger, C. (2010). *Retaling retold. Unfolding the process of image construction in everyday practice*. Lund: Lund Business Press.
Collison, C., and Mackenzie, A. (1999). The power of story in organisations. *Journal of Workplace Learning,* 11(1), s. 38–40.
Corvellec, H. (1997). *Stories of achievement: narrative features of organizational performance*. New Brunswick, NJ: Transaction.
Corvellec, H., and Holmberg, L. (2004). *Organisationers vardag – sett underifrån*. Malmö: Liber ekonomi.
Czarniawska, B. (1992). *Styrningens paradoxer. Scener ur den offentliga verksamheten*. Stockholm: Norstedts.
Czarniawska, B. (1993). Sweden: A modern project, in D. Hickson (ed.), *Management in Western Europe: society, culture and organization in 12 countries*. Berlin: de Gruyter: 229–248.
Czarniawska, B. (2002). *A tale of three cities, or the glocalization of city management*. Oxford: Oxford University Press.
Czarniawska, B. (2004). *Narratives in social science research*. London: Sage.
Czarniawska, B., and Joerges, B. (1996). Travels of ideas, in B. Czarniawska and G. Sevón (eds), *Translating organizational change*. Berlin: de Gruyter, 13–48.
Czarniawska, B., and Rhodes, C. (2006). Strong plots: the relationship between popular culture and management theory and practice, in P. Gagliardi and B. Czarniawska (eds), *Management education and humanities*. Cheltenham: Edward Elgar, 195–218.
Czarniawska, B., and Sevón, G. (1996). Introduction, in B. Czarniawska and G. Sevón (eds), *Translating organizational change*. Berlin: de Gruyter, 1–12.
Czarniawska B., and Sevón, G. (eds) (2005). *Global ideas: how ideas, objects and practices travel in the global economy*. Malmö/Copenhagen: Liber/CBS Press.
Denning, S. (2001). *The springboard: how storytelling ignites action in knowledge-era organizations*. Woburn, MA: Butterworth-Heinemann.

Denning, S. (2005/2011). *The leader's guide to storytelling: mastering the art and the discipline of business narrative.* San Francisco: Jossey-Bass.
Dennisdotter, E., and Axenbrant, E. (2008). *Storytelling: ett effektivt marknadsföringsgrepp.* Malmö: Liber.
Fineman, S., and Gabriel, Y. (1996). *Experiencing organizations.* London: Sage.
Fisher, W.R. (1984). Narration as a human communication paradigm: the case of public moral argument. *Communication Monographs*, 51: 1–22.
Gabriel, Y. (1991). Turning facts into stories and stories into facts: a hermeneutic exploration of organizational folklore. *Human Relations*, 44(8), 857–875.
Gabriel, Y. (2000). *Storytelling in organizations: facts, fictions, and fantasies.* Oxford: Oxford University Press.
Gardner, H. (1995). *Leading minds: an anatomy of leadership.* New York: Basic Books.
Girard, R. (1977). *Violence and the sacred.* Baltimore, MD: Johns Hopkins University Press.
Gisvold, M. (2005/2006). From Scheherezade's divan. Gemini, SINTEF/NTNU, Trondheim, Norge, http://www.ntnu.no/gemini/2002-06e/18-21.htm.
Gold, J. (1997). Learning and story-telling: the next stage in the journey for the learning organization. *Journal of Workplace Learning*, 9(4), 133–141.
Hägg, G. (1983). *Doktor Elgcrantz eller Faust i Boteå.* Stockholm: Wahlström & Widstrand.
Holmes, D.R., and Marcus, G.E. (2006). Fast capitalism: Para-ethnography and the rise of the symbolist analyst, in M.S. Fisher and G. Downey (eds), *Frontiers of capital: ethnographic reflections on the new economy.* Durham, NC: Duke University Press, 33–57.
Jensen, R. (2001). *The dream society: how the coming shift from information to imagination will transform your business.* New York: McGraw-Hill.
Kellaway, L. (1998). The consultant's tale. *Financial Times*, 20 April, p. 11.
Kunda, G. (1992/2006). *Engineering culture: control and commitment in a high-tech corporation.* Philadelphia, PA: Temple University Press.
Labov, W., and Waletzky, J. (1967). Narrative analysis: Oral versions of personal experience, in J. Helm (ed.), *Essays on the verbal and visual arts.* Seattle, WA: University of Washington Press, 12–44.
Larsen, S.E. (2005). Min fortælling – eller vores? Aarhus: VÆRK. http://www.asb.dk/groups/vaerk/aspx.
Latour, B. (1986). The power of association, in J. Law (ed.), *Power, action and belief.* London: Routledge and Kegan Paul, 261–277.
Latour, B. (2005). *Reassembling the social: an introduction to actor-network theory.* Oxford: Oxford University Press.
Martenson, R. (1987). Is standardization of marketing feasible in culture-bound industries? A European case study. *International Marketing Review*, Autumn, 4: 7–17.
Martin, J., Feldman, M.S., Hatch, M.J., and Sitkin, S.B. (1983). The uniqueness paradox in organizational stories. *Administrative Science Quarterly*, 28: 438–453.
McCloskey, D.N. (1990). Storytelling in economics, in C. Nash (ed.), *Narrative in culture: the uses of storytelling in the sciences, philosophy and literature.* London: Routledge, 5–22.
Meyer, J. (2007). Globalization. Theory and trends. *International Journal of Comparative Sociology*, 48(4): 261–273.
Mitroff, I.I., and Killman, R.H. (1975). Stories managers tell: a new tool for organizational problem-solving. *Management Review*, July: 18–28.
Musacchio Adorisio, A.L. (2009). *Storytelling in organizations: from theory to empirical research.* London: Palgrave Macmillan.
Orr, J.E. (1996). *Talking about machines: an ethnography of a modern job.* Ithaca, NY: Cornell University Press.
Polkinghorne, D.E. (1987). *Narrative knowing and the human sciences.* Albany, NY: State University of New York Press.
Rogers, E. (1962/1983). *Diffusion of innovation.* New York: Free Press.
Salmon, C. (2010). *Storytelling: bewitching the modern mind.* London: Verso.

Serres, M. (1974/1982). *Hermes: literature, science, philosophy*. Baltimore, MD: Johns Hopkins University Press.
Sevón, G. (1996). Imitation, in B. Czarniawska and G. Sevón (eds), *Translating organizational change*. Berlin: de Gruyter, 49–67.
Silverman, L.L. (2006). *Wake me up when the data is over: how organizations use storytelling to drive results*. San Francisco, CA: Jossey-Bass.
Simmel, G. (1904/1971). Fashion, in D.N. Levine (ed.), *Georg Simmel on individuality and social forms*. Chicago, IL: University of Chicago Press, 294–323.
Strawson, G. (2004). Against narrativity. *Ratio*, XVII, 4 Dec.
Tarde, G. (1890/1962). *The laws of imitation*. New York: Henry Holt.
Tarim, E. (2009). Tilly's technical accounts and standard stories explored in financial markets: the case of the Istanbul Stock Exchange. Sociological Research Online, http://www.socresonline.org.uk/14/5/21.html.
Tilly, C. (2006). *Why? What happens when people give reasons...and why*. Princeton, NJ: Princeton University Press.
White, H. (1973). *Metahistory: the historical imagination in nineteenth-century Europe*. Baltimore, MR: Johns Hopkins University Press.
Wilkins, A.L. (1984). The creation of company cultures: the role of stories and human resource systems. *Human Resource Management*, 23(1): 41–60.

6

'Re-localization' as Micro-mobilization of Consent and Legitimacy

Renate E. Meyer

Introduction

One of the most interesting and paradoxical aspects of our studies of institutional and organizational change is the phenomenon that, on the one hand, we encounter many similarities in themes, forms, structures, practices, or rhetoric across diverse contexts, and, on the other, we increasingly realize that local, regional, and community characteristics are crucial to understanding the processes and trajectories of change as well as the cultural meanings of these new forms. The two tendencies have often been regarded as opposites: homogenization versus heterogenization, or universalism versus particularism, or global versus local. Trying to go beyond these traditional dichotomies, the concept of 'glocalization' regards globalization and localization as simultaneous processes, as two sides of the same coin. Highlighting this simultaneity, Roland Robertson, one of the earliest proponents of the concept (e.g., 1992 or 1995; Pieterse 1994), describes glocalization as the 'co-presence of universalizing and particularizing tendencies' (Robertson 1995: 25) and refers to the dictionary meaning of the term 'glocal'—'formed by telescoping the global and the local to make a blend' (Oxford Dictionary, cited in Robertson 1995: 28). Similarly, John Meyer has recurrently (e.g., 2000) pointed out that the spread of globally available models actually legitimates the increase of the dramatization of local differences.

Most scholars of glocalization stress that global and local should not be understood in terms of larger and smaller in the sense of nested contexts, nor should they be related to geographic scale at all. Rather, the travel across cultural contexts is the characteristic feature. Defined as a process by which global ideas, models, institutions, or events are interpreted through local frames of reference, and local ideas, models, institutions, or events through global frames (Robertson 1992), glocalization combines two aspects: the de-localization/de-contextualization of a specific cultural 'item' from its original context and its re-localization/re-contextualization in a new context (van Leeuwen and Wodak 1999; Wodak 2010). De-localization or de-contextualization requires that the specificities of the original context be filtered out (for a similar argument see Sahlin-Andersson 2001) and results in the definition of the 'typical' and portable that allows for the 'item' to travel not only across time and space (the ability to flow across time and space is inherent in all institutions), but, more importantly, to overcome meaning boundaries. Re-localization or re-contextualization, then, encompasses the appropriation of the typified construct to the local conditions by creating a new, aligned model. In the conceptual language of institutional theory, theorization (e.g., Strang and Meyer 1993) and translation (e.g., Czarniawska and Joerges 1996) are the corresponding mechanisms.

In this chapter, I focus on the re-contextualization part of the glocalization process. Drawing on literature from institutional theory, social movement research, and political discourse analysis, my overall starting point is that actors, supporters, and opponents alike need to mobilize consent and/or minimize dissent within their local contexts in order to gain support for their interpretations of the global model. Thus, glocalization involves the negotiation of social meaning and legitimation. Both are essentially discursive and political processes (Berger and Luckmann 1967). I start by reviewing theorization and translation as glocalization mechanisms and elaborate the role of accounts as discursive micro-mobilization devices. Drawing on a frame analysis of the translation of shareholder value in the Austrian media discourse from 1991 to 2000 as illustration (for more details on the empirical background and the methodology and methods used, see Meyer [2004] or Meyer and Höllerer [2010]), I describe how different types of accounts can be used in these processes. In particular, I point to two interrelated objectives actors need to attend to when aligning the 'foreign' with indigenous values and beliefs. The first aims at mobilizing support for one's own interpretations. This can be achieved either by linking the new idea to broadly shared 'problems' and/or by engaging in discourse coalitions with local elites (Hajer 1995; Koopmans and Statham 1999). The second objective relates to the capacity to avoid contestation by discursively placing the construct outside known lines of conflict. This can be done by building on ambiguity. Another possibility is to restrict access to the 'politics of signification' (Benford and Snow 2000: 625) by claiming the issue to be a matter for experts. I close with a short discussion of how these types of accounts can contribute new insights into glocalization processes, and outline some topics for future research.

Translation as Re-contextualization of Globally Theorized Models

Theorization, a concept introduced by David Strang and John Meyer (especially 1993 and 1994), refers to the discursive process by which concrete forms or practices are turned into types through the 'development and specification of abstract categories and the formulation of patterned relationships such as chains of cause and effect' (Strang and Meyer 1993: 492). This involves defining a 'problem' and a 'solution' and role identities for a particular cast of actors, as well as placing the practice or form that is theorized in relation to these definitions. According to institutional theory, a concept's theorization provides the quasi ready-made 'bundles' of general accounts to standardize the 'who', 'what', and 'why' (e.g., Strang and Meyer 1993). This generalized language and rationale to account for activities is one of the most important aspects of isomorphism (Meyer and Rowan 1977); it is actually these abstracted theorized models that flow and not copies of the practices (Strang and Meyer 1993).

In the de-contextualization/re-contextualization scheme that underlies the concept of glocalization, theorization refers to dis-embedding. It creates portable abstractions or, in the terminology of Giddens' structuration theory (1984), theorization provides the abstractions that facilitate the distanciation of time and space that is an essential element of institutions. Thus, while all institutions require that a typified, abstracted model be interpreted and enacted in a concrete situation, glocalization includes the overcoming of meaning boundaries. What the glocalization stresses in this regard—and this concern is shared by Scandinavian institutional theory and framing research (see also the concept of *Anschlussfähigkeit* in Luhmann's system theory) and represents a very prominent intersection of these strands of literature—is that meaningful items cannot be transported 'wholesale' from one cultural context to another. Instead, they have to pass through a powerful filter of local cultural and structural constraints to also gain legitimacy in their new local context and can, thus, only spread if they resonate within this context. Thus, for theorizations that leave their cultural contexts (this includes the travel from one institutional sphere [the private sector] to another [the public sector]), a new fit has to be accomplished, a new, adjusted theorization with standardized vocabularies that are aligned with the values and beliefs has to be developed— that is, they have to be translated (see e.g., Czarniawska and Joerges 1996; Sahlin-Andersson 1996; Strang and Soule 1998; Benford and Snow 2000; Campbell 2004; Meyer 2004; Frenkel 2005; Boxenbaum 2006; Sahlin and Wedlin 2008; Meyer and Höllerer 2010).[1]

Re-contextualization involves transformation and may change the form and meaning of the object quite considerably, sometimes almost beyond recognition (Strang and Soule 1998; van Leeuwen and Wodak 1999; Czarniawska 2011). The outcome (both with regard to the meaning as well as the actual practices and material manifestations) reflects the interests and goals of the actors involved as well as the local stocks of knowledge, local mobilizing structures and power constellations and may range from nearly identical to the global type, to hybrids or blends, to almost completely new versions that have only a vague family resemblance with the global template. With global models that travel into many different contexts, a multiplicity of more or less divergent translations provides for considerable variation. When models are contested, various re-contextualizations co-exist within one local context.

Glocalization means that universalizing and particularizing tendencies are simultaneously co-present (Robertson 1995). 'Global' is no particular place and the actual enactment of a global model always has to be effected within in a specific local context. Thus, to put a global model in practice always includes its particularization. At the same time, it is the family resemblance with all the other localized variants that accounts for the underlying universalizing dimension that is equally present in each enactment. Thus, despite all heterogeneity resulting from the existence of multiple local translations, global models and local deviations mutually legitimate each other and it is exactly the increasing celebration of local differences and variations that actually accelerates the global models' spread (e.g., Meyer 2000).

On the level of micro-mobilization, accounts are the central discursive 'tools' of glocalization processes. They are the building blocks of the legitimation strategies (van Leeuwen and Wodak 1999; Vaara, Tienari, and Laurila 2006). Accounts are 'given to neutralize the attribution of deviance' (Scott and Lyman 1970: 91); they are the answers to 'why' questions and are provided in order to 'bridge the gap between the promised and the performed, the expected and the actual, and the surprising and the routine' (Scott and Lyman 1970: 113; see also Mills 1940; Elsbach and Sutton 1992; Lamertz and Baum 1998; Creed, Scully, and Austin 2002; Meyer 2004). As 'reasoning devices', that is, 'pieces of a potential argument that one might make in justifying or arguing for a particular position on an issue' (Gamson and Lasch 1980: 3; see also Gamson 1992), they are, by definition, discursive devices to achieve a fit between the 'foreign' and the 'indigenous'. Accounts 'work' as long as speaker and audience share stocks of knowledge and the categorical systems the accounts are drawn from. Apart from their actual content, accounts, thus, include a claim that the frame of reference they use to interpret a particular situation is legitimate and the 'bridge' they thereby build is appropriate. They can be challenged on precisely these dimensions.

However, not all accounts are equally potent in their capacity to elicit support and eschew dissent in the glocalization process. Their resonance and, thus, mobilization potential depends on how they are located in the broader discourse: how widely the categorizations, frames, and story lines they evoke are shared among relevant audiences, and to what extent coalitions between powerful actors and elites are enabled or impeded. I will, in what follows, develop different types of accounts that were specifically relevant in the context of aligning the globally diffusing model of shareholder value with existing values and beliefs.

Accounts as Central Discursive Micro Re-contextualization Devices

With regard to the resonance that is required for a global model to be successfully translated into a local context, it is useful to separate two objectives: manufacturing consent and avoidance of dissent. The two are obviously closely interrelated, but are addressed in different ways. In my study, I identified different types of accounts that are, for systematization purposes, clustered into two groups according to their primary target. The first set that primarily aims at manufacturing consent contains two types of accounts. A first one—*compliance accounts*—increases the translation's ability to mobilize legitimacy by linking the new model to taken-for-granted 'facts'. The second type—*bridging accounts*—increases the legitimation base by creating a new link to other framings that enables engaging in discourse coalitions with powerful actors.

If consent cannot be achieved, muffling resistance may be the next best option. The second set of accounts aims at avoiding contestation. These two types of accounts both function as neutralizing techniques (Neidhardt 1994). The first works by building on ambiguity (*ambiguous accounts*); the second—*expert accounts*—by restricting the definitional authority to a particular group of actors and silencing potential opposition.

Mobilizing Consent

Compliance Accounts

The ability of an account to connect the problematic and the accepted is, as Scott and Lyman elaborate, dependent on its comprehensibility and acceptance by the audience. An account is likely to resonate '(t)o the extent that everyone in the audience to whom an account is given shares a common universe of discourse and a common basis of beliefs' (Scott and Lyman 1970: 107). On the level of discourse, contestation is manifested through the co-presence of accounts that have a similar argumentative structure, but lead to opposite conclusions with regard to an issue. For example, in the Austrian media debate on Shareholder Value, the pro-account 'Shareholder Value is good because it is based on the rational mechanisms of the capital market and will, thus, lead to overall efficient governance structures that will come to benefit the whole economy', has its argumentative opposite in the idea that 'Shareholder Value is bad, because it is based on the mechanism of an imperfect capital market and the effect will, thus, be a power concentration in the hands of banks, analysts, and managers who will use it to further their particularistic interests'.

Scholars working in the tradition of political and critical discourse analysis (e.g., Ruth Wodak, Teun van Dijk, or Theo van Leeuwen) remind us to not only analyze what is visible in a discourse, but also to pay particular attention to what is absent. Compliance accounts I have called accounts whose argumentative opposites are absent from the actual debate. This means that there is a 'gap' in the discourse in the sense that, although it would be easy to form such an argument, nobody actually uses it.

In the study on the translation of shareholder value, compliance accounts were especially important in the early re-contextualization of the concept. The main problem that the concept was linked to (as solution) by promoters was the low performance of the Austrian capital market. Although this is not a complex argument and, given the structure of the Austrian economy (for more details, see e.g., Barca and Becht 2001; Meyer and Höllerer 2010), it is easy to imagine the inverse account (i.e., considering the structure of the Austrian economy, the inactivity of the capital market is not a serious problem), the necessity to stimulate and revitalize the capital market remained unchallenged in the public debate. It was the most frequently used account in favor of shareholder value in the initial phase. Another compliance account on the pro-side successfully linked shareholder value to the very general and unquestioned statement that owners of corporations have financial interests that need to be taken into consideration. While the 'translators' strongly draw on compliance accounts, resistance to the translation mostly linked with the more encompassing debate on the negative impacts of globalization and the overall Americanization of society—accounts that were not at all unchallenged.

Accounts that have no immediate counter-accounts point to highly legitimate interpretations and are powerful devices when it comes to mobilizing consent. In fact, as social movement scholars (e.g., Gerhards, Neidhardt, and Rucht 1998) have argued, it is often more advisable to switch accounts than to try standing up against them. On the level of discursive re-contextualization strategies, the findings indicate that initial translations of 'foreign' models rely on widely accepted 'facts' as 'springboard for mobilizing support' (Snow et al. 1986: 469).

Bridging Accounts

While compliance accounts locate the issue within widely shared, uncontested definitions, bridging accounts attempt to mobilize consent amidst contradiction and contestation by aligning with other framings and creating new possibilities for coalition formation. This can be done through the addition of new elements to the translations or the deletion of existing elements. Failed attempts to create such bridges are as interesting as successful ones.

Promoting shareholder value by arguing that the free market is also the best instrument to pursue non-economic values and non-monetary objectives (e.g., via ethical investment) is an example of a failed 'offer'. Another example is the attempt to 'sell' the concept as a means to bring to life the Marxist ideal of the people owning the means of production via the investments of their pension funds ('shareholder value suspends the cleavage between workers and capitalists; from shares comes the power of the people'; quote from the media). While these two attempts to build a bridge did not resonate very well (i.e., they were not taken up by the proponents of the respective framings), other accounts were more successful. The 'target' was the traditional Austrian economic elite who were not attracted by the categorical scheme of initial translation. Especially the short-term orientation of the concept and the reduction of their role to a mere shareholder with only financial interests in the corporations, which ran counter to their preferred identity as owner with strategic interests who assumes responsibility for the organization and its stakeholders and prioritizes the organization's long-term survival over short-term profits.

Established elites are powerful allies; their accounts have precedence over those of other groups (Scott and Lyman 1970). Established elites are, however, in general rather conservative with regard to globalization and the change in the institutional framework that is often a result (Höllerer forthcoming). Several bridging accounts were used to appease the traditional economic elites' concerns. One of them downplayed the differences between a shareholder and a stakeholder approach by contending that in the long run, all interests converge. Another one pleaded that the concept was not new, but, in fact, only another name for the 'good old businessmen's tradition' of careful investment and close scrutiny. Yet another redefined shareholder value as a concept aiming at long-term, sustainable growth instead of short-term rises in share prices, thereby absorbing the position of the targeted group. An interesting bridging account in the context of glocalization actively embraced the criticism against globalization and 'Americanization'. It objects to the 'brutal' and 'primitive' Anglo-Saxon version of shareholder value and invents a 'sophisticated' European or Austrian 'alternative' instead. Very often, this account goes hand in hand with the introduction of a new label for the translated model. An anti-globalization account that is used to neutralize local resistance and works as a globalization device is a good micro-level example of how particularizing tendencies actually spur universalistic trends.

Apart from making the global concept compatible with local economic elites' frames of reference and opening the way for a discourse coalition between them and the proponents of shareholder value, this constituted a split in the old truce within the social partnership which was the strongest opponent of the concept at that time. Research into political opportunity structures has amply shown that when elites are divided, the odds for challengers to succeed considerably increase.

Neutralizing Dissent

While mobilizing support aims at active approval of the proposed re-contextualization, the second set of accounts rather tries to circumnavigate expected lines of conflict or to de-emotionalize the debate. In this sense, these types of accounts are a 'neutralization technique' (Neidhardt 1994).

Ambiguous Accounts

Accounts 'work' because they explain and justify by linking to a shared frame. However, they do not always make a link to one particular frame. This may be the result of incomplete reasoning when it remains unclear which account a statement is actually reproducing. On the level of standardized accounts, a similar effect—namely, that a range of interpretations is possible and, if no additional information is provided, it is up to the audiences to fill the argumentative gaps with their own assumptions—may also be produced when the account used resonates in multiple story lines simultaneously. For example, the account that it is important to take into account shareholders' interests leaves open what position in the hierarchy of a company's objectives this implies—that is, whether they are to be prioritized against other stakeholders or regarded as one stakeholder among others. This seemingly small argumentative gap, however, becomes highly relevant when the main line of contestation is the question whether a shareholder value (priority) or a stakeholder value (one among others) orientation is to be pursued. Similarly, distrust in the rationality and efficiency of the market as reason to oppose shareholder value can equally be part in a storyline that calls for state regulation and intervention or in one that sees the balancing power in the ethical orientation and social responsibility of the industrialist.

Ambiguity and multivocality are no 'accidents', but a powerful way to target multiple reference groups and avoid contestation especially in arenas where actors cannot segment their audiences and tailor their claims accordingly (e.g., Pratt and Foreman 2000; Meyer and Höllerer 2011). Equally, Padgett and Ansell (1993) see multivocality as the key to understanding Cosimo de Medici's sphinx-like character and 'robust action', and Leifer (1988) uses the concept of 'local action' to point out that concealing one's actual position in a contestation may be favorable as it ex ante leaves open a range of future moves and ex post does not prove inconstent with any of them. A similar point has been made by Brunsson (1993: 499), when he contends that 'ambiguity implies a reduction in control and the rescue of some consistency'. In the context of glocalization, avoiding dissent through ambiguous, multivocal accounts is an important key to robust local theorizations.

Expert Accounts

The categorical scheme inherent in a concept's theorizations and translations assigns specific subject positions and places the actors differently within the field, thereby authorizing certain actors and perspectives and neglecting others. What makes expert accounts special with regard to the avoidance of dissent in the re-contextualization of a global model is not so much the content of their account but the fact that they link to a domain with restricted access, meaning that they narrowly define who is part of the 'legitimated theorists' (Strang and Meyer 1993) and able to give competent accounts. Equally, once an area is established as domain of a certain type of expert, only other recognized experts are entitled to challenge their accounts (Collins and Evans 2009). This can be a powerful tool to silence opponents without having to engage with their viewpoints. Consequently, expert accounts are often compliance accounts (but see Lefsrud and Meyer 2012 for an example of expert contestation).

For example, to establish shareholder value as a valuation method that is based on the discounted free cash flow and gives a true and fair view of the company's value (better, at least, than all the procedures used before its invention) denies voice to all who are not thoroughly familiar with the respective mathematical and accounting procedures. Such an interpretation invites a totally different cast of competent voices than, for example, a framing as manifestation of a particular ideology. Consequently, speakers who point to shareholder value as expert domain frequently complain that 'shareholder value is heavily contested, but most people don't understand what it is about' (quote from the media).

Reference to authority is a powerful legitimation mechanism. It answers the implicit or explicit 'why' question with 'essentially "Because I say so" or "Because so-and-so says so" where the "I" or "so-and-so" is someone in whom institutionalized authority is vested' (van Leeuwen and Wodak 1999: 104). In the study on shareholder value, the 'true and fair view' account was not a compliance account, but its vis-à-vis (a critic from an accounting perspective, or as one financial analyst in the media put it, 'I could use a crystal ball instead') was very rarely used.

With regard to the theorization and translation of global models, the authority vested in experts is also a central diffusion mechanism. Strang and Meyer point out that the diffusion capacity of a theorized model varies with the degree to which it is built into standard and authoritative interpretations and schemes. They emphasize (1993: 495) that 'one reason for emphasizing the sciences and professions is that these communities are relatively central, prestigious, influential, and so not only construct models but are able to promote them vigorously'. Authorization and diffusion capacity increases with the prominence and prestige of the expert. This type of account stands and falls with the credibility of the expert. This is why fighting expert accounts often involves attacking their expert identity and position rather than actually disputing their claims (Lefrsud and Meyer forthcoming). It is interesting to note that attacks on the other's expert status came almost exclusively from the proponents of shareholder value who criticize their opponents as 'wanna-be economists who, with this silly discussion, display their billowing incompetence in the full light of the public' (quote from the media).

Apart from restricting access to defined authorities, expert accounts often de-emotionalize. As pointed out elsewhere, '[a]n indicator to measure a firm's residual income (e.g., economic value added), for instance, does not mobilize people at the barricades or "put fire in the belly and iron in the soul" (Gamson 1992: 32)' (Meyer and Höllerer 2010: 1256). This is, on the one hand, due to them being regarded as based on objective and superior knowledge (Lefsrud and Meyer 2012); on the other hand, they frequently use a technical language and make use of the objectifying power of numbers and league tables whose legitimacy reflects the global processes of rationalization (Meyer and Rowan 1977).

Conclusion

Transcendence of time and space through typification and enactment is the basic mechanism through which institutions work. Glocalization refers to a specific variant: the typification comes from 'outside'—other geographical scope, other cultural context, other institutional sphere, etc.—and a modified theorization with abstractions and generalizations that are congruent with the local context has to be formed before enactment is possible. In this chapter, I have focused on this re-contextualization that is a prerequisite of glocalization.

On the micro level, accounts are the building blocks of legitimation strategies and the central discursive 'tools' to accomplish this task. Building on literature from institutional theory, social movement theory, and political discourse analysis and, as empirical illustration, on a framing analysis of the translation of shareholder value in Austria, I identified different types of accounts that actors use to align their local translations with existing values and beliefs. They were grouped depending on whether they primarily address consensus mobilization or aim at avoiding contestation.

In the first group, I discussed two types of accounts: a) *compliance accounts*, which are uncontradicted because they reproduce the taken-for-granted 'facts' of a community; and b) *bridging accounts* that provide a link to other framings with the aim to open the way for new discourse coalitions. Three such bridging accounts became relevant in my study: downplaying of differences between positions, denying newness and change, and absorbing the position of the targeted group. In the second group, I discussed the role of c) *ambiguous accounts* and d) *expert accounts*. Both work as neutralizing techniques. I assume that these types of micro-mobilization are not only relevant for the particular context of my empirical study, but also apply more broadly to the early re-contextualization process. More research is required, however, to assess their generalizability. In addition, these types may not cover, in a comprehensive way, all types of accounts that are used in micro-mobilization.

Studies on micro-mobilization like my own can contribute to glocalization research in several ways. First, they draw attention to the opportunities and constraints that the local context holds for actors' interpretative efforts to translate globally diffusing models. Actors are bound by the cultural opportunities and repertoires of accounts provided by their context and available to their own social positions, but they are also creative and strategic. They combine and reinterpret the available 'material' and redefine both the model and the situation. The accounts they use are, as such, 'moves in a social game' (Scott and Lyman 1970: 94).

Closer attention to the micro-mechanisms can contribute to our understanding of success and failure of re-contextualization attempts. In their local translations, actors use several of the types of accounts that I described above. It may be fruitful to gain more systematic insights into the conditions under which certain types or combination of types prove to be more powerful in the re-contextualizing of a global model than others. Moreover, re-contextualization is not a one-time achievement, but ongoing; interesting differences with regard to types of accounts may be found in earlier or later phases of re-contextualization.

A focus on the micro-foundation of glocalization also emphasizes the heterogeneity that surrounds globally diffusing models. The global is no particular 'place,' and global models exist only to the extent that they are enacted in the re-localized variants. Not only are global models translated differently into different local contexts, there may also exist various versions—with varying degrees of similarity to the 'original' model—that compete for legitimation within the same context. Together these variations account for the simultaneous presence of universalizing and particularizing tendencies that are characteristic of glocalization processes.

Note

1 Every enactment of abstract category in a concrete situation (i.e., every enactment of an institutionalized template) is based on sense-making. Thus, every enactment of an institutionalized template requires the actors to mutually define the situation as being eligible. Every enactment will, in one way or another, have to modify the template upon performing (even rituals are never performed exactly the same way). I understand theorization to refer to the development of a template and not its concrete enactment; similarly, translation of theorized models refers to the development of a localized template and not local enactment.

References

Barca, F., and Becht, M. (eds) (2001). *The control of corporate Europe*. Oxford: Oxford University Press.
Benford, R.D., and Snow, D.A. (2000). 'Framing processes and social movements: an overview and assessment'. *Annual Review of Sociology*, 26: 611–39.
Berger, P.L., and Luckmann, T. (1967). *The social construction of reality. A treatise in the sociology of knowledge*. New York: Anchor Books.
Boxenbaum, E. (2006). 'Lost in translation: the making of Danish diversity management'. *American Behavioral Scientist*, 48: 939–48.
Brunsson, N. (1993). 'Ideas and actions: justification and hypocrisy as alternative to control'. *Accounting, Organizations and Society,* 18: 489–506.
Campbell, J.L. (2004). *Institutional change and globalization*. Princeton: Princeton University Press.
Collins, H., and Evans, R. (2009). *Rethinking expertise*. Chicago and London: University of Chicago Press.
Creed, W.E.D., Scully, M.A., and Austin, J.R. (2002). 'Clothes make the person: the tailoring of legitimating accounts and the social construction of identity'. *Organization Science*, 13: 475–96.
Czarniawska, B. (2011). 'Operational risk, translation, and glocalization'. Gothenburg Research Institute Report No. 2011/8. Gothenburg: University of Gothenburg.
Czarniawska, B., and Joerges, B. (1996). 'Travels of ideas', in B. Czarniawska and G. Sevón (eds), *Translating organizational change*. Berlin: Walter de Gruyter, 13–48.
Elsbach, K.D., and Sutton, R.I. (1992). 'Acquiring organizational legitimacy through illegitimate actions: a marriage of institutional and impression management theories'. *Academy of Management Journal*, 35: 699–738.
Frenkel, M. (2005). 'Something new, something old, something borrowed…: the translation of the "family friendly organization" in Israel', in B. Czarniawska, and G. Sevón (eds), *Global ideas:*

how ideas, objects and practices travel in the global economy. Malmo: Liber and Copenhagen Business School Press, 147–66.

Gamson, W. (1992). *Talking politics*. Cambridge: Cambridge University Press.

Gamson, W.A., and Lasch, K.E. (1980). 'The political culture of social welfare policy'. Center for Research on Social Organization Working Paper No. 221. University of Michigan.

Gerhards, J., Neidhardt, F., and Rucht, D. (1998). *Zwischen Palaver und Diskurs. Strukturen öffentlicher Meinungsbildung am Beispiel der deutschen Diskussion zur Abtreibung*. Opladen: Westdeutscher Verlag.

Giddens, A. (1984). *The constitution of society. Outline of the theory of structuration*. Cambridge: Polity Press.

Hajer, M.A. (1995). *The politics of environmental discourse. Ecological modernization and the policy process*. Oxford: Clarendon Press.

Höllerer, M.A. (forthcoming). 'From taken-for-granted to explicit commitment? The rise of CSR in a corporatist country'. *Journal of Management Studies*.

Koopmans, R., and Statham, P. (1999). 'Political claims making: integrating protest event and political discourse approaches'. *Mobilization*, 4: 203–22.

Lamertz, K., and Baum, J.A.C. (1998). 'The legitimacy of organizational downsizing in Canada: an analysis of explanatory media accounts'. *Canadian Journal of Administrative Sciences*, 15: 93–197.

Lefsrud, L.M., and Meyer, R.E. (2012). 'Science or science fiction? Professionals' discursive construction of climate change'. *Organization Studies*, 33: 1477–1506.

Leifer, E.M. (1988). 'Interaction preludes to role setting: exploratory local action'. *American Sociological Review*, 53: 865–78.

Meyer, J.W. (2000). 'Globalization. Sources and effects on national states and societies'. *International Sociology*, 15: 233–48.

Meyer, J.W., and Rowan, B. (1977). 'Institutionalized organizations: formal structure as myth and ceremony'. *American Journal of Sociology*, 83: 340–63.

Meyer, R.E. (2004). *Globale Managementkonzepte und lokaler Kontext. Organisationale Wertorientierung im österreichischen öffentlichen Diskurs*. Vienna: WUV Universitätsverlag.

Meyer R.E., and Höllerer, M.A. (2010). 'Meaning structures in a contested issue field: a topographic map of Shareholder Value in Austria'. *Academy of Management Journal*, 53: 1241–62.

Meyer, R.E., and Höllerer, M.A. (2011). 'Laying a smoke screen: obfuscation and ambiguity as organizational responses to institutional complexity'. Working Paper, WU Vienna University of Economics and Business.

Mills, C.W. (1940). 'Situated actions and vocabularies of motive'. *American Sociological Review*, 5: 904–13.

Neidhardt, F. (1994). 'Öffentlichkeit, öffentliche Meinung, soziale Bewegungen'. *Kölner Zeitschrift für Soziologie und Sozialpsychologie*, Sonderheft 34: 7–41.

Padgett, J.F., and Ansell, C.K. (1993). 'Robust action and the rise of the Medici, 1400–1434'. *American Journal of Sociology*, 98: 1259–319.

Pieterse, J.N. (1994). 'Globalization as hybridization'. *International Sociology*, 9: 161–84.

Pratt, M.G., and Foreman, P.O. (2000). 'Classifying managerial responses to multiple organizational identities'. *Academy of Management Review*, 25: 18–42.

Robertson, R. (1992). *Globalization: social theory and global culture*. London: Sage.

Robertson, R. (1995). 'Glocalization: time-space and homogeneity-heterogeneity', in M. Featherstone, S. Lash, and R. Robertson (eds), *Global modernities*. London: Sage, 25–44.

Sahlin K., and Wedlin, L. (2008). 'Circulating ideas: imitation, translation and editing', in R. Greenwood, C. Oliver, K. Sahlin, and R. Suddaby (eds), *The SAGE handbook of organizational institutionalism*. London: Sage, 218–41.

Sahlin-Andersson, K. (1996). 'Imitating by editing success: the construction of organizational fields', in B. Czarniawska and G. Sevón (eds), *Translating organizational change*. Berlin: de Gruyter, 69–92.

Sahlin-Andersson, K. (2001). 'National, international and transnational constructions of new public management', in T. Christensen and P. Lægreid (eds), *New public management: the transformation of ideas and practice*. Aldershot: Ashgate, 43–72.

Scott, M.B., and Lyman, S.M. (1970). 'Accounts, deviance, and social order', in J.D. Douglas (ed.), *Deviance and respectability. The social construction of moral meanings*. New York: Basic Books, 89–119.

Snow, D., Rochford, Jr., E.B., Worden, S.K., and Benford, R.D. (1986). 'Frame alignment processes. Micromobilization and movement participation'. *American Sociological Review*, 51: 464–81.

Strang, D., and Meyer, J.W. (1993). 'Institutional conditions for diffusion'. *Theory and Society*, 22: 487–511.

Strang, D., and Meyer, J.W. (1994). 'Institutional conditions for diffusion', in W.R. Scott and J.W. Meyer (eds), *Institutional environments and organizations. Structural complexity and individualism*. Thousand Oaks: Sage, 100–12.

Strang, D., and Soule, S.A. (1998). 'Diffusion in organizations and social movements: from hybrid corns to poison pills'. *Annual Review of Sociology*, 24: 265–90.

Vaara, E., Tienari, J., and Laurila, J. (2006). 'Pulp and paper fiction: on the discursive legitimation of global industrial restructuring'. *Organization Studies*, 27: 789–810.

van Leeuwen, T., and Wodak, R. (1999). 'Legitimizing immigration control: a discourse-historical analysis'. *Discourse Studies*, 1: 83–118.

Wodak, R. (2010). 'The glocalization of politics in television: fiction or reality?' *European Journal of Cultural Studies*, 13: 1–20.

7
Competition Regulation in Africa Between Global and Local
A Banyan Tree Story

Marie-Laure Djelic

Introduction

The literature on globalization takes the nation-state seriously, but the issue is generally polarizing. On the one hand, globalization is understood to imply a decline of national polities and their order-creating capacities with a parallel increasing role for markets and market logics (Held and McGrew 1998; Ohmae 1995; Strange 1996). On the other hand, the demise of the nation-state is contested and its role re-affirmed as central in the context of multi-level governance (Boyer and Drache 1996; Hirst and Thompson 1996).

This chapter begins from a different perspective. Globalization is not about the disappearance of rules and order; it comes, in fact, with an increasing density of regulatory and governance activities. On issues as distinct as climate, environment, labor, health, poverty, accounting and finance, competition, corporate responsibility, and more, dense transnational activism over the past decades has resulted in polyarchic and overlapping governance structures, in which multiple actors claim a right to engage in policy-making, rule-setting, and rule-monitoring (Levi-Faur and Jordana 2005; Djelic and Sahlin-Andersson 2006; Graz and Nölke 2008; Tamm-Hallström and Böstrom 2010; Levi-Faur 2012). In the process, nation-states do not disappear; they remain involved but are profoundly transformed. The national rule of law is not displaced by a global runaway market but inscribed in a thick landscape of rules often produced and monitored transnationally. The national rule of law must, in other words, confront and adapt to the progress of a transnational 'law of rules' (Djelic 2011). Globalization always gets localized, but the local also becomes inscribed in and framed through global dynamics—'glocalization' is the right term to describe this circular interplay.

This interplay is often mediated at the level of transnational regions. The European Union (EU), the North American Free Trade Agreement (NAFTA), the Mercado Comun del Sur (MERCOSUR), the Association of South East Asian Nations (ASEAN), or the Common Market for Eastern and Southern Africa (COMESA), amongst others, are such transnational regions. There is rich literature on the EU as a striking exemplar of the complex interplays between the global or transnational and multiple nationals/locals (Héritier 1996, 2001; Hooge and Marks 2001; Sabel and Zeitlin 2010). We know much less, though, about the ways in which glocal dynamics play out in the context of other transnational regions.

In this chapter, I propose to focus on the transnational region we arguably know the least about—Africa. To further our understanding of glocalization, we urgently need to expand our geographical reach to those parts of the world that have tended to escape scholarly attention. For at least two reasons, Africa represents a highly interesting ground for looking at the dynamics of glocalization. Firstly, the African continent is, on the whole, a rule-taker when it comes to the dynamics of globalization and is rarely or marginally involved in the arenas where transnational rules are negotiated and structured (Djelic and Sahlin-Andersson 2006). As a consequence, global norms and rules tend to be superimposed and to confront as clear external forces many actors on the African continent. Secondly, the local–national remains a fluid reality in Africa. National institutions and states do not have the type of hard historical embeddedness that nation-states and institutions have in countries at the core of the world system (Wallerstein 1979).

The empirical setting, in this chapter, is competition and its regulation. I explore the ways in which, in the case of competition regulation in Africa, the global interacts with different nationals/locals, in particular through the structuring mediation of regional initiatives. The first section provides an exploration of the context and identifies important steps in the transnationalization of competition regulation. The second section focuses on the development of regional initiatives, within the African continent. Finally, in the last section of the chapter, I underscore the complexities of global—national/local interactions and the particular dynamics of glocalization that emerge in this case. The image of the Banyan tree captures quite well, I propose, the nature of the dynamics at work in the case of competition regulation in Africa. With respect to competition regulation, regional initiatives in Africa are strongly shaped and steered by global actors and constitutive myths. Competition regulation in Africa, in other words, is a foreign seed grafted upon emerging regional integration regimes. Those regional initiatives, in turn, become mediators, with a clear focus on diffusion, transplantation, and translation of competition regulation nationally and locally. The idea is that the regional trunk, like the Banyan tree, should progressively send roots down towards the national/local ground.

The Context—Competition Regulation and its Transnationalization

Until the mid-1980s, only a handful of geographic jurisdictions, mostly from the developed West, had a preoccupation for competition regulation and the regulatory tools that went with it. With the exception of the European community, most of those jurisdictions were national ones. Competition regulation was contained within each jurisdiction; there was no framework for cross-border collaboration and only rare opportunities for contact. A few initiatives to elaborate common guidelines—within the GATT in 1944, through the OECD in 1967, and within UNCTAD in 1980—were not associated with implementation mechanisms and hence had scant influence.

Geopolitical Conditions and Globalization

From the late 1980s, two developments made it urgent to consider antitrust and competition regulation as a cross-jurisdictional issue. Firstly, many national jurisdictions around the world developed a competition regulation regime. Secondly, the increasing transnational projection of economic activity—often labeled 'globalization'—created multiple opportunities for friction between different jurisdictions.

From a handful of jurisdictions with competition regimes in 1980, there are more than a hundred today. This striking development is in large part the result of diffusion in the context of rapidly changing geopolitical conditions (Djelic 2005). The second half of the 1980s saw the revival of the European construction effort, boosting activity around antitrust at the community level. Old and recent member states developed or modernized their antitrust regimes to follow evolutions at the European level. At about the same time, the world was struck by the fall of the Berlin Wall. The 'extension of the West' was a direct consequence. With respect to antitrust, this triggered a wave of international missionary activity. In the 1990s only, American antitrust authorities organized close to 400 antitrust missions worldwide (Djelic 2005). The European commission was also actively involved, either directly or in a more indirect manner, through UNCTAD. As a consequence, competition authorities were set up and competition laws enacted in many countries around the world.

As Charles James, then Assistant Attorney General, US Antitrust Division (DoJ), liked to put it, 'We sometimes joke that antitrust has been one of the United States' most successful exports' (James 2001). Even though there has been a rapid diffusion process, from two core centers or nodes (the US and the EU), this has not resulted in easy or clear convergence of rules and institutions. The wildfire-like spread of competition regimes has come together with a fair amount of local translation and adaptation. Hence opportunities for friction and contradiction have multiplied in the process. Complexity was only reinforced by the rapid internationalization of economic activity. Globalization and an increasing number of jurisdictions combined to create new challenges for the regulation of competition and its core actors. Risks of inconsistent and/or conflicting decisions became particularly salient. By the mid-1990s, it was clear that the antitrust world was facing a problem more acute every day. Antitrust was 'going global' and it appeared necessary, in that context, to create the conditions for better coordination of existing regimes and jurisdictions.

Different Routes to Cross-jurisdiction Coordination

A first easy strategy was to negotiate bilateral agreements as a forum to ensure reciprocal understanding. In 1991, the United States and the European Union signed an agreement that provided for cooperation—a reciprocal notification system, exchange of information, synchronization of investigations and coordination of enforcement activities. Similar bilateral agreements were then signed in rapid succession. By the end of the 1990s, a dense web of bilateral agreements connected the most developed authorities in the world. While bilateral agreements had positive results, they also rapidly showed their inherent limitations. They did not prevent conflict and tension between the US and the EU on highly visible cases (Boeing in 1998, GE/Honeywell or Microsoft in 2001). They were also highly insufficient when more than two jurisdictions were involved. As a consequence, multilateral initiatives were given serious consideration.

In 1986, and then again in 1995, the OECD revised its 1967 Recommendations. In parallel, the OECD was promoting international discussion of competition policy matters within its long-standing working group, the Competition Law and Policy Committee (CLP). The CLP worked well as a forum-promoting soft convergence; it did not, however, achieve much with respect to rule-making or dispute settlement. In 1999, the Europeans tried to mobilize the WTO to foster the development of a multilateral framework for competition. Reactions to the EU proposition were far from enthusiastic, though. Developing countries were generally skeptical, not recognizing what interest could lie for them in a multilateral framework. The US also insisted that any agreement should be set on a voluntary basis and that it would be difficult to frame competition in a way similar to trade (Pons 2002).

UNCTAD also proved an active forum. The United Nations Conference on Trade and Development (UNCTAD) was held for the first time in 1964 in Geneva, with a focus on developing countries and international trade. Rapidly, UNCTAD connected the weak trading position of developing countries in international trade to restrictive practices in developed countries. In 1980, the United Nations adopted as a non-binding resolution the Set of Multilaterally Agreed Equitable Principles and Rules for the Control of Restrictive Business Practices (the Set) produced by UNCTAD. The Set is a list of recommendations to states, multinational corporations, and regional institutions with the objectives of a) encouraging national states to adopt a competition regime and b) encouraging transnational cooperation in antitrust matters. While the non-binding character of the Set has certainly limited its influence, the role of UNCTAD should not be minimized. In 1995, UNCTAD compiled a 'model law' of competition that could be used to develop national or regional competition regimes. UNCTAD was also very active in technical assistance and capacity-building projects, sending experts to those jurisdictions, mostly in the developing world, that were building competition regimes during the 1990s (UNCTAD 2004).

In parallel to these developments, the US was launching its own initiative in 1997: the International Competition Policy Advisory Committee (ICPAC). After holding extensive public hearings, ICPAC recommended against the development of binding competition rules subject to dispute settlement procedures within the WTO. Instead, it proposed a Global Competition Initiative to foster dialogue not only among antitrust officials but also between officials and broader constituencies with a view to bring about common understandings and a common culture, a greater convergence of laws and principles but also of analyses and implementation (James 2001). The following step was the setting up, in October 2001, of the International Competition Network (ICN). From thirteen founding members, numbers rose quickly, and today the ICN is close to having a global reach, as 98 jurisdictions are represented that together account for more than 90 percent of world GDP. From its early days, the ICN defined and positioned itself as a transnational 'community of interest' structured around issues of competition and antitrust. The ICN is not only a platform for discussion around topics of common interest. It has also become a 'self-disciplining' transnational community with a clear regulatory objective. More precisely, the ICN wants to drive progressive but real homogenization not only of formal rules, but of practices and understandings as well. The 'community of interest' of the ICN has therefore moved to become a 'community of governance,' and it belongs, as such, to the dense web of contemporary transnational governance activism (Djelic and Sahlin-Andersson 2006; Djelic and Quack 2010; Levi-Faur 2012).

Transnational Community-building in Regional Integration Regimes—The Case of Africa

Soon after its creation, the ICN became the dominant template for the transnational coordination and homogenization of competition regimes. In rapid succession, parallel initiatives emerged at the regional level. The European Competition Network (ECN), for example, was set up in 2004. The European Commission, and in particular DG Comp, envisioned the ECN as a governance tool allowing for greater effectiveness and integration of competition regulation in Europe. Other initiatives of the same nature emerged in other parts of the world; I focus here on developments in Africa. I consider, in particular, three community-building projects on the African continent—one within the boundaries of the East African Community (EAC), one within the boundaries of the Common Market for Eastern and Southern Africa (COMESA), and the recent and more inclusive African Competition Forum (ACF).

Competition in the East African Community

The East African Community (EAC) is an intergovernmental organization that brings together five East African countries—Burundi, Kenya, Rwanda, Tanzania, and Uganda. Originally created in 1967, it was dissolved in 1977. It was formally revived in 2000, and Article 75(1) of the EAC Treaty identified competition as one of the priority targets. The protocol setting up a customs union and planning for an East African Competition policy was finally signed in 2004 and took effect one year later. In 2006, an East African Competition Act was enacted that provided for the creation of an East African Competition Authority (EAC 2006). As defined in the 2006 Act, the East African Competition Authority shall have five commissioners, one from each member state. It shall have the power to

> collect information, to investigate and compel the provision of evidence, to hold hearings, to issue legally binding decisions, to impose sanctions and remedies, to refer matters to court for adjudication, to develop appropriate procedures for advocacy, to pursue a research program.
>
> (EAC 2006; Bonge 2010)

The Act identifies prohibited practices—cartels of all kinds—which are clearly associated with punitive provisions (Bonge 2010). Dominance in itself is not illegal; only when a firm abuses its dominant position does it have to incur penalties (predatory pricing, denying market access, use of dominance in one market to enter another, etc.). The EAC Authority will have the power to scrutinize all proposed mergers and acquisitions with cross-border effects. The Act also limits, in theory, the powers of the EAC partner states to unilaterally impose subsidies (Bonge 2010).

Competition within COMESA

The Common Market for Eastern and Southern Africa (COMESA) was established in 1994. With 19 country members, it represents a total population of close to 400 million. Except for Tanzania, all member countries of the EAC are also members of COMESA. Article 55(1) of the COMESA Treaty dealt with competition in a manner that committed member states:

> The Member States agree that any practice which negates the objective of free and liberalized trade shall be prohibited. To this end, the Member States agree to prohibit any agreement between undertakings or concerted practice, which has as its objective or effect, the prevention, restriction or distortion of competition within the Common Market.
>
> (COMESA 1994)

The Treaty, however, did not say much about how members should go about implementing this. It simply indicated that 'the Council shall make regulations to regulate competition within the Member States' (COMESA 1994). Those regulations were finally produced in 2004 (COMESA 2004). They are 'consistent with internationally accepted practices and principles of competition, especially with the "Set" developed by UNCTAD in 1980' (Njoroge 2008).

In December 2008, the COMESA Competition Commission was finally formally appointed. With a total of nine members, it is chaired by Peter Njoroge, former Commissioner of the Monopolies and Price Commission of Kenya and one of the founding fathers of the EAC Competition regime.

Launching the African Competition Forum

A third important initiative is the launch of the African Competition Forum (ACF) on 3 March 2011. The ACF pertains of the same philosophy—to structure in Africa, at the regional level, a competition regime compatible if not homogeneous with Western and global standards. The ACF focuses more specifically on the construction of a transnational regional community—an African counterpart to the ICN—that would be creating the conditions of tighter coordination within the African continent.

The creation of an ACF was initially proposed in the UK 2009 White Paper on International Development 'as a way of taking forward competition policy activities under the British Aid Program' (Joekes 2011). This early proposal suggested that an 'African-led Competition Forum' would help 'governments in the region identify and address obstacles to fair competition' (DIFD 2009: 34). Representatives from 23 national and regional competition authorities from across Africa were present at the formal launch of the ACF in Nairobi, Kenya. Also present were representatives from regional and international organizations such as UNCTAD, OECD, the World Bank, the EU, and the South African Development Community (SADC), as well as scholars and experts in the field from across the world. The scoping phase will be co-financed by DIFD and the Canadian International Development Research Center (IDRC). The ACF will have three main objectives: a) to create awareness and build support for competition policy within/outside national governments; b) to strengthen implementation of competition policies by providing advice and building capacity; and c) to encourage regional integration on the matter of competition regulation (Kaira 2010). In its philosophy (a common 'platform for mobilizing and harnessing experiences and ideas in competition regulation') and in its structure and governance (a 'virtual and flat' organization), the ACF has clearly been modeled on the ICN (Kaira 2010; Kenyatta 2011).

The ACF hence targets community-building at the transnational but regional level with a view to foster coordinated action around competition policy in Africa. As such, the ACF could work in two main directions. It could build up institutional strength in order to have an impact on the structure and development of national competition regimes (Kenyatta 2011). The ACF could also represent a unique opportunity for a group of weak and dispersed actors to gain visibility, power, and influence—this time as an organized collective—within the broader transnational community, delineated in particular by the ICN.

Competition in Africa—Complexities in the Global–Local Interface

Competition and competition regulation have come into Africa only recently. The notion of competition, and the concepts and tools associated with its regulation, have entered this region as foreign objects coming from the global/transnational galaxy. Interestingly, the regional level emerges as pivotal mediator; and glocalization has, in that context, striking features. We explore below the most interesting of those features.

Complex Layers of Transnational Influence

As suggested above, an important mechanism for the transnational diffusion of competition and its regulation has been a multi-layered process of transnational community-building. A first layer has been woven through the active involvement of a small number of older, powerful, and resourceful agencies (the US, Europe, Germany, the UK, and France). This central kernel has played a significant role in the transnational diffusion of competition and its regulation, whether through bilateral technical assistance or through the steering of multilateral fora (Nicholson 2008). A second layer of transnational community-building has been driven by key international organizations—the OECD and UNCTAD, and less so, the WTO. Those organizations have provided models, resources, training, and networking opportunities. UNCTAD has played a particularly significant role in Africa, contributing to the integration of actors from that region into broader communities. The International Competition Network represents a third layer of transnational community building. Initially driven from and by the United States, the ICN has today a nearly global reach—this is at the same time its strength and weakness. Finally, I identified above a fourth layer of transnational community-building that plays out regionally. In the case of Africa, different initiatives with a regional or sub-regional reach are more or less loosely connected to or in interaction with each other.

This multi-layered process of transnational community-building suggests a complex landscape. However, the different layers are not simply juxtaposed; there is, in fact, a fair amount of interconnectedness across layers. Regional initiatives are strongly helped by activities in and around international organizations and/or by the activism of certain core agencies. On the development and advocacy of antitrust, the ICN works in close cooperation with international organizations such as the WTO, UNCTAD, or the OECD. The ICN also explicitly identifies regional initiatives and organizations as privileged partners in its strategy of international coordination.

A Small Group of Bridging Missionaries

In parallel to a complex, multi-layered organizational and community landscape, it is interesting to note that a small group of individuals has played a pivotal role. These few 'bridging missionaries' have been and remain instrumental as they connect global, regional, and, increasingly, national initiatives in favor of competition and competition regulation. This small group includes active African-based champions of competition. But it also involves a small number of foreign (Western) experts and consultants, working for and through international organizations or national public agencies, namely competition agencies or, increasingly, development agencies, such as the British DIFD.

The small group of African-based champions has deployed considerable energy over the past decade to foster a competition agenda. So far, they have mostly worked at the regional level, keeping in mind, though, the importance of reaching the national level. Their active involvement has taken place in a difficult environment, where competition and competition regulation were essentially strange and alien. I have already mentioned Peter Muchoki Njoroge, a Kenyan lawyer, who became the Chairman of the COMESA Competition Commission in 2008. Before that, Njoroge had been Commissioner of the

Kenyan Monopolies and Price Commission and one of the founding fathers of the EAC Competition regime. George Lipimile, who holds an MSc in Law from Queen Mary's College in London and a PhD in Economics from the University of California, also played an important role. Lipimile has been Executive Director of the Zambian Competition Commission, which he helped to establish, as well as a Special Consultant to many African countries on competition issues. He is now a Senior Advisor to UNCTAD and involved, as such, in technical assistance programs that aim to create or stabilize competition regimes in developing countries. He was instrumental in the development of the COMESA Competition Authority and remains the official contact person (COMESA 2012). Francis Kariuki, who followed Njoroge in 2008 as Commissioner of the Kenyan Monopolies and Price Commission, is another regional champion of competition. He coordinated the review and modernization process of the Kenyan Competition Law that was finalized in 2010. He holds an MSc in Economic Regulation and Competition from City University, London. He actively championed the formation of regional competition communities and became, in March 2011, the first Chairman of the African Competition Forum. Finally, Thulasoni Kaira has also been strongly involved. With an MSc from the Norwegian School of Management and an LLB from the University of Zambia, Kaira started his career as a competition analyst in the Zambian Competition Commission. He then followed in the footsteps of Lipimile as Executive Director of the Commission. In 2010, he became the Executive Secretary of the Botswana Competition Commission. In parallel, he was actively championing the creation of an African Competition Forum (Kaira 2010). While the list is certainly not exhaustive, these four men have been key bridging missionaries, contributing in powerful ways to the development of competition regulation within Africa.

All along, this transnational (but regional) small group had the support of international organizations and of powerful agencies in core countries. This support proved particularly significant during the drafting stages (Njoroge 2006, 2008). In 2001, the Secretariat of the EAC appointed a team of consultants with the objective of constructing a competition regime for the regional community. Njoroge was a member of that team and the EAC Secretariat, he recalls, had asked them to 'take into account the best international practices as a way of ensuring that the EAC region shall eventually develop into an internationally competitive single market and development area' (Njoroge 2006). UNCTAD's model law on competition was the main source of inspiration, but the team also looked at the OECD guidelines and at the European competition regime (Njoroge 2006). All along and in other regional initiatives as well, a small group of foreign experts were involved. Some names come up regularly: Carl Buick, Senior Advisor UNCTAD; John Preston, Senior Advisor Department for International Development (DIFD), UK; and Susan Joekes, from the International Development Research Center (IDRC), Canada. UNCTAD played a pivotal role. It provided models, consultants, and training opportunities, and it sponsored and fostered different fora, in which regional actors could meet and create powerful bonds:

> Joint training and attendance at international conferences have allowed most senior staff to develop professional relationships with their corresponding counterparts in the other authorities.
>
> (Njoroge 2008)

UNCTAD also facilitated the development of the Southern and East African Competition Forum (SEACF) as a mechanism for cooperation and dispute settlement between COMESA and the South African Development Community or SADC (Njoroge 2008).

Under the leadership of a small network of strong believers, a regional community has progressively emerged that was from the start deeply embedded within the broader transnational community for competition regulation (Djelic and Quack 2010). This remains, however, a work in progress, as actors themselves acknowledge:

> Through such institutional arrangements under UNCTAD, OECD, ICN, SEACF, both formal and informal relationships should continue to be nurtured, which inevitably have helped in sharing information, joint training sessions, which have enhanced each other's knowledge and assisted in evidence collection and analysis.
>
> (Kaira 2009: 2)

Searching for Translation: Between the Global Myth of Competition and the Grail of Development

A question that comes to mind, when we see the high level of resources and energy spent on the development of competition regulation in Africa, is that of motives and rationale. A functional and utilitarian explanation will not do—competition regulation is not an answer, in Africa, to a well-identified problem. Rather, a garbage-can type of logic seems to be at work—restrictions to competition are becoming a problem in the region only as competition regulation becomes institutionalized (Cohen et al. 1972).

The small group of active missionaries has provided a rationale for its activism. Interestingly, though, the rationale changed during the period explored here (about a decade). What stood out initially was a quest for (global) legitimacy. At a first level, at least, the internationalization of competition regulation, seen from Africa, is a relatively simple 'power and hegemony' story, where solutions and models belonging to a small core become dominant and increasingly taken for granted through broad-based diffusion. The following attempt at justifying competition regulation in Africa, by one of its key champions, clearly illustrates this:

> All successful market economies have in place adequate competition regulation mechanisms … As developing and less developed countries are not expected to reinvent the wheel, I take the position that a successful modern economy requires a robust competition regulation mechanism.
>
> (Njoroge 2004)

Competition regulation and its positive consequences have had, in that period, the status of taken-for-granted and indisputable 'myths' (Meyer and Rowan 1977). The foundation texts of all regional initiatives reflected that (COMESA 2004; EAC 2006). In fact, this 'mythical' dimension remains present today, in spite of the evolution described below. The introductory speech of the then Deputy Prime Minister of Kenya, Uhuru Kenyatta, to the launching conference of the African Competition Forum, is a nice illustration. To justify the development of competition regulation on the African continent, Kenyatta mobilized Adam Smith! In his speech, he quoted two sentences from *The Wealth of Nations* sequentially, which, in the original text, are not associated:

> It is not from the benevolence of the butcher, the brewer or the baker that we expect our dinner, but from their regard to their own interest (Smith 1999: 119) … People of the same trade seldom meet together, even for merriment and diversion, but the

conversation ends in a conspiracy against the public or in some contrivance to raise prices.

(Smith 1999: I, x, 232).

In reality, those two sentences connote very different things. The 'benevolence' sentence is a key foundational moment in *The Wealth of Nations* of the 'myth' of self-regulating markets. The second sentence, in fact, destroys that first 'myth'—competition on the basis of self-interest is not self-sustaining. This second sentence outlines the intellectual foundation for another contemporary 'myth'—that of 'competition regulation.'

The importance of these two global myths has remained strong in the rationale of regional champions; adherence to both myths (even though they could arguably be seen as contradicting each other) ensures global legitimacy. But the rapid progress of competition regulation in Africa owes a lot to a consequential change in framing, the 'story' of competition regulation being told in time in an entirely different way. Over the past decade, competition regulation has progressively been connected to the idea of development and to the poverty alleviation objectives of the Millennium Development Goals (MDGs):

> While some prefer to think of the effects of competition law and policy in terms of efficiency and resource allocation, many senior policymakers in developing countries, aid agencies and leading international organizations, see economic policies through the lens of the Millennium Development Goals.
>
> (Evenett 2006: 3)

This had not always been the case. Evenett goes on to underscore that senior policymakers initially did not promote competition and competition regulation as 'they did not see a strong link between competition and other indicators of development' (Evenett 2006: 3). In the words of John Preston from DIFD, 'to some people, "competition policy" might sound remote from the Millennium Development Goals' (Preston 2004). The MDGs were set in September 2000, with 2015 being the target year. One year later, the UN Secretary General issued a report entitled 'Roadmap towards the Implementation of the UN Millennium Declaration.' The report underscored the importance of 'good governance,' 'sound economies,' and the 'lowering of tariffs.' It made no reference to the role of competition and competition regulation (Evenett 2006: 5).

Here again, UNCTAD was a key change agent. Progressively, throughout the early 2000s, UNCTAD came to weave its long-standing preoccupation for competition regulation with the newly framed MDGs. The official declaration, closing off the 11th Section of UNCTAD in 2004 in Sao Paulo, articulated this redefined approach. This declaration is known as the 'Sao Paulo consensus' and is often said to 'mainstream competition into development policy' (Evenett 2006: 6). The declaration clearly associated competition and competition regulation with development, and in particular, with the triple objective of alleviating poverty, reducing hunger, and spreading the benefits of new technologies:

> The extent to which full economic and social benefits can be derived from FDI is dependent upon, among other things, a vibrant private sector, improved access to international markets, well designed competition law and policy ... Competition policies best suited to their development needs are important for developing countries in safeguarding against anti-competitive behavior in their domestic markets.
>
> (UNCTAD 2004: 9, 16)

The conclusion that Simon Evenett drew in 2006 from a systematic attempt at empirically showing the direct connection between competition and development, was that, in fact, competition regulation should be much more systematically 'sold' by interested parties as a direct mechanism leading in time to the achievement of the MDGs:

> These findings provide a good starting point in making the case for promoting competition to senior policymakers and to the development community in general and for giving more attention to competition policy in national strategies on the MDGs ... With the appropriate expertise and support, in principle, competition law and policy can influence development outcomes but it would seem that, to date, the potential contributions in this regard have not been acknowledged by the broader development community. This may well account for the difficulties faced by competition authorities and their supporters when making their case in developing countries and in certain international institutions and aid agencies.
>
> (Evenett 2006: 11)

This message, strongly relayed by UNCTAD, has now been heard. Arguably, this connection has fueled the rapid expansion of competition regulation in Africa over the past few years. By the end of the decade, development had become the main rationale used to defend the progress of competition regulation in Africa (Qaqaya and Lipimile 2008). In his introduction to the launching Conference of the African Competition Forum, the then Deputy Prime Minister of Kenya, Uhuru Kenyatta, made it clear that 'competition' was the solution to the 'key problem of poverty in Africa' (Kenyatta 2011). By the end of the decade, the most active champions of competition regulation in Africa, along with UNCTAD, were development and aid agencies such as IDRC and DIFD. These agencies have internalized skills and competences on competition regulation and they have been producing large quantities of documents all pointing towards the link between competition regulation and development (e.g., Stewart et al. 2007; DIFD 2009). Local laws and texts, regional and national leaders, and the media are all coming to connect competition regulation with development objectives, stabilizing in the process the legitimacy of competition regimes in the region.

Conclusion: A Banyan Tree Story—The Challenge of Decoupling

Banyan trees are surprising and beautiful multi-trunk trees that are found mostly in Asia and Africa. They grow from seeds that germinate in the cracks of a foreign structure—another tree, a wall, or a building. Once anchored in this pre-existing structure, the Banyan tree will grow a central trunk. In parallel, it will develop a multiplicity of associated trunks by sending aerial roots from the top down. When they reach the ground, those roots thicken and become trunks themselves. The numerous trunks of a single Banyan tree are hence interconnected from 'above,' as it were, through the main trunk structure. The result is a complex and often expansive natural 'cathedral' that produces deep shape.

The image of the Banyan tree captures well, I propose, the dynamics of glocalization associated with the current development of competition regulation in Africa. The legal provisions associated with different regional initiatives all look very similar, at least on paper. They appear, furthermore, to be highly compatible with UNCTAD, OECD, WTO, and even European Union provisions. In light of what was described above, this is, in fact, not surprising. The seeds of competition regulation in Africa are foreign seeds that are grafted upon pre-existing or emerging regional structures. Behind the multiplicity of regional and national initiatives pushing the development of competition regulation within Africa, there is a small and tight network with access to organizational resources. The same individuals are involved and they carry with them the same models and templates produced and diffused by a small number of international organizations. Organizational power and individual activism combine to fuel dynamics on the ground, fostering the development of regional initiatives.

As the regional trunk thickens, the idea is that it will produce aerial roots that should reach down towards the various local/national contexts. There is an explicit rationale or vision that regional competition regimes should/would be spurring (if not forcing), in time, the emergence of national competition regimes (Njoroge 2004). The idea is to start with a regional strategy that should then become a key driver for the development of national competition regimes on the African continent. In time, the aerial roots stemming from the regional trunk should become anchored into the local/national soil and thicken themselves into more solid trunks. Those local/national trunks would then draw their initial sap not from the ground but from the main trunk above—regional initiatives around competition regulation. Once they themselves become stabilized as associated trunks, that is, national competition regimes, they should, in principle, come to play an important role in sustaining and reinforcing the central trunk. Here again, the image of the Banyan tree provides a vivid illustration.

Still, the road towards a regional homogeneous regime in action will not be easy; there are many obstacles (Njoroge 2004). The formal legal provisions, although mainstream, are often weakened by exemptions stemming from political fiat (COMESA 2004; EAC 2006). The implementation of regional regimes and their possible translation into national frameworks are challenging because resources are missing and a competition culture does not exist (Njoroge 2004). Most actors on the ground (whether regional or Western-based) agree that regional regimes will not become fully operational as long as they are not relayed by well-structured national regimes (Bonge 2010). For now, though, the aerial roots of the Banyan tree of competition regulation in Africa remain weak. Many countries involved in regional initiatives still do not have national competition regimes fully in place. In June 2010, the EAC launched a sensitization drive aimed at implementing more systematically the EAC's Competition Act at the national level, in each of its five member countries. By then, only Kenya and Tanzania had operational national regimes. The other three countries were at different stages of preparing or enacting their national regulations (Bonge 2010). The main trunk (transnational regional competition initiatives in Africa) will stay fragile if associated trunks (national competition regimes) do not come to buttress it in time. The local inscription of competition regulation at the national level in Africa remains an important challenge for champions of competition regulation in Africa and elsewhere. If this does not happen, competition regulation in Africa will remain a fragile Banyan trunk with aerial roots that never reach the ground.

Acknowledgments

I want to thank Kerstin Sahlin and members of the SCORE Research Workshop for helpful comments on earlier drafts of this chapter

References

Bonge, G.M. (2010). Towards EAC competitions law and policy. EABC Briefing Paper, Issue 05/10, August.

Boyer, R., and Drache, D. (eds). (1996). *States against markets*. London: Routledge.
Cohen, M., March, J., and Olsen, J.P. (1972). A garbage can model of organizational choice. *Administrative Science Quarterly*, 17(1): 1–25.
COMESA. (1994). *COMESA Treaty*. Accessed 28 January 2012. http://about.comesa.int/attachments/comesa_treaty_en.pdf.
COMESA. (2004). *COMESA Competition Regulations*. Accessed 28 January 2011. http://www.givengain.com/cause_data/images/1694/COMESACompetitionRegulatio.pdf.
COMESA. (2012). *COMESA Competition Commission Website*. Accessed 15 January 2012. http://www.comesacompetition.org/.
DIFD. (2009). Eliminating world poverty: building our common future. *White Paper presented to Parliament by the Secretary of State for International Development*, July.
Djelic, M.L. (2005). From local legislation to global structuring frame: the story of antitrust. *Global Social Policy*, 5(1): 55–76.
Djelic, M.L. (2011). From the rule of law to the law of rules. *ISMO*, 41(1): 35–61.
Djelic, M.L., and Quack, S. (eds). (2010). *Transnational communities*. Cambridge, UK: CUP.
Djelic, M.L., and Sahlin-Andersson, K. (eds). (2006). *Transnational governance*. Cambridge, UK: CUP.
EAC. (2006). *Treaty for the Establishment of the East African Community*. Accessed 15 March 2012. http://www.eacj.org/docs/Treaty-as%20amended.pdf.
Evenett, S. (2006). Competition and the Millennium Development Goals: new 'evidence' from official sources. Paper commissioned by the Competition and Consumer Policies Branch, UNCTAD. Accessed 15 January 2012. www.alexandria.unisg.ch/export/DL/28428.pdf.
Graz, J.C., and Nölke, A. (2008). *Transnational private governance and its limits*. London: Routledge.
Held, D., and McGrew, A. (1998). The end of the Old Order? *Review of International Studies*, 24: 219–44.
Héritier, A. (1996). The accommodation of diversity in European policy-making and its outcomes: regulatory policy as a patchwork. *Journal of European Public Policy*, 3(2): 149–67.
Héritier, A. (2001). New modes of governance in Europe—policy making without legislating? in A. Héritier (ed.), *Common Goods*. Lanham, MD: Rowman and Littlefield, 85–104.
Hirst, P., and Thompson, G. (1996). *Globalization in question*. London: Polity Press.
Hooge, L., and Marks, G. (2001). *Multi-level governance and European integration*. Lanham, MD: Rowman and Littlefield.
James, C. (2001). International antitrust in the 21st century: cooperation and convergence. Address before the OECD Global Forum on Competition, 17 October, Paris, France.
Joekes, S. (2011). African Competition Forum–Scoping Phase. Accessed 28 March 2011. http://publicwebsite.idrc.ca/EN/Regions/Middle_East_and_North_Africa/Pages/ProjectsList.aspx.
Kaira, T. (2009). The competition authority and economic development: the case of Zambia. Paper presented to the Third Annual Competition Conference and 10th Anniversary of the South African Competition Commission, Pretoria, 3 September. Accessed 15 January 2012. http://www.docstoc.com/docs/18570307/Speaking-Notes-for-Thula-Kaira-at-the-10th-Anniversary-of-the.
Kaira, T. (2010). The possibility of establishing an African Competition Forum. Workshop in competition law and policy in African small states, Windhoek, Namibia, 26–27 July.
Kenyatta, U. (2011). Uhuru Kenyatta launching the African Competition Forum, 3 March. Accessed 23 November 2011. http://www.youtube.com/watch?v=UX7LtqGA__w.
Levi-Faur, D. (ed.). (2012). *The Oxford handbook of governance*. Oxford: OUP.
Levi-Faur, D., and Jordana, J. (eds). (2005). *The rise of regulatory capitalism*. Annals of the American Academy of Political and Social Science, 598. London: Sage.
Meyer, J., and Rowan, B. (1977). Institutionalized organizations: formal structure as myth and ceremony. *American Journal of Sociology*, 83(2): 340–63.
Nicholson, M. (2008). An antitrust law index for empirical analysis of international competition policy. *Journal of Competition Law and Economics*, 4(4): 1009–29.
Njoroge, P. (2004). A vision of competition policy: experience and lessons for developing and developed countries – the case of Kenya. Working Paper World Bank. Available online: http://siteresources.

worldbank.org/INTCOMPLEGALDB/Resources/VisionOfCompetitionPolicySAConference.pdf downloaded May 15, 2012.

Njoroge, P. (2006). Regional cooperation on competition policy and law: the East African Community experience—contribution by Kenya on behalf of the East African Community. *Intergovernmental Group of Experts on Competition Law and Policy*, UNCTAD, Geneva 30 October–2 November. Accessed 5 March 2011. http://www.unctad.org/sections/wcmu/docs/c2clp_ige7p25_en.pdf.

Njoroge, P. (2008). Technical assistance and capacity building. Intergovernmental Group of Experts on Competition and Policy, UNCTAD, Geneva 16–18 July. Accessed 28 March 2011. http://www.unctad.org/sections/wcmu/docs/c2clp_ige9p5COMESA_en.pdf.

Ohmae, K. (1995). *The end of the nation state*. New York: Simon & Schuster.

Pons, J.F. (2002). Is it time for an international agreement on antitrust? Speech at Frauenchiemsee, 3–5 June. Accessed 15 January 2012. http://ec.europa.eu/competition/speeches/text/sp2002_027_en.pdf.

Preston, J. (2004). Competition, growth and poverty reduction. Accessed 15 January 2012. http://www.ifc.org/ifcext/fias.nsf/AttachmentsByTitle/ConferencesCompetitionPolicyTanz_John+Preston+2.prn.pdf/$FILE/Conferences_CompetitionPolicyTanz_John+Peston+2.prn.pdf.

Qaqaya, H., and Lipimile, G. (2008). The effects of anti-competitive business practices on developing countries and their development prospects. UNCTAD: UNCTAD/DITC/CLP/2008/2. Accessed 15 January 2012. http://unctad.org/en/docs/ditcclp20082_en.pdf.

Sabel, C., and Zeitlin, J. (eds). (2010). *Experimentalist governance in the European Union*. Oxford: OUP.

Smith, A. (1999 [1776]). *The wealth of nations—Books I–III*. London, New York: Penguin Books.

Stewart, T., Clarke, J., and Joekes, S. (2007). *Competition law in action: experiences from developing countries*. IDRC, Canada.

Strange, S. (1996). *The retreat of the state*. Cambridge, UK: CUP.

Tamm-Hallström, K., and Boström, M. (2010). *Transnational multi-stakeholder standardization*. Cheltenham, UK: Edward Elgar.

UNCTAD. (2004). Draft Sao Paulo Consensus. 11th Session, Sao Paulo, 11–18 June. Accessed 15 January 2012. http://www.unctad.org/en/docs/tdl380_en.pdf.

Wallerstein, I. (1979). *The capitalist world economy*. Cambridge, UK: CUP.

Part III
Ideas, Structures, and Practices

8

Boomerang Diffusion at a Global Bank

Total Quality Management and National Culture

David Strang

Introduction

How do organizational practices fare on the road? With the growth of global firms and professional communities that span national boundaries, it is common for corporate programs—like the total quality management (TQM) initiative studied here—to be exported overseas. These practices often hail from the United States, home not only to many of the world's largest multinationals but also to the greatest concentration of the carriers of management knowledge: business schools, management consultants, and organizational researchers (Sahlin-Andersson and Engwall 2002).

Two opposed perspectives inform most thinking on long-distance diffusion patterns. The first is that organizational practices, especially those that gain great popularity, can express universally valid ideals. This is the perspective of the professional advocates of quality management who refer to fundamental human capabilities such as the desire to learn and the pride of workmanship. Joseph Juran (1974: 4.54) embodied this point of view in explaining the appeal of modern quality control practices: 'The human being exhibits an instinctive drive for precision, beauty, and perfection.' Given universality of appeal, organizational practices are expected to be adopted widely with little modification.

An alternative perspective proposes a 'liability of foreignness,' where national borders impede the routine export of management practices (Kogut and Singh 1988). For example, Steele (1977) finds that American-based organization development clashed with British class antagonism, while Laurent (1983) reports that French managers found the notion of matrix management incoherent. Kostova (1999) provides a broad analysis of the incompatibilities that may arise when practices move across borders. The adoption and institutionalization of corporate innovations by sub-units may be interrupted by national regulatory systems that render them inappropriate, cognitive frames that render them uninterpretable, and corporate culture mindsets that render them unattractive. From this perspective, a complex intervention like TQM involves a culturally loaded vision of the organization whose enactment in a new setting requires translation (Czarniawska and Sevon 1996).

This essay analyzes the spread of a total quality program across the businesses making up Global Financial, a multinational money center based in New York. After providing background on the program and a brief excursus into the global dimensions of the benchmarking program that gave it entrée within the bank, I focus on the diffusion of program activity. To summarize the results and argument developed below, substantial differences arise in the speed and extent to which TQM projects diffused across business units are defined by national location. Surprisingly, however, the empirical pattern of program diffusion observed at Global Financial reverses the one implied by a liability of foreignness. The bank's program resonated better in the bank's periphery than its center and was adopted more vigorously there as well. I link this pattern to total quality's cultural affinities, particularly to collectivism and uncertainty avoidance, and consider how a program ill-suited to American social psychology came to be promulgated by a bank based in Manhattan.

Benchmarking and the Origins of Global Financial's Quality Initiative

This paper draws on a broader study of Global Financial's Team Challenge benchmarking program and the efforts at organizational change that it fostered (Strang 2010). That research approached benchmarking as an opportunity to observe explicit efforts at inter-organizational imitation, to trace the innovation efforts that observation of best practice gave rise to, and to detail the subsequent implementation of these programs. While not centering on debates over globalization, the worldwide scope of Global Financial's operations means that many aspects of the study relate to issues considered in this volume. The managers who conducted benchmarking visits hailed from Europe, Asia, Latin America, and the United States, and their backgrounds influenced the lessons they communicated to the bank's CEO and top leadership team. As a business, Global Financial financed the activities of many of the world's largest companies, provided foreign exchange and related services to a wide range of customers, packaged derivatives and other debt instruments on national and international markets, and invested heavily in the world's most promising emerging markets.

The bank's strategic goals emphasized the organizational realities of a global business as well. How could the bank exhibit the same face in New Delhi and New York, enabling customers to move seamlessly between the two? How could Global Financial become an instantly recognizable global brand? How could best practices be rapidly disseminated across the far-flung national and market segments of the bank, so that a good idea in Cairo would be quickly picked up in Brussels and Manila? These were exactly the challenges (and the rhetoric) that led the bank to a corporate-wide quality program.

Global Financial's Quality Initiative was the major intervention that emerged out of the bank's efforts to learn from corporate best practices. (Other interventions included the establishment of an Internet banking unit, the restructuring of the organization's headquarters, the development of a work/life balance program, and an initiative to expand the cross-selling of financial products.) While many aspects of the Team Challenge program must be passed over here as separable from this essay's concern with the subsequent diffusion of total quality activities, one aspect of benchmarking does bear attention: the global distribution of best practice visits.

The organizations that Global Financial's managers visited as exemplars were overwhelmingly based in the United States. Of the 93 visits conducted to observe best practice, 80 (86 percent) took place in the United States. The great majority of these were private sector firms, although they also included a hospital, a university, and a government department.

Only 13 benchmarking visits, by contrast, took place in organizations headquartered outside the United States. This disparity arose despite the fact that benchmarkers toured the world in their data collection efforts, observing Global Financial's own operations in Hong Kong, Belgium, and elsewhere, and personally interviewed bank executives and personnel in Asia, Latin America, and Europe.

A finer-grained examination is also revealing. The regional location of benchmarking partners within the United States resembles homogeneous mixing, with numbers of visits proportional to levels of economic activity and the distribution of large company headquarters. For example, companies headquartered in New York hosted 8 percent of domestic visits while making up 10 percent of the Fortune 500; the Far West (home to 17 percent of the Fortune 500) received 19 percent of domestic visits. Outside the US, by contrast, benchmarking visits went to firms located in a small set of countries to which the Manhattan-based bank was culturally and historically 'close.' With the one exception of a Japanese manufacturer, all of these 13 visits were to European organizations. And within Europe, Global Financial's benchmarking partners were all based in the North and West: four visits were to Great Britain and the others to Denmark, Germany, Finland, the Netherlands, and Switzerland. None of the BRICS countries were home to any company from which Global Financial sought to learn, and, in fact, no firms based in Latin America, continental Asia, Africa, or the Middle East were visited, despite Global Financial's extensive presence in emerging markets throughout the world.

Homogeneous mixing within the United States suggests that American businesses form a highly integrated community that can be represented by a single national prestige ordering, at least from the perspective of a major money center like Global Financial. The corresponding absence of homogeneous mixing outside the US indicates that a parallel global business community has not yet taken form. If Global Financial, as a bank with worldwide reach, was unaware, unable, or unwilling to access best practices outside its national/cultural niche, it is unlikely that other companies would cast a broader net.

The visits that gave rise to the Quality Initiative were prototypical of the benchmarking program's American-centrism. Benchmarking partners were major US manufacturers and service providers as well as a British transportation giant. More than any other benchmarking area, the focus was on large, well-established corporations, many of which had won the Baldrige, the major US award for excellence in quality management. The limited geographic scope of this search for best practice meant that Global Financial's corporate strategy was strongly molded by the American definition of and experience with TQM.

Following Team Challenge, the bank selected Motorola's Six Sigma approach as its quality framework (Six Sigma subsequently diffused so extensively that its origins at Motorola are often forgotten). Global Financial worked directly with the telecommunications manufacturer to implement its program: a Motorola executive 'on loan' advised the bank's quality director on strategy, Global Financial professional staff were certified by Motorola, and the bank licensed Motorola's proprietary training materials. Over time, the bank modified its approach to better fit its task structure and corporate culture, but the program's basic structure drawn from Motorola remained intact.

The quality initiative was framed within the bank as a 'breakout strategy' that would deliver superior customer service, provide seamless integration across business functions, and increase operational efficiency. The ambition to enhance the bank's global brand—an instantly recognizable consumer interface and transparent dealings across national borders—was key. The program also spoke to the human dimensions of work at Global Financial, seeking the personal commitment of all Globalbankers (the CEO led the way in announcing that he, too, would 'have a few projects on my personal quality'). The program would lead the bank 'to become a better place to work' and in the long run provide opportunities for enterprising bankers to distinguish themselves ('It's going to change a lot of career paths').[1]

Global Financial's quality program is best understood as an orchestrated social movement (Strang and Jung 2005; Strang 2010: 221–2). The Quality Initiative did not require managers to enact specific policies or modify organizational structures. Instead, it encouraged them to take action, with the hope that a self-sustaining cascade would ultimately arise. Managers who placed projects under the quality umbrella allied themselves with the CEO's agenda, nominated themselves and their businesses as potential success stories (the most prominent such managers were recognized and spoke at the bank's annual leadership conference), and gained public credit that might facilitate upward mobility. The possible benefits were enticing but unsure, resting on the precarious staying power of the quality program and its champions at Global Financial. As one quality team member who had been with the bank for 17 years said, 'I was skeptical; I thought this would die on the vine.' Such skepticism was well warranted; despite the strong support of the CEO, the Quality Initiative lasted for three years before a power shake-up at the bank led to its demise.

To capture the diffusion of quality program activity, I focus on the formation of cross-functional performance improvement (CFPI) projects, also known as 'quality teams.' (The other principal operational wings of the program were individual quality training and the development of customer service metrics.) Over 1,200 such teams were formed at Global Financial over the three-year lifecycle of the initiative. These involved a wide variety of activities. For example, quality teams sought to expand check processing capacity in Egypt, designed protocols for cross-selling financial products in Argentina, and aimed to increase the speed of reporting statements in Hong Kong.

The social movement-like character of Global Financial's initiative is significant from a research design standpoint because it makes program activity a good index of compatibility with the intervention. Top-down implementation generally limits variation across units, and links much of the variation that does arise to factors like the vigor of those in charge. In the Quality Initiative, by contrast, corporate staff lacked the authority or capacity to direct quality activities within the bank's businesses and instead played the role of activists who promoted the quality gospel and provided resources for Globalbankers who wanted to get something done. Under these conditions, levels of program activity are likely to vary greatly and to be tied to characteristics of business units that facilitate or impede local mobilization.

From a substantive perspective, the social movement character of the Quality Initiative meant that concrete program activities were necessarily formulated in terms of local objectives and organizational capacities. Adaptation, rather than replication, was built into the structure of the program. Line managers identified the 'critical business issues' that cross-functional process improvement projects would tackle and chose the members (and often leaders) of the quality team. The bank's corporate quality office provided nascent teams with a template organizational structure and action plan, but these could be substantially modified (or discarded) in the course of a team's year-long project. The loose and voluntaristic character of quality improvement efforts meant that managers were empowered and obliged to translate its abstract problem-solving scripts into something that made sense to them and their business.

Quality teams were perceived at Global Financial as a novel vehicle for getting things done. Greater speed of operations and minimization of errors would drive down customer dissatisfaction, enhancing the bank's balance sheet, and proving the utility of the total quality model. Some also saw CFPI projects as offering more indirect benefits. While the bank was known for its competitive culture (some said 'cut-throat competition'), team projects required cooperation among employees who varied in expertise and rank. Several program advocates told me that the real payoff would be to help Globalbankers learn to work together in new ways.

Variation in Quality Team Formation

The major source of variation in program activity was geographic, with large differences in the numbers in quality improvement projects across world regions, as well as smaller differences between countries within regions. Business units in Asia were the fastest to start CFPI projects, doing so at a rate more than twice that of businesses in North America. Singapore's Consumer Bank was the home of more teams than any other business at Global Financial, with Hong Kong, the Philippines, Thailand, Japan, and India not far behind. In addition to Asia, hotbeds of quality team activity included businesses in Latin America (especially Brazil, Argentina, and Colombia) and Eastern Europe. Even Africa and the Middle East, the regions where Global Financial's operations were the youngest and least developed, were the location of considerable activity on a per employee basis.

The diffusion of team-based performance improvement was correspondingly halting in North America and Western Europe. The United States, Canada, the United Kingdom, Germany, and neighboring countries registered low rates of quality team formation. The difference between tepid program activity in these countries versus the rest of the world is particularly striking when we consider the worldwide distribution of bank operations. On a per-employee basis, rates of team formation were an order of magnitude lower in North America and Western Europe than in Asia or Latin America. Fewer teams were formed in Western Europe than in Central and Eastern Europe, where the bank had a considerably smaller footprint. Forty-five percent of Globalbankers were based in the United States, but only 7 percent of its quality teams were located there. At the same time, the United States stood out as the leader in the percentage of quality projects that were terminated.

While national location was the major source of variation in quality team activity, differences linked to task structure arose as well. TQM is a problem-solving modality designed for high-reliability, high-volume production (Sitkin et al. 1994) whose methodology works best where tasks are routine and well-defined. (This orientation is conveyed by the term Six Sigma itself, which indicates the goal of limiting errors to a rate of 3.4 per million—a meaningless concept for a banker who does a few deals a year.) Businesses that performed relatively routine functions for ordinary customers (the 'Consumer Bank') were thus better positioned to utilize quality improvement techniques than were businesses that performed more varied and situation-specific functions for corporations and high net-worth individuals (the 'Corporate Bank' and 'Private Bank'). But these differences based on task structure were small relative to differences based on geography. Not only did the Singapore Consumer Bank pursue more quality projects than the US Consumer Bank, so did Singapore Corporate.

An additional set of factors had to do with the bank's occupational structure (see Strang and Jung 2009 for an extended analysis). Rates of team formation were high where clerical workers received low wages relative to managers and professionals, experienced weak wage growth, were less likely to rise into supervisory positions, and formed a shrinking proportion of bank employment; and where managerial and professional wage gains and employment growth were strong. In businesses where the pink collar/white collar divide was large and expanding, there was much scope for efficiency-minded managers to use CFPI projects to introduce new operational technologies. But these differentials add to, rather than explain, the large effects of country and global region.

Why was geography so critical for the formation of quality teams, and why was the quality program adopted more vigorously in the bank's periphery than in its center? Opportunities for operational improvement form part of the answer. Global Financial's businesses in emerging markets like Poland and Columbia were growing faster than those in mature markets like France and Canada. Growth turned the technological advances sought by CFPI projects into potential big gains and win-win propositions for managers, professionals, and potentially even clerical workers. In stagnant markets, by contrast, potential operational gains were smaller, while the prospect for conflict over potential human costs—layoffs—was greater. (Relatively new units in countries like Poland and the Ukraine may also have felt themselves obliged to take the Quality Initiative seriously as 'what New York wants,' though this does not account for the strong response in Asia and Latin America where Global Financial had long-standing operations.)

While these and other forces were undoubtedly in play, I focus on the role of cultural orientations that vary with national background. Performance improvement 'TQM-style' rests on a distinctive social and cognitive architecture (Anderson et al. 1994; Hackman and Wageman 1995). Behaviorally, total quality is allied to participative management and organizational development, stressing teamwork, employee empowerment, and personal openness to change. Technically, quality approaches endorse systematic measurement, reduction in variance around numerical targets, continuous improvement, and cross-functional engineering. These principles are likely to appeal to some bankers and not others, and to better resonate with some national cultures and not others.

National Culture

To probe cultural influences at the level of individual Globalbankers, 205 members of 14 quality teams from 11 countries (Argentina, Columbia, Egypt, Ireland, Mexico, Nigeria, Saudi Arabia, South Africa, Tanzania, the United States, and Zambia) were surveyed, and meetings in Egypt and the United States were observed. The focus was on cultural orientations that shaped interpretations of the individual's quality team experience and his or her views of the Quality Initiative. Sine and Strang (2001) provide a detailed analysis of survey materials; below, I report some of the most telling relationships.

Surveys measured each team member's position on the four cultural dimensions identified in Hofstede's (1980) pioneering research as showing substantial cross-national variation. These orientations are: power distance (contrasting preferences for more versus less egalitarian relationships), individualism versus collectivism (contrasting individual action and responsibility versus group membership), masculinity versus femininity (contrasting a competitive achievement orientation versus concern for interpersonal relationships), and uncertainty avoidance (preferences for more versus less structured situations). Much work in cross-cultural social psychology is broadly consistent with these distinctions, with most theoretical and empirical development centering on individualism versus collectivism (see Earley 1989; Triandis 1995).

In its formal design and ideology, Global Financial's quality program can be located on three of Hofstede's dimensions (for a related analysis, see Harzing and Hofstede 1996). It is *egalitarian* (low power distance) in emphasizing the contribution of lower-level workers closest to the problem, setting up quality teams where managers and front-line workers should participate without reference to differences in rank, and empowering teams to implement change. It is *collectivist* in its emphasis on teamwork and cross-functional cooperation rather than the achievements of individual experts. Quality is also opposed to *uncertainty avoidance* through its commitment to organizational change and experimentation. The only dimension where total quality appears ambiguous is *masculinity/femininity,* since initiatives are simultaneously results-oriented and concerned with fostering better interpersonal relationships.

To discover if cultural orientations influence individual evaluations of the total quality framework, team members were asked about the effectiveness of eight principles that underlie TQM (Anderson et al. 1994; Hackman and Wageman 1995): 'focus on customer satisfaction,' 'openness to experimentation and change,' 'data-driven decision making,' 'structured problem-solving and statistical tools,' 'group effort rather than individual effort,' 'development of interpersonal skills,' 'empowered to directly implement change,' and 'roles based on expertise, not status.'

There is a strong link between the perceived efficacy of TQM principles and collectivist orientations. Collectivists embraced TQM's support for group effort, development of interpersonal skills, openness to experimentation and change, a data-driven approach, and structured problem-solving (statistically significant correlations ranged from 0.16 to 0.33). To understand these latter connections, it is useful to recall that total quality treats organizational change and problem-solving as a group product. For example, a participant on a Nigerian project praised 'the team approach to problem resolution … brainstorming, theming, process maps.'

While TQM's goal of promoting organizational change suggests it might appeal to 'uncertainty seekers,' core elements of TQM were, in fact, endorsed by 'uncertainty avoiders.' These features all involved the technical side of total quality: uncertainty avoidance was correlated with positive evaluations of TQM's focus on customer satisfaction ($r = 0.33$), its data-driven approach ($r = 0.17$), and structured problem-solving and statistical tools ($r = 0.27$). It appears that uncertainty avoiders are drawn to the structure that well-defined decision procedure imposes on complex, uncertain domains.

Finally, assessments of the principles underlying TQM were unrelated to orientations toward power distance and masculinity/femininity. The latter non-effect is unsurprising given TQM's refusal to choose between achievement and supportive social relationships, but the former runs against TQM's emphasis on the contributions of workers 'closest to the problem' (Zeitz 1996). There was a positive correlation between a preference for democratic/consultative managers and endorsement of TQM's concept of empowerment, but this relationship was modest and not statistically significant. As I note below, the forms of empowerment that actually arose in the Quality Initiative may have been too limited to excite the enthusiasm of egalitarian-minded Globalbankers.

What about evaluations of Global Financial's own quality program? (Employee support for the bank's Quality Initiative measured with a question about the program's significance for the bank; members responded on a 5-point scale from 'not important' to 'critically important.') Collectivism was the one cultural orientation robustly linked to positive evaluation of the Quality Initiative, while power distance, uncertainty avoidance, and masculinity/femininity showed weak effects. Bankers who preferred working on teams, stressed the value of interpersonal relationships, and emphasized collective goals, assessed the Quality Initiative as important. Those who preferred working independently and were more oriented to individual goals regarded Global Financial's program with skepticism.

Collectivist themes also appeared when participants described the benefits of performance improvement projects in their own words:

teamwork, enthusiasm, and honesty [Egypt]
the power of having a common goal among team members [South Africa]
sharing ideas and working together [Mexico].

Finally, an emphasis on cooperation and teamwork were visible in the quality training and project formation sessions I attended. Activities focused on group interaction were compelling to Globalbankers, while formulas for computing organizational defects had to be bolstered by the authority of the company ('Global Financial has decided this will be our common language …').

Observation of quality teams in action helped me better understand why orientations toward power and inequality were weakly related to employee support for the bank's program. One team experienced much conflict. Like other groups, it had a 'sponsor,' a high-ranking banker who defined the team's project, recruited participants, and was then supposed to let the team get to work. But here, the sponsor required that all external communications go out over his signature, insisting that he would not let himself be embarrassed by their possible missteps. Team members balked, demanding real autonomy before committing themselves to the project, and the dispute grew heated enough that as an observer, I was asked to leave the room. While the immediate issue was resolved, the incident illustrates that ownership of team projects was up for grabs, and empowerment was potentially a convenient fiction.

The strong effects of collectivism at Global Financial are consistent with Yu and Zaheer's (2010) comparative analysis of Six Sigma implementation in Korean and US firms, which argues that the conceptual and social aspects of Six Sigma are more context-dependent than the program's technical side. The face-to-face structure of quality teams elicited strong reactions from Globalbankers of all stripes. Some were reluctant to commit themselves to a potential 'time sink,' others were concerned about the political ramifications of organizational change, and still others were energized by the opportunity to work on a challenging team project. Technical aspects of the program were less salient and more likely to be taken for granted, at least at the outset.

While I have emphasized the effects of individual cultural orientations, evaluations of Global Financial's Quality Initiative were also powerfully conditioned by the banker's personal experience (recall that all surveyed employees were members of quality teams and so had a substantial connection to the program). Individuals whose team project had enhanced their skills saw the broader initiative as more important, while those who had learned little were more critical of the program. A personal sense of satisfaction and commitment to the team were also positively related to endorsement of the Quality Initiative, though not as strongly as perceptions of skill development. The addition of measures of team experience more than doubled the explanatory power of models of employee attitudes, raising R^2 from 0.09 to 0.23.

Finally, endorsement of the Quality Initiative was shaped by the volume and success of quality efforts within the Globalbanker's business unit. Participants in North America, where quality teams were few and far between, had a very different sense of the program's significance than did employees where many quality projects were launched. Differences in employee evaluations were thus triply determined: by the collectivism of individual bankers, which led them to value the group-based structure of TQM; by the learning and mutual commitment that arose in teams; and by the positive reality check provided by large numbers of projects operating within one's business.

The effects of collectivism documented here at the individual level are echoed in aggregate differences. Hofstede (1980) found high levels of collectivism in Asia, Latin America, and Africa, exactly those locations where quality teams diffused most rapidly. North America and

Western Europe were, by contrast, dominated by individualist orientations, again consistent with the diffusion pattern, with the United States scoring as the most individualist culture that Hofstede studied. Businesses where the group-centered structure of total quality management were in line with dominant cultural understandings of appropriate and effective action found many problems for quality teams to work on, while those dominated by individualism saw few such opportunities.

Discussion

There are strong regularities in the global diffusion of a multinational's management program. Global Financial's Quality Initiative was most extensively adopted in Asia, Latin America, and by other businesses far from the bank's headquarters in New York, while program activity in the United States and Western Europe was tepid and problematic. A key ingredient underlying this adoption pattern was the cultural resonance of TQM, particularly its appeal for collectivists. Cultural affordances appear both in the aggregate and in the responses of individual Globalbankers who participated on CFPI projects.

Culturally inflected diffusion undercuts claims about the universality of popular management practices. An organizational reform package like TQM does, indeed, seek to appeal to fundamental human capacities like creativity, precision, and hard work. But TQM's commitment to small group participation and structured problem-solving led its appeal to be strongest where individuals possessed particular social psychological dispositions, most notably collectivist orientations, and to diffuse rapidly within societies where these orientations were dominant.

While affirming the notion of cultural contingency, the diffusion pattern at Global Financial reverses the one proposed by a liability of foreignness. If managerial practices reliably reflect the cultural and institutional profile of the adopter, they can be expected to experience difficulty when they are exported. But in the case studied here, the greatest cultural mismatch occurred at the bank's center. While TQM resonates with particular value orientations, it was not well tuned to the social psychology of its American headquarters. Rather than accord with an appetite for change, total quality's methodological commitment to data-driven decisions, structured problem-solving, and customer satisfaction appealed to uncertainty avoiders. Americans endorsed the notion of empowerment, but this is where TQM was least credible and most difficult to pull off. Most importantly, TQM's emphasis on teamwork and group decision-making played badly in a highly individualist society.

Why this disjuncture between the quality program and underlying cultural orientations? Why did an American-sourced program make less sense to managers and staff in the United States than elsewhere? While Motorola was the proximate source of Global Financial's program, the deeper roots of modern quality management lie in Japan. Students of the post-war Japanese firm have emphasized its distinctive organizational practices: lifetime employment, extensive lateral mobility, and modest inequality within and across ranks (Dore 1973; Lincoln and Kalleberg 1990). Reinforced by cultural understandings of the firm as a community and company–union cooperation, these practices are intimately linked to the rich array of autonomous quality programs that flourished and were institutionalized within Japanese firms. The enormous success of Japanese manufacturing in the 1970s and 1980s precipitated widespread borrowing by American companies of Japanese quality practices and their adaptation in the form of schemes like Six Sigma (Cole 1989, 1999).

Some would trace the history back an additional step to contend that Japanese quality techniques were themselves originally imported from the United States. This claim stresses the role of W. Edwards Deming, an applied statistician who gave a series of lectures on sampling and error rates during the American post-war occupation, and whose generous refusal of an honorarium led Japan's quality prize to be named in his honor. But such an account exaggerates the significance of a historical incident and, more importantly, fails to recognize that the key contribution of Japanese quality management is its combination of problem-solving and small-group activity. This mixture of approaches that are historically antagonistic in the United States is visible in Japan as early as the 1920s, when the Japanese National Railway and other firms adopted Taylorist principles but married them to shopfloor participation (Strang and Kim 2005: 182–3).

The notion that Global Financial's Quality Initiative is marked by a characteristically Japanese combination of small-group participation and systematic problem-solving helps us understand why the program was adopted more vigorously in the Pacific Rim and Latin America (which both score high on collectivism) than in the United States or Western Europe. But it also raises new questions. Why would American companies not have found ways to strip quality management of Japanese group-centrism over a period of decades? If Six Sigma does not resonate well with American cultural understandings, why did it become so popular within the United States? Why would Global Financial have adopted a system of management reform that was ill-suited to its large US workforce?

Barley and Kunda's (1992) theory of managerial ideology provides one answer to this puzzle. They argue that organizational theories and associated practices oscillate between two grand visions: the organization as a machine that can be optimized through 'rational control' and the organization as a human community that can be mobilized through 'normative control.' Both visions are attractive but incomplete, articulating with some elements of Western culture but not others. From Barley and Kunda's perspective, the adoption of Japanese total quality management by American firms like Global Financial makes sense in terms of a broad swing towards normative models that began in the 1980s.

This Levi-Straussian conception of culture as a dualistic system affords insight into the complex meanings activated by programs of organizational reform. The focus in Hofstede, and in the Hofstede-inspired survey research reported here, is on identifying a dominant mindset. Are people more liable to view the world in terms of individual rights and interests or in terms of groups and collective benefits? Put in these terms, the prevailing disposition of Americans is individualist, as are the institutional structures of American society (Meyer et al. 1987). From the dualistic perspective that Barley and Kunda invoke, efforts at organizational change wrestle with fundamental cultural dilemmas that can never be satisfactorily resolved.

Total quality management does not fit within Barley and Kunda's notion of oscillation between 'pure solutions,' however. Global Financial's total quality initiative did rely on broad-based employee participation and was presented as a form of cultural change that would build commitment and make work more meaningful. But it also approached the bank as a collection of input–output processes that could be optimized via structured problem-solving. The latter was far from an irrelevant detail—Global Financial's CEO was neither interested in a 'feel-good' program nor able to sell one to the many skeptics at the bank. While Barley and Kunda classify quality management as an effort at normative control, this ignores the operational dimensions of the approach and its technocratic underpinnings.

I would argue that TQM was attractive to American managers precisely because it seemed to transcend the rational–normative divide. In the land of rugged individualism, the notions of group participation, egalitarian empowerment, and commitment to an abstract collectivity possess cultural cachet. But they do so as utopian ideals, which, when made the basis of strong institutional arrangements, appear difficult to put into practice and impossible to maintain over time. (All Western utopias, from Thomas More to Karl Marx, are founded on notions of equality and community and dismissive of self-interest.) These subordinate cultural motifs cannot plausibly stand on their own, but in partnership with a 'scientific' approach towards learning and systematic problem-solving, they make a powerful recipe for an organizational improvement campaign.

The key opposition here is thus not between rational versus normative ideologies, but between highly theorized efforts at organizational reform versus hard-headed everyday management. Six Sigma at Global Financial took the form of a secondary, 'offline' initiative that sought to improve rather than supplant the bank's primary structure of business units, reporting relationships, and profit and loss assignment. Quality teams could dispense with formal roles because these were already built into the bank's division of labor and could promise intrinsic benefits and long-term opportunities for mobility because the bank already paid salaries and bonuses. Quality improvement could take the form of abstract problem-solving because the bank offered powerful countervailing incentives for 'hitting your numbers' in the short run. CFPI projects could be framed as egalitarian teams because the bank's reporting structure was founded on individual responsibility among unequals. Quality management practices that were integrated into the fabric of Japanese firms could be reproduced in the American context, but in the form of a rationalizing initiative that could be self-consciously 'rolled out' and later brought to a close.

In summary, Global Financial's Quality Initiative presents a pattern of periphery-led program diffusion embedded in a broader process of practice translation. It does not reveal a structure of hegemonic dominance, where innovations emerging from a stable center are replicated with or without adjustment for local conditions. We see here a looser system where management models are recycled across national boundaries in all directions. A management approach native to Japan was taken over in the United States, repositioned in light of cultural understandings as an organizational improvement campaign, and exported once again. Management practices are modified as they move, but the translation preserves enough content that when a practice boomerangs back to its source, it is able to spread like wildfire.

Acknowledgments

Thanks to Dong-Il Jung, Young-Mi Kim, and Wesley D. Sine for their research assistance, and to the editors for their suggestions. Financial support was provided by the Citigroup Behavioral Science Research Council.

Note

1 All quotations were drawn from a video interview with the CEO that introduced the quality initiative to Globalbankers.

References

Anderson, J.C., Rungtusanatham, M., and Schroeder, R.G. (1994). 'A theory of quality management underlying the Deming management method'. *Academy of Management Review*, 19: 472–509.
Barley, S.R., and Kunda, G. (1992). 'Design and devotion: surges of rational and normative ideologies of control in managerial discourse'. *Administrative Science Quarterly*, 37: 363–99.
Cole, R.E. (1989). *Strategies for learning*. Berkeley: University of California Press.
Cole, R.E. (1999). *Managing quality fads*. Oxford: Oxford University Press.
Czarniawska, B., and Sevon, G. (eds) (1996). *Translating organizational change*. New York: De Gruyter.

Dore, R. (1973). *British factory, Japanese factory*. Berkeley: University of California Press.

Earley, P.C. (1989). 'Social loafing and collectivism: a comparison of the United States and the People's Republic of China'. *Administrative Science Quarterly*, 34: 565–81.

Hackman, J.R., and Wageman, R. (1995). 'Total quality management: empirical, conceptual, and practical issues'. *Administrative Science Quarterly*, 40: 309–42.

Harzing, A.-W., and Hofstede, G. (1996). 'Planned change in organizations: the influence of national culture', in S.B. Bacharach, P.A. Bamberger, and M. Erez (eds), *Research in the sociology of organizations*. Greenwich: JAI, 297–340.

Hofstede, G. (1980). *Culture's consequences*. Thousand Oaks: Sage.

Juran, J.M. (1974). *Quality control handbook*. New York: McGraw-Hill.

Kogut, B., and Singh, H. (1988). 'The effect of national culture on the choice of entry mode'. *Journal of International Business Studies*, 19: 411–32.

Kostova, T. (1999). 'Transnational transfer of strategic organizational practices: a contextual perspective'. *Academy of Management Review*, 24: 308–24.

Laurent, A. (1983). 'The cultural diversity of western conceptions of management'. *International Studies of Management and Organization*, 13: 75–96.

Lincoln, J.R., and Kalleberg, A.L. (1990). *Culture and commitment*. Cambridge: Cambridge University Press.

Meyer, J.W., Boli, J., and Thomas, G.M. (1987). 'Ontology and rationalization in the Western cultural account', in G.M. Thomas, J.W. Meyer, F.O. Ramirez, and J. Boli (eds), *Institutional structure: constituting state, society, and the individual*. Beverly Hills: Sage, 12–37.

Sahlin-Andersson, K., and Engwall, L. (eds) (2002). *The expansion of management knowledge*. Stanford, CA: Stanford University Press.

Sine, W.D., and Strang, D. (2001). '"On the road again": quality teams and national culture in a global bank'. Paper presented at the annual meetings of the American Sociological Association, Anaheim 2001.

Sitkin, S., Sutcliffe, K.M., and Schroeder, R.G. (1994) 'Distinguishing control from learning in total quality management: a contingency perspective'. *Academy of Management Review* 19: 537–64.

Steele, F. (1977). 'Is culture hostile to organization development? The U.K. example', in P.H. Mirvis and B.N. Berg (eds), *Failures in organization development and change: cases and essays for learning*. New York: Wiley, 23–31.

Strang, D. (2010). *Learning from example: imitation and innovation at a Global Bank*. Princeton: Princeton University Press.

Strang, D., and Jung, D.-I. (2005). 'Organizational change as an orchestrated social movement: recruitment to a "quality initiative"', in G.F. Davis, D. McAdam, W.R. Scott, and M.N. Zald (eds), *Social movements and organization theory*. Cambridge: Cambridge University Press, 280–309.

Strang, D., and Jung, D.-I. (2009). 'Participatory improvement at a global bank: the diffusion of quality teams and the demise of a Six Sigma initiative'. *Organizational Studies*, 30: 31–53.

Strang, D., and Kim, Y.M. (2005). 'Diffusion and domestication of managerial innovations: the spread of scientific management, quality circles, and TQM between the United States and Japan', in S. Ackroyd, R. Batt, P. Thompson, and P.S. Tolbert (eds), *The Oxford handbook of work and organization*. Oxford: Oxford University Press, 177–99.

Triandis, H.C. (1995). *Individualism and collectivism*. Boulder, CO: Westview.

Yu, J., and Zaheer, S. (2010). 'Building a process model of local adaptation of practices: A study of Six Sigma implementation in Korean and US firms'. *Journal of International Business Studies*, 41: 475–99.

Zeitz, G. (1996). 'Employee attitudes toward total quality management in an EPA regional office'. *Administration & Society*, 28: 120–43.

9

Rhetorical Variations in the Cross-national Diffusion of Management Practices

A Comparison of Turkey and the US

Şükrü Özen

Introduction

Growing attention has been paid to the role of rhetorical justifications in the diffusion of management practices across time and space (Abrahamson and Fairchild 1999; Brown, Ainsworth, and Grant 2012; Green 2004; Suddaby and Greenwood 2005). The main premise of this research is that institutional entrepreneurs influence the (non)adoption/abandonment rates of management practices by (de)legitimating them through the instrumental use of language to persuade audiences (i.e., rhetorical strategies) (Abrahamson and Fairchild 1999; David and Strang 2006; Green 2004). Aristotle's three rhetorical strategies—*pathos,* which appeals to the emotions of individuals, *logos*, which appeals to the desire for efficient/effective action, and *ethos*, which appeals to socially accepted norms and mores—have received the greatest attention (Brown, Ainsworth, and Grant 2012). Green (2004: 660) suggested that these three types of rhetoric follow a specific sequence for highly diffused management practices, such as corporate takeover and TQM in North America, starting with pathos (with its emotional emphasis capturing potential adopters' limited attention), followed by logos (appealing to the values of efficiency and effectiveness more admired by management), and ending with ethos (justifications attaching a normative value to the practices that have already lost their logical and emotional appeals).

This research has largely focused on the practices within the nation-states where they *emerged*, and has not distinguished whether the practice in focus is an indigenous practice or a foreign practice transferred from another country (e.g., Abrahamson and Fairchild 1999; Barley and Kunda 1992; David and Strang 2006; Suddaby and Greenwood 2005). Therefore, it has largely neglected the following question: To what extent do the rhetorical strategies for a practice vary when it is transferred from its source country to another country? Overall, the question is how the sequence of rhetorical justifications looks if we compare indigenous and foreign management practices. Comparing the introductory rhetorical strategies used to legitimate TQM in Turkey (receiving country) with those used in the US (source country), Özen and Berkman (2007) found that ethos rhetoric was dominant in Turkey whereas logos rhetoric was dominant in the US. Although Özen and Berkman's (2007) study provides a good starting point, it is far from providing a more complete picture of the variations in the rhetorical strategies for foreign and indigenous practices, since it did not include indigenous practices in the analysis.

In this study, I aim to expand the rhetorical research on diffusion to the cross-national level. In order to understand how the rhetorical strategies change when a practice is transferred from its source country to a receiving country, I first conduct an explorative research that compares the rhetorical strategies for M-form (indigenous) and TQM (transferred) in the US, and holding structure (indigenous) and TQM (transferred) in Turkey. Then, considering the findings of the study, I attempt to explain the variations in the rhetorical strategies by taking into account the diffusion trajectories that a practice follows at its source and receiving countries, and political economic and cultural differences between these countries. I also briefly discuss alternative explanations. In doing so, my ultimate purpose is to contribute to the development of a rhetorical theory for the cross-national legitimation and diffusion of management practices.

Empirical Context and Methodology

The research is designed to compare the frequencies of introductory rhetorical strategies for M-form and TQM in the US with those for holding structure and TQM in Turkey. The reason why I chose the US and Turkey is that the former has been the main producer and diffuser of management knowledge throughout the twenty-first century (Kipping, Engwall, and Üsdiken 2009), though it has also emulated a few countries (e.g., Japan), whereas the latter has usually transferred management practices from the former, particularly since the 1950s (Üsdiken and Wasti 2009).

I chose M-form, holding structure, and TQM because they represent indigenous and foreign practices for each country. However, the labels *indigenous* and *foreign* are relative, to be understood as matters of degree, because every practice combines international insights and local adaptations due to *glocalization* (Robertson 1995). For instance, TQM was originally developed in Japanese companies as 'total quality control' with the help of US experts after World War II, and then reformulated by the US gurus Deming, Juran, and Cosby in the 1980s as a management method that integrates such practices as teamwork, continuous process improvement, and customer orientation (Xu 1999). On the other hand, M-form, which refers to multi-divisional structure, deserves the label 'indigenous' more so than TQM in the US, because it was invented by such US corporations as Du Pont and General Motors during the 1920s and 1930s as a solution to the coordination problems in managing growth and diversity within a centralized structure (Chandler 1962). Holding structure was also developed by an elite Turkish business group, KOÇ Group, by taking insights from the American M-form in the early 1960s to solve similar coordination problems due to diversification, as well as to enforce the control of the owning family over highly diversified businesses (Çolpan and Hikino 2008). Holding structure is different from M-form in the sense that it centralizes both strategic and operational decision-making at the head office where the owning family exercises control. In this respect, it is a more centralized version of M-form, resembling South Korean *chaebols*. TQM in Turkey also deserves the label 'transferred' because it was transferred from the US to Turkey in the 1990s (Özen and Berkman 2007).

In this study, I specifically compare the texts produced by the actors at the early stages of diffusion processes at the national level to legitimate M-form and TQM in the US, and holding and TQM in Turkey. I selected rhetorical texts produced between 1921 and 1950 for M-form, between 1980 and 1992 for the American TQM, between 1963 and 1985 for holding structure, and between 1992 and 1999 for the Turkish TQM. I selected these periods because they are considered by the relevant literature to be the early period of each practice's diffusion. For instance, since its invention in the 1920s, M-form had initially been diffused gradually among large US corporations until the 1950s (Chandler 1962; Fligstein 1985). Then, it became widely diffused in its late adoption period of the 1950s and 1960s due to coercive and normative isomorphism mechanisms (Palmer, Jennings, and Zhou 1993). TQM spread rapidly and extensively in the US throughout the 1980s and the early 1990s (Lawler, Mohrman, and Ledford 1992); however, its diffusion slowed down from the mid-1990s onwards due to the countermobilization effect and the emergence of competing practices (Abrahamson and Eisenman 2008; David and Strang 2006). Holding structure in Turkey was gradually diffused among big family business groups during the 1960s, and since then, it has been more widely diffused, particularly from mid-1985 onwards (Çolpan and Hikino 2008). Finally, TQM has been widely diffused particularly among big businesses in Turkey, as it was strongly promoted by two associations during the 1990s: TUSIAD (Turkish Industrialists' and Businessmen's Association), a group of elite businesses, and KALDER, a quality association (Erçek and Say 2009; Özen and Berkman 2007). However, its diffusion stagnated towards the end of the 1990s, due to the 1999 Marmara earthquake and the following economic crisis (Özen 2002).

I personally selected the text segments that involved rhetorical language for each practice. In selecting the text segments, I adopted two criteria: practice-orientedness (excluding academic journals and books) and openness to the public (excluding intra-organizational reports and memos). However, because the relevant texts for the Turkish case were not sufficient to make a comparative statistical analysis, I had to include the sources relaxing these criteria, such as KALDER's TQM seminar handout, the TQM introductory page on its website, and the company journal of KOÇ Group. The possibility that the different sources may have different genres is a methodological limitation of the study. For M-form, I selected 46 rhetorical texts by examining the news and articles in the *Wall Street Journal*, *Economist*, *Business Week*, *Fortune*, *Forbes*, *Harvard Business Review*, *Management and Administration*, and relevant books such as L.H. Seltzer's *A Financial History of the American Automobile Industry* and A.P. Sloan's *Adventures of a White Collar Man*. For TQM rhetoric in the US, I selected 59 text segments published in the above journals and in the journal *Quality Progress*, as well as relevant books, such as W.E. Deming's *Out of Crisis* and J.M. Juran's *Juran on Planning for Quality*. For holding structure, I chose 41 rhetorical text segments published in the company journal of KOÇ Group, namely *Bizden Haberler*, and the autobiographies of the prominent Turkish business people who adopted holding structure in the earlier period, such as V. Koç's *Hayat Hikayem* and S. Sabancı's *İşte Hayatım*. Finally, I used the same data set of 25 rhetorical texts as Özen and Berkman (2007) for TQM in Turkey, which was selected from the articles published in the national press and in the official journal of KALDER, *Önce Kalite* (*Quality First*), speeches by key figures at the Turkish national quality congresses, a book on TQM authored by one of the pioneers of the quality movement in Turkey, a handout on TQM used in KALDER's training seminars provided to the public, and the TQM introductory page on KALDER's website (www.kalder.org).

Six independent raters and I coded the text segments of three practices (US M-form and TQM, Turkish holding structure) with respect to the themes emphasized in the texts and the respective rhetorical strategies (i.e., ethos, pathos, and logos strategies); for Turkish TQM rhetoric, coded strategies were borrowed from Özen and Berkman (2007). The texts of M-form were coded by two American PhD students at a university in the US. The American

TQM texts were coded by two Turkish PhD students who were fluent in English and had previously studied in the US, but who studied most recently at a Turkish university. Finally, the text segments for holding structure were coded by two other Turkish PhD students at the same university. Thus, three raters coded each of three practices; the author was common to all coding teams. The final agreement rates between raters were 86.3 percent for M-form, 85.3 percent for the US TQM, and 85.4 percent for holding structure. In the Turkish TQM coding that we borrowed from Özen and Berkman (2007), the agreement rate was 85.3 percent.

Examples are given in order to illustrate how each text segment was coded. The following text segment from Alfred P. Sloan, Jr. was coded as logos rhetoric because it attempts to legitimate M-form by referring to its 'rational' (theme) aspects: 'The object of this study is to suggest an organization for the General Motors Corporation which will definitely place *the line of authority* throughout its extensive operations as well as *to co-ordinate each branch of its service…*' The following text was coded as ethos rhetoric since it attempts to legitimate M-form by referring to 'a federal system of government,' which is a widely accepted cultural and political template in the US: 'He [Alfred P. Sloan, Jr.] has set up a management for General Motors that resembles a federal system of government.' Finally, the following text was coded as pathos rhetoric that appealed to a sense of 'following the trend': 'One of the great needs and present trends in industrial organization is toward further decentralization [i.e., M-form].'

Findings

The results of the text analysis are presented in Table 9.1. Since a text segment may include more than one rhetorical strategy, the total number of rhetorical strategies exceeds the number of text segments for each practice. Concerning the variations of the rhetorical strategies *within* each of transferred and indigenous practices, the American TQM is legitimated dominantly by logos justifications (46.4 percent) rather than pathos or ethos appeals, whereas the rhetoric of Turkish TQM involves ethos appeals (55.3 percent) much more than pathos and logos. For both practices, the chi-square goodness-of-fit test shows that the differences between the proportions of the rhetorical categories are statistically significant at the 0.05 level. M-form is legitimated almost entirely by the logos strategy (79.6 percent) as compared with ethos and pathos appeals (significant at the 0.001 level). The legitimating rhetoric of holding structure, on the other hand, contains logos justifications (43.9 percent) just slightly more than ethos justifications (34.8 percent), and is *not* statistically significant at the 0.05 level.

The results of the analysis of the association between the rhetorical strategies and the origin of the practices, controlling for the country effect, are given in Table 9.2. The chi-square

Table 9.1 The rhetorical strategies for management practices

	US TQM		TR TQM		M-form		Holding	
	Count	%	Count	%	Count	%	Count	%
Pathos	23	23.7	11	28.9	6	11.1	14	21.2
Logos	45	46.4	6	15.8	43	79.6	29	43.9
Ethos	29	29.9	21	55.3	5	9.3	23	34.8
Total	97	100.0	38	100.0	54	100.0	66	100.0

Table 9.2 The rhetorical strategies and the origin of the practices

Countries				Rhetorical strategies			Total
				Pathos	Logos	Ethos	
USA	Practice origin	Indigenous (M-form)	Count	6	43	5	54
			% within practice origin	11.1%	79.6%	9.3%	100.0%
		Foreign (TQM)	Count	23	v 45	^ 29	97
			% within practice origin	23.7%	46.4%	29.9%	100.0%
	Total		Count	29	88	34	151
			% within practice origin	19.2%	58.3%	22.5%	100.0%
Turkey	Practice origin	Indigenous (holding)	Count	14	29	23	66
			% within practice origin	21.2%	43.9%	34.8%	100.0%
		Foreign (TQM)	Count	11	v 6	^ 21	38
			% within practice origin	28.9%	15.8%	55.3%	100.0%
	Total		Count	25	35	44	104
			% within practice origin	24.0%	33.7%	42.3%	100.0%

statistics indicate that the associations between the three rhetorical strategies and the origins of the practices are significant for both the US and Turkey at the 0.01 level. The rhetorical strategy of TQM in the US is more ethos (29.9 percent) and pathos (23.7 percent), and less logos-oriented (46.4 percent) than the M-form in the US (9.3 percent and 11.1 percent, and 79.6 percent, respectively). Similarly, the Turkish TQM rhetoric contains more ethos (55.3 percent) and pathos (28.9 percent), and less logos (15.8 percent) strategies than does the Turkish holding structure rhetoric (34.8 percent and 21.1 percent, and 43.9 percent, respectively). These results indicate that the rhetorical strategies for foreign practices are significantly more ethos and pathos-oriented and less logos-oriented than those of indigenous practices in both the US and Turkey.

The results of the analysis of the association between the rhetorical strategies and the countries, controlling for the effect of the practice origin, are shown in Table 9.3. The chi-square tests indicate that the associations between two factors are significant at the 0.001 level. The Turkish TQM rhetoric contains more ethos (55.3 percent), more pathos (28.9 percent), and less logos (15.8) strategies than the US TQM rhetoric (29.9 percent, 23.7

Table 9.3 The rhetorical strategies and the countries

Origin of practices				Rhetorical strategies			Total
				Pathos	Logos	Ethos	
Indigenous (M-form)	Countries	USA	Count	6	43	5	54
			% within countries	11.1%	79.6%	9.3%	100.0%
(Holding)		Turkey	Count	14	v 29	^ 23	66
			% within countries	21.2%	43.9%	34.8%	100.0%
	Total		Count	20	72	28	120
			% within countries	16.7%	60.0%	23.3%	100.0%
Foreign (TQM)	Countries	USA	Count	23	45	29	97
			% within countries	23.7%	46.4%	29.9%	100.0%
(TQM)		Turkey	Count	11	v 6	^ 21	38
			% within countries	28.9%	15.8%	55.3%	100.0%
	Total		Count	34	51	50	135
			% within countries	25.2%	37.8%	37.0%	100.0%

percent, and 46.4 percent, respectively). The rhetorical strategies of holding structure are also more ethos (34.8 percent), more pathos (21.1 percent), and less logos-oriented (43.9) than those of M-form in the US (9.3 percent, 11.1 percent, and 79.6 percent, respectively). These results indicate that the rhetorical strategies of foreign or indigenous practices in Turkey are more ethos and pathos, and less logos-based than those for the practices in the US.

Discussion

The findings of the study show that the introductory rhetorical strategies for legitimating management practices *vary* across *both* the origins of the practices and the countries. One can explain these variations by drawing upon relevant but diverse literatures. However, for pragmatic reasons, I limit myself to explaining the findings of the empirical research in this study, instead of attempting to fully integrate the relevant literatures to construct a rhetorical theory of cross-national diffusion of practices. In this respect, I draw mainly upon the classical diffusion model of new institutional theory (Tolbert and Zucker 1983), the rhetorical theory of diffusion (Green 2004), the translation approach (Czarniawska and Joerges 1996), and business systems and cross-cultural studies (Hofstede 1980; Whitley 1999).

Rhetorical Variations between the Practices

I argue that the main reason for the rhetorical variations between indigenous and foreign practices is that they follow different diffusion trajectories at their source and receiving countries. The classical two-stage diffusion model (Tolbert and Zucker 1983) suggests that a new practice is initially invented to solve a managerial problem and adopted by early-adopters having similar problems for its economic benefits, but as it spreads out among organizations, it is infused with value (i.e., institutionalized) and, therefore, is adopted by late-adopters for its social benefits. Supporting this argument, the indigenous practices in this study, M-form and holding structure, emerged as a solution to 'organizational problems' involved with the effective coordination and control of diverse businesses (Chandler 1962). After its invention in the 1920s, M-form had been *gradually* adopted by some numbers of companies having similar coordination concerns. However, as the translation approach argues, in order for a management idea to diffuse more widely, it must first become objectified, codified, and labeled in its local context (Czarniawska and Joerges 1996). Accordingly, the gradual diffusion of M-form continued until it was materialized into a collective action, becoming a 'public knowledge' (Czarniawska and Joerges 1996: 44) through such publications as Drucker's *The Concept of Corporation,* published in 1946, and particularly Chandler's *Strategy and Structure,* published in 1962. Only after this objectification has M-form started to diffuse widely, through coercive and normative isomorphic mechanisms among US corporations throughout the 1960s and the 1970s (Palmer et al. 1993). As for holding structure, after it was adapted by KOÇ Group in the early 1960s to solve similar coordination and control problems due to unrelated diversification, it slowly diffused among a few big business groups, and only from the mid-1980s onwards has it had a relatively wide diffusion. Holding structure had not been linguistically objectified until the mid-1980s and the early 1990s— until the pioneering business people published their autobiographies and a few academicians published articles on it (e.g., Koç 1983; Buğra 1990). Thus, I argue that in its early period, an indigenous practice is simultaneously being objectified *while* it is diffusing, generally *silently,* in its local context. Only after it reaches a certain threshold of adoption by a recognizable number of organizations (i.e., its mid-stage), does it start to attract the attention of carrying actors such as consultancies, universities, gurus, and associations as their potential 'product' to promote. Then, these carriers begin to promote it to wider audiences by universalizing, commodifying, harmonizing, and dramatizing it (Røvik 2002).

I argue that it is usually by this stage that an indigenous practice is ready to travel across countries. In order to be able to travel cross-culturally, a practice must become relatively well packaged and labeled by carrying actors and diffused relatively widely in its local source context (Czarniawska and Joerges 1996; Røvik 2002). This implies that a practice arrives at a receiving context (i.e., becoming a 'transferred practice') when it has already been established in its source context, as also argued by Hwang, Jang, and Park (chapter 24 in this volume). In other words, an indigenous practice is *less* established at the *early* stage of its diffusion process in its source country as compared with its transferred version at the early stage of its diffusion in the receiving country.

I think that these differences between the diffusion processes of indigenous and transferred practices explain the variations in their rhetorical strategies. Since the availability of information about the practice's performance is relatively low in the early stage of an indigenous practice and, therefore, the concerns about its economic benefits are more prevalent (Ansari, Fiss, and Zajac 2010), it is understandable that logos rhetoric will be greater than that of a transferred practice for the same stage. Ethos and pathos appeals will also enter the scene in addition to logos appeal, particularly when the aforementioned carrying actors begin to enter the field as the practice moves to its mid-stage. However, since an indigenous practice, by definition, diffuses where it emerges (i.e., not 'foreign') in its early stage, it would need *less* legitimation through local cultural norms and values (i.e., ethos appeals) than a foreign practice. This explanation is more valid for M-form, which emerged from scratch in the US, than holding structure, which was a modified form of a foreign practice (M-form). The 'foreign' flavor in holding structure might have caused ethos rhetoric to be equal to logos rhetoric in its legitimation. Finally, since an indigenous practice is already diffused among a number of organizations in its local context, it would need less pathos appeals to trigger the attention of potential adopters in its early stage. As it becomes institutionalized in its later stage of the diffusion process, it is increasingly legitimated with ethos appeals, rather than logos and pathos appeals (Green 2004).

As a result, a management practice is already loaded with ethos appeals, suppressing pathos and logos appeals, when it arrives in a receiving country. In addition to this, an important factor that would make the rhetoric of a transferred practice more ethos-oriented would be its 'liability of foreignness' in the receiving country. To make a foreign practice understandable by local adopters, it has to be 'translated' (Czarniawska and Joerges 1996) and 'contextualized' (Boxenbaum and Gond 2006) with reference to local institutions (i.e., local cultural values, norms, and institutionalized practices). This would be so because a foreign practice can only be understood in relation to what the audiences in the receiving context already know (Czarniawska and Joerges 1996). Therefore, the legitimation of a foreign practice would become rather 'a cultural work' by which local carriers would relate it to broader cultural values (Perkman and Spicer 2008). In the case of TQM in Turkey, for instance, TQM was legitimated dominantly by ethos appeals that related TQM with Turkish cultural values, Islamic practices, Japanese admiration, the official state ideology, and nationalism in order to persuade wider audiences (Özen and Berkman 2007). The ethos rhetoric used for TQM in the US also involved, although to a lesser extent than in Turkey, the references to such American values as mutual trust, world leadership, national pride, participation, and involvement (see also Abrahamson 1997; Barley and Kunda 1992). However, the logos rhetoric is used more than the ethos rhetoric for the American TQM as compared with the Turkish TQM. This discrepancy can be attributed to the fact that, in contrast to the Turkish TQM, the American TQM involves an 'indigenous' part, since it was reformulated within the US. Thus, this 'indigenous' component of TQM in the US may have made its rhetoric more logos-oriented than expected.

Moreover, since a transferred practice is already packaged by global carriers, and the availability of information about the practice's performance is mostly taken for granted right at the beginning in the receiving country, there would be a *lesser* need to legitimate it through logos appeals in the receiving country. These taken-for-granted technical benefits in the receiving country will be most salient where local adopters and carriers have historically endorsed the source country's practices (Kipping et al. 2009), as happened in the TQM case in Turkey (Erçek and Say 2009). Because the performance benefits of the practice are taken for granted, local carriers will tend to legitimize them through ethos and pathos appeals rather than logos appeals. Brown et al. (2012: 310) argue that ethos and pathos appeals may assume significance where logos-based legitimations are confused or insufficient. I think that this is also valid when logos justifications for the practices are perceived as 'too obvious' by local adopters, as happened in the Turkish case. Therefore, local carriers would also use pathos rhetoric for a foreign practice, more than they do for an indigenous one, to complement the lack of logos appeals in order to trigger the attention of potential adopters, where the practice is not yet adopted by a significant number of companies.

There might be another factor influencing the rhetorical strategies: namely, the *content* of the practices themselves. M-form and holding structure only represent 'neutral solutions' for a technical problem (i.e., redesigning organizational structure to minimize transaction costs), whereas TQM addresses an important value of industrialized Western society, namely quality,[1] by suggesting a better management of production process through 'empowering' workers. Thus, M-form and holding structure are expected to have inherently a more rational discourse; TQM, on the other hand, is expected to have both rational and normative discourses (Abrahamson 1997). Then, assuming that a practice's own discourse affects the associated rhetoric to legitimate it, one would expect that M-form and holding structure would be legitimated by more logos but less ethos and pathos rhetoric than the American and Turkish TQMs. As seen in Table 9.1, the findings partially support this expectation. M-form has more logos and less ethos and pathos rhetoric than both the American and Turkish TQMs, as expected. However, holding structure satisfies this expectation when compared with the Turkish TQM, but not to the American TQM; in contrast, it has less logos, more ethos, and almost equally pathos justification as compared with the American TQM. This implies that the effects of the practice contents on their rhetorical strategies interact with the country effects.

Rhetorical Variations between the Countries

I argue that the main reasons for the rhetorical variations between the countries are the political, economic, and cultural differences between them. Using the classification of national business systems (Whitley 1999), the Turkish business system resembles *state-organized* (or *-dependent*) *business systems* despite gradual changes towards liberalization in the last decades, whereas the US represents *compartmentalized business systems*. The Turkish business system is characterized by the dominant developmental state actively coordinating and controlling economic activities and the state-created family business groups (i.e., family holdings) (Buğra 1994). Being dependent on the state in both economic and ideological senses, the owners and top executives of these business groups constitute a group of big-business elites that becomes isomorphic to the state by acquiring its developmentalist and modernizing ideology (Özen and Küskü 2009). Therefore, they perceive contributing to the modernization of the nation as their social obligation largely assigned by the state (Özen and Akkemik 2012), and frequently use this mission as a legitimating tool for themselves (Özen and Berkman 2007). As a vital part of this mission, these organizations become the most important adopters and carriers of 'modern' management practices. For instance, the holding structure and TQM in Turkey examined in this study were developed, or transferred, either directly by these business elites or by their networks of associations (i.e., TUSIAD and KALDER). They are *both* early adopters of modern practices *and* enthusiastic mediators disseminating these practices, which they adopted earlier, to other organizations. They play this dual role of *Actorhood* and *Otherhood*, not only for enhancing and stabilizing their prestige (Meyer 1996: 245), but also for perceiving it as a moral obligation consistent with the developmentalist ideology (Özen and Küskü 2009). Therefore, in legitimating these practices, they frequently exploited the macrocultural discourses of dominant developmental and modernizing ideology. As frequently seen in their rhetoric to legitimate TQM and holding structure, the main themes of these discourses are nationalism, economic development, collective good, and national pride, involving full of ethos appeals. These are the themes to which every social actor who wants to legitimate his/her choice or action tends to refer in Turkey because they are more effective than logos appeals in persuading broader audiences, and particularly the state (Özen and Akkemik 2012; Özen and Berkman 2007). Thus, heavy references to these ethos-based macrocultural discourses in a state-dependent business system make the rhetorical strategies for TQM and holding structure in Turkey more ethos and less logos-based than those for the practices in the US.

On the other hand, the compartmentalized business system in the US is characterized by an 'arm's length' state that establishes the rules of the game and lets market mechanisms work, and by horizontally and vertically integrated large firms that are controlled by financial markets, rather than owning families, banks, or the state (Whitley 1999). This arm's length institutional context discourages collaboration between firms and maintains impersonal market competition (Whitley 1999). Thus, the free market mechanism that encourages the values of rationality, efficiency, innovativeness, and competition is more developed in the US than in Turkey. After all, the US has been one of the centers of the Western cultural account, particularly since World War II, which has shaped the modern world culture with its values of rationality, progression, renewal, and individuality (Thomas, Meyer, Ramirez, and Boli 1987). As a part of such an institutional context, the US also has a well-developed management knowledge market where the supply of (mostly, consulting agencies, gurus, and business media and business schools) and the demand for (mostly, companies) management practices meet on the principles of free market mechanism (Abrahamson 1996). In such a developed management knowledge market, the most salient motive for both the supply and demand sides is the belief that certain techniques are at the forefront of *rational management progress* (Abrahamson 1996). Although the managerial ideologies within this institutional context have historically swung between rational and normative rhetoric, depending on the long waves of economic expansion and contraction, rational rhetoric has always been prevalent throughout all periods (Abrahamson 1997; Barley and Kunda 1992). In conclusion, these institutional factors explain why the rhetorical strategies for both groups of management practices are more logos and less ethos-based than those in Turkey.

These institutional factors are also intertwined with the cultural values dominant in the two countries. Dominant cultural values in a society are both reproduced by the existing institutions (here, business systems characteristics) and, in turn, support their persistence (Hofstede 1980; Whitley 1999). Thus, an explanation with reference to cultural values is not an alternative to, but complementary with, a political economic explanation. According to the findings of Hofstede's (1980) cross-cultural study, Turkey and the US are on the opposite sides in terms of all of the four cultural dimensions: *individualism–collectivism*, *power distance*, *uncertainty avoidance*, and *masculinity–femininity*. Collectivism, high power distance, strong uncertainty avoidance, and femininity are more dominant in the Turkish society, whereas individualism, low power distance, weak uncertainty avoidance, and masculinity are more dominant in the American society. Considering that actors use these cultural values as 'a tool kit' to legitimate their actions or practices (Swidler 1986), legitimating actors are expected to use those rhetorical appeals that are congruent with the dominant values in a society. This explains why the legitimating actors in Turkey use more ethos appeals congruent with collectivistic values of commitment to the collective good, and more pathos appeals consistent with high uncertainty avoidance, but not so many logos appeals congruent with individualism, emphasizing rationality and self-interest. Here, the consistency between pathos appeals and strong uncertainty avoidance needs further elaboration. Strong uncertainty-avoidance societies avoid risk and manifest a higher level of nervousness and emotionality (Hofstede 1980). Thus, emphasizing the global threat to the national survival, the local carriers in Turkey seem to use more pathos justifications that appeal to people's emotions than those in the US.

One may think of an alternative explanation that rhetorical strategies may follow the dominant managerial ideologies prevalent at the periods when management practices are transferred to a country (Barley and Kunda 1992). This kind of explanation sounds plausible because the periods of the rhetorical strategies that were compared in this study are different for both countries. Considering the periods of economic waves and associated managerial ideologies in the US (Abrahamson 1997; Barley and Kunda 1992), both the periods of 1921–1950 for M-form and 1980–1992 for TQM correspond largely to economic contraction periods (1923–1950 and 1980 to present, respectively), paving a way to the dominance of normative ideologies. Thus, if one assumes that the pendulum thesis of Barley and Kunda (1992) was true for the practices in focus, it would be expected that both M-form and TQM would be legitimated by dominantly ethos or pathos appeals congruent with the normative ideology. However, the findings showed that they were not; in contrast, they were legitimated primarily by logos rhetoric. The reason for this discrepancy may be attributed to the fact that although M-form emerged when a normative ideology was more prevalent, it was, in fact, more congruent with the spirit of the structural rationalism ideology that would be dominant at the subsequent period, and TQM was a technique that embraced rational as well as normative ingredients (Abrahamson 1997). For Turkey, how managerial ideologies *in practice* have changed, if at all, according to the long waves of economic conditions, is not known due to the lack of studies. However, we know that the early expansion of holding structure during the 1960s was an outcome of unrelated diversification strategies implemented by Turkish corporations during the economic expansion periods of the 1950s and 1960s (Çolpan and Hikino 2008). We also know that the diffusion period of TQM during the 1990s matched generally with relatively high growth rates in the economy despite several financial crises (Özen 2002). Thus, the diffusions of both holding structure and TQM correspond to relative expansion periods in Turkey. Then, assuming that the pendulum thesis is also true for Turkey, both practices would be legitimated dominantly by logos rhetoric consistent with the rational ideology of the periods. However, they were not: TQM was legitimated by basically ethos appeals, and holding structure was equally legitimated by ethos and logos appeals. One explanation for this discrepancy might be that the pendulum thesis may not be valid for explaining the rhetorical strategies in Turkey due to the overwhelming dominance of nationalistic and developmentalist ideologies over all periods, thus leaving little room for the influence of economic waves on rhetorical strategies. This explanation is consistent with the findings of Seeck and Kuokkanen (2010)—the pendulum thesis may not be valid for the Finnish case since the Finnish management discourse has long been dominated by a rational discourse.

Conclusion

The findings of this study indicate that the introductory rhetorical strategies for legitimating management practices vary across foreign and indigenous practices as well as source and receiving countries. In addition to this empirical contribution, the study also contributes to the literature by conceptually distinguishing the diffusion processes of indigenous and transferred practices and relating this to the variations in their rhetorical strategies in source and receiving countries. Another contribution of the study is to relate the cross-national political economic and cultural differences to the variations in the rhetorical strategies of management practices. These contributions can be expanded by future studies, particularly towards developing a rhetorical theory of cross-national diffusion. First, the future comparative studies may include rhetorical strategies in the later stages of the diffusion process in addition to those in the early stage. Secondly, they can take into account the characteristics of diffusing practices, other than their origin, as a potential factor influencing their legitimating rhetoric. Finally, they can test the generalizibility of the conceptual arguments made in this study by conducting similar studies for various source and receiving countries. Future studies can use the potential of this study, particularly to better understand how the rhetoric and diffusion of management practices vary when they are transferred, especially from the core to peripheral countries.

Acknowledgments

This study was supported by the Scientific and Technological Research Council of Turkey (TÜBİTAK), and its earlier draft was presented in Subtheme 22: Management and Glocalization of the 26th EGOS Colloquium held in Lisbon in July 1–3, 2010. I thank all subtheme participants, particularly Florian Scheiber, Achim Oberg, and Dominika Wruk, for their invaluable comments and suggestions. I am also thankful to Ruth Aguilera and Hüseyin Leblebici for their help and guidance during my research at University of Illinois, Champaign-Urbana. Finally, I thank Umut Koç, and two anonymous reviewers who provided valuable suggestions and insights for further development of the manuscript, and James Andrew Hutchinson for editing the earlier draft of the manuscript. All mistakes are mine.

Note

1   I would like to thank one of the anonymous reviewers who suggested this difference between the practices.

References

Abrahamson, E. (1996). 'Management fashion'. *Academy of Management Review*, 21, 254–285.
Abrahamson, E. (1997). 'The emergence and prevalence of employee management rhetorics: the effects of long waves, labor unions, and turnover, 1875–1992'. *Academy of Management Journal*, 40, 491–533.
Abrahamson, E., and Eisenman, M. (2008). 'Employee-management techniques: transient fads or trending fashions?' *Administrative Science Quarterly*, 53, 719–744.
Abrahamson, E., and Fairchild, G. (1999). 'Management fashion: life cycles, triggers and collective learning processes'. *Administrative Science Quarterly*, 44, 491–533.
Ansari, S.M., Fiss, P.C., and Zajac, E.J. (2010). 'Made to fit: how practices vary as they diffuse'. *Academy of Management Review*, 35, 67–92.
Barley, S.R., and Kunda, G. (1992). 'Design and devotion: surges in rational and normative ideologies of control in managerial discourse'. *Administrative Science Quarterly*, 37, 363–399.
Boxenbaum, E., and Gond, J.-P. (2006). 'Micro-strategies of contextualization: cross-national transfer of socially responsible investment'. Danish Research Unit for Industrial Dynamics, Working Paper No. 06-24.
Brown, A.D., Ainsworth, S., and Grant, D. (2012). 'The rhetoric of institutional change'. *Organization Studies*, 33, 297–321.
Buğra, A. (1990). 'The Turkish holding company as a social institution'. *Journal of Economics and Administrative Sciences*, 4, 35–51.

Buğra, A. (1994). *State and business in Turkey*. Albany: State University of New York Press.
Chandler, A.D., Jr. (1962). *Strategy and structure: chapters in the history of the American industrial enterprise*. Cambridge, MA: MIT Press.
Çolpan, A., and Hikino, T. (2008). 'Türkiye'nin büyük şirketler kesiminde işletme gruplarının iktisadi rolü ve çeşitlendirme stratejileri'. *Yönetim Araştırmaları Dergisi*, *8*, 23–57.
Czarniawska, B., and Joerges, B. (1996). 'Travel of ideas', in B. Czarniawska and G. Sevon (eds), *Translating organizational change*. Berlin: de Gruyter, 13–48.
David, R., and Strang, D. (2006). 'When fashion is fleeting: transitory collective beliefs and the dynamics of TQM consulting'. *Academy of Management Journal*, *49*, 215–233.
Erçek, M., and Say, A.I. (2009). 'Discursive ambiguity, professional networks, and peripheral contexts: the translation of total quality management in Turkey, 1991–2002'. *International Studies of Management & Organization*, 38, 78–99.
Fligstein, N. (1985). 'The spread of the multidivisional form among large firms, 1919–1979'. *American Sociological Review, 52,* 44–58.
Green, S.E., Jr. (2004). 'A rhetorical theory of diffusion'. *Academy of Management Review, 29*, 653–669.
Hofstede, G. (1980). *Culture's consequences: international differences in work-related values*. Beverly Hills: Sage.
Kipping, M., Engwall, L., and Üsdiken, B. (2009). 'Preface: the transfer of management knowledge to peripheral countries'. *International Studies of Management & Organization*, 38, 3–16.
Koç, V. (1983). *Hayat Hikayem*. İstanbul: Çeltüt Matbaacılık.
Lawler, E.E., Mohrman, S.A., and Ledford, G.E. (1992). *Employee involvement in total quality management*. San Francisco: Jossey Bass.
Meyer, J.W. (1996). 'Other hood: the promulgation and transmission of ideas in the modern organizational environment', in B. Czarniawska and G. Sevon (eds), *Translating organizational change*. Berlin: Walter de Gruyter, 191–240.
Özen, Ş. (2002). 'Bağlam, aktör, söylem ve kurumsal değişim: Türkiye'de toplam kalite yönetiminin yayılım süreci'. *Yönetim Araştırmaları Dergisi*, *2*, 47–90.
Özen, Ş., and Akkemik, K.A. (2012). 'Does illegitimate corporate behavior follow the forms of polity? The Turkish experience'. *Journal of Management Studies, 49*, 515–537.
Özen, Ş., and Berkman, Ü. (2007). 'The cross-national reconstruction of managerial practices: TQM in Turkey'. *Organization Studies, 28,* 825–851.
Özen, Ş., and Küskü, F. (2009). 'Corporate environmental citizenship variation in developing countries: an institutional framework'. *Journal of Business Ethics*, *89*, 297–313.
Palmer, D.A., Jennings, D.P., and Zhou, X. (1993). 'Late adoption of the multidivisional norm by large US corporations: institutional, political, and economic accounts'. *Administrative Science Quarterly, 38,* 100–132.
Perkman, M., and Spicer, A. (2008). 'How are management fashions institutionalized? The role of institutional work'. *Human Relations*, *61*, 811–844.
Robertson, R. (1995). 'Glocalization: time-space and homogeneity-heterogeneity', in M. Featherstone et al. (eds), *Global modernities*. London: Sage, 25–44.
Røvik, K.A. (2002). 'The secrets of the winners: management ideas that flow', in K. Sahlin-Andersson and L. Engwall (eds), *The expansion of management knowledge: carriers, ideas and circulation*. Stanford, CA: Stanford University Press, 113–144.
Seeck, H., and Kuokkanen, A. (2010). 'Management paradigms in Finnish journals and literature between 1921 and 2006'. *Business History*, *52*, 306–336.
Suddaby, R., and Greenwood, R. (2005). 'Rhetorical strategies of legitimacy'. *Administrative Science Quarterly, 50,* 35–67.
Swidler, A. (1986). 'Culture in action: symbols and strategies'. *American Sociological Review, 51*, 273–286.
Thomas, G.M., Meyer, J., Ramirez, F., and Boli, J. (1987). 'Institutional structure: constituting state, society, and individual'. Newbury Park: Sage.

Tolbert, P.S., and Zucker, L.G. (1983). 'Institutional sources of change in the formal structure of organizations: the diffusion of civil service reform 1880–1935'. *Administrative Science Quarterly, 28,* 22–39.

Üsdiken, B., and Wasti, S.A. (2009). 'Preaching, teaching and researching at the periphery: academic management literature in Turkey, 1970–1999'. *Organization Studies, 30,* 1063–1082.

Whitley, R. (1999). *Divergent capitalisms: the social structuring and change of business systems.* Oxford: Oxford University Press.

Xu, Q. (1999). 'TQM as an arbitrary sign for play: discourse and transformation'. *Organization Studies, 20,* 659–681.

10

Toward a Multi-layered Glocalization Approach

States, Multinational Corporations, and the Transformation of Gender Contracts

Michal Frenkel

Introduction: From a Single-layered to a Multi-layered Understanding of the Global Transfer and Translation of Ideas and Policies

Refining our understanding of the process of globalization, students of 'glocalization' (Robertson 1995), 'translation' (Czarniawska-Joerges and Sevon 1996; Czarniawska and Sevon 2005; Frenkel 2005), and hybridization (Pieterse, 1995) of ideas and practices across national boundaries have repeatedly pointed to the transformations both state and organizational policies undergo when implemented in a social setting different than the ones from which they originated. In addition, these theories have (to different degrees) underlined the importance of the social actors involved in the cross-national transfer process and the active and creative role these actors are taking in adjusting ideas and practices to meet local needs and traditions. However, while theories of homogenizing globalization (e.g., Meyer, Boli, Thomas, and Ramirez 1997) tend to take for granted the exposure and receptiveness of all influential local institutions in each society to a powerful global idea or practice (therefore predicting very little resistance toward the global isomorphism process), the theories of glocalization, translation, and hybridization tend to focus, at least empirically, on a single social agent seen as primarily responsible for the importation and alternation of the specific foreign idea or practice. Other social actors in the local setting, if accounted for in these studies, are often portrayed as representing local logics and traditions and as embedded exclusively in their local institutional and cultural environment. Beyond the empirical inaccuracy this 'single agent glocalization' perspective implies, it also reproduces the binary distinction between local and global and, therefore, hinders a more complex understanding of the mutual transformation of what we term 'local' and 'global'.

To challenge this 'single agent glocalization' perspective, in the current chapter I draw upon the case of the global transformation of gender contract and work–family (WF) state and organizational policies to develop a *multi-layered glocalization* approach. According to this approach, in the era of intensive globalization, many different actors in each society— including workers (especially professional and knowledge workers), unions, grassroots organizations, state apparatuses, and others that constitute the institutional environment within which states and employers operate—are understood to be simultaneously exposed to foreign and local conceptualizations of social and organizational problems, and as drawing upon local and foreign tools designed to offer at least partial organizational and social solutions to them. Instead of assuming the centrality of the role played by the usual suspects, namely, international organizations and multinational corporations (MNCs) in disseminating ideas and policies across national boundaries or the centrality of the state in imposing such policies upon employers within its legal jurisdiction, this approach adopts a dynamic research strategy, making the identification of dominant actors an empirical question. Likewise, instead of assuming which actors represent local traditions and which serve as agents of globalization or glocalization, the dynamic approach argued for here sees that as an empirical question as well. While, for lack of better terminology, I still use the terms 'local' and 'global' here, 'local' should be understood as 'already institutionalized in a specific environment' and as subjectively understood by actors in this environment as 'local' and traditional, while 'global' is defined as 'foreign' by local actors who introduce it. The distinction between global and local is therefore fluid and contextualized. The ways in which 'foreign' ideas, conceptualizations, and policies, are finding their ways into a society and transforming its social order is seen, from this perspective, as an outcome of an ongoing negotiation between the different actors operating in the local environment, each bringing to the negotiation table its own interpretation and translation of the ideas or policy proposals to which it has been exposed through its independent global network.

This *multi-layered glocalization* research agenda, I argue, may also help us tackle the disturbing discontinuity characterizing the literature on cross-national transfer of ideas and policies—that is, the discontinuity between studies of global transfer of state policies (e.g., Berkovitch 1997; Drori, Jang, and Meyer 2006; Henisz, Zelner, and Guillen 2005; Meyer et al. 1997) and those looking at organizational policies (e.g., Ferner, Almond, and Colling 2005; Guler, Guillen, and Macpherson 2002; Kostova 1999). While both literatures ask similar questions and draw upon similar theoretical schemas, the interrelations between the global transfer of these two types of policy have been largely overlooked. Furthermore, while theories of cross-national diffusion of state policies generally overlook the role of employers in encouraging states to adopt certain policies, most studies of the cross-national transfer of *organizational* practices disregard the independent transformation of host countries' policies as part of a process that facilitates the adoption of new managerial fashions and practices.

The tendency to ignore the transformation of nation-states' institutional and cultural environments—which is partly due to their embeddedness within a global network of states and the fact that they are often subjected to regulatory pressures from international organizations—is specifically salient in studies of international management (IM) and multinational corporations (MNCs). Studies of the globally spread state policies similarly overlook the role of business in transforming state policies, especially when these policies are not specifically business-oriented. Moreover, both literatures often disregard the exposure of workers (and citizens), their unions, and other organization members to global trends. While the top managers at the MNC headquarters and subsidiaries as well as international organizations and states' elites, are seen as cosmopolitan figures, moving and maneuvering between local and global systems of meaning and action, workers and unions are viewed as tied to their local (mostly national) cultural and institutional environment. As such, they are frequently portrayed as naturally opposing any change that represents a different cultural or institutional logic to their own (Harris and Moran 2000; Hofstede 1983, 2001).

A multi-layered perspective, drawing simultaneously upon cultural and economic globalization, highlighting different collective agents and a variety of ways through which these agents are exposed to foreign ideas, highlights the complexity of the transfer process. While avoiding a predetermined assumption about the homogenizing outcomes of the exposure of multiple actors to global pressures may help us construct a better and more complex understanding of the phenomenon under consideration, in what follows, I demonstrate how the *multi-layered globalization* approach sheds new light on one of the burning questions of today's feminist studies—namely, how globalization affects gender relations while bridging the gap between the literature looking at the cross-national diffusion of gender-related state policies, and that looking at the spread of gender-related organizational practices.

States, Multinational Corporations, and Gender Contracts

As mentioned, one field in which the close interrelations between state and organizational policies *at the national level* have been found is the field of diversity and gender equality policies. For at least three decades now, students of gender and organizations have been able to demonstrate the role of organizational structures, practices, and labor relations in shaping not only gender relations and inequalities within the organization (e.g., Acker 1990, 1992; Cohen, Broschak, and Haveman 1998; Ely 1995; Ely, Scully, and Foldy 2003; Ibarra 1997), but also the division of labor in the family and societal discourses about gender in general. At the same time, however, studies have repeatedly shown that these social norms, representing the tacit rules that govern the obligations and rights that in turn define the relations between genders and generations and between the spheres of production and reproduction (Rantalaiho 1993: 2), also known as 'gender contracts', themselves determine the extent to which employers are likely to adopt gender-related practices, such as HR policies regarding work–life balance, diversity, and affirmative action. It has also been shown that the state provision of gender-related policies as part of the general welfare state regime, such as maternity, paternity, and parental leave, has influenced the extent to which employers are willing to voluntarily offer additional family leaves (den-Dulk 2001; Ferner et al. 2005).

These studies, however, have mostly focused on policy construction in a single state and have, therefore, taught us little about the ways in which the increased exposure of individuals, employers, grassroots organizations, and states to global trends affects the shaping of organizational and states' gender-related policies. Introducing the notion of 'multi-layered globalization', this chapter examines how states, organizations, and individuals incorporate, hibernate, and translate global trends in their conceptualization of gender relations and how they reconstruct new gender contracts at the intersections between the different layers of global influence. Specifically, it focuses on one set of gender-related organizational HR policies, namely, those associated with the notion of 'work–family' practices, designed to help workers balance, harmonize, or synergize their work and family responsibilities. The chapter looks at how the cross-national adoption and translation of WF policies and ideologies occurs simultaneously but not necessarily interdependently at the state, organizational, and individual levels. Social actors in each of these three levels are embedded in separate global networks, in which norms and practices associated with balancing work and family are discussed and articulated. The desirable 'gender contract' that these actors develop in response to the norms and practices to which they have been exposed as part of their global network shapes their position as they negotiate WF policies at the state and organizational level.

Gender Contracts between States and Organizations

Comparative studies of gender-related state and organizational policies have tended to highlight the persistent and resilient differences in the ways in which nation-states (or regions), and the individuals and employers within them, conceptualize the desirable gender division of labor (e.g., Carnoy 2000; Crompton and Le Feuvre 2000; Esping-Andersen 1999; Orloff 1993; Pfau-Effinger 2009). This is especially true regarding the role of the nuclear and extended family, community, employers and the state in caring for children and other dependents, and the degree of de-familialization each welfare regime allows for citizens with family responsibilities. Family welfare regimes, as this literature repeatedly demonstrates, are grounded in long-lasting and deep-rooted local traditions and are reconstructed and reproduced through stable local institutions, such as the amount of daycare available, the existence of flexible work arrangements, and sick and other leave days that allow workers to care for their families.

Given the embeddedness of these welfare policies in the national economic system and normative gender division of labor, a cross-national conversion of these different systems had seemed, until recently, an unlikely occurrence. In recent years, however, with the growing intervention of the EU and other international organizations in shaping states' policies in this area, scholars looking at welfare state policies have begun turning their attention to the possibility of a convergence towards a more unified European or even global policy aimed at helping workers to better integrate the two spheres (Gambles, Lewis, and Rapoport 2006; Lewis 2006; Mahon 2006; Walby 2004, 2005; Wang, Lawler, Shi, Walumbwa, and Piao 2008).

While making an important contribution in exposing parts of the role of global forces in shaping and transforming gender regimes, this literature, by and large, follows the 'single layer' approach, presenting the EU and other international organizations as the primary agent behind the transformation of WF state policies in its different members. The member states are mostly seen as complying, to one degree or another, with the imposed new directives. The traditional welfare and gender regimes, along with traditional local power relations and norms, are portrayed as restricting the new spirits of WF, and local forces (especially unions and women's organizations) are mostly seen as embedded in their local institutional environments, rather than playing a role in the cross-national transfer process. Despite the major effect these changes in legislation may have upon them, the potential role of multinational and local corporations in shaping the transformed policies are not treated at all in this line of studies.

In a similar vein, while taking into consideration the role of nation-states' policies and welfare regimes in shaping organizational WF policies (e.g., den-Dulk 2001; Kelly and Dobbin 1998), students of organizational WF policies have not yet accounted for the effect the growing transnational transfer of state policies may have upon the cross-national transfer of these organizational policies. The few studies looking at these policies from the point of view of their cross-national transfer commonly treat nation-states' welfare regimes as a 'constant' and stable part of the institutional environment, hindering the possibility of cross-national diffusion of organizational policies in this field (Ferner et al. 2005).

To demonstrate the potential merit of the multi-layered glocalization perspective, the following sections look at two case studies: the case of the transformation of the Israeli state's WF policy since 2000, and the case of the introduction of WF organizational policy in the South Korean-based global MNC, Samsung Group. In both cases, I briefly present the different actors involved in shaping the WF policy, and the global networks affecting the positions and the ideas they put forward.

State Policies in the Context of Multi-layered Globalization: The Case of Israel

International Organizations, the State, and the Transformation of the State's Maternity Leave Policy

To demonstrate the importance of the multi-layered approach to the understanding of the glocalization of WF state policies in Israel, three short examples are examined: the legal change in the provision of maternity leave, the introduction of pro-work flexibility state policies, and the introduction of family-friendly policies by the state as an employer. At first glance, all three examples seem like clear demonstrations of a cross-national diffusion of state policies in which the state surrenders itself to global isomorphic pressures and adopts a policy proposal promoted by a global power. A closer examination, however, demonstrates that even the simplest importation of state policy involves different actors who bring to the table ideas and arguments to which they are exposed through their global networks.

Maternity, paternity, and family leaves are seen as the backbone of state WF or de-familialization policies. Allowing working parents to care for their newborn children without endangering their jobs, the duration of these leaves, whether they are paid or unpaid, and who takes on the responsibility of providing an income for the length of the leave (the state, the employer or the worker) are all seen as a good proxy for the gender contract or the family welfare regime characteristic of a given society. While in social democratic welfare regimes, the state provides, or forces, employers to provide long and mostly paid leaves for fathers and mothers (encouraging them to share care responsibilities while keeping their jobs), conservative regimes have traditionally offered short, fully paid maternity leaves, complemented by lengthy but low-paying parental leaves, available mostly to mothers. This arrangement, combined with a shortage of quality daycare services, encouraged women under this regime to stay at home with their children until they were three years old, thus reinforcing the traditional division of labor between the male breadwinner and the female caretaker. Finally, the liberal regime is characterized by a minimal availability of state-sponsored and paid leaves, forcing parents of newborn children to go back to work shortly after the birth of their children and to rely either on the market for the provision of care services (nannies or private daycare facilities) or upon their family and individual resources. Alternatively, they may have to withdraw from the labor force.

Seen as a critical tool in facilitating a work–family balance and in integrating mothers and women in general into the labor market, the provision of extended and paid parental leaves has become a central goal for many international and supranational organizations, such as the International Labor Organization (ILO), the EU, and the OECD.

Although Israel is not a member of the EU and is not formally subject to its directives and regulations, the global trend represented in and advanced by the EU and other international organizations' directives and recommendations has led to a policy transformation and to the extension of the duration of maternity leave in Israel as well.

Israel is a particularly interesting case for students of the shaping of WF policies for two main reasons: its unique work–family constellation and its rapid adjustment to the requirements of the global market since the 1990s. To start, Israel has higher fertility rates and a higher proportion of mothers of preschool children working full-time in the labor market than any other industrialized society (Stier, Lewin-Epstein, and Braun 2001). The combination of high fertility and participation in the labor force has been described as contributing to nation-building and the national collective good (Berkovitch 1997). As part of this dual national agenda of increasing productivity and fertility, and due to a strong social democratic tradition, in the 1950s, Israel was one of the first countries to offer a relatively generous package of state-sponsored work–family benefits. The powerful unions helped to protect workers with family responsibilities as part of the general protection of unionized workers.

This facilitating political environment, however, did not last long. While other social democratic welfare regimes extended their maternity leave provisions and pushed for paternity leave as well, attempts to extend maternity leave in Israel and add paternity leave did not gain board support in the Israeli parliament until around the turn of the millennium.

Two important alterations were made to the Israeli parental leave policy in 2007. The first was an extension to mandatory maternity leave from 12 to 14 weeks (amendment No. 37); the second was the expansion of the right for parental leave to men (Employment of Women Law, amendment No. 38). While it is true that the internal political constellation in Israel has clearly turned towards neo-liberalism, with welfare cutbacks constantly on the agenda, it is nonetheless noteworthy that the two amendments to the Employment of Women Law were passed with hardly any debate in the local parliament. In particular, the former registered no opposition whatsoever among members of parliament, despite the extra burden it placed on the national budget (Frenkel, Hacker, and Braudo 2010).

While pro-natalist sentiments and the views of constituents may explain politicians' support for the expansion of parental leaves, they cannot account for the fact that several previous attempts to pass similar amendments had failed, nor can they explain how it is that the newly adopted length of maternity leave and the introduction of paternity leave so closely paralleled the new minimal recommendations made by the International Labor Organization (ILO) and the EU. Analysis of the discussions of the new amendments in the Israeli parliament's Committee on the Status of Women shows that almost all participants— be they representatives of different political parties or women's organizations, experts, or state officials—referred to the recommendations and practices of international organizations and other countries. A document prepared by the parliament's Research and Information Center informed MPs about the prevalent policies in other, mostly European societies, and about international organizations' directives and suggestions. While the different parties and grassroots organizations participating in the debate favored the expansion, they all brought to the negotiating table ideas, practices, and modes of justification taken from other societies and international organizations. Each of them, however, brought in a slightly different view and mode of justification and offered a 'translation' of the global policy that appealed to its own constituency. While left-wing parties and women's organizations presented the new policy as a move toward a better integration of women in the labor force, Arab and Jewish more traditionalist parties presented it as way to increase fertility rates in line with religious imperatives. Against this very wide political and public coalition stood the professional cadre of the Ministry of Finance, the traditional opponents of any welfare budget expansion, drawing on the US case and on the growing neo-liberal resistance towards state expansion. Concerned that the Ministry of Finance would block the amendment, the committee members converged around the minimal expansion that was recommended by any international organization, that of the ILO.

The case of the amendment to the Employment of Women Law in Israel thus demonstrates two of the central elements of the multi-layered glocalization approach. First, it shows how international trends and multinational transfers come to define the general framework within which locally embedded political and public debates are conducted; and second, it demonstrates how all of the different actors in the struggle over policy making come to the table armed with models and examples taken from a gradually globalizing arsenal.

International Donors, Grassroots Organizations, and the Transformation of Pro-flexibility State Policies

On December 6, 2011, the Israeli Women's Network (IWN), a prominent grassroots women's organization, submitted its proposal for new legislation on flexible work arrangements to the Israeli parliament. The proposal had been endorsed by 12 MPs from several different parties across the Israeli political spectrum. While it had been 'translated' to fit the specific features of Israeli society and its legal system, the proposal was basically a copy of the British Employment Act of 2002, which encouraged employers to offer flexible work arrangements to parents of children under 16 whenever such arrangements were congruent with the nature of the job (Israel Women's Network 2011).

Similar to maternity and paternity leaves, flexible work arrangements, such as flex-time, job sharing, and telecommuting, are considered employment practices that contribute to a better balance of work and family. While in the past a degree of flexibility was available to Israeli working parents through the option of part-time work, especially in the state sector, the number of such jobs has been declining significantly since the 1980s, and today, quality part-time jobs are scarce. Flexible work arrangements are offered by private employers, but this proposed law was the first to encourage the state to take an active part in promoting them.

The process by which the IWN became active in promoting the cross-national diffusion of the British law represents another example of the potential importance of the multi-layered glocalization framework by demonstrating how a grassroots organization's independent global network contributes to the shaping of local WF policies.

The proposed law should be understood as part of a broader agenda to offer better WF opportunities to working parents in Israel, an agenda that has been central to the activities of the IWN since 2005. The choice of this agenda is neither random nor unique to Israel. Around the industrialized world, women's and feminist organizations have made work–family and work–life balance a top priority. Learning from parallel organizations within its international network, the IWN has tried to advance the same solutions that have been found useful in other societies. The construction of the IWN's agenda and the specific practices that it endorses and promotes are closely associated with its relationships with foreign donors and collaborators.

However, the willingness of MPs and the state to consider introducing this legislation in Israel, despite the major differences between the legal systems and gender contracts of the two countries, cannot be explained in terms of the efforts of the IWN alone. Here, too, the general calls for greater work flexibility, endorsed by international organizations such as the EU, the ILO, and the OECD, of which Israel is now a member, make both the state itself and its decision makers more open to the implementation of such policies as flexible work arrangements. Thus, while the outcome of the process may be the cross-national transfer (and partial translation) of a British policy to Israel, this transfer is actually facilitated by the independent embeddedness of the state and the IWN—each within their own distinct international networks.

Multinational Corporations and the Adoption of the Business Case Ideology by State Apparatuses

While students of globalization often refer to the power of MNCs to change host countries' policies in order to secure a more advantageous business environment for their local affiliates and subsidiaries, it is less common to think of MNCs as carriers of ideologies of social justice and welfare, especially at the state level. However, the development of the business case ideology for WF policies has turned some large, often US-based, MNCs into fierce advocates of WF policies and their adoption in different countries. The business case ideology for WF policies emerged in the 1990s in the US before traveling to other societies and international organizations. It presents the balance of work and family not as a welfare practice aimed at helping workers, but as a core business strategy aimed at contributing to the firm's bottom line (Rapoport, Bailyn, Fletcher, and Pruitt 2002). Due to their simultaneous contribution to organizational performance and widely celebrated social objectives, some highly visible MNCs have turned the adoption of these organizational policies into part of their flagship corporate social responsibility projects, advocating their dissemination across borders as part of their participation in the global rationalization of the business world.

In 2008, the Israel Civil Service Commission founded a committee tasked with turning the civil service itself into a family-friendly organization. While the original letter of intent presented the project's objective as women's better and more equal integration in the organization, the business case discourse came to dominate the committee's discussions from a very early stage. Led by the Prime Minister's Adviser for Women's Affairs, the committee soon decided to invite representatives of state organizations and large MNCs to share their WF practices with the committee. While state organizations were asked to describe the current situation and the main obstacles to the introduction of WF practices, representatives of large and well-known MNCs were mostly asked to provide a role model for the state to follow, at least partially. In their testimonies, MNCs' representatives repeatedly introduced the business case ideology, convincing many of the committee members that it was the right way to approach the subject and persuading managers in the civil service to adopt WF practices. The committee's final report reflects the adoption of the business case framework, promoting several of the policies seen by MNCs as the best WF solutions for organizations in the public and private sector. While not specified in the original letter of intent, one of the eventual outcomes of the committee's work was a public campaign aimed at encouraging private employers to adopt WF organizational policies. The slogan chosen for this campaign was 'It's good for the business and good for the family,' thus fully embracing the logic and language of the business case framework.

Once again, we can see how the shaping of state-level WF policy was simultaneously stimulated by the changing trends in international organizations' views of desirable WF solutions, as well as by another group of social actors who were embedded in their own international network, namely, US-based MNCs, who took it upon themselves to spread the gospel of the business case for the adoption of WF practices.

While the case of transforming Israel's WF state policies demonstrates the relevance of the multi-layered approach to the understanding of the glocalization of state policies, the following case, that of the adoption of WF policies by Samsung Group, clearly demonstrates the importance of understanding the adoption of organizational HR policies from that perspective.

A Multi-layered Globalization Perspective on the Construction of Organizational WF Policies: The Case of the Samsung Group

Established in Taegu, Korea, in 1938, the Samsung Group has grown into one of the world's leading electronics companies, specializing in digital appliances and media, semiconductors, memory, and system integration, with business affiliates and subsidiaries scattered around the globe. Until 2008, the Samsung Group did not have a formal and detailed WF corporate policy, nor had it published official documents encouraging its foreign affiliates and subsidiaries to adopt, or to avoid adopting, WF policies. However, a series of corporate sustainability reports, published annually since 2008, tells the story of the development and spread of a detailed and formal WF policy, accompanied by a well-articulated ideology combining the rhetoric of the business case with that of the rhetoric of sustainability and corporate social responsibility (Samsung Electronics 2012). Both explicitly and implicitly, these reports tell the story of the emergence of a corporate HR policy in response to different corporate stakeholders.

The Home Country Effect

While prominent US-based, high-tech MNCs have celebrated their adoption of comprehensive and well-publicized work–family or work–life balance corporate policies (see, for example, Intel Ltd. 2012), the lack of interest in developing such policies at the Samsung Group can be attributed, at least partially, to Korea's Confucian gender contract, which held sway until quite recently. According to this gender contract, married women and mothers were expected to stay at home and outside of the labor force, taking on all familial responsibilities, including caring for children and the elderly. The prevalent corporate culture forbade workers from leaving their workplace earlier than their managers, and passing one's after-work hours with colleagues was considered a strong corporate norm. However, like the Israeli state, the Korean state has recently embraced WF policies, such as parental leave schemes (1995) and maternity benefits (2001), following recommendations by the UN, the ILO, and other international organizations, and in accordance with the growing participation of professional women in the workforce (Sung 2003). While it is difficult to determine to what extent this change in the Korean family welfare regime affected Samsung's conceptualization of its own role in improving its employees' work–life balance, the changes in the local gender contract and the growing number of married women and mothers in the labor force have explicitly affected the adoption of global WF policies. In 2009, a document published by Samsung Electronics, entitled 'Integrity Management: Building a Creative Corporate Culture,' presents the introduction of work–life balance benefits to the company and justifies them in reference to changing societal norms:

> Because social norms have changed, an increasing number of female workers are participating in economic activities and retaining high potential employees has become the key to successful business operations. Happiness has become the overarching value of employees' quality of life, giving rise to greater social interest in balancing work and life. Therefore, Samsung Electronics also supports and encourages the employees to balance their work and life.
>
> (Samsung Electronics 2009)

While a rhetoric that combines the integration of women and mothers into the labor market with the business case, and even with workers' satisfaction and happiness, resembles similar statements made by other global corporations in the industry, the timing and the reference to local needs and norms suggest that policies at the level of the state, which was itself affected by global trends and international organizations' recommendations, had a lot to do with the Samsung Group's new-found openness in this regard. It should be noted, however, that while other (Western) MNCs present WF policies as part of their diversity strategy, Samsung has presented it as part of its longstanding sustainability policy, suggesting a wide process of translation and adaptation done by the corporate leadership.

The Global Consultancies Effect

While the impact of the changing family welfare regime and gender contract in the home country on the Samsung Group's adoption of the new WF scheme is hard to pin down precisely, the firm's sustainably reports clearly point to the powerful influence wielded by one particular global institution—the Great Place to Work Institute. The Great Place to Work Institute (GPW) defines itself as 'a global research, consulting and training firm that helps organizations identify, create and sustain great workplaces through the development of high-trust workplace cultures'. The institute serves businesses, non-profit organizations and government agencies in 45 countries on six continents, conducting workplace surveys to estimate worker satisfaction with different aspects of their work. It is important to note that while the institute is global, it applies homogeneous standards to all corporations that it surveys and would appear to be trying to define a standard set of organizational policies across borders. These surveys are used to compile a list of the best places to work in different countries and different industries, as well as to help consultants and managers shape their HR and other organizational policies.

The Samsung Group was first surveyed by GPW in 2006 and scored poorly in the field of work–family and work–life balance. The firm's 2009 sustainability report clearly links these surveys with its adoption of WF policies (Samsung Electronics 2009: 20).

While GPW presents itself as a global institute, Samsung clearly portrays it as American, closely linking the use of a US-based consultancy with the need to provide for a global and diversified workforce.

Global and Local Workforce

GPW's reports are based on employees' responses to their surveys. Because Samsung has to compete for highly skilled workers in the strongly competitive technological sector, employee satisfaction is highly valued by the Samsung Group, both in Korea and elsewhere. In addition, websites such as GlassDoor.com now publish anonymous reviews by workers of their workplace, adding a more subjective and detailed evaluation of the desirability of any specific workplace to that published by GPW. In these reviews, Samsung, and especially its overseas affiliates, are often mentioned as failing to offer a good balance between work and family. According to the corporation's own report, while Korean employees rarely list family considerations as their top reason for quitting the firm, they are the number two reason for resignation among foreign employees. This may be the reason that the firm claims to be investing so much effort in involving employees and their unions in shaping its work–life balance policies.

Thus, much like the shaping of state-level WF policies, the case of the Korean Samsung Group's WF policies suggests that we can better understand the shaping of those policies through the framework of multi-layered glocalization. Similarly to the state, the MNC's headquarters and local affiliates are sites in which different actors are exposed to, articulate, debate, translate, and implement ideas and practices available to them through the different global networks in which they are embedded—networks that are both internal and external to their organizations.

Concluding Remarks: From Global Homogenization to Globalizing Translation

My objective in this chapter has been twofold. First, against the common single-layer conceptualization of the cross-national transfer of state and organizational policies within the MNC that is common to globalization and glocalization studies, I presented the framework of *multi-layered* glocalization, which offers a more complex and dynamic understanding of the transfer process. While most 'transfer' studies focus on international organizations or the MNCs' headquarters as the main generators and key agents of innovative ideas that cross national boundaries, the multi-layered glocalization approach encourages us to observe how different actors both within and outside the corporation draw upon the ideas and practices available to them through their different and independent global networks in their negotiations over and struggles to shape state and organizational policies. It also underlines the importance of understanding the mutual and complex relations between the different global influences on states, employers, and individuals. As both the policies of the Israeli state and the Samsung Group demonstrate, any attempt to present any of these actors as predominantly 'local,' thereby eliminating their independent embeddedness in global networks, means missing out on at least part of the transfer dynamic.

The second objective was to offer a better analysis of the global dynamics that are presently constructing the work–family balance as one of the most burning social problems of our time, as well as of the institutionalization of a globally available repertoire of possible solutions and paradigms through which WF policies may be framed and negotiated. While in most cases, changes to WF policies in the public and the private sectors are treated as distinct entities, and while comparative and global studies of family welfare policies and gender contracts rarely feed back into each other, a multi-layered perspective on the cross-national influences that shape states' and employers' WF policies can help us understand why, despite strong homogenizing pressures by international organizations, multinational corporations, popular culture, and the media, total convergence around a single WF model is not likely.

References

Acker, J. (1990). 'Hierarchies, jobs, bodies: a theory of gendered organizations'. *Gender and Society*, 4(2): 139–58.

Acker, J. (1992). 'Gendering organization theory', in A.J. Mills and P. Tancred (eds), *Gendering organizational analysis*. Newbury Park: Sage Publications, viii, 309.

Berkovitch, N. (1997). 'Motherhood as a national mission: the construction of womanhood in the legal discourse in Israel'. *Women's Studies International Forum*, 20(5–6): 605–19. doi: 10.1016/s0277-5395(97)00055-1.

Carnoy, M. (2000). *Sustaining the new economy: work, family, and community in the information age*. New York: Russell Sage Foundation; Cambridge, MA: Harvard University Press.

Cohen, L.E., Broschak, J.P., and Haveman, H.A. (1998). 'And then there were more? The effect of organizational sex composition on the hiring and promotion of managers'. *American Sociological Review*, 63(5): 711–27.

Crompton, R., and Le Feuvre, N. (2000). 'Gender, family and employment in comparative perspective: the realities and representations of equal opportunities in Britain and France'. *Journal of European Social Policy, 10*(4): 334–48.

Czarniawska, B., and Sevon, G. (2005). *Global ideas: how ideas, objects and practices travel in the global economy.* Malmo: Liber and Copenhagen Business School Press.

Czarniawska-Joerges, B., and Sevon, G. (1996). *Translating organizational change.* Berlin, New York: Walter de Gruyter.

den-Dulk, L. (2001). *Work–family arrangements in organisations: a cross-national study in the Netherlands, Italy, the United Kingdom, and Sweden.* Amsterdam: Rozenberg.

Drori, G.S., Jang, Y.S., and Meyer, J.W. (2006). 'Sources of rationalized governance: cross-national longitudinal analyses, 1985–2002'. *Administrative Science Quarterly, 51*(2): 205–29.

Ely, R.J. (1995). 'The power of demography: women's social constructions of gender identity at work'. *Academy of Management Journal, 38*(3): 589–635.

Ely, R.J., Scully, M., and Foldy, E.G. (2003). *Reader in gender, work, and organization.* Malden, MA: Blackwell.

Esping-Andersen, G.S. (1999). *Social foundations of postindustrial economies.* New York: Oxford University Press.

Ferner, A., Almond, P., and Colling, T. (2005). 'Institutional theory and the cross-national transfer of employment policy: the case of "workforce diversity" in US multinationals'. *Journal of International Business Studies, 36*(3): 304–21. doi: DOI 10.1057/palgrave.jibs.8400134.

Frenkel, M. (2005). 'The politics of translation'. *Organization, 12*(2): 275–301.

Frenkel, M., Hacker, D., and Braudo, Y. (2010). 'Working families in the Israeli law: between neo-liberalism and human rights'. *Studies in Israeli Society and Modern Jewish Society.*

Gambles, R., Lewis, S., and Rapoport, R. (2006). *The myth of work–life balance: the challenge of our time for men, women and societies.* Chichester: John Wiley.

Guler, I., Guillen, M.F., and Macpherson, J.M. (2002). 'Global competition, institutions, and the diffusion of organizational practices: the international spread of ISO 9000 quality certificates'. *Administrative Science Quarterly, 47*(2): 207–32.

Harris, P.R., and Moran, R.T. (2000). *Managing cultural differences* (5th edn). Houston, TX: Gulf.

Henisz, W.J., Zelner, B.A., and Guillen, M.F. (2005). 'The worldwide diffusion of market oriented infrastructure reforms, 1977–1999'. *American Sociological Review, 70*(6): 871–97.

Hofstede, G. (1983). 'The cultural relativity of organizational practices and theories'. *Journal of International Business Studies, 14*(2): 75.

Hofstede, G. (2001). *Culture's consequences: comparing values, behaviors, institutions, and organizations across nations* (2nd edn). Thousand Oaks, CA: Sage.

Ibarra, H. (1997). 'Paving an alternative route: gender differences in managerial networks'. *Social Psychology Quarterly, 60*(1): 91–102.

Intel Ltd. (2012). 'Life and work: two worlds one you'. Retrieved August 17, 2012, from http://www.intel.com/lifeatintel/lifework/.

Israel Women's Network. (2011). 'Work life balance: a national aim'. Retrieved December 2, 2011, from http://www.iwn.org.il/?CategoryID=183andArticleID=141.

Kelly, E., and Dobbin, F. (1998). 'How affirmative action became diversity management—employer response to antidiscrimination law, 1961 to 1996'. *American Behavioral Scientist, 41*(7): 960–84.

Kostova, T. (1999). 'Transnational transfer of strategic organizational practices: a contextual perspective'. *Academy of Management Review, 24*(2): 308–24.

Lewis, J. (2006). 'Work/family reconciliation, equal opportunities and social policies: the interpretation of policy trajectories at the EU level and the meaning of gender equality'. *Journal of European Public Policy, 13*(3): 420–37.

Mahon, R. (2006). 'The OECD and the work/family reconciliation agenda: competing frames', in J. Lewis (ed.), *Children, changing families and welfare states.* Cheltenham: Edward Elgar, 173–200.

Meyer, J.W., Boli, J., Thomas, G.M., and Ramirez, F.O. (1997). 'World society and the nation-state'. *American Journal of Sociology, 103*(1), 144–81.

Orloff, A.S. (1993). *Politics of pensions: comparative analysis of Britain, Canada and the United States, 1880–1940*. Univ. Wisconsin Press.

Pfau-Effinger, B. (2009). 'Cultural foundation of welfare state policies'. *Osterreichische Zeitschrift fur Soziologie, 34*(3): 3–21.

Pieterse, J.N. (1995). 'Globalization as hybridization', in M. Featherstone, S. Lash, and R. Robertson (eds), *Global modernities: 10th anniversary conference: revised papers*. Sage, 46–68.

Rantalaiho, L. (1993). 'Gender system of the Finnish society'. *Social changes in the status of women: the experience of Finland and the USSR*. Tampere: Research Institute for Social Sciences.

Rapoport, R., Bailyn, L., Fletcher, J.K., and Pruitt, B. (2002). *Beyond work–family balance: advancing gender equity and workplace performance* (1st edn). San Francisco, CA: Jossey-Bass.

Robertson, R. (1995). 'Glocalization: time-space and homogeneity-heterogeneity', in M. Featherstone, S. Lash, and R. Robertson (eds), *Global modernities: 10th anniversary conference: revised papers*. Sage.

Samsung Electronics. (2009). 'Building a creative corporate culture'. Retrieved August 9, 2010, from http://www.samsung.com/us/aboutsamsung/sustainability/integritymanagement/download/building_a_creative_corporate_culture.pdf.

Samsung Electronics. (2012). 'Our sustainable development at Samsung Electronics'. Retrieved August 17, 2012, from http://www.samsung.com/us/aboutsamsung/citizenship/oursustainabilityreports.html.

Stier, H., Lewin-Epstein, N., and Braun, M. (2001). 'Welfare regimes, family-supportive policies, and women's employment along the life-course'. *American Journal of Sociology, 106*(6): 1731–60.

Sung, S. (2003). 'Women reconciling paid and unpaid work in a Confucian welfare state: the case of South Korea', *Social Policy & Administration*, 37(4): 342–60.

Walby, S. (2004). 'The European Union and gender equality: emergent varieties of gender regime'. *Social Politics, 11*(1): 4–29.

Walby, S. (2005). 'Introduction: comparative gender mainstreaming in a global era'. *International Feminist Journal of Politics, 7*(4): 453–70.

Wang, P., Lawler, J.J., Shi, K., Walumbwa, F., and Piao, M. (2008). 'Family-friendly employment practices: importance and effects in India, Kenya and China', in J.J. Lawler and G. Hundley (eds), *The global diffusion of human resource practices: institutional and cultural limits* (1st edn). Bingley, UK: Emerald JAI, 235–66.

11

Words Fly Quicker Than Actions
The Globalization of the Diversity Discourse

Iris Barbosa and Carlos Cabral-Cardoso

Introduction

Having to compete in the world market, multinational companies (MNCs) play a prominent role in the process of transferring management knowledge and practices, particularly when they originate in more developed/hegemonic countries and subsidiaries are hosted in peripheral societies (Frenkel 2008). A good example of this process is provided by the diversity agenda and the role played by US MNCs in spreading it to local affiliates and other visible local companies aiming to be seen as innovative.

Less experienced than their US counterparts in dealing with workforce diversity, European organizations are also facing new challenges and pressures to include diversity issues in their agendas. In a context of growing cultural diversity but little knowledge and experience in managing it, the more progressive Portuguese organizations may feel tempted to import the US diversity model as a package. In particular, local subsidiaries of US MNCs are likely to face pressures to adopt the diversity parental policies, which may overshadow specific local issues. Paradoxically, by ignoring the national and organizational specificities of the host countries, these global companies may contribute to silencing differences across the planet (Banerjee and Linstead 2001).

The literature on management knowledge transfer argues that concepts or ideas that travel are more or less intentionally manipulated by carriers and intoxicated by local conventions, rules, and power relations (e.g., Sahlin-Andersson and Engwall 2002), particularly because adopters still have to respond to local expectations. Using the framework of the new institutionalism, this chapter examines how four affiliates of MNCs (two US, one UK, and one Japanese) located in Portugal are dealing with pressures for internal consistency and local isomorphism in the management of workforce diversity.

Conceptual Framework
Spreading the US Diversity Gospel

Like in many other aspects of modern life, management concepts and practices originally developed in the US carry a sense of progress and have been very effective in penetrating foreign contexts. The UK tends to be an early adopter of US management ideas, testing their suitability to European settings, as the enthusiastic welcoming of the human resource management (HRM) model illustrates (Guest 1990). Following this path, the original US diversity models have significantly inspired the European landscapes.

Regarded as the land of opportunities, the US attracted people from all over the world. The initial efforts to deal with workforce diversity took a legalistic approach that largely ignored individual attributes unrelated to the work requirements, as if everyone was exactly the same (Liff and Wajcman 1996). Several European directives, gradually incorporated into national legislations, were issued, aligned with the principles of equal opportunities to prevent discrimination on the grounds of gender, maternity, nationality, religion, physical condition, age, and sexual orientation. In contrast, affirmative action programs were seldom adopted beyond the English-speaking world (Mayer 2007).

The attraction and retention of the most talented people in the fierce competitive environment brought up by globalization requires a more strategic perspective on workforce diversity. The diversity management model argues that each person is unique and that important benefits can result from workforce diversity, particularly for organizations operating in the global market: a wide pool of innovative ideas, great fulfillment of the expectations and needs of diverse customers, and the capacity to deal with change (e.g., Milliken and Martins 1996). To benefit from diversity, organizations are advised to adopt diversity training, mentoring and career-development programs, and work–life balance initiatives, as well as to develop an inclusive culture that values meritocracy, trust, collaboration, free expression, non-discrimination, and appreciation for diversity (e.g., Thomas and Ely 1996). The organization's commitment to diversity is communicated through mission statements, advertising, and public relations, and is reflected in the website's content. A better organizational image and reputation is expected to follow that strengthens the capacity to attract and retain the best talents and to get the preference of customers and shareholders in societies that are increasingly sensitive to diversity issues (Milliken and Martins 1996).

The diversity model seems to combine the key ingredients to become popular in Europe: its voluntary and market-oriented nature and the intimate connection with the widely adopted HRM model. The belief that to successfully compete in the global market, organizations must become more diverse and skilled in dealing with cultural differences, increases its appeal. Good business opportunities also emerge (e.g., training programs on managing and valuing diversity, multicultural workshops, and diversity audits) to be explored by knowledge carriers promoting mimetic and normative isomorphism, mainly consultants and the business popular media (Edelman, Fuller, and Mara-Drita 2001). Supported by such a catalogue of persuasive arguments and the example of successful global corporations with considerable workforce diversity, the diversity model has been exported to different European countries, mainly the UK, Germany, Denmark, Finland, and Belgium (e.g., Point and Singh 2003; Süß and Kleiner 2008).

The Diversity Rhetoric Reaches the Portuguese Shores

Portugal has a unique experience in dealing with cultural differences since the maritime odyssey of the 15th and 16th centuries. But despite the colonial legacy, during most of the 20th century, the ruling class promoted an isolationist ideology aiming to prevent the local society from contamination by foreign ideas and lifestyles. A population with only residual linguistic, religious, and ethnic minorities and a low-qualified and low-wage workforce was a fertile ground for that ideology. In the last two decades, however, a continuous influx of migrant workers, particularly from Brazil, Eastern Europe, and the old African colonies, have put into question the values and traditional self-image of Portugal as a 'homogeneous' society. The ageing of the population and the access of more educated and ambitious women to top positions, as well as the visibility of minority lifestyles, sexual orientations, and religious beliefs, have contributed to a more diverse society. The prevailing market-driven economic policies also contributed to growing social differences, widening pay inequalities, and the gap between those with high and low income. As a result, what was once a rather homogeneous society (for European standards, at least) is now witnessing growing inequality and diversity.

Portuguese equality legislation was a significant first step to prevent discrimination in the workplace, but diversity management is not a familiar concept among local organizations. In universities, diversity issues remain a footnote in most management programs, and research tends to focus on gender matters while national and ethnic diversity are seldom addressed. In one of the few studies available, Barbosa and Cabral-Cardoso (2010) examined the diversity discourse of the most prominent companies operating in Portugal, showing that when it comes to companies of Portuguese ownership, the management of difference and sameness in the workplace tends to stick to the non-discrimination legalistic rhetoric. In contrast, the diversity rhetoric tends to be displayed by affiliates of foreign MNCs (mainly from the US and the UK), thus suggesting their significant role in disseminating the diversity discourse in this part of Europe.

MNCs as Management Knowledge Carriers

Initially suggested by Meyer and Rowan in the 1970s, the New Institutional theory argues that organizations sharing the same environment tend to adopt similar structures and behaviors in order to respond to the common 'institutionalized expectations'. DiMaggio and Powell (1983) distinguish three mechanisms impelling to this 'isomorphic' phenomenon: (1) 'coercive', resulting from impositions of social, legal, and economic authorities; (2) 'normative', associated to perceptions of appropriate behavior shared by occupational groups; and (3) 'mimetic', promoted by the appeal to deal with uncertainty by replicating practices from leading or excellent organizations. Since today's organizations are hardly confined to (and protected by) national boundaries, some of these isomorphic forces can originate abroad. In MNCs' affiliates, isomorphic mechanisms from both the headquarters and the host country challenge the quest for legitimacy, a situation that Kostova and Roth (2002) called 'institutional duality'.

Typically, policies and practices initiated on the MNCs' headquarters tend to be seen as worth replicating on the affiliates. Frenkel (2008) explains that this one-direction transfer process is usually regarded as benefiting the entire MNC with better internal communication, lower development costs, and a superior ability to defeat local competitors. Additionally, MNCs are generally regarded as global management experts (Fairclough and Thomas 2004), thus inspiring other organizations aiming to compete in the international market and/or to be seen as innovative. But more often than not, management models are uncritically imported and presented as panaceas or quick fix solutions (Watson 1994), despite obvious reservations about their relevance and suitability for national contexts with significant cultural dissimilarity. Comparing the US and Portugal, Hofstede (1991) describes the latter as showing considerably higher levels of power distance and uncertainty avoidance, and lower levels of individualism and masculinity. Therefore, US management concepts and models should be wisely assessed and carefully adjusted before being adopted by Portuguese management agents.

The possibility of a non-translated appropriation of foreign management models, including the case of subsidiaries following the headquarters' orientations, is questioned by several authors (e.g., Sahlin-Andersson and Engwall 2002). The argument here is that local affiliates are involved in a continuous interplay between different pressures: (1) to align with parental practices and discourses for internal consistency reasons; and (2) to reveal local isomorphism in order to benefit from legitimacy in the host country (e.g., Geppert, Matten, and Williams 2003). In this process, Frenkel (2008) stresses the role of affiliate managers as interpreters and translators of the MNC's global vision in ways that (should) make sense in the local environment, thus promoting its 'glocalization' (Robertson 1995). Kostova and Roth (2002) add that the employees' judgment about the value of a new practice is mainly influenced by the institutional local environment and strongly affects its internalization.

Distinct functional areas tend to face different levels of pressure for internal alignment vs. local responsiveness. HR practices, for instance, may reveal local isomorphism when resembling local conventions that are highly visible and/or regulated by local legislation (Rosenzweig and Nohria 1994). But Florkowski (1996) argues that subsidiaries of MNCs from more diverse societies, or with more progressive equality legislation (like the US), tend to follow the parental orientation in dealing with the host country diversity. According to Rosenzweig and Nohria (1994), affiliates feel particularly impelled to correct gender inequalities when they are not approved in their country of origin.

On the other hand, while new management labels, discourses, and structures may be enthusiastically adopted (and communicated) for legitimacy/impression management purposes, established practices might not be challenged. This decoupling strategy sounds tempting to affiliates experiencing competing or conflicting pressures from the parental and the host country institutional environments (e.g., Meyer and Rowan 1977). Once involved in a translation exercise that can be interpreted as organizational hypocrisy, organizations will do their best to avoid internal and public scrutiny (Boxenbaum and Jonsson 2008).

Method

This study aims to uncover the way diversity is perceived, discoursed, and practiced by four Portuguese affiliates of foreign MNCs and to unveil how such *modus operandi* reflect the parental pressures and the local concerns and conventions. It seeks to shed some additional light on the contribution of international organizations to the development (and dissemination) of a *glocal* strategy to deal with the increasing social heterogeneity in a peripheral European country.

The Participants

A previous study from Barbosa and Cabral-Cardoso (2010) identified 137 affiliates of foreign MNCs operating in Portugal with websites and integrating the list of the 500 largest companies. The 137 websites were analyzed and only 41 included references to equality/diversity. These affiliates were invited to participate in the current study, but only four accepted to do so. All four are originated in countries where management practices are usually regarded as progressive and/or worth being replicated by more peripheral countries such as Portugal. Table 11.1 summarizes the major attributes of the affiliates participating in the study.

In different ways, the globalization process has benefited and/or challenged the competitive position of the four companies. Besides dealing with very demanding customers

Table 11.1 The affiliates' major attributes

Country of origin and year of establishment	Sector	Global activity	Affiliate's fictional designation	Major attributes of the Portuguese affiliate (in 2008)
UK, 1974	Contract foodservice	70 countries	UK Meal	Established in 1995. About 5,000 workers distributed by 70 units (company restaurants, restaurants, and cafeterias)
Japan, 1941	Automotive components and energy-related equipment	97 affiliates located abroad	Japan Automotive	Established in 1986. A number of downsizing processes gradually reduced the workforce from 3,000 to 900 individuals
US, 1975	Software development and trade	88 countries	US Software	Established in 1990. Employs about 300 workers. Regular presence in The Great Place to Work® Institute annual ranking
US, 1919	High-tech raw materials	More than 100 countries	US Material	Initially a local company acquired in 1970. Employs 250 individuals

in terms of quality and variety of meals, UK Meal also faces strong price competition by both international and local competitors. Since the earlier 1990s, Japan Automotive has been threatened by Eastern European competitors offering lower salaries and lower prices. The prosperity of US Material and the job security of its 250 employees are being seriously challenged by Eastern European and Asian companies. In contrast, US Software seems to be a major beneficiary from globalization. Its success is deeply dependent on the employees' innovation skills and the market expansion allowed by the globalization process. In general, the continuous development of new products and the growing flexibility of their structures are the main responses enacted by these four companies to deal with global competition.

The Procedure

Documents from various sources (websites, magazines, ethical codes, values, and mission statements) were content analyzed, aiming to depict the corporate diversity rhetoric. Additionally, seven semi-structured interviews were conducted in each affiliate (28 in total) with CEOs, HR managers, PR professionals, middle and line managers, and workers. UK Meal was the only affiliate at which no opportunity was given to interview non-managerial staff, since interruptions of their work schedule were considered too costly. In the four companies, both men and women from different age groups, nationalities (mainly Portuguese, but also Indian, Mozambican, and Mexican), ethnicities, and religious faiths were interviewed. The interviews were audio-recorded and lasted from 40 to 180 minutes. With the help of the NVivo 8 software, data were content analyzed into the following categories:

- External and internal corporate diversity discourse (communication means and content);
- HRM policies and practices;
- Managing diversity initiatives;
- Minorities in the organization (identity groups and tasks performed);
- Perceptions of organizational prejudice and discrimination;
- Perceptions of adoption vs. local adaptation of the headquarters' discourses and practices.

Findings

Balancing Parental Orientation and Local Adjustment

Managers from the four affiliates explained that their companies' vision, values, and strategies were mainly determined by headquarters, though with a recommendation to adjust the policies and practices to the local context. The following quotes depict affiliates as active agents committed to such translation process:

> Think globally and act locally is one of the headquarters' guidelines. (…) Of course we can't compare our reality with the reality of other affiliates in another country. Markets are different, cultures are different… The understanding and application of values and strategies is quite different in each country.
>
> (US Material, HR manager)

> We can't adopt something just because it seems to work well in another country. First of all, we must check if that practice also applies to our national reality and business. (…) The major management guidelines come from the headquarters. But there is always some flexibility: we must adapt management orientations to local stakeholders. Otherwise, instead of implementing management tools that help our work, we are implementing things that make it harder.
>
> (UK Meal, HR manager)

> Some rules are mandatory for the entire Group. (…) But other situations are specific for each country and must be managed in ways that meet local needs and resources.
>
> (Japan Automotive, HR manager)

When it comes to diversity, the reported translation efforts seem to lose energy, as examined in the following section.

Discoursing Diversity

US Software exhibits both the diversity and the equality discourses on the local website. The influence of the more progressive headquarters' rhetoric on diversity (enthusiastically displayed on the global website) is apparent in the details describing the benefits of a diverse workforce. But this discourse, quite unfamiliar to Portuguese society, is balanced with the more locally institutionalized ethical and moral arguments. The resulting 'glocal' content highlights the organizational commitment to the development of a fair work environment where all individuals have access to the same opportunities and chances of succeeding. This message is included in the social justice/ethics section, which adds to the view that Portuguese society increasingly values the involvement of corporations in social responsibility initiatives (Guimarães-Costa and Cunha 2008). Therefore, coercive mechanisms from both the headquarters and the local context seem to have influenced the diversity discourse that US Software presents to the Portuguese public. But at the same time, managers declared their willingness to appropriate, translate, and exhibit the headquarters' diversity philosophy in order to improve the affiliate's image in Portuguese society and among more diverse applicants and customers. The appreciation for this discourse points to a mimetic rather than a coercive conformity and is shared by employees:

> A non-Portuguese applicant wants to know if the [local] company also welcomes foreign workers; and the corporate website is a good starting point to check it out. (...) We deal with a very diverse pool of customers who want to be sure that we don't have any kind of prejudice and we treat them properly.
>
> (US Software, foreign worker)

In contrast, the diversity rhetoric that is disseminated among members through intranet statements and training sessions is designed at the headquarters and applied with little evidence of local adjustment. This MNC seems to conceive the whole world as their recruitment pool and take for granted that affiliates will embrace multiculturalism. However, while members seem to agree that every employee has a singular combination of background, thinking style, needs, and skills that bring more ideas and perspectives to the workplace, the issue is seldom debated: 'We don't have to talk about it' (middle manager).

US Material does not have a local website, but the MNC's global website links to a page that presents this affiliate's features (displayed in Portuguese language). According to the managers, local websites are irrelevant since the company is unknown to the general public locally, and creating a good public image in Portuguese society is not a US Material's major concern. The diversity content of the global website is assessed by the local managers as producing a positive impact on global investors and as being particularly relevant in the US context. Some items are also available in the local language of the affiliates, such as the Group's exposed values 'to value and encourage diversity' and 'to understand cultural differences', but these are not followed by translation efforts. Moreover, when attempting to get more details about the MNC's diversity policies and practices, Web surfers are directed to sites that are exclusively related to the US units and alien to other national contexts.

Local managers describe the affiliate as appreciative of the uniqueness of individual employees, but they seem uncommitted to translate that conviction into action. Internal diversity discourses are only marginally mentioned on the intranet, and the Group's list of values do not reveal any adjustment to the local specificities or take into account the culture of the previous (acquired) local company. The workers claim that 'diversity is not a big issue in Portugal' in a context where the disparity between 'haves' and 'have-nots' seems a more sensitive issue in the current economic situation than diversity matters.

UK Meal disseminates the diversity discourse to its external stakeholders through the local website, as the following statement illustrates:

> We develop our workers and value their diversity. We build a work environment that offers challenges, opportunities and support so that everyone can develop, learn and succeed.

This diversity content was developed by the British headquarters, and local concerns have not been taken into account. However, the headquarters' directives seem willingly imported by local managers who believe in their ability to promote the company's reputation in Portuguese society and particularly among customers and applicants:

> We are proud to say that we work with quality, that we value teamwork and that diversity is important to us. (…) There is obviously a business case around here: it is important to show our customers and other people who want to know us better through our website what our values and principles are. And if they agree with such a view, they may prefer us rather than our competitors. It definitely improves our business image. (…) Besides, communicating our values can contribute to make the company more attractive to applicants who value a good work environment.
>
> (UK Meal, top manager)

The diversity rhetoric communicated to the internal constituencies was developed by the British headquarters. However, local managers seem genuinely committed to its diffusion and have made some efforts to make it more meaningful to Portuguese employees. Along the lines of the official discourse, managers seem to share the conviction that 'each person has unique traits that must be taken into account', but a local interpretation of diversity is adopted: while religion, ideology, and sexual orientation are regarded as 'neutral' attributes, cultural diversity is said to produce diverse ideas that are fundamental to deal with the increasing competition. The diversity rhetoric is internally communicated through flyers and notice boards located throughout the premises. A recent issue of the company's internal newsletter also stresses this value: 'The most intelligent companies are the ones that better use their workers' diversity and translate it into better customer service.' Moreover, in recent internal training sessions designed and recommended by the British headquarters, the group's values (including diversity) were further explained to all employees. Efforts were made to make the training content more significant to the affiliate:

> It was an intense training program. (…) We highlighted how these values make sense in our daily work, mostly through real examples. (…).We intended that members truly understand how their attitudes can or cannot promote equality.
>
> (UK Meal, HRM manager)

Japan Automotive has not designed a website targeting the local audience, which seems justified by the characteristics of their clients—mainly foreign big automobile companies that can get information from the group's global website. The global website stresses some diversity initiatives under the title 'Observing human rights and respecting diversity: Creating work environments that respect diversity', included as part of the social responsibility page. The same website indicates a number of practices that are exclusively implemented in the Japanese factories (e.g., the Women's Committee), but the diversity and equality values advocated on the website are apparently extended to the affiliates: 'As a global enterprise that conducts business in 38 foreign countries, the (…) group is working to create systems and environments that respect employee diversity.' A middle manager confirms the requirement to adopt the Japanese headquarters' values:

> There is a clear orientation from the head office in Japan for affiliates to develop and spread a social and environmental awareness, which must guide our decisions and plans.

Local managers believe that the external diversity rhetoric contributes to strengthen the global company's image and reputation in societies that value the corporations' involvement in social responsibility issues and/or that are witnessing a growing diversity. Although these attributes also apply to Portuguese society, local managers do not acknowledge the importance of that discourse to the local context. Moreover, the lack of a local website displayed in Portuguese language limits the impact of the diversity content among local stakeholders.

The diversity and equality discourses are disseminated to the internal audience through the MNC's Code of Ethics. This document argues the moral case for diversity, a rhetoric that is increasingly institutionalized in Portugal. Managers expressed the conviction that every member has particular knowledge and skills from which the organization can benefit. However, the current unemployment threat seems to have alienated workers from diversity concerns, even if wrapped up in the more locally adjusted ethical case for equality. The comment of a worker is representative of this anxiety:

> I didn't know the interview's purpose. The moment my supervisor told me I was selected to an interview, I thought, 'Now they are sending me home.'

In sum, the headquarters' directives have shaped the diversity discourse in the four affiliates. Coercive mechanisms originated abroad are contributing to the diffusion of the diversity discourse in Portugal, a context where these issues are not yet part of daily conversations, despite the growing demographic diversity of the country. Mimetic mechanisms also seem to underline the external diffusion of the diversity discourse coming from headquarters in both US Software and UK Meal; their managers believe it improves the company's image among local stakeholders. The more voluntary adoption of the diversity discourse by these two affiliates seems to instigate the development of more locally adjusted contents. While US Software disseminates a 'glocal' version of the diversity discourse to the external public but found it unnecessary to make such an adjustment when diversity issues are internally communicated, UK Meal seems to take a different route. The distinct recruitment pool of the two companies (global in the case of US Software and local in the case of UK Meal) may justify the contrasting strategies concerning the internal diversity discourse, though not the external one. US Material and Japan Automotive seem uninterested in disseminating the diversity discourse to the local audience, as local websites were not even created. The diversity discourse disseminated internally reflects the headquarters' philosophy and their control over affiliates. The lack of effort to take into account local specificities and current concerns (mainly derived from the economic and social crisis) may explain the little interest that workers seem to devote to the theme. In these two companies, diversity discourses are missing the opportunity to promote a work environment that really supports and benefits from workforce diversity.

Table 11.2 summarizes the diversity discourses displayed by affiliates. They were classified as 'global' when lacking translation efforts, and 'glocal' when benefiting from some local interpretation.

Practicing Diversity ... Sometimes

The affiliates participating in this study have HRM departments that seem to play a significant role in the companies' strategies, a status that is expected to add centrality to diversity management issues. HR managers from the four companies indicated diversity policies and practices as mainly coming from headquarters. They agree that identity attributes

Table 11.2 The affiliates' external and internal diversity discourses

Audience		US Software	US Material	UK Meal	Japan Automotive
External diversity discourse	Global website	Content reflecting the main paradigm of the country of origin			
	Local website	'Glocal'		Global	
Internal diversity discourse	For example, intranet, internal documents, training sessions	Global	Global	'Glocal'	Global (coincidently adjusted to the local context)

are not usually considered in personnel decisions, but exceptions were also found. In order to reduce gender imbalance, for instance, US Software is promoting the recruitment of women to management positions, an initiative that seems inspired by affirmative action. Although also integrating a North American group, US Material does not sufficiently value the contribution of female workers to bother overcoming an old architectural barrier—the lack of female dressing rooms, which is used to justify keeping women out of production lines. And while almost 90 percent of the UK Meal workforce is made up of women, their presence is minimal in management positions, thus suggesting some type of 'glass ceiling' mechanism in place. Middle (male) managers admit their preference for more attractive women and men in functions that require direct contact with customers, a policy that may also raise equal opportunities issues.

Apart from US Software, the other companies show a negligible participation rate of foreign workers in their workforce. Additionally, migrant workers from less developed countries like Angola, Mozambique, and even Brazil and Eastern Europe, are still being relegated to less demanding and less rewarding functions. The following quote is suggestive of that prejudice:

> Someone of African origin would be more easily integrated in a low qualified job than in a more rewarding and challenging one. I have absolutely no doubt about that.
> (US Material, middle manager)

Japan Automotive employs a considerable number of workers with hearing disabilities in their assembly lines. The other three companies have a limited number of members with disabilities, and some barriers to their presence and development were detected in all companies. Managers explain that US Software does not recruit people with visual or hearing disabilities since that would require considerable spending with special working tools. US Material, UK Meal, and Japan Automotive avoid people with limited mobility in the production lines due to the special requirements of those jobs.

To make sure that every employee benefits from the same opportunities to succeed, US Software and US Material develop comprehensive integration programs and design tailor-made training and development programs. However, the integration of new workers in UK Meal is based on the colleagues' good will to offer informal support, a process dependent on the affinity between old workers and newcomers. In such a context, individuals with less common backgrounds and unusual looks may face greater integration difficulties. Managers and technicians from Japan Automotive who are frequently assigned to temporary projects in affiliates of the group located in very distant cultural environments (like Islamic countries) are not offered training to help their adjustment.

Mirroring the corresponding headquarters' policy, US Software and Japan Automotive seem committed to developing work/life policies and family-friendly practices. Both companies provide extended free medical assistance to their employees. US Software work/life balance policies include flexible work arrangements such as part-time work, flexible work schedules, and telework opportunities. To mitigate the workers' domestic concerns, a partnership was established with a local company that offers a number of convenience services (e.g., babysitting, home keeping, takeaway, vet, and pharmacy). Japan Automotive has a kindergarten available to workers' children during school holidays. In contrast, the remaining two companies reveal sporadic work/life practices (almost limited to sick leave) that have to be negotiated between the workers and their supervisors, which may not be the best way to promote equal opportunities.

Despite some conflicting evidence, all managers participating in the study declared being committed to limiting the impact of biased attitudes and discriminatory behaviors that persist in Portuguese society. US Software, US Material, and UK Meal headquarters have created global hotlines for their members' anonymous reporting of unethical behaviors, workplace discrimination, and sexual harassment. But while admitting that whistleblowing mechanisms can help prevent unacceptable conduct, both local managers and workers consider this initiative unadjusted to the Portuguese culture. A top manager explains:

> This American fashion is strange to Portuguese people. To report somebody's bad action through an anonymous mechanism is viewed as a cowardly attitude.

US Software and UK Meal adopted diversity training based on the headquarters' guidelines and educational material, but only UK Meal dared adjust it to the local culture. In both companies of US origin, the annual performance appraisal takes into account the managers' contributions to equality and diversity, a measure that is at the heart of the US diversity model (Milliken and Martins 1996), though unrelated to the local culture.

In sum, while the diversity initiatives applied by the four affiliates have been identified as a major echo of the headquarters' policy, they are beyond what the more exuberant diversity rhetoric would suggest. US Software distinguishes itself from the remaining affiliates by revealing a more comprehensive and sophisticated set of diversity initiatives, thus appearing more committed (and/or persuaded by headquarters) to diversity. Nonetheless, the four companies' demographics reveal little heterogeneity in their workforces. Moreover, diversity initiatives (e.g., diversity training) often miss the necessary adjustment to the Portuguese context or tend to be regarded by employees as being at odds with the local culture (e.g., hotlines). The lack of an effective adjustment and communication of the diversity policies and practices was particularly evident in US Material and Japan Automotive. Their workers revealed little awareness of diversity issues:

> Those questions concerning equality and non-discrimination are handled by the human resources [department], I guess. I'm not very informed about that. But there's no discrimination around here… I think.
>
> (US Material, employee)

Table 11.3 The affiliates' diversity practices

Origin		US Software	US Material	UK Meal	Japan Automotive
Parental context	Promotion of minorities	'Glocal' (Women to management positions)			'Glocal' (Workers with disabilities)
	Integration programs	'Glocal'	'Glocal'		
	Training and development programs	'Glocal'	'Glocal'		
	Work/life policies and practices	'Glocal'			'Glocal'
	Global hotlines	Global	Global	Global	
	Diversity training	Global		'Glocal'	
	Appraisal of managers' support to diversity	Global	Global		
Local context	Acknowledgment of the Portuguese equality legislation	(Limited effect in eradicating workplace prejudice and discrimination)			

Table 11.3 summarizes the diversity practices identified in the four affiliates participating in the study. Practices originated by headquarters were classified as 'global' if the affiliate did not adjust them to the local context, and 'glocal' if some adaptation did occur.

Discussion and Conclusions

This chapter looked at four affiliates of MNCs and how they were discoursing and practicing diversity in a country where growing social heterogeneity has not yet captured significant attention from politicians, academics, and practitioners. The affiliates have two characteristics in common: (1) the multinational group is originated in more developed and diverse societies; and (2) management knowledge and practices produced in their countries of origin are usually seen as progressive and/or able to penetrate foreign contexts. These attributes make it particularly interesting to examine the way affiliates are coping with the 'think globally and act locally' principle when it comes to managing workforce diversity.

Affiliates' managers adopt the diversity perspective originated by headquarters, mainly influenced by parental coercive dynamics. However, since these companies are located in a context where diversity matters tend not to be institutionalized, they do not seem particularly eager, or even concerned with translating the diversity discourse so that it makes sense locally. They seem unaware that by failing to do so, companies risk being viewed as being at odds with the aspirations and interests of local stakeholders and internal constituencies. To a certain extent, such disregard may be explained by the perception that in the current context of economic crisis, individuals may have other priorities, as suggested in the interviews with non-managerial staff. On the other hand, the detachment of Portuguese society from diversity issues and the short-term economic pressures do not foster an atmosphere receptive to 'glocal' diversity management approaches, but rather a decoupled one. Moreover, the more exuberant diversity discourses tend to meet less enthusiastic practices. Such practices were also imported from headquarters but barely or only partly adjusted to the local context, perhaps hoping that would suffice to secure internal consistency and preserve local legitimacy in a less demanding country. This apparent divorce between diversity rhetoric and practice has been described in the diversity literature as an 'empty shell' (Hoque and Noon 2004). Unlike the argument of Florkowski (1996), the results of the current study suggest that this decoupled strategy may be particularly enacted by affiliates operating in host countries with fewer pressures on equality and diversity issues than the parental context. The new-institutional literature presents decoupling as a strategy enacted by organizations that are facing competing institutional pressures (e.g., Meyer and Rowan 1977), as is often the case with MNCs. Apparently, the perception of a less demanding host environment can also tempt affiliates to develop a more superficial response. Employees, on the other hand, seem unaware of the gap between diversity rhetoric and practice, and their companies can hardly be seen as promoting the full potential of every individual or described as discrimination-free environments. And in a context of fewer job opportunities, an effective (and locally adjusted) organizational response to prejudice and discrimination is even more needed.

In sum, when it comes to managing diversity in foreign affiliates hosted in contexts with little institutional pressure towards equality and diversity issues, words seem to fly quicker than actions and some of them appear to be lost in translation. However, exceptions to this pattern were found among the affiliates participating in the study. Three conditions seem to promote the development of a more 'glocal' way to discourse and practice diversity that considers both the headquarters' and the host country's specificities:

1. The affiliate evaluates the headquarters' discourse as having the potential to enhance the corporate image among local stakeholders and distinguish the company from its competitors. When that is the case, affiliates may feel more committed to disseminate such a discourse and to adapt it to the local context.
2. The affiliate believes in the value of parental practices and their contribution to the local results. Therefore, more efforts are dedicated to integrate those (foreign) practices and harmonize them with the local ones already in place.
3. Staff members are aware of diversity issues and the organizational rhetoric–practice gap. In this case, conditions appear to be met for the development of a 'glocal' version of the parental discourse (for internal and external consumption) and the adoption of practices that are consistent with that discourse.

Under the conditions that underline parental mimetic mechanisms, MNCs seem to play a significant role in disseminating management knowledge, and affiliates seem more prompt to locally adjust discourses and practices and to couple them. The perception of headquarters' coercive pressures (not compatible with the affiliates' free will) seems to conduct to a more superficial, decoupled, and locally unadjusted adoption of parental discourses and practices.

A better understanding of the transfer mechanisms of management knowledge and practices and the role played by MNCs in this process requires further research. The field would benefit from the expansion, validation, and refinement provided by studies focusing on issues other than diversity and targeting companies with different degrees of institutionalization in the host country. The effect of the MNC's country of origin in this process also remains unclear, particularly because of the contrasting results found in the two affiliates of US origin. Future studies with a cross-sectional design should address and shed some more light on these issues.

References

Banerjee, S.B., and Linstead, S. (2001). 'Globalizations, multiculturalism and other fictions: colonialism for the new millennium?' *Organization, 8*(4): 683–722.

Barbosa, I., and Cabral-Cardoso, C. (2010). 'Equality and diversity rhetoric: one size fits all? Globalization and the Portuguese context'. *Equality, Diversity and Inclusion: An International Journal, 29*(1): 97–112.

Boxenbaum, E., and Jonsson, S. (2008). 'Isomorphism, diffusion and decoupling', in R. Greenwood, C. Oliver, K. Sahlin, and R. Suddaby (eds), *Organizational institutionalism.* London: Sage, 3–27, 78–98.

DiMaggio, P., and Powell, W. (1983). 'The iron cage revisited: institutional isomorphism and collective rationality in organizational fields'. *American Sociological Review, 48*(2): 147–60.

Edelman, L.B., Fuller, S.R., and Mara-Drita, I. (2001). 'Diversity rhetoric and the managerialization of law. *American Journal of Sociology, 106*(6), 1589–641.

Fairclough, N., and Thomas, P. (2004). 'The discourse of globalization and the globalization of discourse', in D. Grant, C. Hardy, C. Oswick, and L. Putman (eds), *The Sage handbook of organizational discourse.* London: Sage, 379–96.

Florkowski, G.W. (1996). 'Managing diversity within multinational firms for competitive advantage', in E.E. Kossek and S.A. Lobel (eds), *Managing diversity: human resource strategies for transforming the workplace.* Cambridge, MA: Blackwell, 337–64.

Frenkel, M. (2008). 'The multinational corporation as a third space: rethinking international management discourse on knowledge transfer through Homi Bhabha'. *Academy of Management Review, 33*(4), 924–42.

Geppert, M., Matten, D., and Williams, K. (2003). 'Change management in MNCs: how global convergence intertwines with national diversities'. *Human Relations, 56*(7), 807–38.

Guest, D. (1990). 'Human resource management and the American dream'. *Journal of Management Studies, 27*(4), 377–97.

Guimarães-Costa, N., and Cunha, M.P. (2008). 'The atrium effect of website openness on the communication of corporate social responsibility'. *Corporate Social Responsibility and Environmental Management, 15*(1), 43–51.

Hofstede, G. (1991). *Cultures and organizations: software of the mind.* New York: McGraw-Hill.

Hoque, K., and Noon, M. (2004). 'Equal opportunities policy and practice in Britain: evaluating the "Empty Shell" hypothesis'. *Work, Employment and Society, 18*(3), 481–506.

Kostova, T., and Roth, K. (2002). 'Adoption of an organizational practice by subsidiaries of multinational corporations: institutional and relational effects'. *Academy of Management Journal, 45*(1), 215–33.

Liff, S., and Wajcman, J. (1996). '"Sameness" and "difference" revisited: which way forward for equal opportunity initiatives?' *Journal of Management Studies, 33*(1), 79–94.

Mayer, K.U. (2007). 'The paradox of global social change and national path dependencies', in A. Woodward and M. Kohli (eds), *Inclusions and exclusions in European societies.* Oxon, UK: Routledge: 89–110.

Meyer, J.W., and Rowan, B. (1977). 'Institutionalized organizations: formal structure as myth and ceremony'. *American Journal of Sociology, 83*(2), 340–63.

Milliken, F.J., and Martins, L.L. (1996). 'Searching for common threads: understanding the multiple effects of diversity in organizational groups'. *Academy of Management Review, 21*(2), 402–33.

Point, S., and Singh, V. (2003). 'Defining and dimensionalising diversity: evidence from corporate websites across Europe'. *European Management Journal, 21*(6), 750–61.

Robertson, R. (1995). 'Glocalization: time-space and homogeneity-heterogeneity', in M. Featherstone, S. Lash, and R. Robertson (eds), *Global modernities*. London: Sage, 25–44.

Rosenzweig, P.M., and Nohria, N. (1994). 'Influences on human resource management practices in multinational corporations'. *Journal of International Business Studies, 25*(2), 229–51.

Sahlin-Andersson, K., and Engwall, L. (2002). 'Carriers, flows, and sources of management knowledge', in K. Sahlin-Andersson and L. Engwall (eds), *The expansion of management knowledge*. Stanford, CA: Stanford University Press, 3–32.

Süß, S., and Kleiner, M. (2008). 'Dissemination of diversity management in Germany: a new intuitionalist approach'. *European Management Journal, 26*(1), 35–47.

Thomas, D.A., and Ely, R.J. (1996). 'Making differences matter: a new paradigm for managing diversity'. *Harvard Business Review, 74*(5), 79–90.

Watson, T.J. (1994). 'Management "flavours of the month": their role in managers' lives'. *International Journal of Human Resource Management, 5*(4), 893–909.

12
New Public Management and Beyond
The Hybridization of Public Sector Reforms

Tom Christensen

Introduction

New Public Management (NPM) emerged as an important reform wave in Anglo-American countries in the early 1980s, subsequently spreading around the world as the received wisdom to a wide range of political-administrative systems (Pollitt and Bouckaert 2011). NPM contains major elements from management theory and new institutional economic theory and advocates a combination of structural devolution, efficiency, market orientation, and consumer orientation (Boston et al. 1996). A variety of factors, including the failure to produce efficiency gains, an undermining of political control, concerns about coordination, and worries about the ability of public administrations to deal with threats such as terrorism and pandemics and with the global financial and environmental crises, led some of the trail-blazing NPM countries to embark on another set of public reforms in the late 1990s, characterized variously as post-NPM, whole-of-government, or joined-up government (Christensen and Lægreid 2007a; Gregory 2003; Halligan 2006). Post-NPM reforms did not replace NPM reforms, but instead partly merged with them and partly modified them in what can be described as a layering process (Mahoney and Thelen 2010). This layering process represents not only a complex and hybrid development, combining two reform waves, but also a cross between global reform ideas, like NPM and post-NPM, and national/local considerations, for which the term 'glocalization' may be used (Robertson 1995). We might also characterize this as a combination of de-contextualization and contextualization (Røvik 2002). These reform processes and the dynamic relationship between them involve many central aspects of government, but here we will focus on the balance between central political control and institutional autonomy (Christensen and Lægreid 2007b).

In this chapter, we will first discuss what characterizes the concepts of complexity, hybridity, and layering in reform processes, and will then link them to the concept of glocalization. We will then discuss the explanatory factors behind such a development in a comparative perspective, drawing on various strands of organization theory (Christensen, Lægreid, Roness, and Røvik 2007). We will examine some of the main instrumental driving forces and mechanisms behind the development and characterize some of the main ideas behind the reforms, in particular, with respect to balancing political control and institutional autonomy. We will also ask what the cultural preconditions for the development are and what role is played by environmental factors. Second, we will look at examples of hybridity and layering of reforms in countries with different political-administrative systems. Third, and more briefly, we ask what the effects are of this hybridization and layering of reform waves. Do these processes result in a more flexible balance between political control and institutional autonomy, or do they increase conflicts and ambiguity? We analyze the processes and effects using instrumental and institutional theories drawn from the wide world of organization theory (Scott and Davis 2006). The empirical examples are primarily taken from comparative works on public reforms in New Zealand and Australia, China, and Norway.

A Conceptual Basis: Complexity, Hybridity, Layering, and Glocalization

The literature on complexity is very varied (Pollitt 2003), but here, the focus will be on structural and cultural complexity (Anderson 1999; Christensen and Lægreid 2011). Structural complexity in public organizations may be measured along some central dimensions, one of which is vertical specialization and another horizontal specialization; both dimensions have intra- and inter-organizational elements (Egeberg 2003; Gulick 1937; Simon 1957). Vertical, intra-organizational specialization tells us how formal authority is distributed among different levels of the hierarchy within a public organization. Vertical inter-organizational specialization focuses on hierarchical specialization among public organizations. Horizontal intra-organizational specialization means internal specialization within public organizations—the division of an organization into different departments and units, according to principles that Gulick (1937) labels purpose, process, clientele, and geography. Horizontal inter-organizational specialization focuses on specialization among public organizations on the same hierarchical level as, for example, among ministries or agencies. If we look at these dimensions together, we get an indication of how complex a system is. One extreme is strong vertical and horizontal specialization overall, meaning strong fragmentation—a typical feature of NPM reforms (Pollitt and Bouckaert 2011); the other is low specialization on both dimensions, indicating an integrated political-administrative system, like the 'old public administration' in many countries or reflecting the emergence of post-NPM reforms (Christensen and Lægreid 2007a).

Cultural complexity is more difficult to grasp (Selznick 1957). Strong cultural complexity means that there are a variety of informal cultural norms and values in and among public organizations because there are many traditions to attend to, because sub-cultures have developed, or because cultural norms from different types of reforms have been combined. Weak cultural complexity indicates cultural homogeneity and integration (i.e., members of an organization are very committed to its basic cultural norms and values and there is a common sense of purpose and a feeling of being in the same 'cultural boat') (Kaufman 1960; Krasner 1988; March and Olsen 1989).

There is also a dynamic relationship between structural and cultural complexity. On the one hand, structural and cultural factors may be reinforced (for example, if a bid for strong hierarchical leadership is supported by cultural norms), while structural and cultural complexity may also involve a lot of tension (for example, when the political executive tries to implement modern reforms but encounters path-dependency and cultural resistance, which may undermine the reform efforts) (Pollitt and Bouckaert 2011).

One can distinguish between complexity and hybridity (Christensen and Lægreid 2011). The former has a structural dimension addressing vertical and horizontal specialization and a cultural dimension addressing the variety of informal norms and values. The latter addresses the potential *tension* or *inconsistency* between diverse structural and cultural elements in government. Complexity is a precondition for hybridity, meaning that hybridity always implies some form of complexity. Hybrid organizations are multifunctional entities combining different tasks, values, and organizational forms, like ministries organized according to different and inconsistent structural principles, or agencies with professional groups that have diverse cultures. These composite and compounded arrangements and cultures may produce 'peaceful coexistence,' but unstable trade-offs and lasting tensions as well.

So how does the concept of layering or sedimentation work when reform waves are combined (Streeck and Thelen 2005)? The main reasoning is the following. When a new reform wave comes along, elements of its basic structures and cultures developed over a period of time may either be pushed aside/deinstitutionalized or else manage to survive and continue to influence the development of the organization, no matter what the new reform wave brings. Hence, in different reform periods, some structural and cultural elements will be deinstitutionalized, some will be reinstitutionalized, and some will be newly institutionalized. Layering refers to the process whereby new structural or cultural elements and rules are 'introduced on top of or alongside existing ones' (Mahoney and Thelen 2010: 15). These new elements may result in changes, revisions, or amendments to existing elements, but the older elements will also continue to influence the newer ones. This makes public organizations increasingly complex and hybrid, as they combine elements from the 'old public administration', NPM, and post-NPM. So layering is one main reason why complexity and hybridity develop in political-administrative systems.

Robertson (1995: 26, 30, 33, 38, 39) sees glocalization as simultaneity and inter-penetration of the global and local, or the universal and the particular. He points to a main argument in the literature that the global and the local are necessarily in conflict or tension, yet stresses that these elements can also be reconciled, or that there may be more heterogeneity between the global and the local than one might think, so the degree of compatibility may vary. His reasoning is closely connected with complexity and hybridity in reform efforts, while the link with layering is less clear. One important argument that suggests a connection between glocalization and layering is the question of whether reform elements can exist side by side, combining the global and the local in different ways, or whether this involves a transformation into qualitatively new forms (March and Olsen 1989).

Perspectives Explaining Hybridity and Layering

Hierarchical Design by Top Leaders

The first question is to what extent and how political and administrative leaders may design hybridity and layering as a way of achieving a balance between control and autonomy (Christensen and Lægreid 2010). A simple answer is that they see this as the most instrumental solution to the challenges confronting modern public organizations (March and Olsen 1983). Both the internal conditions and the external constraints, for example, in crisis situations, may be so demanding and complex that the executive leadership will want to diversify the structure to try to cater to both control and institutional autonomy at the same time (Aberbach and Christensen 2001). So there may be congruence between complex constraints and complex structure or reforms—at least, that is how leaders argue.

Second, lack of insight and scoring low on rational calculation might mean that complexity is a result of arbitrary processes (cf. Dahl and Lindblom 1953). Leaders may wish to develop the public organization in a systematic way, but they lack the ability to see the connection between means and ends. This limited cognitive capacity could result in complexity in situations where there is a lot of reorganization or patchwork reform. Overall, more comprehensive reforms are the most difficult to design and control, while narrower and more partial ones are often more easily implemented (Wright 1994).

Negotiational Features

Heterogeneity and negotiations inside government, diverse institutionally-based interests, and a tug-of-war between different leaders may create the background for organizational complexity and hybridity (March and Olsen 1983). Heterogeneity and different interests may foster hybridity and layering through compromise, winning coalitions, or 'sequential attention to goals and the quasi-solution of conflicts' (Cyert and March 1963). This characteristic is most typical in non-Westminster parliamentary systems or in presidential systems (Wright 1994). When the NPM reforms began, they were backed in many countries by a winning coalition of different actors, like central politicians, civil servants furthering economic ideas, and business actors (Gregory 2003). When the post-NPM reforms started to emerge, this coalition was partly dismantled and a new one formed (Gregory 2003; Halligan 2006).

Cultural Factors

In principle, the development of common cultures in public organizations should decrease complexity, particularly if culture is the 'institutional glue' that holds the organization together, or if culture means a lot for organizational development (see Selznick 1957). So how might hybridity and layering be related to cultural development? One answer might be that the cultural path and logic of appropriateness developed are complex and hybrid, embracing a variety of informal norms and values, and they are probably more complex the older the public institution is (Boin and Christensen 2008). The cultural complexity of public organizations becomes rather evident when modern reforms are introduced, for NPM reforms represent a challenge to the traditional public sector culture (Christensen and Lægreid 2007a). When post-NPM reforms were introduced, they tried to revive some of the traditional cultural norms and values, but in so doing supplemented rather than replaced the NPM culture. This increased cultural hybridity at the 'cultural cross-roads' and added a layer on top of the NPM measures.

Institutional-environmental Factors

Reform myths coming from the institutional environment are generally believed to make public organizations isomorphic (i.e., more similar in form), at least on the surface because of 'window-dressing' (Meyer and Rowan 1977). NPM was partly based on the myth that a large public sector was bad, that structural devolution and differentiation were good, and that competition and choice were better than control and regulation. When post-NPM came along, a set of counter-myths gained support—namely, that an integrated public system was better than a fragmented one, that coordination was better than competition, that central capacity and standardization were better than institutional autonomy and variety

(Christensen and Lægreid 2007a). This created an even more complex, hybrid, and layered system of ideas, because most NPM ideas were not deinstitutionalized, but continued to exist alongside post-NPM ideas.

Myths may also be seen as manufactured and deliberately spread by certain actors like international organizations from different organizational fields, while institutional standards are imitated and combined from different periods and types of reform (Lægreid, Roness, and Rubecksen 2007; Sahlin-Andersson 2001; Westney 1987). Hybridity could also result from organizations combining different reform elements containing both control and autonomy measures (Røvik 2002). Røvik (1996) asserts that successful imitation may involve combining de-contextualization (i.e., arguing that a broad reform has potential everywhere) and contextualization (i.e., arguing that a given reform fits local conditions).

Hybridity may signal flexibility on the part of leaders, a more loosely coupled organization (March and Olsen 1976), the creation of 'noise' in decision-making processes (Cohen and March 1974), opportunities for leaders to cover their tracks, and generally more opportunities and options (Brunsson 1989). Motives of this kind may result in leaders using myths and symbols to balance control and autonomy, pretending to some audiences that the control side is important, while others will hear the autonomy message. Or, control might be emphasized in certain periods, while autonomy is focused on in others.

Glocalization and Perspectives

Glocalization may result from the dynamic relationship between and inter-penetration of structural, cultural, and symbolic factors, and it may result in different glocal forms, depending on the type of political-administrative structure and culture and the prevalence of certain national and local symbols. Glocalization may also reflect different degrees of homogeneity and heterogeneity depending on structure, culture, and myths.

NPM and Post-NPM Reforms: Hybridity and Layering in Practice

Selected Countries

Australia and New Zealand were the NPM trail-blazers, introducing reforms from the early 1980s, but they also spearheaded the development of post-NPM from the late 1990s (Christensen and Lægreid 2007a). These countries both deliver central ideas to international organizations that spread reform templates and receive and adapt generic templates (Sahlin-Andersson 2001). Norway represents the reluctant reformers and is a typical Scandinavian country in this respect, but some Continental European countries also followed a similar path (Hood 1996). China, by contrast, represents a group of one-party-dominated states often found in Asia that jumped on the reform bandwagon believing that they had the instrumental preconditions for implementing the reforms, although they often lacked the cultural preconditions and did not understand the reforms properly (Christensen, Lisheng, and Painter 2008).

Australia and New Zealand

When New Public Management was introduced in Australia and New Zealand in the early 1980s, it was intended to be an alternative and a challenge to the 'old public administration', which was held to represent a centralized, integrated model of extensive government

(Boston et al. 1996). The NPM entrepreneurs argued that governments and public sectors around the world had to be fundamentally restructured along the principles espoused by the private sector (Self 2000; Wright 1994). The structural model proposed was one of increased specialization and fragmentation, both vertically and horizontally (Christensen and Lægreid 2007a). Vertically, structural devolution was the answer to central capacity problems, allowing leaders to focus on more strategic questions, while leaving the choice of implementation instruments to officials on lower levels (Gregory 2003). The NPM entrepreneurs argued that both control and autonomy would be improved by the reforms.

There were many new forms of structural devolution in those countries. One was to give traditional agencies more leeway (i.e., to move them further away from the political executive and/or to relax rules constraining their activities) (Christensen and Lægreid 2007a). Other measures included establishing more regulatory agencies with stronger autonomy based on professional values (Pollitt et al. 2004), transforming public administration bodies into state-owned companies, giving state-owned enterprises more autonomy (Spicer et al. 1996) and privatizing public activities related to services and the market. NPM was also associated with increasing horizontal specialization inside and between organizations, whereby roles became more specialized in a process of so-called 'role-purification'. Taken together, these NPM reform ideas produced a more fragmented public-sector model.

Studies of NPM in these countries pointed to the fact that in reality, NPM constituted a complex, mixed, and hybrid bag of reform elements based on the global ideas they themselves furthered (Gregory 2003). Boston et al. (1996) showed that the underlying economic ideas of NPM reforms were both ambiguous and contradictory about how to organize the public sector. Over the last two decades of NPM, it has become increasingly clear that devolution and deregulation have come to be coupled with re-regulation and more scrutiny and control. It is also quite easy to show that NPM in reality represents a lot of variety, complexity, and hybridity between and inside countries and policy sectors (Pollitt and Bouckaert 2011). The overall trend has been in the direction of increased autonomy and has hence raised problems of political control. So the dominant glocal template is to move towards more autonomy, but overall glocalization takes many different forms.

When the first post-NPM measures emerged in Australia and New Zealand in the late 1990s, they were primarily seen as a reaction to the effects and implications of NPM-related reforms (Christensen and Lægreid 2007a; Gregory 2003; Halligan 2006). They were designed to allow executive politicians to take back some of their lost control and increase their own capacity to solve cross-sectoral societal problems. Measures were introduced to vertically reintegrate some of the agencies and enterprises and to establish more controls and constraints. Another measure was to strengthen overall administrative or political capacity close to the political executive (Halligan 2006).

The horizontal challenge was seen as even more important than the vertical because a lot of specialized sectoral pillars or silos had been created under NPM that were perceived as obstructing the solution of cross-sectoral and 'wicked' problems (Pollitt 2003). The NPM reforms had led to a lot of horizontal specialization and fragmentation and turf wars among competing public organizations. Several new coordinative measures emerged that were easier to implement than merely reversing structural devolution; more collaboration was introduced in the central government apparatus, among both political and administrative leaders and across sectors. Cross-sectoral programs, projects, and networks were established, and there were even some structural mergers (Gregory 2003; Halligan 2006).

When the post-NPM reforms were introduced, the balance tipped back somewhat towards more control, but it did not restore the situation that had existed under the 'old public administration' (Christensen and Lægreid 2007b). Post-NPM has played out more along the horizontal dimension, with more structural and cultural integration, and has added to and modified the NPM reforms, making the system even more structurally and culturally hybrid and layered. The development has been from simple integration (old public administration) through complex, fragmented, and unbalanced complexity (NPM) to integrated and more balanced complexity concerning political control and autonomy (post-NPM).

Post-NPM reforms are in some ways more culturally oriented than the NPM reforms were (Halligan 2006). This is particularly the case in Australia, where the concept of 'value-based management' has been important. NPM has a much more specialized cultural perspective, while the post-NPM message is that there should be more emphasis on a holistic perspective. The credo now is that civil servants and public institutions should be developing some kind of collective notion that they are in the same boat, and that there should be some kind of ethical standards and a focus on the ethos of civil servants (Gregory 1999).

Summing up developments in New Zealand and Australia, the vertical and horizontal specialization introduced by NPM as a global set of generic ideas made the system much more complex and tilted the balance away from control and towards autonomy (Pollitt and Bouckaert 2011). Nevertheless, Weberian features from the old system were retained and blended with NPM in a layering process, creating more complexity and hybridity. When the post-NPM reforms came along, adding a new layer of global ideas, the 'local' balance tilted back somewhat towards more control, making the system even more complex and hybrid. But this hybridity was different in each of the two reform waves (i.e., more disintegrated in NPM and more integrated in post-NPM), potentially leading to different tensions, challenges, and effects. The glocal forms under post-NPM reflect more heterogeneity and tensions than existed under NPM.

China

A major question in modern public reforms in China is whether the reforms conform with the Chinese tradition and culture or whether they simply imitate the West (Christensen, Lisheng, and Painter 2008). Chinese scholars seem to emphasize the former, while Western scholars point to the fact that a lot of the reforms seen in China in recent decades are pretty similar to central Western reforms (Chan and Suizhou 2007; Ngok and Chan 2003). A third answer would be that Chinese public reforms are a complex, hybrid, and layered combination resulting from instrumental actions by executive leaders, cultural path-dependency, and imitation from the West (cf. Westney 1987). China has a centralized political leadership, making it easier to control the direction public reforms take, but imitation from the West is not easy, for there is internal cultural resistance to reforms and China is a vast and complex country, which also makes reforms difficult to control. This may all result in hybridity and layering related to public reform processes.

When China introduced modern public reforms in the early 1980s, they were designed mainly to 'streamline' (to down-size and avoid overlap). This was clearly NPM-inspired, indicating that China was imitating a set of global ideas (Ngok and Zhu 2007). These reforms met with internal cultural resistance and resulted in few actual changes. Later in the decade, reforms designed to separate the party apparatus from the governmental apparatus were started and one measure was to give state-owned enterprises more autonomy. The reality today is that this organizational form, the state-owned enterprise—on the surface an imitation from the West—is, in fact, subject to much more political control than comparable entities in the West, showing hybridity and ambiguity.

The reforms in China in the 1990s were carried out against the background of Deng's market economy reforms. They added complexity and hybridity and bore many post-NPM features, such as the merger of ministries and agencies, the strengthening of macro-structures for regulating and controlling the market, the strengthening of state-owned enterprises, the establishment of one-stop-shops, and the establishment of a stronger Ministry of Labor and Social Security, showing that market-oriented reforms had brought about social problems and that therefore, compensatory measures were needed (Ngok and Zhu 2007). In addition, the use of symbolism was stepped up in the form of ambiguous political terms like 'socialist market economy' to legitimize economic growth and structural change.

Since 2000, reform in China has added new layers of structural change and cultural norms and values. One trend has been the introduction of even more post-NPM reform measures to strengthen central control over local changes, partly by empowering the provinces (Lan 2001; Yang 2004). The decision on 'super-departments' in 2008 which ushered in a new wave of mergers of central ministries and agencies was also in line with this trend (Lisheng, Christensen, and Painter 2010a). In response to external pressure from the OECD, a system of regulatory agencies was installed, which turned out to be less autonomous than the original global form that it was imitating. Housing, health, and education were three sectors that the central leadership considered important to reform. Reforms in these sectors were characterized by market-like reform measures, a reluctance to accept all the effects of the reforms, and subsequently, the slow development of post-NPM-oriented compensatory policies and a rebalancing of reforms and structures (Lisheng, Christensen, and Painter 2010b).

Summing up, in line with the theory Westney (1987) developed to study imitation in Japan in the Meiji period, China has tried to be a 'rational shopper', seeking to learn from and imitate reform successes in Western countries. Often, China adopts the basic structural forms and administrative cultures from the West, but adapts them to its own cultural path (Christensen, Lisheng, and Painter 2008). In this process, a lack of knowledge about the cultural context of the reforms being imitated leads to a distortion and exaggeration of the reforms, as seen in efforts to privatize the hospital and education sectors. The result of all this is a very complex, hybrid, and layered system, where traditional Confucianist values are blended with command economy elements, NPM reform measures, and post-NPM elements. Up until now, the dominant glocal template, at least on the rhetorical level, has been the rather ambiguous term 'socialist market economy', which is now under a lot of pressure because of problems of increasing social inequality.

Norway

Norway has implemented many public reforms over the past 10 to 15 years, particularly in the hospital, immigration, regulatory, and welfare sectors. All the reforms show active ministers, some of them typical political entrepreneurs, trying to achieve a certain balance between political control and autonomy. In all cases, the main executive leadership had not done a sound rational calculation concerning potential effects, and in all cases, the preferred solutions were later modified as a result of rethinking, negotiations, cultural factors, or because another solution was forced upon them from outside, resulting in even more complexity, hybridity, and layered reforms.

The reform of the hospital administration, completed in 2002, involved transferring ownership of the hospitals from the counties to the central government (post-NPM) and the establishment of regional and local health enterprises run according to the principles of efficiency and performance management (NPM), the latter being more typical for global ideas. The reform was controlled by the political leadership but supported by actors with diverse motives and has resulted in problems of efficiency and in sharp conflicts between political-administrative actors on the one hand and health professionals on the other.

The immigration reform of 2001 established a 'super-autonomous' complaints agency and more freedom for the existing immigration agency, following both a global NPM template and a European standard, but has since then been subject to repeated post-NPM efforts by ministers from different parties and governments who have tried to exert more control over two agencies with a culture of autonomy (Christensen and Lægreid 2009). These efforts came in response to external pressure caused by an increase in the number of immigrants and more blame for problematic cases, but they have not been very successful and have created a much more complex, hybrid, and layered system.

The regulatory reform launched in 2003 by a conservative, neo-liberal minister inspired by OECD reform ideas aimed to give all regulatory agencies strong autonomy from political control (Christensen and Lægreid 2007b). It eventually resulted in a compromise whereby regulatory agencies in some sectors were granted considerable autonomy and independent complaints bodies, while in other sectors, the regulatory function was more integrated into ordinary agencies and controlled by the political leadership. Again, this is definitely a complex, hybrid, and layered system.

The largest public reform ever in Norway, the welfare administration reform, was initiated in 2001, adopted in 2005, and implemented through 2009 (Christensen, Fimreite, and Lægreid 2007). It merged the pensions and employment services (post-NPM) to create a national welfare agency and established local partnerships between this new agency and the social services in the municipalities (post-NPM); this complex and hybrid system was to be run according to the principles of efficiency and performance management (NPM). The resulting hybridity and layering was engendered not only by the structural complexity of combining a central and local government hierarchy, but also by combining three different cultures and professions.

Summing Up

All the countries compared here have tried to imitate global reform templates—both NPM and post-NPM. They have also all combined these global ideas with national/local structural and cultural elements, resulting in different types of complex, hybrid, and layered systems. Concerning the balance between political control and institutional autonomy, Australia and New Zealand score highest on autonomy, China lowest, and Norway somewhere in between. This implies varied forms of glocalization.

Effects of Hybridity and Layering

What seem to have been the overall consequences of increased complexity, hybridity, and layering in the balancing of control and autonomy in public organizations, as discussed in general and illustrated with examples from different countries (Christensen and Lægreid 2011)? One major argument may be that complexity and hybridity are preferable to simplicity built on one-dimensional theories. Structural complexity in public organizations enables them to cope more easily with complex societal problems and heterogeneous interests and demands. Political and administrative leaders thus have a repertoire of responses to complex and diverse problems at their disposal. The legitimacy of government will be related to how well the balance between different considerations is organized. Culturally, complexity may indicate that a hybrid culture, catering to diverse traditions and sub-cultures, has developed, enabling organizations to be flexible in adapting to internal and external efforts to bring about change.

The flexibility of complexity may be enacted in different ways. One way is to compromise and trade off between diverse norms, values, and interests at different points in time. This means that rather than giving priority to one norm, value, or interest, the aim is to reconcile them, if possible, for example, by allowing the broad participation of diverse interests, thereby increasing legitimacy (Mosher 1967). Leaders may then portray this compromise or trade-off in different ways, pointing more to how each interest has received its fair share rather than stressing the need to balance it with other interests. This can be done by double-talk and by using symbols that appeal to different actors, whereas reality is less rosy (Brunsson 1989). Another way is to emphasize certain norms, values, and interests at one point in time, while paying attention to others at other times. As Cyert and March (1963) point out in their seminal work, this is more likely to create consensus and legitimacy, but may suffer from long-term conflicts and inconsistencies, which may, in turn, lead to more hybridity and layering.

A different argument stresses that increasing complexity, hybridity, and layering will make control more problematic for political and administrative leaders, particularly if political priorities remain ambiguous, making it more difficult to influence 'local' activities and implementation. A further argument is that compared with the 'old public administration' NPM-related complexity is tilted towards more autonomy, which makes control even more problematic, even as leaders try to take back control via post-NPM reform measures (Christensen and Lægreid 2001). What is more, hybridity makes more demands on the knowledge base of political leaders. The more hybridity, the more potential capacity and cognitive problems leaders will have, a problem that may be coped with by delegation, making administrative leaders more powerful. Political leaders have to divide their attention and process more information than before, while policy questions may become more technical and complicated, which makes politicians more reliant on experts and more vulnerable to criticism (Brunsson 1989).

Another downside of complexity and hybridity may be that different elements of complexity are incompatible, leading to uncoordinated or countervailing actions and chaos or stalemates (Boston et al. 1996). The ultimate question is whether it is possible for executive leaders to choose many roads at the same time, going in the direction of both control and autonomy, without getting lost or encountering problems. Our examples also illustrate the executive problems related to complexity.

Third, given the fact that leaders have shown themselves more able to control reform processes than to think rationally about them, increased complexity may lead to a steady stream of new reforms being implemented in public organizations (Pollitt and Bouckaert 2011). Since executive leaders decide constantly on new reforms that are difficult to deliver on, but still control change processes quite well, they may try to demonstrate their power and will to change through even more reforms and reorganizations. This may be one reason why such reforms are often symbol-ridden decisions or else shallow reforms that do not last long (cf. Downs and Larkey 1986). Evaluation and scrutiny of reforms will hence tend to become more political processes, where it is important to control the interpretation of effects; in other words, 'image management' becomes more important.

A fourth possibility, and the most pessimistic one, is that the increased complexity, hybridity, and layering resulting from combining NPM and post-NPM reforms will quite simply result in increased institutional confusion and ambiguity (March and Olsen 1976). Increased complexity would step up the pressure to control and increase the demands on actors' attention, making them less able to produce decisions on changes and reforms capable of fulfilling public goals. Going back to the classical distinction between control and rational calculation drawn by Dahl and Lindblom (1953), reforms may lead to both conflicts and confusion concerning participation, but also to acute problems of clear organizational thinking. And the more confusion and ambiguity, the greater the problems of legitimacy and the more difficult it will be to garner support for and acceptance of the reforms by civil servants and external stakeholders. This may also make public opinion more cynical.

Fifth, glocalization as discussed above may mean at least two different things. It may indicate glocal templates capable of combining and reconciling diverse reform elements in a way that furthers goals and fulfills a variety of interests, but it could also reflect loosely coupled glocal templates with elements that are not easy to reinforce.

Conclusion

Summing up, the main argument in the chapter, supported by an analytical discussion of driving forces behind reform processes and empirical examples from diverse countries, is that different reform waves produce a combination of complexity, layering, hybridization, and glocalization, rather than dominance, substitution, and pendulum swings (Christensen and Lægreid 2011). Public administration faces an increasingly complex environment and internal preconditions, reflected in multifunctional organizational forms, and the administrative reforms in the public sector can be understood as compound reforms that combine different organizational principles based on multiple factors working together in a complex mix (Egeberg and Trondal 2009). Compound administrative reforms are multi-dimensional and represent 'mixed' orders and combinations of competing, inconsistent, and contradictory organizing principles and structures, but also cultures that co-exist and balance interests, values, and claims to power.

Multi-dimensional orders are considered to be more robust against external shocks and therefore preferable to uni-dimensional orders (March and Olsen 1989). Compound reforms depend on the mobilization of multiple and complementary sets of institutions, actors, interests, decision-making arenas, values, norms, and cleavages, reflected in what we call a transformative approach to reforms (Christensen and Lægreid 2001, 2007a). In a pluralistic society, where there are many criteria for success and different causal understandings, we have to go beyond the idea of a single organizational principle to understand how public organizations work and are reformed and look at them as composite organizations.

Instead of assuming a linear development towards more and more NPM reform or a cyclical development where tradition makes a comeback and reinstalls the old public administration, our argument is that we face a dialectical development in which the old public administration has been combined with NPM and post-NPM features to create new hybrid organizational forms. The central component in the old Weberian bureaucratic model is sustainable and robust, but in the strong modern state, it has been supplemented with neo-Weberian components such as performance management and user participation and responsiveness (Pollitt and Bouckaert 2011).

Robertson's (1995) term 'glocalization' denotes a dynamic and reciprocal relationship between the global and the local. Our main argument about hybridity and layering goes in the same direction. The global environment, represented by international organizations and entrepreneurial countries, puts strong pressure on countries to accept global ideas and standards that are filtered and layered through cultural compatibility mechanisms and the actions of national political leaders (i.e., made more 'local') (Pollitt and Bouckaert 2011). On the other hand, ideas and standards are initiated and consciously spread by national actors and thereby constitute central parts of global ideas. Our empirical examples show this clearly. The eventual hybridity and layering of the reforms in Australia and New Zealand from the early 1980s on was brought about in a quasi-symbiotic relationship between the national governments and the OECD (Boston et al. 1996; Self 2000). China adapted to and learned from the US, the OECD, and the WTO, while increasingly also spreading its own reform ideas globally. Norway responded to pressure from the OECD and the EU in a reluctant way, but also participated in creating and spreading its own ideas and standards—for example, those of a Scandinavian welfare model.

References

Aberbach, J.D., and Christensen, T. (2001).'Radical reform in New Zealand: crisis, windows of opportunities, and rational actors'. *Public Administration, 79(2)*, 404–22.

Anderson, P. (1999). 'Complexity theory and organizational science'. *Organization Science, 10(3)*, 216–32.

Boin, A., and Christensen, T. (2008). 'The development of public institutions: reconsidering the role of leadership'. *Administration & Society, 40(3)*, 271–97.

Boston, J., Martin, J., Pallot, J., and Walsh, P. (1996). *Public management: the New Zealand model.* Auckland: Oxford University Press.

Brunsson, N. (1989). *The organization of hypocrisy. Talk, decisions and actions in organizations.* Chichester: Wiley.

Chan, H.S., and Suizhou, E.L. (2007). 'Civil service law in the People's Republic of China: a return to cadre personnel management'. *Public Administration Review, 67(3)*, 383–98.

Christensen, T., and Lægreid, P. (eds.), (2001). *New public management. the transformation of ideas and practice.* Aldershot: Ashgate.

Christensen, T., and Lægreid, P. (2007a). 'The whole-of-government approach to public sector reform'. *Public Administration Review, 67(6)*, 1059–66.

Christensen, T., and Lægreid, P. (2007b). 'Regulatory agencies—the challenges of balancing agency autonomy and political control'. *Governance, 20(3)*, 499–520.

Christensen, T., and Lægreid, P. (2009). 'Organising immigration policy: the unstable balance between political control and agency autonomy'. *Policy and Politics, 37(2)*, 161–78.

Christensen, T., and Lægreid, P. (2010). 'Increased complexity in public sector organizations—the challenges of combining NPM and post-NPM', in P. Lægreid and K. Verhoest (eds.), *Governance of public sector organizations. proliferation, autonomy and performance.* London: Palgrave Macmillian.

Christensen, T., and Lægreid, P. (2011). 'Complexity and hybrid public organization—theoretical and empirical challenges'. *Public Organization Review, 11(4)*, 407–23.

Christensen, T., Fimreite, A.L., and Lægreid, P. (2007). 'Reform of the employment and welfare administrations—the challenges of co-coordinating diverse public organizations'. *International Review of Administrative Sciences, 73(3)*, 389–409.

Christensen, T., Lisheng, D., and Painter, M. (2008). 'Administrative reform in China's central government—how much 'learning from the West'?' *International Review of Administrative Sciences, 74(3)*, 351–71.

Christensen, T., Lægreid, P., Roness, P.G., and Røvik, K.A. (2007). *Organization theory and the public sector.* Aldershot: Ashgate.

Cohen, M.D., and March, J.G. (1974). *Leadership and ambiguity: the American college president.* Harvard: Harvard Business School Press.

Cyert, R.M., and March, J.G. (1963). *A behavioral theory of the firm.* Englewood Cliffs, NJ: Prentice-Hall.

Dahl, R.A., and Lindblom, C.E. (1953). *Politics, economics, and welfare.* New York: Harper & Row.

Downs, G.W., and Larkey, P.D. (1986). *The search for government efficiency: from hubris to helplessness.* Philadelphia, PA: Temple University Press.

Egeberg, M. (2003). 'How bureaucratic structure matters: an organizational perspective', in B.G. Peters and J. Pierre (eds), *Handbook of public administration.* London: Sage.

Egeberg, M., and Trondal, J. (2009). 'National agencies in the European administrative space: government driven, commission driven or networked?' *Public Administration 87(4),* 779–90.

Gregory, R. (1999). 'Social capital theory and administrative reform: maintaining ethical probity in public service'. *Public Administration Review, 59(1),* 63–75.

Gregory, R. (2003). 'All the King's horses and all the King's men: putting New Zealand's public sector back together again'. *International Public Management Review, 4(2),* 41–58.

Gulick, L. (1937). 'Notes on the theory of organizations. With special reference to government', in L. Gulick and L. Urwin (eds), *Papers on the science of administration.* New York: A.M. Kelley.

Halligan, J. (2006). 'The reassertion of the centre in a first generation NPM system', in T. Christensen and P. Lægreid (eds), *Autonomy and regulation. Coping with agencies in the modern state.* London: Edward Elgar.

Hood, C. (1996). 'Exploring variations in public management reform of the 1980s', in H.A.G.M. Bekke, J.L. Perry, and T.A.J. Toonen (eds), *Civil service systems.* Bloomington, IN: Indiana University Press.

Kaufman, H.A. (1960). *The forest ranger: a study in administrative behavior.* Oxford: Oxford University Press.

Krasner, S.D. (1988). 'Sovereignty: an institutional perspective'. *Comparative Political Studies, 21(1),* 66–94.

Lægreid, P., Roness, P.G., and Rubecksen, K. (2007). 'Modern management tools in state agencies: the case of Norway'. *International Public Management Journal, 10(4),* 387–413.

Lan, Z. (2001). 'Understanding China's administrative reform'. *Public Administration Quarterly,* Winter: 437–68.

Lisheng, D., Christensen, T., and Painter, M. (2010a). 'A case study of China's administrative reform: the importation of the super-department'. *American Review of Public Administration,* 40(2), 170–88.

Lisheng, D., Christensen, T., and Painter, M. (2010b). 'Housing reform in China: rational interests gone wrong or organizational design failure?' *Journal of Asian Public Policy, 3(1),* 4–17.

Mahoney, J., and Thelen, K. (2010). *Explaining institutional change: ambiguity, agency and power.* Cambridge: Cambridge University Press.

March, J.G., and Olsen, J.P. (1976). *Ambiguity and choice in organizations.* Bergen: Universitetsforlaget.

March, J.G., and Olsen, J.P. (1983). 'Organizing political life. What administrative reorganization tells us about government'. *American Political Science Review,* 77, 281–97.

March, J.G., and Olsen, J.P. (1989). *Rediscovering institutions: the organizational basis of politics.* New York: Free Press.

Meyer, J.W., and Rowan, B. (1977). 'Institutionalized organizations: formal structure as myth and ceremony'. *American Journal of Sociology,* 83, 340–63.

Mosher, F. (ed.) (1967). *Governmental reorganizations.* Indianapolis: Bobbs-Merrill.

Ngok, K., and Chan, H.S. (2003). 'Guest editors' introduction'. *Chinese Law and Government, 36(1),* 5–13.

Ngok, K., and Zhu, G. (2007). 'Marketization, globalization and administrative reform in China—A zigzag road to a promising future'. *International Review of Administrative Sciences,* 73(2), 217–33.

Pollitt, C. (2003). *The essential public manager.* Maidenhead: Open University Press.

Pollitt, C., and Bouckaert, G. (2011). *Public management reform: a comparative analysis* (2nd edn). Oxford: Oxford University Press.

Pollitt, C., Talbot, C., Caulfield, J., and Smullen, A. (2004). *Agencies: how governments do things through semi-autonomous organizations.* London: Palgrave Macmillian.

Robertson, R. (1995). 'Glocalization: time-space and homogeneity-heterogeneity'. In M. Featherstone, S. Lash, and R. Robertson, *Global Modernities.* London: Sage, 25–44.

Røvik, K.A. (1996). 'Deinstitutionalization and the logic of fashion', in B. Czarniawska and G. Sevon (eds), *Translating organizational change*. New York: De Gruyter.

Røvik, K.A. (2002). 'The secrets of the winners: management ideas that flow', in K. Sahlin-Andersson and L. Engwall (eds), *The expansion of management knowledge—carriers, flows and sources*. Stanford: Stanford University Press.

Sahlin-Andersson, K. (2001). 'National, international and transnational construction of new public management', in T. Christensen and P. Lægreid (eds), *New public management. The transformation of ideas and practice*. Aldershot: Ashgate.

Scott, W.R., and Davis, G. (2006). *Organizations and organizing: rational, natural and open systems perspectives* (6th rev. edn). Englewood Cliffs, NJ: Prentice Hall.

Self, P. (2000). *Rolling back the state. Economic dogma and political choice*. New York: St. Martin's Press.

Selznick, P. (1957). *Leadership in administration*. New York: Harper & Row.

Simon, H. (1957). *Administrative behaviour*. New York: Macmillan.

Spicer, B., Emanuel, D., and Powell, M. (1996). *Transforming government enterprises*. St. Leonards, Australia: Centre for Independent Studies.

Streeck, W., and Thelen, K. (2005). *Beyond continuity*. Oxford: Oxford University Press.

Westney, D.E. (1987). *Imitation and Innovation*. Cambridge, MA: Harvard University Press.

Wright, V. (1994). 'Reshaping the state. The implications for public administration'. *West European Politics*, 17, 102–37.

Yang, D.L. (2004). *Remaking the Chinese leviathan: market transition and the politics of governance in China*. Stanford, CA: Stanford University Press.

13
Adoption and Abandonment
Global Diffusion and Local Variation in University Top Management Teams

Danielle M. Logue

Introduction

Over the past century, universities worldwide have experienced a multitude of profound changes. The massification of higher education has seen an explosion of the number of universities around the world and dramatic increases in the number of students enrolled in higher education at undergraduate and graduate levels (Schofer and Meyer 2005). This is situated against broader debates in recent decades on the nature and role of the university in society, coupled with increasing demands from an increasing array of stakeholders for accountability (for example, see Castells 1996; Etzkowitz and Leydesdorff 1997; Arocena and Sutz 2001; Barry, Chandler, and Clark 2001; Enders and Fulton 2002; Lounsbury and Pollock 2001; Frank and Gabler 2006). The fallout from this debate has seen universities worldwide suffer from reduced public funding, diminished public confidence, and financial pressures that require a reconstruction of structural and resource commitments (Gumport, 2000). This has resulted in what some describe as the 'marketization' of higher education (Djelic and Sahlin-Andersson 2006), where students become customers, research needs to be commercialized (Powell and Owen-Smith 1998), and investors want measurable returns and a value-added workforce. Competition from other knowledge-producing institutions shifts the traditional identity of universities, as universities come to be seen not only as educational systems but as economic institutions (Czarniawska and Genell 2002; Bess 2006).

Scholars have described this process in terms of universities being increasingly embedded in transnational processes of diffusion and rationalization of administrative practice, transforming into accountable and coherent organizational actors (Frank and Gabler 2006; Frank and Meyer 2007; Krücken and Meier 2006; Whitley 2008; De Boer, Enders, and Schimank 2008). This process has been described as the 'organizational turn' of universities (Krücken and Meier 2006) and is occurring worldwide. As universities lose their specificity and are considered 'normal' organizations, 'organizational solutions from other organizational contexts, especially business, and general concepts like New Public Management, may be applied' (Musselin 2007: 63). This 'wave of managerialism has washed over universities globally in recent decades, catalyzing the rise of many new administrative, service and management posts' (Frank and Meyer 2007: 288). Yet what does this wave look like, at a university level? How are universities responding to this wave or translating this idea of how universities should be led and managed and by whom? How are universities preserving, accommodating, or transforming their leadership structures?

It perhaps seems unremarkable today that universities have 'Deputy Vice Chancellors' and 'Pro-Vice Chancellors' for Administration, Finance, International Development, Public Relations, and even Technology Transfer. Moreover, it is largely assumed that these leadership positions embody models of good governance and effective administration. However, the emergence of these transformations in key leadership roles is relatively recent in origin, and yet these transformations have diffused widely to universities around the world—universities that are embedded in strategically different environments with widely different configurations of resources and educational traditions. There is a puzzling similarity in the form and timing and the extent of the spread of these elements of governance models, which has made it as likely to find a 'Director for Communications and External Relations' at a university in rural Uganda that suffers from intermittent electricity supply as it is to see a 'Director of Media and Public Relations' at a prestigious university in the United Kingdom. This adoption of new positions is also occurring at the same time as universities are abandoning traditional positions in their leadership teams, such as librarians and deans of academic areas.

Functional explanations would lead one to assume that there would be significant national variations across universities due to differences in resources, history, and culture, yet universities worldwide show a good deal of homogeneity (Drori and Moon 2006; Frank and Gabler 2006; Frank and Meyer 2007; Schofer and Meyer 2005). In this chapter, I explore this process of 'glocalization' (Robertson 1995), the global diffusion and local variation in university top management teams, by tracking the adoption and abandonment of leadership positions. I observe both patterns of global diffusion in regards to the sweeping organizational turn of universities, as well as regional and local variation, as universities preserve, accommodate, and transform their top management teams.

Global Diffusion and Local Variation

There is by now a large literature that investigates the global spread of organizational forms and strategies, models, templates, and ideas (Dobbin, Simmons, and Garrett 2007; Khagram, Riker, and Sikkink 2002; Djelic and Sahlin-Andersson 2006; Meyer, Boli, Thomas, and Ramirez 1997). Most of this literature comes from a broad base of institutional theory, and the fruits of the now decades of study are several (see, for example, reviews by Strang and Meyer 1993; Strang and Soule 1998; Campbell 2004; Drori, Meyer, and Hwang 2006; Dobbin et al. 2007). Yet, there exists a tension in organizational diffusion literature, particularly in transnational and global settings, on understanding processes of change as part of global forces of homogenization (for example, Meyer et al. 1997) and assuming the coherency of world models of management, or in emphasizing the inherently local processes of adoption and a micro level view to reveal translation and editing of global practices (for example, Czarniawska and Sevón 1996, 2005).

Djelic (2008) and Powell, Gammal, and Simard (2005) note that more macro and global studies of diffusion trace the spread and adoption of practices across large populations of organizations or countries. Emblematic of diffusion studies taking this perspective are quantitative analyses using a form of logistic regression that accounts for time, such as event-history analysis. Such techniques and macro level of analysis unsurprisingly lend themselves to seeing broad patterns and change as homogenous. In contrast, studies with smaller numbers of cases can focus on a 'contextualized reception rather than on patterns of diffusion' (Djelic 2008: 548). This more micro perspective and level of analysis is often associated with Scandinavian scholars such as Czarniawska and Sevón (1996, 2005) and Sahlin-Andersson and Engwall (2002). These studies, then, highlight 'the peculiarities of the context on the diffusion path and patterns of appropriation' (Djelic 2008: 548). Processing of editing and translation are a dominant concern of this micro view and 'using a metaphor of travel, these scholars stress the transfer of ideas is highly interactive, with diverse means of transportation carrying ideas from one setting to another' (Powell et al. 2005: 237). Translation 'involves the combination of locally available principles and practices with new ones originating elsewhere' (Campbell 2004: 65), with recipients enacting them in different ways, depending on the local institutional context.

The empirical setting of higher education is a fruitful and generative empirical site for exploring these tensions in the institutional change and diffusion literature (Kraatz, Ventresca, and Deng 2010) and for examining projects of 'glocalization' (Giulianotti and Robertson 2007). In this empirical setting, it seems that diffusion is occurring without a homogenous coherent field (or global) model, yet still providing a pattern of change that is not fully explained by organizational (or local) level variation. Indeed, the composition of university top management teams is in between these dominant views—they do not reveal global uniformity, nor do they reveal infinite variation. There are patterns in these changes that do not place all the explanation with global drivers or with local drivers. I follow Krücken, Kosmützky, and Torka's (2007) idea that 'universities are best understood as historical, time-dependent systems that are strongly embedded in their own national and organizational histories, and that while universities all over the world respond to global trends that may appear standard, they are never standardized in their effects' (2007: 8), as they are adapted, incorporated, or resisted by universities that are ultimately rooted in particular times and places. Looking at both the adoption of leadership positions (traditional approach for global diffusion studies) and the abandonment of leadership positions (a richer picture of the changes occurring), across multiple levels of analysis, gives a more nuanced understanding of how the global wave of managerialism is being translated at the university level and our theoretical understandings of processes of 'glocalization', diffusion, and institutional change. By using this lens of 'glocalization', one can incorporate homogenizing, and often global, trends, yet also extrapolate more meso and micro shifts in meaning and translation at the local level. Adoption of new practices may be at a surface level only, a pragmatic approach to signal legitimacy to a wider audience, or it may be synthesized with existing practices resulting in a hybridity and a new cultural form or practice. Adoption could also lead to a transformation, with the embracing of new practices and the abandonment of existing practices.

Method and Data

I observe the adoption and abandonment of various types of leadership positions at the strategic apex of university management, using a sample of 540 universities from 37 countries of the British Commonwealth over a period of 90 years. The data for this chapter is gathered from the *Commonwealth Yearbook of Universities* and draws upon Logue (2010, 2011). The *Yearbook*, originally known as the *Yearbook of Universities of the Empire*, has been published by the Association of Commonwealth Universities for the past 90 years. In total, 37 countries are covered, in Africa, Asia, Australasia, Europe, Canada, and the Caribbean, comprising 30 percent of the world's people (Frank and Gabler 2006). In essence, it functions as a directory, providing standardized entries about all universities within the Commonwealth; resulting in a rare and continuous picture of a university's development, the people who work there, and the courses taught. It includes the structure of the senior leadership team and the faculties, departments, and research centers in the university. By focusing on the changes of the past 30 years, this coincides with most colonies of the British Commonwealth having secured independence, a prolific expansion in higher education (that is, post-World War II), and captures very recent decades where notions of managerialism, 'mode two knowledge production' (Giddens 1984), and new public management (Ferlie, Ashburner, Fitzgerald and Pettigrew 1996) added to general pressures on universities to be more accountable and relevant to the needs of society (Scott 1995; Frank and Gabler 2006).

Many of the features of corporate directories of executives (such as Standard & Poor's) are comparable with the *Commonwealth Universities Yearbook* (annual publication listing the senior officers with their names, functional titles, and qualifications, amongst other content on university faculties, departments, and lecturers). Several studies (Zorn 2004; Zorn and Dobbin 2003; Power 2007; Kraatz et al. 2010) have demonstrated the value and utility in using occupational titles as a dependent variable in diffusion studies. In this empirical setting, the emergence and presence of (increasingly) corporate occupational titles reflects the increasing importance and pervasiveness of these orientations (as compared with more traditional orientations based in academic specializations). In coding this occupational title data, several homogenizing assumptions were made; for example, if a university had a 'Deputy Vice Chancellor (Finance and Administration)' or 'Director of Finance', this was counted as having a 'Director of Finance'.

Findings

The data from the *Yearbook* enables this diffusion of a 'managerialist wave' to be observed at multiple levels of analysis over historical periods of time, revealing on the one hand homogeneity in this adoption of this more managerialist approach, yet on the other, details of the translation and resulting hybridity occurring.

Global Level of Analysis

Tracing the frequencies of positions and their adoption and abandonment across 540 universities in the sample, from 37 countries, resulted in the identification of five key trends in the composition of university top management teams (TMTs)—all supportive evidence of the organizational turn occurring in universities. Observing the most frequent positions that were adopted or abandoned, this revealed:

1 Abandonment of librarian position
2 Abandonment of academic-area position
3 Adoption of 'external-facing' position (such as communications, marketing)
4 Adoption of student-focused position
5 Adoption of finance position.

These trends speak directly to the notion of 'organizational turn' and ontological claims about the changing nature of university governance. Table 13.1 shows the proportion of universities in the sample at each time point that had each respective position.

One position that appeared to be core to university leadership teams in earlier years has suffered a drastic decline—that of the librarian. In several cases, the librarian has adapted to

Table 13.1 Proportion of universities in sample with position listed in TMT

	1978	1988	1998	2008
Number of universities in sample	245	303	438	540
Number of countries	29	30	37	37
Librarian	65.9%	58.6%	61.3%	35.5%
Academic position	25.7%	16.3%	4.6%	6.0%
External-facing position	10.2%	7.6%	13.1%	26.6%
Student-focused position	8.4%	10.1%	9.9%	23.4%
Finance position	18.6%	22.9%	33.4%	53.1%

Source: Compiled by author from *Yearbook of the Association of Commonwealth Universities.*

become responsible for a new array of materials—for example, 'Director of Library and Media Services'. However, the re-labeling of the librarian position itself into a position responsible for library, information, and media services, still did not counter the overall dramatic abandonment of this position in top management teams of universities in the sample. The abandonment of the librarian position out of the TMT can be considered as evidence of the shift away from the more monastic ideas of the university, towards a knowledge-producing organization.

Across the sample, there is an abandonment of leadership positions relating to specific academic areas or disciplines being included in the TMTs, for example, Deans of Humanities, Sciences, and Law. These positions seem to be subsumed by positions relating to university functions, such as research, finance, human resources, and, in later years, international, quality, and commercial management services. However, this is not to say that universities do not have deans of academic areas. Rather, it indicates that these academic-area leaders are no longer included when the university is outwardly describing its TMT in the ACU *Yearbook*. In 2008, the slight increase appears due to academic positions included in the leadership team that were often for medicine or medical schools (for example, the University of Glasgow in 2008 has a 'Vice Principal for Life Sciences and Medicine' as the only academic-area position listed for that year). This is in contrast to earlier years when it was not uncommon to see leadership structures that included six to ten positions for specific academic areas. I argue that the abandonment of academic-dean positions in the TMT shows a global shift away from collegial governance to formalized management.

Another indicator of the 'organizational turn' occurring in the leadership structures of the universities within the sample is the emergence and proliferation of positions relating to the organization's representation of self (and arguably having to respond to wider societal demands for relevance and accountability). In earlier years, there were more internally focused positions for administration, examinations, and estate management that in later years were corporatized. In 1998 and 2008, one can increasingly observe leadership positions for strategic planning, human resources, and organizational change. Yet, it is the growth in external-facing positions that is quite dramatic. I specifically refer to positions relating to the university's image (such as communications, public relations, marketing, international, community, and partnerships) and positions relating to the relevance of research activities (such as commercialization, technology and development, and industry relations). This may be a direct result of a shift to 'Mode 2' knowledge production (Giddens 1984), where we see the context-driven, problem-focused co-production of scientific knowledge (that now seems to require more specific management and leadership). The adoption of external-facing positions (such as marketing and public relations) not only demonstrates the university's concern with the presentation of its organizational self, but also replaces more collegial and perhaps amateur activity in these areas with professionalized management.

It has been in more recent years that senior leadership positions relating to students (needs, resources, welfare) have appeared in university TMTs. Djelic (2006) described the marketization of higher education, which is arguably contributing to this renewed focus on students as customers, as increasingly powerful stakeholders in evaluation of university performance, and as key components of university ranking criteria (such as their satisfaction ratings).

A striking change in the leadership structure of universities across the sample is the rise of finance. In earlier years, positions relating to finance (if they occurred at all) were located at the bottom of the hierarchy and included positions such as bursar or finance officer. In fact, at the start of the 20th century, the universities of the Commonwealth were worried about the finance function taking importance in university governance. In the foreword of the 1926 proceedings of the Commonwealth Universities Congress, it was described that a new era was upon university leaders: 'the sordid skeleton of finance is out of the cupboard and now sits unashamedly naked at academic board meetings … it cannot be ignored' (1926: ix).

Over time, this naked skeleton underwent a dramatic transformation—from securing a seat at the table, to a formal position and title, to one of the highest and most powerful leadership positions in the university hierarchy. The sample reveals the dramatic emergence and transformation of university bursars and finance officers into Chief Financial Officers (CFOs), from the tail-end to the strategic apex of the university management structure (Zorn 2004). The rise of finance in university management parallels arguments made by other scholars, such as Zorn (2004), who examines the rise of the finance function (specifically the CFO) in Fortune 500 companies and Fligstein's (1990) examination of the emergence and adoption of a finance conception of control. Such trends are arguably supported by and reflective of the broader emergence and rise of a global field of finance (Lounsbury 2002).

When this university level data is aggregated to the global level, there is much evidence of a wave of managerialism washing over universities and transforming and homogenizing their top management teams, consistent with other research and trends on university changes. So does this mean a global model of university management is diffusing? If we remained at the global level (or total sample in this case), we observe fairly consistent changes and trends in top management team composition, demonstrated strongly by the adoption *and* abandonment of leadership positions. I now analyze this same data at another level of analysis—geographical region—to ascertain the strength of this global wave and its translation (or perhaps universality) in different regions.

Regional Level of Analysis

In seeking to examine the diffusion pattern of these positions and essentially the strength of a coherent global model that might be diffusing, I disaggregated the results to the regional level. The regional level is an often neglected yet very interesting level of analysis (see also Djelic, chapter 7), particularly for regions that are rarely the focus of scholarly attention, such as Africa. Here, I grouped universities into one of five regions—Africa, Asia, Europe, North America, and Pacific. In revisiting the adoption and abandonment patterns by region, the substantial regional variation is revealed (Table 13.2).

Table 13.2 Adoption and abandonment of positions by region

		1978	1988	1998	2008
Librarian	Africa	50.0%	61.0%	55.4%	53.7%
	Asia	46.3%	44.6%	59.3%	41.2%
	Europe	77.5%	70.8%	54.7%	10.3%
	North America	76.6%	64.9%	67.3%	35.9%
	Pacific	82.4%	80.0%	78.7%	21.4%
Academic position	Africa	5.0%	5.1%	0.0%	3.2%
	Asia	2.4%	5.8%	0.7%	3.4%
	Europe	10.0%	5.6%	1.1%	7.2%
	North America	72.3%	73.7%	23.1%	15.4%
	Pacific	17.6%	8.6%	10.6%	14.3%
External-facing position	Africa	0.0%	0.0%	4.1%	17.9%
	Asia	4.9%	2.9%	2.9%	8.8%
	Europe	0.0%	5.6%	11.6%	44.3%
	North America	31.9%	35.1%	30.8%	46.2%
	Pacific	0.0%	0.0%	42.6%	73.8%
Student-focused position	Africa	0.0%	1.7%	1.4%	11.6%
	Asia	7.3%	7.9%	3.6%	11.8%
	Europe	5.0%	6.9%	10.5%	42.3%
	North America	19.1%	35.1%	28.8%	35.9%
	Pacific	0.0%	0.0%	19.1%	50.0%
Finance position	Africa	15.0%	16.9%	23.0%	40.0%
	Asia	14.6%	20.1%	34.3%	46.6%
	Europe	20.0%	29.2%	42.1%	72.2%
	North America	29.8%	38.6%	48.1%	61.5%
	Pacific	0.0%	8.6%	14.9%	64.3%

Source: Compiled by author from *Yearbook of the Association of Commonwealth Universities*.

The geographical representations show an adoption of the finance position across the world, yet variation in the other positions. For example, an academic position was initially dominant in North America (Canada) and then abandoned. The external-facing position also seems to originate more in the Canadian universities and then is picked up in other countries, especially Australia and New Zealand. While the librarian is being abandoned across the sample overall, in Asia and Africa this is not so much the case. There seems to be an additive pattern here, where new positions are added to existing positions and so the TMT expands. In disaggregating to the regional levels, we also see in Europe that the adoption of a finance position appears to parallel the abandonment of the librarian position, that is, adopting one means the abandonment of something else, getting closer to a more corporate and organizational model.

It also seems, compared with other regions, that external-facing positions and student-focused positions are adopted as part of a 'package'. In this way, the 'model' seems to be evolving in Europe early, in a rather steady way. An exception to this is the spike in adoptions in Europe in 1998, contributed by the conversion of many polytechnics (colleges) into universities, known as the post-1992 universities. This particular group of universities does appear to wholly embrace corporate leadership positions almost at the very time of their conversion. For example, it is very common in this group to observe Chief Financial Officers (CFO) and Chief Information Officers (CIO), as observed in many Fortune 500 firms. When compared with the Pacific (essentially Australia and New Zealand), there seems to be a late explosion of sorts, as if the model is wholly imported. The changes between 1998 and 2008 are striking in the rapid adoption of finance, external student positions, and abandoning the more traditional positions of librarian and academic deans (in the top management teams). This may also be connected to the reliance of Australia and New Zealand on international students and higher education as an important export sector for GDP growth.

University Level of Analysis

In addition to global and regional levels of analysis, this data provides the opportunity to drill down to the organizational level of analysis—an individual university. In attempting to examine patterns of global homogeneity or local variation, this level reveals finer grained details of the hybridity and translation occurring, as this wave of managerialism sweeps over universities worldwide. Table 13.3, drawing on Logue (2011), provides several examples of the changes in university leadership positions over a 90-year period. These universities were randomly selected from different regions and countries, with different levels of development, age, resources, and prestige, and who provided data for the longue dureé (Pierson 2004)—90 years.

The prominence of national legacies can be observed in positions such as 'Rector Magnificus' in Malta, and yet less obvious is the abandonment of the librarian position or the rise of the finance position in this organizational example. In conducting a detailed micro-analysis of the processes of translation of this managerial wave, this organizational level data could be supported by additional data on individual university histories and development. This could also provide important information on the rationales and motivations behind adoption and abandonment, as demonstrated by Czarniawska and Gennell's (2002) study of the different reasons behind the adoption of marketing approaches, while seemingly similar on the surface level, by particular Swedish and Polish universities.

Discussion

When these changes in titles of university top management teams are situated in the broad, historic changes of university governance, one can observe a shift from faculty-led, collegial administration to professionalized management in the context of the 20th century transformation of the university—from a monastic guild model of education to an axial institution of scientific knowledge production (Kieser 1989; Gumport 2000; Frank and Gabler 2006; Bundy 2004; Scott 1995; Drori et al. 2006). The global trends in the adoption of more corporate positions, such as communications, marketing, and particularly, finance, are striking.

Table 13.3 Examples of leadership positions at individual universities 1918–2008

1918	1958	2008
The University of Sydney, Australia		
Visitor	Visitor	Vice Chancellor and Principal
Chancellor	Chancellor	Provost and Deputy Vice Chancellor
Vice Chancellor	Deputy Chancellor	Deputy Provost (Learning and Teaching) and Pro Vice Chancellor
Warden and Registrar	Vice Chancellor and Principal	Pro Vice Chancellor (Research)
Librarian	Deputy Vice Chancellor	Pro Vice Chancellor (Strategic Planning)
	Assistant Principal	Chief Operating Officer and Deputy Vice Chancellor
	Registrar	Deputy Vice Chancellor (Community)
	Librarian	Deputy Vice Chancellor (International)
		Deputy Vice Chancellor (Research)
		Chair of the Academic Board
		Planning Chief Executive Officer (University College, Sydney Project) and Deputy Vice Chancellor
		Vice Principal (University Relations)
		Registrar
		University Librarian
The University of Malta, Malta		
Visitor	Patron	Rector
President of the General Council	Chancellor	Pro Rector
Rector	Vice Chancellor and Rector Magnificus	Pro Rector
Registrar and Secretary	Registrar	Pro Rector
	Secretary	Director of Finance
	Finance Officer	Director, Library Services
	Librarian	Registrar
The University of Sheffield, United Kingdom		
Visitor	Visitor	Vice Chancellor
Chancellor	Chancellor	Pro Vice Chancellor
Pro Chancellor	Pro Chancellor	Pro Vice Chancellor
Pro Chancellor	Pro Chancellor	Pro Vice Chancellor
Vice Chancellor	Vice Chancellor	Pro Vice Chancellor
Treasurer	Pro Vice Chancellor	Pro Vice Chancellor
Registrar	Treasurer	Treasurer
Librarian	Registrar	Registrar and Secretary
	Bursar	Librarian
	Librarian	
The University of Mysore, India		
Chancellor	Chancellor	Vice Chancellor
Pro Chancellor	Vice Chancellor	Finance Officer
Vice Chancellor	Registrar	Registrar
Registrar	Controller of Examinations	Registrar (Evaluation)
Librarian	Bursar	
	Librarian	
	Director, Oriental Research Institute	

Source: Compiled by author from *Yearbook of the Association of Commonwealth Universities*.

Yet, at other levels of analysis, a coherent model of university governance is not uniformly diffusing across the world. While there is the adoption of finance positions, this may be in the form of a 'Deputy Vice-Chancellor of Finance and Administration' or it could be in the adoption of 'Chief Financial Officer.' While both positions indicate the rise of finance, there may be quite a difference locally in the meaning and impact of these occupational titles. It is important to recognize the homogenizing assumptions made in the data, and avoid stripping 'away potentially interesting variation, masking the nature and extent of diffusion' (Lee 2009: 1248; see also Schneiberg and Clemens 2006).

In analyzing the data at different levels of analysis, it shows that while this pattern of diffusion (and changes in university leadership) is global and dramatic, it is of somewhat a piecemeal emergence (Fligstein 1991), a messy layering and gradual displacement (Streeck and Thelen 2005; see also Christensen, chapter 12), with new ways of managing and leading universities building on the remnants of the existing structures and practices. Dacin and Dacin (2008) argue that efforts to unpack the strategies and dynamics associated with abandonment, deinstitutionalization, and extinction of practices and structures are lacking in institutional studies, yet studies that do look at processes of decline and erosion show that institutionalized practices are rarely ever completely extinguished. This is particularly shown in the regional level of analysis and also the university level of analysis, where the patterns of adoption and abandonment revealed systems of differences. Finance is the most consistent trend across all regions, yet in Asia and Africa, where this is adopted, traditional positions such as librarian are not abandoned in the process, perhaps demonstrating an accommodation of these global trends and expectations. This is in sharp contrast to the Pacific and North America, where in the recent decade in particular, the entire 'model' (adoption of corporate positions and abandonment of traditional positions) is diffusing, transforming top management teams.

This simultaneous analysis of adoption and abandonment provides theoretical and methodological insights and also presents several challenges. Following Mohr (1998), we begin to interpret the presence of finance/external-facing positions and absence of librarian/academic dean positions and their co-presence in university top management teams. Titles can be adopted and abandoned essentially without affecting the adoption and abandonment of other titles. Titles are also cheap to adopt or abandon. Studying both the adoption and abandonment of titles provides a more nuanced understanding of institutional change and shifts in meaning systems.

For example, are there differences in the decision-making processes to adopt as compared to abandon a practice? Both can signal legitimacy, rationality, and status, yet intuitively, there seems to be a difference, in this empirical setting at least. It may be that where the adoption of practices is not associated with the abandonment of other practices (i.e., they are 'added on' to existing structures), adoption may be driven by more reputational, legitimacy concerns and may not be reflective of deeper changes in meaning systems or institutional logics. However, where the more corporate positions are adopted and traditional positions are simultaneously abandoned, this represents a deeper shift in meaning systems and logics (i.e., the university has more fully embraced a new model of governance, priorities, and the organizational turn). This begins to unearth a deeper understanding of glocalization 'projects' (Giulianotti and Robertson 2007), where groups, or in this case, universities, may seek to preserve their institutions, accommodating changes pragmatically yet maintaining key elements of their institutions through hybridization where the adoption and synthesis of global practices produce distinctive, hybrid cultural practices, institutions, and meanings, or through transformation where adoption of new cultural forms and abandonment of existing forms occurs.

Methodologically, this also raises several questions. What designs and statistical models enable the tracking of multiple dependent variables (that track adoption and abandonment)? What other methodological approaches are available to track the reasons for adoption and abandonment per unit of analysis (organization) over time? How can mixed-method approaches be designed to capture and provide a more nuanced understanding of diffusion and institutional change?

Conclusion

In this chapter, I have presented data to show how this global wave of managerialism that is sweeping across universities is being translated at the strategic apex of universities—in their top management teams. There are both global themes and local (and regional) variations in this pattern of diffusion, providing valuable information on both the scale and nature of this change occurring in universities and the interplay between global and local forces. While certain trends in the adoption of corporate positions and abandonment of traditional positions can be observed, disaggregating the data into multiple levels of analysis provides a more nuanced understanding of how this wave of managerialism is being translated in different regions of the world and, indeed, by individual universities.

I have shown the value in tracing the adoption and abandonment of practices in revealing a system of differences (Mohr 1998). This contributes to the broader diffusion literature in institutional theory, where the focus is often on the adoption of a successful practice, with little attention to the diffusion of unsuccessful practices (for an exception, see Soule 1999) or the abandonment of practices (for an exception, see Greve 1995), and certainly no attention to cases of institutional change where adoption and abandonment of practices is co-occurring. In this empirical setting, the presence, co-presence, and absence of positions at multiple levels of analysis provide insights into the understandings and motivations behind these changes, processes of institutional change, and conceptualizations of glocalization.

Acknowledgments

The author would like to thank Green Templeton College, University of Oxford, for the doctoral scholarship awarded to support this research, and also appreciates the academic support and encouragement received from Bob Hinings, Dana Brown, Gili Drori, John Meyer, Lars Engwall, Behlül Üsdiken, Albrecht Blümel, Craig Rawlings, and John Gray.

References

Arocena, R., and Sutz, J. (2001). 'Changing knowledge production and Latin American universities'. *Research Policy,* 30(8): 1221–34.

Association of Commonwealth Universities (1926). *Third Conference of the Universities of The Empire, report of proceedings.* London: Association of Commonwealth Universities.

Barry, J., Chandler, J., and Clark, H. (2001). 'Between the Ivory Tower and the academic assembly line'. *Journal of Management Studies,* 38(1): 88–101.

Bess, J. (2006). 'Toward strategic ambiguity: antidote to managerialism in governance', in J.C. Smart and M. Paulson (eds), *Higher education: handbook of theory and research.* Dordrecht: Springer, 491–593.

Bundy, C. (2004). 'Under new management? A critical history of managerialism in British universities', in M. Walker and J. Nixon (eds), *Reclaiming universities from a runaway world: the society for research into higher education.* London: Open University Press, 160–77.

Campbell, J.L. (2004). *Institutional change and globalization: problems and prospects*. Princeton: Princeton University Press.
Castells, M. (1996). *The rise of the network society*. Maiden: Blackwell.
Czarniawska, B., and Genell, K. (2002). 'Gone shopping? Universities on their way to the market'. *Scandinavian Journal of Management*, 18(4): 455–74.
Czarniawska, B., and Sevón, G. (1996). *Translating organizational change*. Berlin: de Gruyter.
Czarniawska, B., and Sevón, G. (eds). (2005). *Global ideas: how ideas, objects, and practices travel in the global economy*. Copenhagen: Liber and Copenhagen Business School Press.
Dacin, T., and Dacin, P. (2008). 'Traditions as institutionalized practice: implications for deinstitutionalization', in R. Greenwood, C. Oliver, K. Sahlin, and R. Suddaby (eds), *The SAGE handbook of organizational institutionalism*. New York: Sage, 327–52.
De Boer, H., Enders, J., and Schimank, U. (2008). 'Comparing higher education governance', in N.C. Soguel and P. Jaccard (eds), *Governance and performance of education systems*. Dordrecht: Springer, 32–54.
Djelic, M.-L. (2006). 'Marketization: from intellectual agenda to global policy-making', in M.-L. Djelic and K. Sahlin-Andersson (eds), *Transnational governance: institutional dynamics of regulation*. Cambridge: Cambridge University Press, 53–73.
Djelic, M.-L. (2008). 'Sociological studies of diffusion: is history relevant?' *Socio-Economic Review*, 6: 538–57.
Djelic, M.-L., and Sahlin-Andersson, K. (eds). (2006). *Transnational governance: institutional dynamics of regulation*. Cambridge: Cambridge University Press.
Dobbin, F., Simmons, B., and Garrett, G., (2007). 'The global diffusion of public policies: social construction, coercion, competition, or learning? *Annual Review of Sociology*, 33(1): 449–72.
Drori, G., and Moon, H. (2006). 'The changing nature of tertiary education: neo-institutional perspectives on cross-national trends in disciplinary enrollment, 1965–1995'. *International Perspectives on Education and Society*, 7: 157–83.
Drori, G., Meyer, J.W., and Hwang, H. (eds). (2006). *Globalization and organization: world society and organizational change*. New York: Oxford University Press.
Enders, J., and Fulton, O. (2002). *Higher education in a globalising world*. London: Springer.
Etzkowitz, H., and Leydesdorff, L. (1997). *The university in the global knowledge economy*. London: Pinter.
Ferlie, E., Ashburner, L., Fitzgerald, L., and Pettigrew, A. (1996). *The new public management in action*. Oxford: Oxford University Press.
Fligstein, N. (1990). *The transformation of corporate control*. Cambridge: Harvard University Press.
Fligstein, N. (1991). 'The structural transformation of American industry: an institutional account of the causes of diversification in the largest firms, 1919–1979', in W.W. Powell and P. DiMaggio (eds), *The new institutionalism in organizational analysis*. Chicago: University of Chicago Press, 311–36.
Frank, D., and Meyer, J. (2007). 'Worldwide expansion and change in the university', in G. Krücken, A. Kosmützky, and M. Torka (eds), *Towards a multiversity?* Bielefeld: transcript: 19–44.
Frank, D.J., and Gabler, J. (2006). *Reconstructing the university: worldwide shifts in academia in the twentieth century*. Stanford: Stanford University Press.
Giddens, A. (1984). *The constitution of society: outline of the theory of structuration*. Berkeley and Los Angeles: University of California Press.
Giulianotti, R., and Robertson, R. (2007). 'Forms of glocalization: globalization and the migration strategies of Scottish football fans in North America'. *Sociology*, 41(1): 133–52.
Greve, H.R. (1995). 'Jumping ship: the diffusion of strategic abandonment'. *Administrative Science Quarterly*, 40(3), 444–73.
Gumport, P.J. (2000). 'Academic restructuring: organizational change and institutional imperatives'. *Higher Education*, 39(1): 67–91.
Khagram, S., Riker, J., and Sikkink, K. (2002). *Restructuring world politics: transnational social movements, networks and norms*. Minneapolis: University of Minnesota Press.

Kieser, A. (1989). 'Organizational, institutional, and societal evolution: medieval craft guilds and the genesis of formal organizations'. *Administrative Science Quarterly*, 34(4): 540–64.

Kraatz, M., Ventresca, M., and Deng, L. (2010). 'Precarious values and mundane innovations: enrolment management in American liberal art colleges'. *Academy of Management Journal*, 53(6): 1521–45.

Krücken, G., and Meier, F. (2006). 'Turning the university into an organizational actor', in G. Drori, J.W. Meyer, and H. Hwang (eds), *Globalization and organization: world society and organizational change.* New York: Oxford University Press, 241–57.

Krücken, G., Kosmützky, A., and Torka, M. (2007). *Towards a multiversity? Universities between global trends and national traditions*. Bielefeld: transcript.

Lee, B. (2009). 'The infrastructure of collective action and policy content diffusion in the organic food industry'. *Academy of Management Journal*, 52(6): 1247–69.

Logue, D. (2010). 'Top management teams: asking institutional question about who is "in", when and why?' *European Management Review*, 7(1): 71–2.

Logue, D. (2011). 'Understanding 90 years of global organisational change in university leadership', Unpublished doctoral dissertation, Said Business School, University of Oxford.

Lounsbury, M. (2002). 'Institutional transformation and status mobility: the professionalization of the field of finance'. *Academy of Management Journal,* 45(1): 255–66.

Lounsbury, M., and Pollock, S. (2001). 'Institutionalizing civic engagement: shifting logics and the cultural repackaging of service-learning in US higher education'. *Organization,* 8(2): 319–39.

Meyer, J.W., Boli, J., Thomas, G.M., and Ramirez, F.O. (1997). 'World society and the nation-state'. *American Journal of Sociology,* 103(1): 144–81.

Mohr, J. (1998). 'Measuring meaning structures'. *Annual Review of Sociology*, 24: 345–70.

Musselin, C. (2007). 'Are universities specific organisations?', in G. Krücken, A. Kosmützky, and M. Torka (eds), *Towards a multidiversity? Universities between global trends and national traditions*. Bielefeld: transcript, 63–84.

Pierson, P. (2004). *Politics in time: history, institutions, and social analysis*. Princeton: Princeton University Press.

Powell, W.W., and Owen-Smith, J. (1998). 'Universities and the market for intellectual property in the life sciences'. *Journal of Policy Analysis and Management,* 17(2): 253–77.

Powell, W., Gammal, D., and Simard, C. (2005). 'Close encounters: the circulation and reception of managerial practices in the San Francisco Bay Area nonprofit community', in B. Czarniawska and G. Sevón (eds), *Global ideas: how ideas, objects, and practices travel in the global economy.* Copenhagen: Liber and Copenhagen Business School Press, 233–58.

Power, M. (2007). *Organized uncertainty: designing a world of risk management*. Oxford: Oxford University Press.

Robertson, R. (1995). *Glocalization: time-space and homogeneity*. London: Sage.

Sahlin-Andersson, K., and Engwall, L. (eds). (2002). *The expansion of management knowledge: carriers, flows and sources.* Stanford: Stanford Business Books.

Schneiberg, M., and Clemens, L. (2006). 'The typical tools for the job: research strategies in institutional analysis'. *Sociological Theory*, 24(3): 195–227.

Schofer, E., and Meyer, J.W. (2005). 'The worldwide expansion of higher education in the twentieth century'. *American Sociological Review*, 70(6): 898–920.

Scott, P. (1995). *The meanings of mass higher education*. London: Open University Press.

Soule, S. (1999). 'The diffusion of an unsuccessful innovation'. *Annals of the American Academy of Political and Social Science,* 566: 120–31.

Strang, D., and Meyer, J.W. (1993). 'Institutional conditions for diffusion'. *Theory and Society,* 22(4): 487–511.

Strang, D., and Soule, S.A. (1998). 'Diffusion in organizations and social movements: from hybrid corn to poison pills'. *Annual Review of Sociology,* 24: 265–90.

Streeck, W., and Thelen, K.A. (2005). *Beyond continuity: institutional change in advanced political economies*. Oxford: Oxford University Press.

Whitley, R. (2008). 'Universities as strategic actors: limitations and variations', in L. Engwall and D. Weaire (eds), *The university in the market*. London: Portland Press, 23–37.

Zorn, D., and Dobbin, F. (2003). *Too many chiefs? How financial markets reshaped the American firm*. Conference on Social Studies of Finance, University of Constance, May 2003, New Delhi.

Zorn, D.M. (2004). 'Here a chief, there a chief: the rise of the CFO in the American firm. *American Sociological Review*, 69(3): 345–64.

14
Decoding Localization
A Comparison of Two Transnational Life Insurance Firms in China

Cheris Shun-ching Chan

Introduction

The subjects of localization and glocalization that capture the dynamics of global–local interactions have been the focus of an increasing volume of scholarly research and debate (Anderson-Levitt, 2003; Appadurai, 1990; Giulianotti & Robertson, 2004; Ramirez, 2003; Robertson, 1992, 1995). My earlier work on glocalization challenges conventional assumptions that associate localization with cultural divergence (Chan, 2011). This chapter builds on this work to refine the conceptualization of localization in an effort to derive a common ground for more fruitful scholarly debates about global–local dynamics. Because there are many possibilities for defining what is meant by 'local', debates without a common definition could easily talk past each other.

Localization, by definition, is a process by which practices are modified according to the specific conditions of a locale. It is a necessary move of transnational organizations in the course of globalization. Modifications may be initiated by transnational entities as part of their strategies to disseminate their practices, or alternatively, they may occur due to local resistance or constraints. Adopting this definition of localization, this chapter aims to further refine the concept by decoding what 'local' means, and how differences in the definition of 'local' or in the delineation of a 'locale' may lead to different conclusions about the extent and the form of localization of a transnational entity.

The data presented here is derived from a larger project based on a 14-month ethnographic study of the creation of a life insurance market in the People's Republic of China (PRC) between 2000 and 2004. My study focuses on four different life insurance firms in Shanghai, representing a wide range of variation in ownership, product development, and organizational management and culture. These firms include one wholly foreign, one wholly local, and two Sino-foreign joint ventures. Although joint ventures are co-owned by foreign insurers and domestic companies, they are officially listed as 'foreign' insurers because their operations are typically taken over by the foreign partners, whereas the Chinese partners rarely participate in their operations. To capture the localization dynamics on the ground, I participated in each company's activities on a routine basis (such as morning assemblies, group meetings, and training sessions) and interviewed more than 200 people in the field (including managers, administrative staff, sales agents, clients, and prospects).

In this chapter, I focus on the two joint ventures that began their operation in Shanghai at about the same time, but appear to represent opposite poles of the localization spectrum. In the sections that follow, I begin with a reconceptualization of localization by highlighting various possibilities for the definition of 'local' or the delineation of a 'locale.' Then, I compare the localization strategies of these two transnational life insurance firms in Shanghai, by using different definitions of 'local'. These firms include Pacific-Aetna Life Insurance Company, Ltd. (Pacific-Aetna), which is a Sino-American life insurer, and Allianz-Dazhong Life Insurance Company, Ltd. (Allianz-Dazhong), a Sino-German life insurer.

In the early 2000s, the Sino-American Pacific-Aetna appeared to be a highly localized firm, from its managerial composition to its agency management and organizational culture. The Sino-German Allianz-Dazhong, on the other hand, appeared to be the least localized firm in almost every respect. Nevertheless, as I discuss below, Pacific-Aetna only appeared more localized when we define 'local' or the locale as greater China (which includes the PRC, Hong Kong, and Taiwan). If we narrow the scope of 'local' to Shanghai, or mainland China, and then measure the firm's localization, Pacific-Aetna was actually the least localized insurer. The findings reveal that what appears to be highly localized by one definition may actually be less so under another definition, which suggests that localization is a relative concept. Furthermore, the comparison of two transnational life insurance firms in the same locale gives rise to insights about different orders of localization. Specifically, if a transnational organization has been first localized in locale A and then is further localized in locale B, its localization in locale B takes less effort than a corresponding localization that did not go through the first order of localization in locale A. In other words, localization gets progressively easier as organizations expand to multiple locales, especially if these locales share similar cultures.

What is 'Local'?

Current debates about localization often take for granted what 'local' means without clearly defining it (Frank & Stollberg, 2004; Pieterse, 1994; Watson, 1997). Indeed, 'local' can refer to many possibilities (Appadurai, 1990; Robertson & White, 2003). As a case in point, 'local' in my case study can refer to the city Shanghai, the country the PRC, or greater China (including the PRC, Hong Kong, and Taiwan). As I illustrate in the following sections, whether we take Shanghai or greater China to be 'local' will lead to significantly different conclusions regarding the extent to which a transnational entity or event is localized.

In the early 2000s, any observer could plainly see that Pacific-Aetna was the most 'Chinese-oriented' organization among the transnational insurance companies in Shanghai. Aetna Life Insurance Company Limited (Aetna Life) arrived in Hong Kong in 1981, adapting to some extent to the local (Hong Kong) environment in its operation. When Aetna Life set up a branch in Taiwan in 1987, it sent managers from Hong Kong to set up the operation. These managers in turn brought the 'Hongkong model' and modified it to suit the local (Taiwan) environment, giving rise to a 'Taiwanese model' of operation. The 'Taiwanese model' was subsequently introduced in Shanghai with little modification upon the opening of Pacific-Aetna there toward the end of the 1990s. Hence, if we define localization as any modification geared toward any version of 'Chinese-ness,' be it Taiwanese, Hong Kong, or mainland Chinese, then Pacific-Aetna should be considered highly localized.

However, localization can alternatively refer to modifications made according to the institutional and cultural specificities of the PRC or Shanghai. If Shanghai is the locale against which the extent of localization is measured, then Pacific-Aenta is not highly localized. Its organizational and agency management, sales discourse, and product development were brought to Shanghai from Taiwan, rather than locally created. Allianz-Dazhong, on the other hand, has been more localized because it has made considerable modifications, from its staff recruitment to its product development and agency management, since its opening in Shanghai. This Sino-German firm first appeared as the most Westernized company and, thus, has had to make more adaptations according to the local (Shanghai and the PRC) environments. Thus, the term 'localization' should be problematized but not taken for granted. When we say that something is 'localized', we have to be aware of what locale we are referring to.

When Greater China is 'Local'

Pacific-Aetna is Highly Localized

If we define 'local' as greater China, then Pacific-Aetna is indisputably the most localized life insurer in the PRC, whereas Allianz-Dazhong is the least.

Pacific-Aetna was established in Shanghai in October 1998 by the Hartford-based Aetna, Inc. and China Pacific Insurance Company. Because of Aetna Life's success in Taiwan, Pacific-Aetna adopted a full Taiwanese model upon its establishment in Shanghai. The general manager, Mr Chang, and the two deputy general managers were all Taiwanese. They brought a managerial team with them and came directly from Taiwan. Beneath the Taiwanese managers were all locally employed Chinese. The personnel composition of Pacific-Aetna was the simplest among all joint-venture insurers in the PRC.

The organizational structure of Pacific-Aetna did not differ from that of other joint ventures. In fact, the organizational structures of all transnational insurers were more or less the same. Typically, their organizational management is divided into in-house management and sales management. In-house management is composed of a number of highly specialized departments in charge of various operations from product development to investment management, and from agency training to advertising. Sales management focuses on managing the sales force and their sales activities. However, Pacific-Aetna exhibited quite a unique organizational culture that was distinct from other joint ventures in Shanghai. The sales agents of Pacific-Aetna were particularly committed to the company. In my observation, the turnover rate for sales agents was the lowest among all insurers. All of the Pacific-Aetna sales agents I met with or interviewed in 2000 still worked for the company in 2002, whereas various agents at other companies had already left them for other insurers. Likewise, the Pacific-Aetna agents' interactions with the in-house staff seemed very harmonious compared with other companies. The 'Taiwanese model' of agency management seemed to work well for the locally-recruited sales agents in Shanghai.

The differences in agency management between transnational and domestic life insurance firms are best represented by comparing American International Assurance Company (AIA)'s 'professional model' with Ping An Insurance Company of China (Ping An)'s 'massive labor model'. As the first foreign insurer in Shanghai, AIA targeted university degree holders to be their sales agents, and required them to put on 'Western suits and ties'. It trained these agents to go door to door to persuade the local Chinese to buy life insurance by telling stories of misfortune that happened to families without life insurance. In contrast, the locally-founded Ping An put less emphasis on the educational level and the appearance of their sales agents, and instead recruited a large number of middle-aged sales agents, mostly women in their mid-forties, who had good *guanxi* (interpersonal relationship) networks. When Pacific-Aetna arrived in Shanghai, its agency management resembled more that of Ping An than that of AIA. Unlike other transnational insurers, Pacific-Aetna did not place much importance on the agents' educational level. It hired more middle-aged female agents than any of the other joint ventures, and cared less about teaching the agents how to dress in a professional way. Instead, it focused on mobilizing the agents' *guanxi* networks to expand their sales force. In 2001, Pacific-Aetna had 5,168 sales agents, which was the highest number among all transnational insurers (*Almanac of Shanghai Insurance 2002*). The agency system of Pacific-Aetna was structured in a multiple-level marketing system that encouraged the agents to recruit members. Many well-performing agents were promoted to managerial positions within three years. The main task of these agents was to expand their sales groups and increase the sales volumes of their groups. The income levels of these upline agents depended largely on the sales volumes of their groups. This pyramid structure of the sales agents in Pacific-Aetna encouraged the agents to work collectively. The structure was very similar to a direct selling organization (Biggart, 1989).

Aetna Life in Taiwan was renowned for its familial model of labor management. It proclaimed that its corporate culture put human beings and human souls first, by presenting itself as a warm family and striving to empower the sales agents by rhetorically treating them as 'bosses' or 'business partners' (Li, 2001). Pacific-Aetna in Shanghai also adopted this familial management model. It used a number of relational and emotional managerial practices to motivate its agents and to construct their collective identity. Using a logo of a baby angel to symbolize its mission, Pacific-Aetna presented itself as a caring and compassionate institution not only to its clients but also to its sales agents. Like Aetna Life in Taiwan, Pacific-Aetna in Shanghai held regular morning assemblies that were lively, fun, and dramatic. The format of the assembly was designed by the head of the sales and marketing department who came from Taiwan. A typical morning assembly went as follows: At 9:00 a.m., loud and upbeat music was played, signaling that the assembly was to start. The sales agents then rushed to the sides of four long tables in the meeting hall. One of the sales team managers would lead the agents in a 'morning drill', which was an eclectic mix of stretching, dancing, and aerobic exercises. After the morning drill, senior agents and guest speakers shared personal stories about their selling experiences, particularly about their difficulties, and the ways they overcome them.

Despite its unique corporate culture, the commission rates that Pacific-Aetna offered their agents were more or less the same as those offered by AIA and Allianz-Dazhong. And compared with domestic insurers' products, Pacific-Aetna's were not very popular (Chan, 2012). Thus, the monetary rewards the sales agents of Pacific-Aetna received were not particularly high. To motivate the agents and to keep up their morale, Pacific-Aetna applied various relational and emotional strategies based on the familial management model. The entire sales force was described as a *dajiating* (big family) and sales teams and sales groups were called *jiazu* (clans). The heads of the sales teams and the leaders of the sales groups were called *jiazhang* (parents). When agents recruited their own downline agents, they extended the family vertically. If one of the downline agents was promoted to manager and given his or her sales group, the family was extended horizontally. A substantially extended family became a clan. Each family often held its own group meetings, parties, celebrations, and occasional training sessions. Sometimes a few families that belonged to a clan held activities together. Hugs, verbal support, and mutual help were all seen among the agents of Pacific-Aetna, but not among the agents of other companies. Each managerial grade agent was given a small partitioned room (about 50 square feet) with an office desk and a couple of file cabinets. Agents at a similar level at other insurers would only be in a supervisory grade and would not be entitled to use as many facilities as those at Pacific-Aetna. In addition, the managerial agents were granted a certain degree of discretion to manage their downline agents. Although they were under the pressure of meeting their sales targets, they felt empowered as the heads of their sales groups.

Furthermore, the Taiwanese managers strove to downplay their own status in front of the agents in order to make the agents feel flattered. The general manager and other top managerial staff addressed all of the agents as *huoban* (business partners) in their daily routine. In ceremonial activities, they called the agents 'my bosses' and explicitly said that their incomes depended on the agents' sales. The general manager and the deputy general managers repeatedly claimed that none of them was provided with a private car by Aetna (as the top managers of the other insurers were), to show that they were not given any special privileges. They claimed that they rode in a van to work every day and reiterated that they truly had adopted a 'humanized management'. In its Annual Awards Presentation Ceremony in May 2002, the company invited a famous Taiwanese singer, Zhou Huajian, to perform.[1] The top managers told the agents that they spent US$100,000 to invite Zhou simply because they wanted to make the agents happy. In addition, the general managers and a number of top managers wore heavy make-up to entertain the agents at the ceremony. The general manager, Mr Chang, played Snow White, while the head of the sales and agency development manager, Mr Ge, wore a mini-skirt and danced the hula. All of these elicited joyful screams and laughter from the agents.[2]

In terms of products, Pacific-Aetna brought its first policy offering from Taiwan. It was an accident policy with an endowment component. The subsequent products Pacific-Aetna provided, though locally designed, were all similar to its popular products in Taiwan. They were primarily risk management products, such as whole life, accident insurance, and hospital care insurance. These products were not noticeably different from those of other joint ventures, but were quite different from the money management products offered by domestic insurers (Chan, 2009, 2012). Although the local Chinese preferred money management products, such as endowment, annuity, and investment-linked insurance, these products were not as profitable as risk management products were. Transnational insurance firms, thus, were cautious about offering money management products. Nevertheless, Pacific-Aetna framed its products in the vocabulary of local preferences. It framed part of the insured amount as 'repayment of principal' to make the products sound like savings or investment. Knowing that *yanglao* (life during retirement) is a major concern of the local people, it termed its whole life with annuity policies as *yanglao xian* (retirement insurance). Pacific-Aetna came up with this strategy of localizing the features and terminology of the products, without compromising the profit margins of their products as domestic insurers had (Chan, 2012).

Allianz-Dazhong is Least Localized

While the products offered by Allianz-Dazhong were rather similar to those of Pacific-Aetna, this Sino-German insurer was seen as the most 'foreign' to the local public. Its 'foreign-ness' can be largely attributed to its managerial composition and organizational management.

Allianz-Dazhong was jointly founded by the Munich-based German insurer Allianz AG and Dazhong Insurance Company from the PRC in January 1999. It was one of the only two life insurers in China headed by a non-Chinese during my research period.[3] The composition of the managerial personnel of Allianz-Dazhong was least Chinese among all transnational insurance firms. It had the highest proportion of European expatriates in the top managerial body, with most coming from Germany. The operation of the company was headed by a management board, which consisted of two Germans and two Chinese. One of the Germans served as the general manager, and the other as deputy general manager. The two Chinese served as deputy general manager and assistant general manager, respectively. Therefore, the two Germans together were in a higher position than the two Chinese, and because the two Chinese managers had no experience in the life insurance industry, the Germans were in charge of the operation.

In contrast to Pacific-Aetna's soft and emotionally charged image, Allianz-Dazhong represented itself as a sturdy, 'macho man' to the public, and as a modern, Western organization to its sales agents. Dark blue was the color this Sino-German joint venture consistently used as the background for all of its publications. Its mission was symbolized by a picture of the world's sixth largest suspension bridge, the Tsing Ma Bridge in Hong Kong, with strong currents underneath and the word 'risk' on the top. Allianz-Dazhong was the most aggressive among the transnational insurers in advocating a 'Western' managerial model when it started its operation in Shanghai.

This company also had the highest proportion of top managers holding a PhD degree, including the general manager, Dr von Canstein. Dr von Canstein had worked for Allianz AG for more than 20 years, but he had never visited China before heading the joint venture in Shanghai. He took up this challenging job and endeavored to establish an organizational culture that was comparable to the German ideal. He used a Chinese word, *kai*, which means 'open,' to describe his management theory. With the ambition of establishing a democratic management model, he invited his staff from different levels to open their minds to think for the benefit of the company.[4] He wanted to set up a corporate culture in which employees were accountable, responsible, independent, proactive, task-oriented, open, and democratic. He admitted that he had encountered countless cultural shocks in managing the local Chinese. For instance, he had difficulty with the local culture of mixing work with private life and personal feelings:

> There was no such challenge in Germany when I was a manager there. People there separate their business and private lives. Here, people have more of a family-like feeling. They behave differently if 'I like you' or if 'I don't like you'. Their personal feelings and relations affect their work. There's just too much personal distraction here.[5]

This German manager endeavored to teach the Chinese employees to separate their personal life from work, admit mistakes, communicate in an open manner, and be task-oriented and proactive:

> The major challenge for the in-house management here is to get people to be accountable, to get them to be responsible. … In other cultures, people understand better what their tasks are. People in other cultures see that 'OK, this is my task. So, I need to finish it …' We need to enhance communication. And we need to enhance the 'mistake culture.' When you make a mistake, just say, 'Sorry, I made a mistake. I will do it right next time.' We want to establish openness and trust … So, there is a lot of training we have to do … We want them to be proactive, responsible, and accountable. We are using a practical approach of management. We have to keep on controlling, pushing, and initiating … They have this attitude that if I do nothing, then I commit no mistake. Then they are inactive …[6]

The other cultures Dr von Canstein appreciated seem to be primarily 'Western cultures'. He clearly advocated a work attitude and ethos that was instrumental, task-oriented, proactive, democratic, and daring to make mistakes. Yet some of these qualities, particularly the idea that employees should dare to make mistakes and the idea of a democratic ethos, were quite alien to the typical work attitude and habits of the people in the PRC.

When Allianz-Dazhong set up its sales team at the beginning, it recruited only university graduates who had not previously worked for any other insurers. The Sino-German company did not like the way the sales agents in Shanghai were selling and, therefore, preferred to recruit those without any prior experience in insurance sales. In 2001, it had only 934 sales agents (*Almanac of Shanghai Insurance 2002*). Moreover, Allianz-Dazhong wanted to distinguish itself from other insurers by introducing a strictly professional way of selling. Unlike AIA, Pacific-Aetna, and Ping An, which encouraged their agents to go door to door to approach strangers, Allianz-Dazhong did not allow the agents to knock on someone's door without first making an appointment. This was intended to convey to the agents that making an appointment was a sign of respect, whereas walking in without an appointments or consent was a sign of rudeness. Some of its first agents were able to observe this rule, and behaved as professionals. These agents were young university graduates. They dressed well, looked urbane, spoke confidently, and regarded their job as a professional career. They appeared to be closest to the ideal model that Allianz-Dazhong intended to build.

When the PRC or Shanghai is 'Local'

Allianz-Dazhong is Highly Localized

Despite being highly localized with respect to greater China, Pacific-Aetna was actually not as localized as it first appeared to be when the scope of what is considered 'local' is narrowed to the PRC or Shanghai. Instead, under this definition, Allianz-Dazhong appeared most localized, as it had made tremendous efforts to adapt to the PRC's specific institutional and cultural conditions. Like other transnational insurers in Shanghai, Allianz-Dazhong adopted a profit-oriented model in their product designs (as compared with the market share approach by domestic insurers), and was rather reluctant to accommodate to the local preference for money management products (Chan, 2012). However, compared with Pacific-Aetna, Allianz-Dazhong was relatively more willing to localize its products. It was more accommodating to the local preference for investment-related products.

The Shanghai Securities Exchange was opened in December 1990, and a 'stock fever' (*gupiao re*) culture soon sprang up. Anthropologist Ellen Hertz found that basically 'everyone'—peasants, workers, hooligans, intellectuals, and government officials—was getting on the stock market bandwagon in the early 1990s (Hertz, 1998). Toward the end of the 1990s and the early 2000s, the Shanghai integrated stock index was climbing up. This intensified the optimistic investment atmosphere in Shanghai. Capitalizing on stock performance and the popularity of stock exchanges, the domestic insurer, Ping An, launched an investment product in October 1999 called 'unit linked', in which each unit of the premium paid is linked to an investment return. Ping An presented this product as a profitable investment, like a variant on stock. This new concept of insurance as a modern, fashionable means of investment received a feverish response from the public (Chan, 2009, 2012). As investment products were not as profitable as risk management products to insurers, the experienced transnational insurers pushed hard on the traditional idea of insurance. They underscored the risk management function of life insurance in their agency training, blaming Ping An for misleading the public and distorting the concept of insurance. The managers of these foreign insurers repeatedly commented that the market in mainland China was too 'immature' for investment insurance.

Nonetheless, under the pressure of competition, these transnational insurers introduced a new category of products that sounded like investments. A Sino-Canadian insurer, Manulife-Sinochem Life Insurance Company, Ltd., first offered a participating policy in March 2000. As participating insurance entitles policyholders to share in the surplus earnings of the company through dividends, the local people called it 'dividend insurance' (*fenhong xian*). The term 'dividend' was associated with investment, so it corresponded well to the locals' preference for money management products, and participating insurance was rather well received by the public. AIA and Allianz-Dazhong responded quickly to this new product line by launching their own participating products. However, because the profit margins of this kind of product were relatively low, AIA was not very enthusiastic in promoting it. Instead, Allianz-Dazhong's two participating policies, one called Full of Gold and Jade, and the other Fortune God Looking After, became the primary products that the agents of this Sino-German insurer sold in 2001–2002. In 2003, Allianz-Dazhong made further efforts to launch a series of participating products.

While the sales agents of Allianz-Dazhong complained that the company kept changing people, management, and its rules during its first few years there, this instability was in fact due to its attempts to localize its managerial body and approach. The Sino-German insurer began with ten Western expatriates serving in the management team when it was founded in 1999. Three years later, it began to localize the personnel composition. It reduced the number of European expatriates to only three and replaced the British actuary with a Taiwanese. It appointed a Hongkongese from Allianz AG's branch in Singapore to be the head of the sales and marketing department, and a Singaporean to be the sales and marketing operating manager. Although for the local Shanghainese, the Singaporean was still a foreigner whose perspective was seen as very different from the local sales agents', the move was obviously an effort to put more Chinese in the managerial body as part of its localizing strategy.

Another localizing strategy Allianz-Dazhong put in place soon after its founding was to hold morning assemblies for its sales agents. As there was no such practice of weekly or daily morning assemblies for the sales agents in Germany, the German managers at first did not like the idea of holding morning assemblies. They simply did not see a need for it. Nevertheless, their Taiwanese insurance sales management consultancy, Insurance Marketing Magazine International, successfully persuaded the German managers to adopt the morning assembly practice as all other insurers did. The frequency and format of the morning assemblies at Allianz-Dazhong then resembled closely those at AIA and Pacific-Aetna.

The recruitment of sales agents at Allianz-Dazhong also underwent localization. At first, the general manager expressed disapproval of the pyramid, family-tree-like structure of the agency system that created the family group culture. The recruitment of sales agents therefore followed the German model at the beginning. Sales agents were recruited by the company's human resources department, and they were all subject to the supervision of the head of sales. The agents initially all worked independently and individually. Those who had outstanding sales records were then promoted to become sales team managers. The human resources department assigned new recruits to be their downline agents. These managers' incomes were then linked to the sales performances of their downline agents. However, given the inherent difficulty of insurance sales (Leidner, 1993; Oakes, 1990; Zelizer, 1979), especially in the Chinese context where the topic of death is a taboo (Chan, 2009, 2012), it was extremely difficult for Allianz-Dazhong to expand its sales force without mobilizing the sales agents themselves to recruit downline agents. As a result, Allianz-Dazhong had to adopt the pyramid system to encourage agents to recruit downline members. The difficulty of recruiting sales agents also forced Allianz-Dazhong to give up its ideal German model and, instead, to follow other insurers to recruit agents with lower qualifications. The spirited, young, educated sales agents, after all, represented only a minority of Allianz-Dazhong's sales force. The majority, generally in their 40s and 50s, were no different from those working for domestic insurers.

Pacific-Aetna is Least Localized

In contrast to Allianz-Dazhong, Pacific-Aetna was less willing to accommodate local preferences in its product development. Although the local public in Shanghai preferred money management products, Pacific-Aetna at first simply refused to offer these products. It was the least interested of all insurers in offering participating policies, though it finally did, given the keen competition. In November 2000, it offered two products with dividends, one called 333 Incremental and Returning Principal, and the other 888 Returning Principal. Like AIA, Pacific-Aetna did not promote these products. The profit margins on these products were so low that the sales and marketing manager of Pacific-Aetna discouraged agents from selling them. In a morning assembly in October 2001, he explained to the agents why the participating products were not beneficial to the insurance companies, and why they should make an effort to sell traditional life policies:

> We don't compare our products to those offered by the domestic insurers ... You need to have knowledge about the profitability of insurance. It operates like a funnel. The wide, circular top is like the premiums we receive from clients, and the tube is like the money we have to pay out to the clients. (He is drawing a funnel on the whiteboard while speaking.) If the tube is too wide, then we have to pay out more. This is exactly what dividend insurance is like. We receive the premiums, but do you know where this money goes? At least 80% of this will go through the funnel tube back to the clients, leaving very little for our company as profits ...[9]

Like AIA, Pacific-Aetna carried participating insurance under market pressure for cosmetic purposes, but discouraged their agents from selling them, despite the fact that the local public largely favored this kind of product.

Thus, when 'local' refers to the PRC or Shanghai, Pacific-Aetna was not as localized as it first appeared to be. Although its organizational culture departed from the 'legal-rational' image that AIA and Allianz-Dazhong attempted to establish, its culture was 'Taiwanese' rather than 'mainland Chinese.' The top managers of Pacific-Aetna came from Taiwan, where the practice of direct selling was more popular than anywhere else on the globe (Chan, 1999). The predominance of the use of relations and emotions to manage and control the sales labor force in the direct selling industry is well documented (Biggart, 1989; Pratt, 2000; Lan, 2001; Chan, 2001). Therefore, the organizational practices adopted by Pacific-Aetna in Taiwan mainly followed a direct selling organization model.

The managers of Pacific-Aetna arrived in Shanghai with their unique organizational management ideas and techniques that made this insurer substantially different from other foreign players in many respects. Nevertheless, it was also very different from the locally-founded Chinese insurers. The organizational culture of the domestic insurers exhibited a more 'authoritative' character. In contrast to the relational and emotional management approach of Pacific-Aetna, the domestic insurers adopted a paternalistic and punishment-oriented approach to manage their sales agents (Chan, 2012). If Pacific-Aetna had attempted to localize its management according to the management styles of the mainland Chinese firms, it would have followed the domestic insurers' approach. But it did not. Instead, it maintained the Taiwanese approach—an alternative version of 'Chinese-ness' outside the PRC.

Conclusion

One of the important defining characters of glocalization refers to the ways in which a global business adapts to local conditions (Robertson, 1995). But just as organizational studies scholars note the difficulties of overnight reorganization of transnational firms (Bartlett, 1986; Bartlett and Ghoshal, 1991), this case study illustrates that adapting to local conditions, the so-called localization is neither an either–or, nor a linear process. Instead, localization can go through various levels or orders.

As a case in point, Aetna Life had long been in Hong Kong and Taiwan before entering the PRC, despite its American origin. It was first localized in Hong Kong (which I call first-order localization). The 'Hongkong model' was then further localized in Taiwan (second-order localization). The 'Taiwanese model' was then brought to Shanghai through the Taiwanese managers. As the 'Taiwanese model' was already one version of 'Chinese-ness,' Pacific-Aetna did not need to substantially modify its practices to make itself appear Chinese. Moreover, because of the cultural proximity between Taiwan and mainland China, a lesser degree of localization in Shanghai was called for. Although the top managers primarily introduced their Taiwanese approach in Shanghai, such an approach worked rather effectively, particularly in motivating the local sales agents. On the other hand, Allianz AG had no experience in greater China prior to its arrival in Shanghai. Its cultural distance from the Chinese required Allianz-Dazhong to make tremendous efforts to adapt to the conditions in the PRC. Compared with Pacific-Aetna, Allianz-Dazhong adapted even more to the specificities of mainland China, including accommodating more to the locals' preference for investment-related products and implementing various agency management methods that were unpopular in Germany. However, the effectiveness of this first order of localization, though significant in its own right, was far behind Pacific-Aetna's third-order localization. The Sino-German insurer was seen as the most 'Westernized' firm, and its sales agents still complained the most about its agency management. The morale of the sales agents at Allianz-Dazhong was the lowest among the insurers I studied, and their turnover rate was the highest (Chan, 2012). Thus, different orders of localization could lead to different outcomes. The multiple levels of localization inevitably add to the complexity of the concept of glocalization and provide an important dimension for comparative studies of the subject. The idea that a higher order of localization is, as a whole, more effective and effortless than a lower order of localization can be posited as a hypothesis for future research.

Throughout this chapter, I elucidate the importance of defining what 'local' means in scholarly debates. The case of life insurance firms in China has demonstrated that different definitions of 'local' can lead to different conclusions about the extent and the form of localization of transnational entities. For instance, if we consider greater China to be 'local', then Pacific-Aetna is highly localized and Allianz-Dazhong is less localized. However, if the PRC or Shanghai is taken as being 'local', then Allianz-Dazhong is actually more localized than Pacific-Aetna. This finding poses an interesting question, namely, who defines what 'local' is and how do different parties and stakeholders define 'local'? Furthermore, how do different definitions of 'local' impact the diverse conclusions reached by distinct theoretical approaches? These questions await further empirical studies that problematize the concept of 'local' in the first place.

Notes

1. Zhou Huajian was at the time a very popular singer in Taiwan, Hong Kong, and parts of mainland China.
2. I did not have a chance to participate in the ceremony directly, but I watched a video of the entire event, read the details of the ceremony from the monthly magazine of Pacific-Aetna, and interviewed the agents who had attended the ceremony.
3. Another was a Sino-Chinese joint venture, John Hancock Tianan Life Insurance Company, Ltd., which was founded in Shanghai in January 2001, and was headed by an American.
4. Dr von Canstein stated his theory in *Allianz-Dazhong Focus* (Spring 2000), a quarterly newsletter of Allianz-Dazhong.
5. Interview, Shanghai, September 2000.
6. Ibid.
7. From my interviews with the general managers of Allianz-Dazhong and Manulife-Sinochem respectively. Both of them defended the traditional risk management concept of life insurance during the interviews.
8. The agents complained that the Singaporean was too serious, and that she made jokes that nobody laughed at because she lacked 'local knowledge.'
9. Participating observation at the morning assembly of Pacific-Aetna, Shanghai, October 2001.

References

Almanac of Shanghai Insurance (2002). Shanghai: The Editorial House of Shanghai Insurance Yearbook.
Anderson-Levitt, K.M. (2003). *Local meanings, global schooling: anthropology and world culture theory*. New York: Palgrave MacMillan.
Appadurai, A. (1990). 'Disjuncture and difference in the global cultural economy'. *Public Culture*, 2(2): 1–24.
Bartlett, C.A. (1986). 'Building and managing the transnational: the organizational challenge', in M.E. Porter (ed.), *Competition in global industries*. Boston, MA: Harvard Business School Press: 367–404.
Bartlett, C.A., and Ghoshal, S. (1991). *Managing across borders: the transnational solution*. Boston, MA: Harvard Business School Press.
Biggart, N.W. (1989). *Charismatic capitalism: direct selling organizations in America*. Chicago, IL: University of Chicago Press.
Chan, C.S.-c. (1999). 'The socio-economic and cultural contexts for the success of direct selling—using fuzzy-set analysis'. Unpublished paper. Department of Sociology, Northwestern University.
Chan, C.S.-c. (2001). 'Reenchantment of the workplace: the interplay of religiosity and rationality'. *Berkeley Journal of Sociology*, 45: 42–70.
Chan, C.S.-c. (2009). 'Creating a market in the presence of cultural resistance: the case of life insurance in China'. *Theory and Society*, 38(3): 271–305.
Chan, C.S.-c. (2011). 'Divorcing localization from the divergence paradigm: localization of Chinese life insurance practice and its implications'. *International Sociology*, 26(3): 346–63.
Chan, C.S.-c. (2012). *Marketing death: culture and the making of a life insurance market in China*. New York: Oxford University Press.
Frank, R., and Stollberg, G. (2004). 'Conceptualizing hybridization: on the diffusion of Asian medical knowledge to Germany'. *International Sociology*, 19(1): 71.
Giulianotti, R., and Robertson, R. (2004). 'The globalization of football: a study in the glocalization of the "serious life"'. *British Journal of Sociology*, 55(4): 545–68.

Hertz, E. (1998). *The trading crowd: an ethnography of the Shanghai stock market*. London: Cambridge University Press.
Lan, P. (2001). 'Networking capitalism: network construction and control effects in direct selling'. *The Sociological Quarterly*, 43(2):165–84.
Leidner, R. (1993). *Fast food, fast talk: service work and the routinization of everyday life*. Berkeley and Los Angeles, CA: University of California Press.
Li, F. (2001). *Yingde haoxian* [*Winning good insurance*]. Aetna Insurance Research Series. Beijing: Economic Science Press.
Oakes, G. (1990). *The soul of the salesman: the moral ethos of personal sales*. Atlantic Highlands, NJ: Humanities Press.
Pieterse, J.N. (1994). 'Globalisation as hybridisation'. *International Sociology*, 9: 161.
Pratt, M. (2000). 'The good, the bad, and the ambivalent: managing identification among Amway distributors'. *Administrative Science Quarterly*, 45: 456–93.
Ramirez, F. (2003). 'Toward a cultural anthropology of the world?' in K.M. Anderson-Levitt (ed.), *Local meanings, global schooling: anthropology and world culture theory*. New York: Palgrave Macmillan, 239–54.
Robertson, R. (1992). *Globalization: social theory and global culture*. CA: Sage Publications.
Robertson, R. (1995). 'Glocalization: time-space and homogeneity-heterogeneity', in M. Featherstone, S. Lash, and R. Robertson (eds), *Global modernities*. CA: Sage Publications, 25–44.
Robertson, R., and White, K. (eds) (2003). *Globalization: critical concepts in sociology*. London and New York: Routledge.
Watson, J. (ed.). (1997). *Golden arches east*. Stanford, CA: Stanford University Press.
Zelizer, V.A. (1979). *Morals and markets: the development of life insurance in the United States*. Piscataway, NJ: Transaction.

Part IV
Actors and Influences

15
Cosmopolitans, Harlequins, or Frankensteins?
Managers Enacting Local, Global, and Glocal Identities

Giuseppe Delmestri

You wanna be americano,
'mericano, 'mericano
but you were born in Italy!
You want to be 'alla moda'
but if you drink whiskey and soda
then you have a long hangover.
You dance a rock 'n' roll,
you play a baseball,
all cigarettes you smoke
leave 'mamma' broke!
You wanna be americano,
'mericano, 'mericano.
How can people that love you
understand you if you speak half-American?
When you are making love under the moon
how come you say 'I love you'?
From Renato Carosone and Nicola Salerno's *Tu vuò fà l'americano* (1956)

Renato Carosone's song became a hit in Italy despite its strict Neapolitan dialect. Sophia Loren sang and danced its English translation in front of Clark Gable in the American movie *It Started in Naples* (1960) and contributed to its enduring international success. This fortune is surely related to the topical issue of the song. Can different cultural models blend or is their amalgamation an unnatural phenomenon? The person described in the song is less of a versatile cosmopolitan and more of a cultural Harlequin. Is this the unavoidable destiny of all those trying to bridge cultural terrains?

Carosone's own life seems an implicit rejection of this doubt. He had worked in Africa, Europe, and America and had played with foreign musicians; his song *Torero* remained number one for 14 weeks in the US Hit Parade. In contrast to the Neapolitan-Americano described in his song, Carosone appears to have had a real cosmopolite drive: chameleonic adaptability to foreign countries, at ease with people from different cultures, and still proud of his Neapolitan origins.

Why start a chapter on managers in the global economy with a Neapolitan song? Because *Tu vuò fà l'americano* addresses issues that are particularly relevant in multinational firms in an era still under strong American influence (Zeitlin and Herrigel 2000; Frenkel and Shenhav 2003). International mergers and acquisitions, geographically distributed projects, and knowledge transfer across borders are making issues of cultural anxiety, resistance, and escalating conflicts more and more salient (Shimoni and Bergmann 2006; Styhre, Borjesson, and Wickenberg 2006; Frenkel 2008; van Marrewijk 2011; Brumana and Delmestri 2012). Just as the protagonist of Carosone's song is floating 'at the intersection of different institutional domains' (Lam 2010: 333), some individuals feel compelled or seduced to enact alien cultural conceptions, others blend indigenous and foreign ones, while still others resist and affirm their own culture:

> If you want to become a top manager, you have to Americanize yourself because the risk is that you are unable to communicate. I have been influenced in a conscious way, because, as I know the American culture, I decided to voluntarily adopt behaviors which are typical of this culture, and also in an unconscious way because one is embedded in such a deep way that sometimes one uses English words instead of Italian ones. (Italian team leader of German multinational pharmaceutical company, quoted by Delmestri 2006: 1528)

> Last year, I almost quit because of my management … I am a very strong person, I drive everybody … So I sit down and talk to my [American] boss … he is saying … 'there is another management style that you can adopt' … And it's tough for me … I have to change right away, you know, my leadership style … I still believe, even [with] the team work, we must have a leader. (Thai regional operation manager of British communication MNC in Thailand, quoted by Shimoni and Bergmann 2006: 81–2)

> I think we must not be shy to be different from the West. I think it is a combination of both whenever we think we have to adapt we will do it but inherent. We must not be shy and present our way of doing things to the world. (Indian Philips employee in Bangalore, quoted by van Marrewijk 2011: 21)

The music of *Tu vuò fà l'americano* is a successful fusion of swing and jazz with Neapolitan rhythms. The cosmopolitan Carosone created a Harlequin for a successful hit. But do all creatures assembled from alien elements turn out to be amusing Harlequins, and when do we risk ending up with a Frankenstein instead? An Italian manager of a Dutch electronic multinational told me: 'They [the Dutch and their culture] tend to be oppressive and to create androids.' Another manager working in Italy for an American electronic firm reported: 'We are made from the same mold.' The issue was seen ambivalently by these respondents. They recognized the risk of falling into unauthentic behavior, inappropriate for the local context, and, at the same time, they saw also advantages in standardization. As a manager of a US domestic appliance company put it: 'I could work in the same way also in the States.' The real problems emerged when they had to deal with locals not acculturated to or not willing to comply with the supposed global culture of transnational business, especially when, in a career move, they went back to a local firm. In that case, 'you cannot play the Americano;

otherwise you don't survive more than two months. Your boss, your colleagues and your employees will teach you the better way!' (Personnel manager at HQ of Italian MNC).

In this chapter, I treat the above-discussed issues from the standpoint of both individual managers having to navigate the quagmire of intercultural relations of cooperation and conflict, and of organizations having to deal with the complexity of global economic operations. I base the discussion both on existing sparse literature on this subject and on provisional results from an ongoing research I am leading in Austria, Brazil, China, Germany, and Italy, and from an action research I conducted in a multinational European bank. I show how national and global institutions, professional role identities, and personal dispositions interact in defining the enactment of glocalized managerial roles.

Technical versus Managerial Underpinnings of Authority Relations

The starting point of the ideas presented in this chapter were two studies published in the mid-2000s on the social construction of middle management from an institutional point of view (Delmestri and Walgenbach 2005; Delmestri 2006). Peter Walgenbach and I discussed the results obtained for Germany and Great Britain by Stewart and colleagues in the midst of the 1990s (Delmestri and Walgenbach 1994) and compared them with more recent results from Germany and Italy. Those studies showed that a main difference between Germany and Great Britain was the diverse role attributed in each culture to technical-professional knowledge (i.e., knowledge of the substantive areas like production, personnel, or marketing managed by the role incumbents) in order to legitimize positions of authority. Accordingly, in the two countries, 'management' itself experienced varying degrees of professionalization, and the career paths leading to middle management positions were different. In Germany, managerial employees followed mono-functional career paths (so-called chimney paths) and grounded their authority in technical knowledge, while their counterparts in Britain followed multifunctional career trajectories (so-called helicopter promotions) and based their acceptance on social rather than on technical skills. Italian managers resembled their German counterparts more for the important role taken by technical knowledge and chimney careers, and their British colleagues more for the prevalence of in-house informal training as opposed to German-type, externally formalized job definitions and training curricula.

Later, in the early 2000s, I conducted an additional study where I investigated the extent to which Italian middle managers working for Anglo-American firms in Italy switched to an alien conception of management, abandoning vertical mono-functional career paths and the reliance on being the technical expert for justifying positional authority (Delmestri 2006). I found that, in comparison to middle managers working in Italy for Italian or non-Anglo-American international firms, Italian managers working in Italy for Anglo-American firms tended to espouse a non-technical conception of management as a social art and to follow so-called helicopter career trajectories (i.e., circularly moving laterally and up from function to function). The switch was supported by a vast array of HRM management tools (inter-functional career paths, performance management, training, assessment centers, diversity management) interpreted as acculturation practices. Subsidiaries of non-Anglo-American (i.e., German, Finnish, French, or Japanese multinationals) presented a composition of managerial orientations that resembled more the Anglo-American managerial model than the technical one, while headquarters of Italian international firms presented an overtly technical orientation of their managerial work force. In other words, work socialization within the corporate field of foreign multinationals brought the majority of Italian managers to abandon their identification with the native conception of management and to espouse an alien model. The same process did not happen at the headquarters of Italian multinationals where managers' professional socialization confirmed the prevalent native model of technical mastery.

Despite this clear general tendency, in all firms, regardless of their nationality, I could find exceptions: technical-oriented managers were present in American firms and 'Americano' managers were present in Italian ones. Not only exceptions, but also hybrid orientations, emerged from both quantitative and qualitative data. The following questions, therefore, demanded attention:

1. How general is the opposition between technical-oriented and interpersonal-oriented management discovered comparing Great Britain with Germany and Italy first, and local and international firms in Italy later? Or, in other words, is this opposition also confirmed if we look at countries with a different position in the world system, like Brazil or China?
2. What personal factors, beyond the organizational ones, can account for the switching to an alien role enactment at the level of the individual manager?

Anglo-America versus Rest-of-the-World

With regard to the question of the generality of the opposition between technically versus managerially conceived hierarchical relationships in organizations, I present here the results of four research projects replicating and supplementing the design of my above-presented Italian study (Delmestri 2006). The four studies I conducted in cooperation with my students in the mid/late-2000s regarding Brazil, China, Germany, and Italy again, present yet unpublished preliminary findings (Arduini 2007; Brumana 2007; Degasperi 2005; Delmestri 2007). Beyond replicating my early 2000s study in different countries and times, these studies considered additional potential explanatory variables at the individual level of personal dispositions and identities that I present in the next section.

All studies used surveys of middle managers (258 in total), supplemented by interviews, group discussions, and/or open questions with subsets of the samples. The Brazilian study used mixed methods: a survey in the local language of 40 middle managers in local Brazilian firms and of 56 middle managers in eleven foreign firms from Europe, India, Japan, and the United States, supplemented by 38 interviews with middle managers and HR representatives. The Chinese study is based on 46 Chinese managers, of which 37 worked for local and 9 for international firms. All respondents attended a reputed international MBA in Guanzhou (Canton), coming from several regions of that country. They received an English survey, which might have had an influence on the results. However, all respondents had also been selected because of their language skills and had already been attending the English program for a full year. Moreover, administrating the questionnaires in the classroom ensured the correct use and understanding of the terms (see also Zhang, George, and Chan 2006). Fourteen respondents also answered to an open question on how they were influenced by experiences they had had in international firms. The German study is based on the answers of 49 German managers, of which 24 worked for local and 25 for international firms; these answers correspond to a 15 percent response rate to a German language survey sent by email to a casual sample of 315 managers. The Italian study is based on the answers of 71 Italian managers, of which 44 worked for local and 27 for international firms. The survey was in Italian. In about half of the cases, the middle managers attended a management training course where I provided them with the individual scores.

The survey measured the extent to which respondents endorsed a managerial Anglo-American concept of management or a more technical understanding of their role. I developed the measure together with Roberto Moggia (Moggia 2002) and Silvio Arduini (Arduini and Delmestri 2005). The survey items are based on the qualitative interview guidelines used by Stewart et al. (1994) and Delmestri and Walgenbach (2005). For each manager, an index was calculated. The index was developed using data on 418 middle managers in local and international firms in Italy, considering the survey questions that significantly discriminated between clusters of managers in local and international firms; all questions have face validity (for details, see Arduini and Delmestri 2005; Delmestri 2006). Each manager could, therefore, be assigned to one of four clusters: highly technical (Tec+), technical (Tec), managerial (Mgr), or highly managerial (Mgr+).

All four studies confirm the results obtained in the early 2000s (Delmestri 2006). As Figures 15.1 to 15.4 show, both the BRIC countries, Brazil and China, and the European countries, Germany and Italy, present the same pattern: a technical understanding of the role of managers prevailed in locally headquartered firms, while in foreign international firms, the majority of middle managers espoused a relational-managerial conception. Only in the Chinese sample did the majority of middle managers of both local and international firms espouse a technical conception. However, also in the Chinese case, managers working for international firms clearly espoused a higher managerial orientation than those of local firms.

The title of this section should be clear now. For local managers from all countries, the prevailing model of management is closer to what Stewart and colleagues (1994) defined as the German technical conception of authority, while only in subsidiaries of international firms, regardless of the national location of their headquarters, the Anglo-American conception prevailed. In my 2006 article, I proposed this phenomenon to be related to the global prevalence of the American discourse on management over indigenous variants, testified by its inclusion in business education around the world (through the translations of American and British textbooks and the central position of American and British journals in academia) and in management practices diffused by international consulting firms that, on their part, tend to hire graduates of business schools. Because international firms themselves usually employ business school graduates as HR managers and buy the services from the global consulting industry, these firms are subject to internal normative-professional pressures to adopt state-of-the-art practices of American origin, such as performance management, dual careers, and potential evaluation through assessment centers (see also Delmestri and Walgenbach 2009). Such practices favor identification of middle managers with American conceptions of authority relationships. Two models seem, therefore, to confront each other in the countries studied so far: the Anglo-American managerial model spanning its influence on multinational firms of any national origin on the one side, and the rest-of-the-world model emphasizing the foundation of authority on technical knowledge on the other. We tend to interpret what Stewart and colleagues (1994) defined as the German model of management as a more general model anchoring hierarchical position to technical proficiency.

However, hybridization also finds confirmation in these studies. Apart from middle managers working for local firms in Brazil and Germany, in all cases, the majority of respondents espoused in-between conceptions (i.e., moderately technical or moderately managerial). In the next section, I sketch some preliminary results of our studies showing how personal disposition and identity influence identity switching and hybridization.

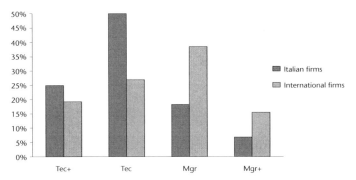

Figure 15.1 Italian managers espousing distinct role identities according to firm nationality

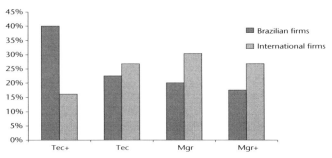

Figure 15.2 Brazilian managers espousing distinct role identities according to firm nationality

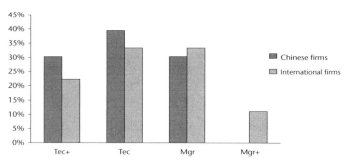

Figure 15.3 Chinese managers espousing distinct role identities according to firm nationality

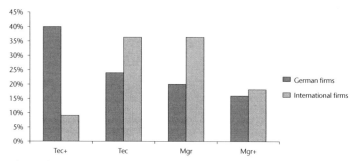

Figure 15.4 German managers espousing distinct role identities according to firm nationality

Identity Switches: Chameleonic Personality and Global Longing

Beyond the HR and organizational meso-factors discussed in the previous sections, the studies I present here concentrate on the individual level constructs of self-monitoring (using the 18-item, true–false version of the Self-Monitoring Scale; see Snyder and Gangestad 1986) and of global/local identities espoused by managers, measured using the 4-item scale developed by Miriam Erez and Efrat Gati-Shokef (Erez and Gati 2004; Shokef and Erez 2006, 2008).

Self-monitoring is a personality dimension denoting the willingness and ability of individuals to adapt their public and self image and their behavior to situational cues deriving from their environment (Snyder 1974, 1987; Gangestad and Snyder 2000). Self-monitoring affects organizationally relevant outcomes, such as leader emergence in groups (Dobbins, Long, Dedrick, and Clemons 1990), and organizational and managerial behavior (Kilduff and Day 1994; Mehra, Kilduff, and Brass 2001). In particular, high self-monitors are more likely than low self-monitors to obtain internal and cross-company promotions, change employers, and move locations (Kilduff and Day 1994). The antecedents lie in the higher need for social appropriateness, higher attention to situational cues, higher social competence in terms of expression control, and higher variability in self-presentation and enactment of social scripts typical of high self-monitors in comparison to low self-monitors. While high self-monitors have a chameleonic disposition to their public and self image, low self-monitors tend to remain true to themselves (i.e., to their self-conception) independent of the situation. In a new situation, high self-monitors would ask themselves, 'What does the situation require me to be?', while low self-monitors would ask, 'How can I preserve my identity in the new situation?' Our expectation was that high self-monitors would more readily enact a foreign institutionalized model when they work for an international firm.

We found that high self-monitors are more likely to espouse an Anglo-American managerial identity that is alien to their national culture, but only in MNCs, where this identity is institutionalized as the proper way of being a manager. In local firms, high self-monitors espouse a technical conception of management in the same way as low self-monitors. This result testifies to the chameleonic character of high self-monitors, as they tend to more easily react to situational cues, understand the situation, and adapt their self-perception to what is consistently expected from them. Apparently, the organizational re-socialization apparatus discussed above is more effective when directed towards individuals with chameleonic personality dispositions.

Shokef and Erez (2006) define global identity as an individual's sense of belonging to and identification with the world society, while local identity is the identification with and the belonging to the national community in which the person has grown up. Identifications with the global and with the local are not conceived as mutually exclusive, giving rise to four possible identities: local, global, marginalized, and glocal. An exclusive local identification represents a segregation type of acculturation, meaning that managers would preserve their own national values but reject the values predominant in world society. Opposite this identification is an exclusive global identification, meaning that managers would assimilate the new culture but reject their own. A marginal identity refers to a situation when individuals are 'lost in transition' (i.e., they are neither attracted to the global culture nor to their native national one). A glocal identity refers to the integration of a strong attraction to the global community paired with the preservation of the native culture. Our interest in middle managers' identification with local and/or global identities lies in the attempt to understand the role of individual processes as compared with organizational HRM-interventions.

Managers working in MNCs are more likely to display a global identity than managers working in local firms, confirming the consistent results reported by Shokef and Erez (2008). However, in our samples, the middle managers displaying a higher identification with a global identity in MNCs are *not* more likely to be chameleonic high self-monitors than true-to-themselves low self-monitors. The missing relationship tells us that the higher number of managers with a global identity in international firms seems not to be due to their peculiar ability to adapt to the values prevalent in that context, which is an often-advanced explanation (Shokef and Erez 2006, 2008). An alternative one seems equally plausible: managers who identify themselves with global values choose international firms as employers because this offers them the possibility to be more true to themselves than if they worked for a local firm. To be sure, more solid evidence would come from longitudinal studies concentrating on change and endurance of identification patterns. However, the plausibility of the interpretation paired with our results can offer new interesting avenues of research. Longing for global values would be the mechanism that drives globally identified managers into MNCs. Once exposed to the institutional apparatus of control typical of multinationals, the more chameleonic among the mangers would be those who more readily switch to an Anglo-American conception of management, abandoning, in the move, the conception of authority assumed during primary cultural socialization. A global identity in itself would not necessarily favor this switch.

Sociologists Berger and Luckmann (1966: 190–1), concentrating on the power of secondary socialization in professions, had already envisioned this possibility. They saw modern individuals as 'those with "hidden selves", the "traitors", those who have alternated or are alternating between discrepant worlds', or as the individualists who emerge 'as a specific social type who has at least the potential to migrate between a number of available worlds and who has deliberately and awarely constructed a self out of the "material" provided by a number of available identities.'

The psychologist Bennett (1986, 1993; for the similar construct of cultural intelligence, see Earley and Ang 2003) similarly addressed the issue of cultural sensitivity in cross-cultural encounters. In the next section, I will abandon the empirical ground of the studies conducted with the aim to replicate and enlarge my early 2000s study (Delmestri 2006) and, on the basis of the findings from an action research, address the issue of cultural sensitivity. I propose a theoretical framework on the processes of hybridization and global acculturation that combines the strands spun so far.

Cultural Sensitivity, Global Identity, and Chameleonic Managers

At the end of 2009, I conducted an action research in one of the divisions of an international bank active in several European countries. The research was aimed at understanding and tackling the problem of reciprocal stereotypization and of conflicts in cross-national working groups. In order to understand and solve the problems, we decided to organize eleven workshops, one with the top management of the divisions, the other ten with the middle managers involved into cross-border operations. All 240 managers were administered the Intercultural Development Inventory (IDI), a measure of cultural sensitivity (Hammer, Bennett, and Wiseman 2003). All of them received individual feedback and participated in a 2.5-day workshop with the aim of reflecting on cultural differences and proposing rules, tools, and attitudes to solve problems related to cultural misunderstandings. The proposals that emerged from the workshops were discussed by top management and some were implemented with the effect that problems due to conflicts in international teams started to subside.

The IDI measures intercultural sensitivity from low (ethnocentrism) to high (ethnorelativism) in five stages. The higher the cultural sensitivity, the more a manager is expected to be effective in dealing with colleagues from other cultures. Low cultural sensitivity ranges from denial (when one's own culture is experienced as the only real one), to defense (when one's own native, or adopted, culture is experienced as the only good one) and minimization (when one's own cultural world views are experienced as universal, and cultural differences are minimized, trivialized, or romanticized). High cultural sensitivity can assume the state of acceptance (when one's own culture is experienced as just one of a number of equally complex worldviews) or adaptation (when the experience of another culture yields perception and behavior appropriate to that culture) (see Bennett 1986, 1993). Particularly interesting is the state of minimization, because it does not simply correspond to a situation of intermediate cultural sensitivity. Minimization is a situation in which one considers all humans being the same, not only in terms of rights, but also of values and needs. A person in minimization recognizes that cultural differences exist, but the latter are considered as not essential, but as romantic or trivial surface expressions, while deep essential elements of humanity are stated as uniform and universal. And, because managers in a state of minimization do not have an elaborated sense of cultural difference, they tend to project their own values on others, implicitly assuming the universality of their own culture.

I have highlighted the state of minimization because the results of our 240 IDI questionnaires showed a prevalence of this stage among the top managers of the bank's division. In the workshop with the top management, the Division Head and his deputy supported the view that the only relevant cultural difference in Europe is language, that all European employees should know how to behave in a business context, and that cultural differences were not an issue. Only after the end of the module and the individual feedbacks, they recognized that their employees worked in countries spanning four out of nine world cultural clusters (see Ronen and Shenkar 1985; Peng, Zhou, and York 2006). In a particular insightful moment, the Head of the Division realized that not acknowledging differences and assuming that all would spontaneously follow the precepts of a common business culture was one of the causes that had led to the conflicts they wanted to resolve. In the subsequent meetings with middle managers, he underscored this issue. Moreover, he created a video interview and posted it on the intranet, in which he put forth the idea that the development of a common culture out of the diverse ones constituting the galaxy of the bank would no more be assumed but had to be proactively realized by all employees during cross-national encounters.

The culture that had caused so many interpersonal problems and conflicts to the bank division was directly related to the Division Head's minimizing attitude towards cultural differences. Paradoxically, this executive was the exemplar of a cosmopolitan, globally minded, and multilingual person, a born-global type: he was born in the Near East, studied in a Germanic country, worked in a Latin country, and was pushing for the expansion of the bank into Central and East Europe. During the initial top management workshop, he maintained that all people should feel part of the same world community without losing touch with their local origins. However, as it became clear later, this was not enough. Identification with the global business culture and with one's native national culture was not enough for successfully navigating the multicultural environment of European society. The specific values of one's own native culture and those of the global world culture did not exhaust the existing values and norms structuring cooperation in different countries. To be at ease at home and in the global business jet set did not mean being at ease in third local cultures as well.

Although we cannot generalize from a single, albeit interesting, case, the findings from the reported action research allow conjecturing a more nuanced model of cross-cultural and cross-institutional encounters. High global and local identification (i.e., the glocal integration of a strong attraction to the global community paired with the preservation of the native culture) (Shokef and Erez 2006) seem not to be a sufficient measure of cultural intelligence. This supposition finds additional support in the missing relationship between global identification and self-monitoring reported above. Endorsing a global identity does not automatically mean being adaptable to unknown cultures.

In the following, I venture to present a theoretical model integrating all of these different strands (see Figure 15.5). Following Shokef and Erez (2006), I do not consider identifications with the global and with the local as mutually exclusive. I consider the dimension of cultural sensitivity as a way to unpack what in their model is not distinguished (i.e., global identification and adaptability to third local cultures). The proposed model conjectures eight possible identities. To illustrate some of these identities, I quote the interviews conducted with middle managers in the four countries. The quotes should be understood as plausible rationalizations or theories in use by respondents confronted with the complexity of intercultural relationships.

A *marginal identity* refers to a situation when individuals are really 'lost in transition', meaning they are neither attracted to the global culture nor to their native national one and they do not have the motivation and the knowledge to understand and learn new cultures. Instead, the situation of missing local and global identification paired with cultural sensitivity can be conceived for managers that act as real *chameleons*, always malleable and adaptable to new cultural contexts. Lacking their own role models and convictions (i.e., the enabling side

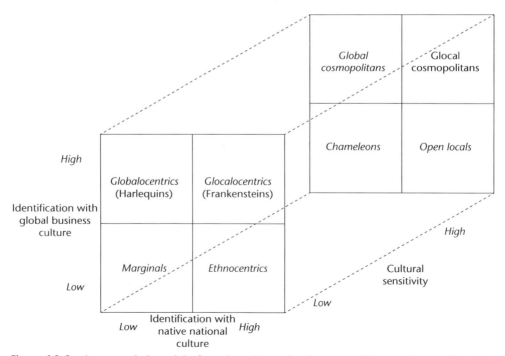

Figure 15.5 An expanded model of acculturation to local communities and the world society

of institutions) would make it unlikely for these managers to become seeds of institutional change. An exclusive local identification represents *ethnocentrism* when managers experience their own native culture as the only good one, as in the following quote:

> Brazilians take it with 'jeitinho', more relaxed, without losing commitment. Americans sometimes do not know the person who sits beside them. In Brazil, we go for the barbecues all together. (Local manager of foreign firm; Arduini 2007: 102)

However, when exclusively local identification is paired with openness and active involvement with other cultures, this can give rise to dynamic identities as *open locals*. This can particularly happen when a sensitive person in middle to lower manager position is exposed to a new foreign work culture without having previously had the opportunity to enter the jet set of global business culture, and when the new culture is not the global business culture itself but a third local culture. This situation happens often to middle managers with high technical expertise who are asked to transfer valuable technical knowledge to a third country. In this case, we are not dealing with the typical milieu of expatriate top managers, but of down-to-earth, cross-cultural encounters, as the following quotation illustrates:

> I worked for 10 years in the German subsidiary of a Japanese corporation. This experience made me more open to the world and, to use an exaggerated word, more cosmopolitan—thanks to travels to the Far East (Japan, Taiwan, China) and to the interaction with foreign cultures ... I am more open to people and I have discarded stereotypes I may have had. (German middle manager working for foreign firm; Degasperi 2005: 82)

The identity of the *glocal cosmopolitan* mostly resembles Shokef and Erez's (2006) glocal identity concept; it refers to the integration of a strong attraction to the global community paired with the preservation of the native culture and a high cultural sensitivity for additional local cultures. The following quote illustrates this nicely:

> The possibility to work internationally is the most exciting thing in the world; you do not have to give up your cultural roots. This becomes even clearer when you have small children: a good mix of internationality and *Bodenständigkeit* [German: being down-to-earth, solid, rooted] is a good approach ... For the kids, it becomes taken for granted that one can work everywhere in the world and that many conversations can take place in a language different from the mother tongue. (German middle manager working for foreign firm; Degasperi 2005: 84)

The last three identities to be presented—the global cosmopolitans, the globalocentrics, and the glocalocentrics—are the most interesting because they represent innovations to existing theory. *Global cosmopolitans* and *globalocentrics* represent a growing group of people in actual world society (Brookfield Global Relocation Services 2011, cit. by Shaffer, Kraimer, Chen, and Bolino 2012). More and more bi-cultural or multicultural children missing local roots, at least in the usual sense of national or regional roots, are born from mixed couples (Piaskowska and Trojanowski 2012). These children are multilingual, attend English-speaking schools together with other children from several nationalities, and I suggest that they have two possibilities in adulthood. The first possibility is they may become attached to the third culture emerging from the multinational and multilingual encounters in a rigid way. In this case, they become a sort of ethnocentric. I suggest, inspired from the evidence collected in the studies summarized above, that the global culture they experience becomes the only good culture, while they develop a sense of discomfort with locals, as narrow-minded people who are not open to modernity. While they long for the missed opportunity to feel local in any place, they also are aloof and ineffective when dealing with people who do not share their same experience. I name this kind of identity *globalocentric* (i.e., global, but in some way, ethnocentric). The intercultural orientation is minimization, and the risk of ridicule is imminent, as the harlequinesque Americano protagonist of Carosone's song exemplifies. The following quotes illustrate how such an identity orientation could find expression:

> There is no real difference between different people, no matter whether you come from the US, Britain or another country, people in every country are self-interested and rational, and this is the foundation of human being ... [N]ationality, or culture, is just the coat of people, that may decorate or make up the inside, may try to draw others' attention, or show the trend or the fashion to show up; in one word, culture is just a tool! ... Maybe the best way for organizations is letting it be what it is. Maybe organization is the same as dis-organization. Just as to love is to harm. (Chinese manager, December 2005)

> An image to describe my company is an oasis: a mess in the streets, but when you enter the IT firms in India it is like Microsoft in the US. It is like moving to another planet. Indian IT firms are islands of excellence. I prefer the oasis. (Local manager of foreign firm; Arduini 2007: 102)

We may further speculate that *glocalocentrics* are managers who, while remaining attached to their local roots, are able to understand the values and norms of the new global culture. However, from a minimization perspective, they consider these values as universal and are not sensitive to third local cultures. This identity may be misunderstood as cosmopolitan, while it represents a false cosmopolitanism, a double-ethnocentric attitude—that the native national local attachment is preserved to give color to a rigidly constructed corset of values of norms of foreign origin. In an admittedly excessive way, I name these as the Frankensteins; the following quotation exemplifies a worldview consistent with this identity:

> The Italian manager works more in emergency with improvisation. The German is slower, everything has to be programmed, but this is a more solid approach. The American to the contrary decides and then changes every week, there is no space for either Italian creativity or German solidity. (Italian marketing manager working for the subsidiary of a German pharmaceutical firm; field notes 2004)

The second possibility for bi-cultural and multicultural people is that they come to terms with their nostalgia for local roots and accept the relativity of the global third culture they experienced in their childhood. In this case, they become *global cosmopolitans*, uprooted but flexible and principled agents of cultural bridging and amelioration through cultural encounter. They may even become glocal cosmopolitans if they decide to manage their identity-portfolio and identify mostly with one of the local cultures they experienced while preserving their attachment to the global culture and their openness to third local cultures.

Discussion and Conclusions

In this chapter, I have expanded the work on the cultural typification of managerial identities and on its influence on the structuring of organizations and on the roles of managers (Stewart et al. 1994; Delmestri and Walgenbach 2005). In this tradition, typified managerial identities are macro institutions connecting micro and meso levels in organizations: the person, the professional role, and organizational structures. Such macro institutions, which have for a long time derived their legitimacy from the national institutional environment, are more and more subject on one side to the process of globalization (i.e., the international diffusion of templates and ideologies on rationalized management roles and functions) (Drori et al. 2006), and to the process of glocalization on the other (i.e., the blending of global and local elements that leads to the co-construction of the global and the local) (Robertson 1992). Through a reflection on existing literature and on preliminary results and findings from my own studies, I have discussed how the glocalization process of managerial identities unfolds and the challenges it poses for the individuals on one side and for the organizations on the other.

The opposition between technical-oriented and interpersonal-oriented management first discovered when comparing Great Britain with Germany seems to be of a very general character. Not only in Italy, but also in Brazil and China and in MNCs of various national origins, this distinction seems of relevance. Particularly owing to the success of MNCs, academia, and consultancies of US origin after the Second World War, a new model of management has spread that spurs imitation, opposition, and hybridization. Not only organizational factors, such as career systems and differentiation of structures, seem to account for the adoption of the American model, but individual personal dispositions also play an important role. In particular, the personal disposition of self-monitoring facilitates the working of the acculturation apparatus of MNCs. Identification with global work values and cultural sensitivity seem, however, to be at play when the role of managers should go beyond that of chameleonic adapters to that of culturally sensitive cosmopolitan agents of institutional innovation. The adoption of an alien model or its hybridization can indeed have negative consequences for organizations, spurring conflicts and misunderstandings when cultural Harlequins and cultural Frankensteins are misunderstood as cosmopolitans. This focus on individual level mechanisms of diffusion and hybridization can enrich neo-institutional sociological perspectives on globalization (Drori et al. 2006).

In this chapter, I also addressed, at least partly, four of the five 'future issues' for cross-cultural organizational behavior identified by Gelfand, Erez, and Aycan (2007: 499). First, my focus moved from intracultural comparisons to the study of the 'dynamics of cultural interfaces' in multicultural and multinational corporations. Second, I pointed towards the importance of studying typified role identities as 'neglected sources of cultural differences'. Third, I highlighted the importance of considering the additional meso level of analysis of the organization and its practices. And finally, I moved from a 'primary emphasis on differences in cultural values and management practices to an additional focus on similarities in values and management practices in the global work context'. The latter point is particularly relevant in advancing our understanding of cross-cultural organizational behavior. Indeed, the classical cross-cultural paradigm (Hofstede 1980) tended to neglect that social identities enacted by managers could vary from their typical national cultural pattern because of the salience of a national culture of another territory, like the United States. Individuals can indeed be bearers of more than one national culture (Hannerz 1996; Haas 2006). Within the cross-cultural paradigm, born in an age, the 1970s, in which nation-states were still the dominant organizing principle of social and political life, this possibility was less thinkable.

In the emerging contemporary globalized and post-disciplinary societies, individuals are better seen as 'dividuals' (Deleuze 1995; cit. by Kallinikos 2003). Contemporary social sciences, indeed, present human beings as assemblages of independent, loosely connected modules of attitudes and behaviors of diverse cultural and institutional origins. Leung et al. (2005) argue that current research in cognitive psychology shows that the human mind is fluid and adaptive and is engaged in active, dynamic interaction with the environment. This conception of the human mind gives rise to a dynamic view of culture and institutions, which contrasts sharply with oversocialized views of individuals equipped with minds programmed once and for all by their local culture and their embedding institutional context. This dynamic view argues that culture is represented by cognitive structures and processes that are sensitive to environmental influences. National culture and institutions are only one of different potential identity strands and, among these strands, opposite cultural and institutional templates also coexist and hybridize. Such was the case for the Neapolitan author and singer Carosone, in contrast to the *Americano* in his song.

References

Arduini, S.C. (2007). 'The organizational role of Brazilian middle managers'. Unpublished dissertation, Bocconi University, Milan (supervisor G. Delmestri).

Arduini, S.C., and Delmestri, G. (2005). 'New paradoxes of management: between global leadership and cultural specificity'. Paper presented at the Academy of Management Conference, Honolulu, 2005.

Bennett, M.J. (1986). 'A developmental approach to training for intercultural sensitivity'. *International Journal of Intercultural Relations*, 10(2): 179–96.

Bennett, M.J. (1993). 'Towards ethnorelativism: a developmental model of intercultural sensitivity', in M. Paige (ed.), *Education for the intercultural experience*. Yarmouth, ME: Intercultural Press.

Berger, P., and Luckmann, T. (1966). *The social construction of reality*. New York: Doubleday Anchor.

Brookfield Global Relocation Services. (2011). *2011 Global Relocation Trends Survey*. Woodridge, IL: Brookfield Global Relocation Services.

Brumana, M. (2007). 'Comportamento manageriale, identità e personalità. Uno studio in aziende locali e internazionali'. Unpublished Bachelor Thesis, Bergamo University, Bergamo (supervisor G. Delmestri).

Brumana, M., and Delmestri, G. (2012). 'Divergent glocalization in a multinational enterprise. Institutional-bound strategic change in European and US subsidiaries facing the late-2000 recession'. *Journal of Strategy and Management*, 5(2): 124–53.

Degasperi, M. (2005). 'Middle managers in Germania: ruolo, carriera e identità globale'. Unpublished Master Thesis, Bocconi University, Milan (supervisor G. Delmestri).

Deleuze, G. (1995). *Negotiations*. New York: Columbia University Press.

Delmestri, G. (2006). 'Streams of inconsistent institutional influences: middle managers as carriers of multiple identities'. *Human Relations*, 59(11), 1515–41.

Delmestri, G. (2007). 'Multiple identities, self-monitoring and careers in MNCs and local firms in China and Germany'. Paper presented at the 3rd New Institutionalism Workshop, Bergamo University.

Delmestri, G., and Walgenbach, P. (2005). 'Mastering techniques or brokering knowledge? Middle managers in Germany, Great Britain and Italy'. *Organization Studies*, 26, 197–220.

Delmestri, G., and Walgenbach, P. (2009). 'Interference among institutional influences and technical-economic conditions: the adoption of the assessment center in French, German, Italian, UK and US international firms'. *International Journal of Human Resource Management*, 20(4): 885–911.

Dobbins, G.H., Long, W.S., Dedrick, E.J., and Clemons, T.C. (1990). 'The role of self-monitoring and gender on leader emergence: a laboratory and field study'. *Journal of Management*, 16: 609–18.

Drori, G., Meyer, J., and Hwang, H. (eds). (2006). *Globalization and organization: world society and organizational change*. Oxford: Oxford University Press.

Earley, P.C., and Ang, S. (2003). *Cultural intelligence: individual interactions across cultures*. Stanford, CA: Stanford University Press.

Erez, M., and Gati, E. (2004). 'A dynamic, multi-level model of culture: from the micro level of the individual to the macro level of a global culture'. *Applied Psychology: An International Review*, 53(4): 583–98

Frenkel, M. (2008). 'The multinational corporation as a third space: rethinking international management discourse on knowledge transfer through Homi Bhabha'. *Academy of Management Review*, 33(4): 924.

Frenkel, M., and Shenhav, Y. (2003). 'From Americanization to colonization: the diffusion of productivity models revisited'. *Organization Studies*, 24: 537–61.

Gangestad, S.W., and Snyder, M. (2000). 'Self-monitoring: appraisal and reappraisal'. *Psychological Bulletin*, 126(4): 530–55.

Gelfand, M.J., Erez, M., and Aycan, Z. (2007). 'Cross-cultural organizational behavior'. *Annual Review of Psychology*, 58: 479–514.

Haas, M.R. (2006). 'Acquiring and applying knowledge in transnational teams: the roles of cosmopolitans and locals'. *Organization Science*, 17(3): 367–84.

Hammer, M.R., Bennett, M.J., and Wiseman, R. (2003). 'Measuring intercultural sensitivity: the intercultural development inventory', in R.M. Paige (guest ed.), special issue on intercultural development. *International Journal of Intercultural Relations*, 27(4): 421–43.

Hannerz, U. (1996). *Transnational connections. Culture, people, places*. London-New York: Routledge.

Hofstede, G. (1980). *Culture's consequences: international differences in work-related values*. Beverly Hills, CA: Sage.

Kallinikos, J. (2003). 'Work, human agency and organizational forms: an anatomy of fragmentation'. *Organization Studies*, 24(4): 595–618.

Kilduff, M., and Day, D.V. (1994). 'Do chameleons get ahead? The effects of self-monitoring on managerial careers'. *Academy of Management Journal*, 37(4): 1047–60.

Lam, A. (2010). 'From "Ivory Tower traditionalists" to "Entrepreneurial scientists"? Academic scientists in fuzzy university-industry boundaries'. *Social Studies of Science*, 40(2): 307–40.

Leung, K., Bhagat, R.S., Buchan, N.R., Erez, M., and Gibson, C.B. (2005). 'Culture and international business: recent advances and their implications for future research'. *Journal of International Business Studies*, 36: 357–78.

Mehra, A., Kilduff, M., and Brass, D.J. (2001). 'The social networks of high and low self-monitors: implications for workplace performance'. *Administrative Science Quarterly*, 46(1): 121–46.

Moggia, R. (2002). 'Conoscenza manageriale e istituzioni nazionali: il caso delle aziende statunitensi in Italia'. Unpublished Master Thesis, Bocconi University, Milan (supervisor G. Delmestri).

Peng, M.W., Zhou, Y., and York, A.S. (2006). 'Behind make or buy decisions in export strategy: a replication and extension of Trabold'. *Journal of World Business*, 41: 289–300.

Piaskowska, D., and Trojanowski, G. (2012). 'Twice as smart? The importance of managers' formative-years' international experience for their international orientation and foreign acquisition decisions'. *British Journal of Management*, article first published online. doi: 10.1111/j.1467-8551.2012.00831.x.

Robertson, R. (1992). *Globalization: social theory and global culture*. London: Sage.

Ronen, S., and Shenkar, O. (1985). 'Clustering countries on attitudinal dimensions: a review and synthesis'. *Academy of Management Review*, 10, 435–55.

Shaffer, M.A., Kraimer, M.L., Chen, Y.-P., and Bolino, M.C. (2012). 'Choices, challenges, and career consequences of global work experiences: a review and future agenda'. *Journal of Management*, 38(4), 1282–327.

Shimoni, B., and Bergmann, H. (2006). 'Managing in a changing world: from multiculturalism to hybridization—the production of hybrid management cultures in Israel, Thailand, and Mexico'. *Academy of Management Perspectives*, 20(3), 76–89.

Shokef, E., and Erez, M. (2006). 'Global work culture and global identity, as a platform for a shared understanding in multicultural teams', in E.A.M. Mannix, M. Neale, and Y. Chen (eds), *Research in managing groups and teams: national culture and groups*. Elsevier Science Press, Oxford.

Shokef, E., and Erez, M. (2008). 'Cultural intelligence and global identity in multicultural teams', in S. Ang and L. Van Dyne (eds), *Handbook of cultural intelligence: theory, measurement, and applications*. Armonk, NY: M.E. Sharpe, 177–91.

Snyder, M. (1974). 'Self-monitoring of expressive behavior'. *Journal of Personality and Social Psychology*, 30: 526–37.

Snyder, M. (1987). *Public appearances/public realities: The psychology of self-monitoring*. New York: Freeman.

Snyder, M, and Gangestad, S. (1986). 'On the nature of self-monitoring: matters of assessment, matters of validity'. *Journal of Personality and Social Psychology*, 51(1):125–39

Stewart, R., Barsoux, J.-L., Kieser, A., Ganter, H.-D., and Walgenbach, P. (1994). *Managing in Britain and Germany*. London: Macmillan.

Styhre, A., Borjesson, S., and Wickenberg, J. (2006). 'Managed by the other: cultural anxieties in two Anglo-Americanized Swedish firms'. *International Journal of Human Resource Management*, 17(7): 1293–306.

van Marrewijk, A. (2011). 'Cross-cultural management: hybridization of Dutch–Indian work practices in geographically distributed IT projects'. *International Journal of Business Anthropology*, 2(2): 15–35.

Zeitlin, J., and Herrigel, G. (2000). *Americanization and its limits: reworking U.S. technology and management in post-war Europe and Japan*. Oxford and New York: Oxford University Press.

Zhang, Y., George, J.M., and Chan, T.-S. (2006). 'The paradox of dueling identities: the case of local senior executives in MNC subsidiaries'. *Journal of Management*, 32(3), 400–25.

16
Personal Rule in Asia's Family-controlled Business Groups

Michael Carney

Introduction

The archetypal corporate form of organization in Asia's rapidly developing economies is the family-controlled business group (FBG). In these organizations, transactions with business partners are governed by norms of relational contracting, and financial control is firmly concentrated into the hands of entrepreneurial founders and their extended families, an authority structure described as personal-rule (Üsdiken 2010). Managerial theories of the firm consider the persistence of personal-rule in large modern corporations as an anomaly, since the progressive bureaucratization of modern industrial economies is expected to depersonalize organizational authority, as represented, for example, by the displacement of founder entrepreneurs as the leaders of large firms and their replacement with professional managers operating at arms-length from shareholders (Claessens et al. 2000). In most of Asia's industrialized economies, neither the separation of ownership and control nor the depersonalization of authority has occurred in most major public corporations, with the notable exception of Japan.

In the wake of the Asian financial crisis of 1997, international organizations, such as the World Bank and the International Monetary Fund, applied substantial pressure on Asian states to implement corporate sector reforms and encouraged firms to adopt global standards of good governance. Subsequently, there has been a substantial increase in firm ownership by institutional investors throughout the region (Carney and Child 2013), who typically demand higher standards of managerial oversight and transparency. Asia's FBGs are also intimately integrated into the global economy as partners to multinational enterprises in a variety of joint ventures and strategic alliances, and more recently, through their own foreign direct investment activities. Despite external pressures and exposure to alternative forms of governance, Asia's FBGs retain their personalized authority structures.

Nevertheless, these organizations have not been immune to the influences of globalization. Asia's FBGs have freely incorporated numerous technologies and management practices originating in Western organizations. FBGs have successfully imitated managerial practices, such as total quality management, process engineering, and Six Sigma production, whose implementation is consistent with the authority relation implicit in personal rule. However, FBGs have not imitated corporate and organizational structures, such as professional management, multidivisional organization, and independent corporate boards, whose implementation depends upon the existence of robust principal–agent relations. The integrity of robust principal–agent relations depends heavily upon the existence of high-quality institutions, such as rule of law and other structural devices that protect property rights and allow individuals to make credible commitments to one another. These institutions and structures are often underdeveloped in emerging markets, a phenomenon frequently characterized as an 'institutional void' (Khanna and Rivkin 2001), and families may be reluctant to put much faith in organizational structures that depend upon robust principal–agent relations. In the following, I outline leading theories of the emergence and functioning of Asia's FBGs. I explain that personally ruled FBGs are likely to remain prevalent in the region because political leaders have made institutional choices that protect their property rights, but institutional choices are inconsistent with the establishment of principal–agent relationships in business and, therefore, inhibit the adoption of organizational practices that depend upon them.

The Emergence and Functioning of Asia's Family Business Groups

Following years of post-colonial conflict and Cold War tensions, newly independent Asian governments sought to enhance their legitimacy by strengthening their economies through strategies of industrialization. The legacy of colonial rule left wariness of foreigners and, in any event, the process of decolonization entailed the departure of the business elite, engineers, and public servants, leaving a vacuum of organizational and technological know-how. Thus, the initial conditions of late industrialization were marked by the absence of the capabilities needed by firms to compete successfully in international markets (Amsden 1989; Hobday 1995).

Theories of late industrialization, along with organizational-based theories, such as transactions cost and the resource-based view, suggest FBGs play several interrelated roles in the process of late industrialization. Not all Asian business groups are family-controlled business groups. Japanese keiretsu are based either upon a main bank or a major corporation, and many of China's business groups are nominally state-owned, but their heavy reliance upon relational contracting and their close identification with a charismatic CEO/leader is strongly suggestive of an underlying 'family-like' character.

Late Industrialization Theory

Based on the premise that private firms acting alone could not accumulate the capital and organizational capabilities to compete successfully with resource-rich Western multinationals, late industrialization theory suggests competent and autonomous states can initiate late industrialization by organizing a 'big push' (Wade 1990). A big push entails the simultaneous creation of large firms and supporting industries with several complementary institutions, including a strong public bureaucracy and the protection of property rights sufficient to induce large-scale private investment. Successive Asian states adopted a version of state-led industrialization (Perkins 1994) in which central planning ministries orchestrated and coordinated the allocation of scarce capital investments to high-return projects. Business groups materialized in these conditions as government sought to co-opt a small number of local business families into their planned economic development.

The diffusion of the idea of business groups as a vehicle for organizing economic development resulted from an institutional process of mimetic isomorphism (Granovetter 2005). In what is no doubt one of the earliest instances of glocalization, Imperial Japan sought to emulate the German model of capitalism. Germany's early industrialization relied upon an organizational innovation called *konzerns*, large, multi-business units that successively developed new industries. The Japanese version of this innovation was called *zaibatsu*, or 'family konzerns', family-controlled business groups that focused on developing technologically dynamic and capital-intensive industries. The *zaibatsu* system provided their affiliated firms with much autonomy to react entrepreneurially to business opportunities and to coordinate the resources needed to grow the firm. The result was a simple division of labor: 'a decentralized network of industrial firms taking care of the complex logistics involved in managing diverse technological and industrial activities and a head office taking on the functions of overall strategic planning and resource allocation' (Gerlach 1997: 263).

The process of imitation continued after WWII, as late industrialization unfolded in Korea, Taiwan, Hong Kong, and Singapore. Granovetter (2005) suggests that in imitating colonial-era Japanese *zaibatsu*, the patriarchs of elite Korean business families wished to appear modern and dynamic, so they mimicked the practices and structures that were standard in their reference group. Similarly, British-owned and controlled business groups were a familiar organizational form from colonial-era Southeast Asia (Jones and Wale 1998). During the 1980s, the late development model was adopted in Southeast Asia, as Indonesia, Malaysia, and Thailand each organized business groups to facilitate export-led development strategies. Later still, business groups became the norm in China and Vietnam (Schneider 2010).

Transactions Cost Theory

When protections for property rights are poorly developed, the execution of complex and long-term transactions, such as those based on credit, across market boundaries, are costly. Fully functioning property rights can take many decades to develop (Campbell 2004). In these institutional conditions, transactions cost theory predicts that FBGs can serve as a substitute for missing property rights protection by establishing communities of trusted business partners in which affiliates can confidently trade with one another. In this respect, business groups serve as a 'haven where property markets are respected' (Khanna and Palepu 1997). The main branch of transactions cost literature focuses upon missing institutions in capital markets. In this perspective, the absence of liquid equity and debt markets is an obstacle to growth, as firms lack sources of external financing to fund profitable opportunities. Business groups can step in to function as a quasi-internal capital market. The group can identify new businesses with good opportunities but lacking in finance, allocate credit, monitor its use, and share risk over a large number of ventures, similar to a venture capitalist in more advanced economies (Almeida and Wolfenzon 2006). The family owners of such groups are particularly efficient and vigilant monitors of capital because their own wealth is often at stake in these investments.

Compared with other types of owners, families enjoy competitive advantages in substituting for missing property rights. Individuals, who are known in their communities for honoring their contracts, are well placed to initiate the group-formation process. Gilson (2007) proposes that reputable families possess the characteristics to undertake relational contracts in jurisdictions where commercial law is weak. The effectiveness of relational contracting depends upon two conditions: mutual expectation of recurrent exchange over an extended time horizon and the ability to observe and detect breach of contract. A family's long-term attachment to its businesses can signal that it will be around in the future and that it will exhibit forbearance from short-term opportunism contractual breaches with partners; if it is detected, it will pay a reputational penalty. The reputational mechanism extends beyond credit markets and is generalizable to all types of factor markets. Several studies show that business groups function as a transactions cost reducing mechanism for markets in entrepreneurial talent, technology, and managerial capabilities (Chang and Hong 2000; Khanna and Rivkin 2001).

Reputational advantages are particularly valuable to firms beyond a particular community. For example, high-technology foreign firms seeking to enter markets where property rights are weak may be deterred from doing so by concerns about opportunism and lack of protection for their intellectual property. In these circumstances, reputable FBGs are attractive business partners for foreign firms because they will typically prefer to trade with a partner with a valuable reputation, as they have stronger incentives to honor their contracts.

Resource-based View of Business Groups

The resource-based view focuses on the organizational process of combining internally and externally available resources. The core idea is that in emerging markets, business group structure more readily facilitates learning about technology and creates a structure for technology spillovers across affiliated firms, as group managers successively transfer the newly acquired knowledge into multiple, quasi-autonomous business affiliates (Guillen 2000). A related idea is that much of the learning in emerging market firms is based upon imitation. When domestic firms have limited technological and organizational capability and when government is encouraging them to enter international markets, firms may grow much faster by importing and assimilating existing know-how from more advanced countries. Because know-how already exists, the major task is to coordinate and combine knowledge flows with available capital and physical resources to perform the investment for successful imitation.

The main organizational process for imitative learning is characterized as developing a 'project management capability' (Amsden and Hikino 1994) that facilitates the efficient combination of relatively generic resources to repeatedly enter new industries, often unrelated to one another. Amsden (1989) describes how the process of repeat industry entry process unfolds at Hyundai Heavy Industries:

> …a new subsidiary would most likely be established by a task force typically formed at the group level and comprising qualified managers, engineers, and even supervisors from existing companies within the group. In the case of Hyundai, for example, managers from its construction arm were transferred to its shipbuilding arm to aid in project management. Later, engineers from its shipbuilding arm, who had knowledge of anticorrosion, were loaned to its automobile affiliates where a new paint operation was coming on stream. (p. 128)

The learning by imitation experience was repeated across Asia's newly industrializing economies. In the first instance, firms acquired basic manufacturing and quality control skills in electronics and medium-tech industries (Hobday 1995). To do so, they formed a variety of inter-organizational linking mechanisms, such as performing subcontracting and original equipment manufacturing (OEM), licensing products and brands, and sending technical personnel on overseas reconnaissance missions. Hobday says, 'OEM and subcontracting systems acted as a training school for (Asian) firms, helping them to couple export market needs with foreign technological learning' (1995: 1172). As Asian firms approached the efficiency frontier, they began to adopt and often improve upon best practice organizational processes. For example, Yu and Zaheer (2010) detail how hierarchical Korean firms adopted and improved upon Motorola's Six Sigma quality assurance process.

The Persistence of Personal Rule

While FBGs successfully imitated and assimilated best practice technology skills from Western firms, they have been far more selective in their imitation and adoption of Western models of organization and corporate governance. FBGs are particularly resistant to three key organizational components that are prevalent in Western organizations, namely, employment of professional managers in senior positions, the adoption of multidivisional organization, and corporate governance practices deriving from the separation of financial ownership and control. In particular, FBGs have not yet adopted the bureaucratic set of checks and balances that is typically applied to senior executives in Western firms.

Personal Rule

The authority structure of the archetypal Western firm tends to be more impersonal. Professionally managed firms in the West, especially those in the UK and North America, make greater use of arm's-length capital (public equity and bonds) than do FBGs. The capital supplied by arm's-length investors is typically mediated through the auspices of institutional investors who are concerned with returns on their portfolios rather than the performance of any particular investment. Both investors and managers will typically view the relationship in very instrumental terms. The instrumentality of depersonalized investor–management relations pervades Western firms' governance structures. For example, accountability to shareholders requires that professional managers rationalize their decisions with reference to shareholder value. More generally, managers are subject to bureaucratic constraints consisting of corporate codes of conduct, performance appraisal processes, and quarterly reporting requirements that check the CEO's discretionary authority.

In contrast, the personal rule of the family patriarch of a large FBG is uninhibited by bureaucratic checks and balances (Üsdiken 2010). The concentration of authority in the family patriarch enables the dominant coalition of trusted associates to exercise control over the firm's resources and make important strategic decisions with 'unlimited jurisdiction' (Biggart 1998: 316) and a 'tight grip' (Tsui-Auch 2004: 718) over the direction of the firm. In a study of the top 100 Taiwanese business groups, Chung and Luo (2008) did not find a single case where the key leader (the most powerful post in the group) was not a family member.

FBGs make extensive use of professional management at the operational level (Tsui-Auch 2004), but professional managers are rarely admitted into the inner circle of the ruling coalition. The few that are admitted will likely have prior social ties or have demonstrated loyalty and long service to the family. Tsui-Auch distinguishes between 'family related managers' and non-family managers. The former include family members and relatives, friends, and employees who the owning family considers to be family members. In some cases, families use marriage and outright adoption to incorporate trustworthy executive talent from outside the family (Mehrotra et al. 2011).

Organization Structure

Multidivisional organization is an efficient structure for firms diversified into multiple geographic and product markets (Chandler 1990). Described by Williamson as the M-form, the structure separates 'operating from strategic decision-making ... and ... the requisite internal control apparatus have been assembled and is systematically employed' (1975). Despite its efficiencies, family firms around the world are typically resistant to its adoption. In the US and Europe, family-controlled firms were slower than managerial and bank-controlled firms to adopt the M-form of organization due to the requirement that family owners decentralize management control and increase the firm's performance visibility and their accountability to outsiders (Mayer and Whittington 2004).

Asia's FBGs are multiproduct businesses, but they have not adopted M-form organization, instead preferring to maintain their personal rule over a loosely coordinated group of businesses. The literature depicts business group structure as a complex web of financial and personal relationships, such as multiple and reciprocated equity, debt, and commercial ties and kinship affiliation where family members or trusted friends are placed in senior positions at affiliate firms. Granovetter (2005) characterizes these ties as an 'intermediate level of binding' located on the middle ground of a continuum between market and hierarchy. Other scholars view business group structure as consisting of pyramidal governance devices that concentrate strategic and financial control of affiliated firms in the hands of a 'peak' organization, typically a privately held firm belonging to a founder entrepreneur and his or her family. In practice, the precise system of vertical and horizontal relationships among affiliated firms varies enormously (Yiu, Lu, Bruton, and Hoskisson 2007), but very few approximate the Williamson ideal of the M-form organization.

Corporate Governance Structures

Western systems of corporate governance are comprised of an interconnected set of external (e.g., stock markets, credit rating agencies) and internal mechanisms (e.g., a board of directors, audit committees) that monitor senior management decision-making on behalf of investors. However, the architects of late industrialization in Asia actively suppressed the functioning of external corporate governance mechanisms and instead sought to control the flow of capital through government planning ministries and state-controlled banks to ensure that it reached their preferred industrialists. External corporate governance mechanisms and the attendant array of specialized financial institutions did eventually materialize, but often lacked independence from state influence and were unable to exercise vigilant oversight that similar institutions performed in the West.

While many benefited from soft loans from state influence banks, FBGs learned to self-finance their activities from internally generated sources. Because FBGs were not dependent upon external financing, both external and internal corporate governance mechanisms developed along lines very different from the West (Carney and Gedajlovic 2002). While many FBG affiliates were listed on public stock exchanges, they have remained firmly in the control of the parent, which would typically acquire a controlling share of the firm's public equity. The exact share ownership required to establish control will depend upon the institutional context. In some cases, effective control may require an absolute majority of voting stock to be concentrated in the hands of the patriarch; in other cases, dual-class shares or covenants that provide a patriarch with special decision rights, such as the right to appoint a CEO or decide the composition of the board of directors, might be used.

Internal governance mechanisms also reflect personal control. Asian authorities espouse 'good governance' principles and 'codes of best practice' that call for independent boards of directors and the separation of the CEO and Board Chairperson's role (van Essen, van Oosterhout, and Carney 2012). FBGs frequently adopt these practices and avow their commitment to high standards of international corporate governance, giving the impression that they have a model system of corporate governance. However, there is a significant gap between *de jure* and *de facto* corporate governance practice (Khanna, Kogan, and Palepu 2003). For example, boards may appear to have a large percentage of independent directors, but for many of these directors, independence is nominal. Directors are frequently appointed from the patriarchs' personal networks or they are executives of group affiliated firms. Independents may be unwilling or unable to stand up to powerful family members and they may carry little influence. Boyd and Hoskisson (2010) conclude that many seemingly independent boards of directors are little more than 'rubberstamps'.

Will FBGs adopt Western Models of Corporate Governance?

There is much empirical support for the thesis that FBGs emerge and profit in the absence of well-developed labor and financial markets institutions (Carney et al. 2011) and that their emergence fosters a country's economic development (Amsden 1989; Guillen 2000). It is also evident that FBGs promoted the adoption of large-scale manufacturing technologies and high-quality production processes (Hobday 1995). Unfortunately, there is much less research on how FBGs will change over time or how economic maturity and institutional development will affect them.

Granovetter encourages business group researchers to 'look closely at how business groups have responded to changes in the economies they inhabit, and at how we understand their capacities and the way they change over time' (2005: 445). Implicit in the argument that business groups arise in response to missing institutions is the corollary that once economic development gains momentum and market supporting institutions emerge, then FBGs will lose their competitive advantage, and we should expect that, relative to freestanding firms, FBGs should restructure and divest their diversified portfolios (Khanna and Palepu 2000). Indeed, Khanna and Palepu (1999) build their policy advice on the expectation that business groups will, in fact, fade away when they advocate 'governments in developing countries must focus on building up those market institutions in the long term. The dismantling of business groups will, we believe, follow naturally once these institutions are in place' (1999: 126).

Yet scholars are perplexed by observations that family-controlled business groups continue to be prominent in many countries, such as Hong Kong, Korea, Singapore, and Taiwan, which have attained high levels of economic development and now have high-quality, market supporting institutions. Morck (2010) suggests the persistence of business groups in highly developed economies is a 'mystery'. Granovetter notes that 'FBGs have typically defied predictions of the imminent demise surviving the conscious attempts by politicians to break them up and the impact of financial crises.' Indeed, the development of market supporting institutions may not erode but strengthen the position of established business groups. For example, Indian FBGs have been beneficiaries of the development of liquid capital markets and liberalization policies, since they offer the freedom and the financing for groups to enter new markets (Siegel and Choudury 2010).

One explanation for the evident persistence of FBGs in advanced economies is a co-evolutionary theory that posits that FBGs not only arise as a response to institutional voids, but they also shape and influence the way in which institutional voids are eventually filled. In particular, institutional voids may be filled in a manner that is consistent with continued existence of large-scale family business groups (Carney and Gedajlovic 2002). In the remaining sections, I outline why FBGs persist in the face of growing economic wealth and institutional development.

Co-evolution of FBGs and Institutions

One consequence of late industrialization in Asian economies is that a few large FBGs emerged to wield disproportionate influence in their domestic economies. Claessens and his colleagues put it succinctly when they say 'a relatively small number of families effectively control most East Asian economies' (2000: 109). This concentration of economic power is in part due to scale economies in the functions performed by business groups. Moreover, concentrated ownership provides opportunities for elite families to entrench their control over the firm. Even if their performance deteriorates, business group affiliates cannot be acquired by better managed firms, nor can their senior management be dismissed (Morck, Wolfenzon, and Yeung 2005). Family patriarchs can and do rule their business empires for decades.

Concentrated economic power is mirrored in the political domain. Asia's economic growth miracles occurred during long periods of political domination by autocrats and conservative political movements. For example, the Liberal Party of Japan ruled continuously between 1955 and 1993. In Taiwan, the KMT ruled without interruption between 1950 and 1994. Since gaining independence in the late 1950s, Malaysia and Singapore have seen a monopoly of power by the United National Malays Organization and the People's Action Party, respectively. An unelected colonial governor ruled in Hong Kong until 1997. In Indonesia, Suharto ruled between 1967 and 1997. Thailand's monarchy, in tandem with the conservative military elite, has provided stability in the face of frequently changing governments. Concentrated economic and political power facilitated cooperation between business elites and politicians. Perhaps most importantly, political leaders were able to assure private investors that their property rights would be protected. For the most part, property rights are based not on the rule of law or impersonal processes of formal-legal institutions, but depend crucially upon the capacity of political leaders to give some kind of credible commitments to private investors that they can confidently invest in and expect healthy returns to their investment.

In this respect, we can separate two elements central to the rule of law (Fukuyama 2011). The first element consists of the establishment and observance of individual property rights as provided for in commercial law. These aspects of rule of law facilitate the execution of complex transactions by private investors. The second element consists of the willingness of a sovereign (i.e., the ruling political party or president, or more generally, 'the ruling class') to abide by the rule of law as provided for in commercial law and in other constitutional rules, which govern the rights and responsibilities of all individuals, including the sovereign. The second element has an important effect on the effectiveness of the first. Specifically, if a sovereign does not feel bound by the established body of law, there will be uncertainty about the security of private property and commercial trade, since the sovereign may feel free to confiscate the property of citizens. In practice, an enlightened sovereign may well recognize that the threats of predation upon citizens will scare away investments, undermine economic development, and reduce the potential stream of wealth accruing to the sovereign. To enjoy the public legitimacy of office as well as the private benefits arising from industrialization, an enlightened sovereign may choose to make credible commitments to uphold property rights. For example, China's Communist Party (CCP) does not consider itself to be constrained by law; however, the CCP's leaders recognize the value of protecting property rights due to its beneficial effects on economic development.

In this sense, it is possible to have a 'second-best' rule of law (Rodrik 2008) that makes economic development possible without the existence of the full meaning of rule of law that limits the discretion of the sovereign and does not depend upon him or her for continued functioning. In an environment of second-best institutions and credible protection of property rights, a balance of power has emerged between strong political leaders and a business sector organized around a few large FBGs. This political–economy compromise has engendered high levels of economic growth and capital accumulation. Nevertheless, many Asian states are now approaching economic maturity and the pernicious effects of second-best institutions are beginning to appear. I will now discuss three related problems: the persistence of relational contracting, generational succession in FBGs, and a middle-income trap.

The Persistence of Relational Contracting

In signaling their commitment to upholding property rights, politicians successfully induced investment from the private sector. There is, nevertheless, a continuing risk to private investors of defection by a patron or by unexpected regime change. These risks mean that the value of relations with government actors can be highly contingent (Siegel 2007). When prominent political figures lose their power, the value of relationships can depreciate rapidly. In these circumstances, the new sovereign may have no interest in upholding existing relationships and may even seek recourse against the beneficiaries of prior regimes. For example, following the overthrow of Indonesia's President Suharto, a new government imposed a $6 billion fine against Indonesia's largest business group, Salim, whose patriarch, Liem Sioe Liong, was a well-known crony of Suharto. The fine was approximately equal to the group's market value (Dieleman and Sachs 2008). Peerenboom (2004) suggests that the rule of law in Asia is often 'politicized', wherein the sovereign may selectively intervene in a narrow range of cases to use the legal system to harass political opponents (2004: 16) or dissuade the business elite from supporting alternative political candidates. From the perspective of a politically connected FBG, the inherent ambiguity of 'second best' rule of law presents long-term challenges to the wealth-preservation goals of family firms. However, it is not so much fear of expropriation by a vengeful state that concerns wealthy families, rather a more pressing problem with difficulties in organizing an orderly transfer of wealth from one generation to another, where an impersonal rule of law does not unambiguously protect property rights.

Problems of Succession

In the context of ambiguous property rights, large family firms are of necessity both wealth-generation and wealth-preservation devices. That founding entrepreneurs often wish to retain control of the firm within the family and ensure that a long-term multigenerational view of their wealth is well-established in the family business literature. But how should the aging patriarch of a large FBG plan for future generations in the context of contingent relational capital and second-best rule of law? Many Asian entrepreneurs have amassed great family fortunes during the recent period of sustained economic growth, but under norms of partible inheritance and an exponential growth in the number of legatees, these concentrations of capital are subject to fragmentation due to conflicting and volatile family relationships, which inevitably attend on second and later generations (Tam 1990).

Succession conflicts are endemic in family business, and founders are often advised to seek the counsel of third-party agents or 'fiduciaries' to manage the succession. The fiduciary function can be played by a trusted family friend, but large fortunes likely depend upon several arm's-length relationships with lawyers, accountants, estate administrators, or a corporation with a large professional staff such as a foundation or corporate trust (Marcus 1983). The fiduciary relationship is the responsibility of an agent to a principal and attaches to numerous professional and commercial relationships, such as those between stockbrokers and their clients, corporate directors and senior officers to stockholders, and lawyers/estate administrators and legatees to their heirs. In its legal form, a fiduciary is expected to uphold norms of disinterestedness and has a duty to employ best professional judgment for the benefit of the principal. However, due to information asymmetries between principal and agent, fiduciary relationships are easily corruptible and they rely for their integrity upon the existence of rule of law as well as structural devices that provide oversight of the fiduciary's performance, including normative socialization to professional standards.

Because rule of law and related oversight mechanisms are often underdeveloped in emerging markets, fiduciary relationships may be too easily compromised and founding patriarchs may be reluctant to put much faith in them (Lee, Lim, and Lim 2003). Accordingly, business relationships that rely upon fiduciary responsibility, such as trusts, independent boards of directors, professional executives, and the use of specialized agents, such as executive search and venture-capital, are likely to be eschewed by family patriarchs. Personally ruled firms will flourish when there is little trust in the fiduciary principle. Trust is the essence of the fiduciary relationship but in low-trust societies (Fukuyama 1995) where principals cannot trust fiduciaries to work in their interests, a cadre of trustworthy fiduciaries may fail to materialize because social capital will be unavailable to support the necessary differentiation and specialization of fiduciary roles.

Family businesses remain important in Western economies, but they rarely dominate the entire economic landscape. This is because Western economies have witnessed the development of institutions that permit personally ruled firms to transcend their inherent limitations. In particular, the institutions of Western capitalism provide a legal context where principal–agent relationships can retain their integrity and where violations of such relationships can be remedied in the courts. While the recent economic crises in the North American and European capital markets may cloud our full appreciation of its functioning, the fiduciary relationship underpins complex intergenerational transfers of economic wealth in Western economies. Under a functioning system of either common or civil law, trusteeships and foundations allow for founders of large fortunes to provide for future generations. In these settings, large business empires may gradually transform or dissolve through immersion into a web of multiple fiduciary relationships. For example, large and liquid equity markets permit the gradual dilution of large equity stakes, while institutional investors in combination with a professional management assume control of major corporations and seek to assure their vitality.

Middle-income Trap

Many commentators believe that second-best institutions are adequate for launching late industrialization and helping latecomer firms reach the technology frontier, but are inadequate to the task of supporting the kind of innovation associated with higher levels of national income. The debate is often couched in terms of the challenge of making the leap from imitation to innovation. Much of the recent business group literature is concerned with the question of their capacity for innovation (e.g., Mahmood et al. 2011). A variety of capitalism literature suggests that innovation in advanced economies can take the form of either radical and discontinuous innovations, as observed in Anglo-American economies, or incremental innovations more commonly observed in Continental systems of capitalism (Hall and Soskice 2001). Both systems of innovation in Anglo-American and Continental varieties of capitalism rest upon complex, complementary institutions of property rights and legal arrangements that are hospitable to robust principal–agent relationships. However, in Asian varieties of capitalism, the archetypal personally ruled family business group typically eschews such relationships, but in so doing, they deprive themselves of the relationships needed to foster complex incentives, organizational processes, and capabilities of which incremental and radical indentation depend (Carney, Gedajlovic, and Yang 2009).

Conclusion

Despite attaining high levels of economic development, many Asian jurisdictions are plagued by property rights that are founded on an unambiguous rule of law. These conditions are inhospitable to the emergence of robust fiduciary institutions. If founders of large fortunes are unwilling to commit their wealth into the anonymous hands of fiduciary agents, they will be compelled to retain their personalized systems' corporate control to transfer wealth and organizational control across the generations. In so doing, they perpetuate the personal rule of the family-controlled firm. Asia's FBGs have contributed to the modernization of their host economies, but have not 'bureaucratized' their organizations or installed impersonal, arm's-length forms of corporate governance. This is perhaps unsurprising, since the wider institutional environment is unsupportive of such bureaucratic practices. For the most part, Asia's FBGs retain organizational structures and corporate governance practices that reflect their personalized characteristics. This governance system is consistent with the adoption of technological and organizational management practices that promote economic catch-up and high levels of efficiency, but are less compatible with organizational practices necessary for the development of innovation capability.

References

Almeida, H., and Wolfenzon, D. (2006). 'Should business groups be dismantled? The equilibrium costs of efficient internal capital markets'. *Journal of Financial Economics*, 79: 99–144.

Amsden, A. (1989). *Asia's next giant: South Korea and late industrialization*. New York: Oxford University Press.

Amsden, A.H., and Hikino, T. (1994). 'Project execution capability, organizational know-how, and conglomerate corporate growth in late industrialization'. *Industrial and Corporate Change*, 3: 111–47.

Biggart, N.W. (1998). 'Deep finance: the organizational bases of South Korea's financial collapse'. *Journal of Management Inquiry*, 7(4): 311–20.

Boyd, B.K., and Hoskisson, R.E. (2010). 'Corporate governance of business groups', in A.M. Colpan, T. Hikino, and J.R. Lincoln (eds), *The Oxford handbook of business groups*. Oxford: Oxford University Press, 670–96.

Campbell, J.L. (2004). *Institutional change and globalization*. Princeton: Princeton University Press.

Carney, R., and Child, T. (2013). 'Changes to the ownership and control of East Asian corporations between 1996 and 2008: the primacy of politics'. *Journal of Financial Economics*, 107(2): 494–513.

Carney, M., and Gedajlovic, E. (2002). 'The co-evolution of institutional environments and organizational strategies: the rise of family business groups in the ASEAN region'. *Organization Studies,* 23(1): 1–31.

Carney, M., Gedajlovic, E., and Yang, X. (2009). 'Varieties of Asian capitalism: toward an institutional theory of Asian enterprise'. *Asia Pacific Journal of Management,* 26(3): 361–80.

Carney, M., Gedajlovic, E., Huegens, P., Essen, M.V., and Oosterhout, J.H. (2011). 'Business group affiliation, performance, context, and strategy: a meta analysis'. *Academy of Management Journal,* 54(3): 437–60.

Chandler, A.D. (1990). *Scale and scope: the dynamics of industrial competition.* Cambridge: Harvard University Press.

Chang, S.J., and Hong, J. (2000). 'Economic performance of group-affiliated companies in Korea: intragroup resource sharing and internal business transactions'. *Academy of Management Journal,* 43(3): 429–48.

Chung, C.N., and Luo, X. (2008). 'Institutional logics or agency costs: the influence of corporate governance models on business group restructuring in emerging economies'. *Organization Science,* 19(5): 776–84.

Claessens, S., Djankov, S., and Lang, L.H.P. (2000). 'The separation of ownership and control in East Asian corporations'. *Journal of Financial Economics,* 58: 81–112.

Dieleman, M., and Sachs, W. (2008). 'Coevolution of institutions and corporations in emerging economies: how the Salim Group morphed into an institution of Suhartu's crony regime'. *Journal of Management Studies,* 45(7): 1274–1300.

Fukuyama, F. (2011). *The origins of political order: from prehuman times to the French Revolution.* New York: Farrar, Straus, and Giroux.

Gerlach, M.L. (1997). 'The organizational logic of business groups: evidence from the Zaibatsu', in S. Takao and M. Shimotani (eds), *Beyond the firm: business groups in international and historical perspective.* Oxford: Oxford University Press, 245–73.

Gilson, R. (2007). 'Controlling family shareholders in developing countries: anchoring relational exchange'. *Stanford Law Review,* 60(2): 633–5.

Granovetter, M. (2005). 'Business groups and social organization', in N.J. Smelser and R. Swedburg (eds), *The handbook of economic sociology* (2nd edn). Princeton: Princeton University Press, 429–50.

Guillen, M.F. (2000). 'Business groups in emerging economies: a resource based view'. *Academy of Management Journal,* 43(3): 362–80.

Hall, P.A. and Soskice, D. (2001). 'An introduction to varieties of capitalism', in P.A. Hall and D. Soskice (eds.), *Varieties of capitalism: the institutional foundations of comparative advantage.* New York: Oxford University Press.

Hobday, M. (1995). 'East Asian latecomer firms: learning the technology of electronics'. *World Development,* 23: 1171–93.

Jones, G., and Wale, J. (1998). 'Merchants as business groups: British trading companies in Asia before 1945'. *Business History Review,* 72: 367–408.

Khanna, T., and Palepu, K. (1997). 'Why focused strategies may be wrong for emerging markets'. *Harvard Business Review,* 75(4): 41–51.

Khanna, T., and Palepu, K. (1999). The right way to restructure conglomerates in emerging markets. *Harvard Business Review,* 77 (July-August): 125–34.

Khanna, T., and Palepu, K. (2000). 'Is group affiliation profitable in emerging markets? An analysis of diversified Indian business groups'. *Journal of Finance,* 55(2): 867–91.

Khanna, T., and Rivkin, J. (2001). 'Estimating the performance effects of business groups in emerging markets'. *Strategic Management Journal,* 22(1): 45–74.

Khanna, T., Kogan, J., and Palepu, K. (2003). 'Globalization and similarities in corporate governance: a cross-country analysis'. *Review of Economics and Statistics,* 88(1): 69–90.

Lee, K., Lim, G., and Lim, W.S. (2003). 'Family business succession: appropriation risk and choice of successor'. *Academy of Management Review,* 28(4): 657–66.

Mahmood, I.P., Zhu, H., and Zajac, E.J. (2011). 'Where can capabilities come from? Network ties and capability acquisition in business groups'. *Strategic Management Journal, 32*(8): 820–48.

Marcus, G.E. (1983). 'The fiduciary role in American family businesses and their institutional legacy', in G. Marcus (ed.), *Elites, ethnographic issues*. Albuquerque: University of New Mexico Press.

Mayer, M., and Whittington, R. (2004). 'Economics, politics and nations: resistance to the multidivisional form in France, Germany and the United Kingdom, 1983–1993'. *Journal of Management Studies, 41*(7): 1057–82.

Mehrotra, V., Morck, R., Shim, J., and Wiwattanakantang, Y. (2011). 'Must love kill the family firm? Some exploratory evidence'. *Entrepreneurship Theory and Practice, 35*(6): 1121–48.

Morck, R. (2010). 'The riddle of the great pyramids', in A.M. Colpan, T. Hikinio, and J.R. Lincoln (eds), *The Oxford handbook of business groups*. Oxford: Oxford University Press.

Morck, R., Wolfenzon, D., and Yeung, B. (2005). 'Corporate governance, economic entrenchment, and growth'. *Journal of Economic Literature, 43*: 655–720.

Peerenboom, R. (2004). 'Varieties of rule of law: an introduction and provisional conclusion', in R. Peerenboom (ed.), *Asian discourses of rule of law: theories and implementation of rule of law*. London: Routledge Curzon, 1–53.

Perkins, D.H. (1994). 'There are at least three models of East Asian development'. *World Development, 22*(4): 655–61.

Rodrik, D. (2008). 'Second-best institutions'. *American Economic Review*, 98: 100–4.

Schneider, B.R. (2010). 'Business groups and the state: the politics of expansion restructuring and collapse', in A.M. Colpan, T. Hikinio, and J.R. Lincoln (eds), *The Oxford handbook of business groups*. Oxford: Oxford University Press.

Siegel, J. (2007). 'Contingent political capital and international alliances: evidence from South Korea'. *Administrative Science Quarterly, 52*: 621–66.

Siegel, J., and Choudhury, P. (2012). 'A reexamination of tunneling and business groups: new data and new methods', *Review of Financial Studies 25*(6): 1763–98.

Tam, S. (1990). 'Centrifugal versus centripetal growth processes: contrasting ideal types for conceptualizing the development patterns of Chinese and Japanese firms', in S. Clegg and R.S. Gordon (eds), *Capitalism in contrasting cultures*. New York: de Gruyter, 155–83.

Tsui-Auch, L.S. (2004). 'The professionally managed family-ruled enterprise: ethnic Chinese business in Singapore'. *Journal of Management Studies, 41*(4): 693–723.

Üsdiken, B. (2010). 'The kin and professional: top leadership in family business groups', in A.M. Colpan, T. Hikino, and J.R. Lincoln (eds), *The Oxford handbook of business groups*. Oxford: Oxford University Press, 696–716.

Van Essen, M., Van Oosterhout, J., and Carney, M. (2013). 'Corporate boards and the performance of Asian firms: a meta-analysis'. *Asia-Pacific Journal of Management, 29*(4): 873–905.

Wade, R. (1990). *Governing the market: economic theory and the role of government in East Asian industrialisation*. Princeton, NJ: Princeton University Press.

Williamson, O.E. (1975). *Markets and hierarchies: analysis and antitrust implications*. New York: Free Press.

Yiu, D.W., Lu, Y., Bruton, G.D., and Hoskisson, R.E. (2007). 'Business groups: an integrated model to focus future research'. *Journal of Management Studies, 44*(8): 1551–79.

Yu, J., and Zaheer, S. (2010). 'Building a process model of local adaptation of practices: a study of Six Sigma implementation in Korea and US firms'. *Journal of International Business Studies, 41*: 475–99.

17
The Glocalization of Academic Business Studies

Lars Engwall

Introduction

Rankings of business schools are today published by a number of media outlets. These rankings provide the image that there is a global competition between business schools with a high mobility of students and faculty. No doubt, this image of globalization has significant repercussions on the field by making the top-ranked schools the role models for the others. In this process, it is quite clear that US institutions have taken a lead, inspiring the strategies of business school deans in other countries. As a result, we can, according to the neo-institutionalists (cf. e.g., DiMaggio and Powell 1983), expect a worldwide homogenization of academic business studies. However, there are also reasons to believe that local circumstances will play a significant role in this process. We can, therefore, also anticipate the occurrence of 'translations' (Czarniawska-Joerges and Sevón 1996), 'editing' (Sahlin-Andersson 1996), 'creolization' (Hannerz 1992), and 'bricolage' (Lévi-Strauss 1962; Duymedjian and Rüling 2010). In other words, even if there are ambitions to copy the top schools, there are various local forces working against homogenization, and as a result, we will see different kinds of compromises leading to a glocalization of the field (i.e., local variations in a globalized world) (Robertson 1994). Needless to say, this is quite in contrast to the usual rhetoric that all business schools compete with each other and that this competition is an open competition with equal opportunities for all the actors. This view will be challenged in the present chapter, which will demonstrate that so far, academic business studies primarily have a glocal character. In the following section, the chapter will first focus on business education and then in a subsequent section turn to business research. A final section will provide conclusions.

Business Education

Obstacles to Globalization

Globalization has indeed become a buzz word in business education. Deans all over the world declare their global ambitions. However, particularly in terms of full programs, there are reasons to believe that most institutions are local rather than global. This is the case because the demand for education is strongly related to reputation, a characteristic that is primarily locally constructed. Four significant properties of education constitute the reason for this:

1   A student should not know the content in advance; otherwise the education would not be selected.
2   A student never takes the same education twice, even if it was extremely good.
3   A student cannot really judge the quality of an education until many years after graduation.
4   Dissatisfied alumni seldom tell bad stories about their education, since that will be disadvantageous to their careers.

As a result, prospective students will be weakly informed and have to use reputation as the main criterion for the selection of education. The reputation is strongly determined by the success of earlier graduates in the labor market, which is still, to a large extent, nationally segmented with a bias for alumni to hire people with the same educational background as their own. This, in turn, implies that there are first mover advantages in education (i.e., old institutions have advantages over younger ones) (Williamson 1975). Thus, although there are high ambitions among politicians and academic leaders to stimulate high mobility of students and faculty between nations, these are still more wishes than reality. Needless to say, language plays an important role in this context. Although English is becoming the *lingua franca* all over the world, there is a very large number of countries where languages other than English are the mother tongue of citizens. And, even if new generations are becoming more fluent in English than their parents, they will, nevertheless, have a disadvantage on the international labor market in relation to native speakers, not to mention the lack of the tacit knowledge acquired by those who have grown up in a particular country.

Even if business education can be expected to be primarily local, it has to be acknowledged that most institutions have strong ambitions to become global players. One important method for this has been and is student exchange, which aims at giving the students of collaborating institutions international experience. Such exchanges are not without problems, however. First of all, it requires caution in the selection of partners, since the sending out of students implies the outsourcing of the most significant activity of an educational institution with high risks of quality losses. Second, in countries where English is not the mother tongue, the teaching language has to change to English in order to communicate with incoming students. It is far from evident that this language shift is to the advantage of the preparation of domestic students, since most of them are likely to spend most of their professional life in the home country. Their ability to 'talk management speak' in their mother tongue is then very crucial.

Globalization in Curricula

Nevertheless, if we measure globalization by means of the use of foreign literature, there is evidence that this is happening—at least in countries that are not Anglo-American. A study of curricula in eight Nordic business schools (Engwall 2000) thus shows that US, UK, and Nordic literature dominated the curricula, with only a tiny portion from other countries (Table 17.1). The influence from the US and the UK is considerable already from these figures. This impression becomes even stronger when looking at the titles used by more than two of the eight institutions (Table 17.2), since the list is dominated by titles from US publishers. On top of that, there are reasons to believe that many of the texts of Nordic

Lars Engwall

Table 17.1 Origin of the literature in eight Nordic business schools in the mid-1990s

Country	Institution	USA	UK	Nordic	Other	Total	Number of titles
Denmark	Copenhagen	29.5	17.8	48.7	4.0	100	149
	Aarhus	44.7	12.1	41.1	2.1	100	95
Finland	Helsinki	48.0	15.2	35.3	1.5	100	224
	Hanken	43.8	16.4	38.4	1.4	100	146
Norway	Bergen	52.0	5.1	40.8	2.1	100	49
	Oslo	50.0	10.0	39.0	1.0	100	99
Sweden	Stockholm	44.9	6.6	42.7	5.8	100	67
	Gothenburg	32.4	8.8	55.6	3.2	100	125
Total		42.2	13.0	42.3	2.5	100	954

Source: Engwall (2000: 12; Table 2).

Table 17.2 Titles that were used most in the eight Nordic business schools in the mid-1990s

Title	Publisher	No. of schools
Brealey and Myers (1991)	McGraw-Hill	6
Porter (1980)	Free Press	5
Arens and Loebbecke (1991)	Prentice-Hall	4
Cooper and Kaplan (1991)	Prentice-Hall	4
Foster (1986)	Prentice-Hall	4
Hull (1993)	Prentice-Hall	4
Stern and El-Ansary (1992)	Prentice-Hall	4
Yin (1984)	Sage	4
Anthony and Govindarajan (1995)	Irwin	3
Bradley (1995)	Prentice-Hall	3
Copeland and Weston (1988)	Addison-Wesley	3
Douma and Schreuder (1991)	Prentice-Hall	3
Drury (1992)	Chapman and Hall	3
Eiteman, Stonehill, and Moffett (1992)	Addison-Wesley	3
Gadde and Håkansson (1993)	Studentlitteratur	3
Grönroos (1990)	Lexington Books	3
Kaplan and Atkinson (1989)	Prentice-Hall	3
Kotler (1994)	Prentice-Hall	3
Lambert and Stock (1993)	Irwin	3
Loustarinen and Welch (1990)	Helsinki School of Economics	3
Morgan (1986)	Sage	3
Ryan, Scapens, and Theobald (1992)	Academic Press	3
Welford and Gouldson (1993)	Pitman	3
Yukl (1989)	Prentice-Hall	3

Source: Engwall (2000: 18; Table 7).

authors are likely to have had Anglo-American inspiration due to having long-developed academic relationships with these countries.[1]

The above implies that business education in the Nordic countries, and most likely in other countries as well, to a considerable extent, has global features through extensive use of literature by Anglo-American authors published by Anglo-American publishers. This globalization is reinforced by teaching in English through exchange students and exchange faculty. Nevertheless, it appears fair to conclude that business education is predominantly glocal rather than global, since most programs are delivered in local settings with mainly local recruitment for careers that will be essentially local. For the US business schools, if we measure globalization by the share of foreign literature, we may even consider them as predominant local, since the literature that is foreign in other countries is in the US local.

Globalization among Global Players

The above picture of restrictions on globalization is somewhat in contrast to the image provided by the ranking exercises mentioned above. However, there may be a possibility that both views are correct, that is, that glocalization is true for a large number of institutions, while globalization is true for a limited number of global schools. Programs listed on the Global MBA Ranking of the *Financial Times* have, therefore, been analyzed, since the schools offering them explicitly present themselves as global and actively take part in the rankings by delivering data. For the European and US schools, the ambition to be global is also manifested by their fulfillment of the requirement to be 'accredited by international bodies such as AACSB International, EQUIS or the Association of MBAs'.[2]

For the 2011 Global MBA Ranking, 158 business schools both met the criteria for inclusion in the Global MBA Ranking and completed the FT survey. Of these, 100 have been ranked: 58 North American (of which 5 were Canadian), 28 European, and 14 operating on other continents (Table 17.3).[3] Among the ranking criteria used, there are two that can be used as indicators of globalization: (1) share of international students, and (2) share of international faculty. If we use these two indicators and employ the modest requirement of globalization that a majority of students and faculty should be international, we find that 80 percent of the Global MBA programs do *not* meet this condition.

Considering the whole population of 100 programs, they have on average 51 percent foreign students and 38 percent foreign faculty (last row in Table 17.3), which are not impressive globalization figures. However, there are clear variations in the population. The four transnational institutions had on average almost only international students and two-thirds foreign faculty in their programs. The latter was also the case for the two Australian programs, which had on average 84 percent international students. A similar high average for students is exhibited by the 26 European programs, although 15 of them have a minority of international students and international faculty (i.e., less than 50 percent). For other areas, as shown in Table 17.3, averages are all below 50 percent. Particularly worth noting is the fact that the North American business programs, the template for the others, have the lowest averages, around 30 percent. Again, they appear more local than global.

Globalization in the Wake of the Bologna Process

Our analysis so far seems to indicate that the globalization of business education, even among institutions that define themselves as global actors, has its limitations. The US institutions do not have a dominance of international students and international faculty, while this is

Table 17.3 Share of international students and share of international faculty for the global MBA programs in 2011 FT Ranking

Area	Countries	Number	Students	Faculty
Transnational	Dubai/Singapore; France/Singapore; UK/Netherlands/Germany; US/UK/UAE/China	4	94%	67%
Australia	Australia (2)	2	84%	67%
Europe	Belgium (1), France (2), Ireland (1), Italy (2), Netherlands (1), Spain (4), Switzerland (1), UK (14)	26	84%	47%
Asia	China (2), India (2), Singapore (2), South Korea (1)	7	47%	44%
South America	Argentina (1), Costa Rica (1), Mexico (1)	3	42%	31%
Africa	South Africa (1)	1	34%	31%
North America	Canada (5), USA (53)	57	33%	30%
Total	North America (57), Europe (26), Asia (7), Transnational (4), South America (3), Australia (2), South Africa (1)	100	51%	38%

the case for a limited number of institutions, among them some European ones. The latter circumstance, and the fact that the Master in Management is the outcome of the Bologna process, makes it appropriate to also analyze the ranking list for this type of program.[4] Again, we can observe limitations in the internationalization: 51 of the 65 institutions have less than 50 percent international faculty and 42 of them have less than 50 percent international students. Only 11 institutions meet our criterion of globalization (i.e., a majority of foreign students and foreign faculty). Of these, one is the multinational cooperation CEMS, six are British, two French, one Dutch, and one Swiss.[5]

A closer look at the 65 institutions reveals that about half the population consists of institutions from the British Isles and four Latin countries (France, Italy, Spain, and Portugal): 14 and 20, respectively. As can be seen in Table 17.4, their profiles differ somewhat. The British institutions have as high an average of international students as the three transnational ones (84 percent) and a slight majority of foreign faculty (51 percent), while the corresponding average for the 20 programs in the Latin countries is about one-third. As a matter of fact, there is a remarkable difference between the programs offered by the transnationals and the institutions from the British Isles, and the rest. The averages in the other countries are all below 50 percent, both for the share of international students and international faculty. The three Asian institutions even exhibit an average below 10 percent for both variables. Again, we have thus observed limitations in terms of the globalization of management education.

Conclusions for Education

The results presented above seem to demonstrate that management education, despite accreditation programs and rankings, is far from global. Although the majority of programs can be considered highly globalized through their use of Anglo-American literature, they are mainly local in terms of student and faculty recruitment. Our further analysis has shown that also among those limited number of institutions that qualify for inclusion in Global MBA

Table 17.4 Average share of international students and faculty by region for the 65 institutions listed in the *Financial Times* 2011 Ranking of Masters in Management

Region	Number	Institutions	Students	Faculty
Transnational	3	Grenoble/Singapore; Graduate; ESCP Europe; CEMS	84%	70%
Ireland, United Kingdom	14	UC Dublin; City; Imperial College; London School of Economics; Strathclyde; Aston; Edinburgh; Durham; Brunel; Bath; Lancaster; Bradford; Warwick; Manchester	84%	51%
Canada	1	HEC Montreal	36%	40%
France, Italy, Spain, Portugal	20	Lyon; Essec; HEC Paris; Edhec; Bordeaux; Skema; ESC Toulouse; Reims; Euromed; Rouen; Nantes; ICN; Tours-Poitiers; Clermont; Aix-en-Provence; Bocconi; Nova, Lisbon; Católica Lisbon; EADA; ESADE	32%	37%
Belgium, the Netherlands	8	Antwerp; IAG-Louvain; Vlerick Leuven Gent; Solvay; Maastricht; Rotterdam, Erasmus; Tilburg: TiasNimbas; Nyenrode	32%	28%
Austria, Germany, Switzerland	7	Vienna, Mannheim; WHU; Cologne, Leipzig; St. Gallen; Lausanne	30%	26%
Denmark, Finland, Norway, Sweden	6	Aarhus; Copenhagen; Aalto, Helsinki; NHH, Bergen; BI Oslo; SSE Stockholm	25%	21%
Czech Republic, Poland	3	Prague; Kozminski Warsaw; Warsaw School of Economics	18%	11%
China, India, Taiwan	3	Shanghai Jiao Tong, Antai; Indian Institute of Management, Ahmedabad (IIMA); National Chengchi	1%	6%
Total	65		43%	35%

and Master of Management rankings, globalization has its limitations. Among the top 100 Global MBA programs, four out of five do not have a majority of both international students and international faculty. None of the US schools, the role models for many schools in the rest of the world, have programs that qualify as global, if this majority criterion is used.

The idea that business schools are operating on global markets thus seems to have limitations, even among those who, through their participation in FT rankings, aim at it. If these have limitations in their globalization, it appears likely that the rest of the world's population of business schools is even much less globalized. This means that they are primarily local, although, in terms of content, they may have a high degree of globalization. It, therefore, seems fair to conclude that business education is glocal with a few global actors and a vast number of local ones working with globally diffused management ideas.

In view of the above, it is relevant to ask why academic leaders are so concerned about accreditations and rankings that primarily address the global competitiveness of business schools. The simple answer seems to be that these efforts are primarily directed towards local markets. The accreditations and rankings constitute means of differentiation against the numerous local actors (i.e., a glocalization marketing strategy).

Management Research

The Globalization of Research

Scientific work has long traditions of being international. Scholars have travelled between universities and made endeavors to diffuse their research results internationally. This started after the Renaissance and has continued to the present. In view of the means of communications at the time, we should be impressed with how our predecessors in academia were so successful in spreading their ideas. At the same time, we have to acknowledge that the internationalization of research has become even stronger in the twentieth and the twenty-first centuries, and has turned into globalization through increasing organizing of the sciences and growth of the publishing industry. This organizing implies a continuous addition of new professional scientific associations for various academic specialties. These, in turn, regularly arrange meetings and colloquia as well as provide outlets for research results in the journals they launch. The latter have developed, to a large extent, in a symbiosis with a publishing industry that combines the publishing of scientific journals with the publishing of educational material, as well as databases for the analysis of the impact of journals, individual researchers, research groups, departments, and universities. In this way, the interaction between the academic field and media field has become very close and extremely important for the evaluation of research. In the same way as rankings treat academic institutions as global players competing with each other, the rhetoric around publishing focuses on the publishing in international top journals. As a matter of fact, this has implied that academic assessments are increasingly outsourced from individual academic institutions to journal editors and the reviewers they choose. Quality control has, to a considerable extent, become an exercise with metrics rather than assessments based on presented material that is read.

Fifteen Journals in Business Studies

Against the above background, we will now analyze the extent to which top journals in the field of business studies are global. The analysis will be based on two earlier studies of publication patterns within the field of business studies. They were undertaken for two periods, 1981–1992 and 2005–2009, and aimed at analyzing the integration of the field as well as comparing European and US researchers in business studies (see e.g., Engwall 1996; Engwall and Danell 2011). In order to cover business studies broadly, fifteen top journals in the areas of general management, accounting, administration, and marketing were selected in the following way:

1. In the first step, as described in Engwall (1998a), a selection was made of pairs of European and US journals dealing with the three subfields: (a) general management (*Journal of Management Studies* and *Academy of Management Journal*), (b) accounting/finance (*Accounting, Organizations and Society* and *Accounting Review*), and (c) organization/marketing (*Organization Studies* and *Administrative Science Quarterly*).
2. In the second step, two marketing journals, *European Journal of Marketing* and *Journal of Marketing Research,* were added to the original sample for a further analysis of the differences in citation behavior between European and US management researchers (see further Danell and Engwall 2001).
3. Due to access problems, the *European Journal of Marketing* had to be excluded in subsequent analyses of Scandinavian and French management scholars (Engwall 1996, 1998b). A co-

citation analysis of the seven remaining journals using the Social Science Citation Index (SSCI) identified eight other journals closely related to those originally selected. This left the fifteen titles in Table 17.5 as the key journals in the area of business studies.

A few features from Table 17.5 are worth mentioning:

1. In 2009, in comparison with 1985, all the fifteen journals had higher, and for some like the *Academy of Management Journal* and *Academy of Management Review* considerably higher, impact factors (the average number of citations per paper published in that journal during the two preceding years). This could be an indicator of increasing integration and globalization.
2. The four general management journals, *Academy of Management Journal*, *Academy of Management Review*, *Journal of Management,* and *Strategic Management Journal*, had higher impact factors than the others. This could be interpreted as another indicator of globalization.
3. For both periods, the three European journals had lower impact factors than their counterparts in the four categories. This seems to indicate segmentation between the continents.
4. Accounting journals, irrespective of origin, have the lowest impact factors, which is an indication of the local embeddedness of the field.

For the analysis, we have identified in the Social Science Citation Index (SSCI) for the fifteen selected journals 6,608 documents for the period 1981–1992 and 4,675 documents for the period 2005–2009.

Table 17.5 Fifteen management top journals with impact factors, 1985 and 2009

Area	Journal	1985	2009
General management	Academy of Management Journal	1.964	6.483
	Academy of Management Review	2.629	7.867
	Journal of Management	1.141	4.429
	Journal of Management Studies	0.500	2.805
	Management Science	1.224	2.227
	Strategic Management Journal	1.303	4.464
Accounting	Accounting Review	0.957	1.938
	Accounting. Organizations and Society	0.681	1.904
	Journal of Accounting and Economics	1.146	2.605
	Journal of Accounting Research	1.200	1.870
Administration	Administrative Science Quarterly	3.044	3.842
	Organization Studies	0.511	2.124
Marketing	Journal of Consumer Research	2.432	3.021
	Journal of Marketing	3.154	3.779
	Journal of Marketing Research	1.276	3.099

Table 17.6 Share of author origin in the fifteen top journals, 1981–1992 and 2005–2009

Country	1981–1992	2005–2009	Difference
United States	76.9%	57.6%	–19.3%
United Kingdom	5.6%	7.9%	2.3%
Israel	1.8%	1.0%	–0.8%
Australia	1.8%	2.3%	0.5%
France	1.1%	2.4%	1.3%
Netherlands	0.9%	4.2%	3.3%
Germany	0.6%	2.1%	1.5%
South Korea	0.3%	1.0%	0.8%
Singapore	0.2%	2.4%	2.2%
Switzerland	0.1%	0.9%	0.7%
Spain	0.1%	1.2%	1.1%
PR China	0.1%	3.6%	3.5%

Author Origins

A first indicator of the globalization of research is the origin of the authors. An analysis of this variable in the fifteen journals reveals a considerable local feature: a dominance of US authors (Table 17.6). In 1981–1992, almost four out of five authors were affiliated with US institutions, leaving about 5 percent for UK authors and very tiny figures for many other countries. In 2005–2009, the situation was a bit more favorable for non-US authors, with around 40 percent of the authors from the rest of the world. However, not even the United Kingdom had gained more than a few percentage points, from 5.6 percent to 7.9 percent. Other countries gaining more than 2 percent were the Netherlands, Singapore, and the People's Republic of China.

The strong position of US authors is demonstrated even more in an analysis of the top institutions represented in the material (Table 17.7). It is then obvious that US universities dominate the scene; among the twenty top institutions, there is no institution outside the US in the first period and just one in the second period (the Hong Kong UST). Interestingly enough, all of the listed institutions, except the University of Minnesota, are listed in the *Financial Times* Global MBA Ranking. The sample of publications studied thus seems to cover the top institutions very well. It is also worth noting that the competition between the top institutions is strong: six institutions in the top twenty list in 1981–1992 (University of Wisconsin, UCLA, UC Berkeley, University of Washington, Ohio State University, and University of Florida; in italics in Table 17.7) have fallen out in 2005–2009 and have been replaced by six others (Duke University, University of Maryland, Penn State University, Arizona State University, Cornell University, and Hong Kong UST; also in italics in Table 17.7).

Even if we extend the list from the twenty top institutions to the fifty at the top, the non-US institutions are easily counted. In 1981–1992, they were three Canadian institutions (University of British Columbia, McGill, and University of Toronto) and one British institution (Manchester University), while in 2005–2009, the following eight institutions

Table 17.7 The twenty top institutions in the fifteen top journals, 1981–1992 and 2005–2009

	1981–1992	2005–2009
1.	University of Texas	University of Pennsylvania
2.	Stanford University	*Duke University*
3.	University of Pennsylvania	University of Michigan
4.	Columbia University	Stanford University
5.	New York University	University of Chicago
6.	University of Michigan	*University of Maryland*
7.	University of Illinois	New York University
8.	Northwestern University	University of Minnesota
9.	*University of Wisconsin*	Columbia University
10.	University of Minnesota	University of Texas
11.	*UCLA*	*Penn State University*
12.	MIT	Northwestern University
13.	Indiana University	University of Illinois
14.	*University of California at Berkeley*	University of Southern California
15.	*University of Washington*	*Arizona State University*
16.	University of Chicago	MIT
17.	*Ohio State University*	Harvard University
18.	Harvard University	*Cornell University*
19.	*University of Florida*	*Hong Kong UST*
20.	University of Southern California	Indiana University

appear: Erasmus University, University of Toronto, INSEAD, University of British Columbia, Tilburg University, London Business School, University of Alberta, and National University of Singapore (i.e. one Asian, one British, three Canadian, two Dutch, and one French).

From the above analysis, it seems fair to conclude that the globalization of the fifteen journals has certain limitations. Although the US hegemony has decreased between the two periods, the concentration of authors to one country—and within it, a limited number of elite institutions—is strong.

Frames of Reference

A second indicator of the globalization of business research is constituted by the top references, which should reflect the frames of reference. An analysis of these provides further evidence of the dominance of North American research (Table 17.8). In the first period, there are among the top 25 references only three non-North American titles, all British (in italics in the table): Burns and Stalker (1961), Child (1972), and Woodward (1965); 88 percent of the titles have authors from the US or Canada. In the second period, the non-North American

Table 17.8 Top twenty-five citations in the fifteen journals, 1981–1992 and 2005–2008

	1981–1992 Title	Citations	2005–2008 Title	Citations
1.	Thompson (1967)	479	Baron and Kenny (1986)	487
2.	Pfeffer and Salancik (1978)	433	Barney (1991)	375
3.	Porter (1980)	396	Aiken and West (1991)	314
4.	Cyert and March (1963)	292	Cohen and Levinthal (1990)	295
5.	March and Simon (1958)	289	Jensen and Meckling (1976)	289
6.	Lawrence and Lorsch (1967)	286	DiMaggio and Powell (1983)	275
7.	Williamson (1975)	274	March (1991)	263
8.	Rumelt (1974)	230	*Kogut and Zander (1992)*	210
9.	*Burns and Stalker (1961)*	230	Pfeffer and Salancik (1978)	250
10.	Miles and Snow (1978)	230	Teece, Pisano, and Shuen (1997)	250
11.	Weick (1969)	193	Nelson and Winter (1982)	207
12.	Hofer and Schendel (1978)	170	Kahneman and Tversky (1979)	203
13.	Meyer and Rowan (1977)	165	Eisenhardt (1989)	195
14.	Pfeffer (1981)	160	Fornell and Larcker (1981)	193
15.	Mintzberg (1979)	159	Cyert and March (1963)	189
16.	Jensen and Meckling (1976)	157	Williamson (1985)	179
17.	Hannan and Freeman (1977)	152	Meyer and Rowan (1977)	178
18.	Peters and Waterman (1982)	149	Porter (1980)	177
19.	Aldrich (1979)	149	Wernerfelt (1984)	174
20.	*Child (1972)*	146	Anderson and Gerbing (1988)	170
21.	Porter (1985)	145	Granovetter (1985)	170
22.	*Woodward (1965)*	141	Heckman (1979)	169
23.	Mintzberg (1978)	140	*Dierickx and Cool (1989)*	165
24.	Chandler (1962)	139	Dyer and Singh (1998)	163
25.	Nunnally (1967)	137	Podsakoff et al. (2003)	157

element is even weaker: one of the co-authors of Kogut and Zander (1992) and both authors of Dierickx and Cool (1989). Of these, Zander was affiliated with the Stockholm School of Economics and Dierickx and Cool with INSEAD.

The concentration to North American institutions is further emphasized if we look at the ten most cited authors in the two periods (i.e., adding all the citations of the works of one particular author) (Table 17.9). In this list, there is, in the first period, only one person affiliated with a non-North American institution: John Child at Aston. In the second period, the top ten persons all belong to US elite institutions: Stanford (3), Harvard (2), UC Berkeley (2), Chicago (1), Columbia (1), and Princeton (1). The patterns we have seen in Table 17.7,

Table 17.9 Ten most cited authors in the fifteen journals, 1981–1992 and 2005–2009 (with institutional affiliation)

	1981–1992	2005–2009
1.	Jeffrey Pfeffer, Stanford University	Eugene F. Fama, University of Chicago
2.	Henry Mintzberg, McGill University	Oliver E. Williamson, UC Berkeley
3.	Michael E. Porter, Harvard University	Kathleen M. Eisenhardt, Stanford University
4.	James D. Thompson, University of Pittsburgh	Bruce Kogut, Columbia University
5.	James G. March, Stanford University	James G. March, Stanford University
6.	Oliver E. Williamson, University of Pennsylvania	David Kahneman, Princeton University
7.	John Child, Aston University	Jeffrey Pfeffer, Stanford University
8.	Karl E. Weick, University of Michigan	David J. Teece, UC Berkeley
9.	Herbert A. Simon, Carnegie-Mellon University	Michael C. Jensen, Harvard University
10.	Paul Lawrence, Harvard University	Ranjaj Gulati, Harvard University

with respect to author affiliation, seem thus to have a correspondence in terms of the frames of reference.

The above seems to indicate that there are also considerable local (i.e., US) elements in business research. In the same way as there are limitations in terms of globalization in education, there seem to exist similar constraints in terms of research as it is measured by means of author origin and frames of reference.

Conclusions

Globalization and internationalization are often mentioned in the speeches of academic leaders. They point out that their institutions are competing worldwide for talent and excellence. Such a view has become particularly common in the field of business studies, where rankings and accreditations of business schools have experienced a considerable expansion in the past decades. Nevertheless, the analysis in the present chapter indicates that most business schools are providing more of a rhetoric of globalization than actually being global players. Such a conclusion is based on the following:

1. Among business schools volunteering to be ranked for their Global MBA and for their Master in Management (that is, schools having high global ambitions), only a small number are really international in terms of the share of international students and international faculty in their programs.
2. Among the world's business schools outside the ranking, there are reasons to believe that the limitations in globalization are even larger than for those in the rankings, since academic education, to a considerable extent, constitutes screening mechanisms in local labor markets, in which trust has been built in established local academic degrees.
3. While most programs of business studies all over the world are embedded in local labor markets, they also have considerable globalization features through extensive use of Anglo-American literature and exchange programs.
4. In the same way as globalization has become an established rhetoric for business education, a similar rhetoric has developed in terms of business research. However,

the analysis above has demonstrated that top journals have a local character through dominance by North American authors and North American frames of reference.
5   The fact that the top journals, which have an international reputation through high impact figures, have domination from one continent makes it likely that the rest of the journals in the field are even less globalized. This can be expected to be reinforced by the fact that business studies, to a considerable extent, are based on empirical studies, for which the local context is important.

Together, the above findings indicate that we should consider management studies as glocalized rather than globalized. This means that the field has high ambitions for globalization, both in terms of education and research. At the same time, most of the education is linked to local labor markets, while the main part of the research is locally embedded and often locally reported.

Notes

1   For Sweden, see Engwall (2009, p. 165), and for France, see Colasse and Pavé (1995, p. 27).
2   See http://www.ft.com/intl/cms/s/2/193b2de8-27af-11e0-a327-00144feab49a.html. This and the other webpages referred to were accessed in November, 2011.
3   See http://rankings.ft.com/businessschoolrankings/rankings.
4   See http://rankings.ft.com/businessschoolrankings/masters-in-management-2011. Unfortunately, the list of European business schools does not provide internationalization data.
5   The institutions were (with rankings in parentheses): St. Gallen (1), CEMS (2), ESCP Europe (3), EM Lyon (5), Imperial College (13), London School of Economics (14), Cass (16), Maastricht (28), Bath (44), Warwick (48), and Durham (59).

References

Aiken, L.S., and West, S.G. (1991). *Multiple regression: testing and interpreting interactions*. Newbury Park, CA: Sage.
Aldrich, H.E. (1979). *Organizations and environments*. Englewood Cliffs, NJ: Prentice-Hall.
Anderson, J.C., and Gerbing, D.W. (1988). 'Structural equation modeling in practice: a review and recommended two-step approach'. *Psychological Bulletin*, *103*(3): 411–23.
Anthony, R.N., and Govindarajan, V. (1995). *Management control systems* (8th edn). Chicago, IL: Irwin.
Arens, A.A., and Loebbecke, J.K. (1991). *Auditing: an integrated approach* (5th edn). Englewood Cliffs, NJ: Prentice-Hall.
Barney, J.B. (1991). 'Firm resources and sustained competitive advantage'. *Journal of Management*, *17*(1): 99–120.
Baron, R.M., and Kenny, D.A. (1986). 'The moderator-mediator variable distinction in social psychological research: conceptual, strategic, and statistical considerations'. *Journal of Personality and Social Psychology*, *51*(6): 1173–82.
Bradley, F. (1995). *International marketing strategy* (2nd edn). Englewood Cliffs, NJ: Prentice-Hall.
Brealey, R.A., and Myers, S.C. (1991). *Principles of corporate finance* (3rd edn). New York: McGraw-Hill.
Burns, T., and Stalker, G.M. (1961). *The management of innovation*. London: Tavistock.
Chandler, A.D., Jr. (1962). *Strategy and structure: chapters in the history of the American industrial enterprise*. Cambridge, MA: MIT Press.
Child, J. (1972). 'Organizational structure, environment and performance: the role of strategic choice'. *Sociology*, *6*(1): 2–22.
Cohen, W.M., and Levinthal, D.A. (1990). 'Absorptive capacity: a new perspective on learning and innovation'. *Administrative Science Quarterly*, *35*(1): 128–52.

Colasse, B., and Pavé, F. (1995). 'Claude Riveline. Une pédagogie medieval pour enseigner la gestion'. *Annales des mines*, *49*: 14–32.
Cooper, R., and Kaplan, R.S. (1991). *The design of cost management systems*. Englewood Cliffs, NJ: Prentice-Hall.
Copeland. T.E., and Weston, J.F. (1988). *Financial theory and corporate policy* (3rd edn). Reading, MA: Addison-Wesley.
Cyert, R.M., and March, J.G. (1963). *A behavioral theory of the firm*. Englewood Cliffs, NJ: Prentice-Hall.
Czarniawska-Joerges, B., and Sevón, G. (1996). *Translating organizational change*. Berlin: Walter de Gruyter.
Danell, R., and Engwall, L. (2001). 'Hello Dolly! The European cloning of U.S. management research', in R. Danell (ed.), *Internationalization and homogenization: a bibliometric study of international management research*. Umeå: Umeå University.
Dierickx, I., and Cool, K. (1989). 'Asset stock accumulation and sustainability of competitive advantage'. *Management Science*, *35*(12): 1504–11.
DiMaggio, P.J., and Powell, W.W. (1983). 'The iron cage revisited: institutional isomorphism and collective rationality in organizational fields'. *American Sociology Review*, *48*(2), 147–60.
Douma, S., and Schreuder, H. (1991). *Economic approaches to organizations*. London: Prentice-Hall.
Drury, C. (1992). *Management and cost accounting* (3rd edn). London: Chapman and Hall.
Duymedjian, R., and Rüling, C.-C. (2010). 'Towards a foundation of bricolage in organization and management theory'. *Organization Studies*, *31*(2): 133–51.
Dyer, J.H., and Singh, H. (1998). 'The relational view: cooperative strategy and sources of interorganizational competitive advantage'. *Academy of Management Review*, *23*(4): 660–79.
Eisenhardt, K.M. (1989). 'Building theories from case study research'. *Academy of Management Review*, *14*(4): 532–50.
Eiteman, D.K., Stonehill, A.I., and Moffett, M.H. (1992). *Multinational business finance* (6th edn). Reading, MA: Addison-Wesley.
Engwall, L. (1996). 'The Vikings versus the world: an examination of Nordic business research'. *Scandinavian Journal of Management*, *12*(4): 425–36.
Engwall, L. (1998a). 'Mercury & Minerva: a modern multinational. Academic business studies on a global scale', in J.L. Alvarez (ed.), *The diffusion and consumption of business knowledge*. London: Macmillan, 81–109.
Engwall, L. (1998b). 'Research note: Asterix in Disneyland. Management scholars from France on the world stage'. *Organization Studies*, *19*(5): 863–81.
Engwall, L. (2000). 'Foreign role models and standardisation in Nordic business education'. *Scandinavian Journal of Management*, *15*(1): 1–24.
Engwall, L. (2009). *Mercury meets Minerva. Business studies and higher education: the Swedish case*. Stockholm: EFI (2nd extended edition. 1st edition: Pergamon Press, 1992).
Engwall, L., and Danell, R. (2011). 'Britannia and her business schools'. *British Journal of Management*, *22*(3): 432–42.
Fornell, C., and Larcker, D.F. (1981). 'Evaluating structural equation models with unobservable variables and measurement error'. *Journal of Marketing Research*, *18*(1): 39–50.
Foster, G. (1986). *Financial statement analysis*. Englewood Cliffs, NJ: Prentice-Hall.
Gadde, L.-E., and Håkansson, H. (1993). *Professionellt inköp* (Professional Purchasing). Lund: Studentlitteratur.
Granovetter, M. (1985). 'Economic action and social structure: the problem of embeddedness'. *American Journal of Sociology*, *91*(3): 481–510.
Grönroos, K. (1990). *Service management and marketing*. Lexington, MA: Lexington Books.
Hannan, M.T., and Freeman, J. (1977). 'The population ecology of organizations'. *American Journal of Sociology*, *82*(5): 929–64.
Hannerz, U. (1992). *Cultural complexity: studies in the social organization of meaning*. New York: Columbia University Press.

Heckman, J. (1979). 'Sample selection bias as a specification error'. *Econometrica*, 47(1): 153–611.

Hofer, C.W., and Schendel, D. (1978). *Strategy formulation*. St. Paul, MI: West.

Hull, J.C. (1993). *Options, futures and other derivative securities* (2nd edn). Englewood Cliffs, NJ: Prentice-Hall.

Jensen, M.C., and Meckling, W.H. (1976). 'Theory of the firm: managerial behavior, agency costs and ownership structure'. *Journal of Financial Economics*, 3(4): 305–60.

Kahneman, D., and Tversky, A. (1979). Prospect theory: an analysis of decision under risk. *Econometrica*, 47(2): 263–92.

Kaplan, R.S., and Atkinson, A.A. (1989). *Advanced management accounting*. Englewood Cliffs, NJ: Prentice-Hall.

Kogut, B., and Zander, U. (1992). 'Knowledge of the firm, combinative capabilities, and the replication of technology'. *Organization Science*, 3(3): 383–97.

Kotler, P. (1994). *Marketing management. Analysis, planning, implementation and control* (8th edn). Englewood Cliffs, NJ: Prentice-Hall.

Lambert, D.M., and Stock, J.R. (1993). *Strategic logistics management*. Homewood, IL: Irwin.

Lawrence, P.R., and Lorsch, J.W. (1967). *Organization and environment*. Boston, MA: Graduate School of Business Administration, Harvard University.

Lévi-Strauss, C. (1962). *La pensée sauvage*. Paris: Plon.

Loustarinen, R., and Welch, L. (1990). *International business operations*. Helsinki: Helsinki School of Economics.

March, J.G. (1991). 'Exploration and exploitation in organizational learning'. *Organization Science*, 2(1): 71–87.

March, J.G., and Simon, H.A. (1958). *Organizations*. New York: Wiley.

Meyer, J., and Rowan, B. (1977). 'Institutionalized organizations: formal structure as myth and ceremony'. *American Journal of Sociology*, 83(2): 340–63.

Miles, R.E., and Snow, C.C. (1978). *Organizational strategy, structure and process*. New York: McGraw-Hill.

Mintzberg, H. (1978). 'Patterns in strategy formation'. *Management Science*, 24(9): 934–48.

Mintzberg, H. (1979). *The structuring of organisations*. Englewood Cliffs, NJ: Prentice Hall.

Morgan, G. (1986). *Images of organizations*. Beverly Hills, CA: Sage.

Nelson, R.R., and Winter, S.G. (1982). *An evolutionary theory of economic change*. Cambridge, MA: Harvard University Press.

Nunnally, J.C. (1967). *Psychometric theory*. New York: McGraw-Hill.

Peters, T.J., and Waterman, R.H., Jr. (1982). *In search of excellence: lessons from American best-run companies*. New York: Harper and Row.

Pfeffer, J. (1981). *Power in organizations*. Marshfield, MA: Pitman.

Pfeffer, J., and Salancik, G.R. (1978). *The external control of organizations: a resource dependence perspective*. New York: Harper and Row.

Podsakoff, P.M., MacKenzie, S.B., Lee, J.-Y., and Podsakoff, N.P. (2003). 'Common method variance in behavioral research: a critical review of the literature and recommended remedies'. *Journal of Applied Psychology*, 88(5): 879–903.

Porter, M.E. (1980). *Competitive strategy: techniques for analyzing industries and competitors*. New York: Free Press.

Porter, M.E. (1985). *Competitive advantage*. New York: Free Press.

Robertson, R. (1994). 'Globalization and glocalization'. *Journal of International Communication*, 1(1): 33–52.

Rumelt, R.P. (1974). *Strategy, structure and economic performance*. Boston, MA: Harvard University Press.

Ryan, B., Scapens, W., and Theobald, M. (1992). *Research method and methodology in finance and accounting*. New York: Academic Press.

Sahlin-Andersson, K. (1996). 'Imitating by editing success. The construction of organizational fields and identities', in B. Czarniawska-Joerges and G. Sevón (eds), *Translating organizational change*. Berlin: De Gruyter, 69–92.

Stern, L.W., and El-Ansary, A.I. (1992). *Marketing channels* (5th edn). Upper Saddle River, NJ: Prentice-Hall.
Teece, D.J., Pisano, G., and Shuen, A. (1997). 'Dynamic capabilities and strategic management'. *Strategic Management Journal*, 18(7): 509–33.
Thompson, J.D. (1967). *Organizations in action*. New York: McGraw-Hill.
Weick, K.E. (1969). *The social psychology of organizing*. Reading, MA: Addison-Wesley.
Welford, R., and Gouldson, A. (1993). *Environmental management and business strategy*. London: Pitman.
Wernerfelt, B. (1984). 'The resource-based view of the firm'. *Strategic Management Journal*, 5(2): 171–80.
Williamson, O.E. (1975). *Markets and hierarchy: analysis and antitrust implications*. New York: Free Press.
Williamson, O.E. (1985). *The economic institutions of capitalism*. New York: Free Press.
Woodward, J. (1965). *Industrial organization: theory and practice*. London: Oxford University Press.
Yin, R.K. (1984). *Case study research*. Beverly Hills, CA: Sage.
Yukl, G.A. (1989). *Leadership in organizations* (2nd edn). Englewood Cliffs, NJ: Prentice-Hall.

18
Gender in Times of Global Governance
Glocalizing International Norms Around Money and Power, Violence and Sex in Peru

Miriam Abu-Sharkh

Introduction

The Problem

How are internationally defined gender rights glocalized in Peru? Glocalization is here understood as any form of adoption, implementation, or syncretization of international treaties. The chapter investigates how global governance mechanisms shape discursive and legal practices regarding four key gender issues in Peru: labor market discrimination, political representation, violence against women, and reproductive rights.

Women's rights are an interesting example of the uptake of human rights more generally as they apply to half of humanity. Women's rights thus cover many different domains. I look at developments in Peru around four emancipatory gender issues laid down in treaties and conventions that have long been foci of women's movements across the world: equality at work, empowerment in political representation, the end of gender-based violence, and reproductive choice.

Examining the pertinent interviews and laws suggests that the more institutionalized the women's issue is on a global level or world regional level, the more adoption and less adaption takes place on a discursive and legal level. In other words, internationally well-defined rights are adopted one-to-one to the national context. Glocalization in these cases means direct implementation of global norms disregarding the syncretization with local circumstances.

This chapter adds to the world society (WS) scholarship in several respects. Regarding gender discrimination, the world society literature shows that most nation states have formally pledged to end all forms of discrimination against women by signing the Convention on the Elimination of all Forms of Discrimination Against Women (CEDAW), and International Labour Organization's (ILO) non-discrimination conventions such as Convention 111 against Discrimination in Employment and Occupation (Abu Sharkh 2008; Min, Wotipka, and Ramirez 2008). WS scholarship has demonstrated the global symbolic acceptance of human rights as defined by the United Nations (UN) system (Meyer et al. 1997b). However, there is no research on proving the implementation of women's treaties. World society scholarship has yet to examine the factors influencing the legislative and discursive uptake of women's rights on a world-regional, national, or local level.

In particular, the role of the world-regional level in the global governance structure is under-examined in the world society literature. In Latin America, the Organization of American States (OAS), the Inter-American Court on Human Rights, and the American Convention on Human Rights took up the gender issue. According to Stacy (2009), world-regional human rights institutions play an increasingly important role in implementing human rights. How does the world-regional level affect the treatment of gender issues in Latin American countries?

The world society literature has also not examined how the conflict between different human rights plays out on these various levels. There is an inherent tension in the international human rights instruments between first generation *individual* human rights norms for women's equity and third generation *collective* human rights norms protecting tribal traditions (Stacy 2009). Many of the latter do not put women on an equal footing with men.

Which human rights prevail under which circumstances? Ethnographic studies suggest that 'international packages' are often unpacked; some elements are accepted, others adapted, and yet others rejected by different factions in society (Elwert 1997). Thus, there may be significant variation in the degree of isomorphism, or one-to-one adoption, of different human rights. Some women's rights may be respected while others may be disregarded at the national or local level by different ethno-linguistic groups.

Peru serves as a fitting case study, as it boasts one of the highest cultural and ethno-linguistic fractionalization indexes in Latin America, occupying ranks 2 and 5, respectively, of 23 Latin American countries (Fearon 2003). It can thus illustrate whether or not different women's rights are adapted to different cultural traditions. I chose three disparate regions within Peru: an agricultural-indigenous region, an industrial-export region, and the capital.

To assess whether there is variation in the implementation across women's rights, I look at four key gender issues canonized by CEDAW. These norms were carved out by different international organizations at different time points and at varying levels of specificity:

1. Money: Dating as far back as 1951, the International Labor Organization (ILO, the UN organizations specialized on work) proclaimed in Conventions 100 and 111 that gender-based pay discrimination was prohibited. Based on these conventions, the ILO pressures states to implement measures ending gender-based salary discrepancies. Do actors in Peru implement these conventions in their entirety or do they point out selective uptake out of principle, citing local requirements? Who are the key actors pushing through these norms?

2. Power: The Convention on the Elimination of all Forms of Discrimination Against Women (CEDAW), adopted by the UN in 1979, put forth special measures to increase women's political participation. Article 4 of CEDAW is interpreted to suggest quotas for women, as it calls for special measures to advance the representation of women. CEDAW was ratified by Peru in 1982 without reservations. This stands at odds with later UN conventions, notably the ILO convention concerning Indigenous and Tribal Peoples (Convention 169). Peru ratified this convention in 1994. Whereas CEDAW promotes women in decision-making bodies, the Indigenous and Tribal Peoples calls for respecting tribal customs and traditions. These traditions, in the case of many Peruvian Amazon tribes, do not foresee the integration of women into political decision-making bodies. How does this tension between first generation and third generation humans play out in Peru?

3   Violence: Outlawing violence against women was a late bloomer on the international stage, only coming to the forefront in the 1990s. In Latin America, the Organization of American States, the Inter-American Court on Human Rights, and the American Convention on Human Rights took up the issue of gender-based violence. Do these world-regional instruments substitute or complement world-level agreements regarding gender-based violence? In other words, do they serve as another platform to further world-level, international agreements, or do they try to adapt these agreements to local circumstances?
4   Sex: Of all gender rights, reproductive rights are the least canonized internationally. CEDAW Article 16 grants women the right to freely choose the spacing of their children, but whether or not this statement can be defined as women having the right to terminate a pregnancy is still embattled (Stacy 2009). As the most embattled of women's rights, what forms do national alliances for abortion take and how do they draw on world-level and world-regional agreements?

Two routes of investigation are pursued to give answers to these questions. First, by interviewing activists and experts in local human rights and feminist NGOs, unions, and employer associations as well as government ministers and legislators, I look at the *discursive* frames utilized surrounding women's equitable societal integration. Second, by looking at landmark laws and judgments on discrimination, the research gives a snapshot of the creation of a *legal* human rights structure.

Literature Review

WS research has empirically demonstrated a pledge of allegiance to human rights norms by nation states. Many empirical studies examine treaty ratification or structural changes in line with world society norms (Meyer et al. 1992, 1997b; Bradley and Ramirez 1996; Ramirez 2000; Ramirez et al. 1997; Thomas and Lauderdale 1988; Finnemore 1996; Frank et al. 2000; Boli 1987).[1] A plethora of international organizations, from the UN to Greenpeace, have emerged in the last century and have pressured states to conform to these standards (Meyer and Ramirez 1998; Meyer et al. 1997b). For instance, the United Nations' Educational, Scientific, and Cultural Organization instructed states about the importance of establishing science policy state machineries (Finnemore 1996). The United Nations' specialized agency for work, the International Labour Organization (ILO), teaches states how to write a proper labor code (Abu Sharkh 2008).

In the concept of WS employed by Meyer et al. (1997b) and Meyer et al. (1997a), 'WS' is understood as a partially integrated collection of world-level organizations, understandings, and assumptions that specify the *legitimate* way nation-states deal with domestic and international issues, therefore conferring legitimacy on nation-states. This conceptualization does not reduce transnational activities to military alliances or economic exchange rationales. Rather, it allows conceptual room for the spread and impact of international ideas and norms. Due to this cultural dimension, Meyer et al. (1997b) speak of a world *society*.

One of the most fervently promoted international norms is the concept of 'human rights', as formulated by the UN and its various specialized agencies. All individuals are cast as equal bearers of these rights regardless of their ascriptive characteristics, such as race or gender (Finnemore 1996; Wobbe 2000). What comprises human rights has expanded substantially over the last half-century. Ending discrimination in all realms against women, particularly, constitutes an increasingly central feature for the many different UN treaties and platforms that deal with this issue (Min, Wotipka, and Ramirez 2008).

The provisions of CEDAW, institutionalized in 1979, are the most important binding international commitments to promote the equality of women.[2] CEDAW states: 'In accepting the Convention, states commit themselves to take a series of measures to eradicate all forms of discrimination against women.' These include measures 'to incorporate the principle of the equality of men and women in their legal systems.'[3]

Almost all nation-states have ratified this convention creating 'isomorphisms' in states with vast economic and cultural differences (Meyer 1987: 42). These structures are externally oriented to gain prestige in the international arena.

However, to what degree do these state-level isomorphisms have internal clout? Studies show a large degree of decoupling between state promises and actual occurrences (Leisering et al. 2006). Human rights violations are still widespread, despite official government declarations against them. In what they term the 'paradox of empty promises', Hafner-Burton and Tsutsui (2007) argue that governments often ratify human rights treaties as a matter of 'window dressing', with the worst offenders signing first.

Ethnographic literature demonstrates significant variation in the degree of isomorphism across domains (Elwert 1997). I chose four under-examined domains of gender issues to examine what affects the degrees of isomorphism: money, power, violence, and sex.

WS research has not focused on labor market issues (except Abu Sharkh 2002, 2005, 2008, 2010), though work is the single most time-consuming activity, as well as the most physically, cognitively, and emotionally intensive one for most individuals. Little WS has been done showing the effects of global governance on political representation (except Paxton et al. 2006). Violence against women has been on the forefront of the international governance agenda since the 1990s, though there are no WS studies.[4] Reproductive rights have long been a divisive issue around the world (Stacy 2009). Though CEDAW Article 12 specifies that women have 'access to health care services, including those related to family planning', it does not explicitly advocate 'pro-choice'.[5] Consequently, nations have considerable leeway in that area. From a WS perspective, it is thus an especially interesting contrast to the more canonized international rights. The following section lays out how I tried to tackle these issues methodologically.

Methodology

My analysis employs expert interviews and participant observations. The interviews give a sense of whether the implemented laws were purposefully designed to align with human rights treaty provisions.

For the interviews, the initial sample of international non-governmental organizations (NGOs) was drawn from the Union of International Associations (UIA). The keywords 'women' and 'human rights' were used. This renders the organizations based in Peru purporting to focus on these issues.

In addition to using the UIA as a sample frame, I relied on the help of long-time activists and Ministers of Women Affairs and Social Development. They brokered contact to the various ministries and many Peruvian NGOs and union leaders. Once these contacts had been established, I conducted snowball sampling among governmental and non-governmental actors.

The interview-based methods of these inquiries are complemented by document analysis. On a national level, relevant documents span from national law and their interpreted texts to parliamentary speeches. On a supra-national level, judgments of OAS bodies and UN commissions provide information on Peru's implementation record. Reports to and from the various UN bodies, notably CEDAW and the ILO, also serve as a source concerning the debates around the implementation of standards. According to CEDAW, Peru is committed to submit national reports at least every four years on measures they have taken to comply with their treaty.

Finally, I look at some exemplary legal cases to see how, when, and by whom the international treaties were applied. There have been landmark judgments regarding the gender issues. Again, this does not prove that all women will benefit from these rulings. However, combined, this investigative trilogy lends some exemplary credence to the acceptance and impact of international treaties.

The three regions selected were Lima and its surrounding areas (Lima), the export-oriented costal region around Trujillo (La Libertad), and the more agricultural Amazonian region around Iquitos (Loreto). The inclusion of Lima was fundamental to the study, as I wanted to interview key government actors, the majority of whom find residence there. The Amazon, in many ways the counterpart to Lima, was chosen because it added to the sample a very remote region, in which tribal structures were still in place, allowing me to investigate the tensions between individual women's rights issues and collective, tribal issues. The coastal region was chosen specifically for its agro-export industry, which features some of the worst, unregulated labor practices against women and the weakest forms of protection such as unenforced laws and disenfranchised unions. This region has a high proportion of internal migration by indigenous people from the mountains.

Results: Four Key Issues

Overview of Non-discrimination Treaties to which Peru is Privy

The National Equal Opportunity Plan for Women and Men 2003–2010 is based on the recommendations in the following conventions, agreements, platforms, and regional plans to which Peru is a signatory: the International Covenant on Civil and Political Rights, the International Covenant on Economic, Social and Cultural Rights, the American Convention on Human Rights, 'Pact of San Jose', the Convention on the Elimination of All Forms of Discrimination against Women (CEDAW), the Optional Protocol to the CEDAW, the Inter-American Convention on the Prevention, Punishment, and Eradication of Violence against Women, 'Convention of Belém do Pará', the Beijing Platform for Action, Fourth World Conference on Women, 1995, the Regional Programme of Action for Women of Latin America, and the Caribbean, ECLAC, 1994, the Programme of Action of the International Conference on Population and Development, Cairo, 1994.[6]

Money: Discourse and Laws on Labor Issues

Are world norms as ratified by the UN organizations applied? As the interviews would indicate, every government official, on a national and regional level, from Lima to the Amazon reported an application of the ILO-norms around gender non-discrimination in the labor market in principle. That is not to say that what the ILO conventions stipulate are actually executed 100 percent on the ground, but that there was no *reported* departure from the norms.

Susana Pinilla, Presidential Advisor, former Minister of Labor, and former Minister of Women's Affairs and Social Development, is working on executing the Equal Opportunity

Act and coordinating these goals with the Ministry of Labor. She points out that women still earn 30 percent less than men for equal work when they have the same training. She argued that ratifying a convention is key to cementing goals, as it provides an international framework that commits the country to fulfill them: 'It protects you by going beyond the time the current government is in power. So even if a law already exists against discrimination, as is the case in Peru since 2007, it is still important that all appropriate conventions are ratified.' She specifically cited the UN and CEDAW as being instrumental to the advancement of women. She was also well aware of the differences between the international organizations on different levels. She pointed out that the different international organizations focused on different aspects of women's advancement.

Emerson R. Levenau Delgado, the Director of Work and Employment Promotion in La Libertad, argued that ILO norms are valid for the entire world. He pointed out that the problem was not the differing goals, but that the ILO norms were not applied properly in informal employment. He cited various attempts to combat informality by examining and keeping track of companies' employment registers. The problem with which many females in the labor force contended was that due to pregnancy, their work tenure tended to be shorter, disabling them from accruing pay based on seniority. Furthermore, they tended to be remunerated by piece.

Dr Luis Rodriguez Benavides of the Anti-Poverty Table in Loreto made the following distinction: 'The goals are the same, but there is a big difference between hearing and implementing. People have difficulty internalizing the goals. For people from Loreto that have never been outside of the region, it is still very hard to accept a woman as a boss.' According to him, it was not that the goals of feminist NGOs were different, but that it was difficult to completely implement them.

The Minister of Labor Affairs, Manuela Garcia, argued that there are no key differences between international and local key strategies: 'Peru respects all the international norms.' She cited the most important goal as ending salary discrimination while explicitly citing the relevant ILO Conventions 100 and 111.

The assessment of the Minister of Labor was echoed by her counterpart in the Amazon, the Director for Labor, Emerson R. Levenau Delgado. He argued that Peru had ratified many labor conventions and pointed out that this included the core conventions regarding discrimination, Conventions 100 and 111.

Manuela Garcia pointed to new legislation prohibiting pregnant women from being discharged from work in line with the new Maternity Protection Convention, Convention 183, passed by the ILO in 2000. Emerson R. Levenau Delgado pointed out that Peru has a domestic law of maternity leave that is in accordance with international provisions, as the domestic law allows for pre- and post-natal leave (90 days in total). Note that this actually falls short of the 98 days mandated by the ILO's convention.

Also, Manuela Garcia argued that the ILO Convention 111 referencing sexual harassment had inspired in the year 2002 new legislation that prohibits sexual advances between men and women on the same level of hierarchy; the previous law merely forbade such advances if the perpetrator was a superior. The agro-export industry in La Libertad was especially ripe with such violations. Carmen Salazar, President of the Women's Regional Coordination Council of La Libertad, pointed out that in Peru's coastal La Liberdad region, the agro-export industry was a large employer. Chilean enterprises take mostly young women under 21 from the mountains to harvest asparagus and such vegetation. These young women were often subject to sexual harassment and labor abuse/neglect/mistreatment.

However, in close examination of the ILO Convention 111, there is no reference to sexual advances. It seems as if the ILO is given more credit than is due, perhaps due to social desirability response.

When asked with which organizations she collaborates, Manuela Garcia first cited international organizations, followed by regional organizations: the ILO, UN, Interamerican Development Bank, International Organization for Migration, USAID, American Federation of Labor, Andean Community of Nations, Canadian International Development Agency, and Japan International Cooperation Agency. This shows the permeability of the nation-state border when working on gender discrimination issues.

Ivan Vasquez, the Governor of Loreto, also professed that the ILO conventions served as a cornerstone for legislation. This does not, however, mean that the actual contents of the conventions are known in detail. Dr Luis Rodriguez Benavides again points out that the domestic law gives women a right to an hour of breastfeeding (*lactancia*) until the child is one year old, and she can choose whether it is the first or last hour of the day in alleged accordance with the Maternity Protection Conventions. However, in the current reincarnation of the ILO Maternity Protection Convention, there is no specified amount of time to breastfeed.

Carmen Salazar, President of the Regional Coordination Council in the Libertad Region, points to breastfeeding rights when she describes how women's rights were eroded during Fujimori's presidency. For instance, he eradicated the hour a day set aside for breast-feeding; after giving birth, women no longer had a month off. She argues that the ILO is important, as they push laws and concepts that help growing indigenous movements

The only voice of dissent came from industry, but not on grounds of principle. Javier Caro, President of the Chamber of Commerce of La Libertad, argues that the conventions are too abstract.

A way to circumvent the ILO labor regime is to set up shop in the coastal agro-export industry. According to Flor Nolasco Peres, Council of the Provincial Municipality of Trujillo, Libertad, this area has one of the worst labor conditions despite her attempts to work with CEDAL, the Center for Rights and Development, and the ILO to improve them.

Gladis Campus, President of ATDANA (Asociacion de Trabajadoras Despertando a un Nuevo Amancer – Association of Workers for Waking Up to an New Dawn), notes that the agro-export industry is governed by a special agro-industry special labor regime since Fujimori. Fujimori made laws for every sector. For example, vacation normally is one month; in the agro-export industry, it is 15 days. The salary is lower. The enterprises only pay half of health care, if at all; one needs a contract that is longer than three months for health care, but the companies keep the 'asparigistas' on renewable one-month contracts. Also, there are many bronchial diseases in the agro-export industry, but these are not covered by the national health care system.

ATDANA is part of FEMUCARINAP (La Federacion Nacional de Mujeres Campesina, Artenanas, Indigenas, Nativas y Asalariasdas del Peru – National Federation of Women Farmers, Artisans, Indigenous and Salaried Workers in Peru) which is part of the network of Alianza por Derechos Laborales en la Agroindustria. More traditional union structures and indigenous movement organizations thus join forces to combat working conditions in the agro-export industry.

One issue that was not mentioned much was that of sexual trafficking. The prevention of sexual exploitation of girls in mines is the responsibility of the Ministry of Agricultural Affairs, but they had not made it a priority on their agenda.

The respondents did not believe that the obstacles to upholding the ILO core conventions were unique to Peru. While perhaps not identical to those of other countries, differences were seen on a graduated scale rather than as distinct. For instance, the Minister of Labor reported that the difficulties women face are very similar to those faced by women in other South American countries, yet he argues that Peru has more protection for women's labor rights.

Discursively, all respondents professed both knowledge and adherence to international labor norms put forth in the relevant ILO conventions. That is not to say all workers benefit from them, but that the respondents' national laws were modeled after the relevant conventions. In Peru, there were no noted deviations from the long-established principles to equality in the labor market.

Power: Quotas in Political Decision-making Bodies

A second key gender issue is the participation of women in key political decision-making bodies. CEDAW recommends quotas. Internationally, a quota of 30 percent has become standard.

The effect of international organizations on the introduction of a gender quota in Peru is pronounced according to the interviewees. The gender quota was extended via regional law to remote corners of the Amazon, where women were traditionally not included in political decision-making. None of the interviewees suggested that quotas should not be implemented if it contradicted traditional culture. On the contrary, they pointed out that now that indigenous women were *regidoras* (district leaders), this afforded opportunities to train them in gender consciousness.

Margarita Sucari, congresswoman and chair of the Parliamentarian Caucus of Women of the Peruvian Parliament that proposes laws to different ministries, argued that 'CEDAW played an important role in Peru for establishing quotas.' The Inter-Parliamentarian Union (IPU) was also fundamental to the introduction of the quota system in Peru: 'The IPU publishes statistics on the percentage of women in parliament. They invite the Peruvian parliamentarians to forums, always publish numbers, and rank Latin American countries by how many female parliamentarians they have. A number of Latin American countries have subsequently introduced quotas: Costa Rica and Argentina in 1991, Peru in 1997.'[7] Introducing quotas had a very large impact on moving various social issues forward. 'About 35 female members of parliament now cooperate across party lines on issues of child labor, sexual exploitation and violence', she adds.

To increase women's participation in political decision-making bodies, the Peruvian State has adopted affirmative action measures, such as election quota laws. Article 116 of the current Elections Act (*Ley Orgánica de Elecciones*) increases the gender-equity quota, and provides that 'lists of candidates for Congress in each electoral district must comprise at least 30% women and at least 30% men. In electoral districts in which there are lists with three candidates, there must be at least one woman and at least one man'. The National Elections Board in plenary session established the number of female candidates that must occupy congressional seats through Resolution 057-2001-JNE (17 January 2001) and established the number of seats for each electoral district for the general elections in Resolution 068-2001-JNE (22 January 2001). Consequently, there was a significant jump in the percentage of women in parliament. Whereas the last uncontested election in 1996 had yielded 11 percent female parliamentarians, in 2001, the number jumped to 18.33 percent, and in 2006, it was 29 percent. In 2011, however, it was down to 21.5 percent, showing that legislated quotas are not always attained.[8]

The Regional Elections Act, Law 27683 (March 25, 2002) regulated for the first time the election of regional authorities imposing a gender quota: 'Regional Council must consist of one candidate from each province in the order in which the political movement or party shall decide, including an alternative in each case; also, no fewer than 30% of men or women, and a minimum of 15% of representatives of native and rural communities in each region where they exist, as determined by the National Elections Board (...).' The results for the 2002 municipal elections were thus that of the vacant positions among the councillors (2,644 out of 10,289); 25.7 percent of those elected were female.

In 2007, the National Equal Opportunity Plan was passed to comply with CEDAW. However, the national plan needed to be executed in regional plans. As of March 2010, only 14 out of the 25 regions had implemented the plan.

The plan had been passed in Loreto, the Amazonian part of Peru, a region where human rights violations abound, as sexual exploitation occurs in mines or through sex tourism. When I visited in early 2010, Ivan Enrique Vasques Valera, the Governor of Loreto, reported that they had just adopted the Regional Equal Opportunity Plan.[9] This had led to the cementation of the gender quota system in the Amazon. Women in tribes across the Amazon, who ten years ago had not been permitted to even partake in the communal meetings, were now *regidoras*. These *regidoras*, or district leaders, were brought to the regional capital to be educated about their rights and assert leadership positions in their communities.

The field research thus revealed that this quota system had extended even into the most remote areas of the Amazon to make women into *regidoras* who otherwise displayed very little feminist or political consciousness in the interviews. The only contact most of the *regidoras* had with 'Western women' were with nuns who had run schools or other literacy programs.

If there was any conflict between the first and third generation of human rights, it was not apparent, or it was resolved in favor of first generation rights. There was no mention by any government official that the adoption of a quota was not promoted due to the fact that Amazonian women had traditionally not held power. The quota was immediately introduced at the internationally customary 30 percent, with training workshops about women's rights—one of which I attended. At the workshop, held with frontal lectures, the somewhat helpless-looking 'rulers' were instructed about their new powers with no adaption to tribal customs. Though the practices of the rule in remote Amazonian villages may well be adopted to fit local realities, the formal appointments paralleled international customs.

Violence Against Women

The issue of violence against women is somewhat of a late bloomer on the international stage. Thus, it is a good opportunity to look at how domestic efforts were futile without international 'moral support'. It demonstrates the rising significance of world-regional bodies, such as the Inter-American Commission on Human Rights.

Margarita Sucari, congresswoman and chair of the Parliamentarian Caucus of Women, spearheaded the effort to modify the domestic violence law since 1988. The goal was to criminalize violence against women and provide victims with compensation. However, according to her, it took the Inter-American Commission on Human Rights' ruling in favor of Maria da Penha to put domestic violence on the agenda in Peru.

Mrs Maria da Penha Maia Fernandes, the Center for Justice and International Law[10] (CEJIL), and the Latin American and Caribbean Committee for the Defense of Women's Rights (CLADEM) had filed a case against the government of Brazil drawing upon Articles 44 and 46 of the American Convention on Human Rights and Article 12 of the Inter-American Convention on the Prevention, Punishment, and Eradication of Violence against Women.

The petition argues that the Federative Republic of Brazil had condoned the domestic violence by her husband, including attempted murder in 1983, which left Maria da Penha a paraplegic. The petition was granted by the Inter-American Commission on Human Rights, which is one of the two mechanisms of the Organization of American States set up for the protection of human rights in April 2001.[11]

The same year, the Peruvian government established the National Program against Family Violence and Sexual Abuse. In 2002, the government adopted a law that makes local authorities responsible for policies around domestic violence. Interestingly, the law stipulates punishments not only for rape but also for spousal rape. Margarita Sucari cited that in 2009 alone, 126 women were murdered by their husbands or former husbands. World Health Organization (WHO) statistics show almost half of all women living in a relationship have suffered violence through their partner. With issues bleeding into each other over time, the combating of domestic violence facilitated the emergence of violence against domestic workers as a national issue.

In January 2010, Anel Townsend, former Minister of Women's Affairs and Social Development and former Congresswoman, together with women leaders of different grassroots organizations of Peru, presented a demand against the Peruvian State at the Inter-American Commission of Human Rights of the OAS in Washington DC, for violating the OAS Convention to eliminate all kinds of violence against women (Belem do Para Convention) and the Inter-American Convention of Human Rights of the OAS.

Note that CEDAW had in the early 1990s written a *Draft Declaration on the Elimination of Violence against Women*, a document that included all extra- and intra-familial forms of violence against women, including domestic violence and spousal rape as one of the forms of violence against women in Article 2. This draft was adopted by the General Assembly in 1993.

Susana Pinilla, Presidential Advisor, former Minister of Labor Affairs, and former Minister of Women's Affairs and Social Development of Peru, pointed out that Peru was part of the Inter-American Convention on the Prevention, Punishment and Eradication of Violence against Women since 1996. However, domestic violence had not been made a criminal offense in Peru until after the decision of the Inter-American Commission on Human Rights.

To take up the discussion of Anyul and Punzo (2001), Boyd (1998), and Stacy (2009), world-level agreements gained more impetus when taken up by world-level INGOs and NGOs. There were, indeed, many references in the interviews to the decision of the Inter-American Commission on Human Rights and how the Brazilian government had been reprimanded. Though no comparable case was brought against Peru, it seemed that government officials were intent on pre-empting this by passing the appropriate legislation.

The laws against gender violence make a case for how the judgments of human rights instruments can linger on the international level and may need to be brought home by organizations on the world-regional level.

Reproductive Rights

Abortion is the key gender issue closest to being an example of being adapted, or 'syncretized', on a national level by the invention of the term 'therapeutic abortion'. Note that CEDAW does not openly advocate the right to abort. Article 10 (Education) states that 'Parties shall take all appropriate measures to … (h) Access to specific educational information to help to ensure the health and well-being of families, including information and advice on family planning.' Article 12 (Health Care) states that 'Parties shall take all appropriate measures to eliminate discrimination against women in the field of health care in order to ensure, on a basis of equality of men and women, access to health care services, including those related to family planning.' As only the right to health is enshrined internationally, this provided the access road to pro-choice family planning.

Peru has come under a great deal of scrutiny concerning its lack of reproductive rights both from governmental organizations, notably CEDAW, and from INGOs. Two cases provide an interesting example of how INGOs and different UN covenants, conventions, and committees are mutually reinforcing. They provide a good example of the 'boomerang effect' (Keck and Sikkink 1998).

The first is the case of *Karen Noelia Llantoy Huamán v. Peru*.[12] Three organizations had brought the case by Karen Noelia Llantoy Huamán in front of the Human Rights Committee, established under Article 28 of the International Covenant on Civil and Political Rights: a Peruvian NGO, DEMUS (Estudio para la Defensa de los Derechos de la Mujer – Study for the Defense of Women's Rights), and two INGOs, CLADEM (Latin American and Caribbean Committee for the Defense of Women's Rights) and the Center for Reproductive Law and Policy.

On 16 August 2001, Ms Amanda Gayoso, a social worker in the Peruvian association of social workers, advised a medical intervention to terminate the pregnancy of Ms Huamán, whose child was not likely to survive due to serious physical or mental defects, 'since its continuation would only prolong the distress and emotional instability of Karen and her family'. However, no intervention took place, owing to the refusal of the Health Ministry medical personnel, and Ms Huamán was forced to carry the fetus to full term. Under Article 119 in Peru, therapeutic abortion was permitted only when the pregnancy would lead to serious and permanent damage to the woman's health. Ms Huamán won the case before the Human Rights Committee in November 2005.

However, the government of Peru did not comply with paying reparations. The discussion in the CEDAW committee provides an interesting example of the interlocking efforts of national world-regional and global governance organizations. The CEDAW committee then took this issue up and chastised the representative of Peru. Ms. Dairiam pointed out that 14 percent of abortions performed on young girls in Peru had lethal consequences. As the State party had ratified the Optional Protocol to the International Covenant on Civil and Political Rights, the failure to cooperate with the Human Rights Committee in *Llantoy Huamán v. Peru* 'struck her as extremely disrespectful'.[13] She urged the government to seek a solution to the problem of abortion.[14] The Peruvian delegate, Mr Chávez, replied to the comment:

He did not wish to give the impression that his Government was unwilling to cooperate with the Human Rights Committee. Nevertheless, there were a number of practical difficulties involved in implementing the Committee's decision in *Llantoy Huamán v. Peru*, particularly regarding reparation for damages. Under Article 119 of the Criminal Code, abortion was permitted only when it was the only way to save a pregnant woman's life or to avoid serious or permanent damage to her health. However, that provision left room for interpretation, and should be further clarified at the legislative level.[15]

In June of 2009, the Center for Reproductive Rights and the Center for the Promotion and Defense of Sexual and Reproductive Rights (the Peruvian partner organization) filed a human rights petition against Peru on behalf of L.C. (only the initials are given for privacy reasons) before the United Nations Committee on the Elimination of Discrimination against Women.

In October 2011, the CEDAW committee ruled in favor of L.C. and mandated that Peru amend its law to allow women to obtain an abortion in cases of rape and sexual assault and ensure the availability of abortion services in those circumstances and when a woman's life or health is in danger.[16] This reinforced the direction of the Human Rights Committee.

Susana Pinilla pointed out that international organizations sometimes opened an interpretative backdoor. The WHO had declared that the emergency contraceptive pill is not abortive, so the Ministry of Health and the 'Women's Ministry' opposed the Cardinal of the Catholic Church in an attempt to legalize the so-called 'morning after pill'.

Irma Ganoza, the Director of the NGO Michaela Bastidas, noted that the lack of progress made on this issue was due to the absence of a second generation of activists. This was the area with the staunchest resistance to implementation and the one most inclined to syncretization, that is, the adaption to local beliefs. While the goal of the various organizations was the legalization of abortion, they chose a stepwise approach by first only insisting that abortion be legal due to rape or sexual abuse. As abortion was already legal when the mother's life was endangered, the other goal was to make abortion actually accessible under these circumstances. It is worth noting that 'pro-choice' is not actually codified as a right internationally. The references to women's choice are vaguely cast as it opens up possibilities of national adaption.

Conclusions

Internationally defined gender rights are glocalized in Peru by both state and non-state actors, such as international non-governmental organizations and trade unions. International norms have strong influence on the discourse and legislation around gender issues on a world-regional, national, and country-regional level, both in the capital and in remote regions.

In Lima, the capital, interviews with ministers, parliamentarians, and NGOs suggested that these different actors were well aware and savvy about the jurisdiction of different international organizations, as well as the content of the relevant non-discrimination conventions. They implemented them on a legal level, nationally reinforcing Frank et al.'s (2000) arguments that they serve as receptor sites. The primary route of influence of international norms was via the foreseen institutional routes. CEDAW was taken as the basis for the passing and refining of the National Equal Opportunity Act. Decisions of the bodies of the Organization of American States also had a marked impact on the national discourse and law regarding gender-based violence.

In the Amazonian region, the top-down approach continued on a regional-local level. The most significant development had been the introduction of a gender quota system. The quota system stemmed from the regional implementation of the National Equal Opportunity Plan into a regional National Equal Opportunity Act for Loreto. Women in tribes across the Amazon, who ten years ago had not been permitted to even partake in the communal meetings, were now *regidoras*. These *regidoras*, or district leaders, were brought to the regional capital to be educated about their rights and assert leadership positions in their communities. This is noteworthy, as it is evidence of world societal influences even in very remote regions regarding very tangible power structures.

In La Libertad, the role of unions was pronounced. As it is part of export processing zones, many national labor protection laws do not apply. Also, due to the high incidence of migrant workers, no traditional organizational structures exist. Unions were the chief organizational spine. Internationally linked unions claimed the implementation of non-discrimination conventions of the ILO. Historically, unions have not been one of the proponents of female equity. However, trade unions now actively campaign for gender equity at work, citing ILO conventions. They are also closely affiliated with the International Confederation of Free

Trade Unions (ICFTU), which, in turn, is affiliated with the ILO. This was incidentally true for unions in both the capital and the export processing zone.

National and regional organizations draw on various human rights instruments when acting as plaintiffs for human rights. Organizationally, it is noteworthy, rather than domestic NGOs appealing, most such cases are brought forth by a chain of national and regional NGOs linking up and world-regional organizations taking charge organizationally.

Women's rights that belong to the liberal tradition that emphasize equal opportunity with men rather than unique rights for women, such as reproductive choice, are clearly delineated in international agreements. Liberal women's rights that are clearly canonized in international agreements exert an effect both top-down through nation-state implementation and bottom-up through trade unions or women's NGO chains.

This chapter set out to examine the glocalization of four gender issues in Peru to ascertain in how the degree of implementation differs by dimension: labor, political representation, violence against women, and reproductive rights.

Regarding labor issues, the ILO conventions were referenced without solicitation. Equal pay for equal work was upheld in discourse and law. In addition, all the current ILO convention themes that are treated in more recent ILO conventions surfaced, such as care work (i.e., caring for children or the elderly).

Regarding questions of political representation, quotas in line with the standard interpretation of CEDAW were implemented, disregarding cultural traditions of normally excluding indigenous women from bodies of authority. Neither respondents nor legislative texts pointed out tensions between first generation universalistic human rights norms of gender equity and third generation human rights norms strengthening tribal or indigenous cultures. The individual women's rights superseded any collective, traditional rights without question.

Regarding violence, no one argued that it was endemic to the Peruvian culture, but rather pointed out the regional resolutions banning violence against women. World-regional agreements on a (Latin) American level complement global, world-level agreements. There was much cross-referencing between the different international conventions both on an international level and on a world-regional level.

Reproductive rights were still highly contested due to the position and strength of the Catholic Church in Peru. Vague international norms regarding the freedom of women to choose position and spacing of children are not interpreted in Peru as the right to choose to terminate a pregnancy. Even the officially recognized right to terminate when the life of the mother is in danger due to the pregnancy, though recognized by law as a 'therapeutic abortion', is not recognized in practice. Women's organizations try to close the gap between de jure and de facto recognition.

The more institutionalized a women's issue, the more isomorphic it becomes. The clear codification on the international level leads to the adoption of an identical provision on the national level without the bastardization of either the text or the spirit of the agreement in even very remote regions.

Another noteworthy finding is the pronounced role that regional human rights instruments of the OAS play a key interlocutor role, in particular, in respect to violence against women. Though the theme had emerged on the international level in the early 1990s, it took the OAS body rulings to put violence against women on the agenda for Latin America around the turn of the millennium. More research is needed in comparable countries to ascertain the generalizability of these findings regarding the glocalization of gender issues in times of global governance.

Acknowledgments

This research was made possible through the European Research Council start-up grant 241069, GloGender and the generous in-kind contribution of the Stanford Center for International Development.

Notes

1. Theoretically, this argument builds on the open systems perspective (Scott 1998) that argues that structures of organizations often do not arise out of functional necessity but rather due to the pressures from the 'organizational fields' that constitute the frame of reference for these organizations (DiMaggio and Powell 1991: 9).
2. http://daccess-dds-ny.un.org/doc/UNDOC/GEN/N04/301/07/PDF/N0430107.pdf?OpenElement, visited October 14, 2010.
3. http://daccess-dds-ny.un.org/doc/UNDOC/GEN/N04/301/07/PDF/N0430107.pdf?OpenElement, visited October 14, 2010.
4. See WHO (2005), the Resolution A/55/2 of the United Nations Millennium Declaration September 2000. (www.un.org/millennium/declaration/ares5552e.htm), 'Declaration on the elimination of violence against women' (UN General Assembly resolution, document A/RES/48/104, UN, New York, 1993). The Fourth World Conference on Women, Beijing, China 1995 (document A/CONF.177/20, UN, New York, 1995).
5. http://www.ipu.org/PDF/publications/cedaw_en.pdf.
6. http://daccess-dds-ny.un.org/doc/UNDOC/GEN/N07/214/57/PDF/N0721457.pdf?OpenElement, visited November 1, 2011, page 11.
7. http://www.ipu.org/parline-e/reports/2251_arc.htm, visited November 14, 2011.
8. http://www.ipu.org/parline-e/reports/2251_A.htm, visited November 14, 2011.
9. Ordenanza Regional Aprobacion Plan Regional de Igualdad de Oportunidades entre mujeres y varones de Loreto 2010–2015.
10. The institutional mission of CEJIL is to contribute to the full enjoyment of human rights in the Americas through the effective use of the tools of the Inter-American System and international human rights law.
11. http://www.cidh.org/women/brazil12.051.htm, visited October 20, 2011.
12. Communication No. 1153/2003, UN Doc. CCPR/C/85/D/1153/2003 (2005).
13. http://www.un.org/womenwatch/daw/cedaw/37sess.htm.
14. Ibid.
15. Ibid.
16. http://reproductiverights.org/sites/crr.civicactions.net/files/documents/CEDAW-C-50-D-22-2009%20English%20(clean%20copy).pdf, page 20.

References

Abu Sharkh, M. (2002). 'History and results of labor standard initiatives: an event history and panel analysis of the ratification patterns, and effects, of the International Labor Organization's First Child Labor Convention'. PhD Dissertation. Berlin: Freie Universität Berlin.

Abu Sharkh, M. (2005). 'Why countries do ratify labour conventions despite possible competitive disadvantages? An event history analysis of the ratification of the minimum age convention 1973-2005'. IFP/SES, International Labour Organization working paper. Geneva: ILO.

Abu Sharkh, M. (2008). 'Cross-coupling of international and national law regarding labor market discrimination against women, 1958 to 2005'. Working paper. Stanford: Center on Democracy, Development, and the Rule of Law [Presented at the American Sociological Association Meeting, Aug. 1–4, 2008].

Abu Sharkh, M. (2010) 'Warum ratifizieren Länder internationale Kinderarbeitskonventionen? Eine Ereignisanalyse der Ratifizierung des Übereinkommens über das Mindestalter für die Zulassung zur Beschäftigung'. *Zeitschrift für Sozialreform* 56(2): 207–31.

Anyul, M.P., and Punzo, L.F. (2001). *Mexico beyond NAFTA: perspectives for the European debate*. London and New York: Routledge.
Boli, J. (1987). *Human rights or state expansion? Cross-national definitions of constitutional rights, 1870–1970*. London: Sage.
Boyd, G. (ed.). (1998). *The struggle for world markets: competition and cooperation between NAFTA and the European Union*. Cheltenham and Northampton, MA: Edward Elgar.
Bradley, K., and Ramirez, F.O. (1996). 'World polity and gender parity: women's share of higher education, 1965–1985'. *Research in Sociology of Education and Socialization*, 11: 63–91.
DiMaggio, P.J., and Powell, W.W. (1991). 'The iron cage revisited: institutional isomorphism and collective rationality in organization fields', in W.W. Powell and P.J. DiMaggio (eds), *The new institutionalism in organizational analysis*. Chicago, IL: University of Chicago Press.
Elwert, G. (1997). 'Schmückendes Gerede und reale Entwicklungsbedingungen—Über soziokulturelle Bedingungen der Entwicklung', in M. Schulz (ed.), *Entwicklung: Die Perspektive der Entwicklungssoziologie*. Opladen: Westdeutscher Verlag, 261–90.
Fearon, J. (2003). *Ethnic structure and cultural diversity around the world: a cross-national data set on ethnic groups*. California: Stanford University.
Finnemore, M. (1996). 'Norms, culture and world politics: insights from sociology's institutionalism'. *International Organization*, 50: 325–47.
Frank, D., Hironaka, A., and Schofer, E. (2000). 'The nation-state and the environment over the twentieth century'. *American Sociological Review*, 65: 127–49.
Hafner-Burton, E.M., and Tsutsui, K. (2007). 'Justice lost! The failure of international human rights law to matter where needed most'. *Journal of Peace Research*, 44(4): 407–25.
Keck, M.E., and Sikkink, K. (1998). *Activists beyond borders: advocacy networks in international politics*. New York: Cornell University Press.
Leisering, L., Buhr, P., and Traiser-Diop, U. (2006). 'Grundsicherung als globale Herausforderung' [Basic income as a global challenge]. *Soziale Grundsicherungssysteme in Entwicklungs- und Übergangsgesellschaften—ein weltweiter Survey*. Bielefeld: Transcript.
Meyer, J.W. (1987). 'The world polity and the authority of the nation state', in G. Thomas, J. Boli, J.W. Meyer, and F. Ramirez (eds), *Institutional structure. Constituting state, society and the individual*. Newbury Park, CA: Sage, 41–70.
Meyer, J.W., and Ramirez, F.O. (1998). 'Dynamics of citizenship development and the political incorporation of women: a global institutionalization research agenda', in C.L. McNeely (ed.), *Public rights, public rules. Constituting citizens in the world polity and National Policy*. New York: Garland, 59–80.
Meyer, J.W., Ramirez, F.O., and Soysal, Y.N. (1992). 'World expansion of mass education, 1870–1980'. Sociology of Education, 65: 128–49.
Meyer, J.W., Boli, J., Thomas, G., and Ramirez, F. (1997b). 'World society and the nation state.' *American Journal of Sociology*, 103: 144–81.
Meyer, J.W., Frank, D.J., Hironaka, A., Schofer, E., and Tuma, N. (1997a). 'The structuring of a world environmental regime, 1870–1990'. *International Organization*, 51: 623–51.
Paxton, P., Hughes, M., and Green, J. (2006). 'The international women's movement and women's political representation, 1893–2003'. *American Sociological Review*, 71: 898–920.
Ramirez, F.O. (2000). 'Progress, justice, and gender equity: world models and cross-national trends', in W. Powell and D. Jones (eds), *Bending the bars of the iron cage: institutional dynamics and processes*. Chicago, IL: Chicago University.
Ramirez, F.O., Soysal, Y., and Shanahan, S. (1997). 'The changing logic of political citizenship: cross-national acquisition of women's suffrage rights, 1890–1990'. *American Sociological Review*, 62: 735–45.
Scott, W.R. (1998). *Organizations: rational, natural, and open systems* (5th edn). New York: Prentice Hall.
Stacy, H. (2009). *Human rights for the 21st century*. Stanford, CA: Stanford University Press.

Thomas, G.M., and Lauderdale, P. (1988). 'State authority and national welfare programs in the world system context'. *Sociological Forum*, 3: 383–99.
Wobbe, T. (2000). *Weltgesellschaft*. Bielefeld, Germany: Universitat Bielefeld.
Wotipka, C.M., and Ramirez, F.O. (2008). 'World society and human rights: an event history analysis of the Convention on the Elimination of All Forms of Discrimination against Women', in B. Simmons, F. Dobbin, and G. Garrett (eds), *The global diffusion of markets and democracy*. Cambridge, Cambridge University Press, 303–43.

19

Europeanization of National Administrations in the Czech Republic and Poland

Assessing the Extent of Institutional Change

Christoph Knill and Jale Tosun

Introduction

In the political science literature, a rich body of research on Europeanization has emerged, which, in its dominant form, sheds light on the various ways in which political integration with the European Union (EU) affects the member states' policy and institutional arrangements (see, e.g., Börzel and Risse 2003; Knill 2001; Knill and Lehmkuhl 2002). A central finding of this research perspective is that national factors, such as the preferences of domestic veto players, are essential for explaining the varying degrees of policy and institutional change in the member states (see, e.g., Mastenbroek and Kaeding 2006; König and Luetgert 2009). Typically, Europeanization studies discuss the occurrence of events of policy and institutional change in the context of effective compliance with EU law. Compliance with EU law is of a high practical relevance since otherwise, the single market—that is, the centerpiece of the European integration project—cannot function properly (Kelemen 2000).

The Europeanization literature shares its emphasis on national factors for understanding the effects of international pressures with a sociological research perspective, namely, the study of glocalization (see, e.g., Robertson 1994; Giulianotti and Robertson 2007). Both strands of research advance the view that processes at the local level are critical for the way in which global phenomena become accommodated. As a consequence, exposure to the same international stimulus may still produce varying local-level outcomes. From this perspective, Europeanization can be perceived as a special case of glocalization, where global pressures within the geographic boundary of the EU encounter national structures, which, in turn, determine to what degree the European influence materializes itself in policy and institutional arrangements. Based on this view, in this chapter, we advance the core argument that it is a promising theoretical strategy to build a conversation between these two concepts. To this end, we rely on the literature on governance modes, which has become increasingly popular in the study of EU policy-making (Kohler-Koch and Rittberger 2009), and merge it with the literature on glocalization strategies.

Empirically, we rely on the analysis of institutional change in two new EU member states, namely, the Czech Republic and Poland. Focusing on new member states seems to provide particularly interesting insights into the mutual effectiveness of the European and the national level, as they are often associated with good transposition records (see, e.g., Dimitrova and Toshkov 2007; Sedelmeier 2008; Zubek 2008), but an insufficient degree of institutional change to make EU law actually work (Falkner 2010). This suggests that EU pressure is not a sufficient condition for bringing about institutional change in these countries.

In fact, even during the accession process, we could observe that domestic factors produced variation in compliance with EU law in the various policy fields, despite the accession candidates' overall commitment to aligning their policy and institutional arrangements with those required by the EU (Cirtautas and Schimmelfennig 2010: 423). Consequently, we aim here to identify the relevant local-level factors by concentrating on two new member states we consider to be representative of the entire group of states joining the EU from 2004 onward.

This contribution provides two main insights. The first one is of a theoretical nature and is about the extent to which Europeanization and glocalization research can be integrated into one analytical framework. The second insight is an empirical one and concerns the understanding of institutional change in new member states after entering the EU. This comparatively recent research perspective, known as 'post-accession' compliance, is essentially interested in evaluating whether new member states show sufficient commitment to complying with EU law (see, e.g., Schimmelfennig and Trauner 2009; Cirtautas and Schimmelfennig 2010; Tosun 2011).

The remainder of this chapter is structured as follows. We first define our conceptualization of institutional change. Subsequently, we discuss how the concepts of Europeanization and glocalization can be integrated, before turning to the theoretical model. We then evaluate the theoretical model on the basis of empirical findings advanced by the literature. In the final section, we present the conclusion.

Defining Institutional Change

We conceive of institutional change as any modification to institutional arrangements, which can entail the adoption of new institutions as well as changes of varying degrees to existing institutions. In so doing, however, we are not interested in events of institutional change per se (see, e.g., Zubek and Goetz 2010), but in their relevance for facilitating compliance with EU legal provisions. From this, it follows that we are predominantly interested in the administrative aspects of institutional change, such as modifications to patterns of ministerial coordination (see, e.g., Goetz 2001). It has often been expressed in the literature that the legacy of state-socialist institutions represents the main challenge that new member states have to address in order to comply with EU law, as well as to be able to act as effective players in the EU's multi-level governance system (see, e.g., Goetz 2001; Lippert, Umbach, and Wessels 2001; Camyar 2010; Cirtautas and Schimmelfennig 2010).

New member states have to pursue different types of institutional change. On the one hand, institutions representing a legacy of the state-socialist system must be reformed fundamentally or even terminated. On the other hand, new institutional structures must be created, which equally involves resources and can lead to opposition, as the institutions to be created might be regarded as competitors by the existing institutions. Yet one of the dominant theoretical perspectives on institutional change (i.e., historical institutionalism) stresses that institutions are likely to remain stable due to 'lock-ins'. Thus, if institutional change occurs at all, it can be expected to entail changes in subtle and gradual ways (Streeck and Thelen 2005). In accordance with this view, we expect the most likely form of institutional change to be incremental adjustments to existing arrangements. In other words, the degree of institutional change in response to EU pressure should be constrained by the characteristics of the existing institutional arrangements.

Europeanization and Glocalization: Towards an Integrated Approach

In the introduction, we argued that Europeanization can be conceived as a special case of glocalization, since both concepts challenge the assumption that international pressures lead to a homogenization of national practices and structures. Europeanization studies tend to concentrate on how the EU affects the national level in order to explain why some member states might experience delays or even entirely fail to comply with EU law. This basic research interest results from two particular characteristics of the EU. The first one is that the main objective of the EU has been the creation of a single market. The single market where goods and services are freely exchanged among member states can, however, only function if relevant national laws become harmonized. With the preservation of different regulatory standards, the member states might be inclined to practice 'regulatory arbitrage', that is, to exploit lower regulatory standards to improve their own competitiveness (Kelemen 2000).

The second, but closely related characteristic of the EU, is that member states are responsible for the implementation of harmonized policies. The European Commission is in charge of monitoring the implementation process, but only recently, it was given a more powerful arsenal of tools for performing this task. Despite the availability of new tools, the European Commission is reluctant to make excessive use of enforcement tools, as this could lower the political support by the national governments for the integration project (Jordan and Tosun 2012). The need to properly implement EU law and the fact that member states are responsible for this point out why Europeanization research regards national factors as a potential disturbance to harmonization and the realization of the single market.

In the case of glocalization, national factors are associated with a neutral or even positive connotation. National factors are seen as being responsible for how exactly global phenomena are embraced by the local level, often suggesting that globalization cannot be set equal to homogenization. This analytical lens is intuitive, since glocalization does not focus on one purposeful integration project but on a range of different processes taking place at the global level.

The different (implicit) perceptions about the desirability of national factors for accommodating international pressures are reflected in the typical research perspectives concerning institutional change. Europeanization studies stress the strong relationship between the effective implementation of EU law and effective institutional adaptation (Knill and Lenschow 2005a, 2005b). Even though EU law is mostly concerned with defining contents and instruments rather than prescribing institutional arrangements, it should not be overlooked that appropriate institutional structures are needed in order to meet the policy goals defined by the EU. Glocalization studies, in contrast, tend to focus more objectively on the fusion of global and local elements. This is predominantly done by adopting a tone that globalization does not pose a threat to national structures and practices (Robertson 1994).

Despite the diverse research interests, the concepts of Europeanization and glocalization can be integrated. To this end, we propose to rely on the Europeanization literature for understanding the interlinkage between EU pressures and institutional change in the member states, and on the glocalization literature to characterize the forms of institutional change. Regarding the latter, we rely on Giulianotti and Robertson (2007: 135), who identify four local-level outcomes for processes taking place at the international level: relativization, accommodation, hybridization, and transformation. Relativization is about preserving local institutions despite global influence. Institutional change in response to international pressures is principally possible but limited in scope. Accommodation refers to absorbing pragmatically the practices and institutions associated with other societies or an international model while maintaining key elements of local arrangements. Hybridization is about synthesizing local and global practices and institutions. Institutional change should mainly consist of inserting international elements into existing national institutional arrangements. Transformation is about favoring the practices and institutions promoted by international processes. Processes of institutional change intend to bring about profound changes in existing structures with the objective of bringing them more in line with a howsoever-defined international benchmark.

Once the local-level outcomes of EU pressures are characterized, the analytical lens provided by Europeanization research comes into play. The corresponding body of literature facilitates the establishment of the causal relationship between EU pressures and institutional change as well as a greater understanding of the implications of the degree of institutional change for an effective implementation of EU law. In this regard, Knill and Lenschow (2005a, 2005b), for instance, suggest a distinction between three levels of EU-induced institutional adaptation pressure. This distinction is based on the reasoning that institutionally grown structures and routines prevent easy adaptation to EU pressures (see, e.g., Pierson 2000). As a result, domestic institutional change should be more likely in cases in which European policies imply incremental rather than fundamental departures from existing arrangements.

In constellations of low adaptation pressure, the institutional implications of EU policies are somewhat in line with the domestic arrangements in place, leading to two possible implications for domestic arrangements: no or only marginal changes. Implementation of EU policies is expected to be rather effective since institutional adjustment requirements are either very limited or completely absent. Therefore, the most likely local-level outcomes are accommodation or hybridization.

Constellations of high adaptation pressure are characterized by EU requirements exceeding the adjustment capacities of national institutions. Such constellations can be expected when EU requirements are in contradiction with strongly entrenched elements of national institutional arrangements. Such contradictions occur, for instance, if EU policies require changes in domestic regulatory styles and structures that are strongly rooted in a member state's political, administrative, and legal system. In terms of glocalization outcomes, this would entail the occurrence of relativization.

Finally, in constellations of moderate adaptation pressure, EU policies require substantive adjustments of domestic institutions, but do not challenge well-entrenched patterns of the political, legal, and administrative system. In terms of implementation effectiveness, when faced with moderate adaptation pressure, the outcome can be a positive one. Yet this depends not only on the existing institutional arrangements, but also on the domestic interest constellations. That said, effective implementation by means of carrying out the necessary institutional changes should be most likely when the relevant domestic actors support them (see, e.g., Knill 2001; Knill and Lehmkuhl 2002; Mastenbroek and Kaeding 2006). In this case, we should be able to observe hybridization or even transformation.

Recapitulating, we can relate the four ideal-typical glocalization outcomes as advanced by Giulianotti and Robertson (2007) to the Europeanization mechanisms identified by Knill and Lenschow (2005a, 2005b). In so doing, the glocalization literature serves the purpose of characterizing the local-level outcomes in a descriptive manner, while the Europeanization literature provides ways of establishing a causal relationship between the international and the national levels. The glocalization perspective surely advances the analytical approach to Europeanization processes, since it provides a way of making the outcomes of EU-induced events of institutional changes more general, and might, therefore, be helpful for increasing the external validity (i.e., the generalizability) of the empirical findings in the corresponding research literature.

Varying Degrees of EU Adjustment Pressure: A Governance Approach

A compelling way to develop a generic categorization of EU-induced adjustment pressure is offered by the concept of governance patterns. Governance patterns correspond to particular steering modes that may imply different institutional prerequisites and hence pose demands or incentives for institutional adaptation (see, e.g., Kohler-Koch and Rittberger 2009; Mayntz 2003; Scharpf 1997). We can distinguish between three patterns of governance: (1) hierarchical governance, which prescribes a concrete institutional model for domestic adaptation; (2) governance by competition, which aims at changing domestic opportunity structures; and (3) governance by communication, which pursues the objective of changing the beliefs and expectations of domestic actors (Knill and Lenschow 2005a, 2005b).

Governance by hierarchy seeks to trigger domestic institutional change by prescribing concrete requirements with which member states must comply. This governance mode stresses the role of formal rules and procedures that are binding for both public and private actors and therefore implies, in the great majority of cases, a high institutional adjustment pressure. In EU politics, many legally binding rules relate to the removal of barriers to trade (i.e., measures associated with 'negative integration' where impediments to trade are abolished), but the field of 'positive integration' is also affected (i.e., new arrangements are introduced) (see Scharpf 1999). Measures aiming at negative or positive integration usually correspond to various types of regulatory policies, which are prone to having institutional impacts as frequently procedural obligations are defined in EU legislation. This may include the creation of new organizations, the centralization of regulatory processes, or demand for horizontal organizational change. National bureaucracies (i.e., the actors responsible for realizing events of institutional change) remain widely autonomous in finding appropriate ways towards compliance with EU requirements. The result is that national bureaucracies are insulated from the European pressure to engage in extensive administrative optimization efforts, which suggests that this administrative rationality typically coincides with rather incremental and gradual adjustments of established routines and procedures (Knill 1999). Consequently, the most likely local-level outcome of EU governance by hierarchy is relativization.

An example of hierarchical governance is the 1985 Environmental Impact Assessment Directive, which obliges planners of public and private projects to pass on information regarding the environmental impact of these projects to a designated public authority. The results of this process must then be taken into consideration by those public authorities responsible for the authorization of the projects in question. Compliance with the Environmental Impact Assessment Directive implies the horizontal integration of administrative control responsibilities. In this regard, Knill and Lenschow (2005b) show that in Germany, for instance, the national administration resisted the adoption of the integrated approach in meeting the requirements of the Environmental Impact Assessment Directive and merely implemented the existing authorization procedures, leading to relativization.

Governance by competition is about stimulating the optimization of institutional arrangements in the member states within a general framework set on the EU-level by employing a limited number of legally binding requirements for institutional change in the member states. Pressure for institutional adjustment is comparatively low and basically emerges from the need to rearrange national structures and procedures to enhance their effectiveness in achieving certain objectives in comparison with the performance of other member states. This implies that European policies do not prescribe any distinctive institutional model of how the new institutional equilibrium should actually look, but leave the member states broad discretion for institutional design (Knill and Lehmkuhl 2002; Héritier 2007: 12).

Examples of EU governance being based on the competition mode can be found in particular in market-making policies of the EU, that is, measures based on the principle of negative integration. These policies basically exclude certain options from the range of national policy choices, rather than positively prescribing distinctive institutional models to be enacted at the national level. Their impact is generally restricted to the abolition of domestic administrative arrangements, which distort the functioning of the single market. Accordingly, the rationale behind institutional change is 'systems competition', implying that there are certain re-distributional effects between member states that are affected by the comparative performance of national regulatory practices and institutions.

Rather than securing institutional persistence, the basic focus is on institutional effects, such as the impact of certain regulatory arrangements on the competitive position of the national industry within the single market. Differing taxation systems in member states, for instance, could trigger moves of capital and investment between countries, bearing far-reaching consequences for national tax revenues, the overall economic development, and the level of employment. This leads to an augmented potential for societal mobilization and politicization, implying that the national bureaucracy is no longer in an autonomous position when adjusting national arrangements to European requirements. Instead, bureaucratic behavior becomes highly contingent on the preferences of and the strategic interaction between political leaders. Perceived in this way, accommodation and hybridization represent the most likely outcomes of EU pressure.

The third pattern of governance aims at the stimulation of information exchange and mutual learning between national policy-makers and the development and promotion of innovative regulatory models or concepts to be applied in the member states. There is no legally binding prescription of institutional models for domestic compliance. Instead, these models offer non-binding suggestions for national policy-makers to guide the search for regulatory solutions to certain policy problems (see, e.g., Knill and Lehmkuhl 2002). This governance approach is currently diffusing from international organizations, such as the Organization for European Economic Cooperation, into the EU repertoire (see also Drori, Höllerer, and Walgenbach, this volume). It is marked by a considerable degree of openness, as policy suggestions leave broad leeway for interpretation and adjustment to domestic conditions. Moreover, the promotion of certain concepts, which have been successfully applied in other countries, is based on 'policy-transfer' rather than on competitive selection (Dolowitz and Marsh 2000).

At the European level, governance by communication is principally pursued through the Open Method of Coordination (Héritier 2003; Rhodes 2010). At present, the Open Method of Coordination is applied to domains like the information society, research and development, enterprises, economic reforms, education, employment, social inclusion, health care, and pensions (i.e., flanking policies for building the economic union with an emphasis on social cohesion). The concrete design of the Open Method of Coordination varies across policy fields, with some emphasizing information exchange (e.g., pensions and health) while others build up stronger adaptation pressure through cross-national and Commission peer reviews (e.g., employment and to a lesser extent also social inclusion).

If communication and information exchange is the predominant governance pattern, institutional change should follow the rationale of securing and increasing the legitimacy of certain institutional arrangements within a transnational discourse (see Meyer, Chapter 29, this volume). In this context, institutional actors typically embrace forms and practices that are widely accepted and valued, triggering processes of institutional 'isomorphism' (DiMaggio and Powell 1991). Striving for legitimacy is analytically distinct from rationalities illustrated by the two previous patterns of governance. It aims at responding to dominant global discourses, which we expect to induce a moderate level of institutional adjustment pressure. Moreover, if necessary, the global or transnational discourse should support far-reaching reforms of existing arrangements to secure the survival of the institution. The bureaucratic interest to protect their institution is pursued not defensively by prioritizing the status quo, but responsively through dynamic adjustment. Moreover, it is not functionality but transnational acceptance of the institutional design that guides this dynamic (Knill and Lenschow 2005a).

The embeddedness of national bureaucrats and policymakers in transnational expert networks and the involvement of 'epistemic communities' (Haas 1992) do not only imply that these actors can observe and learn from developments in other countries. By the same token, they are aware that they are under scrutiny and thus have to demonstrate the quality and legitimacy of their concepts vis-à-vis external actors and members of epistemic communities. Nationally autonomous bureaucracies may well be tempted to protect national practices and structures, but their integration into transnational networks forces them to react to this discourse. It is, therefore, the professional need to legitimize national developments against the background of the international discourse that drives institutional change, which may result in hybridization or even transformation.

In sum, we differentiate between three modes of EU governance that are related to institutional adjustment pressures, the local-level outcomes, and the implication for the effectiveness of EU policy implementation. In this regard, hybridization can occur in situations of governance by competition and communication.

Institutional Change in the Czech Republic and Poland

The theoretical model outlined in the previous section is based on the understanding that Europeanization occurs among relatively homogeneous states. Yet with the accession of the Central and Eastern European states, the EU is composed of the old member states and the new member states, which are associated with different institutional characteristics. In this context, it is also important to note that the EU accession of the Central and Eastern European states was conditional on their ex ante adoption of the complete *acquis communautaire* (i.e., a compilation of about 80,000 pages of legislation) as a condition for EU membership. While grace periods for the implementation of some components of the *acquis* were granted (Sedelmeier 2008; Tosun 2011), the new member states had to undertake a remarkable number of substantive reforms within a very short period of time.

In light of this specific situation of pre-accession conditionality (Schimmelfennig and Sedelmeier 2004, 2005), Bauer, Knill, and Pitschel (2007), for instance, argue that events of EU-induced institutional change occurring in the new member states cannot be compared to those taking place in the old member states, for the behavior of the new member states was driven by the motivation to join the EU (see also Cirtautas and Schimmelfennig 2010: 422). From this perspective, rather than being oriented towards securing domestic institutional models, the new member states should have been more willing to embrace demands for far-reaching institutional change. We now evaluate this basic theoretical argument by performing a meta-analysis of some recent empirical findings.

Governance by Hierarchy

To explore to what extent hierarchical governance can stimulate institutional change in the new member states, the Environmental Impact Assessment Directive provides an ideal case. To recall, we expect that the high adjustment pressures exerted by the EU in this scenario should result in institutional relativization (i.e., the maintenance of local institutional arrangements despite the EU requesting modifications).

The empirical findings on how the Czech government dealt with the Directive draw a very clear picture. It has fully overhauled the institutional arrangements related to Environmental Impact Assessments. In fact, even more generally, the entirety of Czech environmental legislation enacted between 1999 and 2002 aimed to achieve compliance with the European environmental *acquis* (Kružíková 2004: 99). To attain the horizontal integration of administrative control responsibilities, a specific unit within the Czech Environmental Information Agency was created, which has the exclusive task of providing support to the state and public administration in all matters related to Environmental Impact Assessments. This specific unit operates and develops the Environmental Impact Assessment information systems as well as prepares and administers Environmental Impact Assessments. However, some parts of the previous national institutional arrangements are still in place and cause tensions with the requirements of the Directive. In this regard, the limited provisions for public participation pose a serious problem (European Commission 2010).

The Polish government also made changes to the country's Environmental Impact Assessment system. The most important change refers to the creation of the National Environmental Impact Assessment Commission as an advisory body to the Ministry of Environment (Woloszyn 2004: 113). However, again some institutional characteristics have been preserved, indicating that similar to the situation in the Czech Republic, we can speak of hybridization rather than transformation. Nonetheless, the observation of institutional change clearly contradicts the reasoning of the model advanced by Knill and Lenschow (2005a, 2005b).

Governance by Competition

A case in point for illustrating the implications of governance by competition for institutional change is the EU's regulatory framework on electronic communication, which consists of the framework directive 2002/21/EC plus four specific directives (i.e., 2002/20/EC; 2002/19/EC; 2002/20/EC; 2002/58/EC). The objective of this regulatory framework is to promote competition in the provision of electronic communications networks and services. Traditionally, telecommunications governance across Europe was premised on the 'state-centricity' of the sector. The state was the sole operator of networks and services, and international cooperation was limited to technical matters, international tariffs, and accounting rules (Humphreys and Simpson 2008). The new EU regulatory framework, in contrast, calls for a liberalization of the telecommunication sector.

The telecommunication sector in the Central and Eastern European countries has been burdened with the legacy of the past. The Communist economic system gave the telecommunications sector low priority because it was not recognized as a productive sector (Gruber 2001: 21). The Czech government readily embraced the EU requirements for institutional change, and by 2004, the Czech Republic had achieved an almost maximum level of liberalization of telecommunication services (Nemec, Sagat, and Vitek 2004: 351–2).

In Poland, the ruling political parties from 2001 to 2007 did not support the EU regulatory framework's objective of fast liberalization of the telecommunication market and limitation of the state's regulatory power. Their reluctance mainly stemmed from their respective ideologies. Furthermore, the ruling political parties from 2005 to 2007 were distinctly skeptical about the EU and regarded any supranational influence as a threat to national sovereignty. Therefore, the ruling political parties deliberately hampered institutional change. However, the conservative and economically liberal party Civic Platform, which took office in 2007, fostered with its EU-friendly attitude the implementation of a regulatory framework and triggered the necessary institutional changes (Knill, Tosun, and Preidel 2011).

While the events of institutional change took longer to occur in Poland than in the Czech Republic, the eventual outcome can be characterized as a transformation of the existing institutional arrangements. What this case—or more specifically, the finding for Poland—additionally illustrates is that the role of domestic interests might be also important in situations where the institutional adjustment pressure is low.

Governance by Communication

The European Employment Strategy provides an elucidating example for the implications of governance by communication. The launch of the European Employment Strategy marked a radical departure from the existing modes of governance, for it is based on voluntary soft-law instruments, including peer review mechanisms and benchmarking (Rhodes 2010: 294). The major goal of the European Employment Strategy is to maintain the European Social Model by reforming it through a number of measures, for example, higher employment participation. In response to the European Employment Strategy, several member states made changes to existing national employment policy arrangements (Szyszczak 2006). The new member states are no exception to this pattern.

In the Czech Republic, the European Employment Strategy has played an important role in framing the employment policy agenda. In the face of sharply rising unemployment throughout the 1990s, the European Employment Strategy was conceived by the Ministry of Labor and Social Affairs as a welcome model for reorienting Czech employment policy (Schüttpelz 2004). The most important event of institutional change in this regard refers to the institutional organization of the Public Employment Service, originally established in

1991, which has been developed in line with the EU provisions (De la Porte 2009). These institutional changes facilitate cooperation between the Public Employment Service and the Czech Employer Association in the context of the Labor Market Institute Program, which is co-funded by the European Social Fund and the national budget. The program aims to establish labor market institutes that will provide more intensive services to employers (Kalužná 2008: 18). More generally, Schüttpelz (2004) points to three factors that were decisive for institutional change through the European Employment Strategy: the growing unemployment, the entering into office of the new Social Democratic government in 1998, and accession to the EU. Altogether, however, we can confirm the expectation of hybridization, since not all national institutional arrangements were given up. Rather, new institutional structures were adopted to complement the existing ones.

Since 1999, the Polish government has been involved in ongoing dialogues with the European Commission to ensure the implementation of the European Employment Strategy. In this context, Mailand (2008) emphasizes that Polish civil servants felt a certain pressure from the EU to properly implement the provisions of the European Employment Strategy. There are two issues in particular that have been given a far more prominent place in Polish employment policies than they would otherwise have been, had it not been for pressure from the European Commission. One of them is the tax wedge and the other is the financing of pensions. In terms of institutional changes, akin to the Czech case, reforms mainly addressed the Public Employment Services (Ministry of Economic Affairs and Labour 2005: 60). Again, we can speak of hybridization rather than more profound forms of institutional change.

Drawing the Findings Together

The empirical examples provided in this section showed that the theoretical model based on Knill and Lenschow (2005a, 2005b) is not accurate for predicting institutional change in the new member states. In saying this, three observations are rather remarkable. The first one is that institutional change corresponding to hybridization was observed for a situation in which the EU employed hierarchical governance. The second interesting observation refers to the role of domestic actors and their preferences for the effectiveness of governance by competition for moderating institutional change. In the case of Poland, for a certain period at least, governance by competition even resulted in a situation of relativization before more far-reaching institutional reforms were made. This finding clearly provides support for the basic argument put forward by the glocalization literature that domestic factors do matter. The third instructive insight is that governance by communication did not lead to transformation, although it represented the most likely case for observing this outcome. Remarkably, we could only observe transformation in the case of governance by competition.

All of these observations call for a different theoretical approach to how the EU accomplishes institutional change in the new member states. While the elaboration of a new theoretical model would go beyond the scope of this contribution, we think that the three insights previously discussed will provide a useful starting point for theorizing. This means that the theoretical model to be developed must pay attention to the effectiveness of hierarchical governance, the fact that domestic interests also matter in situations of low institutional adjustment pressure, and that governance by communication seems to be less effective than expected for inducing a transformation of national institutional arrangements.

Conclusion

In this chapter, we pursued three objectives. Firstly, we advanced the argument that Europeanization, understood as processes of institutional change induced by the EU, represents a special case of glocalization. Secondly, we integrated a model of Europeanization stressing the differential impact of governance by hierarchy, competition, and communication with four glocalization scenarios, namely, relativization, accommodation, hybridization, and transformation. We expected governance by hierarchy to lead to relativization, governance by competition to give way to accommodation or hybridization, and governance by communication to produce hybridization or transformation. Thirdly, we illustrated the plausibility of this model by investigating the patterns of institutional change in the Czech Republic and Poland. We decided to focus on the new EU member states, as we conceived them to represent the most likely cases to be affected by far-reaching institutional changes because of the effectiveness of pre-accession conditionality (Schimmelfennig and Sedelmeier 2004, 2005). In contrast to our theoretical model, we observed that the new member states did not automatically overthrow their institutional arrangements, but rather combined them with new structures promoted by the EU. Taking into account that the pressure exerted by the EU is particularly powerful compared with other kinds of international pressures, the finding that national institutions are still maintained to a certain extent supports the main argument of the glocalization literature.

Based on these findings, we encourage future studies to pursue two research avenues. The first avenue refers to the need to come up with a modified theoretical model of how the EU leads to institutional change in the new member states. We discussed some empirical insights which may inform such a new theoretical model. Second, this contribution was but a first endeavor to integrate Europeanization and glocalization. While we could show that there is some promise to merging the two concepts, what is still needed is a broader approach that also tackles the causal mechanisms provided by glocalization research.

References

Bauer, M.W., Knill, C., and Pitschel, D. (2007). 'Differential Europeanisation in Eastern Europe: the impact of diverse EU regulatory governance patterns'. *Journal of European Integration, 29*(4): 405–24. doi: 10.1080/07036330701502431.

Börzel, T.A., and Risse, T. (2003). 'Conceptualizing the domestic impact of Europe', in K. Featherstone and C.M. Radaelli (eds), *The politics of Europeanization*. Oxford: Oxford University Press, 57–80.

Camyar, I. (2010). 'Europeanization, domestic legacies and administrative reforms in Central and Eastern Europe: a comparative analysis of Hungary and the Czech Republic'. *Journal of European Integration, 32*(2): 137–55. doi: 10.1080/07036330903274664.

Cirtautas, A.M., and Schimmelfennig, F. (2010). 'The European Union and Post-Communist Eastern Europe: conditionality, legacies and Europeanisation'. *Europe-Asia Studies, 62*(3): 421–522. doi: 10.1080/09668131003647812.

De la Porte, C. (2009). 'The role of the OECD and the EU in the development of labour market policy in the Czech Republic'. *Journal of Contemporary European Research, 5*(4): 539–56. Stable url: http://www.jcer.net/ojs/index.php/jcer/article/view/232/185.

DiMaggio, P.J., and Powell, W.W. (1991). 'The iron cage revisited. Institutionalized isomorphism and collective rationality in organizational fields', in P.J. DiMaggio and W.W. Powell (eds), *The new institutionalism in organizational analysis*. Chicago: Chicago University Press, 63–82.

Dimitrova, A., and Toshkov, D. (2007). 'The dynamics of domestic coordination of EU policy in the new member states: impossible to lock in?' *West European Politics, 30*(5): 961–86. doi: 10.1080/01402380701617381.

Dolowitz, D.P., and Marsh, D. (2000). 'Learning from abroad: the role of policy transfer in contemporary policy making'. *Governance, 13*(1): 5–24. doi: 10.1111/0952-1895.00121.

European Commission. (2010). 'Environment: commission asks Czech Republic to comply with Court ruling on environmental impact assessments'. Retrieved from http://europa.eu/rapid/pressReleasesAction.do?reference=IP/10/1587andformat=HTML.

Falkner, G. (2010). 'Institutional Performance and Compliance with EU Law: Czech Republic, Hungary, Slovakia and Slovenia'. *Journal of Public Policy, 30* (Special Issue 1): 101–16. doi: 10.1017/S0143814X09990183.

Giulianotti, R., and Robertson, R. (2007). 'Forms of glocalization: globalization and the migration strategies of Scottish football fans in North America'. *Sociology, 41*(1): 133–52. doi: 10.1177/0038038507073044.

Goetz, K.H. (2001). 'Making sense of post-communist central administration: modernization, Europeanization or Latinization?' *Journal of European Public Policy, 8*(6): 1032–51. doi: 10.1080/13501760110098332.

Gruber, H. (2001). 'Competition and innovation: the diffusion of mobile telecommunications in central and Eastern Europe'. *Information Economics and Policy, 13*(1): 19–34. doi: 10.1016/S0167-6245(00)00028-7.

Haas, P.M. (1992). 'Introduction: epistemic communities and international policy coordination'. *International Organization, 46*(1): 1–35. Stable url: http://www.jstor.org/stable/2706951.

Héritier, A. (2003). 'New modes of governance in Europe: increasing political capacity and policy effectiveness?' in T.A. Börzel and R.A. Cichowski (eds), *The state of the European Union*. Oxford: Oxford University Press, 105–27.

Héritier, A. (2007). *Explaining institutional change in Europe* (1st edn). Oxford: Oxford University Press.

Humphreys, P., and Simpson, S. (2008). 'Globalization, the "Competition" state and the rise of the "Regulatory" state in European telecommunications'. *Journal of Common Market Studies, 46*(4): 849–74. doi: 10.1111/j.1468-5965.2008.00802.x.

Jordan, A., and Tosun, J. (2012). 'Policy Implementation', in A. Jordan and C. Adelle (eds), *Environmental policy in the European Union: actors, institutions and politics*. London: Earthscan, 247–66.

Kalužná, D. (2008). 'Main features of the public employment service in the Czech Republic'. *OECD Social, Employment and Migration Working Papers, 74*(1): 1–56. doi: 10.1787/230150403603.

Kelemen, R.D. (2000). 'Regulatory federalism: EU environmental policy in comparative perspective'. *Journal of Public Policy, 20*(2): 133–67.

Knill, C. (1999). 'Explaining cross-national variance in administrative reform: autonomous versus instrumental bureaucracies'. *Journal of Public Policy, 19*(2): 113–39.

Knill, C. (2001). *The Europeanization of national administrations. Patterns of institutional change and persistence* (1st edn). Cambridge: Cambridge University Press.

Knill, C., and Lehmkuhl, D. (2002). 'The national impact of European Union regulatory policy: three Europeanization mechanisms'. *European Journal of Political Research, 41*(2): 255–80. doi: 10.1111/1475-6765.00012.

Knill, C., and Lenschow, A. (2005a). 'Compliance, competition and communication: different approaches of European governance and their impact on national institutions'. *Journal of Common Market Studies, 43*(3): 583–606. doi: 10.1111/j.0021-9886.2005.00570.x.

Knill, C., and Lenschow, A. (2005b). 'Compliance, communication and competition: patterns of EU environmental policy making and their impact on policy convergence'. *European Environment, 15*(2): 114–28. doi: 10.1002/eet.376.

Knill, C., Tosun, J., and Preidel, C. (2011). 'Once in the EU Club: which factors account for the transposition performance of the "new" member states?' Unpublished manuscript, University of Konstanz, Germany.

Kohler-Koch, B., and Rittberger, B. (2009). 'A futile quest for coherence: the many frames of EU governance', in B. Kohler-Koch and F. Larat (eds), *European multi-level governance. Contrasting images in national research*. Cheltenham: Edward Elgar, 3–18.

König, T., and Luetgert, B. (2009). 'Troubles with transposition? Explaining trends in member-state notification and the delayed transposition of EU directives'. *British Journal of Political Science, 39*(1): 163–94. doi: 10.1017/S0007123408000380.

Kružíková, E. (2004). 'EU accession and legal change: accomplishments and challenges in the Czech case'. *Environmental Politics, 13*(1): 99–113. doi: 10.1080/09644010410001685155.

Lippert, B., Umbach, G., and Wessels, W. (2001). 'Europeanization of CEE executives: EU membership negotiations as a shaping power'. *Journal of European Public Policy, 8*(6): 980–1012. doi: 10.1080/13501760110098314.

Mailand, M. (2008). 'The uneven impact of the European Employment Strategy on member states' employment policies: a comparative analysis'. *Journal of European Social Policy, 18*(4): 353–65. doi: 10.1177/0958928708094893.

Mastenbroek, E., and Kaeding, M. (2006). 'Europeanization beyond the goodness of fit: domestic politics in the forefront'. *Comparative European Politics, 4*(4), 331–54.

Mayntz, R. (2003). 'New challenges to governance theory', in H. Bang (ed.), *Governance as social and political communication*. Manchester: Manchester University Press, 27–40.

Ministry of Economic Affairs and Labour. (2005). *Poland—2005 Report Labour Market*. Retrieved from http://www.mpips.gov.pl/en/analyses-forecasts/poland-2005-report-labour-market/.

Nemec, J., Sagat, V., and Vitek, L. (2004). 'Privatisation and liberalisation in the utility sector: the case of telecommunications in the Czech and Slovak Republics'. *Public Administration and Development, 24*(4): 345–56. doi: 10.1002/pad.323.

Pierson, P. (2000). 'Increasing returns, path dependence, and the study of politics'. *American Political Science Review, 94*(2): 251–67. Stable url: http://www.jstor.org/stable/2586011.

Rhodes, M. (2010). 'Employment policy: between efficacy and experimentation', in H. Wallace, M. Pollack, and A.R. Young (eds), *Policy-making in the European Union*. Oxford: Oxford University Press, 283–306.

Robertson, R. (1994). 'Globalisation or glocalisation?' *Journal of International Communication 1*(1): 33–52. doi: 10.1080/13216597.1994.9751780.

Scharpf, F.W. (1997). *Games real actors play. Actor-centered institutionalism in policy research* (1st edn). Boulder, CO: Westview Press.

Scharpf, F.W. (1999). *Governing in Europe effective and democratic?* (1st edn). Oxford: Oxford University Press.

Schimmelfennig, F., and Sedelmeier, U. (2004). 'Governance by conditionality: EU rule transfer to the candidate countries of Central and Eastern Europe'. *Journal of European Public Policy, 11*(4): 661–79. doi: 10.1080/1350176042000248089.

Schimmelfennig, F., and Sedelmeier, U. (eds) (2005). *The Europeanization of Central and Eastern Europe* (1st edn). Ithaca: Cornell University Press.

Schimmelfennig, F., and Trauner, F. (eds) (2009). 'Post-accession compliance in the EU's new member states'. *European Integration Online Papers*, Special Issue 2(13). Retrieved from http://eiop.or.at/eiop/index.php/eiop/issue/view/22.

Schüttpelz, A. (2004). 'Policy transfer and pre-accession Europeanisation of the Czech employment policy'. WZB Discussion Paper, SP III 2004-201. Retrieved from https://www.econstor.eu/dspace/bitstream/10419/48952/1/569295963.pdf.

Sedelmeier, U. (2008). 'After conditionality: post-accession compliance with EU law in East Central Europe'. *Journal of European Public Policy, 15*(6): 806–25. doi: 10.1080/13501760802196549.

Streeck, W., and Thelen, K. (eds) (2005). *Beyond continuity. Institutional change in advanced political economies* (1st edn). Oxford: Oxford University Press.

Szyszczak, E. (2006). 'Experimental governance: the open method of co-ordination'. *European Law Journal, 12*(4): 486–502. doi: 10.1111/j.1468-0386.2006.00329.x.

Tosun, J. (2011). 'When the grace period is over: assessing the new member states' compliance with EU requirements for oil stockholding energy policy'. *Energy Policy, 39*(11): 7156–64. doi: 10.1016/j.enpol.2011.08.035.

Woloszyn, W. (2004). 'Evolution of environmental impact assessment in Poland: problems and prospects'. *Impact Assessment and Project Appraisal, 22*(2): 109–19. doi: 10.3152/147154604781765950.

Zubek, R. (2008). *Core executive and Europeanization in Central Europe*. Basingstoke: Palgrave.

Zubek, R., and Goetz, K.H. (2010). 'Performing to type? How state institutions matter in East Central Europe'. *Journal of Public Policy, 30*(1): 1–22. doi: 10.1017/S0143814X09990237.

20

From Historical Roots to Hybrid Identities

The Transformation Challenge of French Grandes Ecoles de Commerce

Farah Kodeih

Introduction

Institutional complexity, or pluralism, refers to a situation where new institutional arrangements develop alongside old ones without pushing the latter underground (Reay and Hinings 2009; Kraatz and Block 2008; Greenwood et al. 2011). Instead, organizations experience multiple and often conflicting institutional logics. Logics are the rules, principles, and belief systems that guide and shape the behaviors, interests, identities, and values of individuals in a particular organizational field (Thornton and Ocasio 2008). Faced with multiple logics, organizations are compelled to simultaneously abide by different "rules of the game" (Kraatz and Block 2008: 243). While long tacit in institutional research, the notion of institutional complexity has only recently received empirical attention, demonstrating the coexistence of multiple logics in a given organizational field (e.g., Reay and Hinings 2009; Meyer and Höllerer 2010). Most empirical studies that recognize the multiplicity of logics are situated at the field level and have focused on the conditions that promote the diffusion and persistence of multiple logics at that level (see Greenwood et al. 2011 for a review). In contrast, very few empirical studies have explored how organizations actually cope with institutional complexity arising from incompatible logics. Thus, there have recently been calls for research that examines "how individual organizations process that complexity" by looking "inside the organization" (Greenwood et al. 2010: 16).

Several researchers propose identity as a vehicle through which organizations process and respond to institutional complexity and advocate a fuller exploration of its role (e.g., Kraatz and Block 2008; Glynn 2008; Greenwood et al. 2011; Kodeih and Greenwood forthcoming). For example, Kraatz and Block suggest that institutional complexity poses problems for an organization's identity and that how organizations cope with complexity is, in effect, how they cope with multiple identities that reflect the contradictions of larger systems themselves. Battilana and Dorado (2010) argue that institutional complexity potentially triggers internal tensions and conflicts, and requires the creation of a common hybrid organizational identity to strike a balance between these multiple incompatible logics.

This chapter builds on and extends this emerging stream of research to understand how identity is impacted when organizations face institutional complexity, or more specifically, when they no longer operate in a single, well-known, local environment but are obliged to adapt to a more plural and less familiar one. To answer this question, this research moves beyond a mere account of the multiplicity of identities within organizations and the subsequent flexibility in compliance with multiple external pressures, and explores how organizations draw on different symbolic systems of meanings and components that emanate from various institutional logics to build "hybrid identities".

For that purpose, this chapter is based on a study of French Grandes Ecoles de Commerce (FGECs). Up until the mid-1990s, FGECs operated in a familiar and monolithic national institutional environment. Recent years have seen a rise in global standards for management education (Takagi and De Carlo 2003; Hedmo et al. 2007), a movement particularly salient in Europe with the proliferation of MBAs (Hedmo et al. 2006; Kumar and Usunier 2001), the development of accreditation and public ranking systems (Hedmo et al. 2006), and the endorsement of the Bologna agreement, aimed at developing a harmonized European higher education system (Mottis 2008). These changes have "launched a new, international perspective on business schools" (Hedmo et al. 2007: 18), but have triggered questions surrounding schools' identities, namely, who they are, who they want to be, and who they can be (Bouchikhi and Kimberly 2007).

The purpose of this chapter is to understand how FGECs coped with the emergence of global standards alongside the ongoing prevalence of traditional national rules. With this in mind, the chapter ascertains the process whereby schools' identities are hybridized in the transition from a monolithic to a pluralistic institutional environment. It explains the transformation process of FGECs from historical roots to hybrid identities—how they attempted to preserve certain core practices that still form a strong basis of national legitimacy while incorporating practices of another form: the international business school. Based on a comparative and longitudinal approach, the chapter shows how four FGECs have gone through hybridization processes in response to both traditional (national) and new (global) demands.

Evolution of the FGEC Environment

French Grandes Ecoles de Commerce: A Very Particular Form of Management Education

Historically, France has developed its own model of business education (Kipping et al. 2004; Kodeih and Greenwood forthcoming), one organized and embedded in French society and history (Kumar and Usunier 2001; De Fournas 2007). The first Grandes Ecoles were engineering schools, known as Ecoles d'Ingénieur (Kumar and Usunier 2001; De Fournas 2007). These were created outside the university sphere in the late 1790s and throughout the 19th century to train and prepare the nation's young elite to run the French empire (Mottis 2008). Schools of commerce, or "Ecoles de Commerce", were created later in the 19th century by business owners and chambers of commerce and industry, again outside the university sphere[1] (ESCP in 1819, HEC in 1881, Essec in 1907). The ambition was to develop business education in France (Fridenson and Paquy 2008). The initial purpose of these schools was to train the children of business owners in accounting and business law and to prepare them for setting up their own businesses:

> Two systems of higher education have come to coexist in France. One (Grandes Ecoles) is oriented almost exclusively towards providing technical or professional training, while the other (universities) is more preoccupied with theoretical and intellectual concerns ...
> (Suleiman 1978: 24)

Given the prestige of engineering schools (especially relative to universities),[2] they served as a source of aspiration and legitimacy for schools of commerce (Engwall et al. 2009). Most notably, schools of commerce adopted the formers' somewhat demanding screening procedure in the 1920s. From this point onward, students were selected on the basis of an intense, nationwide competitive examination (a "concours"), which included written and oral tests, followed by two years of intensive preparatory classes ("classes préparatoires"). Students entered preparatory classes after earning the "Baccalauréat" (after graduation from high school based on their prior educational achievements). Subsequently, students entered schools of commerce based on their performance in the concours, the only criterion for acceptance on the traditional Grande Ecole program (a generalist three-year program that includes mandatory internships).

Interestingly, while admission to a Grande Ecole is difficult and considered to reflect the intellectual capability of the accepted student (Kumar and Usunier 2001), graduation is considered "almost a done deal" for those who are admitted (Mottis 2008: 94). The system is based on an ascriptive-oriented meritocracy that contrasts with the Anglo-Saxon system, characterized by "achievement-oriented meritocracy" (Kumar and Usunier 2001).

From the Grandes Ecoles' perspective, the ability of FGECs to "select" their students created a virtuous circle, in which they came to attract the brightest and most capable students in the country. This has not only resulted in a sizable portion of France's intellectual and technical leaders, but has also served to elevate their status and prestige, which, in turn, has reinforced their ability to attract the best students. This demanding selection process has allowed FGECs to increasingly develop an elitist and bourgeois character, especially as alumni have become leaders and entrepreneurs (Dameron and Durand 2008). These former students are well organized, occupy key positions in companies and public administrations, and tend to recruit graduates from the same schools[3] (Kumar and Usunier 2001). Pierre Bourdieu (1989) referred to Grandes Ecoles as "elite reproduction systems",[4] whose main purpose is to sustain social order and "state nobility".

Given the initial vocational mission of schools of commerce, teaching was mainly provided by practitioners and practicing managers (Locke 1989). During the early 1960s, the "academization" of business schools (and business education in general) in the US had a parallel expression in France under the impulsion of the Ministry of Higher Education. Along with the FNEGE[5] (Fondation Nationale pour l'Enseignement de la Gestion), the state contributed to the creation of a management faculty in France by financing academic training in management (mainly doctoral studies) in North American universities for numerous French students between 1969 and 1973 (Kipping et al. 2004; Dameron and Durand 2008).

While this exposure to the American business school model brought about new practices (most notably curricular changes,[6] innovative programs, and a permanent body of faculty members), FGECs' main concerns remained competing nationally and focusing on the Grande Ecole program (Kodeih and Greenwood forthcoming):

> There were international initiatives, such as professors attending international conferences and students going abroad and so on, but obviously we were still operating in the familiar field of FGECs. (Field Expert)

At this time, FGECs were regulated by a body of national organizations and actors only. While some constituted informal sources of prescriptions (FGECs' network of alumni, evaluations of professors who teach in preparatory classes), the French Ministry of Education and the Conférence des Grandes Ecoles[7] played—and still play—an important role in defining and enforcing local regulations.

The Rise of Global Standards for Management Education in the Late 1990s

In the late 1990s, Europe witnessed significant changes in the management education field. Accreditation bodies have played a significant role in promoting global standards for management education, particularly AACSB, EQUIS, and AMBA, and have become signaling devices for schools wishing to acquire international visibility. They institutionalize standards by "providing assessments, comparisons, and evaluations, and by constructing a global model that providers and observers of management education can follow" (Hedmo et al. 2007: 20). For instance, they have forced schools to perform each aspect of their mission correctly (research, for example), in order to be accredited (Thietart 2009). Consequently, research has become one of the most important indicators of both faculty quality and international status, and one of the most visible outputs for accreditation purposes (Thietart 2009: 714). As a result, a new standardized way of conducting research has been institutionalized: publishing in refereed journals (Sahlin-Andersson and Engwall 2002).

At the same time, a European harmonization process, widely known as "the Bologna Process", was launched to harmonize the very fragmented European academic landscape. As academic traditions varied significantly from one country to another in terms of student selection processes, degrees granted, and corresponding skills (Mottis 2008), the process required European colleges and universities to adopt the LMD[8] format (Thietart 2009), a model structured on three levels, including a bachelor, a master's program, and a PhD (Mottis 2008). It thus required universities and colleges to split their five-year degree programs into a bachelor and a master's program (Kieser 2004). The purpose of this reform was to increase Europe's competitiveness on a world scale by creating an "Open European Higher Education Area" by 2010 (Mottis 2008) and to enhance the international visibility of European educational institutions.

Recent years have also borne witness to the rise of regional and global rankings in daily press and magazines (Thietart 2009). In 1998, *The Financial Times* (*FT*) launched a European ranking of MBA programs, which a year later became the first widely-recognized ranking of business schools and programs in various parts of the world (Hedmo et al. 2007). Following this initiative, many additional rankings appeared.[9]

The Hybridization Challenge for FGECs

Since then, a veritable "internationalization" has undoubtedly occurred in FGECs. Yet, as in most European countries (Mottis 2008; Hedmo et al. 2007), the internationalization of FGECs took place alongside the persistence of national peculiarities. While FGECs simultaneously and gradually incorporated practices of another institutional form—the international business school (IBS)—by enhancing their international profiles, they did so in accordance with standards that did not match their historical identity (De Fournas 2007; Kodeih and Greenwood forthcoming).

The traditional FGEC logic and the IBS logic are sometimes contradictory in the application of the rules they promote. On the one hand, the IBS model enables students with

Table 20.1 Institutional logics in the French Grande Ecole de Commerce (FGEC) field

Dimensions	Traditional French Grande Ecole de Commerce (FGEC) logic	International Business School (IBS) logic
Schools' focus of attention	Emphasis on the GE program Practice-oriented	Running many programs Research-oriented
Source of the schools' legitimacy	Quality of the GE program, difficulty of the competitive examination, the percentage of students recruited through preparatory classes, Membership of the Conférence des Grandes Ecoles (CGE), French employers, national rankings	Graduate placements, alumni networks, international rankings, faculty
Source of legitimacy of graduates	Ascriptive-oriented meritocracy	Achievement-oriented meritocracy
Source of identity of faculty	Traditional FGEC professor as a "Residential", involved in the schools' activities (teaching, lucrative activities…)	IBS professor as a "Cosmopolitan", the international academic community as the reference point
Organizational manifestations		
Schools' core supply	Emphasis on the GE program that does not require professional experience	Bachelor, MBA and PhD programs MBA as the core feature of a business school
Recruitment of students	Mostly students selected through the concours Traditionally French and homogeneous batches of students	Students selected based on personal and professional essays International and heterogeneous batches of students
Faculty profile	Mostly French professors who earned a French Doctorate, and practitioners hired on a per hour basis	International professors, who earned international PhDs
Research values	Practice-oriented Local research in collaboration with local enterprises and publication of books	Academic-oriented Scientific research and publications in academic peer-reviewed journals

Source: Adapted from Kodeih and Greenwood, forthcoming.

diverse backgrounds and professional experience to be accepted on MBA programs—the dominant international standard. Meanwhile, the emphasis for professors is on conducting research and publishing in academic journals. On the other hand, FGECs are still deeply attached to their historical heritage, that is, the student selection process,[10] which guarantees the elitist character of their GE program (the cornerstone of the GE system). Central to this logic is the idea that elite students can continue their education without prior concrete professional experience, while the emphasis for professors is on teaching and creating practical knowledge (see Table 20.1).

Methods

I began by conducting an exploratory study based on secondary data and fourteen interviews with relevant informants in ten different FGECs. I gathered online information on FGECs by looking at school websites and press articles.[11] I then conducted semi-structured interviews, asking informants about their understanding of internationalization in the context of FGECs in general and in their particular school.

The next step was a confirmatory study based on longitudinal, qualitative case studies. The sample includes two Parisian schools (ESSEC and ESCP Europe) that implemented international initiatives earlier than their counterparts. It also includes two regional schools (Grenoble EM and Euromed Management, based in Marseille) that were forced to "catch up", since Grenoble EM was established much later than its counterparts (in 1984) and Euromed ranked behind them. The data included semi-structured interviews (35) conducted between 2008 and 2010, documents (internal and external communication, French and international press), and archival material.

The data was analyzed following an abductive approach, as I repeatedly went back and forth between theory development and empirical analysis (Wodak 2004). I worked iteratively between interviews, archival material, and relevant literature to develop themes and codes to categorize my findings. I analyzed the data in an effort to elaborate on the processes used by members to conserve one identity while developing another in response to the simultaneous national and global institutional demands.

A Comparative Study of Four FGECs

An examination of the FGEC case studies revealed convergence at the macro-level of the institutional field and divergence at a more micro-organizational level. All FGECs have come under pressure to adapt to the growing internationalization of business education and adopt its dominant standards. However, while trying to redefine themselves as international, "fully fledged" business schools, they continue to value their French historical identity, which still forms the basis of their national legitimacy. To do so, they have actively embraced institutional complexity by incorporating practices from the IBS logic, while maintaining the traditional "core" practices of FGECs.

This section presents the integrated results of the four case studies. Four dimensions to the model of identity hybridization emerged from the schools' experiences: (1) experiencing institutional complexity and identity discrepancies; (2) projecting a "new" identity; (3) combining practices through preservation and change; and (4) hybridization of identities.

Experiencing Institutional Complexity and Identity Discrepancies

With the rise of new standards, social referents of FGECs expanded, creating identity discrepancies for school members. These discrepancies represented inconsistencies between members' perceptions of how the national environment saw their school and their awareness of how the international environment perceived it. Prior to the rise of global standards, FGEC referents included schools' local counterparts and respective national rankings. Although local referents were not substituted, the proliferation of assessment and rule-setting activities directed the schools' attention to their international counterparts. Most FGECs enjoy a reputation in their home environment inherent to the legacy of the Grandes Ecoles, which does not really correspond to how they are perceived abroad:

> The most notable change was definitely the decline of the French frame of reference in terms of competition [...]. We started competing with European and international institutions, and this was new [...]. (ESCP Europe)

> In France, when you say "ESSEC", the reference is the GE quality and selectivity. On the international scene, we need to prove that we are a good business school. (ESSEC)

Confrontation with the standards set the basis of the gap between "who we are" and "who we should be", as promoted by the new institutional logic. At this level, variations emerged depending on the width of the perceived gap.

As a school that was internationally-oriented and inclined towards international standards in terms of research values, AACSB's assessment of ESSEC in 1997 was positive: "It was a long process, but the result was positive, they told us that we were excellent and that we met and even exceeded all their criteria" (ESSEC).

The picture was slightly different for ESCP Europe, which was more of a "teaching school". The comparison with the norms was more destabilizing:

> The comparison with the norms was a crucial moment and we wanted to receive EQUIS accreditation in 1998. The accreditation team started asking us a bunch of questions; "how do you deal with this and that"—we quickly understood that some of the things that were relevant before had to be changed. For instance, we used to have practitioners who would teach. We had to stop putting this forward and focus on the academic dimension. Everything we did was under scrutiny ... it was destabilizing. (ESCP Europe)

As for the professionally-oriented Grenoble EM, where research was underdeveloped, the comparison pointed to some deficits that the school needed to address:

> In 1999, we decided that accreditations would help us improve and the criteria they proposed appealed to us. We really did ourselves some harm [...] the first time the accreditation body told us, "it's not that bad, but you don't do enough research" [...] it was like blaming a student and telling him that he can do better [...]. But we were small, recent and fragile, and the only way to exist was to accept the rules, no matter what they were [...]. (Grenoble EM)

Euromed Management's comparison with the norms took place later than its counterparts. Its "local" nature and status deficit nationally triggered a reconsideration of the school's identity.

Projecting a "New" Identity

In all cases, the responses of deans and administrators reflected an all-embracing claim and the projection of a desired future identity of their school as both a national and international one. While continuously asserting the "international character" of their schools, FGECs regularly reassured national constituencies about their "Frenchness" and reiterated their commitment to the GE legacy and core through the Conférence des Grandes Ecoles (CGE). The following comment suggests this:

> While diversifying their recruitment, FGECs seek to preserve the specificities of their model, mainly, the originality of the "preparatory classes" and the "GE program". The schools' legitimacy was built on the notoriety of these. FGECs thus would like to ensure the sustainability of preparatory classes, while making them more attractive for students. (CGE records 2006)

Yet, the projected identities varied from one school to the next, based on their initial identities and the perceived gap with the expectations of the new IBS logic's constitutive norms. ESSEC and Euromed provide compelling illustrations of this pattern. Given the reputation of its GE program, ESSEC was considered one of the most prestigious FGECs in France in the mid-1990s. It was regularly ranked first or second (after HEC) and members perceived their organization positively, describing it as being "innovative", "entrepreneurial" and "closer to a dynamic SME" (since it had previously introduced important innovations in the FGEC field). Senior members, who had both witnessed and contributed to ESSEC's achievements, spoke about its "glorious past". Its activities were considered "internationally-oriented" and it was also one of the few schools in France to produce academic research. These perceptions were broadly shared among faculty members who were "highly recognized by the national environment" and who contributed to the school's prestige.

Conversely, Euromed Management suffered from perceptual issues in the mid-1990s, since it was stigmatized by the national environment and came in poorly in national rankings. Several statements included claims that Euromed's ranking was not indicative of its true stature, while others agreed on the school's poor performance as an FGEC during this period. Members referred to their school as "local", "not internationally-oriented", "very practice-oriented", "bad in communication", and described it as "not independent", suffering from the local chamber of commerce's overwhelming control:

> We had trouble promoting the positive aspects of the school. Moreover, the faculty was not that competent; there were only two people who held a habilitation qualification to supervise research, and those who had French doctorates were mainly external speakers. The school was very local and would only attract students from the region [...] Other schools and the press used to call us the "beach school", i.e., the school where students don't do much work [...]. (Euromed)

Bearing this in mind, and with the transformation of the institutional environment, ESSEC perceived the new international standards as a source of self-verification and a way of enhancing international visibility and enriching the core, while building on strengths and continuing to enjoy a high status in the home field. Alternatively, Euromed's ambition was to simultaneously acquire national and international legitimacy. It regarded internationalization as a means to "renew identity", to restore its status in the FGEC field and to catch up with its counterparts:

> Going for accreditation will allow us to recruit foreign students (who make up only 10 per cent of ESSEC intake at present) and build international skills […], but it won't have any impact on our national recognition. (ESSEC's dean in *The European*, July 1997)

> Back in 2002, the idea was to rely on international standards to reinvent the school and refine its status and position in France. We aimed to become a Top 10 school in France by conforming to international standards, and ultimately, to become a recognized and specific school in Europe. (Euromed)

Combining Practices through Persistence and Change

All FGECs studied incorporated practices from the IBS logic: recruiting international students, running international programs, hiring and socializing international professors, and emphasizing and rewarding academic research. At the same time, all remained true to their traditional core by retaining the attachment to the student selection process and the GE program's centrality within the curriculum. The following section describes how FGECs (1) incorporated changes in core graduate GE programs, and (2) introduced changes to research agendas and faculty hiring practices.

The Core Graduate GE Program

Up until the late 1990s, schools primarily focused on the GE program—their "raison d'être". Without this program—and the recruitment of students via concours—these schools could not be considered FGECs. Thus, the GE program remained a central feature:

> The centrality of the GE program is still very salient at ESCP Europe today. We are very attached to this program. But some faculty and students who are on our European campuses don't really feel the same. They think of it as only one of the school's programs and certainly not the most interesting. (ESCP Europe)

Yet, each school has hybridized its core GE program in its own way, as outlined below.

ESSEC: Innovating by Turning the GE into an MBA of a Different Kind

In 1999, ESSEC chose to reposition its GE program by redesigning its curriculum to create an MBA of a different kind. Building on the "strengths of its core", ESSEC thus created a different model among MBA formats, rather than adopting the pure MBA standard program.

As many informants suggested, this decision was based on the will to distinguish the value of the GE program and to "internationalize the school without downgrading the ESSEC GE program by calling it a mere Master in Management". It was also based on AACSB's official recognition that ESSEC's GE program was "equivalent to an MBA", as stated in their accreditation letter. Considering the acknowledgment of this legitimate body and the entrepreneurial character of the school, the decision was taken to create a program "halfway between the traditional GE program and the American MBA":

> We wanted to create harmony and not suffer from cognitive dissonance between the flagship program of FGECs—the GE program and that of any other university in the

world—the MBA program. Our French counterparts, namely HEC, followed a different strategy—copying the existent MBA model, and not fitting it into the school's history and purpose. This creates a cognitive dissonance [...]. (ESSEC)

Unfortunately, ESSEC was left alone to promote an atypical MBA program, unable to be classified in the *FT* MBA ranking:

It is very irritating not to be able to get this program recognized through the ranking system, especially the *FT* MBA one ... The main issue for us, then, on an international level, is the rankings. (ESSEC)

For ten years, ESSEC strove unsuccessfully to legitimize its Grande Ecole-MBA model as a true MBA in order to access the *FT* rankings:

It is true that over the years, this decision has triggered questions and tensions. Our executive MBA is well positioned and recognized by the external environment; our specialized MBAs and PhD, as well. But this Grande Ecole-MBA program is not. (ESSEC)

In response, ESSEC has recently decided to realign itself with the dominant norms, by repositioning its GE program as a Master in Management to qualify for the *FT* Masters rankings, and by creating a standard post-experience MBA for submission to the *FT* MBA ranking.

ESCP Europe: Merging with an International School

Although considered a national elite in the late 1990s, ESCP was perceived as remaining in the shadow of more prestigious Parisian schools (HEC, in particular). ESCP's main concern was to address its international deficit and enhance its prestige in relation to its Parisian counterparts, while building on the strengths of its core GE program. In 1999, ESCP thus merged with EAP, a European school with an important contingent of international students and professors, and campuses in France, Germany, and the UK. This merger resulted in a slightly different version of the GE program, which allowed students to spend three years in three different countries. The school's strategy thus focused on strengthening and enhancing the core by adding an international component. The core program is submitted to both national and the *FT* rankings:

In the late 1990s, the leaders set an objective of 50% international students. We are not that far off today. It is striking to see how the GE program, which was historically the most homogeneous—as all students came from preparatory classes and had the same background—is today extremely diverse; they come from everywhere, they go everywhere, and they have very different backgrounds. (ESCP Europe)

The high ranking of the core program in the *FT* Masters ranking (1st in 2010) proves the strategy's success. Furthermore, ESCP has recently consolidated its European positioning by changing its name to ESCP *Europe*: "We decided to capitalize on ESCP's history, while adding the European dimension [...]". (ESCP Europe)

Grenoble EM: Creating an International School within the School

As a recently established school, Grenoble EM was striving to build national legitimacy and become an FGEC of consequence:

> During the first 10 years, we clearly focused on building national legitimacy. Our concern was to get our GE program to be recognized by the Conférence des Grandes Ecoles, students of preparatory classes and the national rankings. And for that purpose we had to rely on the established network of FGECs. (Grenoble EM)

Its leaders perceived the school as young and fragile, yet one that was rapidly expanding and enjoying a relatively fair status in the FGEC field for a recent school. According to the dean, the school's strategy was to "stick to the rules of the game no matter what they were" and to build on the strength of pure international standardized programs. Interestingly, after building the national legitimacy of the core GE program, Grenoble EM did not leverage it to compete internationally (as ESCP Europe or ESSEC), but focused instead on creating pure international programs that fit with international standards. Consequently, the GE program—the basis of the *national* school—was submitted to national rankings, while master's and MBA programs were implemented to form the basis of the *international* school. These international programs "imposed themselves in the *FT* rankings as they sounded better and conformed better to the rules of the rankings":

> The GE program is anchored in the French tradition of Grandes Ecoles; it is ranked in national rankings under the name ESC. It has a fair amount of internationality. GGSB is a school that adheres to global tradition and standards, so its programs appear in international rankings. Sometimes we are told that our GE program is not international enough because there aren't enough overseas students in it. This is paradoxical, since we have more than 1,000 foreign students in our international programs next door. (Grenoble EM)

Euromed Management: Reinventing the School

Given its initial low status in the FGEC field, Euromed's response strategy was to reinvent its core in 2002, positioning itself as a "Euro-Mediterranean" school, relying on both national and international standards:

> The Chamber of Commerce desperately wanted to create a school worthy of the city's ambitions and expectations ... and that would rank at least among the top 10 schools in France—this was the challenge taken up from 2002 to 2004. (Euromed)

Consequently, Euromed started recruiting international students for their GE program, 50 percent of courses were taught in English, and international experience for students became compulsory. When queried about the initial changes implemented when he was put in charge of the programs, the previous dean stated:

> We started implementing changes in the GE program because it is the flagship of the French GE. This program was way behind other GE programs in France, so we had to begin with this [...].

The program appears in both national and *FT* rankings for Masters in Management. Euromed's response, then, entailed redefining the school's core based on the new standards promoted by the new logic at stake.

Faculty and Research

With the rise of accreditations and rankings that set norms and "policies guiding faculty in the production of intellectual contributions",[12] most schools' focus of attention has shifted from a practitioner and professional dimension (inherent in the traditional GE logic) to an academic dimension (inherent in the IBS logic). However, a generation of French professors more oriented towards French research, who have developed national networks and who mostly conduct applied research and publish books, has remained important. These professors are "well recognized in the French environment" (ESSEC).

In all cases, the decision was taken to build on existing faculty members and offer the possibility for those members whose profile did not match the expectations of the new logic's constitutive norms to improve. This was primarily the case for Euromed and Grenoble EM, where the initial stage entailed helping certain faculty members become better researchers by contributing to their doctoral studies, prior to recruiting international professors:

> The most unethical and yet the most effective solution to reduce the gap would have been to lay off everyone and build from scratch, but that was not our philosophy [...] Our plan was to help our body of professors become better researchers. We [...] contributed massively to their doctoral studies. Every professor who decided to earn a PhD was able to do so and now we can start recruiting competent international researchers. The gap is acceptable. One of our new rules is to recruit only senior competent researchers. (Grenoble EM)

At ESSEC and ESCP Europe, the rise of international standards accelerated the recruitment of international professors who published in academic journals and who considered themselves members of worldwide networks. Although in both schools a hybrid contingent of French professors who published in international journals emerged, certain French professors were nostalgic about the previous embeddedness within one logic—the GE logic. Hence, they strived to preserve the centrality of the GE program to their schools' identities and rejected certain aspects of the new logic (such as an extreme focus on publications in top journals):

> Several years ago, some of the faculty members reacted to new faculty management measures by voting for a dean who stood for the traditional values of the school, mainly the emphasis on the GE program. It was getting more and more difficult for them to see how those who were long considered as the "kings" in this field, were being ignored. Suddenly the most important thing was the number of articles you publish in international journals! (ESCP Europe)

Outcome: Hybridization of Identity

In all schools, informants reflected on this transformation process by comparing "who we were" to "who we have become", emphasizing their "hybrid" identity as both FGECs and international business schools with clear national and international anchors:

> I am, myself, an alumnus of this school. In the 1980s the school was the GE program … it was only French at that time and there were almost no international students [...]. It is a totally different school today [...]. Nowadays, we communicate both the international dimension [...], and what has contributed to our excellence today, i.e., the professional dimension of the French GE [...]. Always this twofold vision. (ESSEC)
>
> We were a very local school but we managed to bet on both sides: we have simultaneously earned the credibility and the legitimacy in the FGEC field, and enhanced our international profile [...]. (Euromed)
>
> Running for accreditations was a very good idea because not only has it allowed us to expand nationally [...], it has also put us directly on the international map; suddenly we exist in this international environment [...] we are already both an FGEC and an international BS. (Grenoble EM)
>
> If we hadn't accepted the new international standards, we would have become a second or third-tier school in France, whereas today, not only have we sustained our position in France, we also belong to the prestigious group of International Business Schools. (ESCP Europe)

For these schools, entering a new environment with different rules and developing an international identity has provided an alternative to completely changing the previous rules of the game. Institutional complexity has thus expanded the schools' jurisdiction, allowing them to escape a sometimes-constraining national institutional environment and embark on actions they would not otherwise have been authorized to take:

> Being an FGEC, there are many local rules we need to abide by. For instance, we need to keep recruiting students from preparatory classes, pay attention to national rankings and deliver a diploma that is recognized by the Ministry of Education. We have developed an international identity that minimizes the impact of these commitments. That's why, today, we consider ourselves an international school that happens to be in France, and not the other way around. (Euromed)

Hybridization has also allowed these schools to remain true to their traditional core, which serves to secure the financial and symbolic support of their domestic constituencies and signal that the FGEC logic is still legitimate and robust:

> Alumni and companies constitute important sources of funding for our school … so we need to handle them carefully. (ESCP Europe)
>
> Employers are very willing to accept GE students and are satisfied with this model. I don't think they will encourage any radical change in the model because … I think we are making our way and that you will not see any radical change in that. (ESSEC)

Discussion and Conclusion

This chapter explains the transformation process of French Grandes Ecoles of Commerce (FGECs) from historical roots to hybrid identities. It answers calls to combine institutional theorizing and organizational identity (Glynn 2008; Greenwood et al. 2011) and explores how identity is hybridized when organizations simultaneously face local and global logics. The analysis affords two important insights into the phenomenon of hybridization.

First, hybridization is a way of simultaneously coping with local constraining (and yet still legitimate) institutional pressures and new global ones. This contributes to the growing body of research on organizational coping with institutional complexity and the particular role of identity therein (Greenwood et al. 2011; Battilana and Dorado 2010; Glynn 2008; Kodeih and Greenwood forthcoming). Four stages of the hybridization process are developed:

1   Confrontation with institutional complexity, which resulted in identity discrepancies primarily due to a shift in focus to a comparison with international business schools. Indeed, institutional complexity posed a challenge for schools, as both logics had to be accommodated because of the resource and legitimacy implications of not doing so.
2   Projection of a "new" identity which is reflected in the schools' intentions to seize the opportunity created by the changing institutional environment to shape an alternative hybrid identity. These intentions reflected different meanings depending on the schools' initial identities.
3   Combining practices through preservation and change, describing how each school infused practices from the new logic while remaining true to the traditional core.
4   Hybridization of identities, which explains how the accommodation of two logics has ultimately fed back identities that are not static, but impacted by organizational responses to institutional complexity. Active accommodation of a hybrid identity proved helpful, when displacing a historical identity was not an option. This new identity was not constructed in a vacuum and did not necessarily require renouncing the traditional core (Sahlin and Wedlin 2008).

Second, the process depicted in this chapter shows homogeneous trends at a macro-level of analysis, and variation at the more micro-organizational level. While both logics were enforced in all schools, accommodation occurred in different ways based on the perceived gap between the initial and projected identities. To respond to the growing pressures of the complex institutional environment, FGECs have preserved certain core practices that continue to form a strong basis of national legitimacy, all the while incorporating practices of another form—the international business school. They have translated the global pressures to fit both their national and organizational contexts, which has ultimately resulted in the hybridization of their identities. Hence, the process of organizational coping with local and global demands is ultimately an idiosyncratic process that delves into the unique identity of the organization, reflecting "specific organizational meanings" (Pedersen and Dobbin 2006: 4414). By adding an organization-centric perspective, this chapter brings together the intra-organizational and institutional levels of analysis (e.g., Battilana and Dorado 2010; Kraatz and Block 2008) by accounting not only for external influences and global dissemination of standard models, but also for how organizational factors can influence the accommodation process. Consequently, it contributes to the growing body of research on organizational variation, taking issue with the previously totalizing view of isomorphic diffusion (Marquis and Lounsbury 2007), and highlights the variety of ways in which organizational accommodation of multiple logics occurs. Future research could explore whether or not the variation in the schools' response to institutional pressure constitutes a temporary adjustment before they converge and adopt similar processes.

Acknowledgments

I would like to thank Royston Greenwood, Hamid Bouchikhi, Lars Engwall, Diane-Laure Arjaliès, and both the convenors and attendees of the 2010 EGOS Colloquium in Lisbon for their helpful comments on previous versions of this manuscript. I would also like to express my sincere thanks to all the informants (i.e., business school professors, deans, administrators, and members of other organizations) who opened their door to me and shared their enthusiasm and experience.

Notes

1. This is unlike the American model where business schools were created within universities under the impulsion of industrials such as Joseph Wharton.
2. Suleiman (1978: 53) states, "The creation of these specialized institutions, Grandes Ecoles, relegated universities to second-class status."
3. This is still the case today. As stated in *Le Figaro* (July 2010), "Based on the principle of elite reproduction, directors of companies who are themselves GE graduates, mainly recruit and select young graduates of the same FGEC."
4. According to Bourdieu (1989), 46% of HEC graduates are from upper-class families. Traditionally, these families push their children towards the GE system (Kumar and Usunier 2001).
5. The FNEGE was created by the French government following the publication of *The American Challenge* by J.J. Servan-Schreiber in 1968, which stressed the management gap between France and the United States: "Its role was to close the perceived gap between the outdated training of the future management elite of French companies and what seemed to be required to face the economic challenge of American multinationals in Europe" (Thietart 2009: 713).
6. Such as business-oriented courses and the Harvard Business School case study paradigm.
7. The Conférence des Grandes Ecoles (CGE) was created in 1973 to develop relations between its member schools (Takagi and de Carlo 2003). It plays an important role in bringing together Grandes Ecoles and promoting the GE system, both nationally and internationally (Dameron and Durand 2008). CGE membership serves an accreditation function and authorizes member schools to use the prestigious "Grande Ecole" label (Takagi and Cerdin 2004).
8. License, Master, Doctorate, or BA, MBA/Master, PhD.
9. *Business Week* launched an international ranking in 2000, *The Wall Street Journal* in 2001, and *The Economist* in 2002 (Hedmo et al. 2007: 18). In 2005, *FT* introduced the European Ranking of Master in Management Programs, institutionalizing the Masters degree norm. This ranking was presumably promoted by FGECs to allow their GE program, rebranded as a "Master in Management", to acquire international visibility (De Fournas 2007).
10. Through concours and preparatory classes.
11. Mainly articles in influential magazines and rankings, such as *l'Etudiant* and *The Financial Times*.
12. AACSB website.

References

Battilana, J., and Dorado, S. (2010). 'Building sustainable hybrid organizations. The case of commercial microfinance organizations'. *Academy of Management Journal*, 53(6): 1419–1440.

Bouchikhi, H., and Kimberly, J.H. (2007). *The soul of the corporation: how to manage the identity of your company*. Upper Saddle River, NJ: Pearson Education–Wharton School Publishing.

Bourdieu, P. (1989). *The state nobility: Elite schools in the field of power*. Cambridge: Polity Press.

Dameron, S., and Durand, T. (2008). 'Management education and research in France', in T. Durand and S. Dameron (eds), *The future of business schools: scenarios and strategies for 2020*. Basingstoke: Palgrave Macmillan Press.

De Fournas, P. (2007). 'Quelle Identité pour les Grandes Ecoles de Commerce Françaises'. Thèse de doctorat en sciences humaine et sociales, Ecole Polytechnique.

Engwall, L., Kipping, M., and Üsdiken, B. (2009). 'Public science systems, higher education and the trajectory of academic disciplines: business studies in the United States and Europe', in W. Richard, G. Jochen, and L. Engwall (eds), *Reconfiguring knowledge production: changing authority relationships in the sciences and their consequences for intellectual innovation*. Oxford, UK: Oxford University Press.

Fridenson, P., and Paquy, L. (2008). 'Du haut enseignement commercial à l'enseignement supérieur de gestion (Xixe–Xxe Siècles)', in P. Lenormand (ed.), *La Chambre de commerce et d'industrie de Paris (1803–2003)*, t. II: *Études thématiques*. Genève: Droz.

Glynn, M.A. (2008). 'Beyond constraint: how institutions enable identities', in R. Greenwood, C. Oliver, R. Suddaby, and K. Sahlin-Andersson (eds), *The Sage handbook of organizational institutionalism*. Los Angeles: SAGE Publications.

Greenwood, R., Diaz, A.M., Li, S.X., and Lorente, J.C. (2010). 'The multiplicity of institutional logics and the heterogeneity of organizational responses'. *Organization Science*, 21: 521–539.

Greenwood, R., Raynard, M., Kodeih, F., Micelotta, E., and Lounsbury, M. (2011). 'Institutional complexity and organizational responses'. *Academy of Management Annals*, 5(1): 317–371.

Hedmo, T., Sahlin-Andersson, K., and Wedlin, L. (2006). 'The emergence of a European regulatory field of management education', in M.L. Djelic and K. Sahlin-Andersson (eds), *Transnational governance: institutional dynamics of regulation*. Cambridge: Cambridge University Press.

Hedmo, T., Sahlin-Andersson, K., and Wedlin, L. (2007). 'Is a global organizational field of higher education emerging? Management education as an early example', in G. Krucken, A. Kosmutzky, and M. Torka (eds), *Towards a multiversity? Universities between global trends and national traditions*. Bielefeld, Germany: transcript-Verlag.

Kieser, A. (2004). 'The Americanization of academic management education in Germany'. *Journal of Management Inquiry*, 13(2): 90–97.

Kipping, M., Usdiken, B., and Puig, N. (2004). 'Imitation, tension and hybridization: Multiple "Americanizations" of management education in Mediterranean Europe'. *Journal of Management Inquiry*, 13(2): 98–108.

Kodeih, F., and Greenwood, R. (forthcoming). 'Responding to institutional complexity: the role of identity'. *Organization Studies*.

Kraatz, M.S., and Block, E.S. (2008). 'Organizational implications of institutional pluralism', in R. Greenwood, C. Oliver, R. Suddaby, and K. Sahlin-Andersson (eds), *The Sage handbook of organizational institutionalism*. Los Angeles: Sage Publications.

Kumar, R., and Usunier, J.-C., (2001). 'Management education in a globalizing world. Lessons from the French experience'. *Management Learning*, 32(3): 363–393.

Locke, R.R. (1989). *Management and higher education since 1940: the influence of America and Japan on West Germany, Great Britain and France*. Cambridge, UK: Cambridge University Press.

Marquis, C., and Lounsbury, M. (2007). 'Vive la résistance: competing logics and the consolidation of US community banking'. *Academy of Management Journal*, 50(4): 799–820.

Meyer, R.E., and Höllerer, M.A. (2010). 'Meaning structures in a contested issue field: a topographic map of shareholder value in Austria'. *Academy of Management Journal*, 53(6): 1241–1262.

Mottis, N. (2008). 'Bologna and business education: far from a model, just a process for a while…', in *European Universities in Transition*. Cheltenham (UK): Edward Elgar.

Pedersen, J.S., and Dobbin, F. (2006). 'In search of identity and legitimation: bridging organizational culture and neoinstitutionalism'. *American Behavioral Scientist*, 49: 897–908.

Reay, T., and Hinings, C.R. (2009). 'Managing the rivalry of competing institutional logic'. *Organization Studies*, 30(6): 629–652.

Sahlin, K., and Wedlin, L. (2008). 'Circulating ideas: imitation, translation and editing', in R. Greenwood, C. Oliver, K. Sahlin, and R. Suddaby (eds), *The Sage handbook of organizational institutionalism*. London, UK: Sage Publications.

Sahlin-Andersson, K., and Engwall, L. (2002). *The expansion of management knowledge. Carriers, flows and sources*. Stanford: Stanford University Press.

Suleiman, E. (1978). *Elites in French society*. Princeton: Princeton University Press.

Takagi, J., and Cerdin, J-L. (2004). 'What strategy for internationalization for French management education?', in C. Wankel and R. DeFillippi (eds.), *The cutting-edge of international management education*, Research in Management Education and Development, volume 3. Charlotte, NC: Information Age Publishers.

Takagi, J., and de Carlo, L. (2003). 'The ephemeral national model of management education: a comparative study of five management programmes in France', in R.-P. Amdam, R. Kvalshaugen, and E. Larsen (eds), *Inside the business schools: the content of European business education*. Oslo, Norway: Abstrakt Press.

Thietart, R.A. (2009). 'The research challenge of the French business schools: the case of the Grandes Ecoles'. *Journal of Management Development,* 28(8): 711–717.

Thornton, P.H., and Ocasio, W. (2008). 'Institutional logics', in R. Greenwood, C. Oliver, R. Suddaby, and K. Sahlin-Andersson (eds), *The Sage handbook of organizational institutionalism*. Los Angeles: Sage Publications.

Wodak, R. (2004). 'Critical discourse analysis', in C. Seale, J.F. Gubrium, and D. Silverman (eds), *Qualitative research practice*. Thousand Oaks, CA: Sage.

21
Governance of Science in Mediatized Society
Media Rankings and the Translation of Global Governance Models for Universities

Josef Pallas and Linda Wedlin

Introduction

As several chapters in this book have already suggested, the field of higher education and research constitutes an attractive area in which the process and dynamics of glocalization can be observed and studied (Sahlin; Logue; Engwall; Kodeih, in this volume). The field is undergoing major transformation influenced by the development and proliferation of new governance models and managerial practices across the world (Wedlin 2011b). One of the core features of current changes is the construction of a global model for universities, a model for management and governance of universities worldwide that compete and interact on an international—even global—'market' for higher education and research. This model holds recognition of the university as an organizational 'actor', making it subject to increasing managerialism and rationalization of work practices and routines (cf. Witley 2007; Paradeise et al. 2009). Supported by the development of international standards and quality assurance systems, the global model for universities has also become linked to the notion of 'excellence', and thus, to a normative model for how universities in a variety of contexts and settings should be managed. This way, the model has come to serve as a primer for further reform and transformation at both national and local levels.

The proliferation of managerial practices and models in the academic field is subject to much research and debate. In this chapter, we pay particular attention to the role of the media in constructing and diffusing a global model of universities, beginning to link the spread of managerial models and ideals in this field to a significant contemporary transformation of society—that of mediatization. In this field, researchers have noticed increasing media coverage of science, both in the general and specialized outlets, where it tends to be mainly presented on the basis of controversies (Brossard 2009), sensational discoveries (Lewenstein 1995), and with focus on individual researchers/research projects and their results. But media has also, and perhaps more importantly, become more explicit in articulating and discussing/questioning the way academic research and educational activities are organized, performed, and evaluated. The media plays here an important and integral part in shaping the general perception of science, its results, and its activities, which, in turn, constitutes an inspiration for changes in policies, regulations, and other normative pressures around and within academia (Weingart 1998; Weingart et al. 2000; Kepplinger 2002; Peters et al. 2008; Engwall forthcoming). Paralleling these changes, scientists, research groups, universities, and other academic institutions have started to prioritize and allocate more resources to their media activities (Nisbet et al. 2003; Engwall and Wearie 2008). Among the popular media-oriented efforts, we find expanded responsibilities and status of communication and PR departments with a clear intensification of activities, such as organizing of press conferences, a professionalization of writing and distributing press releases, and an increasing media training of vice-chancellors, heads of departments, and other front figures. The increased media orientation can also be observed in the priorities of university boards and management teams, as they assign significant material and administrative resources dedicated to activities such as marketing, branding, promotion, and reputation management (Weingart 1998, 2007; Peters et al. 2008; Rödder 2009; Besley and Tanner 2011).

Whereas the changes in the media coverage of scientific activities and the more profound orientation of science towards the media have been discussed relatively frequently, we have limited understanding of how such processes shape the governing conditions for science and scientific activities. What is the role of media in creating and diffusing global models for organizing and governing in the academic field? We will in this chapter discuss one particular aspect of this process—the role of media in creating and diffusing global rankings of universities as a way to promote global ideas for university governance.

Understanding glocalization as a process in which global ideas and models get translated, theorized, and mixed as they move between cultures and spaces (Djelic and Quack 2003) not only opens a door for studying how these ideas acquire hybrid forms as they are adjusted to local prerequisites and expectations in the national academic contexts, it also emphasizes the role and importance of actors involved in proliferation, translation, and theorization of these normative stands as they travel across different parts of the social landscape (cf. Sahlin-Andersson and Engwall 2002). Among such intermediary actors, we have earlier seen and studied a variety of governmental bureaucracies, NGOs, private organizations, and trans/national regulatory bodies (Neave 1998; Guston 2000). Also in the university field, intermediary organizations, such as ranking and accreditation organizations, have been shown to be instrumental in introducing, spreading, and implementing global models for governance (Hedmo and Wedlin 2008).

The rest of the chapter is organized as follows. First, we address the relationship between media and the science in terms of mediatization and its role in proliferation of managerial knowledge. We also introduce the notion of media logic—that is, taken-for-granted journalistic norms, values, and working practices—as a guiding principle for presentation and evaluation of organizations. In the subsequent section, the discussion focuses on how the construction, proliferation, and use of rankings can be understood as a mediatized tool for describing, comparing, and assessing academic institutions. We thereafter elaborate on the role that these mediatized 'tools' function as a translation of local practices and procedures into global forms. We will argue that these processes entail three forms of translation procedures: simplification, or a translation from complex to simple measurements and assessments of scientific value and worth; standardization, or a translation from diffuse or unclear to exact and precise standards for comparisons; and popularization, or translation of disparate assessment results in easily accessible and relative judgments of position, standing, and 'worth' among global universities. We close with some thoughts on mediatization and glocalization as global processes of change in contemporary academic field.

Mediatization of Science, Media Logic, and Media Rankings

A conventional view on the relationship between science and the media is based on the understanding of the (news) media as facilitating communication between science and society, where the media is involved in spreading and popularizing scientific knowledge and discoveries in order to increase 'intellectual public support for scientific way of thinking and material public support for scientific work' (Brossard and Lewenstein 2010; see also Nelkin 1995). This is based on what has been termed as the linear diffusion/deficit model, in which science relates to the media from a position of a closed and relatively independent sphere of knowledge production (cf. Ekström 2004; Trench and Bucchi 2010). The result of scientific work is simply transmitted, communicated, and disseminated to the surrounding world by the work of (among others) the media, where it is received and interpreted (cf. Wynne 1995). The role of media is in such a view mainly connected to disseminating information about organizational attributes, which, in turn, contributes to the perception of science in terms of legitimacy and reputation (cf. Deephouse and Suchman 2008).

However, other parts of the society, on which science is dependent for political, economical, and moral support, have also undergone severe organizational and communicative changes related to their increased reliance on and orientation towards the media. We should, therefore, nuance our understanding of the media as not mainly influencing our knowledge about and perception of science directly through news coverage. The media has also an indirect effect on science by way of changing the organizational and institutional prerequisites for interactions between science and its audiences/other social actors (Irwin 2008: in Buthci and Trench). The media is more to be understood as involved in creating conditions as well as tools for translating and leveling out the different requirements, ideas, and expectations the different parties have on each other. Thus, rather than seeing the media as merely providing information about science for individual audience members to make sense of, the media—alongside other institutional intermediaries such as academia, consultants, and industry associations—is to be seen as central for building normative, regulative, and cognitive bases on which science is assessed and evaluated (cf. Scott 2001; Sahlin-Andersson and Engwall 2002).

Such an institutional perspective on relationship and increasing interdependence between science and the media has been described as a progressive 'mediatization' of science (Weingart 1998; Rödder 2009). Mediatization as a concept has been discussed in a variety of studies, where the media is addressed as involved in changing conditions and *modus operandi* of different parts of our society. Sociology of science (Weingart 1998; Rödder 2009), journalism and media studies (Asp 1986; Lundby 2009), political studies (Cook 1998; Altheide 2004; Strömbäck 2011), and organizational research (Kjaer and Slaatta 2007; Raviola 2010; Pallas and Strannegård 2010/forthcoming) are just some of the examples of parts of society where mediatization has been addressed in terms of prevailing societal changes that influence—alongside other institutional forces such as marketization, scientification, or individualization—activities of individuals and organizations in different societal sectors (cf. Schulz 2004). Hjarvard describes mediatization as a process where the media 'intervene into, and influence the activity of other institutions, such as the family, politics, organized religion, etc., while they also provide a "commons" for society as a whole, that is, virtual shared fora for communication that other institutions and actors increasingly use as arenas for their interaction' (Hjarvard 2008: 115).

What this definition suggests is that the way science and the media relate to and deal with each other also needs to be addressed in relation to mediatization of other parts of society.

Specifically, with the increased mediatization of politics (cf. Strömbäck 2008) and business (cf. Pallas and Strannegård 2010), there is an increased pressure on the academic organization to understand and use the media and their working procedures in order to relate to and influence the audiences within the political and economical systems. The political and market actors, in turn, tend to more extensively articulate their expectations on academic institutions sectors publicly. Moreover, these expectations are increasingly shaped by the rationales and values of the media. This suggests that mediatization of science is not limited to changes in communication activities between science and media representatives, but also includes changes in the way science and its different stakeholders understand and interact with each other (cf. Schrott 2009; Pallas and Fredriksson 2011).

One concrete example of how mediatization shapes the institutional context of science is the emergence and proliferation of media products, such as rankings and public assessments of scientific activities and organizations (cf. Fombrun 1998; Power et al. 2009). Rankings are often mentioned as major drivers of the way science is perceived, evaluated, and acted upon (Sauder 2008; Wedlin 2006; see also Fombrun 1998; Pollock and Rindova 2003). But rankings are not only designed to evaluate organizations on the basis of their qualities relevant to their field of affiliations or spreading and proliferating moral and professional norms, values, and expectations. Rankings also translate these qualities in accordance with prevailing media preferences that emphasize the media products to: (1) reduce complexity (i.e., simplicity); (2) introduce elements supporting general validity (i.e., standardization); and (3) create a sense of relevance to a variety of audiences (i.e., popularity) (cf. Rödder 2011; Mazza 1998). In order to be competitive in the ongoing struggle to capture people's attention, rankings need to translate/format the qualities they measure in accordance with established patterns of orientation and interpretations for public communication—that is, patterns that are based in journalistic values, activities, and practices, or, if put in the words of Altheide and Snow (1979), the *media logic* (see also Lundby 2009). Thus, rankings are constructed so they enable presentation and communication of their results by way of media dramaturgy—building on things such as simplification, polarization, intensification, personalization, visualization, and stereotypization (cf. Asp 1986). This includes the propensity of media products to be formulated so they can be understood as a part of a general, and therefore important, event or phenomenon that can engage the audience ('How does this relate to the context of which I'm a part?'). At the same time, the media needs to focus on and emphasize specific aspects of an event to make it easier for the audience to identify it as personally relevant (Hamilton 2004; Caroll and Deephouse forthcoming). While not all of these characteristics are present in the case of rankings, we can still argue that rankings can be regarded as carrying distinctive media insignia. Let us illustrate this by showing how rankings package and translate models of science governance into a mediatized form.

Rankings as a Mediatized 'Tool'

Since the mid-2000s, rankings of universities and scientific fields have come to occupy an important role in shaping means of comparison and assessment of academic activities across the world. We have, in less than a decade, witnessed an increase in rankings in many countries and continents, and most significantly, a proliferation of international comparisons and rankings that have received both global recognition and coverage (Kehm and Stensaker 2009; King 2009; Wedlin et al. 2009). The first university rankings that gained global attention were the Shanghai-produced Academic Ranking of World Universities (ARWU)[1] (2003) and *The Times Higher Education Supplement* ranking[2] (2004). These rankings were highly influenced, however, by previous rankings that had first appeared in the United States in the 1980s, most prominently the *US News and World Report* rankings. In addition, before rankings of global universities became widespread, there were numerous rankings of professional schools within specific fields, such as those of business schools (Wedlin 2006) and law schools (Sauder 2008). While an increase in the ranking and assessment of universities is only one recent development in the area of higher education, these mechanisms have been important in creating the appearance of an international and unified educational market, in which universities compete for attention and recognition on a global scale (Hedmo et al. 2006; Wedlin 2011a).

While not the first ranking of universities, the publication of the Shanghai ranking caused considerable discussion in the field. Suddenly, universities all over the world became interested in rankings—how they were structured, what they did, and how to do well in them. With this development, universities appear to have become active organizational reformers: they are developing new and advanced forms of governance, performance measurements, and marketing techniques and activities (Hazelkorn 2007; Locke et al. 2008). But rankings have very quickly moved from being the concern of individual universities, to becoming an element in the construction of global models for organizing and governing higher education and research. Conferences where rankings are discussed are now held regularly all over the world, including, for example, the World-Class Universities Conference in Shanghai in November 2007, and the Leiden Ranking Conference in the Netherlands in February 2009. Special organizations and groups dedicated to discussing and developing rankings have also been formed, such as the International Rankings Expert Group (IREG), founded in 2004 on the initiative of the UNESCO European Centre for Higher Education (UNESCO-CEPES) in Bucharest and the Institute for Higher Education Policy in Washington. In 2008, the organization developed a permanent structure with the establishment of the *IREG/ International Observatory on Academic Ranking and Excellence* (IREG 2009). In addition, nation-states, such as Sweden (Wedlin et al. 2009) and France (Siganos 2008), and international organizations, such as the EU (van Vught and Westerheijden 2010), are discussing and investigating rankings as elements in new or revised governance schemes for higher education and research.

Packaging Global Governance Models in Media Form

This development has been clearly interrelated with an expansion of other forms of quality assurance mechanisms, most prominently perhaps accreditation systems (Schwarz and Westerheijden 2005) and accountability principles and practices (Stensaker and Harvey 2010), making rankings a particular element of partly new systems of governance for universities and other higher education organizations. Based on a reformed relationship between higher education and national governments, including deregulation of direct rule systems and an increasing focus on ex-post evaluations and assessments (Paradeise et al. 2009), new, and to a large extent global, models for managing and governing universities have developed (King 2009). Such new governance systems rest on 'private' authority of regulation (King 2009) and give significantly more room for 'soft' regulatory modes and mechanisms (Djelic and Sahlin-Andersson 2006; Hedmo et al. 2006), including accreditation and ranking practices (Hedmo 2004; Wedlin 2006).

With the rankings clearly an element in a larger transformation of governance systems for science and universities, they embody a global governance model, building on ideals of transparency and accountability, answering to political and public demands—in a new public management tradition—of increasing information and justification of taxpayer money spent on higher education and research (Paradeise et al. 2009). Rankings also embody beliefs and ideals about competition, based on neo-liberal ideas of markets and market models for steering (Djelic 2006), as well as supporting the increasing interest of public officials to identify, and to create, 'excellence' in higher education and research systems. In what is increasingly considered educational 'markets', rankings are presented and rationalized as 'consumer tools' that help audiences, particularly prospective students, to make informed judgments about the quality and worth of educational offerings (Altbach 2006; Harvey 2008; Kehm and Stensaker 2009).

In attempting to serve these transparency, accountability, and information functions, an important characteristic of rankings is their public nature. 'Wide and simplified dissemination' (King 2009: 140) is one of the keys to the impact and proliferation of rankings, and here, the media obviously plays an important role. The most influential ranking systems are produced and/or extensively reported on by the media across the world. The clearest examples are the internationally recognized rankings produced by the *Times Higher Education*, the *US News and World Report* rankings of colleges and universities in the United States, and the *Business Week* and *Financial Times* rankings of business schools and management education programs around the world (Wedlin 2006). While a large number of other organizations have also engaged in producing and publishing rankings, such as universities (e.g., Shanghai Jiao Tong University, Leiden University), quality assurance agencies (e.g., the German CHE, the Higher Education Evaluation and Accreditation Council of Taiwan), and commercial educational organizations (e.g., QS), most of these are published in or extensively reported on in the media as well as on the Internet (Wedlin 2011a).

Mediatized Standards for Ranking Communication

To place these governance models into the media and to disseminate them to a wide audience place further demands on how the rankings are to be presented and packaged—that is, in order to become a part of public discourse, rankings have been formulated and communicated to relate to the practices, preferences, and procedures of news producing organizations covering scientific activities (cf. Ryfe 2006). To fit the needs and expectations of its (often highly media literate) audiences, media rankings have come to be formed according to media logic, thus packaged and presented in a media format.

The embodiment of media logic in rankings is evident in the guidelines set up by IREG and jointly agreed upon among a large set of ranking and media organizations. In a declaration of sixteen general principles for good ranking practice—what has become known as the Berlin Principles on Ranking Higher Education Institutions (IREG 2006)—ranking organizations have agreed on a set of guidelines for how rankings should be developed and improved. These are largely intended as a 'framework for the elaboration and dissemination of rankings' that will lead to 'a system of continuous improvement and refinement of the methodologies used to conduct these rankings' (IREG 2006). These guidelines are part of the efforts of this group to solidify and create a more coherent practice of rankings as an element in a global governance model for universities.

Translating a Global Model for Universities

In order to make the evaluations of universities more assessable to and useful for disparate audiences, the rankings are constructed so they translate the general properties of high academic quality and performance into coherent, specific, and sometimes detailed standards and procedures. This translation has, as suggested earlier, three main parts: (1) simplifying complex measurements and assessments of scientific value and worth; (2) introducing partly new and standardized measures and criteria for assessment and comparison; and (3) transforming and combining various academic criteria and measures into partly non-academic and popular understandings and measures. Specifying these processes of translation in more detail, we can look at some of the features and current developments of existing ranking practices in the global field.

Simplification

Current rankings display a plethora of approaches to methodology and criteria on which to compare and assess universities and academic performances. Whereas some, like the ARWU ranking, measure mainly research output (in the form of the number of Nobel prizes and Field Medals, as well as citations in journals such as *Science* and *Nature*), others, like the *Times Higher Education* (*THE*), incorporate educational aspects more prominently, combining citation and research criteria with assessments of teaching and the 'learning environment'. The former focuses exclusively, or to a great extent, on statistical methods and data, such as publication and citation records and databases (most prominently the Web of Science), while the latter also incorporate reputational survey data and other measurements in their final rankings.

While perspectives and methodological choices differ, there appears to be a movement—along the lines of the desire for 'completeness' as expressed in the Berlin Principles—to incorporate different features and aspects of university performance into the rankings. A clear example of this is the *THE*, which proudly claims on its webpage to '[e]xamine all core missions of the modern global university—research, teaching, knowledge transfer and international activity'. To do this, the ranking includes thirteen different performance criteria, grouped into five main categories: teaching, research, citations, industry income, and international outlook (Baty 2011). The criteria include statistical measures of citations, staff–student ratios, research income, number of published papers, and the like, but aspects of teaching and research also rest on a reputation survey of academics worldwide.

Another example of this development is the EU-initiated U-Multirank project, which aims to create 'a multi-dimensional, user-driven ranking tool, addressing the functions of higher education and research institutions across five dimensions: research, education, knowledge exchange, regional engagement and international orientation' (Richardson 2011). This ranking attempts to overcome the limit of other rankings that oversee most of the diversity of mission and aims for higher education organizations across the world by not producing an overall ranking list of all universities according to a common set of criteria. Instead, the ranking will be presented through an interactive and visual tool that will be able to display 'performance profiles' of the chosen schools as well as ranking results showing the institutions' performance in all, or specifically chosen, ranking criteria. The ranking here is not numbered, but color-coded according to the relative score on each ranking criteria/category (green, yellow or red) (see www.u-multirank.eu).

One of the effects of the attempts to combine a large set of different performance criteria into a single ranking, whether numerical or color-coded, is that it creates a strong focus on the institutional level (i.e., the university) as the main unit for comparison. While there are attempts by ARWU and the *THE* (and will perhaps also be a feature of U-Multirank) to also create sub-rankings of academic fields and subject areas, their main rankings and those that receive the most attention are the institutional rankings of 'global' universities.

This type of translation of the global university model performed by the mediatized rankings has two important elements, making the inherently complex and multidimensional characteristics and quality of higher education and research into something assessable and comprehensible for a wide audience, and making the tacit and often vague or undefined features of status and position into something concrete and explicit. Through a process of commensuration, which includes the transformation of qualities into quantities, and the specification of common metrics for what is usually considered disparate characteristics or units, this helps to reduce and simplify information. This, in turn, allows people to 'quickly grasp, represent, and compare differences' (Espeland and Stevens 1998: 316) as well as highlight similarities and comparable features. At the same time as rankings produce comparability, they also produce and construct differences, particularly in a hierarchical sense.

Standardization

In defining and setting criteria to assess the 'global university', we can also note a second form of translation, in that the global rankings are taking part in shaping what has been described by some as a 'global definition of academic quality' (Dill and Soo 2005), or a standardization of the practices by which academic units are compared and assessed. In their analysis of global rankings, Dill and Soo (2005) conclude that particularly input measures, focused on the characteristics and quality of students, faculty, and financial resources, are prominent in many of the rankings, along with measures of 'reputation' of universities and other academic units. Although, as noted above, the criteria and approaches applied in different rankings vary greatly, these measures seem to be present in the majority of global rankings.

As a more pronounced element of this translation, however, we can also note an increasing attention to relatively 'new' measures of academic performance being included in the rankings. As witnessed by the *THE* and the U-Multirank rankings described above, measures of 'internationality,' expressed as international activity and international orientation, respectively, have become important elements in these assessments (see also Engwall, chapter 17). This has also been noted as one of the important features of global rankings in business education (Wedlin 2007). Another important feature is the increasing attention to output measures, which, in the business school field, has meant a prominent role for criteria that assess the 'employability' of graduates, including various measures of salary, salary increase, employment opportunities, recruitment efforts, and the like (see Wedlin 2006).

The increasing role of rankings means that standards for and procedures for quality assessment and comparison are becoming increasingly standardized and made to serve a specific purpose—to compare educational offerings across contexts and settings. As global comparisons and rankings have proliferated and standards are being set for how these rankings are to be presented as 'legitimate' and trustworthy, these systems are increasingly forming perceptions of a unified and global field of universities and of academic activity (particularly higher education). The implication of this is that the same criteria and procedures to evaluate performances of higher education and research can be used across the world.

Popularization

A significant part of the translation of academic performance to the public through rankings is the interest in and attention to research criteria that are prominent in all of the major international rankings (ARWU, *THE*, U-Multirank, Leiden, HEEACT). Through a widespread and accepted use of bibliometric measures (publication and citation analysis), research performance has been transformed from a largely academic criteria and evaluation procedure into a public measure to assess the relative standing of universities across the world. Bibliometric researchers have argued that a commercialized, often simplified, construction and use of bibliometric measures, as used in rankings and in many other contexts, has become a quick, relatively cheap, and popular way to create seemingly objective measures of academic performance (Weingart 2005; Taylor et al. 2008; van Raan 2005).

The notion of popularization is also related to the media rankings' ability to provide easily accessible and comprehensible hierarchical orderings of universities or other entities to non-academic audiences. The conception of rankings as an indicator of past and future performance influences the status and reputation positions and relations among actors by punishing those ranked low and rewarding those positioned high in the rank order (Martins 2005; Sauder 2006, 2008). As the rankings are highly visible and widely spread, they have become an accepted and dominant element in the public evaluation of science and scientific activity, suppressing the more substantial and complex assessments measures (Adler and Harzing 2009).

Discussion

A wide number of organizations—both national and transnational—are currently actively involved in creating and proliferating norms, standards, and measurements for assessing and comparing the quality of the research results achieved by individual scientists and their organizations. Media rankings are one of these measurements.

In this chapter, we have argued that the way in which rankings are constructed gives evidence of media logic. Not only have these assessments become a popular media product, as they, in a very simplified manner, introduce a basis for evaluating and grading educational and scientific standards of universities, but politicians, research funders, and universities themselves, as well as their existing and potential students, employees, and partners are also relying on the media products in forming their opinions and subsequent decisions concerning their relationships and engagements in the academic institutions and research activities (Wedlin 2011b; Weingart and Maasen 2007). Moreover, the media (logic) and its influence on the assessments tools and processes is also assumed to influence political processes among nations to defend, construct, or revise the 'geo-political pecking order' of higher education systems across the world (Kivinen and Hedman 2008). Thus, in the context of governance, the emergence of different ranking systems is a fitting example of the role of the media—both in its institutional form (i.e., mediatization) and as a news producer (Wedlin et al. 2009; cf. Eide and Hernes 1987)—in shaping both the local and global context in which science and its representatives interact with the rest of society.

Such a constitutive role of the mediatized rankings and media logic, we believe, is related to the way rankings translate the global model for universities between the global and the local. First, rankings entail a process of translating something that has traditionally been considered—and perhaps, to a great extent, still is (see Engwall, chapter 17)—inherently local and contextual, into something that is perceived as global and abstract. This process implies making the specific (higher education and research) general, and thus comparable across contexts and settings. Here, rankings construct and help to diffuse and translate a global, largely decontextualized model for academic assessment and comparison and, in part, to construct the imagery of an international field for higher education and research (Wedlin 2006). Second, the rankings also help to translate this model into specific governance ideals and models for universities to use locally. Using the simplified, standardized, and popularized model for academic assessments as the input, the model for a global university is increasingly becoming the template for reform for universities across the world.

We believe, given the arguments provided in this chapter, that the media and its logic should be carefully reconsidered as enabling other actors to publicly participate in forming conditions under which science conducts and organizes its activities. Our illustrations also indicate that including the effects of mediatization on the processes in which models and ideas are translated from one context to another can enhance the notion of glocalization. Relating to the discussion on editing rules (Sahlin-Andersson 1996), there is reason to suggest that the processes and outcomes of glocalization are governed by rules and norms that bear witness of the media's emphasis on simplicity, standardization, and popularity. The future research can, therefore, benefit from testing whether such mediatized editing rules can also be observed in other contexts where glocalization is at work.

Notes

1 Developed by the Center for World-Class Universities and the Institute of Higher Education of Shanghai Jiao Tong University, China. From 2009, produced by the independent organization the 'Shanghai Ranking Consultancy'.
2 Since 2010, the *Times Higher Education* World University Ranking.

References

Adler, N., and Harzing, A.-W. (2009). 'When knowledge wins: transcending the sense and nonsense of academic rankings'. *Academy of Management Learning and Education*, 8(1): 72–95.

Altbach, P. (2006). 'The dilemmas of ranking'. *International Higher Education*, 42.

Altheide, D.L. (2004). 'Media logic and political communication'. *Political Communication,* 21(3): 293–96.

Altheide, D.L., and Snow, R.P. (1979). *Media logic*. Beverly Hills: Sage.

Asp, K. (1986). *Mäktiga massmedier. Studier i politisk opinionsbildning*. Stockholm: Akademilitteratur Stockholm.

Baty, P. (2011). 'Rankings methodology fine-tuned for 2011-12'. Retrieved 13/9/2011, from http://www.timeshighereducation.co.uk/story.asp?storycode=417368

Besley, J.C., and Tanner, A.H. (2011). 'What science communication scholars think about training scientists to communicate'. *Science Communication,* 33(2): 239–63.

Brossard, D. (2009). 'Media, scientific journals and science communication: examining the construction of scientific controversies'. *Public Understanding of Science* 18(3): 258–74.

Brossard, D., and Lewenstein, B.V. (2010). 'A critical appraisal of models of public understanding of science: using practice to inform theory', in L. Kahlor and P.A. Scout (eds), *Communicating Science*. New York: Routledge, 11–39.

Carroll, C., and Deephouse, D. (forthcoming). 'What news is fit to print? A multi-level framework explaining the production of news about organizations', in J. Pallas and L. Strannegård (eds), *Organizations and the media: organizing in a mediatized world*. New York: Routledge.

Cook, T.E. (1998). *Governing with the news: the news media as a political institution*. Chicago: University of Chicago Press.

Deephouse, D., and Suchman, M. (2008). 'Legitimacy in organizational institutionalism', in G. Royston, C. Oliver, K. Sahlin, and R. Suddaby (eds), *The Sage handbook of organizational institutionalism*. Thousand Oaks: Sage, 49–77.

Dill, D., and Soo, M. (2005). 'Academic quality, league tables, and public policy: a crossnational analysis of university rankings'. *Higher Education,* 49: 495–533.

Djelic, M.-L. (2006). 'Marketization: from intellectual agenda to global policy-making', in M.-L. Djelic and K. Sahlin-Andersson (eds), *Transnational governance. Institutional dynamics of regulation*. Cambridge: Cambridge University Press, 53–73.

Djelic, M.-L., and Quack, S. (eds) (2003). *Globalization and institutions: redefining the rules of the economic game*. Cheltenham: Edward Elgar.

Djelic, M.-L., and Sahlin-Andersson, K. (2006). *Transnational governance. Institutional dynamics of regulation*. Cambridge, Cambridge University Press.

Eide, M., and Hernes, G. (1987). *Død og pine: om massemedia og helsepolitikk*. Oslo: FAFO.

Ekström, A. (2004). *Den mediala vetenskapen*. Nora: Nya Doxa.

Engwall, L. (forthcoming). 'Academia, trust and the media', in G. Hermerén, K. Sahlin, and N.-E. Sahlin (eds), *Aspects of trust and confidence in scientific research*. Stockholm: Royal Swedish Academy of Letters, History and Antiquities.

Engwall, L., and Wearie, D. (2008). *The university in the market*. London, Portland Press.

Espeland, W., and Stevens, M. (1998). 'Commensuration as a social process'. *Annual Review of Sociology*, 24(1): 313–43.

Fombrun, C. (1998). 'Indices of corporate reputation: an analysis of media rankings and social monitors' ratings'. *Corporate Reputation Review*, 1(4): 327–40.

Guston, D. (2000). *Between politics and science: assuring the integrity and productivity of research*. Cambridge: Cambridge University Press.

Hamilton, J.T. (2004). *All the news that's fit to sell: how the market transforms information into news*. Princeton: Princeton University Press.

Harvey, L. (2008). 'Rankings of higher education institutions: a critical review'. *Quality in Higher Education*, 14(3): 187–207.

Hazelkorn, E. (2007). 'The impact of league tables and ranking systems on higher education decision making'. *Higher Education Management and Policy*, 19(2): 87–110.

Hedmo, T. (2004). *Rule-making in the transnational space: the development of European accreditation in management education*. Uppsala: Uppsala University.

Hedmo, T., and Wedlin, L. (2008). 'New modes of governance: the re-regulation of European higher education and research', in C. Mazza, P. Quattrone, and A. Riccaboni (eds), *European universities in transition: issues, models and cases*. Cheltenham: Edward Elgar Publishing, 113–32.

Hedmo, T., Sahlin-Andersson, K., and Wedlin, L. (2006). 'The emergence of a European regulatory field of management education', in M.-L. Djeclic and K. Sahlin-Andersson (eds), *Transnational governance. Institutional dynamics of regulation*. Cambridge, UK: Cambridge University Press, 308–28.

Hjarvard, S. (2008). 'The mediatization of society: a theory of the media as agents of social and cultural change'. *Nordicom Review*, 29(2): 105–34.

IREG (2006). 'Berlin principles on ranking of higher education institutions', downloaded from www.ireg-observatory.org, 24 Aug 2011.

IREG (2009). 'Programme. 4th Conference of the International Ranking Expert Group', downloaded from www.ireg-observatory.org, 24 Aug 2011.

IREG (2010). 'Programme. 5th Conference of the International Ranking Expert Group', downloaded from www.ireg-observatory.org, 24 Aug 2011.

Irwin, A. (2008). 'Risk, science and public communication: third-order thinking about scientific culture', in M. Bucchi and B. Trench (eds), *Handbook of public communication of science and technology*. New York: Routledge.

Kehm, B., and Stensaker, B. (2009). *University rankings, diversity, and the new landscape of higher education*. Rotterdam/Boston/Taipei: Sense Publishers.

Kepplinger, H.M. (2002). 'Mediatization of politics: theory and data.' *Journal of Communication*, 52(4): 972–86.

King, R. (2009). *Governing universities globally. Organizations, regulation and rankings*. Cheltenham: Edward Elgar.

Kivinen, O., and Hedman, J. (2008). 'World-wide university rankings: a Scandinavian approach'. *Scientometrics*, 74(3): 391–408.

Kjaer, P., and Slaatta, T. (2007). *Mediating business: the expansion of business journalism in the Nordic countries*. Copenhagen: Copenhagen Business School Press.

Lewenstein, B. (1995). 'Science and the media', in S. Jasanoff, G.E. Markle, J.C. Peterson, and T. Pinch (eds), *Handbook of science and technology studies*. Thousand Oaks: Sage, 343–60.
Locke, W., Verbik, L., Richardson, J., and King, R. (2008). *Counting what is measured or measuring what counts? League tables and their impact on higher education institution in England*. Bristol, Higher Education Founding Council for England.
Lundby, K. (2009). *Mediatization: concept, changes, consequences*. New York: Peter Lang.
Martins, L. (2005). 'A model of the effects of reputational rankings on organizational change'. *Organization Science*, 16(6): 701–20.
Mazza, C. (1998). 'The popularization of business knowledge: from academic knowledge to popular culture? The diffusion and consumption of business knowledge', in K. Sahlin-Andersson and L. Engwall (eds), *The expansion of management knowledge. Carriers, flows, and sources*. Stanford: Stanford University Press, 164–81.
Neave, G. (1998). 'The evaluative state reconsidered'. *European Journal of Education*, 33(3): 265–84.
Nelkin, D. (1995). *Selling science: how the press covers science and technology*. New York: Freeman.
Nisbet, M.C., Brossard, D., and Kroepsch, A. (2003). 'Framing science'. *International Journal of Press/Politics*, 8(2): 36–70.
Pallas, J., and Fredriksson, M. (2011). 'Providing, promoting and co-opting: corporate media work in a mediatized society'. *Journal of Communication Management*, 15(2): 165–78.
Pallas, J., and Strannegård, L. (2010). *Företag och Medier*. Malmö: Liber.
Pallas, J., and Strannegård, L. (eds) (forthcoming). *Organizations and the media: organizing in a mediatized world*. New York: Routledge.
Paradeise, C., Reale, E., Bleiklie, I., and Ferlie, E. (2009). *University governance: Western European comparative perspectives*. Dordrecht: Springer.
Peters, H.P., Heinrichs, H., Jung, A., Kallfass, M., and Petersen, I. (2008). 'Mediatization of science as a prerequisite of its legitimization and political relevance', in D. Cheng, M. Claessens, N.R.J. Gascoigne, J. Metcalfe, B. Schiele, and S. Shi (eds), *Communicating science in social context*. New York: Springer, 71–92.
Pollock, T., and Rindova, V.P. (2003). 'Media legitimation effects in the market for initial public offerings'. *Academy of Management Journal*, 46: 631–42.
Power, M., Scheytt, T., Soin, K., and Sahlin, K. (2009). 'Reputational risk as a logic of organizing in late modernity'. *Organization Studies*, 30(2–3): 301–24.
Raviola, E. (2010). *Paper meets Web: how institutions of news production works on paper and online*. (Doctoral), Jönköping: Jönköping University.
Richardson, M. (2011). 'A "democratization" of university rankings: U-Multirank'. *Research Trends*, 24.
Rödder, S. (2009). 'Reassessing the concept of a mediatization of science: a story from the "book of life"'. *Public Understanding of Science*, 18(4): 452–63.
Rödder, S. (2011). 'Science and the mass media—"medialization" as a new perspective on an intricate relationship'. *Sociology Compass*, 5(9): 834–45.
Ryfe, D.M. (2006). 'The nature of news rules'. *Political Communication*, 23(2): 203–14.
Sahlin-Andersson, K. (1996). 'Imitating by editing success: the construction of organizational fields', in B. Czarniawska and G. Sevón (eds), *Translating organizational change*. Berlin: Walter de Gruyter.
Sahlin-Andersson, K., and Engwall, L. (2002). *The expansion of management knowledge. Carriers, flows, and sources*. Stanford: Stanford University Press.
Sauder, M. (2006). 'Third parties and status position: how the characteristics of status systems matter'. *Theory and Society*, 35(3): 299–321.
Sauder, M. (2008). 'Interlopers and field change: the entry of the US news into the field of legal education'. *Administrative Science Quarterly*, 53(2): 209–34.
Schrott, A. (2009). 'Dimensions: catch-all label or technical term', in K. Lundby (ed.), *Mediatization: concept, changes, consequences*. New York: Peter Lang, 41–62.
Schulz, W. (2004). 'Reconstructing mediatization as an analytical concept'. *European Journal of Communication*, 19(1): 87–101.

Schwarz, S., and Westerheijden, D. (2005). *Accreditation and evaluation in the European higher education area.* Dordrecht: Kluwer.

Scott, W.R. (2001). *Institutions and organizations.* London: Sage.

Siganos, A. (2008). 'Rankings, governance, and attractiveness of higher education: the new French context'. *Higher Education in Europe,* 33(2): 311–16.

Stensaker, B., and Harvey, L. (2010). *Accountability in higher education: global perspectives on trust and power.* New York: Routledge.

Strömbäck, J. (2008). 'Four phases of mediatization: an analysis of the mediatization of politics'. *International Journal of Press/Politics,* 13(3): 228–46.

Strömbäck, J. (2011). 'Mediatization of politics: toward a conceptual framework for comparative research', in E.P. Bucy and R.L. Holberg (eds), *The sourcebook for political communication research: methods, measures, and analytical techniques.* New York: Routledge, 367–82.

Taylor, M., Perakakis, P., and Trachana, V. (2008). 'The siege of science.' *Ethics in Science and Environmental Politics,* 8: 17–40.

Trench, B., and Bucchi, M. (2010). 'Science communication: an emerging discipline.' *Journal of Science Communication,* 9(3): 1–5.

Van Raan, A.F.J. (2005). 'Fatal attraction: conceptual and methodological problems in the ranking of universities by bibliometric methods'. *Scientometrics,* 62(1): 133–43.

Van Vught, F., and Westerheijden, D. (2010). 'Multidimensional ranking: a new transparency tool for higher education and research'. *Higher Education Management and Policy,* 22(3): 1–26.

Wedlin, L. (2006). *Ranking business schools.* Cheltenham: Edward Elgar.

Wedlin, L. (2007). 'The role of rankings in codifying a business school template: classifications, diffusion and mediated isomorphism in organizational fields'. *European Management Review,* 4(1): 24–39.

Wedlin, L. (2011a). 'Going global: rankings as rhetorical devices to construct an international field of management education'. *Management Learning,* 42(2): 199–218.

Wedlin, L. (2011b). 'Crafting competition: international rankings and the creation of a global market for business schools'. *Education Inquiry,* 2(4): 563–80.

Wedlin, L., Sahlin, K., and Hedmo, T. (2009). 'The ranking explosion and the formation of a global governing field of universities', in L. Wedlin, K. Sahlin, and M. Grafström (eds), *Exploring the worlds of Mercury and Minerva. Essays for Lars Engwall.* Uppsala: Acta Universitatis Upsaliensis, 315–31.

Weingart, P. (1998). 'Science and the media'. *Research Policy,* 27(8): 869–79.

Weingart, P. (2005). 'Impact of bibliometrics upon the science system: inadvertent consequences?' *Scientometrics,* 62: 67–85.

Weingart, P. (2007). 'Communicating science in democratic media societies', in H. Tiessen, M. Brklacich, and G. Breulmann (eds), *Communicating global change science to society—an assessment and case studies.* SCOPE Series, 55–6.

Weingart, P., and Maasen, S. (2007). 'Elite through rankings—the emergence of the enterprising university', in R. Whitley and J. Gläser (eds), *The changing governance of the sciences.* Dordrecht: Springer, 75–99.

Weingart, P., Engels, A., and Pansegrau, P. (2000). 'Risks of communication: discourses on climate change in science, politics, and the mass media'. *Public Understanding of Science,* 9: 261–83.

Whitley, R. (2007). 'Changing governance of the public sciences: the consequences of establishing research evaluation systems for knowledge production in different countries and scientific fields', in R. Whitley and J. Gläser (eds), *The changing governance of the sciences.* Dordrecht: Springer, 3–29.

Wynne, B. (1995). 'Public understanding of science', in S. Jasanoff, G. Markle, J. Petersen, and T. Pinch (eds), *Handbook of science and technology studies.* Thousand Oaks: Sage, 361–88.

Part V
Processes and Mechanisms

22
Micro-strategies of Contextualization
Glocalizing Responsible Investment in France and Quebec

Eva Boxenbaum and Jean-Pascal Gond

Introduction

Decades of research on the global spread of business practices suggest that adaptation to the local context is imperative. The label may remain intact, suggesting that the practice is unchanged, yet it is often necessary to adapt it to the local political, technical, and societal context in order to facilitate its implementation in organizational practice (Ansari, Fiss, and Zajac 2010). Such adaptations tend to occur as organizational members make sense of an ambiguous concept as they implement it in practice (Edelman 1992). Our aim is to specify some components of this local adaptation process, which we refer to as 'glocalization' (Latour 1993; Robertson 1992).

Glocalization alludes to the emerging consensus among researchers that business practices are adapted to the local context through an intensive work of contextualization (Djelic 1998; Hall and Soskice 2001; Latour 2005). Glocalization entails, for instance, the combination of imported business practice with local elements that enable a global concept to take root in a local setting. Business practices may, in this process, be entangled with elements from a new context, which change their shape and meaning and ultimately 'provide them with their context' (Latour 1996: 133). Our analytical work consists in integrating two streams of literature on glocalization processes. One stream is discursive in orientation (e.g., Greenwood, Oliver, Sahlin-Andersson, and Suddaby 2008; Vaara, Tienari, and Laurila 2006), while the other emphasizes materiality (e.g., Latour 2005). We integrate findings from these two streams of research and refine the results through an empirical study of *responsible investment* (RI).

RI refers to the act of investing in companies whose business practices are deemed to be socially responsible (Kurtz 2008). This practice, which has a fairly long history in the United States (d'Antonio, Johnsen, and Hutton 1998), has, in the past decade or two, spread globally. This global spread has not, however, led to the establishment of identical RI practices in all localities (Eurosif 2010). We illustrate the making of two different RI practices that both result from the glocalization of RI, one in a French social rating agency and another in a

Quebecois RI fund. Our focus is the processes through which early adopters in France and Quebec contextualized the concept of RI to fit their respective localities, resulting in different glocalized versions of RI. The analysis illuminates commonalities in the two processes of contextualization, which are expressed in the form of a repertoire of micro-strategies. We propose that these micro-strategies, which we label filtering, reframing, and bricolage, apply beyond the context of RI and account more generally for how individuals engage with local elements as they contextualize a concept or business practice that is spreading globally.

We begin this chapter with a review and integration of two streams of literature on processes of globalization and contextualization. The next section introduces the empirical context of the study. We subsequently present our method, which explains how we proceeded to develop the three micro-strategies of contextualization. The following section illustrates how entrepreneurial individuals employed these micro-strategies to adapt the globally diffusing concept of RI to a specific local context in, respectively, France and Quebec. We conclude with a discussion of the contribution of these three micro-strategies to the existing literature on glocalization and contextualization.

Glocalization and Processes of Contextualization

Discursive and Symbolic Approaches

The discursive and symbolic perspective on glocalization is treated within organizational institutionalism and related literatures (Boxenbaum and Jonsson 2008; Greenwood et al. 2008). Researchers tend to examine two processes: (1) how local practices are packaged to facilitate their global diffusion, and (2) how the resulting globalized concept is subsequently translated to fit the institutional context in local host settings. As an example of the former process, Kerstin Sahlin-Andersson (2001: 55–7) proposes three editing rules that enhance the global flavor of a local practice. When *editing for context*, individuals strip business practices of elements that seem to be too unique or specific to the local context. When *editing for logic*, individuals assign effects to certain activities or present practices as efficient solutions to recognized problems to render them rationally justified. When *editing for formulation*, individuals cast practices in a narrative form that dramatizes them and makes them more appealing. These three editing rules serve to discursively translate a context-specific practice into a global concept with general appeal and wide applicability.

In terms of adapting foreign business practices to new local contexts, empirical research shows that rejection may occur if an adaptation fails to make sense to members of the host society (Biggart and Guillén 1999: 726). Rejection can occur if a foreign business practice is considered immoral, irrational or irrelevant (Biggart and Beamish 2003: 448). Subsequent research has identified five legitimation strategies that help to enhance the local perception of a foreign business practice (Vaara et al. 2006). These and other discursive and symbolic processes can alter the meaning and improve the local legitimacy of a global concept without necessarily changing practices or material artifacts such as evaluation grids or decision-making tools (Brannen 2004; Zilber 2006).

Practice-related and Material Approaches

Another stream of glocalization research emphasizes changes to practices or material artifacts. It includes Actor Network Theory (ANT) (Latour 2005) and other glocalization literatures that emphasize practice (e.g., Djelic 1998; Westney 1987). Common to them is a focus on how practices change in response to new contexts of implementation. For instance, actors are said to engage in *selective emulation* when they 'choose not to adopt certain features of the original model because they conflict with local patterns' or when they try to legitimize changes in the host society by transferring only desired features of a foreign business practice (Westney 1987: 27). Other studies further point out that actors engage in *hybridization* when they combine a foreign practice with local elements to make it meaningful or legitimate in the host society (Pieterse 1994). Empirical studies confirm that practice adaptation at the time of initial adoption facilitates local implementation (Boxenbaum 2006; Djelic 1998; Lippi 2000; Westney 1987).

The ANT tradition goes one step further in emphasizing ongoing local adaptations of a practice and its material manifestations (Latour 2005). The notion of contextualization, which is key to this literature, consists in actively and creatively integrating a globally diffusing business practice with objects and practices that are well established in the local context in order to secure support for it (Akrich, Callon, and Latour 1988; Latour 1996, 2005). It is, thus, individuals who *create* a new context for the diffusing practice by constantly integrating it with local practices and artifacts. According to Bruno Latour (1996), the success of a new practice depends on the capacity of actors to entangle specific dimensions of the practice with the local context of adoption. Entanglement consists in coupling and uncoupling various practices and material artifacts in a constant process of contextualization (Latour 1996, 2005).

Combining Two Streams of Literature

Relatively scant attention has been paid to linking the discursive, material, and practice-related dimensions of glocalization. A notable exception is the work of Barbara Czarniawska and Bernward Joerges (1996), which proposes that contextualization processes can be understood as a set of three consecutive steps: selection, objectification, and materialization. *Selection* occurs when individuals choose an idea that seems promising for alleviating an organizational problem. *Objectification* consists in assigning a label to a selected idea so that it may be understood collectively. Ideas crystallize somewhat when they acquire a fixed terminology. *Materialization,* 'this magic moment when words become deeds' (Czarniawska and Joerges 1996: 41), is the act of turning objectified ideas into quasi-objects, such as an RI assessment tool that transforms an idea into a practice. Individuals select, and discard, material and practice components from a range of available ones, which they combine with conceptual components to create a unique glocalized version of a business practice. This approach stresses the creativity of individuals who engage in glocalization (Ansari et al. 2010), but it also locks glocalization into a set of processual steps. We propose that the discursive, material, and practice-related dimensions of an adaptation unfold simultaneously and, as such, we advance a more comprehensive and multi-dimensional approach to glocalization.

Both streams of literature recognize that the removal, or addition, of undesirable elements from a global concept or foreign business practice can increase its local appeal and adoption. They differ primarily on the *nature* of these elements, for which reason we maintain a distinction between discursive/symbolic elements and practice-related/material elements. Four processes can thus be distinguished theoretically: the removal or addition of a discursive/symbolic element and the removal or addition of a practice/material element. These processes are not mutually exclusive, yet their distinction is important because implications may differ. We further refine and illustrate them in the following empirical study of RI.

Empirical Context: Responsible Investment

RI refers to 'a set of approaches which include social or ethical goals or constraints as well as more conventional criteria in decisions over whether to acquire, hold or dispose of a particular investment' (Cowton 1999: 60; d'Antonio et al. 1998). As a practice, RI refers to the assessment that financial investors make of the social responsibility of corporations, using data made available by firms. This data is interpreted in light of certain principles, norms, and conventions that are related to RI. The roots of RI stretch back to the 17th century, when the Quaker community in United States and the United Kingdom opposed investment in activities that contradicted their values, such as war-related activities or slavery (d'Antonio et al. 1998). The RI movement was revitalized in the United States in the 1970s and 1980s in response to the Vietnam War and Apartheid in South Africa (Giamporcaro 2004). From 1984 to 1988, investments in RI products in the United States increased from USD 40 billion to USD 400 billion (SIF 2010). They continued to increase during the 1990s, while the concept of RI began to spread globally.

The global spread of RI is reflected in assets. In 2002, American RI assets amounted to about USD 2 trillion, approximately two-thirds of RI assets worldwide (Committee of Public Finance 2002). Today, RI represents a sizable proportion of investments in the US and in Europe: an estimated 12 percent and 10 percent, respectively, of total assets under management in these markets in 2010 is invested in some form of RI. The growth of RI has been sustained over the last 15 years, and has influenced mainstream investment through signaling the significance of social and environmental risk (Eurosif 2010; SIF 2010). As such, RI represents a well-established glocalized concept and business practice, yet it differs across local contexts.

Methodology

Case Selection

The two cases we have selected for in-depth analysis of glocalization represent early initiatives of RI in France and Quebec. Early initiatives are interesting because they unfold in relatively uncharted territory. Without local exemplars to copy, actors need to anchor global concepts and foreign business practices locally. Variation in the type of initiating organization and societal context ensures difference in the resulting 'glocalized' form of RI. Our two cases represent first-movers in unrelated settings, which allow us to identify shared processes that actors engage in during glocalization.

Our two case studies are drawn from independent RI initiatives in France and Quebec. The French case, ARESE, was a small entrepreneurial company created in 1997 to measure the corporate social performance of companies that were quoted on the stock market. The mission of ARESE was to provide structured, quantified information to RI fund managers to help them select the most ethical or responsible companies for their investment portfolio (Igalens and Gond 2005). ARESE was the first formal initiative to quantify and legitimize the notion of corporate social responsibility within the French financial community (Déjean, Gond, and Leca 2004; Giamporcaro 2004). They contextualized RI in the late 1990s.

The Quebec case is that of *Fonds d'Investissement Responsable* (FIR), a social RI fund that was created in 2003 (the name has been altered). FIR's mission was to evaluate the financial, social, and environmental sustainability of small and medium sized enterprises (SMEs) in Quebec and make investments in the most promising ones, using risk capital. Half of the capital was provided by two labor pension funds in Quebec. The other half came from public funds for environmental protection that was transferred from a non-governmental organization. FIR's contextualizing of RI started in 2002.

Data Collection

Our main data source is interviews, which is one of the best ways to gain access to individual perceptions and strategies (Yin 2003). We first identified key individuals involved in the import of RI, including internal members of the firms (e.g., the CEO, financial analysts, and board members) as well as external constituents (e.g., sustainable development managers of evaluated companies, socially responsible fund managers, and managers of partnering organizations). The interviews inquired about their interest in implementing RI, their perception of difficulties, and their strategies for overcoming obstacles. In total, we conducted 24 semi-structured interviews. All interviews were tape-recorded and transcribed.

Data Analysis

Our data analysis consisted in inductively identifying initiatives aimed at 'glocalizing' RI, that is, of adapting the practice of RI to the local context. We coded all instances of glocalization according to the type of action (removal or addition of element) and the nature of the element (symbolic/discursive or material/practice-related). We then compared our findings with the theoretical literature through a systematic process of iteration between data and theory (Orton 1997), which led to the identification of three micro-strategies. Since discursive/symbolic elements were often removed and added simultaneously, we retained a single symbolic/discursive micro-strategy, which we call *reframing*. The distinction between removing and adding components was more obvious in the realm of materiality/practice; hence, we retained two micro-strategies: *filtering* depicts the removal of components of a practice and/or material artefacts, while *bricolage* reflects the addition of a new practice-related or material component. In choosing terms, we sought to not complicate the conceptual landscape unnecessarily and, therefore, selected well-established concepts rather than introducing new labels whenever possible; only filtering is a new concept. We also sought conceptual coherence across micro-strategies and with our main argument. The selected terms, all visually expressive, allude to human manipulation of physical objects. In contrast, the notion of hybridization makes reference to reproductive processes that are normally beyond human reach. Table 22.1 represents the three micro-strategies of filtering, reframing, and bricolage that actors deployed to contextualize RI to their local setting.

Micro-strategies of Glocalization

In what follows, we show how actors employed the three micro-strategies to adapt RI to their local context. In Quebec, the resulting RI practice developed into one of investing in local entrepreneurial initiatives to develop and market green technologies. The local RI practice consisted in developing and using a Life Cycle Assessment tool to assess and finance investment applications from green technology producers in the social economy sector. This sector is a local hybrid between SMEs and non-profit organizations (Neamtam 2005). The RI fund in question was created to invest in, rather than to subsidize, the social economy sector. This mandate implied lower profit expectations than were the case for other investment funds.

Table 22.1 Micro-strategies of contextualization: definition and illustrations

Micro-strategy of contextualization (label and definition)	Illustrative example from the French case	Illustrative example from the Quebec case
(1) Filtering		
Removal or downplaying of elements in the globalized construct that could be perceived as 'incongruent' with the new context.	Downplay of the moral and religious connotations of RI to present it as a neutral and objective investment in firms with long-term profitability.	Downplay of the profit-making elements of RI to better align with the history and values of Francophone Quebec.
(2) Reframing		
Discursive alignment with local myths, past history, social movements, or current trends in order to make the globalized concept more acceptable in the new context.	Alignment of RI with a current reform of the financial investment sector in France.	Alignment of RI with the discourse of the Quiet Revolution in the 1960s in Quebec.
(3) Bricolage		
Integration of a widely accepted practice or object from the new context in order to increase the perceived usefulness and/or acceptability of the globalized construct in this context.	Integration of a positive screening methodology (instead of moralistic negative screening) into the tools employed to practice RI.	Integration of the Life Cycle Approach (LCA) into the evaluation tool developed to guide the practice of RI.

In France, the local RI practice consisted in creating a system for quantitative evaluation of corporate performance in the non-financial domain, which resulted in the creation of ARESE, a pioneer 'social rating agency' in this country (Igalens and Gond 2005). This agency has had an important influence on the development of the RI market in France (Déjean et al. 2004). It merged in 2002 with a competing project to become Vigeo, which is still the most prominent non-financial rating agency in France today and one of the most important actors in this domain at the European and global scale.

Filtering

Filtering occurs when individuals eliminate or downplay features of the original practice that may block its entry into the host society. These features may be specific practices, beliefs, or values that carry negative connotations in the host society. Filtering serves to eliminate or downplay practice-related features that may block the adoption of a foreign concept or business practice. Much like uncoupling (Latour 2005) and selective emulation (Westney 1987), filtering disentangles practice-related or material elements that in the local setting may be perceived as illegitimate or unattractive. This micro-strategy was employed to open the door for RI in both France and Quebec.

France

One of the original features of the RI construct is its moral(istic) undertones of investing in something inherently good as opposed to the presumed irresponsibility of ordinary investments. Entrepreneurs in the French case relied extensively on filtering to develop an evaluation tool for social investment in France because mainstream investors on the French market perceived moral, and even religious, claims related to RI with some suspicion. Prior to the formal creation of ARESE, the CEO had travelled to the United States and other European countries to deepen her knowledge of RI. She identified some dimensions of the American RI practice that she deemed culturally incongruent with French society:

> I realized that the model was extremely militant ... and really difficult to export. The model of [*responsible*] investment was marked by values directly inherited from puritanism or civil rights engagement. So, it was something really embedded in the American and Anglo-Saxon culture. On the religious side, it was the Quakers; on the civil side, it was related to the problem of minority discrimination and inspired by Martin Luther King; on the consumer side, it was Ralph Nader. The three leverages were a racial leverage, a consumerist leverage and a religious leverage ... With these approaches, the evaluation method was not of importance, and this value-based legacy was really not exportable. On the contrary, the financial leverage of pension funds appeared very credible to me.
> (CEO of ARESE)

Some of these associations to moral and religious traditions in the United States needed filtering before the entrepreneurs could hope to develop an RI evaluation tool that would be construed as legitimate and attractive on the French financial market. When preparing the business plan of ARESE, she and her team carefully removed the overtly moral and religious elements in the American RI construct, highlighting instead the technical dimensions of corporate evaluation. As an ARESE analyst reported:

> She [the Founder/CEO of ARESE] always told us: "We cannot sell that [RI] in the name of ethics, we have to sell it as a financial product. This is a tool that will be put to use. Our goal is to inform investors, not to convey ideological or moral convictions."
> (ARESE, Analyst B)

They developed a quantitative methodology for RI that was susceptible to pass as morally neutral in French society, an emphasis that resonated well with French investors and facilitated their acceptance of RI (Déjean et al. 2004).

Quebec

In contrast to the French context in which actors perceived the RI practice of the United States as 'too' moral or religious and not sufficiently business-oriented, actors in the Quebec context regarded the US concept of RI as excessively profit-oriented. They expressed skepticism toward the idea of creating synergy between profit-making and social gains (i.e., simultaneously making profit from investments and producing societal benefits). This conceptual feature of RI encountered some resistance in Quebec where profit-making and societal benefits are traditionally construed as being in opposition to one another. For historical reasons, the Francophone population of Quebec tends to associate profit-making with social oppression and exploitation of unskilled workers in industrialized factories that, at least until the 1960s, were primarily owned and managed by the Anglophone community. The Francophone community has since then made significant progress in terms of managing and developing their own society, not least during the Quiet Revolution of the 1960s, but the opposition between profit-making and societal benefit remains emotionally imprinted in collective cognition. An entrepreneur engaged in the introduction of RI into Quebec society explains the situation in the following words:

> The reality of this country [Quebec society] is that no Francophones had power, nor money, for that matter. There were priests, notaries, doctors and liberal professions who did, but the rest of us did not touch money. They were dirty. They served to exploit others. I felt that way myself when I was 10 years old and wanted to be a communist. Now, at 38, I tell myself, I want to take charge of money myself.
>
> (CEO of FIR)

The idea of inherent synergy between profit-making and societal benefits had to be filtered in order for RI to become attractive and meaningful in this local context. The entrepreneur in question proceeded by minimizing the prominence of profit-making in the RI concept. She reformulated profit as a resource for new societal investments, that is, as a tool for social development rather than as a desirable outcome in its own right. She gives an example of this filtering in the following quote:

> When this project starts to make money, the part of that money that belongs to the environmental organization will be reinvested in environmental groups and educational projects. The money we generate will sustain the survival of the environmental organization.
>
> (CEO of FIR)

This subordination of profit-making to social goals fitted better than the synergy formulation with collective cognitive templates in Quebec. The filtering made RI more legitimate and desirable in this societal context.

As we see from these two examples, filtering served to remove certain components of RI that entrepreneurs deemed to hinder the adoption of RI in, respectively, France and Quebec. By filtering the concept, they developed a locally appropriate version of RI that carried sufficient legitimacy and attraction to be implemented locally. Interestingly, actors from each context pushed RI in radically opposite directions through filtering: downplaying its morality in France and downplaying its profit dimension in Quebec.

Reframing

Reframing assigns new positive meaning to a globalized concept or transforms its purpose without altering the practice itself. The concept is reformulated to make it reflect local values and beliefs (Brannen 2004; Vaara et al. 2006; Zilber 2006). Reframing assigns a new rationale to a global concept (Kelly and Dobbin 1998) and occurs when individuals use the mobilizing force of a myth, a societal problem, a social movement, or a current trend to facilitate the acceptance of a globalized concept or foreign business practice without making any substantial changes to practice. Reframing simply infuses a globalized concept with new symbolic energy, orienting it toward new directions or purposes.

France

The entrepreneurs employed reframing from the very launch of ARESE in 1995. For instance, the decision to name ARESE a 'social rating organization' contributed to adapting RI to the new context. The notion of *rating* captures the standard logic of financial markets. Outside France, providers of extra-financial information used fuzzier labels, such as 'research offices' and 'social information provider'. The term 'social rating organization' is clearly aligned with the financial domain and facilitated communication with investors.

Moreover, RI was reframed through association with elements of financial market liberalization, a reform that was taking place in France at the time. Newspaper reports from the late 1990s made explicit links between RI and the reform. In a newspaper article, published in *Le Monde,* RI professionals expressed that they 'feel ready to provide an answer to the demand for socially responsible pension funds [if they are created]' (*Le Monde* 1998). The founder/CEO organized a business trip for financial executives from *Caisses de Dépôts et Consignation* (CDC) and the *Caisses d'Epargne* (CE), two French banks associated with the public sector, to introduce the financial executives to innovative ideas and techniques in the American financial market. The last day was devoted entirely to RI, and executives responded with enthusiasm. They perceived the notion of RI as an opportunity to reconcile social concerns (social welfare in a public service ideology) with institutional investment (new commercial products and profitable markets), two dimensions that until then had proven difficult to reconcile in the liberalization of the French financial markets (Schmidt 2003). The alignment of RI with the pending reform of French pension funds also led the two financial institutions to show interest in developing the emerging market of employee savings. By means of reframing, RI was discursively aligned with values and reforms in French society, which greatly facilitated its local adoption.

Quebec

Reframing also facilitated the adoption of RI in Quebec, where the global market was generally perceived to be a destructive force. There was widespread resistance to liberal market forces and all practices associated with them, including RI. This negative perception of RI required a reframing, as explained here by the initiator of FIR:

> I'm scared that people will say that I'm corrupt because I'm not choosing resistance. When I presented the project to the board of the environmental organization of which I was in charge, one of the board members said that he was not in favour of it. I asked why, and he answered that, "Well, okay, because you buy into the establishment." He had strong principles on this. He is anti-globalization, anti, anti, anti.
>
> (CEO of FIR)

The CEO responded to resistance with two types of reframing. First, she associated RI with the World Summit on Sustainable Development, held in Johannesburg in August 2002, shortly before the launch of FIR. The World Summit carried positive connotations as a social movement for environmental protection and helped to reframe RI as a business practice that would help protect the world against exploitation by multi-national corporations. Second, she represented RI as an extension of the strategy adopted during the Quiet Revolution: a collective effort to appropriate tools that would help restore social order and economic autonomy to Quebec. She reframed RI as an act of 'empowering people for a common social cause', asserting that 'abuse, lies, and exploitation of children make me really angry. I want to restore justice; I want to change the power balance', echoing the Quiet Revolution. Framed as a means to protect the social and natural world and to gain autonomy and independence from global power structures, RI became legitimate and desirable in Quebec society.

Bricolage

Bricolage consists of adding a new material or practice-related component to a globalized concept. Individuals engage in bricolage when they attach a well-established practice or material device from the local context to the globalized concept to make it more useful, familiar, or legitimate in this context. Much like hybridization (Zeitlin and Herrigel 2000), bricolage consists of combining elements of practice, including persons or organizations (Campbell 2004; Duymedjian and Rüling 2010). In contrast to reframing, which infuses the construct with new symbolic value, bricolage alters the practice by adding material or practice-related components to the practice.

France

The team that launched ARESE in the mid-1990s perceived threats to the development of RI in France. All the interviewees who were employed at ARESE in its early stage of development agreed that there was uncertainty around RI in France in 1997 and 1998. In fact, a market study conducted by the founder/CEO prior to the launch of ARESE concluded that the French market was not yet ready for RI. They engaged in various forms of bricolage to overcome this situation.

Firstly, ARESE adopted positive screening instead of negative screening. Positive screening identifies firms that perform best on a set of social and environmental criteria in any given industrial sector and encourages investors to include these firms in their portfolio. In contrast, negative screening, which is dominant in the United States (SIF 2010), seeks to identify firms that make profit in industries that are considered immoral (e.g., alcohol and tobacco) and encourages investors to exclude these firms from their portfolio (Giamporcaro 2004). Negative screening reflects the religious and political elements of RI that are also conveyed in social movements that aim to change corporate behavior and ultimately society. By combining RI with positive screening instead of negative screening, the entrepreneurs at ARESE transformed RI from a moral device to a managerial tool, adapted to France.

Secondly, the RI construct was combined with elements that were familiar to French managers and that helped solve technical problems. Elements such as the *European Framework for Quality Management* (EFQM), the well-established principles from *Total Quality Management* (TQM), and a very basic description of firms' stakeholders were used to construct the methodological tool for corporate social evaluation. The combination of RI with TQM and financial concepts facilitated acceptance of RI in the evaluated firms, especially by managers trained in TQM. Some of them decided to use ARESE's questionnaires to design their own internal CSR policy:

> Personally, I found the ARESE referential [RI evaluation tool] to be well designed. As the underlying framework of that approach was satisfying, we decided to use it! You can consider social rating to be an external constraint and adopt a compliance attitude by simply providing the requested information. Well, we decided to adopt a positive

attitude and use rating as a managerial exercise ... So, we use the ARESE referential as an internal management tool.

(Director of Quality Management, Bank of the CAC 40)

Through bricolage, RI was adapted substantially to actors, trends, and traditions in France.

Quebec

In the case of FIR, bricolage was used extensively to legitimize the concept of RI. One form of bricolage consisted in creating strategic alliances with key actors. At the preliminary stages of FIR, the CEO contacted a number of stakeholders that could either facilitate the transfer by associating with the project or, alternatively, actively distance themselves from it and hence block its adoption. She identified local elements of importance to each stakeholder, such as small and medium sized enterprises (SMEs) and environmental technologies, and combined them with RI through bricolage to gain support from key stakeholders. The strategic selection of board members helped legitimize RI and prevent its rejection:

> We made an agreement with the Responsible Investment Network of Quebec and all the community organizations in Quebec to develop a common approach to sustainable development. The government officials who were most reluctant to support the project saw immediately that we were reinforcing an organization that they wanted to abolish.
>
> (CEO of FIR)

The bricolage with local organizations and practices facilitated the adoption of RI in Quebec.

Another form of bricolage took place when the CEO of FIR combined RI with the Life Cycle Approach (LCA). LCA is a tool for calculating the pollution that a product generates during its entire life cycle. Already familiar with this approach, she adopted it as a way to implement RI in organizational practice:

> I first heard about the Life Cycle Approach two years ago, but I did not explore it that much. Now I am facing a real problem because sustainable development is really huge. People tell me "it can mean anything", so I asked myself which tool I can use to avoid that. I want to be able to explain why we say yes, why we say no [to applications for investment]. And the Life Cycle Approach is rigorous. It is a model and when you apply it, you definitely do sustainable development. You prevent problems.
>
> (CEO of FIR)

FIR subsequently introduced LCA as a technical measure in its evaluation tool for RI. An integration of stakeholders and an established practice like LCA was thus instrumental in adapting the concept of RI to the local setting. More substantial in nature than reframing, bricolage played an important role in 'glocalizing' the practice of RI in Quebec.

Revisiting Contextualization

Micro-strategies represent the nitty-gritty of how individuals adapt globally diffusing constructs and business practices to their local context. We juxtaposed two streams of literature on this topic, one emphasizing the discursive and symbolic dimension of glocalization (Greenwood et al. 2008; Vaara et al. 2006) and the other focusing on changes in practice and material elements (Latour 2005). Through this work, we identified two dimensions of importance in glocalization processes: (1) whether an element is being added or removed, and (2) whether the nature of the element is symbolic/discursive or material/practice-related. These options fit into a matrix, where a symbolic or discursive element can be added or removed, just like a material or practice-related element can be added or removed. We subsequently compared this theoretical matrix with the empirical findings from our France and Quebec cases. Through iteration between the two streams of literature and our case studies, we identified three micro-strategies that entrepreneurial individuals in the two cases used to contextualize RI to fit their local organizational and national settings. *Filtering* refers to the removal (or downtoning) of a practice-related or material component, *reframing* to a replacement of the discursive frame without changes to practice, and *bricolage* to the addition of a new practice or material component. We propose that these three micro-strategies of contextualization apply beyond the empirical domain of RI and beyond the societal contexts of France and Quebec. However, additional empirical research would be needed to ascertain the validity of this proposal.

We also illustrated the three micro-strategies in action, using findings from our double case study of responsible investment (RI) in France and Quebec. This illustration shows that individuals applied the same three micro-strategies to adapt RI to their respective local settings, yet, since they removed and added different components, their local RI constructs differed from one another. Other glocalized forms of RI could probably have been developed in the same local contexts. This potential local variety in outcomes represents an interesting topic for future research.

We contend that the three micro-strategies contribute with new insight into processes of glocalization. The integration of the symbolic/discursive dimension with the material/practice dimension of glocalization adds an important distinction to the widely recognized distinction between adding or removing components (Westney 1987). Our study contributes to identifying a specific structure of contextualization beneath the apparent freedom of association and desociation. This structure is characterized by an interplay of discursive, symbolic, material, and practice-oriented contextualization that can take many different forms in practice. Relative to previous studies of such processes (Boxenbaum 2006; Djelic 1998; Latour 2005; Westney 1987), our study parses out micro-strategies that operate simultaneously in the symbolic, practice-related, and material realms. As such, it opens a broader scope of action than that offered by either symbolic/discursive approaches (Vaara et al. 2006) or practice/material types of adaptation (Latour 2005) alone.

Another contribution lies in our conceptualization of glocalization as a creative space where actors, relatively unconstrained by stepwise progression (Czarniawska and Joerges 1996) or institutional determinants (Hall and Soskice 2001), develop unique local versions of globally diffusing business practices. Most importantly perhaps, our study shows how individuals engage creatively and strategically with locally available practices and material objects to produce the kind of glocalized outcomes that have been identified in previous research (Djelic 1998). As such, the repertoire of micro-strategies makes explicit the practice of contextualization, which is often taken for granted in studies of glocalization. Our illustrated account of micro-strategies can be valuable to managers who engage in the practice of transferring practices across societal and organizational divides. For instance, within the domain of RI, our empirical findings may provide insights into the processes through which programs and practices on corporate social responsibility or corporate social citizenship can be adapted for the purpose of intangible asset creation.

Additional studies of glocalization may contribute to refining the repertoire of micro-strategies, including its uses and effects. It would be worthwhile to investigate which contextualization strategies are best suited for a given situation, and whether the same repertoire of micro-strategies apply to subsequent contextualizations of a glocalized business practice in the same organization or society. Glocalized business practices do undergo change over time, including within the same organization (Boxenbaum, Gjuvsland, and Leon 2011), yet it is unclear if the same micro-strategies are in play in later modifications. The dimension of time may add interesting new insights into processes of contextualization and glocalization, which hold significant promise at a time of growing disenchantment with globalization.

Acknowledgments

We are grateful to Peer Fiss, Martin Kornberger, Magnus Larsson, Dirk Matten, Jeremy Moon, Sidney Winter, an anonymous reviewer, and the editors of this volume for helpful comments and suggestions on earlier versions of this chapter. Data collection in Quebec was made possible by financial support from Kai Houmann Nielsens Fund in Denmark.

References

Akrich, M., Callon, M., and Latour, B. (1988). 'À quoi tient le succes des innovations? Premier épisode: l'art de l'intéressement'. *Gérer et Comprendre. Annales des Mines,* June 4–17.

Ansari, S.M., Fiss, P.C., and Zajac, E.J. (2010). 'Made to fit: how practices vary as they diffuse'. *Academy of Management Review, 35(1)*: 67–92.

Biggart, N.W., and Beamish, T.D. (2003). 'The economic sociology of conventions: habit, custom, practice, and routine in market order'. *Annual Review of Sociology, 29(1)*: 443–64.

Biggart, N.W., and Guillén, M.F. (1999). 'Developing difference: social organization and the rise of the auto industries of South Korea, Taiwan, Spain, and Argentina'. *American Sociological Review, 64(5)*: 722–47.

Boxenbaum, E. (2006). 'Lost in translation: the making of Danish diversity management'. *American Behavioral Scientist, 48(7)*: 939–48.

Boxenbaum, E., and Jonsson, S. (2008). 'Isomorphism, diffusion and decoupling', in R. Greenwood, C. Oliver, K. Sahlin-Andersson, and R. Suddaby (eds), *Handbook of organizational institutionalism*. London, UK: Sage, 78–98.

Boxenbaum, E., Gjuvsland, M., and Leon, C.E. (2011). 'Diversity management in Denmark: evolutions from 2002 to 2009', in S. Gröschl (ed.), *Diversity in the workplace: multi-disciplinary and international perspectives*. Farnham, UK: Gower Publishing, 101–18.

Brannen, M.Y. (2004). 'When Mickey loses face: recontextualization, semantic fit and the semiotics of foreignness'. *Academy of Management Review, 29(4)*: 583–616.

Campbell, J. (2004). *Institutional change and globalization: exploring problems in the New Institutional Analysis*. Princeton, NJ: Princeton University Press.

Committee of Public Finance (2002). 'Corporate social responsibility and socially responsible investment'. Consultation document. Quebec, CA: National Assembly of Quebec.

Cowton, C.J. (1999). 'Playing by the rules: ethical criteria at an ethical investment fund'. *Business Ethics: A European Review, 8(1)*: 60–9.

Czarniawska, B., and Joerges, B. (1996). 'Travels of ideas', in B. Czarniawska and G. Sevón (eds), *Translating organizational change*. Berlin: Walter de Gruyter, 13–48.

d'Antonio, L., Johnsen, T., and Hutton, B. (1998). 'Socially responsible investing'. *Business and Society, 37(3)*: 281–306.

Déjean, F., Gond, J.-P., and Leca, B. (2004). 'Measuring the unmeasured: an institutional entrepreneur strategy in an emerging industry'. *Human Relations, 57(6)*: 741–64.

Djelic, M.-L. (1998). *Exporting the American model: the postwar transformation of European business*. Oxford, UK: Oxford University Press.

Duymedjian, R., and Rüling, C.-C. (2010). 'Towards a foundation of bricolage in organization and management theory'. *Organization Studies, 31(2)*: 133–51.

Edelman, L.B. (1992). 'Legal ambiguity and symbolic structures: organizational mediation of civil rights law'. *American Journal of Sociology, 6*: 1531–76.

Eurosif (2010). *European SRI study*. Retrieved from www.eurosif.org.

Giamporcaro, S. (2004). 'L'investissement socialement responsable en France. Un outil au service d'une action politique par la consommation?' *Sciences de la Société, 62*: 169–89.

Greenwood, R., Oliver, C., Sahlin-Andersson, K., and Suddaby, R. (eds). (2008). *Handbook of organizational institutionalism*. London, UK: Sage.

Hall, P.A., and Soskice, D. (2001). 'An introduction to varieties of capitalism', in P.A. Hall and D. Soskice (eds), *Varieties of capitalism: the institutional foundations of comparative advantage*. New York: Oxford University Press, 1–68.

Igalens, J., and Gond, J.-P. (2005). 'Measuring corporate social performance in France: a critical and empirical analysis of ARESE data'. *Journal of Business Ethics, 56(2)*: 131–48.

Kelly, E., and Dobbin, F. (1998). 'How affirmative action became diversity management: employer response to anti-discrimination law, 1961–1996'. *American Behavioral Scientist, 41(7)*: 960–84.

Kurtz, L. (2008). 'Socially responsible investment and shareholder activism', in A. Crane, A. McWilliams, D. Matten, J. Moon, and D.S. Siegel (eds), *The Oxford handbook of corporate social responsibility*. Oxford, UK: Oxford University Press, 249–67.

Latour, B. (1993). *We have never been modern*. Cambridge, MA: Harvard University Press.

Latour, B. (1996). *Aramis, or the love of technology*. Cambridge, MA: Harvard University Press.

Latour, B. (2005). *Reassembling the social. An introduction to Actor-Network Theory*. Oxford, UK: Oxford University Press.

Le Monde (1998). 'Concilier l'éthique et la finance'. September 5, 14.

Lippi, A. (2000). 'One theory, many practices. Institutional allomorphism in the managerialist reorganization of Italian governments'. *Scandinavian Journal of Management, 16*: 455–77.

Neamtam, N. (2005). 'The social economy: finding a way between the market and the state'. *Policy Options,* July/August: 71–6.

Orton, J.D. (1997). 'From inductive to iterative grounded theory: zipping the gap between process theory and process data'. *Scandinavian Journal of Management, 13(4)*: 419–38.

Pieterse, J.N. (1994). 'Globalization as hybridization'. *International Sociology, 9(2)*: 161–84.

Robertson, R. (1992). *Globalization: social theory and global culture*. London: Sage.

Sahlin-Andersson, K. (2001). 'National, international and transnational constructions of new public management', in T. Christensen and P. Lægreid (eds), *New public management: the transformation of ideas and practice*. Aldershot, UK: Ashgate, 43–72.

Schmidt, V.A. (2003). 'French capitalism transformed, yet still a third variety of capitalism'. *Economy and Society, 32(4)*: 526–54.

Social Investment Forum (SIF) (2010). *Socially responsible investment trends in the United States*. Retrieved from www.ussif.org.

Vaara, E., Tienari, J., and Laurila, J. (2006). 'Pulp and paper fiction: on the discursive legitimation of global industrial restructuring'. *Organization Studies, 27(6)*: 789–810.

Westney, E.D. (1987). *Imitation and innovation: the transformation of Western organizational patterns to Meiji Japan*. Cambridge, MA: Harvard University Press.

Yin, R.K. (2003). *Case study research: design and methods* (3rd edn). Applied social research methods series, vol. 5. Thousand Oaks: Sage.

Zeitlin, J., and Herrigel, G. (eds). (2000). *Americanization and its limits. Reworking US technology in post-war Europe and Japan*. Oxford: Oxford University Press.

Zilber, T. (2006). 'The work of the symbolic in institutional processes: translations of rational myths in Israeli high tech'. *Academy of Management Journal, 49(2)*: 281–303.

23

Projecting the Local into the Global

Trajectories of Participation in Transnational Standard-setting

Olga Malets and Sigrid Quack

Introduction

Stakeholder participation and inclusiveness are increasingly becoming global ideas that shape contemporary national, international, and transnational standard-setting. It is believed that open, fair, and equal participation of various stakeholder groups in decision-making increases standards' public acceptance, legitimacy, and effectiveness, and helps solve problems associated with democratic deficits of global governance institutions (Black 2008; Buchanan and Keohane 2006; Hale 2008; Quack 2010). Stakeholders are individuals, organizations, and groups that have a stake in a specific issue and/or are affected by the (lack of) rules or by an issue. Participation and inclusiveness turn into an institutional force (to use Djelic and Sahlin-Andersson's [2006] term) that pushes governance institutions into a more participatory direction (Tamm Hallström and Boström 2010). In line with the world polity theory (e.g., Thomas et al. 1987) and neo-institutionalist theory of isomorphism in organizational fields (e.g., DiMaggio and Powell 1983), it is expected that governance arrangements are likely to converge on a more participatory model of rule-making (Dingwerth and Pattberg 2009).

Yet a review of existing literature (Auld 2009; Botzem 2012; Fransen 2011; Fransen and Kolk 2007; Mayntz 2012; Reinecke et al. 2012; Sell and Prakash 2004; Bartley 2007) suggests that the accounts emphasizing isomorphic processes have difficulties explaining variation in the adoption of global ideas across and within governance fields. They tend to overlook that political struggles between different groups with distinct goals and interests may sustain and enhance rather than reduce differentiation and competition (Fransen 2011). They also often neglect that the ambiguity inherent in abstract categories such as 'participation' may bring about clashes between goals and perceptions of locally situated 'stakeholders' and globally operating governance organizations.

The concept of glocalization helps address both convergence and variation in transnational governance fields. It refers to the diffusion and tailoring of global products, services, ideas, and practices to suit particular cultural contexts, and emphasizes '*co-presence* of both universalizing and particularizing tendencies in globalization; that is, the commonly interconnected processes of homogenization *and* heterogenization' (Giulianotti and Robertson 2007: 134, emphasis in the original; Robertson 1995). We borrow the concept of simultaneous homogenization and heterogenization from the glocalization literature to explain (1) the diffusion of global ideas of participation across governance fields, and (2) the variation in the forms these global ideas take as they settle in two governance fields. Yet, we modify and extend the concept in three ways.

Firstly, we extend the glocalization framework from products and practices to transnational governance institutions which govern markets. Secondly, we study the interactions between locally and globally situated actors within differentiated global governance fields. Thirdly, we emphasize the temporal dimension of universalizing and particularizing processes in transnational governance that give rise to different trajectories of how the local becomes built into transnational governance initiatives.

We argue that whereas many governance fields are increasingly shaped by a global idea of participation and inclusiveness (homogenization as one component of glocalization), they evolve along different trajectories (heterogenization as another component of glocalization). In this chapter, we concentrate on two trajectories of transnational governance—monopolistic and pluralistic (Quack 2012)—which can be considered as two options within a wider range of trajectories. We identify them by focusing on key standard-setting organizations within emerging and developing governance fields. As standard-setting has become an ever more prevalent mode of transnational governance, it provides a good entry point into studying governance trajectories.

The monopolistic trajectory implies that despite global diffusion of participation as normative framework, an emerging global elite of actors succeeds in institutionalizing organizational structures and procedures, as well as categorizing certain types of knowledge as expertise, which tend to reinforce their influence and maintain their privileged position over time. Despite being formally transparent, such governance institutions become increasingly difficult to penetrate for locally embedded actors who cannot claim the relevant expertise and competence. In contrast, the pluralistic trajectory implies that a variety of stakeholders and constituencies from different local contexts struggle over and establish organizational structures. They also struggle over what type of knowledge is relevant for standard-setting. While such governance trajectories undoubtedly may also display tendencies of social closure, institutionalized participation and grievance rights nevertheless establish a social and political space for the articulation and negotiation of countervailing perceptions and goals, as well as different types of knowledge, in standard-setting and governance.

In order to understand these trajectories, we build on the literature that emphasizes the dynamic and contested nature of transnational governance fields populated by actors (e.g., standard-setters, constituencies, and standard users) with diverging identities, interests, power resources, and action repertoires (Auld 2009; Bartley 2007; Djelic and Sahlin-Andersson 2006; Dobusch and Quack 2012). The trajectories are historically rooted and evolve as a result of repeated interactions between actors in a specific historical and socio-geographic context. In the case studies below, we trace how global and local actors institutionalize ideas about participation and membership in organizational structures and procedures of global standard-setters, how they blend together and recombine global and local discursive and structural elements (Djelic and Quack 2003, 2008; Malets 2011), and how institutionalized structures, in turn, start mediating and shaping interactions among actors over time (Djelic and Quack 2010, 2011).

We propose three sets of factors that shape the trajectories of transnational governance fields. These factors may be at work during different phases; yet we do not suggest that they occur in any linear sequence. They rather intersect and interact over time. The first set of factors is represented by the *initial design* of standard-setting organizations. We consider early decisions for specific organizational structures, procedures, and operation principles related to membership and participation as not only informed by the global norms prevailing at a given point in time, as the world society theory would predict (e.g., Meyer et al. 1997), or as a result of actor constellations and pre-existing institutions, as historical institutionalism would suggest (e.g., Steinmo et al. 1992); instead, we argue that they are also shaped by anticipations of future consequences of certain organizational models and the role of participation of different constituencies. As Beckert (2011: iii) points out, '[A]ctors are motivated in their actions by the imagined future and organize their activities based on these mental representations' (see also Mische 2009). In turn, the initial design related to the degree of stakeholder participation in decision-making is critical in shaping further organizational development and fostering participation and inclusiveness.

Two remaining sets of factors continue to influence the governance fields' development during later stages. The second set of factors we propose relates to *challenges and contestation* that organizations face. External challenges may bring about critical situations (e.g., crises). Equally, recurrent tensions may arise from within the field and lead to conflicts over a standard-setter's performance and legitimacy. Whereas the initial design of standard-setting organizations shapes future interactions within a governance field, it does not determine them. Actually, institutionalized forms of membership and participation may be reconfigured because of exogenous shocks or endogenous tensions bringing about new struggles and conflicts between competing standard-setters, users, or other constituencies challenging existing institutional settlements.

The third set of factors we propose is related to the degree of *responsiveness* of standard-setting organizations to such challenges. How standard-setters react depends, among other factors, on their susceptibility to external and internal pressures. In addition to the initial design and the availability of alternatives, we also consider organizational identities and inter- and intraorganizational power struggles as influencing the responsiveness of standard-setters to challenges occurring at a given point in time.

In order to illustrate our conceptual framework, we present two in-depth case-studies. We examine why and how standard-setting organizations in two transnational governance fields adopted and developed different forms and procedures of membership and participation, and how this influenced the interactions between global and local actors. Since transnational standard-setting by definition requires commensuration across a variety of particular circumstances, it provides a paradigmatic case for studying interactions between the local and the global. Based on our own research, document analysis, and secondary literature, we trace the development of two central standard-setting initiatives in their respective governance fields: the Forest Stewardship Council (FSC) in the field of forest management governance, and the International Accounting Standards Board (IASB) in the field of financial reporting. We have chosen two very different cases to maximize variation. Both standard-setting initiatives vary significantly in the number and type of actors involved, relations between global standard-setters and local constituencies, and types of knowledge considered appropriate for standard-setting.

The Pluralistic Trajectory: The Forest Stewardship Council

The Forest Stewardship Council (FSC) was established in 1993 by a coalition of conservation activists and business representatives, partly as a reaction to a perceived failure of intergovernmental organizations to tackle the issues of tropical deforestation. It was inspired by the success of activists' campaigns against the use of tropical timber, which targeted large retailers that subsequently became interested in developing a program that would enable them to trace timber in their supply chains and improve their reputation (Synnott 2005). FSC operates as an international, non-profit, standard-setting and accreditation organization with a goal of promoting responsible forest management worldwide through an international third-party certification program. By 2007, 23 percent of the world's forests allocated for production had been certified (Auld 2009: 304).

The FSC certification program is based on a set of substantive rules (standards of good forest management), procedural rules (decision-making rules and accreditation standards), and a system compliance assessment by independent compliance assessment bodies, or certifiers. Complying industries can place an FSC logo on their products and use it for marketing. Certifiers must comply with accreditation rules in order to be able to assess compliance and issue FSC certificates. FSC was a pioneer in environmental and social certification and has become a powerful model for several certification organizations that emerged later in forestry and other sectors.

The Initial Design

From the very beginning, people with very different backgrounds and institutional affiliations and from different countries—both the global North and South—were working on the idea of FSC: environmental NGOs, tropical timber traders, individual activists, large do-it-yourself retailers, manufacturers, scientists, and foresters (Synnott 2005). They all had one goal of establishing an international standard-setting, accreditation, and monitoring organization. Deliberately excluding any of these actors was probably hardly thinkable at that point of time. FSC founders were also influenced by an emerging sustainable development paradigm in international environmental policy-making that emphasized the need for consideration of multiple interests in the environment and the involvement of various non-state actors, including industries and activist groups.

In addition, the FSC founding group felt there was a need for broad consultations on draft proposals for FSC statutes and forest management principles and criteria. There were two purposes: one was to spread information and create broad support for FSC; the second was to collect ideas (Synnott 2005: 20). Through 1992, consultations took place in Brazil, Canada, Ecuador, Ghana, Malaysia, the US, Papua New Guinea, Peru, Sweden, Switzerland, and the UK. The results of this consultative process suggest that FSC was projected as an organization global in scope, but committed to broad consultations with national and local stakeholders, as well as based on global principles of forest stewardship, but locally defined in a set of ecosystem-specific standards. The consulted stakeholders also emphasized the need for an equal consideration of economic, environmental, and social issues. This equality was appealing and enabled the participation of diverse interests in the decision-making process (Synnott 2005: 20–21), which, in turn, provided for the inflow of local ideas into the global project.

The impression may emerge that FSC was predestined to become a strong participatory organization. However, this was not 'entirely expected' (Synnott 2005: 23). The founders also considered making FSC an organization run by a small board of directors responsible for decision-making and with a consultative body instead of members with decision-making rights (Synnott 2005: 23). Yet the successful examples of the International Union for Conservation of Nature and International Federation of Organic Agriculture Movement, both membership organizations, made the founders feel that strong participatory models were feasible (Auld 2009: 246–7). The founding assembly voted for a model in which they would have a voice in the future—a membership-based organization (Auld 2009: 247; Synnott 2005: 24).

During the first years of FSC, the issue of participation of economic stakeholders in decision-making was also controversial. At the founding assembly, several environmental NGOs opposed giving voting rights to industry (Synnott 2005: 24). The compromise was to structure FSC membership into two chambers: an environmental and social chamber with 75 percent of voting rights, and an economic chamber with 25 percent of voting rights. Each chamber was divided into northern and southern sub-chambers to ensure parity between stronger and less strong stakeholder groups. In 1996, FSC divided the environmental and social chambers into two separate ones. Each of the three chambers were given one-third of the voting rights. Although several actors exited relatively soon, in particular, producers and some NGO-affiliated members opposing industry membership (Auld 2009: 247–8), this structure provided FSC with 'an enormous endorsement' (interview, FSC official, 2007) because having an internal voice to shape the organization was appealing (Gulbrandsen 2010: 84).

Challenges and Contestation

The crystallization of the FSC multi-stakeholder participatory governance system should not mask the struggles over FSC identity and legitimacy. There was an agreement on the broad principles of a new organization, but it was not clear how they should be implemented. The first years of the FSC history were marked by the search for its own identity, as well as tensions and conflicts with stakeholders.

One of the tensions concerned the role of local and national stakeholders in FSC. Synnott reports (2005: 29) that the 1993 draft statutes envisioned FSC as an organization registered in one country, with contracts and partners in other countries because some parts of FSC, including national specification of standards, were thought to be better addressed by local people with their knowledge and networks. Initially, national chapters—or national initiatives—were planned as informal working groups consisting 'of people working speedily, without much need for protocols and centralized rules' (Synnott 2005: 29). There was a lot of enthusiasm about FSC, and in several countries, FSC working groups emerged spontaneously. Many people felt they were FSC and were making significant progress. However, the early informality and relative independence of national working groups from the FSC international office caused tensions. The international staff was worried that national activists made decisions on its behalf without prior consultations, whereas national activists felt that their efforts to promote FSC were taken with distrust and were frustrated by the attempts of the international staff to set restrictions (Synnott 2005: 30). By 1997, the need to formalize the relationship between the national initiatives and FSC became clear.

Another recurrent challenge for FSC was the performance of certifiers assessing forest operations' compliance with FSC principles. Early controversies emerged in 1997–1998 (see Auld 2009: 274–5; Synnott 2005: 50). In the early 2000s, the debate about the certifiers' performance became prominent, in particular, after the Rainforest Foundation published a report entitled 'Trading in Credibility' (Counsell and Terje Loraas 2002). The authors claimed that FSC certifiers enjoyed too much discretion, that FSC had been unwilling or unable to control certifiers, and that the needs and grievances of local stakeholders had been systematically ignored. In 2006, a large group of environmental and social NGOs signed a letter to FSC in which they complained about systemic flaws (Gulbrandsen 2010: 83). In 2008, a group of NGOs published a statement in which they again criticized the lack of control of FSC over certificate holders and the poor performance of certifiers and urged FSC to improve its complaints mechanisms (FERN et al. 2008).

Responsiveness of FSC

FSC has been very responsive to these challenges. FSC developed several organizational elements and new rules that were not originally envisioned, at least not in their current form. This includes a formalized system of relations with national initiatives, a set of measures to control certifiers' performance, and a dispute-resolution mechanism.

National Initiatives

In 1997, a meeting with the national initiatives' representatives took place (Synnott 2005: 31). It featured strong debates on many issues that led to several major steps in formalizing the status of national contact persons and working groups. The first formal contract with a national initiative was signed in Bolivia in 1998. In the same year, most FSC contract persons responsible for forming and coordinating national initiatives also signed contracts with FSC (Synnott 2005: 32). The guidelines and protocols concerning the national initiative that emerged over the years were formalized into a manual for the national initiatives approved in 1998.

Synnott (2005: 33) recalls that by 1999–2000, the central authority of the FSC board of directors and international staff was recognized, whereas the 'vital importance' of the work of the national initiatives was established. National initiatives became responsible for developing national standards. The board of directors and the international staff focused on developing global standards, manuals, and policies, as well as managing the network of members and national initiatives and acting on behalf of the whole organization. Accreditation of national initiatives and national standards and formal contracts between FSC and national initiatives and contact persons became central control and feedback mechanisms. As Synnott (2005: 33) suggests, all in all, the participation of national initiatives played a critical role in the success of FSC, even though the specific format of the national involvement was projected differently during the early years. Similarly, Gulbrandsen (2010: 84) observes that strengthening national initiatives and giving them the right to develop national standards fostered democratization of the program, making participation a more attractive option than exit (cf. Auld 2009).

Certifiers' Performance

FSC responded to concerns over certifiers' performance by a wide range of measures introduced gradually starting in 2006. In that year, FSC founded Accreditation Services International (ASI), an organization responsible for the assessment of certifiers', national initiatives', and national standards' compliance with FSC standards and manuals. The idea was to introduce an accreditation body independent from FSC as a standard-setting organization in order to avoid any conflict of interest and improve the quality of accreditation (Gulbrandsen 2010: 83). ASI intensified additional short-notice surveillance inspections. Suspending certificates and certifiers' accreditation became a more common practice.

Dispute Resolution

One of the major controversies was the inclusion of stakeholder grievances and other types of input into decision-making. A formal dispute-resolution procedure was introduced in 2009 in order to address the questions of the FSC system's transparency and accessibility for stakeholders at all levels. The dispute-resolution system enables all stakeholders, including certifiers, to file a complaint or an appeal and receive a response within 60 to 90 days. It specifies clearly who is responsible for handling complaints and how a complaint or an appeal should be handed in and dealt with. Similar dispute-resolution systems were also introduced by many national initiatives to handle complaints at the national level. Certifiers also moved to develop a rigorous dispute-resolution system. This has provided an additional channel for a flow of local voices into the system.

The Monopolistic Trajectory: The International Accounting Standards Board

The International Accounting Standards Board (IASB), established in 2001, and its precursor, the International Accounting Standards Committee (IASC), founded in 1973, have been developing international standards for financial reporting of public companies since the 1970s (Botzem 2012: 63). Financial statements, which are a legal requirement for corporations in most countries, are meant to inform market actors, public authorities, and the public more generally and to provide information for their economic and regulatory decision-making. International Financial Reporting Standards (IFRS) are formulated as one-for-all principles—that is, they are meant to be sufficiently abstract to be applied to all kinds of possible circumstances in whatever economic and social environment. Since about 2000, IFRS has become the dominant international standard in accounting. More than 100 jurisdictions permit or require IFRS for domestically listed companies, including the European Union (EU). The EU made IFRS legally binding for all consolidated accounts of listed companies in its jurisdiction from 2005 (Botzem 2012: 15f.). Among the G20, the US and India are the two exceptions that have not yet decided to adopt or harmonize, though discussions are under way (IASplus 2012).

The Initial Design

The founders of IASC, in stark contrast to those of FSC, emphasized professional expertise and collegial self-regulation as prerequisites for effective international standard-setting. These principles became inscribed in membership, consultation, and participation procedures, which produced strong insider–outsider distinctions. The British, Canadian, and US accountancy bodies that initiated IASC in 1973 considered themselves as representing 'best practice'. Hence, their claim to spearhead international accounting standard-setting was meant to prevent others, particularly public authorities, from doing so (Botzem 2012: 38–40). Consequently, their initiative was exclusively directed towards the accounting profession, and more specifically, towards high-status national professions. Along these lines, professional accountancy bodies from Australia, France, Germany, Japan, Mexico, and the Netherlands were invited to join IASC.

Professional collegiality and status hierarchy were the leading principles that shaped IASC during its early years. The 1973 constitution considered only founding bodies as full members. By way of co-optation, the founding members could admit a national accountancy body as an 'associate member' if it had 'standards and resources which would enable it to contribute towards the work of the Committee' (Camfferman and Zeff 2007: 500–2). Associate members, however, were not entitled to attend committee meetings or to vote. Even following the admission of all members of the International Federation of Accountants (IFAC) as full members in 1982, distinctions between a small core of dominant members and a large number of more peripheral members were maintained by informal means.

Consensus-building and collegiality towards the inside went hand-in-hand with confidentiality towards the outside. Decisions of the IASC Board were typically taken unanimously; dissenting votes were rare and never made public. While the ultimate aim was to develop universal accounting standards that would be applicable everywhere around the world, the founding members of IASC recognized that there was still a long way to go to reach this end. Collegial decision-making in IASC's early period was reflective of local diversity in so far as reasoned arguments of professional colleagues from other countries were taken into account. Yet, local diversity was seen as something to be vanquished in the future rather than to be projected into global standards, as in the case of FSC.

The universalistic orientation of IASC was reflected in the relative neglect of implementation issues in the initial design. Members of IASC were well aware that the voluntary nature of its standards made it important to convince potential users to adopt them. Yet, there was no clear plan on how that should occur. While the constitution required national accountancy bodies to act as IASC's ambassadors of goodwill in their home countries, this did not work out in practice (Camfferman and Zeff 2007: 146). By the mid-1980s, IASC had to realize that its standards were only rarely used by firms or regulators.

Challenges and Contestation

The establishment of IASC as a standard-setter claiming authority based on professional expertise did not remain unchallenged. During the four decades following its foundation, IASC and its successor IASB faced three types of recurrent challenges. First of all, there was the problem of dissemination and adoption of standards. As IASC gradually assembled a comprehensive set of international accounting standards, questions arose of how to convince preparers, users, and regulators of the advantages of international accounting standards as compared with widely used national standards. At least in the early period, IASC was not widely known and its authority and legitimacy remained fragile (Tamm Hallström 2004).

Secondly, the expansion of the IASC's membership to developing countries and emerging economies raised criticism about the weak representation of these countries in decision-making bodies and standard-setting committees. Often, the lack of resources seriously limited the participation of those countries in the standard-setting of IASC and its successor IASB. In the 2000s, there was pressure to increase the representation of emerging economies, including India and China.

Thirdly, the more global rule-setting authority IASC obtained, the more critique it received for the perceived lack of transparency and accountability. Already in the 1980s, the OECD and United Nations pressed IASC to better liaison with regulators, flanked by the Securities Exchange Commission (SEC) in the US and the International Organization of Securities Exchanges (IOSCO). Criticism focused on the incompleteness and the lack of detail of international accounting standards and the absence of any kind of public oversight of the organization's rule-setting (Camfferman and Zeff 2007: 299). In the 1990s and early 2000s, the European Parliament and European Commission advocated for more influence of public actors in the organization's governance (Nölke 2009). Public scrutiny of the IASB's role as a standard-setter resurged in the context of debates over possible pro-cyclical effects of international accounting standards during the financial crisis of 2007–2008 (Lagneau-Ymonet and Quack 2012).

Responsiveness of IASC/IASB

IASC and its successor IASB responded to these challenges. Yet they responded in ways that protected the power of a small group of international accountants, predominantly from large accounting firms (Botzem 2012: 138). Three factors played a role here: co-optation of other international organizations, establishment of due process and consultation procedures, and a reconfiguration of the links to national accounting bodies and regulators.

Formal and Informal Co-optation

In order to promote their standards, IASC and its successor IASB co-opted powerful organizations into newly established advisory and consultative committees (Tamm Hallström 2004), and eventually also admitted the most powerful capital market regulators as members of the standard setting process itself. One example is the Comparability Steering Committee, established in 1987, together with representatives of IOSCO to revise existing international accounting standards to make them more compatible with investor perspectives in financial markets. Another example is the Expert Advisory Panel, established in 2008, together with financial market regulators to investigate the effects of international accounting standards on banks during the crisis (Lagneau-Ymonet and Quack 2012: 224). By including representatives of powerful international organizations in advisory and expert committees, and eventually granting the most powerful of them voting rights, IASC/IASB was able to enhance its own credibility and legitimacy. In exchange for granting them a certain degree of influence, it could lean on their reputation and public standing. The establishment of a Monitoring Board in 2010, which apart from representatives of the European Commission includes predominantly security market regulators, continues this tradition, since it allows for sharing responsibility with public authorities—though predominantly of the kind typically concerned with capital market efficiency.

Due Process and Consultation

When confronted with demands for more transparency and accountability, IASC and its successor IASB developed a due process, including consultation and information procedures. The first steps in this direction were undertaken in the 1980s in response to the SEC's critique of the informality and opaqueness of the IASC's decision-making. From 1989 onward, Board meetings were open to the public (Camfferman and Zeff 2007: 91, 232). Following the transition from IASC to IASB, procedures were formalized and documented. Moreover, videos and podcasts of meetings were made available through the Internet. IASB also initiated regional roundtables to enhance the input from local constituencies into the standard-setting process. Richardson and Eberlein (2011: 235–6) conclude that IASB has an 'innovative set of due process practices', including a high level of 'digital accessibility'. However, reforms of the due process have not solved all legitimacy problems. While formal transparency has been improved, high epistemic barriers for participation persist. The board and staff retain discretion on how to proceed with the comments received, and no complaint procedure exists for constituents who feel that their input has been neglected (Botzem 2012: 177; Pelger 2011).

Re-configuring Links to National Bodies

The year 2001 marked an important point in the trajectory of international accounting standard-setting. IASC, founded as a federation of national accounting bodies, was transformed into a foundation of which the reconstituted IASB became the standard-setter. In essence, this organizational reform completed a more long-lasting shift from a 'constituency model' to an 'independent expert model.' As Camfferman and Zeff (2007: 492) comment, it was 'a victory for the SEC and those of the board members who preferred the independent expert model. Likewise, it was a defeat for those, like the European Commission, who preferred the constituency model.' Standard-setting is now in the hands of the IASB Board members who are recruited by Trustees as 'a group of people representing, within that group, the best available combination of technical expertise and diversity of international business and market experience in order to contribute to the development of high quality, global financial reporting standards' (IASC constitution 2010, para 25, cited in Botzem 2012: 105f).

Overall, the move towards an investor perspective, combined with the institutionalization of the independent expert model, has led IASB to focus increasingly on the universalizing characteristics of its standards. Local constituencies are increasingly considered as information providers to be consulted, rather than constituencies which should have granted decision-making rights. However, the remote possibility of a 'unified high-quality standard' fostered by the G20 and the Financial Stability Board following the financial crisis, has paradoxically pushed IASB to intensify its liaison with national standard setters and regulators in order to achieve enforcement of its standards.

Conclusion

Our two case studies demonstrate that two standard-setting organizations in two governance fields had to respond to the claims of participation, inclusiveness, and fair representation, but they did it in two different ways, generating different trajectories (pluralistic and monopolistic) for transnational governance fields. This has had a profound effect on how local ideas have been incorporated into a global product: transnational standards and organizational structures and procedures. In the pluralistic trajectory, FSC gradually developed a tripartite governance system and introduced public consultations and a dispute-resolution mechanism. FSC strengthened participation at all levels of the certification program and constructed channels for the direct inflow of local ideas into a global certification project. Certainly, FSC's system is not perfect and does not remain uncontested (Dingwerth 2008; Gulbrandsen 2010). However, it uses stakeholder participation and transparency not only as a means to achieve legitimacy and a source of substantive input, but also as 'ends unto themselves' (Auld and Gulbrandsen 2010: 98).

In the monopolistic trajectory, despite calls for 'appropriate representation' by various constituencies, IASB chose to retain an exclusive organizational structure with a small board and to grant voting rights to a rather exclusive group of constituencies, predominantly linked to financial markets. The response to claims of participation was increasing transparency by introducing due process practices, increasing digital accessibility, and opening for public comments, but without providing claimable rights of who should be heard or how obtained information should be processed. Moreover, high epistemic barriers for meaningful participation continued to persist. Transnational accounting standard-setting followed a self-reinforcing trajectory of expert-based governance. To sum up, we observe a homogenization tendency across governance fields towards more participation and inclusion and a heterogenization tendency in the specific forms and procedures of participation.

We argue that these differences are explained by the political and temporal dynamics in the respective governance fields, and in particular, by three sets of factors unfolding and interacting with each other over time.

Initial Design

Whereas the FSC founding members sought to bring in as many stakeholders as possible, IASC founders included only like-minded accounting professionals. FSC founders were influenced by an emerging paradigm of sustainable development emphasizing the need to take various interests and groups into consideration, as well as by the necessity to design a program acceptable for producers, retailers, environmentalists, workers, and indigenous groups. Such an encompassing paradigm was missing at the time when IASC was founded. The dominant idea was that addressing the problems of compatibility of national accounting systems required professional expertise.

Early on, FSC envisioned itself as an organization that developed global standards that would be later adapted to local circumstances and worked to involve people from different parts of the world in standard-setting. IASC envisioned itself as an organization of experts striving for a single set of standards that could be used across diverse national contexts. These early decisions about the organizational design shaped the trajectories of both organizations and the governance fields around them, since they empowered different sets of actors (broad stakeholder groups vs. a relatively small group of experts) that were unwilling to exclude certain groups from decision-making (FSC) or include other groups into decision-making (IASC).

Challenges and Contestation

Early decisions were far from deterministic. Persisting differences of interests and conflicts over organizational legitimacy and performance influenced both trajectories in unexpected and different ways. FSC faced the resistance of national initiatives that felt that their efforts to promote FSC were not appreciated by the international office. Moreover, conflicts over the performance of FSC and its certifiers intensified over time. In the case of IASC and its successor IASB, various constituencies in the financial reporting field felt excluded from standard-setting while being affected by it. In contrast to FSC, an important motivation for IASC and IASB to improve their consultation procedures was the perceived need to foster adoption and implementation of its standards.

Responsiveness

The ways both standard-setters addressed concerns of their constituencies depended on their organizational structure and culture and the kind of legitimacy they strived for. FSC reacted to a growing concern of the national initiatives by formalizing the relationship between the international office and national initiatives and establishing their right to design national standards. FSC also introduced a formal dispute-resolution procedure to ensure that all grievances and conflicts could be dealt with in a fair and predictable way. It strengthened pre-existing and created new structures for considering local voices. In contrast, IASB introduced a set of procedures (e.g., open consultations and public display of documents) that allowed constituencies' feedback to flow in their decision-making, but without ensuring claimable rights for consideration. A small group of experts retained control over standard-setting, even though alternative proposals for more democratic structures were discussed.

To sum up, early on, FSC was dependent on a broad consensus among its numerous stakeholders. Failing to address their critique and demands for more transparency and to consider their interests would have led to significant legitimacy losses. Moreover, FSC's decision-making system gave stakeholders considerable voting power, so that stakeholders could push for more participation and transparency. In the case of IASB, the incumbent group of accounting experts was not interested in giving more power to other stakeholders and was able to appeal to its expertise and experience as a source of their legitimacy and authority, even though it had to respond to pressures from other organizations in the field of financial reporting in order to foster constituencies' support for adaptation and implementation of the standards.

We suggest that the two analytical types of trajectories we identify may be useful for future studies of standard-setters in other governance fields. In many of them, standard-setting organizations appear to have evolved along the monopolistic trajectory based on professional or technical expertise, including the Basel Committee, international regimes for intellectual property rights, commercial law, management standards, and financial market regulation (Cohen 2008; Quack 2007; Morgan 2010). However, there are also fields in which governance initiatives have developed along the pluralistic trajectory. FSC is one of the pioneers and still has probably the most extensive participation system, but in environmental sustainability and labor rights fields, many other organizations have adopted similar participation and transparency procedures. The Marine Stewardship Council, for example, adopted several of FSC's organizational features but opted for a different organizational structure with a non-voting consultative body (Gulbrandsen 2010).

Finally, while we admit that governance fields are shaped by global norms, we highlight the importance of anticipated and real global–local interactions. We suggest that contextualized design choices during the initiation period shape the subsequent development of fields in two major ways: through history and through anticipated future. While we agree with historical institutionalists that history matters, we argue that the anticipated future matters, too. The notion of 'projected futures' (Mische 2009) provides conceptual space for integrating a pragmatic understanding of contingent social action into more long-term, historically shaped trajectories of institutional emergence and development.

Acknowledgment

We thank the editors for their very helpful comments on an earlier draft.

References

Auld, G. (2009). 'Reversal of fortune: how early choices can alter the logic of market-based authority'. PhD Dissertation. New Haven: Yale University.

Auld, G., and Gulbrandsen, L.H. (2010). 'Transparency in nonstate certification: consequences for accountability and legitimacy'. *Global Environmental Politics*, 10: 97–119.

Bartley, T. (2007). 'Institutional emergence in an era of globalization: the rise of transnational private regulation of labor and environmental conditions'. *American Journal of Sociology*, 113: 297–351.

Beckert, J. (2011). 'Imagined futures: fictionality in economic action'. MPIfG discussion paper 11/8. Cologne: Max Planck Institute for the Study of Societies.

Black, J. (2008). 'Constructing and contesting legitimacy and accountability in polycentric regulatory regimes'. *Regulation and Governance*, 2: 137–64.

Botzem, S. (2012). *The politics of accounting regulation: organizing transnational standard setting in financial reporting*. Cheltenham: Edward Elgar.
Buchanan, A., and Keohane, R.O. (2006). 'The legitimacy of global governance institutions'. *Ethics and International Affairs*, 20: 405–37.
Camfferman, K., and Zeff, S.A. (2007). *Financial reporting and global capital markets: a history of the International Accounting Standards Committee 1973–2000*. Oxford: Oxford University Press.
Cohen, E.S. (2008). 'Constructing power through law: private law pluralism and harmonization in the global political economy'. *Review of International Political Economy*, 15: 770–99.
Counsell, S., and Terje Loraas, K. (2002). 'Trading in credibility: the myth and reality of Forest Stewardship Council'. Report with case studies. London: The Rainforest Foundation UK.
DiMaggio, P.J., and Powell, W.W. (1983). 'The iron cage revisited: institutional isomorphism and collective rationality in organizational fields'. *American Sociological Review*, 48: 147–60.
Dingwerth, K. (2008). 'Private transnational governance and the developing world: a comparative perspective'. *International Studies Quarterly*, 52: 607–34.
Dingwerth, K., and Pattberg, P. (2009). 'World politics and organizational fields: the case of transnational sustainability governance'. *European Journal of International Relations*, 15: 707–43.
Djelic, M.-L., and Quack, S. (eds). (2003). *Globalization and institutions: redefining the rules of economic game*. Cheltenham: Edward Elgar.
Djelic, M.-L., and Quack, S. (2008). 'Institutions and transnationalization', in R. Greenwood, C. Oliver, R. Suddaby, and K. Sahlin (eds), *The Sage handbook of organizational institutionalism*. Los Angeles: Sage, 299–323.
Djelic, M.-L., and Quack, S. (eds). (2010). *Transnational communities: shaping global economic governance*. Cambridge: Cambridge University Press.
Djelic, M.-L., and Quack, S. (2011). 'The power of "limited liability": transnational communities and cross-border governance', in C. Marquis, M. Lounsbury, and R. Greenwood (eds), *Communities and organizations: research in the sociology of organizations*, Vol. 33. Bingley, UK: Emerald, 79–109.
Djelic, M.-L., and Sahlin-Andersson, K. (2006). 'Introduction: a world of governance—the rise of transnational regulation', in M.-L. Djelic and K. Sahlin-Andersson (eds), *Transnational governance: institutional dynamics of regulation*. Cambridge: Cambridge University Press, 1–28.
Dobusch, L., and Quack, S. (2012). 'Framing standards, mobilizing users: copyright versus fair use in transnational regulation'. *Review of International Political Economy*. doi: 10.1080/09692290.2012.662909.
FERN et al. (2008). 'Regaining credibility and rebuilding support: changes the FSC needs to make to ensure it regains and maintains its credibility. A joint statement'. 30 October 2008.
Fransen, L. (2011). 'Why do private governance organizations not converge? A political–institutional analysis of transnational labor standards regulation'. *Governance*, 24: 359–87.
Fransen, L.W., and Kolk, A. (2007). 'Global rule-setting for business: a critical analysis of multi-stakeholder standards'. *Organization*, 14: 667–84.
Giulianotti, R., and Robertson, R. (2007). 'Forms of glocalization: globalization and the migration strategies of Scottish football fans in North America'. *Sociology*, 41: 133–52.
Gulbrandsen, L.H. (2010). *Transnational environmental governance: the emergence and effects of the certification of forests and fisheries*. Oxford: Edward Elgar.
Hale, T.N. (2008). 'Transparency, accountability, and global governance'. *Global Governance*, 14: 73–94.
IASplus. (2012). Adoption of IFRS by country. Retrieved 5 May 2012 from http://www.iasplus.com/en/resources/adoption-of-ifrs.
Lagneau-Ymonet, P., and Quack, S. (2012). 'What's the problem? Competing diagnoses and shifting coalitions in the reform of international accounting standards', in R. Mayntz (ed.), *Crisis and control: institutional change in financial market regulation*. Frankfurt am Main: Campus, 213–46.
Malets, O. (2011). 'From transnational voluntary standards to local practices: a case study of forest certification in Russia'. MPIfG discussion paper 11/7. Cologne: Max Planck Institute for the Study of Societies.

Mayntz, R. (ed.). (2012). *Crisis and control. Institutional change in financial market regulation*. Frankfurt am Main: Campus.

Meyer, J.W. et al. (1997). 'World society and the nation-state'. *American Journal of Sociology*, 103: 144–81.

Mische, A. (2009). 'Projects and possibilities: researching futures in action'. *Sociological Forum*, 24: 694–704.

Morgan, G. (2010). 'Legitimacy in financial markets: credit default swaps in the current crisis'. *Socio-Economic Review*, 8: 17–45.

Nölke, A. (2009). 'The politics of accounting regulation. Responses to the subprime crisis', in E. Helleiner, S. Pagliari, and H. Zimmermann (eds), *Global finance in crisis*. New York: Routledge, 37–55.

Pelger, C. (2011). 'Decision-making on stewardship: an analysis of the standard-setters' process of identifying the objective of financial reporting'. Discussion paper. Department of Financial Accounting and Auditing. Cologne: University of Cologne.

Quack, S. (2007). 'Legal professionals and transnational law-making: a case of distributed agency'. *Organization*, 14: 643–66.

Quack, S. (2010). 'Law, expertise and legitimacy in transnational economic governance: an introduction'. *Socio-Economic Review*, 8: 3–16.

Quack, S. (2012). 'Regime complexity and expertise in transnational governance: strategizing on regulatory uncertainty'. Paper presented at the workshop on law, contestation, and power in the global political economy, Onati International Institute for the Sociology of Law, Spain. 7–8 June.

Reinecke, J., Manning, S., and von Hagen, O. (2012). 'The emergence of a standards market: multiplicity of sustainability standards in the global coffee industry'. *Organization Studies*, 33: 791–814.

Richardson, A.J., and Eberlein, B. (2011). 'Legitimising transnational standard setting: the case of the International Accounting Standards Board'. *Journal of Business Ethics*, 98: 217–45.

Robertson, R. (1995). 'Glocalization: time-space and homogeneity-heterogeneity', in M. Featherstone, S. Lash, and R. Robertson (eds), *Global modernities*. London: Sage, 25–44.

Sell, S., and Prakash, A. (2004). 'Using ideas strategically: the contest between business and NGO networks in intellectual property rights'. *International Studies Quarterly*, 48: 143–75.

Steinmo, S., Thelen, K., and Longstreth, F. (eds). (1992). *Historical institutionalism in comparative politics: state, society, and economy*. Cambridge: Cambridge University Press.

Synnott, T. (2005). *Some notes on the early years of FSC*. Bonn: Forest Stewardship Council.

Tamm Hallström, K. (2004). *Organizing international standardization: ISO and the IASC in quest of authority*. Cheltenham: Edward Elgar.

Tamm Hallström, K., and Boström, M. (2010). *Transnational multi-stakeholder standardisation: organizing fragile non-state authority*. Cheltenham: Edward Elgar.

Thomas, G.M. et al. (eds). (1987). *Institutional structure: constituting state, society, and the individual*. Newbury Park: Sage.

24

The Changing Factors of ISO 9001 Adoption among Korean Firms

Hokyu Hwang, Yong Suk Jang, and Ki Tae Park

Introduction

What shapes organizational responses to globally diffusing practices? Traveling to far-flung corners of the world, globally legitimated models and ideas spread and interact with local circumstances to generate varying patterns of institutional dynamics in particular national settings. Early institutional studies depicted the spread of an organizational practice as a process in which adopters' motivation to gain technical and economic gains or to fulfill functional needs gradually gives way to legitimacy concerns (Tolbert and Zucker 1983; Westphal, Gulati, and Shortell 1997; Jang 2000). While this two-stage model of institutionalization emphasizes the shifting motivation for adoption, the literature on translation has highlighted the changes in diffusing ideas and models and how organizations actively interpret, edit, and reshape foreign objects for local circumstances (Czarniawska and Sevón 1996, 2005; Sahlin-Andersson 1996; see also Strang and Soule 1998). The combined insight of the two prominent lines of research in institutional theory establishes the standard account of institutionalization. As an increasing number of organizations adopt an innovative idea, the status and meaning of that diffusing material change in the course of diffusion and institutionalization.

Scholars have recently advanced the view that technical/economic and social motivations are not as distinct as the two-stage model would suggest, and, under certain conditions, organizations may pursue both at the same time (Kennedy and Fiss 2009). Both efficiency and legitimacy concerns motivate early- and late-adopting firms, although the former are driven by the prospect of economic and social gains, while the latter, by economic and social losses (Fiss, Kennedy, and Davis 2012). Diffusing practices also undergo significant transformation in the course of institutionalization (Ansari, Fiss, and Zajac 2010; Lounsbury 2007). Institutionalization is a complex process in which different motivations for adoption co-exist and influence post-adoption behavior and performance to produce organizational heterogeneity. The revised model points to a significant level of heterogeneity in the processes, mechanisms, and consequences of diffusion and institutionalization.

While recent scholarly efforts have developed much more nuanced accounts of diffusion and institutionalization (Colyvas and Jonsson 2011), globalization has expanded the terrain of diffusion (Drori, Meyer, and Hwang 2006). Globalization constructs markets and institutional fields at the global level, and management knowledge and models flow across national and industry boundaries (Meyer 2002; Sahlin-Andersson and Engwall 2002). Global models, at the same time, encounter locally embedded organizations whose legitimacy and identities depend on both local and, increasingly, global culture (Robertson 1994). Consequently, the process, shape, and outcome of diffusion are contingent on the interaction of global influences and local circumstances.

In this chapter, we analyze the process of glocalization by utilizing a longitudinal dataset on a sample of the 300 largest Korean corporations. More specifically, we examine how the factors associated with the adoption of ISO 9001 shifted over the course of diffusion. The expansion of the international standardization movement into management started in 1987, and, by the mid-1990s, the diffusion of quality management certificates became global in scope. Conformity to the globally legitimated practice endorsed by elite consulting firms, the International Organizations for Standardization (ISO), and multinational corporations signaled the modern, rational, and legitimate organization. In this global context, the Korean government exerted pressure on corporations to keep pace with the global trend. Korean chaebols (large, diversified conglomerates) were quick to pursue ISO 9001 certificates, and other Korean firms followed suit. The spread of ISO 9001 in the early period exhibited familiar institutional processes. The main driving forces, however, shifted after the Asian financial crisis of 1997. While Korean firms continued to adopt ISO quality management certificates, in the changed economic environment, institutional influences receded into the background. Managers started to cast doubt on the efficacy of standardization certificates and began to calculate the costs and benefits of ISO certificates. Manufacturing and exporting firms, which saw economic benefits in certification, were more likely to adopt after the economic crisis. While the standard account of institutionalization suggests the shift in the sources of adoption from technical to symbolic concerns, the glocalization pattern of ISO 9001 in Korea more or less reversed the standard pattern, punctuated by an external shock.

The Diffusion of ISO 9001 among Large Korean Firms

The International Organization for Standardization (or ISO) was founded in 1947 and has published over 9,000 sets of standards in over 500,000 documents. In a rapidly globalizing world in which there is no central regulatory authority, ISO became a significant source of global governance and coordination (Loya and Boli 1999; Mendel 2001, 2002). Guler, Guillen, and Macpherson (2002) also observed that 'quality certification has emerged as a key organizational practice helping countries worldwide establish rationalized production processes' (2002: 208–9). The family of ISO 9000 and its related certificates are perhaps the most pervasive quality practice in the world. Between the first introduction of ISO 9000 Quality Certification in 1987 and 1999, over 400,000 organizations in 158 countries and territories were certified. ISO 9001:2000, the most representative certification, had been adopted by 1,064,785 organizations in 178 countries by 2009.

ISO 9001 guarantees that goods and services, including public administration services, offered by certified organizations follow standards through evaluation by a third party. ISO 9001 applies to all production processes undertaken by certified organizations, from design to after-sales service and the whole system of production process. By contrast, national industrial standards, such as those of the American National Standards Institute (ANSI), warrant only the quality of a single product and limit their coverage to manufacturing industries (Guler, Guillen, and Macpherson 2002). Further, ISO 9001 covers non-manufacturing industries

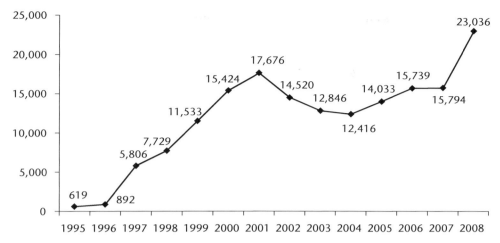

Figure 24.1 The number of companies adopting ISO 9001 in Korea

like the service industry as well. The enormous success of the family of ISO 9000 certificates attests to their perceived benefits, especially given that corporations must spend up to $100,000 and take more than six months to be examined for certification (Martinez-Costa and Martinez-Lorente 2003; Guler et al. 2002).

Since the first adoption by Yeonghwa Metal Co. in 1989, approximately 23,000 Korean firms were certified by 2008. While the family of ISO 9000 standards was known as the quality management system mainly for manufacturing firms, firms from other industries such as service, transportation, and even primary education adopted them in droves (Guler et al. 2002). The Korean Accreditation Board reported that over 85 percent of Korean firms adopted. An ISO report published in 2010 ranked Korea among the top ten countries in the world based on the number of certificates. Figure 24.1 presents the annual count of companies adopting ISO 9000 certificates in Korea since 1995.

Several factors contributed to the spectacular success of ISO standards and certification in Korea. One of the driving forces, particularly for small- and medium-sized firms, was the Korean government, which actively promoted the practice for efficiency gains expected from adopting international standards. The state, moreover, required ISO certification for companies competing for government contracts as well. Certification was instantly seen as an essential license for entry into global markets. The ISO 9000 series was eventually enacted as the national, KS standard in 1992 and replaced the *Poom* (national, quality) mark in 1997. If the legitimacy of ISO standards and certification arose from the fact that certified companies did so voluntarily (Loya and Boli 1999), the Korean state added a coercive dimension and aided the diffusion by subsidizing certification costs, easing the financial burden on corporations.

Diversified conglomerates, known as chaebols, also played a significant role, as they aggressively pursued ISO certification early on. Over time, chaebols expanded both horizontally and vertically, expanding into both related and unrelated lines of business and industries as well as up and down the value chains across diversified industries (Evans 1995; Chang 2003). They have been the backbone of the Korean economy since the beginning of rapid industrialization in the 1960s that led to the country's rapid economic growth. Chaebols often compete in the same industries and product categories in both domestic and foreign markets. More importantly, chaebols collectively constitute a tangible social clique that serves as a reference group for one another and for other smaller firms in Korea (i.e., White 1981; Porac et al. 1995; Fligstein 1996).

In the race for certification, Samsung was the leader among the elite chaebol groups, as 82 percent (or 40 out of 49) of its affiliated companies were certified by 1995. Forty-two of LG's 55 affiliates (76 percent) adopted, and the Hyundai Group's certification rate reached 74 percent by the same year. The diffusion among chaebols quickly spread to small- and medium-sized enterprises. The proportion of small- and medium-sized enterprises among the newly certified increased from 25 percent in 1992 to 54 percent in 1994, and again to 64 percent in the first quarter of 1995. In short, the enthusiastic embrace of ISO 9000 standards and certification facilitated by state pressure and support characterized the early phase of ISO diffusion in Korea. The country's heavy reliance on exporting as a main growth strategy and the centrality and high visibility of chaebols in the Korean business system further fueled the spread.

The tone of the media coverage reflected the overall enthusiasm for the practice. Newspaper articles in the early period tended to be descriptive, factual, and positive. The Korean business press reported government policy and high-profile certification cases such as 'first-in-the-industry' adoptions. An executive of a chaebol affiliate recognized as a leading innovator said that ISO certification was 'a requirement in the era of total quality management'. His company adopted Total Quality Management (TQM) with the assistance of a leading American management consultancy, and it had adopted the recommended model without any modification. As for its affiliates, the ISO 9000 series of standards were required as other chaebol groups and their affiliates were subjected to similar pressure (Hankyoreh 1993). In his interview, aptly titled 'Everyone's Doing It', published in the *Seoul Newspaper* in 1992, the director of the Administration of Industrial Promotion, a government agency overseeing industrial standards, attested to the popularity of ISO 9000: 'Already more than 60 companies have been certified this year, and there are still 200 companies that are in the process of being certified' (Seoul Shinmun 1993).

The early enthusiasm for ISO standards and certification waned precipitously, however, in the aftermath of the Asian Financial Crisis of 1997. The foreign exchange crisis that started with a sharp decline in the value of the Thai Baht quickly spread to Indonesia, Malaysia, and then to South Korea by the end of 1997. Foreign investors started withdrawing their funds from Korea, and the value of the Korean currency dropped from 864 to 1,695 won per dollar between January and December of 1997. The Korean stock index plummeted to 390 from 669 and the bankruptcy rate increased by 3.5 times. Sea-Jin Chang (2003: 4–5) quipped, 'The Korean economy, which had created the miracle on the Han River from the ashes of the Korean War, returned to ashes.'

The shock of the financial crisis reverberated through the economy. The changing mood could be observed from the press coverage of ISO 9001. First, after 1997, media interest in ISO started to decline, as shown in Figure 24.2. Moreover, the initial positive coverage turned more critical, reflective, and analytical. For instance, the *Maeil Business Newspaper* (December 20, 1998) critically reported a few months after the beginning of the financial crisis that 'Korean firms were blindly following management fads such as ISO 9000 and TQM without critically evaluating their benefits. Further, these management practices were mainly used as a public relations and marketing tool.'

Changing Dynamics of Diffusion and Institutionalization

The standard institutional explanation of practice diffusion and institutionalization is the two-stage model, which, initially introduced in Tolbert and Zucker's (1983) pioneering

The Changing Factors of ISO 9001 Adoption among Korean Firms

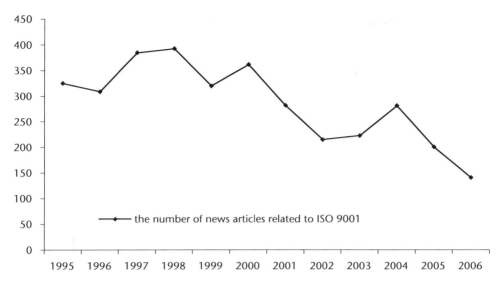

Figure 24.2 The number of newspaper articles on ISO standards and certification

work, has been fruitfully utilized in many different empirical settings (Strang and Soule 1998; Boxenbaum and Jonsson 2008). Tolbert and Zucker (1983) showed that initially civil service reforms diffused slowly across US municipal governments when civil service procedures were not required by the state and not yet legitimated, and the internal characteristics or requirements of cities accounted for early adoptions. However, as civil service reforms became widely adopted, the underlying factors of adoption changed from internal functional needs or technical efficiency to social gains associated with the increased legitimacy of the practice. Meyer and his colleagues (1992) showed that the early expansion of mass education systems in the 19th century was related to internal characteristics of nation-states, but the expansion in the post-war period was enhanced by the institutionalization of the nation-state model as an organizing principle of the post-war global order. Jang (2000) showed that the diffusion of science and technology ministries was driven initially by internal characteristics of nation-states, but later by external institutional influences such as the amount of international science discourse and memberships in international science organizations. In a similar vein, Westphal, Gulati, and Shortell's (1997) study of TQM adoption among hospitals showed that early adopters of TQM did so mainly for efficiency gains and, therefore, customized TQM practices. Later-adopting hospitals, on the other hand, conformed closely to the normative model of TQM programs for the purpose of legitimacy gains.

The standard account suggests that the motivations for adoption shift in the course of diffusion and institutionalization. Functional needs and technical considerations are dominant in the initial phase of practice diffusion when the diffusing practice's legitimacy is yet to be established. However, legitimacy concerns and social gains emerge as motivating factors once the density of adopters reaches a certain threshold and the diffusing practice has been institutionalized. The correspondence between adoption timing and the shifting motivation for adoption from efficiency to legitimacy depends on the extent of legitimacy of the diffusing practice.

Recent scholarly efforts have also demonstrated that motivations for both technical and social gains co-exist throughout the process of diffusion and institutionalization, and early and late adopters alike are concerned with both economic and social gains (Kennedy and Fiss 2009). Early adopters aim to take advantage of performance benefits of new innovations. At the same time, new innovations bring social benefits to early adopters who are looking to differentiate themselves *vis-á-vis* their competition (Abrahamson 1991). Staying a step or two ahead of peers may be one way to signal and maintain high status (Podolny 2005). If early adopters are motivated by the prospect of getting ahead, late adopters are pressed not to fall behind and not to look illegitimate or inappropriate (Kennedy and Fiss 2009). While these studies showed how the motivations driving the consumers of management practices shift in the course of institutionalization or diffusion, David and Strang (2006) demonstrated that in the life cycle of TQM, generalist consultancies, often lacking relevant expertise, entered the market for TQM service during TQM's boom, but later exited the market when TQM became less fashionable. Quality specialists, with the declining presence and exit of generalist consultancies, increasingly made up new cohorts thereby populating the TQM market.

Current studies have also moved beyond idiosyncratic, case-based studies of translation and practice variation and have begun to examine more systematically how practices vary as they are interpreted, enacted, and implemented, moving from one place to another (Ansari, Fiss, and Zajac 2010; Fiss, Kennedy, and Davis 2012). These new developments in the study of diffusion and institutionalization offer an important insight in understanding the dynamics of glocalization or the local institutionalization of global ideas and models.

Globalization generates managerial models and practices that are universal(istic) in application and global in scope and reach (Sahlin-Andersson and Engwall 2002; Czarniawska and Sevón 2005; Drori, Meyer, and Hwang 2006). Some managerial ideas and models are more resonant with rationalistic sensibilities and, therefore, spread more easily (Rovik 2002). Successful managerial models and innovations travel worldwide (Sahlin-Andersson and Engwall 2002). Managerial ideas flow easily and penetrate previously affected organizational populations and become part of management fads and fashion (Abrahamson 1991). During earlier phases of institutionalization, potential adopters may also assess the usefulness or efficacy of a new innovation before adopting. Once institutionalized, however, no such verification occurs, at least among the members of a population for which the innovation is theorized as appropriate (Strang and Meyer 1993; Tolbert and Zucker 1996). Global management models enter specific local territories at a particular time in the course of *global* institutionalization. Glocalization, therefore, produces a variety of diffusion processes, mechanisms, and outcomes at different junctures in worldwide diffusion.

Diffusing ideas, while reshaping adopting organizations and localities, take on particular meanings and roles in different local contexts, and, therefore, evolve in the course of diffusion. For instance, in their comparative study of ISO 9000 standards in the German and French automobile industry, Casper and Hancké (1999) showed that ISO 9000 standards, while modernizing certain organizational features and practices, by and large reproduce the existing institutional arrangements in both countries. Similarly, Özen and Berkman (2007) documented how legitimating agencies used ethos justifications or rhetoric to render TQM congruent with the dominant cultural sensibilities. In this way, TQM was reconstructed, at least at the level of national discourse, as a 'blueprint … for solutions to problems at all levels (individual, organizational, and societal)' (p. 841).

The Logic of Economic and Technical Efficiency

Opportunities for economic and technical benefits contributed to the success of ISO among Korean firms. ISO certificates are concerned not with the quality of final products, but with processes within organizations, and may provide performance benefits or operational efficiency for organizations dealing with particular technical problems such as manufacturing firms. ISO was initially devised mainly for manufacturing companies to improve the quality of manufacturing processes (Mendel 2002). Therefore, we state:

Hypothesis 1: Manufacturing firms are more likely to adopt ISO 9001 than non-manufacturing firms.

Moreover, the family of ISO 9000 certificates was seen as an essential component for the firms engaged in foreign trade and competing in foreign markets. The European Union, for instance, requires ISO certification for foreign companies interested in operating in the European market. Erel and Ghosh (1997: 1244) reported that the initial impetus came from 'export considerations'. ISO certification may be used as a means to overcome the trade barriers of and to help ease entry into advanced markets (Anderson, Daly, and Johnson 1999). Especially for upstart Korean firms that lacked global presence and brand recognition, certification could partially soften the blow of this liability of 'foreignness' in global markets. Thus, we expect:

Hypothesis 2: Exporting firms are more likely to adopt ISO 9001.

Further, given the perceived benefits associated with ISO 9001 in overcoming entry barriers and the lack of brand recognition, exporting firms will be more likely to use ISO certification as a way to increase their foreign trade and export. Therefore, we hypothesize:

Hypothesis 3: Corporations that have a lower exporting ratio will be more likely to be certified.

The Logic of Legitimacy

While the perceived technical and economic benefits motivated Korean firms to rush to ISO certification, institutional factors also played a significant role. By the early 1990s, when Korean companies started to pursue certification, ISO standards were already well established. For instance, ISO standards had become incorporated into the European Union's directives as part of the single market project and harmonization efforts (Guler et al. 2002; Mendel 2002, 2006). The Korean government actively created an environment in which ISO standards and certification diffused with relative ease, in many ways as a response to these global developments. In addition to the state provision of positive incentives for certification (such as tax breaks and subsidization of certification costs), the Industrial Standardization law, which enacted ISO standards as the national standards, was passed in 1992, while the external legitimacy of ISO standards and the sponsorship by the Korean government provided the institutional basis for the diffusion of ISO quality certification in Korea. With the rising number of certified companies, the legitimacy of that practice increases over time. Therefore,

Hypothesis 4: The number of recently certified companies is positively associated with the likelihood of adoption.

The appearance of appropriateness is an important source of motivation that drives adoption behavior. High status and elite firms are quick to adopt new innovations to signal their position in a social structure. The laggards, on the other hand, are also conscious of social consequences of inappropriate structures and behaviors. In the Korean context, chaebols represent the top echelon of the Korean corporate hierarchy and are quicker to adopt innovative management practices. Moreover, given the top-down decision-making structure, they are likely to do so early on and quickly. Therefore, we expect:

Hypothesis 5: Chaebol-affiliated companies are more likely to be certified than organizations that are not related to chaebols.

The Shifting Motivations of Adoption

The standard account in the study of diffusion and institutionalization suggests that multiple motivations or logics of adoption exist. Recent developments in this area contend that these different logics of adoption may co-exist in any given moment, but the nature of those logics changes in the course of diffusion and institutionalization. The watershed moment in the Korean context was the Asian financial crisis, which precipitated a thorough re-examination of existing practices and soul-searching for the country as a whole. The main critique of ISO standards and certification was that these practices mainly served public relations and marketing functions rather than improving operational or organizational efficiency. In the period following the financial crisis, technical and functional considerations would motivate companies to adopt ISO certification, but not social and legitimacy gains. Thus,

Hypothesis 6: Economic and technical factors are significantly related to the likelihood of certification in both periods. Social and legitimacy factors are related to certification only in the first period.

Data, Methods, and Results

Sample

We collected both the financial and organizational information on the 300 largest corporations (based on the amount of sales in 2006) from 1992 to 2006. The first case of adoption in our sample occurred in 1992. The dependent variable (whether certified or not) was coded directly from each sample company's website. We recorded the timing of certification. Figure 24.3 presents the annual count and cumulative number of adoptions in our sample of 300 organizations between 1992 and 2006. Among the organizations in our sample, Samsung Electronics and Daewoo Heavy Industries were the first to be certified in 1992. The number of adoptions peaked at over 45 in 1995, and by the end of 2006, 204 companies were certified.

Control Variables

The organizational age variable is calculated annually by subtracting the year of founding from the year of observation. The dummy variables for younger and older corporations were constructed using the age variable and grouped into quartiles. The dummy variable for 'Young Group' indicates the sample organizations that are younger than 12 years old, and the dummy variable for 'Old Group' denotes the sample organizations that are older than 36

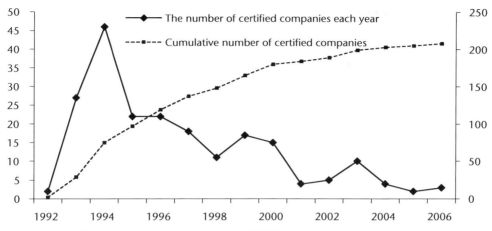

Figure 24.3 The adoption pattern among the 300 Korean firms in the sample

years. Organizational size was measured using the number of employees. We include both profit and indebtedness measures to control for the effects of performance and financial capacity. In addition, we control for the length of membership in the Federation of Korean Industries (also known as KFI) using the information published in the KFI website since management practices could easily travel through professional networks. Finally, we include the amount of academic discourse on ISO standards and certification in Korea to control for the effect of management discourse.

Explanatory Variables

We include the dummy variable for manufacturing firms to see whether manufacturing firms, which would benefit from performance improvement due to process improvements, are more likely to be certified. ISO certification may compensate for the lack of brand recognition for Korean firms in developed markets. Therefore, we include the dummy for exporters and the exporting ratio (measured as the proportion of the amount of sales generated from exporting in the total revenue). We also counted the number of annual certifications over time and lagged the measure by one year to see the effect of mimicry. Finally, the dummy variable for chaebol-affiliated firms indicates whether a firm belongs to a chaebol network or not. Each year, the Korean government agency (the Fair Trade Commission) publishes the list of chaebol companies. We relied on the publication by the Fair Trade Commission to create this variable. Organizational and financial data were collected from KISVALUE, which provides information for 18,000 Korean corporations. Table 24.1 provides the names and descriptions and descriptive statistics of the variables included in the analyses.

Model Estimation

The unit of analysis in this study is the individual corporation, and the dependent variable is whether an organization is certified or not. The first year of observation is 1992, when the first event occurred. Organizations drop out of the risk set once they are certified. The data were structured in the form of event histories. Event history analysis allows an analyst to incorporate information on life history of social units and information on time-varying

Table 24.1 Variable description and descriptive statistics

Variable	Description	Type	Mean	SD
Adoption	Adopt: 1, non-Adopt: 0	Dummy	.092	.289
Age	Age	Logged	2.92	.941
Size	Number of Employees	Logged	7.29	1.40
Profit	Annual Profit Ratio	Continuous	318.3	3573.2
Debt	Annual Debt Ratio	Continuous	2616.4	15664.9
Young Group	Younger than 12 years: 1	Dummy	.248	.432
Old Group	Older than 36 years: 1	Dummy	.267	.442
Membership	Membership Duration in FKI	Continuous	9.25	12.07
Academic Discourse	The number of ISO Articles in Last Year	Continuous	14.1	9.39
Manufacturing	Manufacturing: 1, non-Manufacturing: 0	Dummy	.303	.459
Exporter	Exporter: 1, non-Exporter: 0	Dummy	.523	.499
Exporting Ratio	Annual Exporting Ratio-to-Sales	Continuous	62.8	1124.5
Mimicry	Number of Adoptions in Last Year	Continuous	14.1	13.9
Chaebol	Chaebol: 1, non-Chaebol: 0	Dummy	.388	.487

covariates in investigating the time-dependent rate of occurrence of various events (Tuma and Hannan 1984). We use a 'piecewise exponential model with period-specific effects' (Blossfeld and Rohwer 1995). This model allows both the baseline rate (given by period-specific constants) and covariates or independent variables to vary across time periods. This model is appropriate for this particular study because we distinguish the periods before and after the Asian financial crisis in 1997 and are interested in examining whether the effects of explanatory variables change across the two time periods.

Results

Table 24.2 reports the results of the event-history analyses. Model 1 reports the coefficients of the covariates included in the analyses for the entire observation period from 1992 to 2006. Model 2 splits the period into two—before and after the Asian financial crisis—and shows whether the effects of the covariates change between the two periods.

Among the control variables in Model 1, only the dummy variable for the organizations that are older than 36 years is significantly associated with the likelihood of certification. Model 2 shows the effect is significant only in the first period, suggesting that when ISO standards and certification were relatively new in the Korean corporate environment, older firms were resistant or slower to adopt. However, in the later period, when certification became more prevalent, age differences subsided. While not significant in Model 1, the effect of the number of academic articles, reflecting scholarly attention on the subject and also the volume of discourse on ISO standards and certification, shifts from the early to the late period. The number of publications on ISO standards and certification is negatively associated with

Table 24.2 Factors associated with the adoption of ISO 9000 among Korean firms, 1992–2006

Variable	Model 1 Whole period (1992–2006)	Model 2 Early (1992–1997)	Late (1998–2006)
Size	.085 (.063)	.098 (.076)	.016 (.124)
Age	.173 (.212)	.451 (.321)	.111 (.298)
Young Group	.279 (.358)	.496 (.467)	.352 (.599)
Old Group	−.417* (.236)	−.496* (.293)	−.500 (.445)
Profit	.000 01 (.000 02)	0.000 02 (.000 01)	−.0001 (.0001)
Debt	−.000 08 (.000 06)	−.000 03 (.000 04)	−.0008** (.0004)
Membership	.005 (.008)	.007 (.009)	−.005 (.015)
Academic Discourse	.004 (.009)	−.044** (.023)	.028* (.014)
Manufacturing	.486*** (.183)	.206 (.213)	1.15*** (.364)
Exporter	1.32*** (.248)	1.35*** (.318)	.865** (.419)
Exporting Ratio	−.007*** (.003)	−.004 (.003)	−.012** (.005)
Previous Adoptions	.024*** (.005)	.045*** (.011)	.050 (.037)
Chaebol	.472*** (.164)	.500*** (.193)	.408 (.339)
Constant	−5.26*** (.807)	−6.12*** (1.14)	−4.79*** (1.34)
Number of spells	2042	1092	950
Log likelihood	−263.2	−198.4	−106.3

*$p < .1$, **$p < .05$, ***$p < .01$

the rate of certification in the earlier period, but the effect changes its direction in the second period. This perhaps suggests that in the early period, the spread of ISO certificates in Korea did not depend on the normative or scientific validation from the academic community, attesting the legitimacy of ISO standards at the time of its introduction in Korea. In the later period, however, academic discourse and adoption became more aligned as the reversal of the coefficient's direction in the second period suggests.

The amount of debt, while not significant in Model 1, reduces the likelihood of certification in the later period, but there is no significant relationship in the early period. That is, even the highly indebted firms were equally likely to embrace the costly adoption of ISO standards. However, in the post-crisis period, Korean firms were tightening their belts, and ISO was, it seems, seen as a luxury, especially when the country as a whole was deep under heavy indebtedness. The effect of debt on adoption is particularly revealing because the significance of debt changes drastically after the crisis. Before the crisis, large chaebols aggressively pursued diversification strategies—both vertical and horizontal—with borrowed money. After the financial crisis, Korean firms came under increasing pressure as part of the IMF conditionality to drastically restructure the debt-to-equity ratio. Consequently, the debt-to-equity ratio was substantially reduced in the period immediately following the crisis (Chang 2003). Even with the reduction in the overall level of debt, the variable is negatively associated with the likelihood of adoption. Moreover, in this context, costly certification might have contributed to indebted firms' reluctance to take on addition costs.

We included three variables that represent the functional and economic motivations for adoption. The dummy variable for manufacturing firms has a positive and significant effect in Model 1. However, in Model 2, the manufacturing dummy has a positive and significant effect only in the second period. Before the Asian financial crisis, manufacturing firms were no more likely to be certified than other types of firms, suggesting the wide prevalence of the practice across a wide variety of industries. It was the manufacturing firms that could benefit from technical efficiency that pursued ISO 9001 certificates in the later period. The dummy variable for exporters is positive and significant for both periods, suggesting that exporting firms continued to see the benefits of ISO standards and certification. The proportion of revenues from exporting has a negative and significant effect for the whole period. However, when the time axis is split into two, the variable is significant only in the second period. In other words, firms that were drawing higher portions of their revenues from exporting are less likely to be certified. Controlling for the effect of being an exporter and other factors, it is the firms that were performing relatively poorly that adopted ISO 9001 in the later period. These findings on the economic and technical rationales are broadly consistent with the current development in the studies of diffusion and institutionalization that postulate that concerns over economic and technical benefits exist throughout the entire period of a diffusion process. The analyses, therefore, support Hypotheses 1, 2, and 3. Hypothesis 6 is also partially supported.

The effect of the number of previous adoptions has a positive and significant effect for the whole period. However, in Model 2, the variable is significant only in the early period. ISO 9001 spread in Korea in the early period as large corporations imitated other corporations. In the post-financial crisis period, mimicry no longer served as a diffusion mechanism. Lastly, chaebol-affiliated companies were more likely to be certified, but only in the first period. Highly visible, status-conscious chaebol firms adopted ISO 9001 early on. In the second period, this was no longer the case, probably because most chaebol-affiliated firms had been certified. Given that our sample consists of the 300 largest corporations in Korea, both the effects of the previous adoptions and also of the chaebol dummy suggest that in the early period, chaebol-affiliated firms were quick to get on the bandwagon and were imitating one another in a competitive fashion. The analyses, therefore, support Hypotheses 4, 5, and 6.

Summary and Conclusion

We have examined a specific instance of glocalization in which the motivations for adopting a globally legitimated management practice shift in the course of diffusion and institutionalization. In understanding the glocalization of ISO 9001 in Korea, we have drawn from the insights of both the standard and recent accounts of institutionalization. The standard account portrays a rather mechanical process in which the main motivation for adoption shifts from functional gains to social gains (e.g., Tolbert and Zucker 1983; Westphal, Gulati, and Shortell 1997; Jang 2000). Our study showed that the standard account has been useful, but does not exhaust all the possible scenarios, particularly in the context of glocalization of management practices. The recent, more nuanced approach provides a flexible framework to understand glocalization by acknowledging that both types of motivations may coexist and shape organizational responses. Our study adds to this approach (Kennedy and Fiss 2009; Fiss, Kennedy, and Davis 2012).

We have shown that global diffusion and institutionalization take place in particular local settings in which both global and national influences are at work. While our analysis is on a particular national episode of diffusion, there are general themes that speak to the processes, mechanisms, and consequences of glocalization.

First, global models enter national settings at a particular point in time in the course of *global* institutionalization. Both economic and functional motivations co-existed with social, legitimacy concerns in the earlier period. When ISO 9001 arrived in Korea, it had already become a widely accepted practice globally, and the Korean state actively promoted its diffusion and large Korean firms embraced the practice without much resistance. Exporting and manufacturing firms were more likely to be certified because of enhanced marketing opportunities in advanced markets and operational efficiency gained from doing so. At the same time, chaebol firms, conscious of being at the cutting edge of innovative management practices, were quick to adopt; and large firms imitated other large firms' behavior. However, the Asian financial crisis of 1997 inaugurated a more austere environment in which corporations started to be much more cautious and judicious in their operational and strategic decisions. It was the technical gains and economic motivations that facilitated the diffusion.

Second, global models interact with local contexts to shape adoption motivations and patterns, and the diffusion of the same practice nonetheless reproduces cross-national variation (Casper and Hancké 1999; Djelic 2001). This particular episode of diffusion revealed the role of the Korean state in the economy as well as the centrality of large diversified conglomerates (Evans 1995). When ISO standards and certification entered the Korean market, they were seen as highly legitimate, but at the same time, were immediately recognized as particularly helpful for firms exporting to advanced markets. Given the importance of foreign trade, the state actively promoted the practice. Moreover, large conglomerates that dominated the Korean economy were also influential as role models to other smaller firms, further facilitating the spread. In addition, it was the external shock precipitated by the Asian financial crisis that ushered in a different environment where functional gains became the dominant motivation while social and institutional concerns subsided.

The observations suggest that glocalization may have taken a very different shape in another context. In a political economy characterized by a weak state and small and medium-sized firms, things might have been different (e.g., Dobbin 1994). The unique trajectory of diffusion we document here clearly illustrates the contingent nature of glocalization. Globalization means that states and firms come under similar pressures and influences, which, in turn, interact with local contexts to generate and/or maintain heterogeneity at the local level (Casper and Hancké 1999; Kostova 1999; Djelic 2001; Czarniawska and Sevón 2005; Jung 2006; Özen and Berkman 2007).

References

Abrahamson, E. (1991). 'Managerial fads and fashions: the diffusion and rejection of innovations'. *Academy of Management of Review, 16*: 586–612.

Anderson, S.W., Daly, J.D., and Johnson, M.F. (1999). 'Why firms seek ISO 9000 certification: regulatory compliance or competitive advantage?' *Production and Operations Management, 8(1)*: 28–43.

Ansari, S., Fiss, P., and Zajac, E. (2010). 'Made to fit: how practices vary as they diffuse'. *Academy of Management Review, 35(1)*: 67.

Blossfeld, H., and Rohwer, G. (1995). *Techniques of event history modeling: new approaches to causal analysis*. Mahwah, NJ: Lawrence Erlbaum Associates.

Boxenbaum, E., and Jonsson, S. (2008). 'Isomorphism, diffusion and decoupling', in R. Greenwood, C. Oliver, K. Sahlin, and R. Suddaby (eds), *The Sage handbook of organizational institutionalism*. Los Angeles, CA: Sage, 78–98.

Casper, S., and Hancké, B. (1999). 'Global quality norms within national production regimes: ISO 9000 standards in the French and German car industries'. *Organization Studies, 20(6)*: 961–85.

Chang, S.J. (2003). *Financial crisis and transformation of Korean business groups: the rise and fall of chaebols*. Cambridge: Cambridge University Press.

Colyvas, J.A., and Jonsson, S. (2011). 'Ubiquity and legitimacy: disentangling diffusion and institutionalization'. *Sociological Theory 29(1)*: 27–53.

Czarniawska, B., and Sevón, G. (eds). (1996). *Translating organizational change*. Berlin: Walter de Gruyter.

Czarniawska, B., and Sevón, G. (eds). (2005). *Global ideas: how ideas, objects, and practices travel in the global economy*. Liber & Copenhagen Business School Press: Gothenburg.

David, R., and Strang, D. (2006). 'When fashion is fleeting: transitory collective beliefs and the dynamics of TQM consulting'. *Academy of Management Journal, 49*: 215–33.

Djelic, M.-L. (2001). *Exporting the American model: the post-war transformation of European business*. Cambridge: Oxford University Press.

Dobbin, F. (1994.) *Forging industrial policy*. Princeton, NJ: Princeton University Press.

Drori, G.S., Meyer, J.W., and Hwang, H. (eds). (2006). *Globalization and organization: world society and organizational change*. Oxford, UK: Oxford University Press.

Erel, E., and Ghosh, J. (1997). 'ISO 9000 implementation in the Turkish industry'. *International Journal of Operations and Production Management, 17(12)*: 1233–46.

Evans, P. (1995). *Embedded autonomy: states and industrial transformation*. Princeton, NJ: Princeton University Press.

Fiss, P.C., Kennedy, M.T., and Davis, G.F. (2012). 'How golden parachutes unfolded: diffusion and variation of a controversial practice'. *Organization Science, 23(4)*: 1077–9.

Fligstein, N. (1996). 'Markets as politics: a political-cultural approach to market institutions'. *American Sociological Review, 61*: 656–73.

Guler, I., Guillen, M.F., and Macpherson, J.M. (2002). 'Global competition, institutions, and the diffusion of organizational practices: the international spread of ISO 9000 quality certificates'. *Administrative Science Quarterly, 47*: 207–32.

Hankyoreh (1993) 'The era of total quality management', September 27.

Jang, Y.S. (2000). 'The worldwide founding of ministries of science and technology, 1950–1990'. *Sociological Perspectives, 43(2)*: 247–70.

Jung, D.I. (2006). 'The social construction of management fashion: analysis of exit from the TQM consulting market in the U.S., 1992–2003'. *Korean Journal of Sociology, 40(6)*: 187–225.

Kennedy, M., and Fiss, P. (2009). 'Institutionalization, framing, and diffusion: the logic of TQM adoption and implementation decisions among U.S. hospitals'. *Academy of Management Journal, 52(5)*: 897–918.

Kostova, T. (1999). 'Transnational transfer of strategic organizational practices: a contextual perspective'. *Academy of Management Review, 24(2)*: 308–24.

Lounsbury, M. (2007). 'A tale of two cities: competing logics and practice variation in the professionalization of mutual funds'. *Academy of Management Journal, 50(2)*: 289–307.

Loya, T.A., and Boli, J. (1999). 'Standardization in the world polity: technical rationality over power', in J. Boli and G.M. Thomas (eds), *Constructing world culture: international nongovernmental organization since 1875*. Stanford, CA: Stanford University Press, 160–97.

Martínez-Costa, M., and Martínez-Lorente, A.R. (2003). 'Effects of ISO 9000 certification on firms' performance: a vision from the market'. *Total Quality Management and Business Excellence, 14(10)*: 1179–91.

Mendel, P.J. (2001). 'Global models of organization: international management standards, reforms, and movements'. Unpublished Dissertation. Department of Sociology, Stanford University.

Mendel, P.J. (2002). 'International standardization and global governance: the spread of quality and environmental standards', in A.J. Hoffman and M.J. Ventresca (eds), *Organizations, policy, and the natural environment: institutional and strategic perspectives*. Stanford, CA: Stanford University Press, 407–31.

Mendel, P.J. (2006). 'The making and expansion of international management standards: the global diffusion of ISO 9000 quality management certificates', in G.S. Drori, J.W. Meyer, and H. Hwang (eds), *Globalization and organization: world society and organizational change*. Oxford, UK: Oxford University Press, 137–266.

Meyer, J.W. (2002). 'Globalization and the expansion and standardization of management', in K. Sahlin-Andersson and L. Engwall (eds), *The expansion of management knowledge*. Stanford, CA: Stanford Business Books, 33–44.

Meyer, J.W., Kamens, D.H., and Benavot, A. (1992). *School knowledge for the masses: world models and national primary curricular categories in the twentieth century*. Washington DC: Falmer Press.

Özen, Ş., and Berkman, Ü. (2007). 'Cross-national reconstruction of managerial practices: TQM in Turkey'. *Organization Studies, 28(6)*: 825–51.

Podolny, J.M. (2005). *Status signals: a sociological study of market competition*. Princeton, NJ: Princeton University Press.

Porac, J.F., Howard, T., Wilson, F., Doublas, P., and Danfer, A. (1995). 'Rivalry and the industry model of Scottish knitwear producers'. *Administrative Science Quarterly, 40(2)*: 203–27.

Robertson, R. (1994). 'Globalisation or glocalisation?' *Journal of International Communication, 1(1)*: 33–52. doi: 10.1080/13216597.1994.9751780.

Rovik, K.A. (2002). 'The secrets of the winners: management ideas that flow', in L. Engwall and K. Sahlin-Andersson (eds), *The expansion of management knowledge, carriers, flows and sources*. Stanford, CA: Stanford Business Books.

Sahlin-Andersson, K. (1996). 'Imitating by editing success: the construction of organizational changes', in B. Czarniawska and G. Sevón (eds), *Translating organizational change*. Berlin: Walter de Gruyter, 69–92.

Sahlin-Andersson, K., and Engwall, L. (eds). (2002). *The expansion of management knowledge: carriers, flows, and sources*. Stanford, CA: Stanford University Press.

Seould Shinmun (1993). 'Everyone is doing it', December 3.

Strang, D., and Meyer, J. (1993). 'Institutional conditions for diffusion'. *Theory and Society, 22*: 487–511.

Strang, D., and Soule, S.A. (1998). 'Diffusion in organizations and social movements: from hybrid corn to poison pills'. *Annual Review of Sociology, 24*: 265–90.

Tolbert, P.S., and Zucker, L.G. (1983). 'Institutional sources of change in the formal structure of organizations: the diffusion of civil service reform, 1880–1935'. *Administrative Science Quarterly, 28(1)*: 22–39.

Tolbert, P.S., and Zucker, L.G. (1996). 'The institutionalization of institutional theory', in S.R. Clegg and C. Hardy (eds), *The handbook of organization studies*. Los Angeles, CA: Sage, 175–90.

Tuma, N.B., and Hannan, M.T. (1984). *Social dynamics: models and methods*. New York: Academic Press.

Westphal, J.D., Gulati, R., and Shortell, S.M. (1997). 'Customization or conformity? An institutional and network perspective on the content and consequences of TQM adoption'. *Administrative Science Quarterly, 42(2)*: 366–94.

White, H.C. (1981). 'Where do markets come from?' *American Journal of Sociology, 87*: 517–47.

25

The Localization of Carbon Markets

Negotiated Ambiguity

Anita Engels and Lisa Knoll

Introduction

Carbon trading is the globalized management theme par excellence. Companies throughout the world anticipate a carbon-constrained business future, and in the following chapter, we analyze how this global idea is adopted by companies and public sector organizations in a process of local negotiations of legitimate forms of carbon management. The dominance of market-based approaches to global carbon emissions control is often seen as the triumph of neo-liberalism (Bailey 2007a; Lohmann 2009; Lipschutz and Peck 2010) and as a hegemonic form of global environmental governance (Clémençon 2010; Newell and Paterson 2010). The price of carbon is understood to be a universal and global signal that serves to provide the unambiguous basis on which companies in various local economic contexts develop and evaluate carbon management strategies.

This chapter aims at providing a different view by advancing the following arguments. The diffusion of market-based policy instruments to govern the earth's atmosphere draws on a universal image of rationalized actorhood (Meyer and Jepperson 2000). Yet this diffusion process lacks a clear orientation for companies and other organizations with respect to the day-to-day duty of managing carbon emissions. Even a market tool as clear-cut as the EU Emissions Trading Scheme (EU ETS) is under-determined in terms of local sense-making at the organizational level. The price of carbon that emerges through this market is *not* an unambiguous and easy-to-decipher signal, and companies vary tremendously in the ways in which they relate the price signal to other relevant information and assign a company-specific meaning to it. Companies are confronted with a heterogeneous, contradictory, and fragmented institutional universe that is far from self-explanatory (Hoffman 2001). It leaves the companies with a great deal of decision-making uncertainty and requires processes of societal sense-making. Berger and Luckmann have been very clear in differentiating between the *institutional world* and the processes of sense-making by which society ascribes *legitimacy* to institutions: 'the institutional world requires legitimation, that is, ways by which it can be "explained" and justified' (Berger and Luckmann 1966: 79). Accordingly, the first section highlights the complexity organizations face due to regulations and expectations stemming from the global, national, sectoral, and professional institutional worlds, with brief case descriptions. In the second section, we suggest that local negotiations over legitimate forms of carbon management are the key processes through which carbon emissions become manageable and through which the dominant mode of global environmental governance is 'localized' (Svendsen 1999). We use the French Convention School of Economics to show that different orders of worth are used to justify economic action in equal measure. 'Glocalization' (Robertson 1995) is understood as specific processes of how people in organizations find their 'way in social space' (Boltanski and Thévenot 1983) under the condition of a constant evaluative ambiguity. Agents are presumed to be—as Eymard-Duvernay puts it—'interdisciplinary' (Eymard-Duvernay 2002: 72); that is to say, they are capable of referring to various and different extra-situational orders of worth and to objects available in a situation (visible in arguments such as 'there is no alternative') to make a claim generally valid. Under the condition of heterogeneity, actors are constantly forced to actively explain, legitimate, and justify structures, actions, and opinions.

This perspective can enhance the new institutional research on institutional heterogeneity, which challenges the strong claim for institutional homogenization in organizational fields (DiMaggio and Powell 1983). Drawing on the work of Friedland and Alford (1991), who argue in favor of an inter-institutional system located on the analytical level of society, new institutionalists understand ambiguity in organizational decision-making in terms of conflicting or contradicting belief systems (Scott 1994) or institutional logics (Thornton and Ocasio 1999, 2008; Thornton 2002; Lounsbury 2007). Similarly, the French Convention School of Economics draws on a variety of orders of worth that may justify the world in the face of criticism (Boltanski and Thévenot 2006). However, the French Convention School has two advantages we highlight in this chapter. First, it provides a methodological answer to the question of the consequences of heterogeneity (a constant need for situational sense-making and justification). Second, it offers an alternative to the ontological unambiguousness often ascribed to *economic* institutions. Economic modes of rationalization comprise at least two different orders of worth: the market order *and* the industrial order (Boltanski and Thévenot 2000: 226). The market order remunerates price gaps, opportunities, and the short-term maximization of profit, whereas the industrial order appreciates functionality, measurements, technique, and middle- and long-term planning horizons. Furthermore, economic processes sometimes entail other 'non-economic' orders that can nonetheless constitute the economic—for example, the civic, the domestic, and the green order. The civic order values solidarity, equality, the collective interest, democratic representation, resolutions, and services for the public. In the domestic order tradition, of which patriarchal leadership and family-owned enterprise are typical illustrations, kinship, trust, and reciprocity are valued. Lafaye and Thévenot (Lafaye and Thévenot 1993; Thévenot, Moody, and Lafaye 2000) show a green order of worth that remunerates sustaining and conserving nature as an end in itself. This image of a heterogeneous *economic* sphere challenges the notion of a market and price signals as clear objects to which companies can easily relate (Knoll 2012).

The argument is based on qualitative case studies of several organizations from different countries and industrial branches that were conducted towards the end of the EU ETS's first trading period (2005–2007)—at a time when the preparation for the second trading period (2008–2012) had just started.[1] The case studies aim at investigating how evaluative ambiguity over a company's or a public sector organization's carbon management is resolved. In this chapter, we emphasize processes of local ambiguity management at the organizational level. We draw on group discussions in which the organizational members talked about the how and why of their organization's specific emissions trading behavior (we use the term 'behavior' because not all companies have a clear, dedicated strategy).

The Institutional Horizon of Carbon Management Ideas

Environmental governance ideas are located at various institutional layers. Taken together, these floating ideas constitute an institutional universe in the sense of a horizon of possible orientations that companies and other organizations can refer to in the process of local sense-making. In political science these different layers are often depicted as a hierarchically ordered world in which policy formation emerges, be it in a top-down or a bottom-up manner (Benz and Papadopolous 2006). In this section, we show the various segments of the institutional universe in which carbon emissions appear as a management object. In two case studies, we analyze how these segments create fragmented, overlapping or contradictory layers of institutional signals and how companies need to create a hierarchy and set their own priorities (Hoffman 2001).

Carbon Governance at the Global Regime Level

International climate negotiations are a well-documented and thoroughly analyzed example of global regime formation. The Framework Convention on Climate Change (1992), the Kyoto Protocol (1997) and several amendments to the latter provide the legal framework in which policy formation takes place (Messner 2010; Bulkeley and Newell 2010). Carbon markets have become a dominant policy instrument, and the EU ETS is the most prominent of them (Skjærseth and Wettestad 2008; Bailey 2010). The ETS, which was established in 2005, requires the operating companies of approximately 10,000 plants and installations to surrender emission allowances for each ton of CO_2 they emit in the course of one reporting year. Companies are also required to establish a CO_2 emission monitoring system and to allow for a yearly verification by a state-approved surveyor. The allowances can be freely traded across the EU. Commentators have regularly reified the universal idea of creating a price for carbon (Convery and Redmond 2007: 89). For European companies, it is possible to combine the opportunities provided by the EU ETS with projects in developing countries or economies in transition. Companies can establish elaborate risk-management strategies with regard to their carbon emissions, creating complex hedging instruments and developing carbon portfolios, but it is also possible to outsource the management of carbon emissions to external service providers. Although the EU ETS is mandatory for all member states and is becoming more inclusive over time, it allows considerable freedom for companies under the scheme to determine how to manage their carbon emissions.

National Policy Formation

Even in the EU ETS, which is created by a common European Directive, we find a great variety of national approaches to the implementation of the legislation and to the way in which this market scheme is institutionally embedded (Engels, Knoll, and Huth 2008). The most important differences stem from three sources. First, among EU member states, one can find quite different regulatory styles and traditions, which create path dependencies in spite of all indicators of European policy harmonization (Wurzel 2002; Bailey 2007b; Holzinger, Knill, and Sommerer 2011). In particular, member states vary in the degree of former exposure to and experimentation with market-based policy instruments (for the British case, see, e.g., Nye and Owens 2008) and the stringency of their national allocation plans (Ellerman et al. 2007). Second, the structural composition of each economy (e.g., with regard to import or export orientation, dominant industries, net energy seller or buyer) creates a unique pattern of exposure to carbon legislation and to the need for carbon management. Third, companies experience national variations in terms of the dominant forms of, for example, corporate governance, corporate finance, network relations, educational systems, and labor relations. These differences are summarized in the literature on the varieties of capitalism, with the most important ideal typical distinction existing between coordinated market economies and liberal market economies (Hall and Soskice 2001; Campbell, Hall, and Pedersen 2006). These institutional sources have created distinct national patterns of carbon management ideas.

Industrial Sectors

As carbon emission levels vary enormously across industrial branches, the problem of how to manage carbon emissions can range from a seemingly life-threatening experience in parts of the mineral industry to a promising new business opportunity in the regenerative energy industry or in certain service industries. In sectors such as the chemical industry that have long-standing confrontational relationships with environmental regulations and the general public, the problem of carbon emissions occurs in a different institutional environment than in industries that do not have this kind of institutional history (Hoffman 1999; Scott and Meyer 1991). Moreover, even organizations that are not private companies at all are included in the EU ETS because they operate power plants. Universities and large hospitals are generally public sector organizations, yet some of them have to address the management of their carbon emissions and do so in a completely different institutional environment than their corporate counterparts.

Carbon Service Industries

With the emergence of carbon markets, we observe the creation of a new service industry that sells financial, technical, legal, insurance, and management services to the companies and public sector organizations that have to manage their carbon emissions (Voß 2007; Labatt and White 2007). The availability of support and advice from external consultancies can lead to quite different outcomes in terms of management concepts and general orientations towards the question of how to deal with carbon emissions at the company level. The broad orientations of these carbon service industries might even vary by national context. For example, consulting firms in the UK often have a background in law and finance, whereas many consulting firms in Germany provide technical services and are instead rooted in the German engineering culture (Engels, Knoll, and Huth 2008).

Professional Logics

Professions are seen to be 'the great rationalizers of the second half of the twentieth century' (Meyer and Rowan 1977: 344; DiMaggio and Powell 1983: 147). In this respect, for example, accounting associations and financial institutions attract the attention of social scientists (Froud et al. 2000; Greenwood, Suddaby, and Hinings 2002; Botzem and Quack 2006). During the long process of professional socialization, individuals are imprinted with worldviews and standard operating procedures on how to do their jobs properly. The professions are responsible for the creation of technical standards and for sanctioning rule-breaking among their members. Companies can be viewed as a combination of different departments or organizational units in which different professional logics dominate. For example, they can include the accounting versus the sales department or the environmental management unit. However, carbon management remains far from being a profession. The EU ETS does not give any direction about which department inside a company should be in charge of dealing with emission allowances. As a consequence, we find a huge variety of solutions to this question (Engels 2009). It is plausible to assume that an energy trader will develop a different understanding of carbon management than a plant manager, a risk manager, or an environmental manager.

We call this combination of different institutional segments the institutional context in which the formation of a local carbon management strategy takes place. Two examples from our case studies illustrate that different and often conflicting signals come from these various institutional layers and how organizations struggle with the ambiguity and openness of the institutional horizon.

A Public University in Great Britain

The university operated a power plant that fell under the EU ETS. For the manager of the power plant, the institutional horizon was constituted by the national emissions trading authorities, by a network of universities, by brokers and verifiers specialized in carbon trading or carbon management, and by students. At the time of the case study, the national authorities had not developed any particular guidance for how public universities should deal with the problem of carbon management. Therefore, the plant manager tried to get a sense of what needed to be done from his fellow energy managers at other universities in the university network. They decided, as a group, to hire experts from the carbon service industry. The situation became complicated as the plant manager had to buy additional allowances because he anticipated a shortage of allowances for the compliance period. He had to negotiate with the university administration to be assigned a budget from which he could purchase allowances from the market. As he did not know how to buy allowances himself, he turned to a specialized broker to strike a deal with a seller on the market for emission allowances. However, when the broker found a company willing to sell, the university's energy manager needed to make sure that this company complied with the university's standard requirements for ethical purchasing, a requirement that was strongly supported by the students of that university.

A Refinery (Chemical Industry) in Great Britain

This company struggled with contradictory signals coming from its own industry association, national carbon regulations, the EU ETS rules, the carbon consulting industry, and an international private equity fund that became the new owner of the company while its carbon management strategy was formed. On the one hand, the chemical industry was exempt from the EU ETS in Phase I. On the other hand, some installations were not exempt due to combustion activities and the burning of fossil fuels. When the EU ETS started, the refinery's management was not sure whether it would be exempt because it belonged to the chemical industry, or whether it would fall under the EU ETS legislation because of the type of activity practiced in some of its installations. Because the company was sold to an international private equity fund, the company had been evaluated by a number of consultants focusing on risk management and on identification and establishment of an overview of the most critical risks of the company. Thus, unlike refineries in other countries, the company decided to participate in the EU ETS as soon as possible to make sure it was compliant. However, the refinery was already subject to a sector-specific Climate Change Agreement (CCA) that granted an 80 percent reduction from the national Climate Change Levy in exchange for agreeing to meet certain energy efficiency targets. This CCA was partly at odds with the EU ETS. While the UK CCA remunerated energy efficiency, the EU ETS was orientated towards the totality of the energy consumption and the totality of the CO_2 emissions (Boemare, Quirion, and Sorrell 2003). This conflict led to a situation in which the temporary shutting down of a plant would have been remunerated by the EU ETS because it reduced total emissions, but would have been penalized under the CCA because it worsened energy efficiency levels.

These two examples illustrate how organizations find a rich source of institutional clues from which they can develop a sense of what carbon management means. However, the institutional horizon does not create clarity and lack of ambiguity for the companies. On the contrary, the more 'orientation' these institutional segments provide, the more the companies need to prioritize and choose among different options and interpret the site-specific meaning, as the signals they receive are heterogeneous, refer to many different aspects of the management problem, and are occasionally contradictory. The institutional horizon does not provide a substitute for local sense-making, but requires a very active process of negotiation, legitimation, and stabilization. The institutional orientation remains ambiguous for at least three reasons. First, the institutional prescripts are *under-determined*, given the complexity of the legal rules for the emissions trading scheme, their organizational implementation, and the technical requirements. Second, recommendations coming from different segments of the institutional horizon (e.g., the specific domestic interpretation of the common European directive, the policies and lobbying activities promoted by sector-specific associations, and the standard practices of verifiers, brokers, and other companies from the carbon service industry) are often *conflicting*. Third, there is *no obvious hierarchy* in the various segments of the institutional horizon: the importance of institutional clues does not rise from sector level to the EU regulatory level (or vice versa). The companies need to prioritize, and there is no predefined ranking of institutional orders; some will choose their industrial association as the most important point of orientation, and others may choose national authorities or a specialized consulting firm that belongs to the carbon service industry.

Negotiating ambiguity: 'finding one's way in social space'

In day-to-day organizational economic life, neither 'efficiency' nor 'legitimation' is achieved in an easy or unproblematic manner. This is the case not only because organizations are surrounded by a diverse *institutional* universe consisting of national, transnational, legislative, professional, associational, and advisory input (as the two cases in the previous section have demonstrated), but also because such a heterogeneity causes a permanent need for explanation and legitimation. The institutional world can easily be questioned and criticized under such evaluative ambiguity. The Convention School of Economics offers a methodological answer to the question of what follows from institutional and evaluative heterogeneity. By drawing on what Knorr-Cetina called 'methodological situationalism' (Knorr-Cetina 1981: 2), the Convention School of Economics focuses on the local processes of doing and undoing legitimation through which actors collectively struggle to orient themselves under the condition of ambiguity:

> We intend to deal here with legitimacy as part of the competence of actors. We indeed make the hypothesis that actors are capable of distinguishing between legitimate arguments and arrangements and illegitimate ones. Legitimate means that when

arguments and arrangements are confronted with criticisms they can be the subject of justifications that are valid in all generality, and that they can be used to support universalizable agreements. Illegitimate means that they cannot be justified, and that they cannot support agreements that concern the generality of the common good, even if they can be mobilized by the actors in certain situations to support certain arrangements to the advantage of the parties.

(Boltanski and Thévenot 2000: 215)

Economic actors have to determine what the common problem is before they can find a collective solution to a problem (whether it be in a concordant, conflictive, or compromising manner). Furthermore, they can do so by referring to abstract orders of worth that may be objectified in the contradictory institutional universe surrounding the organization. Under the condition of heterogeneity, it is necessary to constantly prepare for critique. Agreements have to be actively achieved, and compromises have to be negotiated. Compromises may be stabilized by objective and institutionalized forms that bridge the gap between disparate logics, like 'new public management' or organic mass production (Thévenot 2001). The institutional world (made up of a variety of objects and objectifications) may help to back up an argument with plausibility. Nevertheless, as we have shown, the institutional universe does not present itself in a clear-cut way and leaves room for interpretation.

The analysis of group discussions allows for studying evaluative ambiguity (Knoll 2012). Under the condition of heterogeneity, a group is likely to constantly resolve inconsistencies, like those that Meyer and Rowan (1977: 356) referred to in their groundbreaking article. The participants do so at a moment-to-moment level by talking about, arguing over, and justifying diverse topics (e.g., their emissions trading behavior). In group discussions, actors refer to a variety of orders of worth, explaining their understanding of appropriate measures and suitable behavior to the attendant professionals, colleagues, experts, and to the sociologist. Over the course of the discussion, legitimation will be expressed, assigned, and, possibly, denied by the group. The processes of legitimation can thus be observed as an *interactive* process.

While conducting and analyzing the company case studies, we acquired a strong sense of how hard employees and professionals struggle for legitimation in the course of their everyday action. How a company translates the (global) CO_2 price information into a (local) trading decision or most ideally into a (local) decision to reduce CO_2 emissions is a rather complex process full of preconditions that depend on processes of sense-making that arise from negotiations and the collective search for orientation. 'What's going on?' 'What problems do we have?' These are questions that have to be answered prior to solving a problem. An excerpt from a group discussion at a municipal utility provides detailed insight into the negotiation of an appropriate and correct mode of heat generation with reference to various global principles of rationalization through which the meaning of the price of CO_2 is negotiated. The chief of the power plant operation begins the excerpt by stating:

Power Plant Operator: When heat from the district heating network is required, the CO_2 price is irrelevant!
Power Trader: One could play around a little bit by shifting between the combined heat and power plant and the other stations.
Power Plant Operator: This is digital again. If I am able to generate heat in the combined heat and power plant, I do it there and not with primary heat. Finito!
Moderation: And the CO_2 price is completely irrelevant for this decision?

> *Power Plant Operator:* Absolutely! The CO_2 price is completely irrelevant, because we generate heat as and when required. When heat is required, we have to deliver the heat. That's it! No one cares about the price. The important thing is that we deliver the heat.
> *Power Trader:* But you do have the possibility of driving various heat plants according to price signals.
> *Power Plant Operator:* Yes, but when it comes to this decision, I chose the combined heat and power plant over the primary heat because of the better efficiency factor.
>
> (Translation of group discussion at a German municipal utility)

What can be observed here is a situational blending of references through citation of a variety of orders of worth, each of which claims universal prevalence. This brief excerpt illustrates how a demand orientation (industry)—which is based on the need to deliver energy 'as and when required', which in turn reflects a perception of energy as a public good (civic)—implies a very specific way of running an energy plant. The use of the term 'digital' by the power plant operator is interpreted as a critique of the financialization of the power market that detaches power generation from technical needs. In the end, the demand-orientation is additionally justified with an argument for environmental friendliness, in terms of the 'efficiency factor', referring to the climate change mitigation debate (green). This discussion demonstrates, first, that the group is referring to different orders of worth that serve as reason-generating backgrounds concerning the 'good', the 'just', or the 'rational' way of running the process of heat generation. Second, we see how a hierarchy of different logics is reflected in the negotiation process. The power trader mentions that 'one could play around a little' by shifting heat generation between the power plants according to price signals (market), but he has to do so in a defensive way. The demand orientation (industry) and the public good orientation (civic) serve as strong arguments against the market logic and are further justified later in the excerpt by arguments of environmental friendliness. One could conclude that market liberalization and the implementation of an emissions trading scheme, where allowances can be traded on European energy exchanges, do not automatically induce an unquestioned diffusion of the market logic in the field of municipal energy generation. On the contrary, the market logic faces numerous legitimation problems.

In a similar manner, the chief of the sourcing department for energy and the environmental manager of a Dutch food company discuss the question of whether and how the CO_2 price is affecting the emission levels of the company:

> *Environmental Management:* When our position is long, so we don't need to reduce energy, because of the emission trade.
> *Energy Sourcing Department:* Oh, that's not true! That's more technical think. When we reduce them, we have a long position, I can sell them. So that's not true, what he said now. (*both laughing*) The LESS we emit we have a certain right, when we reduce our energy (*cell phone ringing*) volume I can make money of it!
> (Energy Sourcing Leader answering cell phone)
> *Environmental Management:* We have energy reduction plans and what we see is that our annual reduction possibility is more than about one or two percent. So, in fact, that doesn't influence our position much.
>
> (Group discussion at a Dutch food company)

Here, we observe two different understandings of how price information might influence the emission levels of the company. Two different understandings of emission trading, a 'technical think' and a financial way of understanding, are negotiated, implying that two modes of interpreting the question of 'what is going on' are at stake. One position argues that the company's emission reduction policy is *decoupled* from trading due to small technical reduction possibilities (industry), while the other position argues in favor of a *tight coupling* of trading and emission reduction measures due to the potential for profit, which captures the company's ongoing attention to carbon management (a translation of the price-information into a driver for technical emission reductions). Interestingly, those positions reflect different modes of dealing with heterogeneity. The first position argues for the incompatibility of logics that remain disconnected (although the idea of the trading scheme presumes the link between trading and emission reductions). The second position argues for the possibility of a fruitful compromise between industrial, green, and market logics. The French Convention School of Economics treats agreement, compromise, and conflict as equally valid. The situation illustrates a conflict over the question of whether a compromise makes sense or whether the differences between the market logic and an industry-green CO_2 reduction are insurmountable (decoupled). The organizational compromise between industry and market logics is the central condition for a trading scheme that effectively leads to technical emission reductions. This link between the carbon market and a company's CO_2 performance has to be configured and achieved at the organizational level (Knoll and Engels 2012).

Another negotiation of how to understand emission allowances and their cost impact can be found in a discussion between the power trader and the accountant in another German municipal utility. The accountant took part in a qualifying course to learn how to account for carbon.[2] The right to emit one ton of the harmful greenhouse gas CO_2 is a company's asset in the eyes of the accounting department. At the workshop, he learned to address one emission right as a production unit that has to be stored and that is used at the end of one trading phase, when emission rights need to be surrendered to the German emissions authority. At the same time, the power trader established a sourcing strategy for emissions rights that was contrary to this approach and that forced him to buy allowances during the year, during the same months when CO_2 was emitted, both to avoid the price risk at the end of one trading phase and to avoid the 'speculative component' (power trader) of a volatile carbon market. The expenditure that the power trader reports is the actual market price that he paid for the allowances. The expenditure that the accountant captures refers to the annual obligation to return allowances to the national registry at the end of one trading period. The coexistence of two ways of understanding and rationalizing emission rights led to confusion; the power trader reported the actual costs of the allowances he bought according to his monthly buying strategy to the reporting system, while the accountant reported numbers that stemmed from his trading-year-oriented understanding of allowance consumption. In the following excerpt, the accountant argues for his solution (which he found to be less labor-intensive), while the power trader intervenes by referring to the decision to establish a company-wide monthly reporting system to enhance the internal control structure.

> *Accountant:* There are companies that account for carbon differently than we do. For example, municipal utility XY, I think they found another solution. (*looks at marketing manager*)
> *Marketing:* I don't know either.
> *Accountant:* I read in some internal strategy paper that they say we do have a certain stock of emission rights at the beginning of one trading year, and we depreciate them during the year until they are finished. From a bookkeeping perspective, we don't have operating expenses stemming from accrued liabilities before that. But as I said before,

at the end of one trading year it doesn't matter which solution one decides upon. It's important to make a decision.

Power Trader: And we decided to set up a monthly reporting system to report and control our expenditures and revenues monthly. Because we get data every month, it was the most useful approach to have one number every month, always! And we agreed to do it all in the same way.

(Translation: group discussion at a German municipal utility)

This excerpt clearly demonstrates the need for *talking* processes of organizational coordination to establish a common understanding of what an 'expenditure' is. Organizational decisions are the outcome of complex and heterogeneous negotiation processes that involve a variety of technical calculation schemes that do not impose their logics in a clear-cut way. As Carruthers put it: 'Technical criteria may constrain organizational structure, but they cannot determine a unique point of optimality, because no such point exists' (Carruthers 1995: 320). Both the accountant and the power trader argue for a 'rational' way of operating emissions rights: (1) the monthly internal reporting system aiming at the enhancement of the organization's control structure, and (2) the bookkeeping standard that had been established in the organizational field that the accountant learned during his qualification course. The organization and the field suggest different calculative solutions for the same problem. Both technical standards aim at enhancing the organization's planning and measurement system and thus can be interpreted as following an industrial logic dedicated to organizational planning, measurement, functionality, and efficiency. Furthermore, one could argue that it is not only negotiation that is at stake here, but also status, tied to the question of which person is finally able to push his/her position through. In this case, the accountant does the subordinate work that is secondary in importance compared with the power-trading department. Nevertheless, even in this case of a clear hierarchy, solutions need to be justified and founded in general arguments (Boltanski and Thévenot 2000: 212). In this case, the general argument consists of a reference to a past *organizational decision*: every department calculates one number and reports one number every month. However, an organizational decision is not set in stone. It remains open to question. Inconsistencies can be resolved for the moment via interactive strategies of situational subordination, but they cannot be resolved once and for all. Because of the complexity of the institutional and symbolic universe, agents must constantly re-evaluate certain solutions or decisions in day-to-day work. Conflicts are likely maintained and postponed on an interactive basis, most of the time without loss of face (Goffman 1959).

Summary and Conclusion

Anthropogenic climate change is a globalized policy field in which market-based regulation has imposed itself as the most rational policy solution. A global problem is addressed by a not-quite-but-potentially-global market. Emissions rights are tradable across national borders, and the price mechanism is supposed to indicate a universal informational basis for companies' carbon management in very different economic contexts. In this chapter, we examine the process through which this global theme is localized, starting from the institutional ambiguity and contradictions that companies have to deal with when they are exposed to the need to manage their carbon emissions. Drawing from case studies of companies in the European Emissions Trading Scheme, we seek to demonstrate that these companies' institutional environment can be described as an institutional horizon in which many different layers overlap or co-exist, each providing a number of signals and points of orientation. However, each of these layers is under-determined, and often there are contradictions between the different layers. There is no clear or pre-established hierarchy of institutional logics. On the contrary, companies have to prioritize among them. Organizations are exposed to a constant need for local sense-making under the condition of institutional ambiguity. By focusing on the situational and collective struggle for orientation under the condition of a constant and unresolvable ambiguity, the French Convention School of Economics provides an interesting theoretical toolkit for studying how companies account for carbon. Finding an appropriate solution to the new decision-making problem—'finding one's way in social space' (Boltanski and Thévenot 1983)—is a demanding task for energy managers, power traders, environmental managers, and accountants. Three excerpts from group discussions illustrate different ways in which contradictions and conflicts can be resolved on an interactive basis. Inconsistencies can be resolved via interactive subordination and the interactive acknowledgment of supremacy. The power trader in the first case demonstrates the subordination of his price argument in a subservient way. Hierarchy is not pre-given; rather, it has to be made visible and activated during interaction. In a similar manner, the accountant in the third case acknowledges the organizational decision ('one reporting solution for the company'), without refraining from advocating for his favorite alternative solution again. Here, organizational solutions serve as a powerful argumentative focal point, but they do not render a justification superfluous. Inconsistencies can be resolved *for the moment* via reference to organizational decisions. The second case shows not only that different orders of worth are at stake but also a conflict about the question of a suitable compromise between different orders of worth: do price signals induce CO_2 reduction measures on the company's sites? Two positions, that of a possible and fruitful coupling between different logics and that of an unaffected co-existence of CO_2 trading and CO_2 emissions management, confront each other. Organizational life is full of those micro-processes through which ambiguity is managed. We hope we have shown that negotiated legitimation is a central process through which global carbon management concepts are localized. Neither hegemonic nor diffusion processes can account for the many different local outcomes of carbon management, not only in terms of different technical solutions found but also in terms of the different orders of worth or combinations thereof. The French Convention School provides a useful approach to understanding ambiguities in the economic world and the complex and multifaceted processes of economic rationalization. Any political project to construct a global market for carbon rights should take these local variations into account.

Acknowledgments

We would like to thank Peter Walgenbach, John Meyer, and two anonymous reviewers for valuable comments.

Notes

1. The case studies stem from a project funded by the German Research Council (DFG) 2006–2009 on companies in the European market for CO_2 emission allowances, which combined them with a quantitative survey of all companies covered by the EU ETS in these four countries. The sample includes organizations from Germany, the UK, Denmark, and the Netherlands to permit a cross-national comparison of company behavior in the EU ETS (Engels, Knoll, and Huth 2008).
2. See the literature on carbon accounting (Busch and Hoffmann 2007; Günther 2006; Bowen and Wittneben 2011).

References

Bailey, I. (2007a). 'Neoliberalism, climate governance and the scalar politics of EU emissions trading'. *Area*, 34(1): 431–42.
Bailey, I. (2007b). 'Market environmentalism, new environmental policy instruments, and climate policy in the United Kingdom and Germany'. *Annals of the Association of American Geographers*, 97(3): 530–50.
Bailey, I. (2010). 'The EU emissions trading scheme'. *WIREs Climate Change*, 1(1): 144–53.
Benz, A., and Papadopolous, I. (2006). *Governance and democracy–comparing national, European and transnational experiences*. London: Routledge.
Berger, P.L., and Luckmann, T. (1966). *The social construction of reality. A treatise in the sociology of knowledge*. New York: Doubleday.
Boemare, C., Quirion, P., and Sorrell, S. (2003). 'The evolution of emissions trading in the EU: tensions between national trading schemes and the proposed EU directive'. *Climate Policy*, 3(2): 105–24.
Boltanski, L., and Thévenot, L. (1983). 'Finding one's way in social space: a study based on games'. *Social Science Information*, 22(4/5): 631–80.
Boltanski, L., and Thévenot, L. (2000). 'The reality of moral expectations: a sociology of situated judgment'. *Philosophical Explorations*, 3(3): 208–31.
Boltanski, L., and Thévenot, L. (2006). *On justification: economies of worth*. Princeton, NJ: Princeton University Press.
Botzem, S., and Quack, S. (2006). 'Contested rules and shifting boundaries: international standard-setting in accounting', in M.-L. Djelic and K. Sahlin-Andersson (eds), *Transnational governance. Institutional dynamics of regulation*. Cambridge University Press, 266–86.
Bowen, F., and Wittneben, B. (2011). 'Carbon accounting: negotiating accuracy, consistency and certainty across organisational fields'. *Accounting, Auditing and Accountability Journal*, 24(8): 1022–36.
Bulkeley, H., and Newell, P. (2010). *Governing climate change*. London: Routledge.
Busch, T., and Hoffmann, V.H. (2007). 'Emerging carbon constraints for corporate risk management'. *Ecological Economics*, 62: 518–28.
Campbell, J.L., Hall, J.A., and Pedersen, O.K. (eds) (2006). *National identity and varieties of capitalism. The Danish experience*. Copenhagen: DJOF.
Carruthers, B.G. (1995). 'Accounting, ambiguity, and the new institutionalism'. *Accounting, Organizations and Society*, 20(4): 313–28.
Clémençon, R. (2010). 'Pushing past neo-liberalism: rethinking global climate change negotiations', in C. Lever-Tracy (ed.), *Routledge handbook of climate change and society*. New York: Routledge, 453–72.
Convery, F.J., and Redmond, L. (2007). 'Market and price developments in the European Union Emissions Trading Scheme'. *Review of Environmental Economics and Policy*, 1(1): 88–111.
DiMaggio, P.J., and Powell, W.W. (1983). 'The iron cage revisited: institutional isomorphism and collective rationality in organizational fields'. *American Sociological Review*, 48(April): 147–60.
Ellerman, A.D., Buchner, B., and Carraro, C. (eds) (2007). 'Allocation in the European emissions trading scheme: rights, rents and fairness'. Cambridge: Cambridge University Press.
Engels, A. (2009). 'The European Emissions Trading Scheme: an exploratory study of how companies learn to account for carbon'. *Accounting, Organizations and Society*, 34(3–4): 488–98.
Engels, A., Knoll, L., and Huth, M. (2008). 'Preparing for the "real" market: national patterns of institutional learning and company behaviour in the European Emissions Trading Scheme (EU ETS)'. *European Environment*, 18(5), 276–97.
Eymard-Duvernay, F. (2002). 'Conventionalist approaches to enterprise', in O. Favereau and E. Lazega (eds), *Conventions and structures in economic organization: markets, networks and hierarchies*. Cheltenham: Edward Elgar, 60–78.
Friedland, R., and Alford, R.R. (1991). 'Bringing society back in: symbols, practices, and institutional contradictions', in W.W. Powell and P. DiMaggio (eds), *The new institutionalism in organizational analysis*. Chicago: University of Chicago Press, 232–63.

Froud, J., Haslam, C., Johal, S., and Williams, K. (2000). 'Shareholder value and financialization: consultancy promises, management moves'. *Economy and Society*, 29(1), 80–110.

Goffman, E. (1959). *The presentation of self in everyday life*. New York: Doubleday.

Greenwood, R., Suddaby, R., and Hinings, C.R. (2002). 'Theorizing change: the role of professional associations in the transformation of institutionalized fields'. *Academy of Management Journal*, 45, 58–80.

Günther, E. (2006). 'Accounting for emissions rights', in R. Antes, B. Hansjürgens, and P. Letmathe (eds), *Emissions trading and business*. Heidelberg: Physica, 219–40.

Hall, P.A., and Soskice, D. (eds) (2001). *Varieties of capitalism: the institutional foundations of comparative advantage*. Oxford: Oxford University Press.

Hoffman, A.J. (1999). 'Institutional evolution and change. Environmentalism and the US chemical industry'. *Academy of Management Journal*, 42: 351–71.

Hoffman, A.J. (2001). 'Linking organizational and field-level analyses: the diffusion of corporate environmental practice'. *Organization Environment*, 14(2): 133–56.

Holzinger, K., Knill, C., and Sommerer, T. (2011). 'Is there convergence of national environmental policies? An analysis of policy outputs in 24 OECD countries'. *Environmental Politics*, 20(1): 20–41.

Knoll, L. (2012). *Über die Rechtfertigung wirtschaftlichen Handelns. CO_2-Handel in der kommunalen Energiewirtschaft*. Wiesbaden: VS Verlag für Sozialwissenschaften.

Knoll, L., and Engels, A. (2012). 'Exploring the linkages between carbon markets and sustainable innovations in the energy sector: lessons from the EU Emissions Trading Scheme', in D. Jansen, K. Ostertag, and R. Walz (eds), *Sustainability innovations in the electricity sector*. Heidelberg: Springer, 97–116.

Knorr-Cetina, K. (1981). 'The micro-sociological challenge of macro-sociology: towards a reconstruction of social theory and methodology', in K. Knorr-Cetina and A.V. Cicourel (eds), *Advances in social theory and methodology. Toward an integration of micro- and macro-sociologies*. London: Routledge and Kegan Paul, 1–47.

Labatt, S., and White, R.R. (2007). *Carbon finance: the financial implications of climate change*. Hoboken: Wiley and Sons.

Lafaye, C., and Thévenot, L. (1993). 'Une justification écologique? Conflits dans l'aménagement de la nature'. *Revue Francaise de Sociologie*, 34(4): 495–524.

Lipschutz, R.D., and Peck, F.A. (2010). 'Climate change, globalization, and carbonization', in B. Turner (ed.), *Handbook of globalization*. London: Routledge, 182–204.

Lohmann, L. (2009). 'Neoliberalism and the calculable world: the rise of carbon trading', in S. Böhm and S. Dabhi (eds), *Upsetting the offset: the political economy of carbon markets*. London: MayFlyBooks, 25–40.

Lounsbury, M. (2007). 'A tale of two cities. Competing logics and practice variation in the professionalizing of mutual funds'. *Academy of Management Journal*, 50(2): 289–307.

Messner, D. (2010). 'Globale Strukturanpassung: Weltwirtschaft und Weltpolitik in den Grenzen des Erdsystems', in H. Welzer, H.-G. Soeffner, and D. Giesecke (eds), *KlimaKulturen. Soziale Wirklichkeiten im Klimawandel*. Frankfurt am Main: Campus, 65–80.

Meyer, J.W., and Jepperson, R.L. (2000). 'The "actors" of modern society: the cultural constitution of social agency'. *Sociological Theory*, 18(1), 100–20.

Meyer, J.W., and Rowan, B. (1977). 'Institutionalized organizations: formal structure as myth and ceremony'. *American Journal of Sociology*, 83(2): 340–63.

Newell, P., and Paterson, M. (2010). *Climate capitalism. Global warming and the transformation of the global economy*. Cambridge: Cambridge University Press.

Nye, M., and Owens, S. (2008). 'Creating the UK Emissions Trading Scheme: motives and symbolic politics'. *European Environment*, 18: 1–15.

Robertson, R. (1995). 'Glocalization: time-space and homogeneity-heterogeneity', in M. Featherstone, S. Lash, and R. Robertson (eds), *Global modernities*. London: Sage, 25–44.

Scott, W.R. (1994). 'Conceptualizing organizational fields. Linking organizations and societal systems', in H.-U. Derlien, U. Gerhardt, and F. Scharpf (eds), *Systemrationalität und Partialinteresse: Festschrift für Renate Mayntz*. Baden-Baden: Nomos, 203–21.

Scott, W.R., and Meyer, J.W. (1991). 'The organization of societal sectors: propositions and early evidence', in W.W. Powell and P. DiMaggio (eds), *The new institutionalism in organizational analysis*. Chicago: University of Chicago Press, 108–40.

Skjærseth, J.B., and Wettestad, J. (2008). *EU emissions trading: initiation, decision-making and implementation*. Aldershot, Hampshire: Ashgate.

Svendsen, G.T. (1999). 'The idea of global CO_2 trade'. *European Environment*, 9(6): 232–7.

Thévenot, L. (2001). 'Organized complexity. Conventions of coordination of economic arrangements'. *European Journal of Social Theory*, 4(4): 405–25.

Thévenot, L., Moody, M., and Lafaye, C. (2000). 'Forms of valuing nature: arguments and modes of justification in French and American environmental disputes', in M. Lamont and L. Thévenot (eds), *Rethinking comparative cultural sociology: repertoires of evaluation in France and the United States*. Cambridge: Cambridge University Press, 229–72.

Thornton, P., and Ocasio, W. (1999). 'Institutional logics and the historical contingency of power in organizations: executive succession in the higher education publishing industry, 1958–1990'. *American Journal of Sociology*, 105(3): 801–43.

Thornton, P.H. (2002). 'The rise of the corporation in craft industry: conflict and conformity in institutional logics'. *Academy of Management Journal*, 45(1): 81–101.

Thornton, P.H., and Ocasio, W. (2008). 'Institutional logics', in R. Greenwood, C. Oliver, R. Suddaby, and K. Sahlin (eds), *The Sage handbook of organizational institutionalism*. Los Angeles: Sage, 99–129.

Voß, J.-P. (2007). 'Innovation processes in governance: the development of "emissions trading" as a new policy instrument'. *Science and Public Policy*, 34(5): 329–43.

Wurzel, R.K. (2002). *Environmental policy-making in Britain, Germany and the European Union. The Europeanisation of air and water pollution control*. Manchester: Manchester University Press.

26

Managing Illicit Flows

The Formation of Global Anti-money Laundering Regulations

Anja P. Jakobi

Introduction

Since the late 1980s, anti-money laundering activities have become a widely disseminated means to fight different sorts of crime, ranging from drug trafficking to corruption or terrorism financing.[1] As one consequence, financial institutions and related professions are currently confronted with strict regulations related to, for instance, due diligence or auditing. While states and firms are pressured to introduce and implement these standards, it is less known that these actually originate mainly from a United States effort to internationalize its national regulations. Anti-money laundering standards were thus transferred from a specific national context to the international level, to be subsequently implemented in other places. Like many other managerial ideas, anti-money laundering policies have since become daily practice in organizations around the world (Drori, Meyer, and Hwang 2006).

While the prevention and prosecution of crime is rarely brought together with studies of globalization and management, global crime governance has become a growing domain of international activity and includes many processes that institutionalist researchers know from other domains (e.g., Djelic and Quack 2010; Djelic and Sahlin-Andersson 2006; Meyer, Boli, Thomas, and Ramirez 1997). Policies and practices related to crime diffuse along professional communities and via international organizations. For instance, police cooperation has led to common professional principles and working methods, widely irrespective of official diplomatic agreements (Andreas and Nadelmann 2006; Deflem 2002; Nadelmann 1993). Crime has also become an increasingly important topic in the United Nations and other international forums, signifying world society formation in this field (Jakobi 2013). Important ideas in this context are transparency, accountability, control, and oversight. Like other social activities, crime is to be managed and handled along templates of best practice. Current crime control thus shows both a rationalization paradigm and an inherent globalization tendency (Drori 2008; Drori and Krücken 2009). Consequently, the worldwide spread of anti-money laundering policies is a prime example of a globalizing managerial idea related to crime, and against an institutionalist background, it represents yet another example of worldwide diffusion and convergence.

However, given a broad variety of adopters and the restricted uniformity of fighting money laundering, the regionalization of anti-money laundering efforts in particular represents an international translation and editing process, leading to partly different emphases in implementing regulations on the national level (Sahlin and Wedlin 2008: 219–20). Moreover, and unlike many other contributions that analyze worldwide diffusion primarily with regard to the consequences, I also emphasize the sources of institutional change, outlining how a regulation was transferred from a national to an international standard, disseminated across world regions, and implemented on the national and organizational level. Colleagues have shown in detail how difficult the editing process is on the level of banks, and how actors struggle in sense-making and conforming to the expected standard (Svedberg Helgesson 2011; Svedberg Helgesson and Mörth 2012). Yet, focusing on the interaction of regional and global activities tackles a level that is often neglected in diffusion-related research, whose focus is often either on the global or the national level. International regions, however, can act as a translating and editing device to global standards, too.

Central elements of the global diffusion process have been the United States and the Financial Action Taskforce (FATF). The taskforce represents a networked form of meta-organization (Brunsson and Ahrne, chapter 3), assembling different states, regional organizations, and other public bodies relevant in the fight against money laundering. While the United States used the FATF to establish a global standard, the organization has since delivered prototypes of how money laundering should be fought. These models, in turn, have been used as templates for regional action. Editing and translation processes occur at different levels; on the one hand, regional organizations try to translate their global rules to the regional context, editing the templates. Moreover, specific countries need to translate these rules to national regulations and oversight mechanisms, while banks and other financial institutions need to translate and edit these national and regional regulations into their daily practice. Therefore, fighting money laundering also provides an important case of global–local regulatory interactions (see Quack, chapter 23).

Anti-money Laundering as a Global Managerial Idea

In its basic form, money laundering represents the process by which the criminal origin of money is hidden by converting it to an income that seems to be generated by licit activity (Reuter and Truman 2004). Managerial ideas related to prevention and prosecution of money laundering mainly concern banks, related financial institutions, and professions. These are subjected to a growing number of due diligence requirements, 'know your customer principles', risk assessments, and the obligation to report suspicious activities. Money laundering typically takes place in three steps: placement, layering, and integration. In the placement phase, the origin of the money transferred to the legal economy is hidden. In the layering phase, the money is transferred across different bank accounts in several countries, preferably those with lax banking regulations. In the integration phase, the money appears fully detached from its origin and use, and related transactions do not raise any suspicion.

These money-laundering schemes can be highly complex and typically involve several jurisdictions. International efforts have thus been targeted at increasing information exchange about money laundering, criminalizing such activities worldwide, and enhancing the cooperation of authorities. While the regulations used to fight money laundering have been expended significantly over time, the very definition of what money laundering is has also changed. Early discussions on money laundering analyzed it mainly as a 'support crime' linked to predicate offenses like drug trafficking. This strategy aimed to diminish the economic revenue of illicit activities, thus making them less attractive (Levi 2002; Reuter and Truman 2004; Tsingou 2010). Since 2001, the notion of money laundering has been enlarged to cover the financing of terrorism (Gardner 2007). Today, international mandates related to money laundering also include work on proliferation financing, tax evasion, maritime piracy, or human trafficking (FATF, 2008, 2010, 2011a, 2011b). Fighting money laundering, therefore, has become a nearly universal weapon in fighting other crimes, too. Accordingly, the implementation of these regulations is accompanied by a sense of urgency, as money laundering became 'securitized' (e.g., Svedberg Helgesson and Mörth 2012).

The basic managerial idea related to anti-money laundering aims to bring transparency and accountability in a formerly widely unregulated global banking system. Illicit flows are to be prevented or to be found worldwide, and any national regulatory loophole would threaten the success of the overall regulatory aim. In that sense, anti-money laundering policies are intrinsically linked to worldwide organizational change and to the globalization of common standards in the financial sector. Studies of global governance have frequently analyzed anti-money laundering policies as a crucial case for global public policy (Reinicke 1997: 135–72). Some analyses present the FATF primarily as a forum that disseminates policy problems (Hülsse 2007; Hülsse and Kerwer 2007), while others point to its creation and the important influence of powerful states (Simmons 2000; Drezner 2007; Roberge 2009). Recent work analyzes the activities of the FATF, for example, with regard to persuasion processes, but also on how power is executed within the network (Kerwer and Hülsse 2011; Nance 2011; Sharman 2008). As research shows, there is an important linkage between power and policy diffusion, which implies that powerful states coerce smaller countries to adopt the new standard (Sharman 2011). Anti-money laundering, thus, is not only a managerial idea but is also related to criminal law and backed by governmental support. States introduce policies and organizations for oversight. At the same time, banks and other financial institutions are required to implement these standards, supporting the governmental aim to prevent crime. The management of financial flows and the governmental aim of crime control thus go hand in hand. The study of globalizing anti-money laundering regulations needs to consider the attractiveness of rationalized managerial ideas and the coercive power of nation states. This twinning is already visible in the very first stages of the rising global standard against money laundering, starting in the United States.

From National to International Standards

The process by which global anti-money laundering standards were set up actually provide a typical case of institutional entrepreneurship, known from other cases in which large-scale change is triggered by specific actors and their strategic activity (e.g., Beckert 1999; Bernard Leca, Battilana, and Boxenbaum 2008; Leca and Naccache 2006). The first and most visible step in international standard-setting was the establishment of the FATF in 1989 by the G7 countries. Formally proposed by the French who had the presidency of the G7, the meeting was preceded by background preparation of the Americans, including visits of foreign delegations to Washington. The FATF was financed by special contributions, leaving the United States contributing around 25 percent of the budget. From the very beginning, the country played a crucial role in the establishment and development of the FATF (see e.g., Roberge 2009; Simmons 2000). The United States has a history of engagement against transnational organized crime, which also enhanced its standing as a serious and powerful country in this respect; examples are the war against drugs, but also law enforcement exchange, anti-corruption, and many other policy areas (Abbott and Snidal 2002; Andreas and

Nadelmann 2006; Friesendorf 2007). The country's willingness to change the global field with regard to money laundering, its resources, and expertise were important preconditions of successful institutional entrepreneurship.

The American efforts against money laundering date back to the 1970 Bank Secrecy Act, which established customer identification measures for all bank accounts (Levi 1991: 249). Since the Money Laundering Control Act in 1986, money laundering has been criminalized; this was followed by several other acts that aim at fighting this offense (Alford 1993/1994; Reuter and Truman 2004: 45–105, 118). Part of the 1986 legislation was the requirement that the Chairman of the Federal Reserve Bank had to consult with other central banks about the problem of money laundering and the responsibility of banks. After initial reluctance on the part of other banking chairmen, the Basel Committee on Banking Supervision finally issued a statement in 1988 that mentioned the importance of knowing the customer, avoiding suspicious transactions, and cooperating with law enforcement (Reuter and Truman 2004: 80). The US Federal Bank initiated and prepared this statement (General Accounting Office 1991: 61). Throughout these years, Congress also pressured the government to establish an effective, worldwide regulation regarding banking secrecy and money laundering.

The United States aimed to establish an international level of fighting money laundering, at times when very few other countries were actually concerned with this issue. Multilateral efforts were needed because bi-lateral treaties would not provide enough regulatory convergence to American laws. Also, sanctions within such treaties would be highly problematic to be enforced effectively, even if they were considered necessary (General Accounting Office 1991: 56). Since the banking sector operates internationally, financial transactions are directed to the place that offers the most favorable conditions. Burdens that result from anti-money laundering regulations are less confidentiality and bank secrecy, as well as costs linked to the surveillance process (Alford 1993/1994). Both factors may result in clients opting for countries with another regulatory regime. Fighting money laundering is thus not necessarily appreciated, and countries with a large banking sector, like offshore financial centers, may profit significantly from less strict regulation. This results in difficulties for regulators and banks in other countries.

Moreover, the internationalization of standards was perceptible to the United States, since it had a history of unsuccessful trials to enforce its national laws in other territories. In the early 1980s, the country attempted to apply its anti-money laundering regulations—particularly access to financial information—to banks with branches in the Caribbean region. After denial, an American court fixed nearly USD 2 million as court charges, combined with a threat to freeze American assets of the bank. International protest at that time prevented the country from establishing this strategy. However, the United States made tariff concessions in the framework of the Caribbean Basin Initiative dependent on cooperation against money laundering (Helleiner 1999: 73). By setting a global standard, anti-money laundering issues would no longer be perceived as a national regulation only, but as a global concern. Any sanctions, in consequence, would be multilateral in terms of underlying reasons and applicable instruments.

Reaching such multilateral agreement against money laundering has been a core function of the FATF. In crime governance and other fields of foreign policy, the United States follows a pragmatic and case-specific approach, choosing multilateral strategies when they appear to be reasonable and picking those forums that seem to be most promising for its policy goals (Foot, MacFarlane, and Mastanduno 2003: 266; Luck 2003: 27–8, 47). Crime has been a major policy issue in the United States, from Nixon's War on Drugs onward, gaining further momentum throughout the 1990s. The case of initiating anti-money laundering regulations in the American-dominated G7 was a case of pragmatism and strategic reasoning, using a soft governance form of networking to establish a wide-ranging global regulation in those countries that are close to or even hosting large banking centers. At the same time, crime prevention and prosecution was not an entirely new topic for the G7. The meetings had already worked on crime governance during the 1980s. Internal working groups, most prominently the so-called Lyon Group and the Rome Group, developed policy proposals against transnational crime, also with a view to spreading these to other international forums (Scherrer 2009).

In addition, the US also found a field that was particularly perceptive to anti-money laundering issues. The establishment of global anti-money laundering regulations is connected to the late 1980s and early 1990s, in particular the growth and integration of global financial markets. These markets not only provide opportunities for capital with licit sources, but also for gains derived from illicit activities, in particular, organized crime. This problem became particularly obvious in the early 1990s, with a major scandal linked to the Bank of Credit and Commerce International (Simmons 2000: 244–5249).

Global Standard-setting: Managerialism and Prototypes

As a central body for discussing and developing anti-money laundering measures, the G7 countries established the FATF in 1989. Today, the organization has 34 country members—mostly of the industrialized world—plus the European Union and the Gulf Cooperation Council. The basic instruments of the FATF are standard-setting, coordination, and the dissemination of ideas on how to counter money laundering. The standards are the so-called 'Forty Recommendations', a set of guidelines for how countries and the private sector should fight money laundering. Initially published in 1990, they have been revised several times and have been supplemented by nine 'Special Recommendations' that deal with the financing of terrorism (Gardner 2007: 329–32). The recommendations cover four main areas. They are concerned with the legal system, targeted at criminalizing money laundering nationally. They also list measures to be taken by financial institutions and the related non-financial sector. Moreover, they elaborate on institutional preconditions and further measures to prevent money laundering, and they regulate international cooperation (FATF 2003). Following new trends and political aims, the recommendations have been revised several times, most recently to include tax evasion.

Like the FATF itself, the recommendations are a soft form of governance because they are formally non-binding. However, they have become the central reference source for other international attempts to fight money laundering (e.g., by the European Union or the United Nations) and they are linked to a rigorous review process. FATF members are required to submit self-assessments and to undertake peer reviews by other members. Sanctions include reporting on the deficiencies in FATF meetings, missions sent to the country, or even the binding request to banks to pay special attention to all financial transactions related to a specific country. Finally, membership status can be revoked (FATF 2008: 2; Gardner 2007: 333; Levi and Gilmore 2002: 96). However, not just members are targeted: FATF members monitor all countries for compliance to these standards, culminating in the non-cooperative countries and territories (NCCT) process, whose first report was issued in 2000 and included a list of countries that seemed non-compliant to the recommendations. The process was a public 'naming and shaming' approach towards non-members, supplemented by counter-measures and sanctions (FATF 2000: 7–9). While the FATF justified the monitoring through the global nature of the money laundering problem and the vulnerability of the financial system to only a few non-compliant countries, the process essentially meant that a club of countries assesses non-member compliance to its own rules (FATF 2000: 1; Levi and Gilmore 2002: 103–4). In particular, the obvious political component in judging countries was a key point (Tsingou 2010: 623).

In addition, the FATF studies trends and methods in international money laundering and publishes typologies, a collection of incidents that are assumed to represent typical money laundering schemes (FATF 2005: 1–2). By doing so, the regulations against money laundering are supplemented with narratives about money laundering, and templates to fight this crime are developed. Several plenary sessions take place during the year, where the FATF discusses regulations, implementation, and reports. Attendees are financial regulators, law enforcement representatives, and civil servants from national Treasury or Justice Departments (Levi and Gilmore 2002: 95). The different audiences bring in their experiences on money laundering, but are themselves part of a professionalization exercise, given that professional norms and knowledge are developed and disseminated on these meetings.

In fact, by creating the FATF, the US and its allies created a central body that promotes global anti-money laundering standards. By choosing a forum—the G7—where countries would not deny support, a legitimate international authority was created that worked on an issue where knowledge was sparse, linked to other severe crimes (drugs), which was difficult to counter, even for OECD countries with huge banking sectors. The formally non-binding work of the FATF secured the influence of those countries that were particularly interested in pushing the issue forward by expertise and financial support. Additionally, the uncertainty but urgency linked to money laundering has been an important precondition for establishing an international body against money laundering. Strategies like framing—linking money laundering to serious crimes—or the use of alliances and cooperation, as well as the authority and legitimacy of the United States in preventing and punishing crime, all supported the creation of the FATF.

Regionalization and Translation

While the FATF set a global standard, the establishment of so-called FATF-style regional bodies (FSRBs) led to further implementation efforts at the regional level. FSRBs are regional networks of states in which the implementation of FATF recommendations are monitored, in a similar style as is done in the FATF itself. The regional networks have been established since the 1990s, with a growing number and increasing coverage of countries in any region of the world. In almost all cases, they are single standing organizations or formalized networks. Usually, being a member country of the FSRB goes hand in hand with acknowledging the 'Forty Recommendations' and the procedures of the respective regional organization. It represents a one-way street, in which the FATF sets regulations which are subsequently implemented by regional bodies under consideration of local specificities.

The differentiation of the global FATF and the regional FSRBs allows for an effective and regionally differentiated strategy in implementing universal standards. By this regional expansion, the original small group of countries concerned with establishing the global standard against money laundering successively grew over time and now involves nearly every state worldwide. And even if new states come into existence, like the former Netherlands Antilles Curacao and St Martin, they are connected to these regional bodies within weeks (CFATF 2010a). All in all, these organizations work as a translating device to discuss the implementation of the global standards in a regional context, and for this purpose, some regional bodies have also issued additional recommendations. Table 26.1

Table 26.1 Global and regional standard-setting against money laundering

Organization	Region	Year established	Member countries
FATF	Global	1989	34
APG	Asia	1997	41
CFATF	Caribbean	1990	29
EAG	Eurasia	2004	9
ESAAMLG	South-East Africa	1999	15
GABAC	Central Africa	2000	6
GAFISUD	South America	2000	12
GIABA	West Africa	1999	15
MENAFATF	Northern Africa and Middle East	2004	18
Moneyval	Europe	1997	30

Notes: Based on the organizations' websites. Data refers to December 2011 (GABAC: June 2012).
Multiple memberships are possible.
Moneyval is a committee of the Council of Europe.

shows the global expansion of anti-money laundering standards by the growing number of regional organizations. Today, nearly all countries worldwide are members of one or more of these organizations, and they are regularly added as associates or observers to the FATF, most recently the GABAC (FATF 2012b).

This regionalization is interesting in two different, yet interrelated respects: translation and strategy. While the FATF recommendations aim to represent the global standard, regional differences exist that make implementation of some recommendations more difficult than others. For instance, many African countries do not have formal banking systems but rely on informal Hawala banking (Lindley 2009; Sharma 2006). In such cases, money is transferred without clear receipt and is completely trust-based. Such systems represent a great challenge to the Western idea of transparency and accountability embodied in global anti-money laundering standards. Accordingly, while FATF regulations aim to manage Hawala systems, too, actual specification work is much more pronounced in the African region than in others (e.g., MENAFATF 2005).

With a view to strategy, regionalization represents a top-down strategy aimed to implement regionally what has been decided on the global level, not as some sort of bottom-up process. Regional organizations are influenced by FATF members through a variety of means, like formal decision-making, financing, or technical assistance. The Caribbean regional organization provides a particularly suitable example of such influence. This organization has been supported from its very beginning by non-member countries. Its founding meeting was attended by five FATF members that were also donors to the process of building the organization: the United States, Canada, the Netherlands, France, and the United Kingdom (CFATF 1995: 5). A meeting in Aruba gave rise to the organization two years before its official founding in 1992 (Richards 1999: 233–7). As the US General Accounting Office (1991: 62) reported:

> [...] the United States is cooperating with several countries in a Caribbean region anti-money-laundering initiative. Participants at a June 1990 conference agreed to propose

that their governments adopt the 40 Financial Action Task Force recommendations, supplemented with 21 draft recommendations (tailored to the region) developed at the conference.

The CFATF was thus based on an external initiative. Given repeated attempts to cooperate with Caribbean countries in the 1980s, the United States had a strong interest in the formation of such a group and the acknowledgement of common standards against money laundering. Over many years, the United States and other donor countries funded the secretariat and its operations, often providing funds that exceeded the annual membership contributions multiple times (CFATF 1999: 11). Nonetheless, the organization has long had difficulties in raising membership fees, which resulted in a shortfall of around USD 300,000 in 2007 (CFATF 2007: 24). While this has led some to doubt about the commitment to anti-money laundering, countries have pointed to their stressed economies and their status as developing countries (CFATF 2009: 49–50). After a crisis in its operations in 2010, the organization decided to introduce sanctions if members did not fulfill their obligations (CFATF 2010b).

CFATF and its donor countries provide an important example of how regional efforts are widely dependent on external support. Donors have financed the organization and provided technical assistance, personnel, and policy advice. Other cases, like the Asian Pacific regional organization, show that the large share of organizational funding and sponsoring of events is paid by those countries that have supported the establishment of the global regulation in the first place. Active participation, in whatever form, is an important element in institutional entrepreneurship. Contributing resources and expertise, as well as coalition-building and burden-sharing with like-minded states, are elements of such a strategy. The United States and other countries have effectively placed anti-money laundering on agendas worldwide by first creating a global standard and then making significant investments in its regional implementation and oversight.

Implementing Anti-money Laundering in Countries and Organizations

It is an interesting twist to the global regulation of money laundering that these global standards are formally non-binding; they do not represent 'hard law' in the classical sense of inter-state contracts. All global, regional, and national managerialism related to money laundering has sprung from a voluntary initiative. Yet the reliance on these 'soft' rules nonetheless bears important consequences, based on informal information exchange among countries and, ultimately, banks. One example of this process has been the case of the Banco Delta Asia in Macao. Relying on anti-terrorism law, the United States accused the bank—by reference to classified data—of supporting the North Korean government in acquiring weapons of mass destruction. In 2007, international banks were voluntarily called not to trade any dollars with the institute, which they stopped and which quickly led the bank to near collapse and marked it as an international pariah of the financial system within a few weeks (Gaylord 2008). The globalization of anti-money laundering standards thus also meant that enforcement of criminal regulations is greatly enhanced, even in cases where guilt is not proven. Global rules are applied locally and cross-nationally and can be effective even if they are not obligatory.

However, the implementation of anti-money laundering standards goes far beyond these single cases. Looking at the world today, anti-money laundering efforts are abundant. Related legislation or institutions are part of nearly all states worldwide, as customers have to fill

Managing Illicit Flows

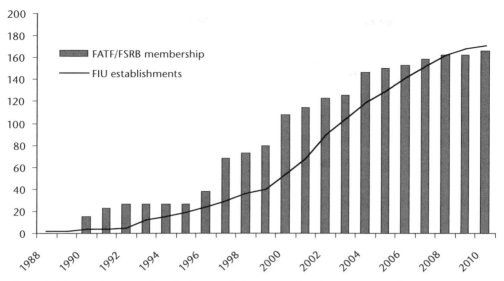

Figure 26.1 Anti-money laundering regulations and related organizational change

out forms and banks submit suspicious transaction records. An important element of these implementation efforts is the establishment of Financial Intelligence Units (FIUs). These organizations are established as oversight bodies, for example, to ensure that banks follow anti-money laundering regulations, or to investigate suspicious transactions.

Figure 26.1 shows the change of national regulations and related organizational innovation. FATF or FSRB membership is accompanied by the acknowledgement of the recommendations and subsequent translation into practice. At the same time, the spread of Financial Intelligence Units shows that these regulations are not only law in books, but triggered new regulatory oversight in countries worldwide. In line with the growth of anti-money laundering efforts, these units have spread worldwide with an accelerating speed. They were first established in Australia and Norway in 1998, followed by the United States and France in 1990, later increasing to 173 countries by 2010.

While Financial Intelligence Units are diffused worldwide, they can follow four different models in how they actually execute surveillance of the financial sector (International Monetary Fund and World Bank 2004: 10–17). The administrative model provides a buffer between financial institutions and law enforcement, channeling financial information received to different agencies that are responsible for regulatory implementation or punishment. A second type is the law enforcement model. In this case, the organization is attached to an existing police unit, relies on its own policing capacities, and investigates money laundering attempts and crimes. The third model is a judicial unit, which is more common with a continental law system. Prosecutors in this case have direct access to the information on financial activities and can initiate and oversee investigations. The fourth type of Financial Intelligence Units is hybrid and embodies different elements of the other three types. The early units of Australia, the United States, and France have been set up following an administrative model, and to date, this category is the predominant model.

The establishment of Financial Intelligence Units was initially only a by-product of anti-money laundering efforts, but since 2003, FATF recommendations refer to the operation of such an organization. Their operation and establishment is an important organizational innovation in countries around the world and are nowadays also mentioned in binding international conventions relating to terrorism, transnational organized crime, or corruption. Their significance has been reached due to the so-called Egmont group as well (International Monetary Fund and World Bank 2004: 19). This group is the worldwide organization of Financial Intelligence Units, formed in Brussels in 1995, at a joint American and Belgian initiative (Gilmore 2004: 71). The group represents a further global network in which practices related to anti-money laundering are developed, exchanged, and translated into daily practice.

However, the widespread introduction of FIUs suggests a homogenization that is not fully justified. While major changes in banking are clearly visible, like the abolishment of anonymous bank accounts that used to exist in Switzerland or Austria, there is still much variance in country compliance. Even as many FATF reviews report, countries still vary widely in how extensively they actually implement the standards in legal and practical terms. For instance, although being a FATF member, Turkey has repeatedly been reported to be non-compliant. The FATF also still publishes a list of countries that are seen as being problematic in terms of effective implementation; this list is currently headed by Iran and North Korea because of loopholes in tracing financing of terrorism and proliferation (FATF 2012a).

But the implementation of global anti-money laundering policies does not stop at the level of countries and their translation of global and regional rules. Equally important, FATF standards directly affect financial institutions and professions. While it is difficult to compare all addressees that are formally affected by the changing legislative environment, research has shown that anti-money laundering standards, often in interplay with the national surveillance by Financial Intelligence Units, provoked important changes within banks (Bergström, Svedberg Helgesson, and Mörth 2011; Svedberg Helgesson 2011). In particular, the so-called risk-based approach, a concept according to which financial institutions need to monitor whether clients show suspicious behavior, has led to high insecurity in banks. In fact, the local implementation of anti-money laundering regulations means that banks take over policing tasks that go far beyond their usual business and might even infringe customer relationships with non-criminal clients. The global regulations against money laundering are actually implemented by people whose core competence is not policing and risk assessment with regard to criminal activity, but banking and risk assessment of financial opportunities. The translation of ideas related to crime prevention in business contexts is challenging and causes high insecurity at the individual and organizational level. And such difficulties only concern banks that are actually eager to employ these standards. In many other cases, interest in large amounts of money can actually prevail over the regulatory aims (Sharman 2011). As in other cases of glocalization, the implementing organization faces a variety of choices to be made when dealing with the external regulation (see Abu-Shark, chapter 18; Knill and Tosun, chapter 19; other contributions in part IV of this volume).

Conclusions: globalizing anti-money laundering

All in all, we can distinguish different phases of globalizing anti-money laundering as management practice. In the first phase, American practices were transferred to the international level, resulting in global standards promoted by the FATF. In the second phase, these standards were expanded by regionalizing them in different forums. In a third stage, implementation has led to changes on the national level (like Financial Intelligence Units) and the very local level (banks). While the earlier stages appear to be a 'success story' of globalization, implementation shows the typical problems related to translation and contextualization. This implies that globalization of local management practices could be less difficult than the local implementation of global management regulations (see Quack, chapter 23). The abstractness of global templates is likely to support the latter, while the specific need to act in a concrete situation makes conflicts more apparent.

Resuming the international activities against money laundering, the large-scale change is obvious. Within only 20 years, the global field has changed massively, from only some countries that aimed to prevent money laundering, to a global network and wide-ranging policy change. The outcome is a growing awareness of banks and other financial institutions concerning money laundering, related monitoring of transactions, and the worldwide proliferation of Financial Intelligence Units. It has taken about two decades, financial investment, and many other tools for establishing international exchange, regulation, and enforcement to the current level, but it has ultimately been highly successful in terms of change. Unlike many cases of diffusion via different channels, global anti-money laundering regulation follows a clear pattern of strategic activity. The attractiveness of a managerial ideal—the oversight of financial flows—has been brought together with the American aim to establish such regulation across countries. As a result, anti-money laundering practices have been globalized and today represent a worldwide managerial template backed by criminal law.

Yet, the case of the FATF also shows a further limit of globalized managerial efforts. While global networking, increased information exchange, and visible policy change might look like a success story, it is not necessarily guaranteed that money laundering is nowadays easy to prevent and detect. The issue of reliable data on money laundering remains salient. The current FATF mandate contains references to cost-benefit analyses and global threat assessments (FATF 2008: 3). The mandate's first version even called explicitly for 'the FATF [to] also increase its efforts to become the authoritative source of data/information on money laundering and terrorist financing issues' (FATF 2004: 3). So far, then, all activities have led to a highly developed structure, but it is still unclear how much this actually helps prevent money laundering or how large the problem of money laundering actually is. From a theoretical perspective, this indeterminacy has an important side effect. As organization sociologists acknowledge, organizations are influenced by diffusion processes in the field that have unclear goals, as well as outcomes that are difficult to assess (DiMaggio and Powell 1983). From such a perspective, the success of establishing an anti-money laundering structure might be closely linked to its insecure outcomes. We could expect those areas to flourish on the global level, where the actual policy outcome is most difficult to detect—and perhaps not even exist. These conditions are likely to provide important reasons for ongoing managerialism. The relationship between globalization and management ideas thus deserves further attention.

Note

1 This chapter partly draws on research presented in Jakobi (2013).

References

Abbott, K.W., and Snidal, D. (2002). 'Values and interests: international legalization on the fight against corruption'. *Journal of Legal Studies, 31*(1): S141-S178.
Alford, D.E. (1993/1994). 'Anti-money laundering regulations: a burden on financial institutions'. *North Carolina Journal of International Law and Commercial Regulation, 19*: 437–68.

Andreas, P., and Nadelmann, E. (2006). *Policing the globe. Criminalization and crime control in international relations*. Oxford: Oxford University Press.

Beckert, J. (1999). 'Agency, entrepreneurs, and institutional change. The role of strategic choice and institutionalized practices in organizations'. *Organization Studies, 20*(5): 777–99.

Bergström, M., Svedberg Helgesson, K., and Mörth, U. (2011). 'A new role for for-profit actors? The case of anti-money laundering and risk management'. *Journal of Common Market Studies, 49*: 1–22.

CFATF. (1995). *Annual Report 1994–1995*. Online at http://www.cfatf-gafic.org/reports-a-documents/cat_view/22-english/23-annual-reports.html?start=10, last access in February 2011.

CFATF. (1999). *Annual Report 1998–1999*. Online at http://www.cfatf-gafic.org/reports-a-documents/cat_view/22-english/23-annual-reports.html?start=10, last access in February 2011.

CFATF. (2007). *Annual Report 2006–2007*. Online at http://www.cfatf-gafic.org/reports-a-documents/cat_view/22-english/23-annual-reports.html?start=10, last access in February 2011.

CFATF. (2009). *Annual Report 2008–2009*. Online at http://www.cfatf-gafic.org/reports-a-documents/cat_view/22-english/23-annual-reports.html?start=10, last access in February 2011.

CFATF. (2010a). *Curacoa and St. Maarten joins the CFATF*. Online at http://www.cfatf-gafic.org/component/content/article/18-content/419-curacao-and-st-maarten-joins-the-cfatf.html, last access in February 2011.

CFATF (ed.). (2010b). *Media release November 2010*. Online at http://www.cfatf-gafic.org/press-releases/425.html?task=view, last access in February 2011.

Deflem, M. (2002). *Policing world society: historical foundations of international police cooperation*. Oxford: Clarendon.

DiMaggio, P.J., and Powell, W.W. (1983). 'The iron cage revisited: institutional isomorphism and collective rationality in organizational fields'. *American Sociological Review, 48*(April): 147–60.

Djelic, M.-L., and Quack, S. (eds). (2010). *Transnational communities: shaping global economic governance*. Cambridge: Cambridge University Press.

Djelic, M.-L., and Sahlin-Andersson, K. (eds). (2006). *Transnational governance. Institutional dynamics of regulation*. Cambridge: Cambridge University Press.

Drezner, D. (2007). *All politics is global*. Princeton, NJ: Princeton University Press.

Drori, G.S. (2008). 'Institutionalism and globalization studies', in R. Greenwood, C. Oliver, K. Sahlin, and R. Suddaby (eds), *The Sage handbook of organizational institutionalism*. Thousand Oaks: Sage, 449–72.

Drori, G.S., and Krücken, G. (2009). 'World society: a theory and a research program in context', in G. Krücken and G.S. Drori (eds), *World society. The writing of John W. Meyer*. Oxford: Oxford University Press, 3–35.

Drori, G.S., Meyer, J.W., and Hwang, H. (eds). (2006). *Globalization and organization. World society and organizational change*. Oxford: Oxford University Press.

FATF. (2000). *Report on non-cooperative countries and territories*. Retrieved from http://www1.oecd.org/fatf/pdf/NCCT_en.pdf.

FATF. (2003). *The forty recommendations. 20 June 2003 (with the amendments of 22 October 2004)*. Paris: FATF.

FATF. (2004). *Mandate for the future of the FATF (September 2004–December 2012)*. Online at http://www.fatf-gafi.org/dataoecd/14/60/36309648.pdf, last access August 2008.

FATF. (2005). *Money laundering and terrorist financing typologies 2004–2005*. Paris: FATF/OECD.

FATF. (2008). *FATF revised mandate 2008–2012*. Online at http://www.fatf-gafi.org/dataoecd/3/32/40433653.pdf, last access August 2008.

FATF. (2010). *Consultation paper: the review of the standards–preparation for the 4th round of mutual evaluations*. Paris: FATF/OECD.

FATF. (2011a). *FATF report: organised maritime piracy and related kidnapping for ransom*. Paris: FATF.

FATF. (2011b). *Money laundering risks arising from trafficking in human beings and smuggling of migrants*. Paris: FATF.

FATF. (2012a). *FATF public statement. 16 February 2012*. Online at http://www.fatf-gafi.org/topics/high-riskandnon-cooperativejurisdictions/documents/fatfpublicstatement-16february2012.html, last access in June 2012.

FATF. (2012b). *Outcomes of the plenary meeting of the FATF, Paris, 15–17 February 2012*. Online at http://www.fatf-gafi.org/documents/repository/outcomesoftheplenarymeetingofthefatfparis15-17february2012.html, last access in June 2012.

Foot, R., MacFarlane, S.N., and Mastanduno, M. (2003). 'Conclusion: instrumental multilateralism in US foreign policy', in R. Foot, S.N. MacFarlane, and M. Mastanduno (eds), *US Hegemony and International Organizations*. Oxford: Oxford University Press, 265–72.

Friesendorf, C. (2007). *US foreign policy and the war on drugs. Displacing the cocaine and heroine industry*. London and New York: Routledge.

Gardner, K.L. (2007). 'Fighting terrorism the FATF way'. *Global Governance, 13*(3): 325–45.

Gaylord, M.S. (2008). 'The Banco Delta Asia affair: the USA Patriot Act and allegations of money laundering in Macau'. *Crime Law and Social Change, 50*(4–5): 293–305.

General Accounting Office. (1991). *Report to the chairman, subcommittee on terrorism, narcotics and international operations, committee on foreign relations, U.S. Senate: money laundering. The U.S. government is responding to the problem*. Washington: GAO.

Gilmore, W.C. (2004). *Dirty money. The evolution of international measures to counter money laundering and the financing of terrorism* (3rd edn). Strasbourg: Council of Europe.

Helleiner, E. (1999). 'State power and the regulation of illicit activity in global finance', in H.R. Friman and P. Andreas (eds), *The illicit global economy and state power*. Lanham: Rowmann and Littlefield, 53–90.

Hülsse, R. (2007). 'Creating the demand for global governance: the making of a global money-laundering problem'. *Global Society, 21*(2): 155–78.

Hülsse, R., and Kerwer, D. (2007). 'Global standards in action: insights from anti-money laundering regulations'. *Organization, 14*(5): 625–42.

International Monetary Fund and World Bank. (2004). *Financial intelligence units: an overview*. Washington: World Bank.

Jakobi, A.P. (2013). *Common goods and evils? The formation of global crime governance*. Oxford: Oxford University Press.

Kerwer, D., and Hülsse, R. (2011). 'How international organizations rule the world: the case of the financial action task force on money laundering'. *Journal of International Organization Studies, 2*(1): 50–67.

Leca, B., and Naccache, P. (2006). 'A critical realist approach to institutional entrepreneurship'. *Organization, 13*(5): 627–51.

Leca, B., Battilana, J., and Boxenbaum, E. (2008). 'Agency and institutions: a review of institutional entrepreneurship'. Harvard Business School Working Paper. Cambridge, MA: Harvard Business School.

Levi, M. (1991). Pecunia non Olet: cleansing the money launderers from the temple. *Crime Law and Social Change, 16*(3): 217–302.

Levi, M. (2002). 'Money laundering and its regulation'. *The Annals of the American Academy of Political and Social Science, 582*(1): 181–94.

Levi, M., and Gilmore, W. (2002). 'Terrorist finance, money laundering and the rise mutual evaluation: a new paradigm for crime control?' in M. Pieth (ed.), *Financing terrorism*. Doordrecht: Springer, 87–114.

Lindley, A. (2009). 'Between "dirty money" and "development capital": Somali money transfer infrastructure under global scrutiny'. *African Affairs, 108*(433): 519–39.

Luck, E.C. (2003). 'American exceptionalism and international organization: lessons from the 1990s', in R. Foot, S.N. MacFarlane, and M. Mastanduno (eds), *US hegemony and international organizations*. Oxford: Oxford University Press, 25–48.

MENAFATF. (2005). *Best practices on Hawala*. Online at http://www.menafatf.org/Linkcounter.asp?rid=646andattached=best%20practices%20on%20Hawala.pdf, last access in May 2010.

Meyer, J.W., Boli, J., Thomas, G.M., and Ramirez, F.O. (1997). 'World society and the nation-state'. *American Journal of Sociology, 103*(1): 144–81.

Nadelmann, E.A. (1993). *Cops across borders. The internationalization of U.S. criminal law enforcement*. University Park, Pennsylvania: University Press.

Nance, M. (2011). 'The power of persuasion'. Manuscript. Raleigh, February 2011.

Reinicke, W.H. (1997). 'Global public policy'. *Foreign Affairs,* 76(6): 127–38.

Reuter, P., and Truman, E.M. (2004). *Chasing dirty money. The fight against money laundering.* Washington: Institute for International Economics.

Richards, J.R. (1999). *Transnational criminal organizations, cybercrime and money laundering. A handbook for law enforcement officers, auditors and financial investigators.* Boca Raton: CRC Press.

Roberge, I. (2009). 'Bringing the United States back in: a response to Rainer Hülse's "Creating demand for global governance"'. *Global Society,* 23(2): 177–81.

Sahlin, K., and Wedlin, L. (2008). 'Circulating ideas: imitation, translation and editing', in R. Greenwood, C. Oliver, K. Sahlin, and R. Suddaby (eds), *The Sage handbook of organizational institutionalism.* Thousand Oaks: Sage, 218–42.

Scherrer, A. (2009). *G8 against transnational organized crime.* Farnham: Ashgate.

Sharma, D. (2006). 'Historical traces of Hundi, sociocultural understanding, and criminal abuses of Hawala'. *International Criminal Justice Review,* 16(2): 99–121.

Sharman, J.C. (2008). 'Power and discourse in policy diffusion: anti-money laundering in developing states.' *International Studies Quarterly,* 52(3): 635–56.

Sharman, J.C. (2011). *The money laundry. Regulating criminal finance in the global economy.* Ithaca: Cornell University Press.

Simmons, B. (2000). 'International efforts against money-laundering', in D. Shelton (ed.), *Commitment and compliance: the role of non-binding norms in the international legal system.* Oxford: Oxford University Press, 244–49.

Svedberg Helgesson, K. (2011). 'Public-private partners against crime: governance, surveillance and the limits of corporate accountability'. *Surveillance and Society,* 8(4): 471–84.

Svedberg Helgesson, K., and Mörth, U. (eds). (2012). *Securitization, accountability and risk management. Transforming the public security domain.* London: Routledge.

Tsingou, E. (2010). 'Global financial governance and the developing anti-money laundering regime: what lessons for the international political economy'. *International Politics,* 47(6): 617–37.

27

Subsidiary Initiative-taking in Multinational Corporations

The Role of Issue-selling Tactics

Christoph Dörrenbächer, Florian Becker-Ritterspach, Jens Gammelgaard, and Mike Geppert

Introduction

Subsidiary initiative-taking occurs when subsidiaries of multinational corporations engage in entrepreneurial activities independent of their headquarters' will. This common occurrence is a bottom-up complement to the many headquarters-inspired transfer processes and accounts for many of the dynamics that characterize contemporary multinational corporations (MNCs). At the same time, subsidiary initiative-taking is one of the main vehicles that allow local elements to find their way into the emerging global strategies of MNCs.

Surprisingly, the bi-directional nature of cross-border interaction in MNCs (headquarters-inspired transfer processes and subsidiary initiatives) has long escaped the attention of mainstream international business (IB) theory. Most traditional IB theories (e.g., Dunning 1979; Johanson and Vahlne 1977; Vernon 1971) view MNCs as headquarters-dominated entities that basically intend to globalize their existing firm-specific advantages. As a result, local subsidiaries have traditionally been viewed as simple transmission belts established to facilitate this process with, at best, the capability to introduce some local adaptations.

In reality, however, subsidiary activities and this picture never entirely matched. One well-documented historical example of this gap between theory and reality is a case from the second half of the nineteenth century involving Siemens' headquarters in Berlin and its UK subsidiary. Werner von Siemens, the founder of the Siemens group, was convinced that technical excellence was vital to Siemens' international competitiveness. To transfer and utilize this resource, he sent his brother, Wilhelm, to the UK. However, Wilhelm's stance on the matter was soon affected by local circumstances. In a letter dated 16 January 1862, Wilhelm recommended that his brother not impose his understanding of technical excellence on the UK operations (as cited in Ehrenberg 1906: 164). At the same time, Wilhelm objected to source components produced by Siemens' German operations and he proposed engaging in business areas other than those recommended by headquarters (Feldenkirchen 1992).

As this historical example illustrates, foreign subsidiaries are not necessarily able or always willing to limit their activities to simply fulfilling what headquarters perceives as their roles.

In fact, several recent surveys on subsidiary development confirm that the subsidiary roles initially assigned by headquarters are soon abandoned by subsidiaries (e.g., Delany 2000; Dörrenbächer and Gammelgaard 2006; Morgan and Kristensen 2006). Subsidiaries take their own routes, try to adapt to the local environment, see business opportunities other than those highlighted by headquarters, and build their own resources and competences. In sum, they engage in idiosyncratic strategic processes that reflect their particular local situations. Of course, as MNCs are hierarchies, such local initiatives need to be tolerated or supported by headquarters if they are to be successful. Therefore, subsidiaries invest a significant amount of effort into selling their initiatives to headquarters.

This latter phenomenon is the focus of this chapter. After discussing some initial considerations regarding the definition of 'subsidiary initiative' and the drivers of such initiatives, the chapter centers on the instruments and tactics subsidiaries and their key managers use to integrate their local initiatives with the global strategy-making processes that take place in the MNC. The instrumental aspects of subsidiary initiative-taking have hardly been dealt with in the literature so far. To address this gap, the chapter first takes stock of the literature on politicking in organizations in general. Based on those findings, the chapter then analyzes recent qualitative empirical work the authors have undertaken on subsidiary initiative-taking among German subsidiaries in France and among French subsidiaries in Germany. The chapter closes with several remarks on the implications of the empirical findings presented here on the debate about globalization, localization, and glocalization.

Subsidiary Initiative-taking: Definition, Types, and Driving Factors

Given the relatively recent conceptualization of MNCs as intra-organizational networks (Hedlund 1986; Ghoshal and Bartlett 2005), subsidiary initiatives have been the subject of growing academic interest. In the most basic definitions, subsidiary initiatives are described as 'entrepreneurial activities carried out by foreign subsidiaries of multinational corporations' (Birkinshaw and Ridderstråle 1999: 14). Such initiatives typically start with the identification of opportunities by subsidiaries, followed by the development and formalization of these initiatives and negotiations with headquarters on the commitment of resources to these opportunities. Subsidiary initiatives can be directed at the local, global, or internal MNC markets (Birkinshaw 1997).

Delany (2000) focuses on the subsidiary's perspective and distinguishes between domain-defending, domain-consolidating, and domain-developing initiatives. Domain-defending initiatives aim to prevent the loss of a current mandate (e.g., by looking for new customers). Domain-consolidating initiatives aim to stabilize the systems position of a subsidiary in the MNC (e.g., through performance improvements). Domain-developing initiatives go beyond current mandates. For example, subsidiaries may pursue new business opportunities in the local market.

While these types of initiatives highlight various purposes for subsidiary initiative-taking, three more profound factors explain the enduring existence and the everyday occurrence of subsidiary initiatives in MNC (Dörrenbächer and Gammelgaard 2011). First, subsidiaries regularly come across lucrative business opportunities in their environments. The local economic and natural environments, specific customer behaviors, institutional idiosyncrasies, and the like, breed opportunities that are unique to local subsidiaries. Second, subsidiaries have a strong interest in enhancing their systems position in the MNC and/or safeguarding their long-term survival. To that end, subsidiaries pursue business strategies that do not necessarily match headquarters' expectations. For instance, subsidiaries need to adapt to changes in their particular local environments to stay competitive. This goal is not always paramount to headquarters, which have other options – they might draw on other subsidiaries or locations. Third, some subsidiary managers do not view their role as restricted to meticulously implementing orders from the headquarters; their entrepreneurial personalities lead them to engage in initiative-taking.

This discussion leads to the assumption that headquarters are flooded by subsidiary initiatives rather than being short of them (Birkinshaw and Ridderstråle 1999). Some contingency research provides general insights into elements that support or hamper subsidiary initiative-taking. For example, a review by Verbeke et al. (2007) refers to various factors at work in the MNC context (e.g., the level of decentralization of decision making in the MNC), the subsidiary context (e.g., the entrepreneurial culture of the subsidiary) and the local environment context (e.g., the overall strategic importance of the host country for the MNC).

Politicking in MNCs: Means and Tactics

As highlighted above, subsidiaries are intrinsically motivated to take initiatives. Given a certain stage of development and the economic importance of such initiatives, subsidiaries need to involve headquarters for either approval of those initiatives or for additional resources to support those initiatives. As a consequence, headquarters can be inundated with such initiatives and need to filter out the promising ones. Headquarters are entitled to do so as, by definition, they possess legal authority over subsidiaries.

According to a study by Birkinshaw and Ridderstråle (1999), headquarters, spurred by resistance to change, ethnocentrism, and the fear of the unknown, tend to apply a rather fine-meshed corporate immune system that filters out many valuable subsidiary initiatives. Moreover, Ambos et al. (2010) provide evidence that those subsidiaries taking initiatives are subject to more intense monitoring by headquarters, which has negative effects on subsidiary autonomy. Therefore, subsidiary initiative-taking requires careful political maneuvering by subsidiaries vis-à-vis their headquarters. An exception might occur in situations where subsidiaries possess resource dependency power over their headquarters because they control certain resources the headquarters requires (Dörrenbächer and Gammelgaard 2010). However, careful political maneuvering might still be important for subsidiaries, as headquarters might make decisions that negatively affect subsidiaries. Such decisions might entail corrective actions, efforts at deterrence, or retaliation for unwanted subsidiary behavior.

Political maneuvering in organizations has been discussed in the literature to some extent. Pfeffer (1981) suggests that a fundamental task of actors in organizations is 'to develop explanations, rationalizations and legitimation' (p. 181) for desired activities or for actions already taken. To mobilize support or quiet opposition in relation to such activities (e.g., initiatives), actors use political language and engage in various tactics to achieve influence. These include strategies of rational persuasion or legitimacy, inspirational, or personal appeals, involvement in consultation and exchange, the formation of coalitions with internal and external stakeholders, the exertion of pressure, and the introduction of strategies of ingratiation, such as other-enhancement, opinion conformity, or self-promotion.

More recently, political maneuvering in organizations has been conceived of as 'issue selling' (Dutton and Ashford 1993; Ling et al. 2005). Dutton and Ashford (1993) define 'issue selling' as the 'individual's behaviors that are directed towards affecting others' attention to and understanding of issues' (p. 398). For subsidiaries that intend to sell an initiative to their headquarters, the issue-selling process involves three interrelated aims: (1) attracting the parent company's attention to the subsidiary and to the initiative, (2) making the parent company understand the initiative, and (3) engaging in interest-based lobbying at headquarters and with other relevant stakeholders (Gammelgaard 2009).

Attracting Headquarters' Attention

The first aspect of selling an initiative to headquarters consists of attracting headquarters' attention to the subsidiary and the initiative. MNCs are often large and complex entities in which headquarters typically face constraints in fully approaching and linking up with all subsidiaries (Nohria and Ghoshal 1997). However, as shown by Birkinshaw et al. (2006), a subsidiary can attract attention by pointing at distinguishing external elements, such as the subsidiary's location in an important market. Another means of attracting headquarters' attention is image control. Here, the subsidiary actively manages its image of being credible, reputable, and high performing through a strategic information policy that it relies on over a longer period of time. Furthermore, a good track record for previous initiatives might spur positive attention from headquarters for a new initiative. Finally, Dutton and Ashford (1993) suggest framing the issue at stake to fit headquarters' preferences. For example, an initiative to obtain a new mandate can be framed as a human resource, a cost, a technical feature, or some alternative issue (Cowan 1991).

Helping Headquarters Understand the Issue

The need to make headquarters understand an issue relates to the asymmetric distribution of information. Subsidiaries can use formal channels, such as monthly or annual reports, to convey information about an initiative. They can also provide detailed project descriptions that back up their requests for approval and resources. This activity always involves personal contact and face-to-face meetings, as information about initiatives is tacit to a certain extent, and therefore difficult to fully document and report in a codified way (Nonaka and Takeuchi 1995). Moreover, initiatives that are specific to the local context might trigger follow-up questions depending on the familiarity of the headquarters manager with the particular context (Sperber and Wilson 1995; Gammelgaard and Ritter 2008). In the process of making headquarters understand an issue, subsidiaries choose which subjects and attributes they wish to emphasize, and which aspects they wish to downplay. This has been labeled 'issue packaging' (Dutton and Ashford 1993: 419).

Lobbying for the Initiative

Subsidiaries lobby for an initiative when they 'exercise a voice' (Cantwell and Mudambi 2005: 1109) in order to promote a particular initiative. Lobbying is important, as headquarters might be overloaded with initiatives or be reluctant to consider new ideas (Birkinshaw and Ridderstråle 1999). Thus, lobbying to promote an initiative involves 'personal appeals, behind the scenes negotiations, or discussions in halls' (Dutton and Ashford 1993: 419) with all of the actors who can have an impact on the initiative. Network centrality in the form of close, frequent, and, in many cases, personal contact with decision-makers in headquarters has been shown to positively affect the promotion of initiatives (Dörrenbächer and Gammelgaard 2010).

The extent to which these theoretically derived aspects and tactics of political maneuvering are adopted by subsidiaries in the process of initiative-taking has hardly been explored. Furthermore, little is known thus about the factors that impact the choice of tactics. Therefore, in the remainder of the chapter, we start to explore these questions by looking at the tactics used in initiative-taking processes at German subsidiaries in France and at French subsidiaries in Germany, and the use of such tactics in different types of MNCs.

Data and Methods

Given the lack of knowledge on this subject to date, we adopted a qualitative approach in order to better explore and understand the issues at hand. In total, we studied fifteen cases, five of which involved French subsidiaries in Germany (all active in the services sector) and ten of which involved German subsidiaries in France (two in the service sector and eight in manufacturing). Subsidiary size varied widely in the sample, which included large, medium-sized, and small subsidiaries. In terms of ownership, the subsidiaries originated from family-owned MNCs as well as large, multidivisional MNCs with dispersed share ownership. Detailed information on the sample is provided in Table 27.1.

In each case, one or two in-depth interviews (each lasting about two hours) were undertaken in the subsidiary. Every interview involved the subsidiary CEO. All of the types of initiative-taking mentioned above were detected (domain defending, domain consolidating, and domain developing initiatives, as well as local, global, and MNC-internal initiatives). In all cases, data on the interviewees (e.g., career paths, organizational identification, and career orientation), the overall organizational setting (local institutional setting, situational context, and nature of the headquarters–subsidiary relationship), and processes in situations of initiative-taking and corresponding actor behaviors were gathered. Biographical and context-related questions were checked for plausibility during the interviews, while information regarding the initiative-taking behaviors of the CEOs was internally validated by approaching the topic from different angles using a variety of back-up questions. Where possible, interview data was triangulated in other interviews. All interviews were prepared and triangulated using extensive 'company profiles' that were drafted on both the subsidiaries and their parent MNCs.

All interviews were carried out in German and were translated for the purpose of this chapter. Notions in square brackets were added by the authors to ensure readability. In many cases, such brackets indicate that although the quote is not exact, the essence/content of the original has been maintained.

Tactics Used

Overall, we found that subsidiaries selling initiatives to headquarters engage in all three aspects of issue-selling discussed above.

Attracting Headquarters' Attention

With regard to attracting headquarters' attention, many respondents indicated that good performance was vital for gaining headquarters' attention and support for initiatives. This was, for instance, expressed by the CEO of a French subsidiary in Germany that had successfully sold a domain-developing initiative to its headquarters:

Table 27.1 Detailed information on the cases mentioned (cases A–I) and the remaining cases in the sample (cases J–O)

Subsidiary	Subsidiary location	Subsidiary CEO	Subsidiary size*	MNC size**	MNC incorporation	MNC ownership type	Industry
A	France	Local manager	Large	Large	Germany	Dispersed share ownership	Telecommunications equipment
B	France	Expatriate	Medium	SME	Germany	Family ownership	Agricultural machinery
C	France	Expatriate	Small	SME	Germany	Family ownership	Machine building
D	France	Expatriate	Small	SME	Germany	Family ownership	Chemicals
E	France	Expatriate	Medium	Large	Germany	Dispersed share ownership	Automotive
F	France	Expatriate	Large	Large	Germany	Dispersed share ownership	Telecommunication services
G	Germany	Local manager	Large	Large	France	Dispersed share ownership	Transportation services
H	France	Expatriate	Large	Large	Germany	Dispersed share ownership	Chemicals
I	Germany	Local manager	Medium	Large	France	Dispersed share ownership	Construction
J	France	Local manager	Medium	SME	Germany	Family ownership	Agricultural machinery
K	France	Expatriate	Medium	Large	Germany	Dispersed share ownership	Fashion
L	Germany	Local manager	Medium	Large	France	Dispersed share ownership	Airline
M	France	Expatriate	Medium	SME	Germany	Family ownership	Brewery
N	Germany	Expatriate	Small	SME	France	Dispersed share ownership	Consulting
O	Germany	Expatriate	Large	Large	France	Dispersed share ownership	Energy supply

* Large > 500 employees, medium 20–499 employees, small < 20 employees.
** SME < 5,000 employees.
Source: based on interview data, annual reports

> If we had not performed properly in recent years and failed to do this job in a particular and reasonable way, then a discussion would have come up [at headquarters]: 'Why are we locating this activity in Germany at all?'
>
> (CEO, subsidiary A)

In another case, attracting headquarters' attention to an initiative required not only that the subsidiary could show good performance with regard to its usual business activities, but that it could also demonstrate excellence in developing new capabilities:

> Our new product initiative was only acceptable [to headquarters] because we could show that we have developed the background to produce this new product with a high level of precision and quality. Previously, we have produced with coarse technology and we mainly employed unskilled foreign workers ... Metaphorically speaking, a few years ago we were still working with hammers and chisels. A major shift was needed ...We had to organize a change in outlook, train workers, get more skilled people, improve production processes, and introduce a sound quality management system.
>
> (CEO, subsidiary B)

For another company, the reputation of the subsidiary with regard to previous initiatives was considered important for attracting headquarters' attention to new initiatives:

> We enjoy a good reputation at headquarters. If we come up with new ideas or innovations, people in headquarters say: 'Oh, yes, that is from [our subsidiary in] France. They always have good ideas.'
>
> (CEO, subsidiary C)

Outside actors were sometimes involved in attracting headquarters' attention to a subsidiary initiative. In one case, the CEO let the headquarters know that the initiative was highly regarded by the subsidiary's main customer (a large MNC) with which headquarters was interested in doing more business. Another example involved a German subsidiary in France, where the manager enlisted the help of the subsidiary's chartered accountant to attract headquarters' attention to his ideas:

> When my CEO recently came to Paris, I organized a dinner with our chartered accountant. He is one of my best allies when it comes to my idea of growing our business in France. As discussed with him in advance, he mentioned to our CEO that the subsidiary had a lot of money that would be best invested in taking over some competitors.
>
> (CEO, subsidiary D)

Making Headquarters Understand the Issue

We found clear indications that subsidiaries use both formal communication channels, such as reporting, and personal contacts to help headquarters understand an issue. However, examples of 'issue packaging' as a means to help headquarters understand an issue were scarce. Only in one case did the CEO of a German subsidiary in France openly admit that he packaged an issue in a particular way to ensure that it was understood by headquarters. This CEO was motivated by a recent wave of management reorganization at headquarters, which was associated with a change in the overall orientation of the MNC from a long-term-oriented, technology-driven company to a relatively short-term-oriented company driven by financial factors:

> Headquarters has had so many changes in leading positions recently. Each one of those new managers is gathering a group of controllers around him or her ... They are not experts but bureaucrats that need to be talked to in an appropriate way.
>
> (CEO, subsidiary E)

Despite efforts to cater to headquarters' special requirements in this respect, this initiative failed. Headquarters was unsatisfied with the financial expectations associated with the initiative:

> They [headquarters managers] want to see cash in one and a half years rather than in three years.
>
> (CEO, subsidiary E)

However, the scarcity of subsidiaries using issue packaging to help headquarters understand an issue does not necessarily mean that this tactic is unimportant. Obviously, a tactic like issue packaging may be associated with manipulation on some level, as was confirmed by the responses in many of our interviews. When asked directly about issue packaging, interviewees – even those who had been relatively open to our questioning – tended to respond evasively.

Lobbying

Lobbying was mentioned in virtually all of the interviews and all interview partners were willing to talk openly about their lobbying activities. Overall, lobbying was considered to be a very important, if not the single most important, tactic used to sell an initiative. One interviewee mentioned:

> If I were to give percentages, I would say about 80% of the decisions [in favor of the initiative] were due to factual matters – we had the best organization, we had the customers, we could finance it, and we had the right people to implement it. All the rest, however, were due to skillful lobbying [at headquarters].
>
> (CEO, subsidiary A)

There was a great coincidence among the interviewees views on what are important prerequisites of skillful lobbying. One aspect always mentioned was the necessity of personal relationships. One interviewee expressed this as follows:

> [Skillful lobbying] means taking a seat at the right tables, taking part in the right talks, and having better 'feelers' out in the company.
>
> (CEO, subsidiary A)

Other aspects frequently mentioned were the socially skillful handling of personal relationships and, to a certain degree, persistence, as expressed in the following quote:

> From a theoretical perspective, one would assume that a corporation as large as ours follows a rational, strategic approach [when evaluating a subsidiary initiative], but the

opposite is the case. It is a highly political process where who you know, who trusts you, and what reputation you have count. *Antichambrer* [walking the corridors of power] is exactly what you have to do – you have to talk to people, you have to convince them and you must not annoy them ... That takes time and continual effort. For me, it is a bit like 'small strokes fell big oaks'.

(CEO, subsidiary F)

Tactics by MNC Type

Throughout our interviews, it was clear that there was a close relationship between MNC type and the tactics used to sell an initiative. This was not surprising, given the rather strong hierarchical relationship typically found for MNC headquarters and subsidiaries. The MNCs in our sample varied in terms of size (large versus small), type of ownership (family-owned versus listed), and country of origin (German versus French). Often, these categories had overlapping impacts on issue-selling tactics.

In many small and medium-sized family-owned MNCs, the selling of an initiative was just another topic in a permanent and intense exchange process between the subsidiary CEO and the owner/CEO of the MNC. Subsidiaries did not have to use tactics to attract headquarters' attention, as they had its attention anyway. Nor did subsidiaries have to work hard to help headquarters understand an initiative, as headquarters were already closely involved in the subsidiary's day-to-day operations. Lobbying was also of minor importance, as there was often a trust-based relationship between the subsidiary manager and the owners or headquarters managers that had developed over many years. This situation is expressed in the following statement made by a CEO of a German subsidiary in France:

> Our company is family-owned, with the family putting a lot of emphasis on a close and long-lasting relationship with subsidiary management. We feel we are taken very seriously and there is a continuous exchange. [Coming up with an initiative] does not trigger a conflict. We talk about the initiative and then they usually say, 'If you are convinced that this will work out, then go ahead and try.'

(CEO, subsidiary C)

While this flexibility probably only applies to initiatives within reasonable limits, the situation in such family-owned MNCs is nevertheless clearly different from the setting experienced in large, diversified MNCs. In the latter contexts, subsidiary CEOs have to actively engage in tactical behaviors to gain headquarters' attention and they have to lobby extensively for their initiatives:

> To get a positive decision [on a subsidiary initiative] in a big multinational, you have to form a large coalition of supporters from your internal and external networks. [For initiatives that require a decision from the board of directors], you have to get the support of about 20 people. That is basically everyone on the management level just below the board of directors, plus everyone in management one level further down, plus some important consultants and investment bankers. Only if you have the support of all of these people and nobody objects you can approach the board of directors.

(CEO, subsidiary F)

Despite the generally more demanding organizational setting, which requires subsidiaries in large, diversified MNCs to follow more intense and more politically minded issue-selling strategies, some noteworthy differences were also observable. Headquarters in some large diversified MNCs were rather initiative averse in that they only allowed subsidiaries to lobby for initiatives that referred to their local markets. This was highlighted in a comment made by a CEO representing a French subsidiary in Germany:

> We are basically tied to the German market. There is still a lot to do here. We are not entitled to come up with initiatives that go beyond our national market. This is strictly top-down according to the patriarchal French system. Everything relating to such matters is decided in Paris and – I say this very frankly – not according to rational criteria that consultants such as Roland Berger would suggest. This is strictly a matter of the leading managers and their fiefdoms.
>
> (CEO, subsidiary G)

In other cases, such restrictions did not exist. Some MNCs systematically supported subsidiaries in their initiatives to use their local insights, knowledge, and experience in other countries. This led to a higher level of issue-selling activities:

> Previously, headquarters only said, 'What is good for the German market must be good for the French market too.' Today, they think beyond that … If I have a new product idea, I try to excite subsidiary CEOs in other countries, too.
>
> (CEO, subsidiary D)

Some MNCs went further, supporting subsidiary initiative-taking as a system for stimulating intra-firm competition. This led to competitive lobbying:

> If a discussion arises within the group on a particular global mandate, then every local subsidiary CEO checks which competencies his subsidiary has with regard to that mandate and whether it makes sense to lobby for that mandate.
>
> (CEO, subsidiary H)

Unfortunately, our interviews revealed little information on the structure of such competitive lobbying strategies.

Finally, some differences were apparent with regard to the MNC's country of origin. At first glance, issue-selling strategies in French and German MNCs did not differ radically. This is hardly surprising, as both German and French MNCs are considered to be rooted in similar institutional environments that have significant effects on the internal organization of firms. Furthermore, traditional German and French firms are assumed to be technology driven, long-term-orientated, and relatively bureaucratic. One notable difference, however, relates to the social constitution of German and French firms. Traditional German firms exhibit a social partnership attitude and are characterized by a rather broad social stratification among top managers, whereas French firms are characterized by fierce class conflicts and a closed group of *Grandes Écoles* alumni in top management positions.

These differences were found to have two effects on issue-selling strategies. First, managers of German subsidiaries in France maintained that their headquarters often did not understand the efforts needed to manage labor relations, so that rather negative (instead of positive) attention was drawn to the subsidiary. Thus, many interviewees indicated that they regularly communicated with headquarters to explain the difficulties associated with organized labor in France. This was viewed as a matter of image control:

> I belong to the people who say [to the headquarters] that we need to get an additional 1,000 points on Hay's Job Evaluation scheme due to our responsibilities with regard to labor issues.
>
> (CEO, subsidiary H)

Second, the fact that top management positions in French firms are generally restricted to *Grandes Écoles* alumni that exhibit a particular way of administration requires some adaptations in issue-selling tactics. The peculiarities common to *Grandes Écoles* alumni administration are well described in the following comments made by a German CEO of a French subsidiary in Germany. A first aspect refers to the necessity of mastering French as a prerequisite for successfully selling an initiative to headquarters:

> When we come to headquarters to give our monthly report together with all of the other subsidiaries, we speak English. However, when we go to lunch, we speak French … It is always a long lunch, as the French people love it. They are planned for two and a half hours and often last for three. That is where [we talk to our counterparts from the headquarters and] get a lot of feedback.
>
> (CEO, subsidiary I)

The second aspect is that status differences are important and need to be respected when selling an initiative to headquarters:

> You can feel the importance of the status differences. Even if you look at the organizational chart [of the MNC], you will find that the *Grande École* a manager attended is always indicated.
>
> (CEO, subsidiary I)

Given these considerations, the CEO of subsidiary I did not dare to engage in selling initiatives to the headquarters alone. Instead he joined forces with his headquarters counterpart:

> I only talk through my headquarters contact, the one who is responsible for us at headquarters … It is company philosophy that we have private contact with these people – that the families visit each other and that you invite your counterpart to your birthday party … My headquarters contact directs me with regard to whom I need to talk to and where to send a proposal.
>
> (CEO, subsidiary I)

Concluding Remarks

Subsidiary initiatives in MNCs are bottom-up complements to the many top-down transfer processes initiated by headquarters. While such initiatives are generally in the interest of headquarters, headquarters must evaluate and make a decision on all of the initiatives that their subsidiaries present. Local subsidiaries undertaking an initiative can enhance their chances of obtaining support by carefully selling the initiative to headquarters. Based on a recent conceptualization suggested by Gammelgaard (2009), which distinguishes among three aspects of issue selling (attracting headquarters' attention to the initiative, making headquarters understand the initiative, and lobbying for the initiative), this chapter undertook an empirical exploration of these aspects at a number of German subsidiaries in France and French subsidiaries in Germany.

Our findings offered strong evidence that subsidiaries engage in all three aspects of issue-selling. Our investigation also revealed that local subsidiaries' issue-selling strategies differ widely with regard to different types of MNCs. Clearly, issue-selling strategies are more necessary in large diversified MNCs than in family-owned SMEs. Within the group of large diversified MNCs, we found initial evidence for the idea that the extent to which subsidiaries engage in issue-selling tactics depends on the level of intra-firm competition stimulated by headquarters (Becker-Ritterspach and Dörrenbächer 2011).

We also found that the country of origin has an impact on the tactics used. This was especially obvious with regard to tactics used in French MNCs, where the social constitution is characterized by conflict-ridden labor relations and a closed group of *Grandes Écoles* alumni in top positions with a particular way of handling administration. Beyond these national idiosyncrasies, which clearly have an effect on issue-selling tactics, we assume that our findings may be generalizable to ventures that touch upon two coordinated market economies, as this type of capitalism typically exhibits a network type of coordination. How issue-selling unfolds in settings that touch upon two liberal market economies, which are typically characterized by arm's-length economic coordination, or in settings that include both types, remains to be seen.

Even though further research is needed, we can conclude that subsidiary initiative-taking and attempts to sell initiatives to headquarters are important vehicles for incorporating local elements into emerging global strategies of MNCs. This is especially the case in MNCs following a strongly centralized approach where strategies and practices developed in headquarters are diffused throughout the global organization. Ironically, selling local subsidiary initiatives is also important in cases where headquarters are receptive to such initiatives. Hence, many initiatives contend for headquarters' attention and approval.

Finally, not all successful local subsidiary initiatives introduce a particular local logic into a global strategy in the sense of more locally responsive 'glocal' strategies. Although many initiatives do enhance the viability of global strategies, some locally developed initiatives simply aim to replace the global logic of headquarters with another global logic, one developed in a subsidiary with ambitions beyond its local scope. What follows is that the overall strategies of MNCs – whether they are global, glocal, or local – are negotiated constructs of headquarters' will and subsidiaries' issue-selling tactics and bargaining power.

References

Ambos, T., Andersson, U., and Birkinshaw, J. (2010). 'What are the consequences of initiative-taking in multinational subsidiaries?' *Journal of International Business Studies,* 41: 1–20.

Becker-Ritterspach, F., and Dörrenbächer, C. (2011). 'An organizational politics perspective on intra-firm competition in multinational corporations'. *Management International Review,* 51(4): 533–59.

Birkinshaw, J. (1997). 'Entrepreneurship in multinational corporations: the characteristics of subsidiary initiatives'. *Strategic Management Journal,* 18(3): 207–29.

Birkinshaw, J., and Ridderstråle, J. (1999). 'Fighting the corporate immune system: a process study of subsidiary initiatives in multinational corporations'. *International Business Review,* 8(2): 149–80.

Birkinshaw, J., Bouquet, C., and Ambos, T. (2006). 'Attention HQ'. *Business Strategy Review*, Autumn: 4–9.

Cantwell, J., and Mudambi, R. (2005). 'MNE competence-creating subsidiary mandate'. *Strategic Management Journal,* 26: 1109–28.

Cowan, D. (1991). 'The effect of decision-making styles and contextual experience in executives' descriptions of organization problem formulation'. *Journal of Management Studies,* 28: 462–84.

Delany, E. (2000). 'Strategic development of multinational subsidiaries through subsidiary initiative taking'. *Long Range Planning,* 33: 220–44.

Dörrenbächer, C., and Gammelgaard, J. (2006). 'Subsidiary role development: the effect of micro-political headquarters – subsidiary negotiations on the product, market and value-added scope of foreign-owned subsidiaries'. *Journal of International Management,* 12(3): 266–83.

Dörrenbächer, C., and Gammelgaard, J. (2010). 'Multinational corporations, inter-organizational networks and subsidiary charter removals'. *Journal of World Business,* 45(2): 206–16.

Dörrenbächer, C., and Gammelgaard, J. (2011). 'Subsidiary power in the multinational corporation: on the subtle role of micro-political bargaining power'. *Critical Perspectives on International Business,* 7(1): 30–47.

Dunning, J.H. (1979). 'Explaining changes in international production: in defence of the eclectic theory'. Oxford *Bulletin of Economics and Statistics,* 41: 269–95.

Dutton, J.E., and Ashford, S. (1993). 'Selling issues to top management'. *Academy of Management Review,* 18(3): 397–428.

Ehrenberg, R. (1906). 'Die Unternehmungen der Gebrüder Siemens'. Erster Band bis zum Jahr 1870, Jena.

Feldenkirchen, W. (1992). *Werner von Siemens.* Bad Godesberg.

Gammelgaard, J. (2009). 'Issue selling and bargaining power in intrafirm competition: the differentiating impact of the subsidiary management composition'. *Competition and Change,* 13(3): 214–28.

Gammelgaard, J., and Ritter, T. (2008). 'Virtual communities of practice: a mechanism for efficient knowledge retrieval in MNCs'. *International Journal of Knowledge Management,* 4(2): 46–61.

Ghoshal, S., and Bartlett, C.A. (2005). 'The multinational corporation as an inter-organizational network', in S. Ghoshal and D.E. Westney (eds), *Organization theory and the multinational corporation.* Houndmills, Basingstoke: Palgrave MacMillan, 68–92.

Hedlund, G. (1986). 'The hypermodern MNC – a heterarchy?' *Human Resource Management,* 25(1): 9–35.

Johanson, J., and Vahlne, J.E. (1977). 'Internationalization process of firm – model of knowledge development and increasing foreign market commitments'. *Journal of International Business Studies,* 8(1): 23–32.

Ling, Y., Floyd, S.W., and Baldridge, D.C. (2005). 'Toward a model of issue-selling by subsidiary managers in multinational organizations'. *Journal of International Business Studies,* 36(6): 637–54.

Morgan, G., and Kristensen, P.H. (2006). 'The contested space of multinationals: varieties of institutionalism, varieties of capitalism'. *Human Relations,* 59: 1467–90.

Nohria, N., and Ghoshal, S. (1997). *The differentiated network: organizing multinational corporations for value creation.* San Francisco: Jossey-Bass.

Nonaka, I., and Takeuchi, H. (1995). *The knowledge-creating company – how Japanese companies create the dynamic of innovation.* Oxford: Oxford University Press.

Pfeffer, J. (1981). *Power in organizations.* Marshfield, MA: Pitman.

Sperber, D., and Wilson, D. (1995). *Relevance: communication and cognition.* Oxford: Blackwell.

Verbeke, A., Chrisman, J.J., and Yuan, W. (2007). 'A note on strategic renewal and corporate venturing in the subsidiaries of multinational enterprises'. *Entrepreneurship Theory and Practice,* July: 585–99.

Vernon, R. (1971). *Sovereignty at bay: the multinational spread of U.S. enterprises.* New York: Basic Books.

28
Cosmopolitanism and Banal Localism
The Domestication of Global Trends in Finnish Cities

Pertti Alasuutari

Introduction

Originally depicting the marketing strategy in which a product is customized to local markets on a global scale, the concept of glocalization has become a prevalent referent to the fascinating ways in which the 'global' and the 'local' are intertwined and construct the meaning of one another (Robertson, 1992, pp. 173–4). The fact that it has become one of the marketing buzzwords of the last few decades tells us a lot about people's lived experience of the global world. Although quite aware of the homogenizing maelstrom of global capitalist mass production, people want to retain a sense of locality, rooted in products, brands, and artifacts that they are used to and which they identify with a local place.

This identification with a local community is interesting when placed against the central argument in globalization literature that the world is becoming a single place and people are becoming increasingly conscious of it (Robertson, 1992). Related to that, there is also discussion about cosmopolitanization (Beck & Sznaider, 2006) and cosmopolitization (Beck, 2003), according to which institutions of global governance are becoming increasingly important and a consciousness of world citizenship is growing. Yet it seems obvious that identification with a nation or a smaller community, such as a city, is not a gradually fading remnant of the past. Rather, it is something that nation-states reproduce by invented traditions (Hobsbawm & Ranger, 1983) or commemorative rituals (Spillman, 1997). According to Michael Billig, national identity, or 'banal nationalism' as he calls it, is also and most successfully reproduced through mundane 'flaggings' of the nation in routine everyday communication:

> Banally, they [the flaggings] address 'us' as a national first person plural; and they situate 'us' in the homeland within a world of nations. (…) Cumulatively, such flaggings provide daily, unmindful reminders of nationhood in the contemporary, established nation-state. It is no wonder, then, that national identity is seldom forgotten.
>
> (Billig, 1995, p. 174)

The reproduction of such banal nationalism or localism amalgamated with an equally banal cosmopolitan consciousness (Regev, 2007; Szerszynski & Urry, 2006) is not only or primarily the work of the state. It is something that people do in their mundane activities.

Of particular interest in discussions and research on this phenomenon, also referred to by several other concepts,[1] has been the fascinating way in which actors may be engaged in actively constructing a 'local' culture in a 'global' framework and yet conceive of it as 'authentic' and as an important part of their identity. For instance, in constructing their cultural 'home base', people do not want to be too different from the rest of the world. That is why the distinctiveness of 'local culture' is often expressed as a variant of a genre that is also recognizable elsewhere, thus both celebrating the uniqueness of local culture and emphasizing that the local people withstand international competition. For instance, national culture may be expressed and promoted by international musical genres such as classical music (Adams, 1999; Alasuutari, 2009) or rock (Regev, 2007).

This question of authenticity in people's lived experience has also been discussed in glocalization research. For instance, Giulianotti and Robertson (2006, 2007) point out in their study on North American-based supporters of Scottish football teams that, although being an expatriate fan is particular in many respects, to mark their regular Scottish identity, the members of the supporters' clubs are keen to emphasize that their supporter identity is no different to that of fans in Scotland. They also differentiate themselves from other transnational fans who are perceived to possess a more consumerist penchant for 'glamour' teams (2006, p. 181).

When talking about the global linkages of policymaking, mainstream research, however, ignores actors' conceptions or consciousness at the expense of its emphasis on how actors are constituted by world cultural principles and ideals. Policy diffusion is typically defined as a process within which a policy is either adopted or rejected in a given country. That leaves little space for reflection on how and whether global policies are introduced and implemented in forms that are customized to the local conditions that make people retain a local identity.

This chapter aims to rectify that neglect by focusing on how the local and the global are enmeshed in policymaking. I particularly aim to address the paradox that although adopting new policies often synchronizes local discourses and practices with global trends and may, in fact, be justified by comparison to other polities, a banal local identity is maintained or even enhanced. What are the means by which this is accomplished in the local policymaking process? To unpack the ways in which such a process of domestication works, this chapter focuses on the discourses within which the report of a Finnish local government cultural activities development project was introduced and discussed in Finnish newspapers. The idea of that analysis is to scrutinize the process triggered in the local contexts by the release of the report—the process that makes it understandable how the news stories on comparative information on Finnish cities drew on and enhanced banal localism instead of strengthening a consciousness of a policy convergence regarding cultural policy.

As will become evident, this article shows that the production of isomorphic social change, dependent on cosmopolitan consciousness, and the reproduction of banal nationalism or localism are not separate processes or competing, contradictory trends. Rather, they can be considered as upshots of a single process, domestication of global trends, whereby local trajectories of social change constantly converge or are near each other, but exogenous elements are tamed so they are experienced as domestic within each polity. While the origins of the concept of glocalization imply that such customization to the local conditions is the work of the one who sells a product or an idea to another place, the concept of domestication refers to the active role of local actors, who bring a foreign object home and civilize it so that it becomes seen as a domestic creature.

The Domestication Framework

The theoretical framework of this paper is based on neoinstitutionalist world polity theory (Boli & Thomas, 1997, 1999; Lechner & Boli, 2005; Meyer, Boli, Thomas, & Ramirez, 1997), which emphasizes that cultural principles and institutions shape the action of states, firms, individuals, and other subunits. For instance, the nation-state as an idea and as an institutional arrangement is considered as a creation of the international community and 'world culture', and policy makers and other actors in various governmental and non-governmental organizations are viewed as 'Babbitts' (Meyer, 2004), conformists who adopt and hence spread worldwide models.

However, world polity theory scholarship has not paid much attention to the processes that the enactment of worldwide models triggers at the local level–processes that actually help us understand why actors end up being 'conformists,' although they do not conceive of themselves that way. The question of how it is that the same ideas and fashions are adopted worldwide and yet that does not unsettle banal nationalism or localism has not been addressed either. For these reasons, world polity theory is here complemented with the concept of domestication.

While world polity scholarship approaches isomorphic social change from a top-down perspective by studying how distinct models spread throughout the world, the domestication framework assumes a bottom-up perspective by scrutinizing the way policy decisions are made in local polities and how actors in the opinion formation and decision-making make use of international comparisons and exogenous policy models. This perspective allows us to see that adopting foreign influences does not equal mindless implementation of a model. Rather, references to comparable entities' policies and performance measures are levers that local actors use to justify and thus advance their views and interests. Synchronization with policies adopted elsewhere is a side effect rather than the main thing. Because of that, a particular decision-making process cannot be reduced to the adoption of a singular exogenous model. Instead, actors appeal to several models and policies of different countries in addition to evoking a number of timely concepts, and the end result may mean that some of them become increasingly squarely rooted in local practices.

The point that local actors play a key role in adapting global ideas to local conditions has already been made in several research traditions. For instance, when talking about policy diffusion or transfer, or about the localization of international norms, it has been pointed out that they always entail complex processes by which domestic actors build congruence between exogenous models and local beliefs and practices (Acharya, 2004, p. 241) and in which models are re-embedded into, and reshaped in, the new context (Cook, 2008, p. 777). Similarly, Kjaer and Pedersen (2001) talk about a process of translation. By that concept, they take distance from the notion of diffusion and emphasize that translation does not assume that there exists a fully developed and easily identifiable idea or paradigm that is transferred unchanged over time and from one country to another. Rather, when concepts and conceptions derived from a different social context are introduced, they trigger a shift in the existing order of interpretation and action in that context, resulting in practices that differ considerably from those used as the model case (see also Dahl, 2009; Noerreslet, Larsen, & Traulsen, 2005).

While other concepts that depict this process, such as creolization, hybridization, localization, translation, and vernacularization, refer to the difference between the 'original' and the modified version, the concept of domestication employed here calls attention to the lived experience of the actors. As Tobin (1992, p. 4) points out, domesticate has meanings such as tame, civilize, naturalize, make familiar, and bring into the home, which all capture people's experience of the outcome of the process as indeed a genuinely 'domestic' phenomenon. Considering the fact that policies are justified precisely by referring to comparative information and to what others are doing, this amnesia of the global links of local practices is really like a magic trick.

How such amalgamation of cosmopolitan and local imagination actually happens has received little attention. If elements considered as distinguishing features of the area or policies implemented by the regional state are composed of global ideas or models, how is banal localism preserved? When talking about the domestication of policy models, earlier research and the empirical evidence to be discussed in the following sections suggests that two factors are crucial in this process. One is the cultural framework of competition, which the introduction of comparative data evokes and to which those introducing cross-national comparisons or policy models justified by them appeal; it constructs the citizens of the state or other regional entity as a team with shared interests. Therefore, doing what others do is not presented as conformism or imitation, but rather as part of the local competition strategy (see Alasuutari & Rasimus, 2009). Because of its success, it is no wonder that measuring and benchmarking states' or other polities' performance in a particular area is deliberately used as a method of governance, a means to make different states voluntarily adopt similar policies.[2] The second factor or mechanism is the local political struggle that the introduction of comparative data or reforms justified by them triggers. When local actors are the key players both in introducing a model and in taking part in the struggles, the whole process is commonly perceived as part of domestic politics, and the eventual forms that potential reforms assume are attributed as victories or losses to the domestic powers involved.

The Construction of Cities as Strategic Actors

As was stressed in the previous section, a particular process—for instance, introducing a cross-national comparison or establishing a new institutional practice—in which global ideas are made familiar to the local discourses and practices, cannot be reduced to importing a distinct idea or model to the local polity. Rather, such a process may involve spreading or evoking several up-to-date ideas or transnational models at various levels. That is also the case with the object of my case analysis, the project that aimed to develop local government cultural activities by providing Finnish towns and cities with comparative data. First, the creation of comparable data serves performance measurement in local government, which is a global trend (Ammons, 1995; Lever, 2002; Pollanen, 2005). Furthermore, the willingness of the Finnish towns and cities to take part in the project shows that the idea of cities as strategic actors and the notion of the creative city are well known to the actors involved. Because of the familiarity of those timely ideas, actors utilized and evoked them, and hence, the project had the effect that they became increasingly proverbial in the local settings. Let us now contextualize the project in this global framework of ideas.

Developing the Creative Economy

As one example of the spread of worldwide models, the idea that states and regions compete against each other in attracting businesses, capital, tourists, and well-educated residents has been applied to cities (see e.g. Boddy, 2003; Schneider, 1989) all over the world, at least from the 1960s onward, and in this activity, cultural policy has played an important role (Coaffee, 2008; Evans, 2009; Grodach & Loukaitou-Sideris, 2007; Mommaas, 2004). In the 1960s and 1970s, the idea was to revitalize declining industrial cities or areas in a city (Bianchini, 1988;

Gale, 1987) and to boost tourism by, for instance, creating more spaces where artists could perform (Paquette, 2008). Gradually, such strategic thinking on the part of city leadership became more and more systematic so that in advanced economies, practically every city is supposed to have a strategy by which they enhance economic activity within their borders—for instance, with the means of sports, arts, entertainment, and heritage industry. Thus, it has become commonplace to conceive of cities as competing market actors for whom enterprises make bids or that play a mediating role in invigorating the local economy (Jensen-Butler, 1999; Mossberger, 1998; Oatley, 1998).

The nowadays self-evident, central role of art and culture in cities' strategies is probably due to a plethora of underlying assumptions. For instance, art and popular culture are viewed as a means to express the uniqueness of the nation or region in question; they are supposed to make the region or city special in the eyes of visitors (see e.g. Angus & Jhally, 1989). Excellent and successful local artists are also considered to be a source of pride for the residents, and in that way, they make local people feel that they belong to a local community (Throsby & Withers, 1983). Furthermore, art is considered as a tool in the citizens' behavior modification, as an instrument capable of 'lifting' the cultural level of the population (Bennett, 1995; Miller & Yúdice, 2002). In recent years, this idea has taken up a new form in the assumption that art instills creative thinking. As it is formulated by cultural economists, it is believed that art has innovative value: 'The practice of the arts makes an essential contribution to the development of *creative thinking* in a society, to improvements in the capacity for critical evaluation and to the creation of aesthetic standards that ultimately affect most individuals positively' (Frey, 2003, p. 113, italics in the original). The importance of creativity for cities has been promoted especially by Charles Landry (1989), who argues that it is not only artists and those involved in the creative economy who are creative, although they play an important role. In Richard Florida's (2004) idea of the creative class, that assumption is further developed by arguing that lively cultural life in a city not just cultivates creativity among the residents, but attracts members of the creative class from elsewhere.

This shift from seeing cultural policy servicing democratic access to art and social cohesion of the people to conceiving of culture as a tourist attraction and as a means to enhance 'creative economy' has swept throughout the advanced economies, and the creative city is now a standard catchword that can be found in the strategy documents of almost any city in the world. For instance, in the documents of Copenhagen, Denmark, it is said that its cultural policy now serves economic and employment objectives and related inward investment of tourists, skilled workers, and capital through a wider experience and creative economy (Bayliss, 2007). The city also targets the creative class; its strategy mentions that technology, creativity, and tolerance are the driving force behind the city's economic growth and development (OECD, 2009b, p. 192).

Nowadays, every city has its own strategy, even in Finland (see e.g. Hautamäki, 1995; Oulun kaupunki, 2002; Rovaniemen kaupunki, 2006; Sotarauta, 1995), and the strategies recycle the same slogans and key concepts. For instance, the competitiveness strategy of the Helsinki metropolitan area says:

> The Helsinki Metropolitan Area is a dynamic world-class center for business and innovation. Its high-quality services, art and science, creativity and adaptability promote the prosperity of its citizens and bring benefits to all of Finland. The Metropolitan Area is being developed as a unified region close to nature where it is good to live, learn, work and do business.
>
> (Economic Development Working Group, 2009, p. 2)

In a similar vein, the city strategy of Tampere is crystallized by saying, 'Tampere is an attractive international business environment and cultural city' (Tampere, 2009).

In such strategy documents, authors typically want to identify something unique in the city in question, and commonly, that uniqueness is related to the 'local culture', which simultaneously refers to cultural products such as art and popular culture on display in the city and to culture as a way of life of the local people, with a special emphasis on history. On the other hand, the uniqueness of the city in question is represented in standard ways, quite like the whole idea of the city or regional strategy. And it is no wonder, because devising them is recommended and promoted by actors such as the OECD or the European Union. For instance, the OECD has a particular Urban Development Programme, under which performance indicators are created (OECD, 2009a), recommendations and 'best practices' are published, and competitiveness reviews are produced. The European Union also gives financial support to cities or regions that build their own competitiveness strategies.

Since cities are constructed as strategic actors that compete against each other for creative residents, tourists, and footloose capital, various measures and instruments have been created to compare and benchmark the performance of cities and regions (Ammons, 1995; Lever, 2002; Malecki, 2007; Pollanen, 2005). Competitions for fame and attraction of tourists have also been organized; for instance, the European Union has a program in which each year they elect a European capital or capitals of culture (Europa, 2011).

On the other hand, the increasingly influential framework of competition, linked with culture and cultural activities through the creative city hypothesis, is actively utilized by actors who defend the interests of artists and culture lovers. Hence, cultural policy, which has traditionally been justified by art as valuable in its own right, is now commonly justified by the claim that it is beneficial for business and economy.

The Finnish Cities' Cultural Activities Development Project

The research and development project launched by the Association of Finnish Local and Regional Authorities (AFLRA) to create a statistical standard about how to calculate the costs and profits of cultural activities in Finnish towns and cities, is a prime example of the way in which the transnational ideas about the competitive and creative city spread throughout the world and are translated into local practices. It certainly did not introduce the global ideas concerned, but through projects like this, general ideas and abstract models are saturated throughout the local organizational structures.

With the scientific expertise provided by the Finnish Foundation for Cultural Policy Research (CUPORE), whose researchers were responsible for the bulk of data collection and reporting, the aim of the project was to help the participating towns and cities better manage their cultural policy activities.[3] Taking part in the project was voluntary and required resources from the participants, but it became quite popular. Altogether, 23 Finnish towns and cities participated in the project to collect data on local government cultural activities.

The report sticks strictly to the local level. For instance, although the idea of creativity as a key element in city strategies is mentioned in the main report and in one of the newspaper articles, there are no references to the international literature in the report. Likewise, the introduction of the report motivates the project by the need for the collection of comparable data on cultural activities, which functions as a tool for strategic planning and management, but the text only alludes to a general domestic trend. The same is true of possible international models behind the classification scheme; when one studies the pilot report and the final report (Ruusuvirta, Saukkonen, Selkee, & Winqvist, 2008a; Ruusuvirta et al., 2008b), one cannot find any references to international authorities or to standards adopted elsewhere. The definitions and decisions appear to be locally made. Only in a background report on the project (Saukkonen & Ruusuvirta, 2008) does one find references to the work done in UNESCO and in the European Union. In that report, the project is considered as part of the international enterprise with the aim to guide the collection of comparable data in the area of cultural statistics (see e.g. UNESCO Institute for Statistics, 2009). This does not mean that any of the categories in the statistical scheme were directly copied from foreign sources; they only share the idea and goal of collecting comparable data, which is to help actors to assess the effectiveness of their culture spending and hence develop and learn from good practices.

Newspaper Media Coverage

When the main report of the project was published, it attracted a good amount of attention in the media. At least 27 news stories, newspaper articles, editorials, or columns were published soon afterwards, primarily in the local newspapers in the cities and towns that took part in the project. The media was particularly interested in the tables and figures in which the expenditures of various cultural activities in different municipalities were compared. One figure from the report is shown here as an example (see Figure 28.1).

The Ranking of a City

In the media coverage, there is a single predominant frame that provides the format for the news stories, most of which came out the very next day after the main report was published. *Helsingin Sanomat* published a news story based on the pilot report, which came out nine months earlier, but that story also follows the same format. It is as if the format was jointly agreed on by the journalists working in the different local newspapers. Yet, it is obvious that the articles published in different newspapers were devised by the journalists independently,

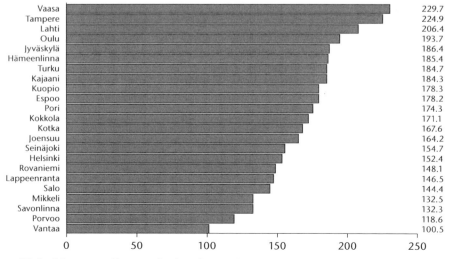

Figure 28.1 Net expenditures of cultural activities in 2007, € per citizen

which shows well how self-evident the framework was. Its self-evidence could be based on the vernacular competition state or competitive city (Schneider, 1989) thesis, according to which nowadays states and other places need to attract enterprises and footloose capital (Fougner, 2006) as well as creative residents (Florida, 2004) to do well in global competition. Following their instinct, the journalists thus made use of this framework to make the report meaningful for their local readers. For instance, instead of questioning the validity of the report,[4] the articles in local newspapers concentrated on relating the ranking of the newspaper's domicile to other municipalities in the study (i.e., how well a city or town did in comparison). For instance, the newspaper *Karjalainen*, which is published in Joensuu, reports that Joensuu invests in culture moderately:

> In Joensuu, the net expenditures of cultural activities are 164 euro per citizen. In seven other cities, the sum remains below 150 euro.
> (*Karjalainen* 26.11.2008)

To take another example, the headline of *Uusimaa*, a newspaper that is published in Porvoo, states that Porvoo and Vantaa are bottommost in culture spending. On the other hand the story goes on to say that in one sector Porvoo is better than all others: the city spent most on basic art education.

Some of the news stories are simple and short, hard news, in which the ranking of the local city or town is characterized, followed by more information about the study, for instance which cities are uppermost and bottommost in it. However, in many articles, local actors, such as the city's cultural director, are interviewed to comment on the results of the comparison. For instance, the cultural director of the city of Kotka says in an interview in *Kymen Sanomat* that the results of the report are important because they show how Kotka is situated in culture-spending compared with other cities.

The league table listing the money spent on culture in different towns and cities can be read in different ways. Depending on what esteem one puts on art and cultural activities, it can be interpreted as a ranking list in which the biggest spenders are the best, the most 'culture friendly', or they may quite as well be seen as the most extravagant and the least economical in their cultural policy. Yet the predominant reading was to consider the topmost municipalities as the best. The bottommost cities, on the other hand, were given negative epithets; for instance, the article in Helsingin Sanomat says that 'Vantaa is the stingiest sponsor'.

This interpretation of the biggest spenders as the best is factualized by a number of positive values associated with art and culture in the news stories—for instance, *Uusimaa* quotes the project coordinator from the AFLRA, who stresses that local government cultural activities are focal from the viewpoint of the well-being of the local citizens.

> Good, well-functioning cultural services are a sign of an exuberant city, Winqvist states.
> (*Uusimaa* 26.11.2008)

Referring to changes underway in which many small municipalities have been merged into larger ones, Winqvist continues by saying that to succeed, big reforms require social activities that create 'togetherness, interaction and bridges between individuals'. Many other classical justifications of culture spending are also used. For instance, the editorial of *Aamulehti* (26.11.2008) refers to the need to educate the next generations as cultured individuals while arguing that libraries should get more money in Tampere. The same editorial also refers to Richard Florida, 'who has emphasized the role of a creative, open and broadminded cultural environment also as the cornerstone of economic success'. In a similar vein, *Helsingin Sanomat* (13.2.2008) quotes the cultural director of Vantaa, who acknowledges that Vantaa has not spent that much, but that the situation will get better: 'We have understood the meaning of culture in the city marketing'. Furthermore, in *Pohjalainen*, the cultural director of Vaasa justified culture spending by saying that according to a number of studies, money spent on culture saves much more money from the expenses in social and health services.

It is noteworthy that the report itself does not discuss the importance of culture or refer to the discussion on cultural economy in any way; it strictly focuses on describing the different ways in which the municipalities have organized their cultural activities and reporting the comparisons. The justifications for culture spending stem from the journalists, probably those responsible for culture sections, from the cultural directors of municipalities interviewed in the articles, and from the project coordinator of AFLRA.

Anticipating the Local Political Battle

A closer look at the interpretations of the results of the comparison reveals a distinct pattern. Although it appears as if the topmost municipalities are unanimously honored and the bottommost are despised, doing particularly well in the comparison has attracted extra accounting on the part of the municipalities and their cultural directors in question. In addition to justifying culture spending particularly vigorously, typically the results of the comparison are interpreted in such a way that the high ranking is questioned or explained away. For instance, the cultural director of Vaasa uses a lot of energy to deal with the fact that the city is number one in terms of money spent on culture per inhabitant. The cultural director, Tarja Hautamäki, from Vaasa, is relaxed with the report, even though she is obviously pleased with Vaasa's top ranking:

> 'In fact, I don't think we should compete about who spends most money on culture,' she says, and points out that this study does not tell anything about quality or how well the cultural producers reach their public.
>
> What the study shows is that cities like Vaasa that own big cultural institutions like museums and theaters spend more. In smaller towns cultural life is to a greater degree dependent on the activities of the third sector.
>
> 'A better way to measure is to compare the shares of cultural activities of the total budget. It tells more about the structure in the city,' says Hautamäki.
>
> In this comparison with its 4.8% Vaasa comes next after Tampere, which spends 5.2% of its total budget on culture.
>
> 'These are good figures,' says Hautamäki.
>
> (*Vasabladet* 26.11.2008)

Similar attempts to explain away the topmost ranking can be seen in *Aamulehti*, the newspaper from Tampere. As was quoted in the previous section, in the editorial the importance of culture is justified in a number of ways, after which the high ranking of Tampere is presented as a positive thing.

> Tampere (…) spent second to most money on cultural services both in absolute figures and per capita. Related to the income it even rises to the top of the comparison.

The biggest amount of money is spent on culture by the country's biggest city, Helsinki, but Tampere is well placed as number two. In per capita figures, Vaasa and Tampere are clearly leading compared with other cities.

(*Aamulehti* editorial 30.11.2008)

In the same editorial, the director responsible for cultural activities in Tampere is also given a voice. She says that she is in principle pleased with the situation in Tampere, but complains that the city spends clearly less than many other cities on basic art education. She also points out that more money should be spent on library services, for which Tampere spends less than many other big cities. In similar vein the cultural director of Kotka says that the city could do better in basic arts education and in library services (*Kymen Sanomat* 26.11.2008).

These kinds of comments and interpretations by the culture people are clearly meant as statements for local cultural politics, making the best possible use of the comparative data. In *Pohjalainen*, the cultural director of Vaasa even takes the issue up openly; she expresses her satisfaction with Vaasa's topmost position, but adds, 'Of course there is the small doubt that someone wants to turn it negative. The proportion of culture of the total expenditure is, however, really small' (*Pohjalainen* 26.11.2008).

Discussion

The analysis of the case example, the Finnish cities cultural activities development project, illustrates well how global ideas are domesticated in local contexts. Unification of accounting standards and, hence, the ability to describe the differences and similarities in the ways Finnish cities have organized their cultural activities, was part and parcel of the project. The report of the project also mentioned fashionable global ideas, such as the creative city as a key to success and comparable data as a management tool. In that sense, the final report of the project presented the cultural activities in different cities in a global or cosmopolitan framework. Yet the newspaper coverage did not highlight the global links or the convergence of local cultural policies as a potential effect of the project. Rather, the comparative data made available to the media were immediately interpreted in terms of the cultural framework of competition. Independently of each other, local newspapers uniformly presented the ranking of their city as the headline news. The newspaper media coverage of the report also reveals how local actors capitalize on the comparison for their political goals and power play; policies are justified by the results and statements made in anticipation of others' demands based on them. In that way, the attention was drawn to the local political battle that the introduction of comparative data or reform demands based on them typically triggers (Rautalin & Alasuutari, 2007; Takayama, 2008).

The results thus show that two factors, the cultural framework of competition between polities and the capitalization of comparative information in local politics, are crucial in sustaining and reinforcing people's lived experience of themselves as members of a local community. It could, of course, be considered as a self-evident fact that local newspapers report on any issue from the viewpoint of its relevance for the city in question, but as Billig (1995) stresses, that is exactly how the ubiquitous flaggings of the nation work. Like the nation in the case of banal nationalism, here, the citizens of each city are addressed as 'us', as a community with supposedly shared interests, arguing amongst themselves how to best advance their wealth and well-being. Although arguments in this political battle often appeal to comparative data and global models, paradoxically, this banal localism is effective in hiding from sight the fact that the same battle synchronizes local paths of change with global trends.

Acknowledgments

An earlier version of this chapter has been published with the title 'Spreading global models and enhancing banal localism: the case of local government cultural policy development' in *International Journal of Cultural Policy*, 19(1), 2013: 103–119. The support from the Academy of Finland funded project 'The Moderns: A Study on the Governmentality of World Society' (code 218200) is gratefully acknowledged.

Notes

1 At least terms such as indigenization (Friedman, 1999), creolization (Hannerz, 1987), vernacularization (Appadurai, 1996; Levitt and Merry, 2009) and hybridization (Pieterse, 1995) have been used.
2 The evaluation and monitoring of member states' behavior and the exertion of peer pressure on that basis, 'naming, blaming and shaming,' has been the main method used by the OECD for decades (Mahon and McBride, 2008; Woodward, 2004), and in recent years the technique has been adopted by the European Union. Within the EU, it goes by the name of open method of coordination (OMC), and it has been defined as an instrument of the Lisbon strategy (European Parliament, 2000).
3 Under the project, data on the revenues and expenditures for cultural activities were collected from the 2007 final accounts of the participating towns and cities. Data were collected by sending a questionnaire to the participating towns and cities. The following areas of cultural activities were surveyed: art and cultural institutions, libraries, cultural houses and centers, art schools, basic art education, and other cultural services provided by departments of cultural services and other administrative sections (Ruusuvirta, Saukkonen, Selkee and Winqvist, 2008b; Saukkonen and Ruusuvirta, 2008).
4 In this respect there was only one exception. The editorial of *Kainuun Sanomat* argues that the figures are misleading because the cultural activities produced by private actors are not included. The researchers sent the paper a rejoinder but it was not published.

References

Acharya, A. (2004). How Ideas Spread: Whose Norms Matter? Norm Localization and Institutional Change in Asian Regionalism. *International Organization*, 58(2), 239–75.
Adams, L.L. (1999). Invention, Institutionalization and Renewal in Uzbekistan's National Culture. *European Journal of Cultural Studies*, 2(3), 355–73.
Alasuutari, P. (2009). Art and Cultural Policy in the World Culture of the Moderns, In Pyykkönen, M., N. Simanainen and S. Sokka (ed.), *What About Cultural Policy? Interdisciplinary Perspectives on Culture and Politics* (pp. 99–115), Helsinki: Minerva.
Alasuutari, P. and A. Rasimus (2009). Use of the OECD in Justifying Policy Reforms: The Case of Finland. *Journal of Power*, 2(1), 89–109.
Ammons, D.N. (1995). Overcoming the Inadequacies of Performance Measurement in Local Government: The Case of Libraries and Leisure Services. *Public Administration Review*, 55(1), 37–47.
Angus, I.H. and S. Jhally (1989). *Cultural Politics in Contemporary America*. New York: Routledge.
Appadurai, A. (1996). *Modernity at Large: Cultural Dimensions of Globalization*. Minneapolis, MN: University of Minnesota Press.
Bayliss, D. (2007). The Rise of the Creative City: Culture and Creativity in Copenhagen. *European Planning Studies*, 15(7), 889–903.
Beck, U. (2003). Toward a New Critical Theory with a Cosmopolitan Intent. *Constellations: An International Journal of Critical & Democratic Theory*, 10(4), 453–68.
Beck, U. and N. Sznaider (2006). Unpacking Cosmopolitanism for the Social Sciences: A Research Agenda. *British Journal of Sociology*, 57(1), 1–23.

Bennett, T. (1995). *The Birth of the Museum: History, Theory, Politics*. London; New York: Routledge.
Bianchini, F. (1988). *City Centres, City Cultures: The Role of the Arts in the Revitalisation of Towns and Cities*. Manchester: Centre for Local Economic Strategies.
Billig, M. (1995). *Banal Nationalism*. London: Sage Publications.
Boddy, M. (2003). *Urban Transformation and Urban Governance: Shaping the Competitive City of the Future*. Bristol: Policy Press.
Boli, J. and G.M. Thomas (1997). World Culture in the World Polity: A Century of International Non-Governmental Organization. *American Sociological Review*, 62(2), 171–90.
Boli, J. and G.M. Thomas, (ed.). (1999). *Constructing World Culture: International Nongovernmental Organizations Since 1875*. Stanford: Stanford University Press.
Coaffee, J. (2008). Sport, Culture and the Modern State: Emerging Themes in Stimulating Urban Regeneration in the UK. *International Journal of Cultural Policy*, 14(4), 377–97.
Cook, I.R. (2008). Mobilising Urban Policies: The Policy Transfer of US Business Improvement Districts to England and Wales. *Urban Stud*, 45(4), 773–95.
Dahl, H.M. (2009). New Public Management, Care and Struggles about Recognition. *Critical Social Policy*, 29(4), 634–54.
Economic Development Working Group (2009). Prosperous Metropolis: Competitiveness Strategy for the Helsinki Metropolitan Area. http://www.culminatum.fi/en/tiedostot/uutinen_60/kilpailukykystrategia_engl.PDF. 20.1.2011.
Europa (2011). *European Capital of Culture*. European Union.
European Parliament (2000). *Lisbon European Council 23 and 24 March 2000 Presidency Conclusions*. European Union.
Evans, G. (2009). Creative Cities, Creative Spaces and Urban Policy. *Urban Studies*, 46, 1003–40.
Florida, R.L. (2004). *The Rise of the Creative Class: And How It's Transforming Work, Leisure, Community and Everyday Life*. New York: Basic Books.
Fougner, T. (2006). The State, International Competitiveness and Neoliberal Globalisation: Is There a Future Beyond 'the Competition State'? *Review of International Studies*, 32(01), 165–85.
Frey, B.S. (2003). *Arts & Economics: Analysis & Cultural Policy*. 2nd edn. New York: Springer.
Friedman, J. (1999). Indigenous Struggles and the Discreet Charm of the Bourgeoisie. *Australian Journal of Anthropology*, 10(1), 1–14.
Gale, D.E. (1987). *Washington DC: Inner-city Revitalization and Minority Suburbanization*. Philadelphia: Temple University Press.
Giulianotti, R. and R. Robertson (2006). Glocalization, Globalization and Migration. *International Sociology*, 21(2), 171–98.
Giulianotti, R. and R. Robertson (2007). Forms of Glocalization: Globalization and the Migration Strategies of Scottish Football Fans in North America. *Sociology*, 41(1), 133–52.
Grodach, C. and A. Loukaitou-Sideris (2007). Cultural Development Strategies and Urban Revitalization. *International Journal of Cultural Policy*, 13, 349–70.
Hannerz, U. (1987). The World in Creolization. *Africa*, 57(4), 546–59.
Hautamäki, A. (1995). *Kaupunkiko Yritys? Kaupungin Strateginen Johtaminen ja Konserniajattelu* [*City is an Enterprise? The Strategic Leadership of a City and Consolidated Corporation Thinking*]. Helsinki: Helsingin kaupunki.
Hobsbawm, E.J. and T.O. Ranger, (ed.). (1983). *The Invention of Tradition*. Cambridge: Cambridge University Press.
Jensen-Butler, C. (1999). Cities in Competition: Equity Issues. *Urban Studies*, 36(5/6), 865–91.
Kjær, P. and O.K. Pedersen (2001). Translating Liberalization: Neoliberalism in the Danish Negotiated Economy, In Campbell, J.L. and O.K. Pedersen (ed.), *The Rise of Neoliberalism and Institutional Analysis* (pp. 219–48). Princeton: Princeton University Press.
Landry, C. (2000). *The Creative City: A Toolkit for Urban Innovators*. London: Earthscan.
Lechner, F.J. and J. Boli (2005). *World Culture: Origins and Consequences*. Malden: Blackwell.
Lever, W.F. (2002). Correlating the Knowledge-base of Cities with Economic Growth. *Urban Studies*, 39(5/6), 859–70.

Levitt, P. and S. Merry (2009). Vernacularization on the Ground: Local Uses of Global Women's Rights in Peru, China, India and the United States. *Global Networks*, *9*(4), 441–61.

Mahon, R. and S. McBride, (ed.). (2008). *The OECD and Transnational Governance*. Vancouver: University of British Columbia Press.

Malecki, E.J. (2007). Cities and Regions Competing in the Global Economy: Knowledge and Local Development Policies. *Environment & Planning C: Government & Policy*, *25*(5), 638–54.

Meyer, J.W. (2004). The Nation as Babbitt: How Countries Conform. *Contexts*, *3*(3), 42–7.

Meyer, J.W., J. Boli, G.M. Thomas and F.O. Ramirez (1997). World Society and the Nation-State. *American Journal of Sociology*, *103*(1), 144–81.

Miller, T. and G. Yúdice (2002). *Cultural Policy*. Thousand Oaks: Sage.

Mommaas, H. (2004). Cultural Clusters and the Post-industrial City: Towards the Remapping of Urban Cultural Policy. *Urban Studies*, *41*(3), 507–32.

Mossberger, K. (1998). European Cities in Competition/Cities in Transformation—Transformation in Cities: Social and Symbolic Change of Urban Space. *Urban Affairs Review*, *34*(1), 168–70.

Noerreslet, M., J.B. Larsen and J.M. Traulsen (2005). The Medicine User—Lost in Translation?: Analysis of the Official Political Debate Prior to the Deregulation of the Danish Medicine Distribution System. *Social Science & Medicine*, *61*(8), 1733–40.

Oatley, N. (1998). *Cities, Economic Competition and Urban Policy*. London: Chapman.

OECD (2009a). *Governing Regional Development Policy: The Use of Performance Indicators*. Paris: OECD.

OECD (2009b). *OECD Territorial Reviews: Copenhagen, Denmark*. Paris: OECD.

Oulun kaupunki (2002). *Oulun Kaupungin Strategia ja Visio 2011* [*The Strategy and Vision of the City of Oulu*]. Oulu: Oulun kaupunki, keskusvirasto.

Paquette, J. (2008). Engineering the Northern Bohemian: Local Cultural Policies and Governance in the Creative City Era. *Space & Polity*, *12*(3), 297–310.

Pieterse, J.N. (1995). Globalization as Hybridization, In Featherstone, M., S. Lash and R. Robertson (eds), *Global Modernities* (pp. 45–68). London: Sage.

Pollanen, R.M. (2005). Performance Measurement in Municipalities: Empirical Evidence in Canadian Context. *International Journal of Public Sector Management*, *18*(1), 4–24.

Rautalin, M. and P. Alasuutari (2007). The Curse of Success: The Impact of the OECD PISA Study on the Discourses of the Teaching Profession in Finland. *European Educational Research Journal*, *7*(4), 349–64.

Regev, M. (2007). Ethno-National Pop-Rock Music: Aesthetic Cosmopolitanism Made from Within. *Cultural Sociology*, *1*(3), 317–41.

Robertson, R. (1992). *Globalization: Social Theory and Global Culture*. London: Sage.

Rovaniemen kaupunki (2006). *Rovaniemen matkailustrategia* [*The Tourism Strategy of the City of Rovaniemi*]. Rovaniemi: Rovaniemen matkailu ja markkinointi.

Ruusuvirta, M., P. Saukkonen, J. Selkee and D. Winqvist (2008a). *Kulttuuritoiminnan Kustannukset 14 Kaupungissa Vuonna 2006: Raportti Tiedonkeruun Pilottihankkeen Tuloksista* [*The Expenditures of Cultural Activities in 14 Cities in 2006: A Report on the Results of the Pilot Project*]. Helsinki: Cupore ja Suomen kuntaliitto.

Ruusuvirta, M., P. Saukkonen, J. Selkee and D. Winqvist (2008b). *Kuntien Kulttuuritoiminta Lukujen Valossa: Kulttuuritoiminnan Kustannukset 23 Kaupungissa Vuonna 2007* [*The Cultural Activities of Municipalities in the Light of Figures: The Expenditures of Cultural Activities in 23 Cities in 2007*]. Helsinki: Cupore and Suomen Kuntaliitto.

Saukkonen, P. and M. Ruusuvirta (2008). *Kuntien Kulttuuritoiminnan Menojen ja Tulojen Tiedonkeruu: Raportti Tiedonkeruun Pilottihankkeen Toteutuksesta, Siitä Saaduista Kokemuksista ja Toiminnan Kehittämismahdollisuuksista* [*Collecting Data on the Expenditures and Revenues of Municipalities' Cultural Activities: A Report on the Realization of the Pilot Project, Experiences Gained from it and on the Possibilities to Develop the Activity*]. In *Cuporen verkkojulkaisuja 4*. Cuporen verkkojulkaisuja 4. Helsinki: Cupore.

Schneider, M. (1989). *The Competitive City: The Political Economy of Suburbia*. Pittsburgh: University of Pittsburgh Press.

Sotarauta, M. (1995). Sivistääkö Strategia Suomen? [Does Strategy Make Finland Civilized?]. *Futura*, *14*(1), 53–7.

Spillman, L. (1997). *Nation and Commemoration: Creating National Identities in the United States and Australia*. Cambridge: Cambridge University Press.

Szerszynski, B. and J. Urry (2006). Visuality, Mobility and the Cosmopolitan: Inhabiting the World from Afar. *British Journal of Sociology*, *57*(1), 113–31.

Takayama, K. (2008). The Politics of International League Tables: PISA in Japan's Achievement Crisis Debate. *Comparative Education*, *44*(4), 387–407.

Tampere, C.O. (2009). Tampere Flows. http://www.tampere.fi/material/attachments/t/5m6qNiRLy/kaupunkistrategia_tiivistelmaENG_final.pdf (20.1.2011).

Throsby, C.D. and G.A. Withers (1983). Measuring the Demand for the Arts as a Public Good: Theory and Empirical Results, In Shanahan, J.L. (ed.), *Economic Support for the Arts* (pp. 37–52). Akron, OH: Association for Cultural Economics.

Tobin, J.J. (1992). Introduction: Domesticating the West. In Tobin, J.J. (ed.), *Re-made in Japan: Everyday Life and Consumer Taste in a Changing Society* (pp. 1–41). New Haven: Yale University Press.

UNESCO Institute for Statistics (2009). The 2009 Unesco Framework for Cultural Statistics. http://www.uis.unesco.org/template/pdf/cscl/framework/FCS_2009_EN.pdf (2.8.2010).

Woodward, R. (2004). The Organisation for Economic Cooperation and Development. *New Political Economy*, *9*(1), 113–27.

Part VI
Concluding Remarks

29
Empowered Actors, Local Settings, and Global Rationalization

John W. Meyer

Introduction

Much modern thinking about organizations follows a rough outline called *institutional theory* (Greenwood et al. 2008). Broad cultural and organizational environments provide templates for local settings, structuring these in standardized and sometimes isomorphic ways. Supported or constrained by these templates, local social organizational structures arise and are stabilized by their environmentally provided exoskeletons. Sometimes, the conformity to the environment and the organizational forms it provides is superficial, with local realities decoupled from the wider standards, and commonly, the standards themselves vary and make room for much local variation. Thus, a frequent research focus is to assess the degrees of isomorphism or variation in a set of social organizations. A common idea is that the variation is a product of strategic action by local participants (e.g., Oliver 1991). But in other cases, variation is thought to result from differences in linkages to environmental institutions, which themselves vary.

For example, many standards operating in the modern world define what a school is to be like, and what it is to do. These are laid out in hard and soft laws (as in the globally-specified Education for All movement [Chabbott 2003]; or a host of national rules), in professional customs and norms, and in what is now a common world culture of schooling (Meyer and Ramirez 2000). As a consequence, one can travel anywhere in the world and find schools—local social structures made with a serious effort to look and act like schools everywhere else. But of course, these schools vary from place to place, and many researchers want to emphasize the variation rather than the global standardization (e.g., Anderson-Levitt 2003). There is a taste in the field to see local variations as resulting from local factors like choice, culture, or historical path dependence, rather than from variations in exogenous linkages; the studies in this book, as I stress in this chapter, give a very different impression. They consider local cultural differences, to be sure, but also give great emphasis to variations in environmental contexts and in linkages to such contexts.

The issue is sometimes discussed in a rather naïve way. Virtuous or oppressive effects of supra-local pressures, often seen as worldwide, are contrasted with virtuous or oppressive customs or interests operating in more local societies (in some instances, national locales). More sophisticated formulations, which lie at the center of this book, follow Roland Robertson (1992, 1995) and his term *glocalization*. The idea emphasizes that global forces shape the interests and customs of local people and worlds. Thus, the same world forces that construct exoskeletal models of proper organizational structure also construct local people as empowered actors, under human rights norms or standards supporting the customs and interests of local societies, to put forward their own distinctive identities. Of course, the same norms that empower the local identities also shape these identities. Thus, it is legitimate for locals to assert their distinctiveness, but wise to shape the distinctiveness they present so that it is acceptable to a wider cultural frame. Few advocates for locals, around the world, find it advantageous to emphasize local cultural rights to infanticide, ethnic stratification, environmental destruction, or corruption. In the modern world, *the local* often refers to a distinctive political order, as national states have not entirely lost their sovereignty. But it often refers to harmless expressive customs—distinctive food, dress, music, art, holidays, and the like. Most importantly, it refers to local rights and interests as certified and legitimated by standardizing global institutions: even tribesmen go to the United Nations for protection under legitimating rules protecting indigenous people. In doing this, they are well advised to formulate their indigeneity in ways that seem proper to their wider audiences.

Thus, the studies in this book examine globalization, and the way it forces reconstruction of local organizational settings, with the idea in mind that the local participants and settings reacting to globalization are themselves legitimated, supported, and constrained by the emerging rules of the wider system (i.e., glocalized). Both conformity and variation, in other words, are shaped by a rapidly expanding global system. This turns out to be of great importance to the chapters in this book, and to my reflections on them; to a striking extent, the local settings and actors that appear in the research reported here are themselves creatures of a globalizing world. There are rubes and rednecks in the world, but not in the arenas reported in this book. Essentially, everyone here is some version of an educated modern actor.

An additional, and more latent, theme lies behind the research reported here. I call attention to it because it defines the distinctive character of the globalizing world, and of the analyses of that world presented here. This book is about aspects of the modern world that appear in formal organizations. Other social structures, like families, ethnic communities, gender solidarities, or communities of taste, are not the focus here. Organizations are. This might seem, from a broader point of view, an arbitrary selection of social structures to analyze. But that would be mistaken. A core feature of modern global society is that organizations of all sorts explosively expand (Drori, Meyer, and Hwang 2006). They expand in every country and in every social sector, from public to private, to a myriad form of what are now called *nonprofits* (a term that includes schools, churches, recreational associations, medical clinics, think tanks, and charities). Correspondingly, the modern globalization that supports rationalized formal organizations built up around entitled individuals also undercuts more traditional authorities—corporate family groups, ethnic communities, landowning structures, and in some measure, even the sovereignty of the national state.

Thus, the studies here describe a world in which pressures create much organization, structure the organization created, and seem to impose these forms on local settings. But these pressures also construct, reconstruct, and empower (i.e., glocalize) the local participants and settings that react to the forces of globalization.

The outcome is that the world of modern organization, while highly variable, is nonetheless quite stylized. A resultant feature of the studies reported here is that, in a sense, they are too easy for a reasonably informed reader to understand; almost everyone involved could be a neighbor, friend, or colleague. This is by no means a property of defective analyses, but is rather a characteristic of the world on which these analyses report. This is a special world from which the bizarre, the exotic, and the opprobrious—routinely found in the empirical world—are, in good part, edited out. When activity comes to be structured as a formal organization, it tends to take on the appearance of blandness.

Three component elements dominate the studies reported here. The following sections discuss them in turn. First, there are the forces associated with the term *globalization*. These, built into supra-national organization and discourse, provide the stimulus and stage for action. Second, there are the local arenas of power, interest, and culture, which adapt to globalization, but function to introduce some variation into a world that is often standardizing. And third, there are the people on whom global forces impinge, who mediate between these forces and their own locales. They are actors in the theatrical sense, and usually play the roles of 'actors' in the social scientific sense (Meyer and Jepperson 2000). In this book, given its focus on formal organization, they are often managers or advisors of managers—of firms, of subsidiaries, of schools, or of public agencies and national states.

Globalization and Rationalization

We need to consider what the term *globalization* means in the context of the organizational analyses reported here because it functions to provide core independent variables. It turns out that there is a good deal of practical coherence to the notion as it is used in this book. This is by no means inevitable. The idea that social interdependencies and cultural conceptions increasingly take on world-wide dimensions does not, in itself, specify the nature of the ideas or structures involved. Globalization could mean, and in some perhaps-distorted analyses does mean, the rise of a world dominated by ogres like the United Nations or the European Union; or the organizations and ideologies of world capitalism; or the West, bent on yet one more crusade; or expanding Islam; or the spread of a destructive set of poisons, diseases, and pollutants destroying the earth. These meanings are very far from those involved in this book.

More positively, globalization could mean the rise of common world doctrines of human rights, environmental sustainability, and social transparency, and the organization of all these in networks reaching around the globe. These meanings are much closer to those underlying the studies here, but not quite close enough.

In the studies reported here, globalization generally means expanded rationalization in organizations and ideologies operating in very widespread environments, like Europe or the whole world (Drori, Meyer, and Hwang 2006). And, it reflects expanded participation and empowerment by at least some local participants in these environments. None of the studies reports a form of globalization that involves domination or centralization with lowered rationalization. This reflects the character of the modern world, not a bias in the research considered here. In a stateless but integrating world society—and one in which older forms of cultural or racial domination are highly stigmatized—rationalized control systems built on expanded actorhood of subunits are natural products (Meyer 2010). This makes a good deal of sense in a world dominated by the West (and especially, the United States), by a strong rationalistic academic culture, and by great international organizations carrying models of rationalized modernity.

Expanded rationalization is the order of the day, built into 'global ideas' (Ahrne and Brunsson; Carney; Engwall) and the global organizations that are the central loci of influence for the studies in this book. Public organizations now come under soft law pressures to manage art and culture as well as sewers, water, forests, education, and the overall environment (Alasuutari; Knill and Tosun; Malets and Quack; Pallas and Wedlin). There are somewhat harder pressures to control money laundering, competition, or carbon (Djelic; Engels and Knoll; Jakobi), and to implement rational management in public or private orders in general (Christensen; Delmestri; Djelic) and in universities (Engwall; Kodeih; Logue; Pallas and Wedlin; Sahlin). Local private organizations come under the scrutiny of their rationally organized multinationals (Chan; Dörrenbächer et al.; Frenkel; Özen; Strang). There are pressures for standardization (Hwang et al.) and for rationalized approaches to diversity (Abu-Sharkh; Barbosa and Cabral-Cardoso; Frenkel). Everywhere there are pressures for expanded and improved organization and management (Christensen; Knill and Tosun; Özen); a rationalized global environment demands the expansion of local management.

Strikingly, in the wider worlds reported here, there are no clear instances of institutional pressures toward lowered rationalization—and, for instance, to simple heightened dependence or to local communalism. Perhaps the closest any chapter gets is in the work of Czarniawska on the resurgent activation in at least some contexts of an older—or, anyway, less rationalized—narrative form of advice and policy. Similarly, Carney sees global pressures for rationalized and managerialized organization, but emphasizes the rationale for, and success of, local Chinese resistance.

Thus, in a stateless but integrating world, liberal or neoliberal models involving a great deal of rationalization have pride of place. Progress is the order of the day, and progress involves expanded and globalized rationalization. Other forms of social order are seen as traditional or reactionary or only local in character, though they sometimes form the backbone of localistic reactions to the global order. Thus, an economy based on family organization is local but not global (Carney), and national customs of gender relations (Barbosa and Cabral-Cardoso; Frenkel), business education (Engwall; Kodeih), or management (Delmestri; R. Meyer) are seen as, in part, parochial.

The degree to which rationalization dominates the environmental scene is striking. And, of course, this helps account for the extraordinary expansion of formal organization in every society and sector of the modern world. An environment filled with pressures of rationalization is one in which formal managerial organizational structures arise and take their place as the proper form for local social life. The chapters here, thus, certainly support two core propositions of the institutional theory of organizations:

Prop. 1:   Rationalization is rapidly expanding in the supra-national or global environment.

Prop. 2:   Rationalization in the wider environment increases local formal organization.

The specific forms rationalization takes vary across the analyses here, though it always has a strongly cultural content, characteristic of developments in an integrating but stateless world society (Meyer 2010). Sometimes, as in the chapters discussing multinational corporations and their local impacts, the rationalization is mainly organizational, with clear structures (perhaps varying depending on national origins as in Chan or Dörrenbächer et al.) carrying modern global policies. Similar organizational pressures send global norms to national states (Christensen; Djelic; Knill and Tosun). Sometimes, the pressure is mainly about substantive or ideological issues—diversity (Abu Sharkh; Barbosa and Cabral-Cardoso; Frenkel), transparency (Boxenbaum and Gond; Hwang et al.; Jakobi), or sustainability (Engels and

Knoll; Malets and Quack). Often, however, it is carried—in classic liberal ways—by rather content-free cultural processes of market-like rankings and prestige; this seems especially characteristic of the studies on the managerial reconstruction of education (Engwall; Kodeih; Logue; Pallas and Wedlin; Sahlin).

Overall, globalization in the studies here means the rise of institutional structure in world society, but structure of a particular kind: organizational and discursive rationalization. New rules emerge, calling for new penetrative social controls over an expanding array of topics everywhere. And new organizations arise, including the modern multinationals, to discipline local arenas under the new rules. The theory here is not about institutions of all sorts, but aggressively expansive rationalistic ones.

Global rationalization, as depicted here, is quite a coherent cultural frame, carried along in the world's educational systems and the knowledge these systems produce and transmit. Almost all the people who create and promulgate the culture, as well as those who diffuse it to local contexts, have a great deal of education in a rather standardized schooling world (Schofer and Meyer 2005). So, any good student in the social sciences, or their applied arenas in business and public policy schools, could give 'correct' answers in evaluating the globalizing institutions at issue here. The student would know that good organizational policy supports diversity and environmental protection. Obviously, countries need improved management and control over issues like money laundering, economic policy, and transparency, and firms and schools clearly need expanded and transparent management. All the questions discussed here have right answers, though there may be reasons to avoid them in China (Carney) or Sweden (Czarniawska), and there are reasons to edit and reinterpret them in many places (e.g., Boxenbaum and Gond; R. Meyer). The right answers celebrate the core values of modern society: rational purposive action towards legitimated goals, respect for the environment and individual human rights, and so on. These are values deeply built into educational institutions that are now central to global stratification, and to the culture depicted in the studies here.

The Partially Tamed Local Reality

Global diversity on many dimensions is undoubtedly decreasing in the current period. But a great deal of variation remains, not to mention ways in which modern rationalization can increase variability with differentiation. In any case, there is still enough cultural diversity to permit the *National Geographic* to survive, and to provide shocking stories in the world press about the offensive dietary customs, family practices, or political structures obtaining in distant places. There is a great deal of extreme inequality—far beyond that obtaining in most specific national societies. One can easily find people to interview or observe whose incomes are in the neighborhood of one-thousandth of the income of those at the Western academic top.

These sorts of diversity do not much appear in the chapters of this book. No multinational human relations officer discussed here is managing the hybridization of global human rights policies with the practices of local head-hunters or practitioners of female circumcision (Abu-Sharkh comes closest). And, while there are large income differences between the global and local worlds discussed here, they are not really extreme. Overall, the local societies discussed here vary, and vary from global society, but not dramatically.

Thus, the modern organizational structures that are the focus of this book are found in locales that are, in good part, prepared for them. They are in national contexts—or parts of them—already tuned to the rationalized global order. They are, to use Robertson's term, glocalized, with properly legitimated identities, and structural and cultural arrangements. The parts of the world, and of national societies in the world, that are not tuned to global culture are not, it seems, locales of much formal organization. So, if the chapters here are about local organizations and the factors affecting them, their subjects are already substantially tamed. The few remaining head-hunters in the world are probably not the foci of much formal organization, and remain structured in much more traditional terms. They are selected out of this book by our focus on formal organizations.

Thus, it turns out that the locals in this book, reacting to global rationalizations, are substantially modernized. They may reflect quite distinctive national cultural patterns as with Chinese or Austrian familial or business forms (Carney; Chan; R. Meyer), or other cultural arrangements (Boxenbaum and Gond; Delmestri; Frenkel; Hwang et al.; Knill and Tosun). World centrality may be at issue (Özen; Strang), or simply previously established educational patterns in nation-states (Engwall; Kodeih; Logue; Pallas and Wedlin; Sahlin). Often, the locals are, in fact, local managers or managerial theorists (Engwall; Delmestri; Knill and Tosun; R. Meyer; Özen), or they may be already rational organizations varying among countries and sectors (Alasuutari; Christensen; Djelic; Engels and Knoll; Jakobi; Malets and Quack; and in part Abu-Sharkh). Sometimes, there is variation in taste or choice (Czarniawska; Delmestri), but these variations are among already modernized managerial establishments.

In practically all cases discussed in this book, the locals and their interests are quite highly legitimized in terms of many wider world norms. Sometimes, broad global norms of rationalization are differently institutionalized in national societies or industries (Chan; Delmestri; Dörrenbächer et al.; Engwall; Knill and Tosun; Kodeih; Malets and Quack; R. Meyer), but in a sense, they are variations on a broad theme. So, when conflicts arise, they have something of a subdued character—some normative issues are on the table, but many others are already resolved, at least in principle. In the future, it might be useful to have studies in which much more is at stake. A researcher could consider, for instance, ways in which large Mexican criminal organizations, or reactive religious movements around the world, deal with the pressures of the principles of global environmentalism, human rights, and transparency.

Overall, there is strong support for further core propositions in institutional theory:

Prop. 3: With globalization, local identities are attuned to the wider rationalized culture.

Prop. 4: Glocalized identities facilitate expansion of isomorphic rationalized organization.

Prop. 5: Glocalization supports local variations, but within legitimated boundaries.

Thus, we have the pressures of expansive global rationalization reaching down into national societies and cultures that are already prepared for them. Much organization-building occurs, of course, under these conditions. And presumably, in less properly glocalized settings, the penetration of global rationalization is lower, and much lower levels of isomorphic organizational formalization result. Such settings, in other words, are less likely to provide chapters for a book like this one.

In any event, readers of the studies here will learn, and presumably need to learn, rather little in substance about any distinctive local settings, anywhere in the world. Boxenbaum and Gond depict some particular modern business postures in France and Quebec that account for adaptations of more global models of responsible investment. Carney goes into detail in defining cultural and organizational circumstances that sustain family business structures in China. Barbosa and Cabral-Cardoso note distinctive elements of some traditionalism in Portugal, and Frenkel discusses the distinctiveness of Israel (and to some extent Korea). Delmestri notes similar variations among countries. Kodeih emphasizes a special French educational history. Strang emphasizes a general core-periphery distinction, as does Özen. Renate Meyer depicts a distinctive business culture in Austria. But, in general, the effective conventional tourist would need to know, and would know, more about Brazil, Italy, New Zealand, Austria, Australia, Norway, Africa, Korea, Finland, Turkey, Poland, or Czechoslovakia as these places display presumably tasteful cultural difference. A student of management no longer needs much instruction of this sort in a glocalized managerial world.

Further, when national or other distinctions are emphasized, in the chapters here, they are generally not deep or primordial cultural matters. Rather, they are differences among local forms of rationalized modernization, or among what are called 'national business systems'. Centers differ from peripheries (Djelic; Jakobi; Özen; Strang), economic interest and structural differences among industries may affect roles (Engels and Knoll; Malets and Quack), or simple path-dependent variations in historical forms of rationalization may be at issue (Boxenbaum and Gond; Christensen; Kodeih; Logue; Malets and Quack; R. Meyer; Sahlin).

The Highly Schooled Mediating Actors

Between global rationalization and local social structure lie the people who manage the relationships involved. Usually, in this book, they are components of local structures—managers of public or private organizations—but, sometimes, they are consultants or interpreters (Ahrne and Brunsson; Czarniawska; Djelic; R. Meyer; Özen; Pallas and Wedlin). In any case, they play mediating roles between the global and local or glocal. Who are these people?

In practically all the cases discussed in this book, they are professionals and managers. They are very highly schooled people, often in professionalized fields like business or law; uneducated people do not appear in this book. As properly schooled professionals, they are imbued with the modern worldwide schooled culture that celebrates matters like the environment, human rights, and organizational rationality (Frank and Gabler 2006). And, as proper schooled professionals, they play active roles as actors, rather than more passive and conforming adapters. Perhaps exceptions to these generalizations might be the family business group elites discussed by Carney (whose core status may be familial rather than educational), some Korean managers discussed by Hwang et al., and some of the local groups in Abu-Sharkh's case who have rather limited schooling.

In any event, the core actors who manage the relationships between global rationalization and glocal social structure are themselves deeply infused with standardizing global rational ideology. Some are substantial civil servants (Alasuutari; Christensen; Djelic; Jakobi; Knill and Tosun). Others are academic leaders and managers (Engwall; Kodeih; Logue; Pallas and Wedlin; Sahlin). Most are business managers (Barbosa and Cabral-Cardoso; Chan; Czarniawska; Dörrenbächer et al.; Engels and Knoll; Frenkel; Hwang et al.; Strang). Consultants, media professionals, and NGO leaders are sometimes involved (Alasuutari; Boxenbaum and Gond; Malets and Quack; Özen; Pallas and Wedlin). Everybody involved, it seems, has spent much time in the university, and is deeply familiar with the global culture of higher education.

Clearly, if we assembled all these people in a room, they could communicate with each other with great ease, and probably in English. They share, to a great extent, a common culture, rooted in eighteen to twenty years of modern schooling—all the way through higher education. The schooled culture involved clearly includes the theory and ideology of rationalized formal organization, incorporating global standards on matters like management, human rights, the environment, and transparency. Thus, whatever private experiences and ideas these people have, they can clearly display their knowledge of globally-correct standards on a great many topics. Such capacities, of course, facilitate their ability to mediate between the global and the local.

Equally clearly, most of these people are also familiar with their local and national contexts, and the glocalized forms these contexts, at least superficially, take on. They are agents of glocalization, indeed, and can explain and justify modest local variations in legitimating global terms. As agents, they can also explain to less glocalized locals the ways in which expansive global rationalization makes sense, or is in any case a good set of arrangements to which to give deference.

In the course of doing their business, the legitimated and schooled actors of modern management, of course, further the glocalization process. That is, they help formulate local distinctiveness in terms acceptable to global norms, and at the same time, help reorganize local cultural and political arrangements to be (or appear to be, at least) within the boundaries of proper global acceptability.

Thus, we have support for more core ideas in modern institutional theory of organizations:

Prop. 6: Schooled management facilitates the translation of global norms into local settings.

Prop. 7: Schooled management facilitates the glocalization of the local in acceptable ways.

Prop. 8: Schooled management facilitates the expansion of rationalized organization.

Schooling expands very rapidly in the modern world, and does so essentially everywhere. Over 20 percent of the appropriate global cohort is enrolled in higher education, and about 30 percent benefit from its blessings (Schofer and Meyer 2005). These are the people who live in and manage modern rationalized organizations, and who populate the tales told in this book. In the same way that older organizational forms relied on the expansion of mass education (Stinchcombe 1965), contemporary formal organizations presume higher education. The university not only produces personnel for managerial roles, but also generates knowledge that renders formerly uncertain, opaque, and parochial matters rationally organizable.

Rationalizing the Opaque

Classically, when we thought of formal organizations, we had two main types in mind. First, especially in centralized countries where organization devolves from the state, we followed Weber in conceptualizing bureaucracies: top-down hierarchical structures enforcing conformity on subject populations and activities. Second, following Barnard and others, theorists in more liberal societies envisioned organizations as managed divisions of labor, producing something for markets. Other structures (religious, educational, charitable, and so on) could be seen as partial or incomplete organizations (as discussed here by Ahrne and Brunsson), and much of social structure was not 'organization' at all.

This has now changed; formal organization can be found in many new domains, and organization in the old domains broadens to cover activities and functions previously unrecognized. The chapters in this book capture the extended rationalization involved. A number of them, for instance, are about higher education, reflecting the rise of what were once traditional universities as standardized modern 'organized actors' (Kodeih; Krücken and Meier 2006; Pallas and Wedlin; Sahlin). The cultural policy of cities can be analyzed, managed, and rated (Alasuutari). Nation-states can have competition regimes (Djelic) and manage money laundering (Jakobi). Multi-national firms, once rare, are now common and widespread; variations among them in their local impacts are frequently considered in the studies here (e.g., Chan; Delmestri; Dörrenbächer et al.).

Further, traditional business organizations can come under pressure to take on completely new functions, far beyond production for markets. They should manage diversity (Barbosa and Cabral-Cardoso; Frenkel), carbon accounting (Engels and Knoll), and proper investment practices (Boxenbaum and Gond), and maintain high and transparent standards (Hwang et al.; Knill and Tosun).

Over and above organizations expanding their functions, or new organizations managing old functions, the chapters in this book reflect the dominance of another element in modern rationalized society. Organizations are to be real actors (not passive bureaucratic structures, for instance) making decisions and behaving accountably. Thus, they are to be managed (not owned as property or subordinated to a sovereign). Many chapters here are about the diffusion, not of particular activities or roles, but of actorhood itself: that is, management (Brunsson and Sahlin-Andersson 2000). Thus, everywhere we have something diffusing, like a CEO or a technology of management (Christensen; Delmestri; Dörrenbächer et al.; Logue; Sahlin; Strang; and less rationalistically, Czarniawska).

As a consequence of these expansions in rationalization, many of the activities that come under regulation are hard to assess in terms of efficiency or effectiveness. If so much effort goes into being an organized actor, and taking on the extended plumages of actorhood, perhaps clarity about effective action disappears. In any event, few of the chapters in this book account for aspects of organizations that have a real bottom line. Outputs tend to be global or local legitimacy, not the effective production of something.

What makes it possible to organize, under rationalistic norms, so many opaque matters? In the background here is the great cultural rationalization carried in the global knowledge system, principally organized in schools and universities. In scientific and social scientific theories, unclear causal relationships are made clear, standards of human and environmental requirements are articulated, and norms of transparent and informed decision-making are rationalized. Rationality, thus, is achieved by rules—embedded in legal and accounting principles—more than by experiential knowledge. The world depicted in this book is a very highly schooled place. Ironically, the schooling involved now feeds back to demand the rational reconstruction of the schools themselves (Engwall; Kodeih; Logue; Pallas and Wedlin; Sahlin).

Reading the Cases

I illustrate the aforementioned points with examples of several of the case studies in this book. Most of these studies can be seen from the point of view suggested here. A few, noted here, fit less well, and may call for reflection.

Hwang et al. discuss ISO 9000 adoption by Korean firms, in an account that fits the form put forward here. The rise of the ISO system, of course, is an outstanding instance of institutional rationalization in a stateless world, involving extended soft-law regulation. In presenting their case, the authors do not need to tell us very much about the Korean state, culture, or society—their locale is quite highly glocalized, of course. The actors of their drama are managers, and probably quite highly schooled ones, adapting their glocalized local structure to high global rationalization.

Similarly, Alasuutari discusses city cultural policy in Finland. Globally, the idea that cities should manage their cultural life through rational policy is well established, and many ratings have appeared. The author discusses the ways in which these ratings impact local officials and observers, who clearly are highly schooled in the matter, and who try to transmit wider standards into local policy. Almost nothing distinctive about the locales involved needs to be said—they vary, but all seem to be highly glocalized already. This is quite ironic because the culture that cities are to display and market, according to global principles, is supposed to be a somewhat unique local one. The author notes the banality of this point, and in no case reports anything distinctive about any of the local cultures that are to be displayed.

Engels and Knoll discuss the management of carbon in response to highly rationalizing global and national policies. The people transmitting the wider rules, and responding to them locally, are very sophisticated and obviously highly schooled. In this chapter, in contrast to some others, there is intense local variation among countries, industries, and firm situations (see also Kodeih; Malets and Quack). But, this variation itself occurs under conditions of great glocalized rationalization, with highly codifiable differences in interests from firm to firm, country to country, and industry to industry. This is not localization in any romantic sense, reflecting some traditional or tribal communal life. It is a set of interests in, not against, the highly rationalized modern order. Corrupted tribes or conspiracies are not involved.

Barbosa and Cabral-Cardoso report a rather canonical case. The rationalized global culture celebrating human resources management for diversity is carried by a set of highly rationalized multinationals to Portugal, varying in national origin and somewhat in diversity policy. The mediating participants are the local subsidiary managers, presumably highly educated in modern actorhood. The issue is how global policy (often American in origin) is adapted to the Portuguese setting, about which surprisingly little needs to be said by the authors. They briefly note late Portuguese modernization, some general traditionalism, a work force only recently diversified in practice, and some discriminatory customs about gender and ethnicity. The local context, apparently, is glocalized enough so that dramatic conflicts do not appear, and a bit of inattention to diversity policy is good enough to localize matters.

Not every study here fits the model of this chapter so well. Carney gives an analysis of how and why Chinese family firm groups succeed and are likely to continue to do so. Local cultural elements are at issue in his account, as are features of a political system weak in the rule of law. In the same way, local consequences vary (Dörrenbächer et al.). Similarly, Frenkel notes both cultural and political elements of Israeli society that have limited the penetration of a rationalized gender regime. Czarniawska discusses the spread of narrative stories as a clearly rationalized form of structuring organizational reality; here, there is a celebration of the unique and distinctive that takes the center of the stage. Finally, Ahrne and Brunsson emphasize that in some respects, less rationalized forms—such as meta-organizations and partial organizations—have advantages for diffusion in the modern global system. These structures, in important respects decoupled, permit a good deal of localization under the umbrella of global rationalization.

Conclusion

The studies in this book add substance to the story of the influences of globalization on organizations and societies around the world. They are not really about the bloodless notion of globalization. They are about the rapid global emergence of a wide range of forces of rationalization, often rooted in the global knowledge system. New rating systems subject universities to nominally universalistic standards. Global ideology and supranational organizations force expanded managerial roles on local structures to supervise new functions: diversity in the work force; responsibility in investment; cultural development in town; improved attention to quality, transparency, and competition; and national regulation of currency flows and carbon outputs.

All these forces impact diverse local settings, varying in political structure, organizational history, and cultural inclinations. But the local and national worlds are themselves modified in tune with world society, or glocalized, so the clashes of local and global are more muted than naïve theories might expect. There is plenty of conflict in the world, but much of it is not between the glocalized realities which sustain formal organization and the wider world that communicates with such organizations. It is between much less rationalized and globalized components of local society outside the domain of this book.

Between local and global lie the mediating actors. They are mostly managers, almost always highly schooled in modern knowledge, and highly professionalized. They are centrally parts of both local and global worlds. They can fluidly participate in world society, and their conferences, media linkages, and schooling and professional connections, by and large, keep them well informed on current global policy fashions. Thus, they are perforce cosmopolitans. At the same time, they are participants and leaders in more local and national settings, linked to particular and distinctive organizational and cultural matters.

Importantly, world integration is not simply organizational, and top-down, in character. It is, indeed, transmitted organizationally (through multinationals or conforming national states), but also in the global construction—substantially through education and the knowledge system—of the identities of the local participants, now reconstructed as actors in a global scheme. As with all forms of actorhood, the roles involve empowerment, but also constraint in terms of world standards of various sorts; modern managers learn to accomplish goals, but also which goals are proper to accomplish. Moreover, they can learn all this in educational programs designed for that purpose: broad ones in the abstract social sciences and more pointed ones in the world's rapidly expanding network of business and public policy schools.

Future Prospects

The studies here reflect a particular liberal period in world history. Aggressive rationalization goes on in global culture and organization. High levels of world stratification create incentives for locals to adapt to global pressures and models. And the schooled actors playing managerial roles have a great deal of credibility. Thus, great models of organization and action spin out of central world institutions like the UN, the World Bank, the EU, or the OECD. Most of the models discussed in this book seem to have some origins in the dominant West, and especially the United States.

It is easy to imagine that all this can and will change in the future. In a less liberal world, perhaps large-scale solidarities will provide very different basic structures than the structures that now characterize models for social organization. Communism is now gone, but alternative religious or cultural forms could become more dominant. They would activate very different forms of local realities than the glocalized ones that are at the center of this book. Then, alternatives other than managerialized formal organization might be the structures that stabilize relations between an altered global and a local—tuned in very different ways than at present.

References

Anderson-Levitt, K. (ed.). (2003). *Local Meanings, Global Schooling: Anthropology and World Culture Theory*. New York: Palgrave Macmillan.

Brunsson, N., and Sahlin-Andersson, K. (2000). 'Constructing Organizations: The Case of Public Sector Reform'. *Organizational Studies*, 21: 721–46.

Chabbott, C. (2003). *Constructing Education for Development: International Organizations and Education for All*. New York: Routledge/Falmer.

Drori, G., Meyer, J.W., and Hwang, H. (eds). (2006). *Globalization and Organization: World Society and Organizational Change*. Oxford, UK: Oxford University Press.

Frank, D., and Gabler, J. (2006). *Reconstructing the University: Worldwide Shifts in Academia in the 20th Century*. Stanford, CA: Stanford University Press.

Greenwood, R., Oliver, C., Sahlin, K., and Suddaby, R. (2008). *The Sage Handbook of Organizational Institutionalism*. London, UK: Sage.

Krücken, G., and Meier, F. (2006). 'Turning the University into an Organized Actor', in G. Drori, J. Meyer, and H. Hwang (eds), *Globalization and Organization*. Oxford, UK: Oxford University Press, 241–57.

Meyer, J.W. (2010). 'World Society, Institutional Theories, and the Actor'. *Annual Review of Sociology*, 36: 1–20.

Meyer, J.W., and Jepperson, R. (2000). 'The "Actors" of Modern Society: The Cultural Construction of Social Agency'. *Sociological Theory*, 18: 100–20.

Meyer, J.W., and Ramirez, F. (2000). 'The World Institutionalization of Education', in J. Schriewer (ed.), *Discourse Formation in Comparative Education*. Frankfurt, Germany: Peter Lang, 111–32.

Oliver, C. (1991). 'Strategic Responses to Institutional Processes'. *Academy of Management Review*, 16: 145–79.

Robertson, R. (1992). *Globalization: Social Theory and Global Culture*. London, UK: Sage.

Robertson, R. (1995). 'Glocalization: Time-Space and Homogeneity-Heterogeneity', in M. Featherstone, S. Lash, and R. Robertson (eds), *Global Modernities*. London, UK: Sage, 25–44.

Schofer, E., and Meyer, J.W. (2005). 'The World-wide Expansion of Higher Education in the Twentieth Century'. *American Sociological Review*, 70: 898–920.

Stinchcombe, A.L. (1965). 'Social Structure and Organizations', in J. March (ed.), *Handbook of Organizations*. Chicago, IL: Rand McNally, 153–93.

Index

Page numbers in italic refer to figures and tables

abortion 257–9
abstraction, in the process of glocalization 10
Academic Ranking of World Universities (ARWU) 53–6, 298. *See also* rankings
accountability 332–3
accounting 327, 331–4
accounts: ambiguous 84–5; bridging 83–4; compliance 82–3; expert 85–6
ACF (African Competition Forum) 95. *See also* community building
Actor Network Theory (ANT) 312–13
actors: cities as 399–401; mediating 419–20
adoption motivations 351
advertising, view of the relation between the local and the global 29
AFLRA (Association of Finnish Local and Regional Authorities) 401–5
Africa: Banyan tree metaphor 100–1; bridging missionaries 96–8; community building in 93–5; competition in 95–100; development policy in 98–100
African Competition Forum (ACF) 95. *See also* community building
AGL (Association Globus et Locus) 26
Allianz-Dazhong, and localization 193–7
ambiguity: negotiating 360–4; and universities 59–62
ambiguous accounts 84–5. *See also* dissent
American National Standards Institute (ANSI) 340

'Americano' managers 204–6
ANSI (American National Standards Institute) 340
ANT (Actor Network Theory) 312–13
anti-money laundering policies 369–79
ARESE 314–23
Aristotle, rhetorical strategies 119
arm's length 128
Armstrong, David M. 68
arts, role in society 399–401
ARWU (Academic Ranking of World Universities) 298
Asia, family-controlled business group (FBGs) 219–29
Asociacion de Trabajadoras Despertando a un Nuevo Amancer – Association of Workers for Waking Up to an New Dawn (ATDANA) 254
assessments 296, 298–9, 301–2
Association Globus et Locus (AGL) 26
Association of Finnish Local and Regional Authorities (AFLRA) 401–5
Association of Workers for Waking Up to an New Dawn (ATDANA) 254
audiences, construction of 29
Australia, NPM reforms 165–7
Austria, media debate on Shareholder Value 82
authenticity, question of 31–2, 397
autonomy, of universities 58–9
Axenbrant, Emma 71–2

banal nationalism 396–7

Index

Bang & Olufsen (B&O), use of storytelling 69
Bank Secrecy Act (US 1970) 372
Benavides, Luis Rodriguez 253
benchmarking initiatives 108–11
bibliometrics 55. *See also* rankings
Bologna Process 235–6. *See also* business education
bricolage 320–1. *See also* contextualization
bridging accounts 83–4. *See also* consent
bridging missionaries 96–8
"business case" 140
business education: glocalization of 232–7; management research 238–43; standards for 281
business systems 124, 127

carbon management: case studies 359–60; and the institutional world 357–9
Carosone, Renato 203–4
CEDAW (Convention on the Elimination of all Forms of Discrimination Against Women) (1979) 249, 251–2, 255, 257
CEMS (Commaunauté Européenne de Management Schools) 47
CFPI (crossfunctional performance improvement) projects. *See* quality teams
chaebols, role in Korean economy 341–2
China: globalization in 28; life insurance firms in 189–99; localization in 191–9; NPM reforms 167–8
CIETT (International Confederation of Private Employment Agencies) 46
CIS (Commonwealth of Independent States) 46
cities, as strategic actors 399–401
climate change. *See* carbon management
CLP (Competition Law and Policy Committee) 92–3
collectivism, effects of 114–15
colonialization, and globalization 66
Commaunauté Européenne de Management Schools (CEMS) 47
Common Market for Eastern and Southern Africa (COMESA) 94–5
Commonwealth of Independent States (CIS) 46
Commonwealth Yearbook of Universities 177–8
communications, and meta-organizations 46
community building: in Africa 93–5; transnational 96
compartmentalized business systems 127–8

competition: in Africa 95–100; myth of 98–100
Competition Law and Policy Committee (CLP) 92–3
competition regulation, and transnationalization 91–3
complexity, concept of 162–3
compliance accounts 82–3. *See also* consent
consent: mobilizing 82–4. *See also* dissent
construction of equivalency, in the process of glocalization 10
consultancy firms 142
contextualization, micro-strategies of 316–21
Convention on the Elimination of all Forms of Discrimination Against Women (CEDAW) (1979) 249, 251–2, 255, 257
convergence, and divergence 4–6
corporate culture: concept of 72. *See also* storytelling
corporate governance, FBGs 224–6
corporate storytelling. *See* storytelling
creative thinking, role in society 399–401
crime control 369–79
cross-cultural leadership 212–13, 215
crossfunctional performance improvement (CFPI) projects. *See* quality teams
cultural complexity 162
cultural diversity 417–19
cultural sensitivity 210–14
cultural values, variations in 128
culture, role in society 399–401
CUPORE (Finnish Foundation for Cultural Policy Research) 401
Czech Republic: Europeanization of 264–74; in the institutional change 270–4

Delgado, Emerson R. Levenau 253
Denning, Stephen 68
Dennisdotter, Emma 71–2
developmentalist ideology 127, 129
diffusion: dynamics of 342–6; and translocalization 66
diffusion of ISO 9001 among Korean firms 340–3
dissent: neutralizing 84–6. *See also* consent
divergence, and convergence 4–6
diversified conglomerates, role in Korean economy 341–2
diversity: cultural 417–19; in MNCs 146–9
dochakuka 28
domestication, concept of 397–9

donors 139
Du Pont 120
due process 333

EAC (East African Community) 94. *See also* community building
East African Community (EAC) 94. *See also* community building
ECN (European Competition Network) 93–4
economic contraction 129
economic expansion 128–9
editing rules, 312 312
education: business 232–7. *See also* universities; French Grandes Ecoles de Commerce (FGECs) study 278–91. *See also* universities
employees 141–2
enactment, in the process of glocalization 10
Environmental Impact Assessment Directive (EU 1985) 268–9
ESCP Europe 283–90
ESSEC 283–90
ethnocentrism 213
ethos 119, 122–9
EU (European Union): characteristics of 266–8; degrees of adjustment pressure 268–70; Environmental Impact Assessment Directive (1985) 268–9; as a meta-organization 45
EU Emissions Trading Scheme (EU ETS), and carbon management 357–60
Euromed Management 283–90
European Competition Network (ECN) 93–4
European Union (EU): characteristics of 266–8; degrees of adjustment pressure 268–70; Environmental Impact Assessment Directive (1985) 268–9; as a meta-organization 45
Europeanization, integration with glocalization 266–8
Evenett, Simon 99–100
expanded rationalization 415–17
expert accounts 85–6. *See also* dissent
experts, as legitimated theorists 9–10

family-controlled business group (FBGs): overview 219; and corporate governance 224–6; emergence and functioning 220–3; organizational structure 224; resource-based view 221–2

fashion, notion of 66–7
FATF (Financial Action Taskforce) 370–9
FATF-style regional bodies (FSRBs) 374–7
FBGs (family-controlled business group): overview 219; and corporate governance 224–6; emergence and functioning 220–3; organizational structure 224; resource-based view 221–2
Fédération Internationale de Football Association (FIFA) 45
Federation of Korean Industries (KFI) 347
femininity 128
FEMUCARINAP (La Federacion Nacional de Mujeres Campesina, Artenanas, Indigenas, Nativas y Asalariasdas del Peru – National Federation of Women Farmers, Artisans, Indigenous and Salaried Workers in Peru) 254
Fernandes, Maria da Penha Maia 256
FGECs (French Grandes Ecoles de Commerce) study 278–91
FIFA (Fédération Internationale de Football Association) 45
filtering 316–18. *See also* contextualization
Financial Action Taskforce (FATF) 370–9
Financial Intelligence Units (FIUs) 377–8
Finland, global trends in 396–405
Finnish Foundation for Cultural Policy Research (CUPORE) 401
FIR (Fonds d'Investissement Responsable) 314–23
FIUs (Financial Intelligence Units) 377–8
flexible work schedules. *See* work-family (WF) policies
Fonds d'Investissement Responsable (FIR) 314–23
foreign practices 119–20, 123, 125–6
Forest Stewardship Council (FSC) 327–31
France, responsible investment (RI) 311–23
French Grandes Ecoles de Commerce (FGECs) study 278–91
FSC (Forest Stewardship Council) 327–31
FSRBs (FATF-style regional bodies) 374–7

Ganoza, Irma 259
Garcia, Manuela 253–4
Gardner, Howard 68
GE (Grande Ecole) programs 283–90
gender contracts, between states and organizations 136–43
gender rights, in Peru 248–60
General Motors 120

Index

global, vs. local 4–6
global cosmopolitan identity 214
global diversity 417–19
Global Financial, benchmarking initiatives 108–11
global identity 209–14
Global MBA Ranking 235. *See also* business education
globalization: in business education curricula 233–5; and organizations 39–41; and rationalization 415–17; as translocalization 66–7; as Westernization 29
globalocentric identity 214
glocal cosmopolitan identity 213
glocalization: agents 12–13; in China 28 concept of 163; dimensions 7–12; integration with Europeanization 266–8; issues 4–7; multilayered 139; overview 30; as a process 10–12; reflexive 30–2; themes 12–13; use of term 3–6, 26–7
governance models 295–6, 298–9
Grande Ecole (GE) programs 283–90
grassroots organizations 139
Great Place to Work Institute (GPW) 142. *See also* work-family (WF) policies

headquarters-subsidiary relationships: and issue selling 386–90. *See also* multinational corporations (MNCs)
heterogenization 326, 335
higher education. *See* education
holding structure 120–9
home-country effect 141–2
homogenization 143, 326, 335
horizontal axis of glocalization 8–9
Huamán, Karen Noelia Llantoy 258
hybridity: concept of 163–5; effects of 169–71
hybridization 207, 209–10, 289–90, 313

IASB (International Accounting Standards Board) 331
IAU (International Association of Universities) 45
IB (international business) theory 383
ICC (International Chamber of Commerce) 45
ICPAC (International Competition Policy Advisory Committee) 93
ideas, travel of 41–2
identity: global 209–14; hybridization of 289–90; national 396–7; projected 285–6

IDI (Intercultural Development Inventory) 210–11
IFA (International Fertilizer Industry Association) 45
IFRS (International Financial Reporting Standards) 331–4
IKEA: as a symbol of rapid globalization 42–3; use of storytelling 71
ILO (International Labour Organization) 48, 249, 252–5
indigenous practices 119–20, 122, *124*, 129
individualism 128
Industrial Standardization law (Korea 1992) 345
initial design 327–9, 331–2
institutional change: in the Czech Republic 270–4; definition of 265–6; in Poland 270–4
institutional logics 278
institutional theory 413
institutional transformation, and ambiguity 59–62
institutional world 355–6
institutionalism: dynamics of 342–6; and universities 52–3; and workforce diversity 148–9
Intercultural Development Inventory (IDI) 210–11
International Accounting Standards Board (IASB) 331
International Association of Universities (IAU) 45
international business (IB) theory 383
International Chamber of Commerce (ICC) 45
International Competition Policy Advisory Committee (ICPAC) 93
International Confederation of Private Employment Agencies (CIETT) 46
International Fertilizer Industry Association (IFA) 45
International Financial Reporting Standards (IFRS) 331–4
International Labour Organization (ILO) 48, 249, 252–5
International Organization for Standardization (ISO) 340
International Ranking Expert Group (IREG) 56, 175–85, 299. *See also* rankings
International Telecommunications Union (ITU) 46
Inter-Parliamentarian Union (IPU) 255

428

IREG (International Ranking Expert Group) 56, 175–85, 299. *See also* rankings
ISO (International Organization for Standardization) 340
ISO 9001: adoption of 345–6; diffusion among Korean firms 340–3; research study 346–50
Israel, maternity leave policy 137–40
Israeli Women's Network (IWN) 139
issue selling 386–90
ITU (International Telecommunications Union) 46

Japan: business practices 28; coffee consumption in 31; and the concept of glocalization 30; workforce diversity *150*, 153, *155*–7

KALDER 121, 127
Karen Noelia Llantoy Huamán v. Peru 258
KFI (Federation of Korean Industries) 347
knowledge management 73. *See also* storytelling
KOÇ Group 120–1, 125
Korea: Industrial Standardization law (1992) 345; and ISO 9001 340–3

La Federacion Nacional de Mujeres Campesina, Artenanas, Indigenas, Nativas y Asalariasdas del Peru – National Federation of Women Farmers, Artisans, Indigenous and Salaried Workers in Peru (FEMUCARINAP) 254
labor issues 252–5
Larsen, Svend Erik 74–5
late industrialization theory 220–1. *See also* family-controlled business group (FBGs)
layering: concept of 163–5; effects of 169–71
LCA (Life Cycle Approach) 321
Leading Minds: An Anatomy of Leadership (Gardner 1995) 68
legitimated theorists 9–10
legitimation 355–6, 360–4
Liberal International 48
Life Cycle Approach (LCA) 321
lobbying 386, 390–2
local, vs. global 4–6
localization: in China 191–9; definition of 190–1; increasing stress on 30
logics, institutional 278
logos 119, 122–9

macrocultural discourses 127–8
management behavior 204, 209, 211

management education, standards for 281
management practices: hybridization 207, 209–10; models of 206–16
management reforms, universities 56–9
management research 238–43
management tools, storytelling 67–70
managerial ideologies 128–9
managerial knowledge, role of media 297–8
Managing by Storying Around: A New Method of Leadership (Armstrong 1992), 67-70 68
marginal identity 212–13
marketing tools, storytelling 73
masculinity 128
Master of Management rankings 236–7
maternity leave policy. *See* work-family (WF) policies
McDonaldization thesis 30–2
McDonald's, as a symbol of rapid globalization 42–3
MDGs (Millennium Development Goals), poverty alleviation objectives 99
media, relationship with science 297–8
mediating actors 419–20
mediatization 295–300
meta-organizations: overview 45–8; and partial organization 48–9. *See also* organizations
methodological glocalism 28
M-form: FBGs 224; research on 120–9
Millennium Development Goals (MDGs), poverty alleviation objectives 99
MNCs. *See* multinational corporations
modernization: process 28, 66, 97, 229; rationalized 419
modernizing ideology 127
money laundering 369–79
Money Laundering Control Act (US 1986) 372
monopolistic trajectory of transnational governance 326, 331–4
multi-divisional structure 120
multilayered glocalization 139
multinational corporations (MNCs): diversity in 146–9; expansion of 42–3; in multinational corporations (MNCs) 391–3; subsidiary initiative-taking in 383–94; work-family (WF) policies 135–43
multiversity: expression of 60. *See also* universities

narrative knowledge 73. *See also* storytelling
national business systems 127

429

national culture, and TQM 112–17
National Federation of Women Farmers, Artisans, Indigenous and Salaried Workers in Peru (FEMUCARINAP) 254
national identity 396–7
needs, construction of 29
new institutionalism: framework/theory 146; and universities 52–3
New Public Management (NPM): in Australia and New Zealand 165–7; in China 167–8; emergence of 161; in Norway 168–9
New Zealand, NPM reforms 165–7
Njoroge, Peter Muchoki 95–7
non-discrimination treaties 252
normative rhetoric 128
Norway, NPM reforms 168–9
NPM (New Public Management): in Australia and New Zealand 165–7; in China 167–8; emergence of 161; in Norway 168–9

Occupy movement 30
Organisation for Economic Co-operation and Development (OECD) 92–3
organizational institutionalism, and universities 52–3
organizational politics 385–7
organizations: and globalization 39–41; ideas within 41–2; institutional theory 413; meta-organizations 45–9. *See also* multinational corporations (MNCs)
organizations and partial organization 43–5

Pacific-Aetna, and localization 191–3, 197–8
partial organization: overview 43–5; and meta-organizations 48–9. *See also* organizations
participation, in standards-setting 325–36
particularization 6–7
pathos 119, 122–9
pendulum thesis 129
People's Republic of China (PRC). *See* China
Peres, Flor Nolasco 254
personal rule 223. *See also* family-controlled business group (FBGs)
Peru, gender rights in 248–60
Pinilla, Susana 252–3, 257, 259
place, concept of 28–9
pluralistic trajectory of transnational governance 326–31

Poland: Europeanization of 264–74; institutional change in 270–4
policymaking, global linkages of 397
political reforms, and universities 57
politicking 385–7
polity scholarship 398–9
Polyethnicity and National Unity in World History (McNeill 1986) 27
Portugal: study of MNCs 149–59; workforce diversity 147–8
poverty alleviation 99
power distance 128
PRC (People's Republic of China). *See* China
primus inter pares, ideals of 57–8
production, view of the relation between the local and the global 29

quality teams, formation of 110–12
Quebec, responsible investment (RI) 311–23

rankings: Global MBA Ranking 235; as a mediatized tool 298–300; of universities 53–6. *See also* business education; universities
rational rhetoric 128
rationalization, and globalization 415–17
rebound, in the process of glocalization 10
receiving country 119–20, 125–6
re-contextualization: and mobilizing consent 82–4; and neutralizing dissent 84–6
reflexive glocalization 30–2
reform processes, conceptual basis 162–3
reframing 318–20. *See also* contextualization
reproductive rights 257–9
research community: engagement with narrative 69–70. *See also* storytelling
resource-based view 221–2
responsible investment (RI) 311–23
responsiveness, of standards-setting organizations 330–1, 333–4
rhetorical strategies 119–29
rhetorical theory of diffusion 124
The Road to Academic Excellence. The Making of World-Class Research Universities (Altbach and Salmi 2011) 53
Robertson, Roland 5

Samsung Group, work-family (WF) policies 141–3
Sao Paulo consensus (UNCTAD) 99
science, mediatization of 297–8

sedimentation: concept of 163–5; effects of 169–71
selective emulation 312–13
Self-Monitoring Scale 209
Shanghai, localization in 195–8
Shanghai rankings. *See Academic Ranking of World Universities (ARWU)*
shareholder value, debate on 82
Sloan, Alfred P., Jr. *124*
Smith, Adam 98–9
social sciences, concepts for analyzing globalization 39–40
source country 119–20, 125–6
The Springboard: How Storytelling Ignites Action in Knowledge-era Organizations (Denning 2001) 68
stakeholder participation, in standards-setting 325–36
standards: adoption motivations 351; anti-money laundering policies 369–79; as an example of partial organization 43–4; Industrial Standardization law (1992) 345; and ISO 9001 340–3; setting 325–36
standards-setting organizations: American National Standards Institute (ANSI) 340; challenges and contestation 329–30, 332–3; Forest Stewardship Council (FSC) 327–31; initial design 327–9, 331–2; International Accounting Standards Board (IASB) 331; International Financial Reporting Standards (IFRS) 331–4; International Organization for Standardization (ISO) 340; responsiveness of 330–1, 333–4
state 139–40
state-dependent business systems 127
storytelling: as a communication tool 72–3; as a management tool 67–70; as a marketing tool 73; other uses 72–3; types of 74–5
Storytelling: An Effective Marketing Concept (Dennisdotter & Axenbrant 2008) 71–2
strategic actors, cities as 399–401
strategic authenticity 31–2. *See also* authenticity
structural complexity 162
subsidiary initiative-taking: overview 384–5; in multinational corporations (MNCs) 383–94; and political maneuvering 385–7; research study 387–91
Sucari, Margarita 255–6
Swedish labor market, deregulation of 46
Swedish organizations, and storytelling 70–2

'Taiwanese model' of operation 190
temporal axis of glocalization 9
theorization, as a glocalization mechanism 80–2
therapeutic abortion 257–9
time, definitions of 9
Times Higher Education Ranking 54. *See also* rankings
The Times Higher Education Supplement ranking 298
top management teams (TMTs) *179, 181, 183*
total quality management (TQM): adoption of 343–4; diffusion of 11; and ISO certification 342; and national culture 112–17; quality teams 110–17; research on 120–9; and responsible investment (RI) 320
Townsend, Anel 257
transactions cost theory 221–2. *See also* family-controlled business group (FBGs)
transcendence, and the axes of glocalization 7–12
transference, approach to globalization studies 5
transferred practices 119–20, 122, 125–7, 129
transformation, approach to globalization studies 5
translation: as a glocalization mechanism 80–2; notion of 66–7; process of 300–3
translocalization, globalization as 66–7
transnational community-building 96. *See also* Africa
transnational governance: monopolistic 326, 331–4; pluralistic 326–31
transnational standard-setting 334
transnationalization, and competition regulation 91–3
transparency 332–3
Turkey, management practices 120–9
TUSIAD 121, 127

uncertainty avoidance 113
Union of International Associations (UIA) 251
unions 134, 138, 142
United Cities and Local Governments (UCLG) 45, 47
United Kingdom, workforce diversity 152–7

431

Index

United Nations Conference on Trade and Development (UNCTAD) 93, 99
United Nations (UN) 45
United States (US): Bank Secrecy Act (1970) 372; management practices 120–9; Money Laundering Control Act (1986) 372; workforce diversity 146–7
Universal Postal Union (UPI) 46
universality principle 6–7
universities: autonomy of 58–9; business education 232–7; global model for 295–304; management and governance of 52–3; management reforms 56–9; and 'multiversity' 60; political reforms 57; *primus inter pares* 57–8; privatization of 58; ranking 53–6; top management teams (TMTs) 175–85. *See also* education; rankings
US News and World Report rankings 299. *See also* rankings

Vasquez, Ivan 254
vertical axis of glocalization 8
violence against women 256–7
voluntary standards 332
Volvo, use of storytelling 70–1

Westernization, globalization as 29
women: in Peru 248–60; reproductive rights 257–9; violence against 256–7
work-family (WF) policies: cross-national adoption of 135–43; Israel 137–40; Samsung Group 141–3
workforce diversity, in MNCs 146–9
world polity theory scholarship 398–9
world society (WS), concept of 250–1
World Trade Organization (WTO), demonstrations against 30

zaibatsu 221